Greatness and Ruin:
Self-Reflection and Universalism Within
European Civilization

GREATNESS AND RUIN

SELF-REFLECTION AND UNIVERSALISM WITHIN EUROPEAN CIVILIZATION

RICARDO DUCHESNE

ANTELOPE HILL PUBLISHING

CONTENTS

INTRODUCTION

Greatness and Ruin is an attempt to explain, within the same theoretical framework, the far higher accomplishments of Europeans in all the endeavors of human life than any other people, and their current ethnocidal path. More specifically, it aims to demonstrate that:

1) Throughout their history Europeans attained the highest levels of knowledge, artistic originality, philosophical reflection, and literary expression—more than all the other peoples of the world combined.

2) The ultimate source of the immense creativity of Europeans was the realization, starting in ancient Greece, that humans have a mind capable of generating standards or criteria upon which it can decide what constitutes knowledge, morality, and beauty, through introspection and self-reflection.

3) The peoples of China, the only cultural contender to the West, remained embedded in kinship-based institutions and Confucian traditions, barely attaining a sense of selfhood, and never discovering the faculty of reason as an independent legislator of values and knowledge.

4) The current scholarship on the comparative study of civilizations, the "rise of the West" and the "Great Divergence," is deeply marred by its preoccupation with mere economic markers and its unexamined ideological commitment to multiculturalism and racial equality.

1

5) The current promulgation of diversity across the West is rooted in the attempt
   of Europeans to generate, out of their autonomous individual minds, freed
   from compliance to kinship norms and traditions, universal principles that
   hold true for all humans, such as equal liberty in the choice of one's cultural
   beliefs, and equality of opportunity.

The central argument sustaining all these aims is that the cultural greatness of
Europeans and their current ethnocidal path are both rooted in their discovery of
the faculty of reason, the emancipation of the self from the continuity of traditional roles, and their belief that their societies must be grounded on principles
valid for humanity as a whole within a liberal pluralist setting that affords equal
rights to everyone regardless of religion, nationality, and race.

This discovery of the mind is encapsulated, in its embryonic apprehension, in
the maxim *Know thyself* carved into stone at the entrance to Apollo's temple at
Delphi in Greece sometime between 525 and 450 BC. Socrates is the name most
often associated with this maxim because of his insistence that in order for us to
claim that we have knowledge, we must first engage in serious *self*-reflection to
find out the unexamined preconceptions we hold to be true.[1] In asking others in
his dialogues to think more deeply about why they hold certain things to be true,
Socrates was personifying a strong sense of selfhood about his own mental states,
thoughts, and feelings, and implying that introspection, reflecting on one's own
feelings, sensations, and thoughts, is the path to knowledge.

When we reach Plato, we have a more formalized meaning of the Delphic
phrase in his belief that it means "know your soul." Plato concluded that, in order
for men to have true knowledge, they had to know that they had an immaterial
spirit within as the source of their reasoning abilities, and that only through intense cultivation of their reasoning powers would they learn to be responsible for
their beliefs and actions. To speak of knowledge entailed an awareness of one's
self as "nothing other than" one's soul, and of one's soul as the source of true
knowledge. The cultivation of one's soul required asking, as Plato did in *Theaetetus*, "Why should we not calmly and patiently review our own thoughts, and
thoroughly examine and see what these appearances in us really are?" By "appearances," Plato meant beliefs that humans acquire through their senses, or as they
appear to the senses, without any introspection about the nature of these appearances.

---

[1] Moore, 2015.

Plato's famous theory of the tripartite soul in Book IV of *The Republic* divided the forces that motivate humans into three parts: 1) *logos*, which he believed to be located in the head and the source of the capacity of humans to regulate the other two parts of their soul, which consist in; 2) the "spirited" or "thymotic" part, which refers to the emotions, and which Plato believed to be located in the chest (and which he implied existed in a very intense way among aristocratic men obsessed with the pursuit of glory and the attainment of superior recognition among their peers); and 3) appetitive drives, which Plato believed to be located in the stomach, and which pertain to the mundane animalistic instinct humans have for bodily pleasures and survival.

The argument I am proposing, however, is not Platonic, but Hegelian. I agree that the essence of the mind or consciousness is incorporeal, but I disagree with Plato that the soul of each person is occupied by an eternal being that exists outside ourselves, and that as human bodies die the soul is continually reborn in subsequent bodies. The breakthrough to the discovery of consciousness occurred in ancient Greece, but from then on, we can detect in the West a long-drawn-out movement characterized by increasing self-consciousness about our place in the world, and how our notions of what constitutes beauty, the good life, and knowledge, are shaped by our own historically evolving consciousness.

This movement reached a high level of self-comprehension in post-Enlightenment German idealism and historicism, with its claim that authorization for one's beliefs, what can be admitted as having universality and objectivity, cannot be seen as inherent, naturally given features of consciousness, or as products of some pre-established authority based on "natural laws" commanded by a divine being, but must be found within a community that realizes that diverse humans will always reach conflicting and irreconcilable doctrines open to challenge, and that individuals must therefore be free to adjudicate for themselves their own values.[2] This view would culminate in the post-World War II decades with the liberal multicultural belief that the only way we can coexist under the inescapable social reality of plurality is to create a political setting which provides "universal" rules allowing for the equal free expression of multiple perspectives in a state of mutual tolerance.[3]

Becoming conscious of their consciousness, starting in ancient times, was the breakthrough mark that allowed Europeans to generate their superlative levels of

---

[2] Pinkard, 2014.
[3] Rawls, 2005.

cognition and artistic creativity. Due to their lack of selfhood and introspection, non-Western peoples were unable to achieve high levels of cognition and artistic creativity, but instead stagnated considerably after attaining some degree of reflexivity and transcendence over tribal-kinship modes of thinking during the Axial Age (700–200 BC). Non-Western thinking barely rose above "first-order thinking," or the general type of thinking involved in the everyday life of humans as they go about surviving, making tools, predicting the behavior of others, or behaving in ways that conform to the expectations of their cultures. Only in ancient Greece do we witness for the first time "thinking about thinking," the examination of the nature of thought itself, or what some call "second-order thinking,"[4] which presupposes a transcendental capacity to stand back from the conventions of one's culture, in order to generate universally valid claims based on criteria decided by reason, and by what Kant would call our "aesthetic judgment."

While the biological-neurological preconditions for consciousness emerged over the course of millions of years of evolution, and we can correctly talk about the "proto-conscious" behaviors of complex animals[5] and the relatively sophisticated levels of cognition attained by civilizations generally,[6] discussions about consciousness as a "human . . . awareness or consciousness of one's self" and "personal identity" were uniquely the purview of European thinkers, rarely addressed in non-Western civilizations, except in a rudimentary way.[7]

The higher cognitive levels achieved by Europeans in logic, mathematics, and philosophy generally were not initial products of a higher intelligence, or products of a cosmopolitan atmosphere, or a polemical democratic culture found in the assemblies of city-states. In the first instance, the difference between Greek and non-Western mathematics, for example, was not a higher problem-solving capability, but a higher awareness of the thinking involved in mathematics. The axiomatic method that Euclid systematized in geometry was made possible thanks to the emergence of a self-conscious mind, which presupposes a consciousness of the "I" as the agent that establishes what is truthful and what is not, and is thus capable of identifying or differentiating "undefined terms and axioms" as "self-evidently true," and the basis upon which it, the mind, can then deduce theorems, as "incontrovertible" mathematical statements.

---

[4] Elkana, 1986; Donald, 2001.

[5] LeDoux, 2019.

[6] Bellah, 2011.

[7] Thiel, 2011.

This "discovery of the mind" in Greece came along with the emergence of characters in literature showing incipient signs of introspection and selfhood, that is, characters "conscious of their individuality" and capable of separating their internal feelings from the accepted norms, which had hitherto been largely undifferentiated, writing poetry expressing "inwardly felt emotions."[8] During the modern era, the new literary form known as the "novel" would emerge, containing characters with greater inner depths, authenticity, and highly differentiated personalities inclined to self-examine their feelings, beliefs, and actions, away from all ready-made character typologies.[9] Through the modern era, music would see the development of more sophisticated, refined, and specialized musical instruments in order to express the wider range of personal feelings and experiences of European individuals relatively detached from collective traditions and inhabiting a world of civic or voluntary associations.

It was this attainment of self-consciousness that allowed Western Civilization to exhibit a relatively continuous sequence of novelties, a high number of renaissances, a sustained creativity in science and technology after 1500, along with the discovery and mapping of the world, ongoing sequences of new philosophical outlooks, artistic and architectural styles, including the development of all the disciplinary fields of knowledge, archaeology, botany, economics, sociology, anthropology, history, biology, chemistry, genetics, physics, geology, philosophy, and geography. It was the lack of self-reflection that kept China and other major civilizations stuck in their Axial Age intellectual achievements, barely cultivating transcendental values, barely originating new styles of painting, architecture, literature, and philosophy, and barely reaching what Jean Piaget identified as the level of "formal operational thinking."

Western consciousness (or individualism) is not a one-time occurrence emerging in complete form during one historical period, as academic specialists are predisposed to argue. Rather, Western selfhood developed over the course of many centuries, with many identifiable periods, emergent qualities, and modes of expression depending on whether one is examining the history of painting, literature, science, philosophy, or music.

Through these movements and successive epochs, we can identify an emerging self-authorizing agent that strives to construct universal concepts, moral principles, and aesthetic standards relatively freed from kinship/traditional norms.

---

[8] Snell, 1960.
[9] Watt, 2001.

Europeans were the only people to become aware of the downside of kinship ties, starting in ancient Greece and Rome, through to the decision by the Catholic Church in the Middle Ages to mandate nuclear families as superior over polygamous-cousin marriages,[10] with Greeks and Romans constructing city-states grounded on civic identities above clannish ties, and medieval peoples constructing institutions and voluntary associations (chartered towns, guilds, universities, monasteries, and representative institutions) above tribal natural bonds.

This "liberal" world socialized Europeans to further extend their trust to anonymous strangers, to think in a less contextual way, and to judge objects and humans in terms of universal principles and rules impartially applicable according to rationally-based criteria.[11] Evolutionary theory is very good at explaining "human universal" traits similarly found among all peoples in history, such as the inclination for music, story-telling, division of labor, religious rituals, status differentiation, bodily adornment, incest taboo, and rules of hygiene. But evolutionary theory has great difficulties explaining the virtuosity of the great artists and the continuous creativity of Europeans in their painting, music, and literature. The relative autonomy of European high culture over evolutionary pressures is one of its defining features. This does not mean that natural selection ceased to play a role, or that Darwinian pressures were not long active in the selection of certain behavioral-individualistic tendencies and racial characteristics in the continent of Europe.[12] It means that European cultural activities were "de-Darwinized" to a much higher degree than the activities of other peoples.

It was this ability to generate universal concepts validated by the self-authorizing aesthetic, moral, and epistemological judgments of European individuals that eventually led to the rise of liberal pluralism and the current ethnocidal path of Europeans. The cultural history of Europeans is characterized by "culture-transcending" longings.[13] We see this in the Aristotelian idea that truth can only arise if the mind frees itself from particular contexts and learns to provide reasons based on abstract-analytical categories (substance, quantity, quality, relationship, place, time, state). We see it in the Stoic notion that human beings are linked together worldwide as "citizens of the world," a cosmopolis, because of the common spark of reason they all share.[14] We see it in the mathematized geography started

---

[10] Witte, 2015.
[11] Henrich, 2020.
[12] See MacDonald, 2019.
[13] Gellner, 1992.
[14] Nussbaum, 1997.

by Ptolemy which "posited a continuous and essentially uniform surface to the globe."[15] We see it in the Roman legal principle of *ius gentium* or a law which "natural reason" establishes for all men;[16] and in the Christian idea that "every human being possessed an equal dignity" and that all humans regardless of their ethnicity "were equally redeemed by Christ."[17] We see it in the modern notion that humans are created equal in certain inalienable rights for life, liberty, and the pursuit of happiness; and we see it in the multicultural idea that Western liberalism should be neutralized and delinked from any particular ethnocentric cultural markers in favor of a political setting within which individuals regardless of religion, race, and nationality have equal rights to choose their cultural preferences as long as such preferences do not violate the equal rights of others.

Europeans have long been driven to generate rational principles and moral values with universal validity through introspective examination of their inner thoughts. The fact that European mathematics, logic, and sciences have produced methodologies and capacities for technologies which have been accepted as valid by cultures around the world points to their "culture-transcending" quality. In the realm of social life and politics, the cultures of the world have also accepted European modernity when it comes to industrialization, creation of modern systems of transportation and communication, standardization of their systems of education, and rationalization of their institutions. While some prominent nations have been reluctant to accept liberal-democratic values, Europeans envision these values as "culture-transcending" in judging them to be values that human beings as human beings prefer when given the opportunity to choose, and in assiduously trying to export them to the world.[18]

The dominant ideology in the West is liberalism, and the current key principle of this ideology is cultural-pluralism,[19] and cultural pluralism is inherently culture-transcending. The Western establishment currently holds that only a political setting which grants value-pluralism is compatible with the equal liberty of individuals. While there have always been efforts among intellectuals to argue that liberalism is guided by the absolutist goal of bringing about the actualization of what is best in human nature,[20] the view currently institutionalized across the

---

[15] Headley, 2008, 41.

[16] Tierney, 2004

[17] Holland, 2019, 494.

[18] See Fukuyama, 1992; Mearsheimer, 2018.

[19] Rawls, 2005.

[20] Taylor, 1979.

West is that humans are sufficiently rational to enjoy equal liberty as moral agents capable of deciding what to believe and which way of life to choose based on personal conscience, as long as they do not seek to undermine the political setting within which this pluralism is possible.

In other words, the belief now prevails that Western governments should no longer take it upon themselves to mandate any cultural values other than the values of tolerance and respect for the decisions of equally free individuals to choose their values. This means, therefore, that Western nations are obligated to transcend any cultural prejudices they may have from the past about the priority of the Christian religion, or the priority of European ethnic identity, customs, and traditions. The equal liberty of everyone—a tenet Europeans drew out of their self-authorizing minds—precludes the imposition of a collective set of beliefs upon the population. Academics today have a hard time thinking properly about the uniqueness of Europeans because their societies and their universities are committed to "diversity, inclusiveness, and equity," and thus they have been curtailed in their ability to engage in true critical thinking about the comparative achievements of civilizations.

My answer to the question of why Europeans discovered the mind, rather than the older, more populated, urbanized, and developed peoples of China, Mesopotamia, or Egypt, starts with the argument that the decision by Europeans to draw out their ideas and values by way of an examination of their inner mental states, in differentiation from the external world, their bodily impulses, and the norms of their kinship group, was a historical achievement, rather than a product of natural selection on its own. The formation of the ego and individuality in history should be contrasted to the reality that through much of our history, the consciousness of humans was at the mercy of their instincts and embedded to a tribal collective consciousness. Humans were in awe of the primal, self-creating force of nature, identifying it with the cyclic fertility of the earth and women's reproduction.

The development of consciousness and civilization entailed, in the first instance, the detachment of the male ego from the unconscious world of fertility goddesses.[21] The rise of ego-consciousness was a phenomenon initiated by men trying to demonstrate their male nature by overcoming the demands of the body and their "effeminate" desire for comfort and fear of death through the performance of heroic acts. Consciousness first begins to differentiate itself from the

---

[21] Neumann, 1973.

surrounding context when men experience the "masculine" character of their consciousness as "peculiarly" their own. The hero is a character that shows incipient signs of differentiation with the formation of male hunting groups. Moreover, as men began to subjugate Mother Earth with agriculture and to establish some control over the cycles of fertility, they started to break down the hegemony of the primal fertility spirits.

But the opportunity to achieve individual heroic renown became increasingly difficult and rare as non-Western cultures moved towards centralized state governments, in which the King, the Pharaoh, the Emperor, or the Sultan came to be seen as the only decision-making individual with the upper classes in a state of relative subservience. It is with Indo-Europeans, a predominantly pastoral people originally located in the Pontic Steppes, who developed in prehistorical and ancient times the most mobile way of life, driven by wheeled vehicles, horse-riding, and then chariots, that we first encounter a true aristocratic people coexisting in a state of equal liberty relative to their acknowledged leader, determined to act according to their self-chosen heroic immaterial ends.[22] Indo-Europeans migrated out of their steppe homeland in the third millennium, both eastward to the Altai Mountains and westward into the Hungarian Plain and south-eastern Europe, and across the European continent, establishing a major part of the genetic and linguistic ancestry in modern Europeans, as well as imposing their aristocratic way of life. It is essentially among Indo-Europeans that we find mythologies, sagas, and epic poems of the heroic deeds of men with identifiable names, proto-differentiated personalities and private internal spaces.

It was not the cognitive part of the brain, passively thinking, without desires, that initiated a feeling of selfhood; it was, rather, the thymotic part of the soul (as differentiated later by Plato, and as embodied intensively by aristocratic men in the pursuit of glory). But for men to really start generating knowledge from their minds, the hyper-masculine aggression of Homeric Greeks needed to be sublimated into civilized activities. While the *Iliad* recognizes many of the superior qualities of Achilles, his braveness and relentless pursuit of glory, Homer also describes him as being unable to control his *thymos*, consumed by anger and overweening pride, and thus mindless in some of his actions. There is already in the *Odyssey* a self-awareness that man's *thymos* needs to be properly harnessed by thought or reason, if it is to be properly channeled into civilized behavior, and that

---

[22] Duchesne, 2011; Kristiansen, 2023.

doing so requires self-control through the introspective faculty of the mind.[23]

It was the Presocratics, however, who started to think universally about the nature of things and rise above ideas based on mere assertions, religious authority, or sensory observations, offering general explanations for the causes of things. Their key idea was that there is a *logos*, a ratio, a principle, a measure in the world that can be accounted for by human reason through explanations and arguments, and that one can apprehend this rational order in the world, not with the senses or by accepting what gods supposedly commanded, but by looking within one's mind, and discovering therein the presence of this *logos*, which is common to all things. As Hegel wrote in the opening paragraph of his *Philosophy of Mind*:

> The significance of that "absolute" commandment, *know thyself*, whether we look at it in itself or under the historical circumstances of its first utterance is not to promote mere self-knowledge in respect of the particular capacities, character, propensities, and foibles of the single self. The knowledge it commands means that of man's genuine reality—of what is essentially and ultimately true and real—of mind as the true and essential being.[24]

The interpretation I am offering here does not at all preclude the role of a whole range of factors, long and short term, geographical, demographic, economic, biological, and political, including unintended consequences, many of which I surveyed in my book *The Uniqueness of Western Civilization*. It implicitly recognizes, or takes as a given, the inescapable complexity of history, the permanent presence of background conditions—environment and racial characteristics—the influence of other civilizations, and accidental occurrences.

This book does not argue either that the discovery of consciousness or that the possibility of generating universal values for humanity necessarily entailed, since ancient times, the current ethnocidal tendencies of Europeans. It does suggest, nevertheless, particularly in Chapters X and XI, that there is an immanent "emancipatory" logic in Western culture, in its drive to create "self-determining" humans freed from all pre-given norms and collective constraints; and it does argue that we can't explain the current diversity regime without understanding the West's unique emphasis on the generation of "unbiased" and "unprejudicial"

---

[23] Zeruneith, 2007.
[24] Hegel, 1830/1971, 1.

values. The phrase *Know thyself* works well as the gravitational point around which to understand both the unparalleled cultural creativity of Europe, and why this civilization is now exhibiting ethnocidal tendencies.

The approach taken in this text can be identified as historiographical and scholastic, meaning that the arguments are developed by way of a rigorous textual analysis of the major sources used in support of the thesis, and of the major sources and arguments that must be disputed to make way for the validity of my thesis. Key components of the thesis expressed in this book, and related subsidiary arguments, are immanent or implicitly contained in various known scholarly books, with my task consisting in drawing these ideas out in a conscious and systematic fashion, as well as re-interpreting these texts/ideas within the larger explanatory framework outlined above. The problem with these scholarly sources is that they either have a very limited time-scale grasp of the rise of the West, or their preoccupation is not with the West as such, but with other subjects, such as the evolution of autonoetic consciousness, the Presocratic discovery of *logos*, the origins of the modern self, the rise of the novel, the contribution of Christianity to the rise of liberalism, or the theory of liberal pluralism. For this reason, they tend to miss the big picture, how their ideas and findings can be connected to construct a more comprehensive account.

The questions this text addresses inherently require a long-term perspective, unafraid to crisscross many disciplinary fields. Too many subjects remain the purview of specialized scholars who, rather arrogantly, believe that one needs to remain a specialized expert to make sense of what they do, and in order to acquire a proper perspective of the whole. For many decades they have been telling us that we need to accumulate more specialized studies to understand the bigger picture. The actual scenario today is that specialized experts on the history of the West can barely make sense of their own findings beyond the narrow confines of their field. What is needed is a synthesis. The "great divergence" of the West occurred in all the spheres of cultural life with deep roots in history and continuously through many centuries. This is not to endorse a reductionist approach that reduces what comes later to what happened earlier. The argument presented here is fully cognizant of newly emergent cultural traits and what I call the "continuous discontinuities" of Western cultural history. My hope is that Europeans will re-appreciate what it means to *Know thyself*, and seek thereby to understand their own history, in order that they may learn to know what is driving them to reject this history and find solutions therein before it is too late.

I

ON THE NATURE AND ORIGINS OF CONSCIOUSNESS

Reflection is, as the word indicates, the power acquired by a consciousness to turn in upon itself, to take possession of itself as of an object . . . no longer merely to know, but to know that one knows. . . . The being who is the object of his own reflection, in consequence of doubling back upon himself, becomes in a flash able to raise himself into a new sphere. In reality another world is born. Abstraction, logic, reasoned choice and inventions, mathematics, art, calculation of space and times, anxieties and dreams of love—all these activities of inner life are nothing else than the effervescence of the newly-formed center as it explodes onto itself.

– Teilhard de Chardin, *The Phenomenon of Man*

Current State of the Debate

What is consciousness? This is possibly the most intriguing question one can ask. How could mental states, or deeply felt subjective feelings, such as hunger, fear, love, regret, depression, boredom, be produced by physical brain processes? When in evolutionary history did living organisms exhibit behaviors suggesting they had "minds" with an awareness that there is a boundary between "me" experiencing these feelings and thoughts, and, on the other, "not-me" or an "out there beyond my internal states"? Philosophers of the mind use the term "qualia" to

13

refer to these bodily sensations (having a stomach ache), or to these emotions (feeling remorse). No one quite denies that there are qualia, or that people are sincere when they say: "I am conscious of my feeling jealousy." But philosophers agree that it is precisely their nature as qualia—that we can only know about our mental states and feelings introspectively—that generates complicated or even insurmountable epistemological and ontological questions.[25] To be aware of one's own feelings and thoughts is to be aware of something that is private and subjective, pure mental stuff unobservable by the public, and thus lacking a reality that is amenable to the third-person point of view that scientific knowledge requires.

This is the source of the perennial mind-body problem: how can we even have a proper discourse about immaterial, first-person mental states, when the acquisition of objective knowledge requires that the phenomena studied be completely objective? How could one get the qualitative content of such conscious experiences as seeing red and feeling pain out of a collection of chemical neural firings in the brain? Given this ontological gap between *res cogitans* and *res extensa*, many philosophers over the centuries have tended to embrace the hypothesis of dualism, which asserts that the universe consists of two distinct but closely joined substances, matter and consciousness, without quite explaining how these two very different substances interact with each other.

However, the most popular approach over the last decades has been to cast doubt on the very existence of subjective mental states. Our vocabulary of belief, desire, fear, hope, they tell us, has misguided us into believing that these words actually stand for a reality that is intrinsically immaterial or subjective. Qualitative, first-person states, are really expressions of brain states, which scientists will eventually explain. This perspective is known as eliminative materialism or physicalism, which is the idea that "all of reality is objective," and that there are no mental processes, just brain processes.[26] These brain processes are yet to be known with precision and completeness, and that is why we think they are subjective and accessible only through introspection. With new research in evolution, genetics, and neuroscience, this school argues, it will be possible eventually to demonstrate that mental states are reducible to physical processes.[27] The notion that we have mental states is derived from folk psychology, or from habitual ways of speaking and ways of making sense of our mental states due to a lack of scientific knowledge

---

[25] Tye, 2021.
[26] Armstrong, 1968.
[27] Churchland, 1988.

of brain states. With the development of neuropsychology, everyday notions like "beliefs" or "feelings" will be abandoned among experts for more evidence-based physiological accounts.

Yet, after decades of research about the nature of neural transmissions (notwithstanding the enormous gains attained in our understanding of the structure of the brain), no one has been able to capture the qualitative content of a person's conscious experience from the study of that person's publicly observable causal relations between neurons in his/her brain. Another influential materialist research project developed by cognitive psychologists over the last decades is that we should think of the mind, in the words of Steven Pinker, as a "a neural computer, fitted by natural selection with combinatorial algorithms for causal and probabilistic reasoning about plants, animals, objects, and people."[28] Qualia, it is argued, are "ineffable" and cannot be communicated, measured, and studied objectively with the methods of the sciences. Therefore, the appropriate scientific stand, according to materialists such as Daniel C. Dennett, is to take a computational view of the human mind, wherein consciousness is defined as a "system of virtual machines" that evolved genetically and then culturally, and is amenable to scientific-mathematical analysis from a third-person perspective. We shall see that this perspective is incapable of recognizing how uniquely important was the European act of reflectively looking inward into one's consciousness and examining one's own thoughts and feelings.

John Searle on the "Irreducibly Subjective Ontology" of Mental States

Let's dig deeper into this debate by evaluating the major perspectives on the nature of consciousness, its undirected evolution by natural selection involving competent or cognitive organisms, and its cultural evolution through purposeful self-examination of one's interior self. An excellent starting point is John Searle, famously known for his "Chinese Room Argument."[29] The mental states of

---

[28] Pinker, 1997, 524.

[29] This argument, first presented in 1980, is intended to refute the theory that human minds are computer-like information processing systems. Searle imagines being in a room by himself without any knowledge of the meaning of Chinese symbols, yet with tools that allow him to manipulate Chinese symbols in a correct syntactical manner, just like a computer that takes a string of symbols as inputs, follows the instructions of the computer program, and then responds correctly with symbols as outputs. Does Searle really understand Chinese merely because he uses

humans, Searle argues, "have an irreducibly subjective ontology" entailing a first-person point of view, which is utterly lacking in computers. As he writes in *The Rediscovery of the Mind*:

> Because mental phenomena are essentially connected with consciousness, and because consciousness is essentially subjective, it follows that the ontology of the mental is essentially a first-person ontology. Mental states are always somebody's mental states. There is always a "first person," an "I," that has these mental states.[30]

Searle, however, does not endorse a dualist position. He believes that "mental states and processes are as much part of our biological natural history as digestion, mitosis, meiosis, or enzyme secretion."[31] "Humans are continuous with the rest of nature," and "their greater intelligence, their capacity for language, their capacity for extremely fine perceptual discriminations, their capacity for rational thought, etc.—are biological phenomena like any other biological phenomena."[32] The only difference is that "conscious mental states . . . have a special feature not possessed by other natural phenomena, namely, subjectivity." This subjective quality makes the study of consciousness "recalcitrant to the conventional methods of biological and psychological research."[33]

Nevertheless, Searle adds, since consciousness "is a biological feature of human and certain animal brains," and "it is caused by neurobiological processes," its origins can be explained in terms of the evolution of animals and humans—so long as it is understood that at some point in this evolutionary history, conscious mental states, which are inherently "first person" features of the brain, did emerge.[34] But Searle does not get into the question of when consciousness emerged, or when in the course of evolution it would be reasonable to say that we have first person experiences. His preoccupation is with thoroughly refuting physicalist and computational treatments of the mental as objective phenomena, and to insist that mental phenomena are intrinsically and irreducibly subjective,

---

syntactic rules to manipulate symbol strings without understanding the meaning or semantics of the Chinese language? See Searle, 1980.

[30] Searle, 1994, 20.

[31] Ibid, 1.

[32] Ibid, 90.

[33] Ibid, 93.

[34] Ibid, 90.

ontologically different from every other natural phenomenon we know about, inaccessible to an external third person observer.

Searle, however, never really considers whether there are different degrees of consciousness in the evolutionary timescale of organisms, or, indeed, in the cultural evolution of humans themselves. Sometimes he gives the impression that we can speak of consciousness as long as we can intuit that a living being has inward sensory experiences involving tastes, smells, and pains. He does not emphasize the importance of conscious intentions and awareness of the act of reasoning in his description of first-person acts of consciousness. He does not distinguish explicitly, as neuropsychologist Nicholas Humphrey does in his book, *A History of the Mind: Evolution and the Birth of Consciousness*, between consciousness as raw sensation, or as sentient responses to external stimuli, and conscious insight into our subjective feelings and sensations, and thoughts about thoughts. Humphrey identifies the latter as "second order mental faculties" that involve "abstract reasoning, language, self-identity, social intelligence."[35] In contrast, he identifies raw sensations such as tastes and sounds as "first order" inner experiences that can be attributed to organisms generally, not just humans, as sentient beings.

Still, Searle recognizes that "any introspection" of one's conscious state "is itself that conscious state."[36] In other words, consciousness necessarily entails consciousness of one's feelings and thoughts, thoughts about thoughts. It is "the ultimate absurdity," he writes, "to treat consciousness independently of consciousness,"[37] that is, to treat it without postulating an "I" that is conscious of his subjective states. He recognizes, moreover, that "the structure" of our conscious states is such that "they come to us as part of a unified sequence."[38] We are not aware of isolated sensory feelings and thoughts each standing on their own, but are aware of ourselves as a unitary "I" that is experiencing a sequence of mental states through a temporal dimension; and we are also simultaneously aware "of all the diverse features of any conscious state." He mentions in this respect Kant's concept of "transcendental unity of apperception," a concept that points to a unified sense of self as the agent of many simultaneous inner experiences differing in both time and topic. Consciousness, in other words, entails a sense of awareness as the same identical self or person that persists through time experiencing a continuous sequence of mental states.

---

[35] Humphrey, 1992, 18
[36] Searle, 97.
[37] Ibid, 20.
[38] Ibid, 129.

However, as will be argued in this chapter, and elaborated at length in subsequent ones, the existence of a self that is not only having first person mental states, but is conscious of being a person having first person mental states, and is thus conscious of his consciousness, is a cultural achievement of Western peoples, which should not be projected onto humans as such. Consciousness becomes "explicitly or for itself the concept of itself," to use Hegel's language, when humans acquire personhood, and are thus aware of themselves as the agents doing the thinking about their consciousness. Humans are not automatically or naturally conscious of their mental states as *their* mental states. They are not naturally aware that their mental states are their own subjective internal experiences. Consciousness is not merely "a biological feature of the human brain," or a mere product of evolution, as Searle claims, but a product of cultural evolution, and a peculiarly Western cultural product.

Udo Thiel on Modern Self-Consciousness

I can't think of one expert in the study of consciousness who has ever pondered over this historical possibility: that only Europeans, a select few at the top, in the course of time, in varying degrees and ways, became conscious of their conscious states as their own internally generated states. Even academics writing about consciousness and selfhood "within a historical context" are unmindful of how singular this discussion is to the West and how this discussion changed over the course of Western history. The discussions are framed instead as if they were philosophical debates among different philosophers with different viewpoints about the nature of consciousness and personhood.

We will be encountering here quite a few of these academics; consider for now Udo Thiel's book *The Early Modern Subject: Self-Consciousness and Personal Identity from Descartes to Hume*. This well-grafted, scholarly book argues that discussions about "human . . . awareness or consciousness of one's self," and of one's own self as the same identical self or person that persists through time emerged, in varying and contesting ways, in the writings of modern philosophers, most prominently Descartes, Locke, Leibniz, Hume, Spinoza, Berkeley, Malebranche, Bayle, and Pufendorf, starting in the seventeenth century through to the first half of the eighteenth century. It is not that Thiel is unaware that interest in self-consciousness and personhood have been peculiarly Western discussions, characteristic of the modern era. Thiel explicitly says that discussions during this period are always about self-consciousness in the sense of consciousness of one's mental states. He contrasts these discussions to ancient and medieval notions of the person as an "individual substance of a rational nature," and of a person as a role or function.[39] He identifies Locke's view in particular as revolutionary. For Locke, personal identity entails "a thinking intelligent Being that has reason and reflection, and can consider itself as itself, [as] the same thinking thing in different times and places."[40] This view of personal identity, Thiel judges, was a direct challenge to the old Platonic (and even Cartesian) conception of man defined as an unchanging soul, or immaterial substance. Personal identity, for Locke, involved thinking self-reflectively and knowing oneself as the thinking being within a particular spatial-temporal location.

Yet Thiel, like the other academics we have mentioned, and others to be mentioned below, thinks of discussions about the emergence of self-consciousness as if they were philosophical positions among other positions expressed by different philosophers, without apprehending the strictly European context out of which these discussions emerged and developed over time. Thiel gets into all sorts of specialized debates as to whether Leibniz, for example, was an immaterialist or a realist, or both; or whether Hume was dissatisfied with the whole section on personal identity, or whether Locke's theory is compatible with the transitivity of identity. But he never stops to consider why it was that Europeans were reaching these new views about the self in the 1600s and 1700s. He writes about "philosophers" thinking about "human" consciousness in the abstract. This is also how the philosophers he examines in his book approach the subject, using the terms "human," "man," and "consciousness" as such. But this is not how we, today, after a thorough comparative awareness of the respective historical paths of the civilizations of the world, should think about this debate on consciousness.

The Evolution of Consciousness by Natural Selection

Every academic involved in this debate lacks this historical perspective about the unique consciousness of Western man. They assume that discussions about first person awareness are natural to humans *qua* humans, or natural to humans in all cultures, without realizing, or daring to realize, that these discussions

---

[39] Thiel, 2011.
[40] Gordon-Roth, 2020

occurred only in the West, and that Westerners discussed these issues in different terms depending on the historical context, namely the degree to which Westerners themselves had become aware that consciousness entails awareness of what passes inside one's own mind. The historical awareness exhibited by academics who discuss this issue is limited to the biological evolution of consciousness. I agree that this genetic evolutionary perspective is crucially necessary, but it is hardly sufficient.

There is indeed a growing, if not already well-established belief, that the only way to explain the nature of consciousness is to look back at how it evolved naturally, step by step, from its beginnings. Since the brain is a product of evolutionary processes, it is argued, and consciousness is impossible without a brain, or some kind of complex cellular structure, it is possible to start to understand the nature of consciousness by thinking of it as an evolutionary adaptation that evolved in complexity in the degree to which increasing "self-awareness" conferred greater coordination and flexibility to the behavior of organisms in their struggle for survival and reproduction. There is no consensus, however, as to when the biological capacity for consciousness likely appeared in the evolutionary timeline, because there is no generally accepted theory as to when animals started to think about their mental states, or what consciousness really entails. There is a major divide between those who identify consciousness with a mere "first-order representation" and those who identify it with second order or higher order mental activities. But the difficulty does not end there, for there are varying levels of complexity (in the evolutionary history of living things) of first order representation and higher order mental states.

Some evolutionary psychologists, such as Arthur Reber and František Baluška, have posited a "cellular-based model" according to which "life and consciousness are coterminous."[41] All organisms from unicellular to humans are "sentient" beings capable of sensing "inwardly" the external world and responding to it. While human consciousness is more complex, it is not "special and epistemically distinct from the forms of cognition expressed in other species." "Consciousness denotes a continuum of subjectivity, awareness—and not a mental state that only (or mainly) humans are privy to."[42] The most basic cell, prokaryotes, known to have evolved some 3.5 years ago, were sentient beings with "the first minds" marked by feelings of attraction or aversion, perceptual functions, with "stable memories"

---

[41] Reber and Baluška, 2019.
[42] Reber and Baluška, 2023.

and a capacity to "learn" simple patterns, anticipate upcoming events and "communicate with each other using distinct molecular messengers that are modified to match the circumstances." They also had a capacity to "evaluate the nutrient content of molecules," to react adaptively to toxic substances, and to make a "distinction between a subjective interior and objective exterior."[43]

But there are other first order theorists who believe that an organism can be said to exhibit consciousness only when it has a centralized nervous system, or a sufficiently developed cranial capacity to combine and process multiple sensory inputs, capable of storing and "memorizing" patterns of information from past experiences, modifying behavior through conditioning, and engaging in "deliberation" over different behavioral responses and outcomes. This is the basic argument that Todd Feinberg and John Mallatt articulate in *The Ancient Origins of Consciousness: How the Brain Created Experience*. They agree, in part, that the seeds of consciousness lie in the very origins of life on Earth; and that single-celled creatures behave as if they have a sense of bodily integrity which allows them to detect the difference between themselves and something that is "not-self." But they insist that this is "sensory consciousness," not real consciousness. Consciousness comes with the emergence of primitive brains combining a previously dispersed nervous system into a tight cluster of interconnected nerve cells with a capacity to store and recall experience, which they believe is evidence of real learning and memory. They date this transition to the great "Cambrian explosion" of novel life forms that occurred about 520 to 560 million years ago.

Consciousness emerged as new life forms (predatory carnivores in particular) evolved beyond earlier life forms, which were essentially vegetarian, grazing on the great oceanic beds of algae. The new life forms of the Cambrian period hunted for food, which required new skills and sharper senses, which exerted evolutionary pressures for new defense mechanisms among the vegetarians. This evolutionary arms race selected for bigger and better brains, enhanced senses, and faster motor coordination, leading to the rise of brains and consciousness. Feinberg and Mallatt believe that all vertebrates (fish, reptile, amphibian, and bird) are conscious, though they suggest that arthropods (including insects) and cephalopods (including the octopus) meet many of the criteria for consciousness, which they define as the ability of an animal to have a unified inner world of perceptual experiences, and thus a sense of a unified "self" as distinct from the external world.

High order theorists, however, believe that conscious awareness occurs only

---

[43] Ibid.

when first-order sensory information is "re-represented by the higher-order network involving areas of the prefrontal cortex," which is the forward-most area of the human brain. This is the argument of Joseph LeDoux's extensively researched book, *The Deep History of Ourselves: The Four-Billion-Year Story of How We Got Conscious Brains.*

One of the best qualities of this deservedly praised book is that it accepts the key claims of "first order" theorists as it goes about explaining major evolutionary steps from the first living organisms to the origins of early humans some two hundred and fifty thousand years ago. He does not underestimate the "robust behavioral life" exhibited by single-cell organisms, despite lacking a nervous system: their ability to "even learn from experience what is useful and harmful in their world," with evidence showing that bacteria are capable of memory-like "internal molecular representations of environmental conditions (temperature, oxygen levels)" to predict future environmental conditions "so that they can respond appropriately." "Learning and memory do not require a nervous system."[44] But while LeDoux says that this behavior by microorganisms (and plants) "can be said to be cognitive," since it "involves information processing," which one may define as "intelligent," he carefully explains why human consciousness, defined as "reflective self-awareness," is fundamentally different.

LeDoux is not persuaded either by the claim that consciousness is evident with the advent of nervous systems during the Cambrian period, even as he acknowledges that the integration and storage of exogenous signals in nerve cells (to be recalled in response to new or unrelated stimuli) "made learning much more sophisticated and flexible." He contrasts as well the "goal-directed instrumental cognition and model-based cognitive deliberation" found among mammals and primates with the conscious deliberation of humans, with their capacity for language. While the goal-directed responses of mammals, which involve "the learning of a novel behavior on the basis of the value of its consequences," is on a higher level than the Pavlovian stimulus-response habits of reptiles, the deliberation of humans is on "another level altogether."[45]

Primates do have "greater facility with deliberation to solve problems," but without language they lack the capacity to "categorize objects and events" and organize their mental processes with syntax, or grammar, and "the capacity to flexibly use sounds or visual symbols to spontaneously indicate things about the

---

[44] Ledoux, 2019, 3, 42–43
[45] Ibid, 225–233.

present, past, and/or future." Although language is not required for cognition, cognition with language makes possible "abstract conceptual thought, hierarchical relational reasoning, and pattern processing."[46] And it is the prefrontal area of the brain, which is uniquely human, that is responsible for language. Studies in cognitive neuroscience have shown that this area of the brain underlies higher-order awareness, with neural states of first-order networks in the non-prefrontal areas "viewed as nonconscious representations that are rendered conscious when re-represented by the higher-order network involving areas of the prefrontal cortex."[47] Expressed differently, the prefrontal cortex, which is engaged "in the highest levels of abstract conceptualization of any brain area . . . actively *re-represents* the sensory cortex information and transforms the non-conscious sensory representation into a conscious experience."

The prefrontal cortex affords humans with "an awareness of you, the experiencing person, as part of the experience."[48] It is likewise the basis for the conceptualization of the difference between self and the not-self, and thus for self-awareness, "knowing that an 'I' exists and the sensations and images exist within 'me.'"[49] This capacity is what allows humans to talk in terms of first-person experiences. LeDoux uses the term "autonoetic consciousness" to designate this "awareness of one's self as the subject and owner" of one's subjective feelings and mental states, and the ability to envision "one's self in different possible future scenarios."[50] Primates may have some high order representation in having some awareness of perceptual or memory representations, but they lack autonoetic consciousness or the ability to mentally place their selves in the past and future, and in alternative outcomes or counterfactual situations, which is crucial to the formation of a conception of selfhood.

My disagreement with LeDoux is that a concept of self and a capacity for autonoetic consciousness is to a considerable measure a Western cultural achievement, rather than a mere product of natural selection and the evolution of *Homo sapiens*. Only momentarily, or in passing, does LeDoux seem to recognize that "the concept of 'self' one has is dependent to a significant degree on the psychological conceptions that are embedded in his or her culture and native language." But after this brief remark, he quickly reaffirms his central argument that "culture

---

[46] Ibid, 236.
[47] Brown et al., 2019.
[48] Ibid, 296.
[49] Ibid, 298.
[50] Ibid, 329.

is made possible by the unique human cognitive system" with its "autonoetic consciousness."[51] In other words, all cultures exhibit the same "autonoetic consciousness." One can say that culture, broadly defined, is made possible by the evolutionary abilities of humans, but, as we will see, there are fundamentally different levels of intellectual attainment, which are reflective of different levels of consciousness. Only in the West, starting in ancient Greece, do we witness an extremely rich written culture with an emerging conception of self and a relatively high degree of autonoetic consciousness.

LeDoux is willing to identify increasing levels of mental complexity and sophistication in the evolution of species, but when it comes to culture, he follows the mandated view that all cultures are more or less the same. Yet, unbeknownst to him, he imposes a Western conception of self-consciousness on cultures generally. While he frequently warns us about the need to avoid an "anthropocentric" perspective that imposes our human mental and inner emotional attributes onto animals, he falls prey to what Joseph Henrich observes in *The WEIRDest People in the World*: the prevailing assumption in psychology that the "patterns and dimensions of personality observed" among Americans and Europeans "represent the human pattern."[52] This book by Henrich, even though it is not a discussion of the nature of consciousness or the mind-body problem, is packed with *cross-cultural* experimental studies demonstrating that the psychological profiles of Westerners are dramatically different from that of non-Westerners in degree of analytical thinking, awareness of the distinction between self and kinship group, ability to distinguish internal mental representations from objects, and other key traits. Henrich's book will be the subject of a long discussion in Chapter VII.

It may be countered that LeDoux's book is strictly about "tracking the chain of the evolutionary timeline" and the origins and nature of human autonoetic consciousness, without any concern about intellectual achievements among civilized peoples. This is not true. The implicit argument (and sometimes explicitly stated view) of his book is that the emergence of human consciousness "made our greatest achievements as a species possible"—in "art, music, architecture, literature, science."[53] It is his view that humans with "new capacities and ways of existing and interacting with one another—language; hierarchical relational reasoning; representation of self versus other; mental time travel," were already existing

---

[51] Ledoux, 2019, 296.
[52] Henrich, 2020.
[53] Ledoux, 2019, 372.

sometime "between fifty thousand and two hundred thousand years ago." Yet, the historical reality is that humans barely accomplished much intellectually for thousands of years after this capacity supposedly emerged via natural selection.

Steven Mithen and the Origins of Cognitive Fluidity

What's the point of having consciousness if it merely allows for the invention of a few tools and elementary symbolic forms of communication without any actual writing and, indeed, without any textual or literary evidence showing that humans were actually self-aware of themselves as the agents of their thoughts and actions, but were instead mentally "childlike," as shown by the cross-cultural empirical research of Jean Piaget and his followers? We shall see in the next chapters that the cognitive level of humans even in "advanced" agrarian civilizations (except the West) remained at the perceptual level, that is, bound up with the sensory appearances of the world, barely transcending context-bound experiences, incapable of counter-factual reasoning, and even without the ability to disentangle mental from bodily functions, subjective feelings about things from their objective properties, and without any awareness that one's inner thoughts are separate from the collective representations of the tribal group.

What makes Steven Mithen's book, *The Prehistory of the Mind: The Cognitive Origins of Art and Science* (1996), very important is that it immediately frames the question on the emergence of human cognition in terms of actual cultural accomplishments. We will see, nevertheless, that Mithen refuses to go beyond the Upper Paleolithic period in his effort to identify when the distinguishing features of the human mind arose. He refuses to rank the cognitive abilities of cultures thereafter, but instead wants us to believe that among Upper Paleolithic humans we may have witnessed the highest "cognitive fluidity" in history, above that of modern Westerners!

Mithen is a renowned Professor of Archaeology, Fellow of the British Academy, and author of the popular book, *The Singing Neanderthals: The Origins of Music, Language, Mind, and Body* (2007). But it is his theory of cognitive fluidity in *The Prehistory of the Mind* that has attracted the attention of scholars interested in the nature of consciousness. Although this book is not about the mind-body problem, or the nature of consciousness as a first-person attribute, his view of cognitive fluidity presupposes consciousness of one's thoughts. It synthesizes a considerable body of literature to argue that humans became conscious sometime between 60,000 and 30,000 years ago. *Homo sapiens,* the first modern humans, appeared 100,000 years ago, but only 40,000 years later did human consciousness arise. Mithen infers that consciousness emerged in this period, the Upper Paleolithic era, because of the incredible cultural and technological efflorescence witnessed during this relatively short period after some million years of stagnation since *Homo erectus* invented the handaxe.

Between 2 and 1.5 million years ago, *Homo habilis, H. rudolfensis,* and *H. ergaster* managed to create stone hand choppers with a brain size between 500 and 800 cc. Between 1.8 and 400,000 years ago, *H. erectus,* with a brain ranging between 750 and 1250 cc, managed to create stone handaxes. This handaxe would remain the core technology until the Upper Paleolithic revolution. Between 400,000 and 100,000 years ago, archaic *H. sapiens* and *H. heidelbergensis,* with a larger brain size of about 1100–1400 cc, continued to create the same stone handaxes. So did *H. neanderthalensis,* who appeared in Europe about 150,000 years ago, with a brain size of 1200–1750 cc, though the handaxes were built with a new "Levallois" technique for removing flakes. And so did modern *H. sapiens,* who appeared around 100,000 years ago, with basically the same brain size—he, too, used handaxes, though there are "hints of something new," the "very first tools of materials other than stone and wood."[54]

It was only about 60,000 years ago, "with no apparent change in brain size, shape or anatomy in general," that humanity, in Mithen's estimation, witnessed a "cultural explosion." Blade production started on a "systematic scale," often chipped as projectile points, and bone was carved to make points and awls, harpoons and needles, designed for specific purposes. The first art objects also appear after 40,000 years ago: beads, necklaces, and pendants are made from ivory; figurines are carved, and abstract and naturalistic images are painted and engraved on cave walls.

Why this sudden explosion if brain size remained the same and human beings, modern *H. sapiens,* had already been around for tens of thousands of years? Mithen draws on the findings of cognitive psychologists to argue that the Upper Paleolithic revolution was the result of a change in the architecture of the mind, characterized by a new ability to make connections between previously separate cognitive modules. Mithen relies heavily on Howard Gardner's popular 1983 book, *Frames of Mind: The Theory of Multiple Intelligences*; Jerry Fodor's well respected idea in *The Modularity of the Mind* (1983), that the human mind is

---

[54] Mithen, 1996.

composed of "modular" domains of intelligence; Jerome H. Barkow, Leda Cosmides, and John Tooby's 1992 book, *The Adapted Mind*, a foundational text
known for its integration of evolutionary biology and cognitive psychology; and
on Nicholas Humphrey's *The Inner Eye* (1986)—to construct the argument that,
in the course of evolution, starting with the ancestral ape some 6–4.5 million years
ago, through the first australopithecines dating to 4.5–1.8 million years ago, to the
first members of the *Homo* lineage 2 million years ago, all the way to *H. sapiens*, a
variety of intelligences evolved in complexity.

Mithen first sees a "general intelligence, which includes modules for trial-and-
error learning, and associative learning" among ancestral apes (and contemporary
chimpanzees).[55] This is an all-purpose intelligence used for survival involving for-
aging decisions, tool use, and basic sensory perception of the environment. In the
course of evolution, specialized modules of intelligence began to emerge over and
above the all-purpose intelligence: social (managing interpersonal relationships),
linguistic (production and comprehension of language), natural history (understanding cause and effect in the natural world), and technical (manipulation of
objects) intelligences.

Mithen agrees with evolutionary psychologists Cosmides and Tooby that "we
can only understand the nature of the modern mind by viewing it as a product of
biological evolution." He likes their metaphor of the human mind as a Swiss army
knife "with a great many, highly specialized blades," each of which was "designed
by natural selection to cope with one specific adaptive problem." These blades or
modules are "hard-wired into the mind at birth and universal among all people."[56]
But this Swiss knife metaphor, he thinks, can only take us so far in understanding
the *H. sapiens* mind that emerges during the Upper Paleolithic era. This was a
mind with a new architecture capable of making analogical connections between
the linguistic, social, natural history, and technical intelligences.

The first specialized intelligence Mithen detects among our ancestral apes is
an emerging module for "social intelligence," defined as the ability to predict the
behavior of others in order to augment our reproductive success. Among primates, this social intelligence module was already highly evolved, in the way primates actually use "deception and the construction of alliances and friendships"
in the pursuit of reproductive success, exhibiting "extensive social knowledge
about . . . allies and friends, and the ability to infer the mental states of those

---

[55] Ibid, 88.
[56] Ibid, 42–43.

individuals."[57] Mithen draws this idea from Humphrey's book, *The Inner Eye*. This short, insightful book argues that the onset of consciousness can be traced back to the ability of monkeys and apes to read the behavior, feelings, or mental states of other members from within their groups, in the pursuit of status and mating. Humphrey thinks that the ability to read the minds of others necessarily entails imagining what it is like to be in the shoes of other members of the group, and that it therefore entails a capacity to self-examine one's interior thoughts and feelings.[58] This "social intelligence" was selected by nature because it enhanced the ability of primates (he emphasizes monkeys and gorillas) to survive within social settings characterized by "endless small disputes about social dominance, about who grooms who, about who should have first access to a favourite food, or sleep in the best site." In dealing with these issues, primates "have to think, remember, calculate, and weigh things up inside their heads."[59] They have to learn to read the brains of other gorillas by looking inside their own brains, which means that they have to be "introspective."

We can see indeed that this concept of social intelligence is close to the idea that consciousness is all about being aware of one's subjective mental states, and that the act of introspecting one's mental states is, by its very nature, an act of self-consciousness. However, while Mithen agrees with Humphrey that our ancestral apes already had a "conscious awareness of their own minds," he believes that full self-awareness only comes with modern *H. sapiens*, when all the other modules are fully evolved and the mind acquires an ability to make analogical connections between all the intelligences.

There are signs of an incipient natural history intelligence among chimps. This intelligence is about perceiving the migratory movements and behavioral traits of other animals, and predicting resource locations and scavenging opportunities. Chimps have detailed knowledge of the spatial distribution of resources and the ripening cycles of many plants; however, they don't exhibit a "creative or insightful use of that knowledge." Their natural history intelligence appears to flow out of "rote memory," or what LeDoux would identify as habitual cognition, without language and without autonoetic consciousness. Mithen thinks that tool use by chimpanzees suggests that they had evolved a specialized module for technical intelligence; however, this intelligence was still rooted in their all-purpose general

---

[57] Ibid, 82–83.
[58] Humphrey, 1986, 65.
[59] Ibid, 37–39.

intelligence, characterized by trial and error. True technical intelligence is exhibited in the ability to manipulate and transform natural objects into manufactured tools with a conceptual grasp of the physical properties of objects.

Once we get to the Neanderthals, we have highly specialized modules for all the intelligences, including a brain with the same size as contemporary humans. But there is a dilemma: Neanderthals remained extremely conservative in their technology. Why did they ignore bone, antler, and ivory as raw materials? Why did they fail to makes tools for specific purposes, and multicomponent tools? Why did they lack any beliefs in supernatural beings and art? Mithen's answer is there was no "cognitive fluidity" between their social, technical, linguistic, and natural intelligences. Only during the Upper Paleolithic era did the intelligences begin to function seamlessly together. Neanderthals could not make tools from bone, antler, or ivory because they had conceptualized only stone objects (transformed into handaxes) within the domain of technical intelligence. It was only after the domains of natural and technical intelligences began to communicate with each other, that modern *H. sapiens* came to conceptualize the idea that animal materials could be subjected to cognitive processes previously limited to the technical domain. Making specific tools for specific tasks—say, projectiles to kill deer—required not only technical intelligence, but also natural history thinking about the deer's anatomy, migratory movements, and hide thickness. Likewise, Neanderthals did not make artifacts for body decoration, such as beads and perforated animal teeth, because their minds lacked fluidity between the social and the technical/natural history modules, and thus they lacked the ability to understand that body decoration could be used to communicate social status and group affiliation.

Social Intelligence = Introspection = Cognitive Fluidity

H. erectus, Neanderthals, and other early humans were as socially intelligent and as Machiavellian in their tactics to gain social advantage as modern humans. But what's revealing is that, according to Mithen, it was the integration of social intelligence with the other intelligences that eventually allowed for the rise of cognitive fluidity, which shows that Humphrey was on the right track to emphasize social intelligence as the module where consciousness is located, even though the research on animal intelligence does not seem to support his view that primates evolved a capacity for self-recognition and self-examination of their mental states.

This capacity for self-examination of one's inner thoughts, Mithen explains, is first found among Upper Paleolithic peoples when all the intelligences were combined under the leadership of a social intelligence with an evolved capacity for self-examination. From *Homo habilis* through to the Neanderthals, social intelligence remained isolated from the intelligence needed to manufacture tools or to interact with the natural environment. Without the combination of an introspective social intelligence with the other intelligences, the other modules could only exhibit a fleeting form of consciousness, for only when individuals started to self-examine their own mental processes, say, about their methods of making tools or hunting, did they really start to reflect critically about these behaviors beyond habitual repetition or simple associative learning.

Now, the emergence of a social intelligence that goes beyond a capacity for recognizing others, as is the case with primates, towards a capacity for recognizing one's internal thoughts, Mithen adds, is intimately associated with the emergence of linguistic intelligence or language, which evolved as the size of hominid groups increased and as social interactions became more complicated. Individuals with better communication skills were selected for their advantage in developing better sounds of communication; that is, better ways to acquire social knowledge about other individuals and about allies and enemies in the pursuit of sexual favors and status. This linguistic aspect of social intelligence allowed for deeper communication and reasoning with others, as well as introspection, about the domains of technical and natural history intelligence, which is what the Neanderthals lacked. This explains "the monotony of industrial traditions, the absence of tools made from bone and ivory, the absence of art" among Neanderthals. But once the domains of technical and natural history intelligence were opened to the domains of social intelligence, with its introspective nature, there was a "cultural explosion," a "frenzy of activity, with more innovation than in the previous 6 million years of human evolution."[60]

We may indeed infer, though Mithen does not do so, that the natural history and technical intelligences are examples of cognition, not consciousness per se, and that it was only the growth of social intelligence and linguistic competence (leading to the emergence of introspection) that brought these two cognitive capacities to a state of consciousness and fluidity. As Searle says, consciousness should not be confused with cognition, or intelligent behavior. Many organisms exhibit complex information processing behaviors, as LeDoux shows, which can

---

[60] Mithen, 1996, 150–152.

be categorized as "intelligent behavior," and observed from a third person per-spective, analyzed with the methods of the natural sciences, but they are not con-scious, insofar as these organisms don't direct their consciousness at their own mental/cognitive states. The same is true of artificial intelligence and the neuronal structure of the brain. Their cognitive mechanisms can be studied from a third person perspective. But the self-examination of one's mental states and feelings is irreducibly subjective.

Now, I am persuaded by Marc Hauser's research in *Wild Minds: What Animals Really Think* (2000), that primates lack a "capacity to understand what it's like to have a sense of self, to have unique and personal mental states and emo-tional experiences."[61] But I also believe that Upper Paleolithic peoples also lacked this capacity. Of course, the biological-neurological preconditions for conscious-ness emerged over the course of millions of years, and one may use the word "proto-conscious" behaviors in reference to many animals and certainly in refer-ence to *Homo sapiens*. Consciousness does not emerge in one shot, at one point in time, in complete form, but very slowly, and it continues to develop after Upper Paleolithic peoples. If Mithen hangs everything on the creativity of the Upper Paleolithic period to infer the full emergence of cognitive consciousness, why not make additional differentiations in degrees of consciousness to explain the even more dramatic contrast between ancient Greece and illiterate peoples lacking any logic, philosophy, and mathematics?

Consciousness Emerges in Degrees Over the Course of History

This inclination to identify one period/stage in the evolution of consciousness, or in the history of civilizations, as the breakthrough transformation, pervades the scholarly world for a variety of reasons. Those who believe that the mission of all organisms, including humans, is to acquire nutrients and energy so that life can be sustained long enough to reproduce itself, are inclined to witness consciousness in the "intelligent" survival behavior of the first organisms. They are inclined to believe that from the first organisms 3.5 billion years ago to the present day, no fundamental difference in the structure and behavior of intelligent beings has oc-curred. There are others, such as Searle, LeDoux, and Mithen, who insist that there are different degrees of cognitive behavior and consciousness, but once they see

---

[61] Hauser, 2000, 113.

humans, either before or during the Upper Paleolithic, they assume an equally developed capacity for introspection.

We will see other scholars (in Chapter III) who hold that a "reflexive consciousness" with an increasing awareness of historical time, and an ability to generate universal moral ideals beyond the conventions of the time, is a unique achievement of civilizations during the Axial Age period between 800 to 200 BC. For others, whom we will start to examine in Chapter II, consciousness really emerges in ancient Greece with the "discovery of the mind," with the emergence of characters in literature showing incipient signs of introspection and selfhood, and/or with the rise of philosophers who consciously go about examining the nature of thinking itself and truths based on rational criteria. I am inclined to accept the latter view, except that I see ancient Greece as the beginning of many subsequent levels or "orders of consciousness"—all of which occurred in the West.

Among most researchers there is a strong reluctance to attribute the origins of consciousness to Europeans if only because in the "inclusive" Western world of today this amounts to "cultural supremacism." Mithen is a typical case. He is so keen to be inclusive, and avoid the charge of racism (about which he warns in the closing pages of his book) that he actually suggests that Upper Paleolithic peoples (and "traditional non-Western cultures" generally) evinced a higher level of cognitive fluidity than the specialized cultures of the contemporary West, because they viewed "their natural world as if it were a social being."[62] This is nonsense. Increasing cognitive fluidity does not preclude further specialization of the intelligences, but actually encourages it.

The history of knowledge, which is almost entirely a history of European knowledge, given that Europeans, as I will argue in chapter six, are responsible for the development of all the specialized disciplines taught in our universities, is proof of this. There can be no modernity, as we learn from Max Weber, without differentiation of functions, laws, offices, disciplines, and so on. This differentiation was made possible by the greater cognitive fluidity of the Western mind. Knowing that there are separate faculties and separate worlds requires a higher level of awareness within each of the domains of intelligence, of one's own reasoning within that domain, and of what particular methodologies are appropriate to employ in one domain as contrasted to another domain.[63]

---

[62] Mithen, 1996, 233.

[63] Mithen even criticizes the claim that science is primarily a product of the West, citing someone claiming that "science is a genuine universal, characteristic of all advanced life-forms" (261). So, even animals who happen to be "advanced" are scientists; this is how far academics are willing

Some may say that this is unnecessarily politicizing this debate by bringing issues external to it, criticizing multiculturalism and the like. But that is precisely the problem: cross-cultural debates about the accomplishments of different peoples are now inherently politicized. As we will explain in Chapters X and XI, this politicization, this inability to recognize the far higher accomplishments of the West, cannot be divorced from the very unique historical trajectory of this civilization, which includes the eventual establishment of a liberal pluralist cultural setting. This is a complex argument that must be bracketed off for the time being for the sake of not overburdening our present discussion. Suffice it to say for now that Western elites, by reaching the conclusion that the best political society is one based on values that are universal in granting equal individual rights to all humans to choose their own values, regardless of nationality and race, have created a scholarly climate that demands the inclusion of all peoples in the accomplishments of "humanity."

Danniel C. Dennet on the Cultural Evolution of Human Mental Capacities

Daniel Dennett is the foremost exponent of the case that only a scientific approach, and the disciplines of biology and computer science, can teach us what the nature of the mind is, and how a "comprehending mind" could have emerged from natural selection and cultural evolution. *From Bacteria to Bach and Back: The Evolution of Minds* (2017), which puts together arguments Dennett has been making "for half a century," may indeed be the best effort to defend a materialistic, evolutionary, and computational view of consciousness. Our mental states, he explains, may "seem so different, so private, so intimately available to us in a way unlike any other phenomena in our living bodies,"[64] as to mislead us into thinking that these are strictly subjective phenomena, but, in reality, our ability for introspection, for thinking about our mental states, is more appropriately seen as a biologically and culturally evolved cognitive "tool kit" wherein humans self-examine their thoughts in order to design their actions intelligently.

Dennett is adamant that the evolved ability for introspection does not justify the claim that there is an immaterial substance called "consciousness." The mind

---

to go in their effort to avoid being labelled racist, or to conform to the government mandate that whites must welcome their replacement by immigrants.

[64] Dennett, 2017, 18.

can be explained from a third person scientific perspective. Humans evolved both genetically and culturally, and we are now (in the modern era) the "only species with an elaborate kit of thinking tools" by which "to know how minds evolved, and even to know how these tools enabled them to know what minds are."[65] When we introspect, we may think we are experiencing subjective experiences, which an immaterial "I" or "self" apprehends. But the experiences so encountered are not properties of inner conscious experiences; for, in reality, what we think are subjective experiences are brain processes which we can now examine with the development of sophisticated cultural "tool kits."

Microorganisms, plants, and animals evolved many "competences that permit them to deal appropriately with the affordances of their environments." Organisms need not be conscious of their cognitive competences to benefit from them. We can explain the emergence of these non-human competences in strictly Darwinian terms, and we can also explain the evolution of humans and the beginnings of human culture from a strictly Darwinian perspective. But, as humans evolved culturally, their cultural evolution was "gradually de-Darwinized," evolving "away from undirected or 'random' searches toward more effective design processes, foresighted and purposeful and dependent on the comprehension of agents: intelligent designers."[66]

Dennett draws on Richard Dawkins' concept of meme. Dawkins defines the term meme "to refer to the ways of doing and making things that spread through cultures." This concept, they believe, allows one to explain cultural changes in terms of "new selective pressures" created by culture itself. Human cultural activity has changed the environments humans respond to, creating thereby "cognitive niches" or "cultural niches" with very different selective pressures. Pinker believes that humans evolved sufficient genetic capacities to be able to select the best memes and discard culturally inefficient or dysfunctional memes. Dennett sees no reason why we need to postulate a first-person view of the mind when we can objectively understand the culturally (and publicly) developing ability of humans. We must learn to think of what goes on inside the brain in the same way we think of computers performing competent tasks without postulating a computer with a "self" examining its conscious awareness. If we are to offer scientific reasons or explanations for the selection of competent memes, we should do it in the same way that we offer explanations for every other purely physical process.

---

[65] Ibid, 3.
[66] Ibid, 412.

The counter-argument is very simple: the first-person point of view can't be explained without explaining the discovery of selfhood, the identification of the faculty of the mind, and the differentiation of the "I" from the "non-I" that is unique to the cultural development of Western civilization. This development is what allowed Europeans to develop, in the first place, thinking tools to attempt to explain the mind from a third person perspective. It is not accidental that whenever Dennett writes about how "minds evolved and created thinking tools . . . to know how those tools enabled them to know" he refers only to tools invented by European philosophers and scientists. Every major technology he mentions, such as the "compass, telescope, microscope, camera, the Internet," as examples of cognitive tool kits, was either originated, or made into a proper tool, by Europeans. The other thinking tools he associates with "cultural development," namely, writing, arithmetic, navigation, mapmaking, were also developed in a continuous way in the West. Similarly, every thinker he mentions who studied the nature of consciousness, the mind-body problem, from Plato to Descartes to Darwin, and countless modern cognitive psychologists and scientists he refers to, either happen to be Western or educated in the West. It is only in reference, indeed, to men like "Socrates and Plato and Aristotle" that he writes about the origins of "talking about talking, thinking about thinking."[67]

Dennett has a habit of writing "of our practice of explicit self-questioning" or "how this human talent for self-questioning gave us our unique cognitive powers,"[68] as if self-questioning, analyzing and reasoning about one's thoughts were a general intellectual activity across the world. He is projecting a uniquely Western way of thinking about thinking onto non-Western cultures, where thinking, as we will see in Chapters III and IV, barely rose above first-order thinking, or above the type of thinking involved in our everyday survival activities and social interactions. Only in classical Greece do we witness for the first time thinking about thinking, or what some call second-order thinking, as in the geometrical proofs of Euclid, which entail a systematic justification for its claims so as to rationally persuade others about the correctness of one's thinking, rather than to mandate a truth prescribed by gods or inscribed in the kinship norms of one's ingroup.[69]

---

[67] Ibid, 331.

[68] Ibid, 296–7.

[69] Revealingly enough, in a 2020 review Dennett wrote of Joseph Henrich's book, *The Weirdest People*, which I mentioned above, he admits that "one of the first lessons that must be learned from this important book is that the WEIRD mind is real," that is, a mind which is unique to the history of Western cultural development. Dennett correctly says that "we must stop assuming

Camille Paglia and the Apollonian "Light" of Male Consciousness

The emergence of self-consciousness was not merely a product of evolutionary processes driven by natural selection. We can thus agree with those who emphasize cultural evolution without assuming, however, that it was bound to produce humans across the world thinking about their own thinking, and aware of themselves as individuals with their own selves in differentiation from their kinship groups. Reaching the level of cultural development of ancient Greece alone entailed a huge struggle for the emancipation of the male ego from the cult of fertility goddesses, from the enveloping world of natural processes, and from the collective representations of the tribal group.

The starting point in our efforts to understand the origins of self-conscious humans should come by way of the question: why were men behind almost all the achievements in human history? From which point we should then ask: why were Western men responsible for almost all human achievements? Camille Paglia infuriated feminists for stating in her spirited book, *Sexual Personae: Art and Decadence from Nefertiti to Emily Dickinson* (1990), that "all the genres of philosophy, science, high art, athletics, and politics were invented by men." This is a question Anthony Esolen addresses directly in his *No Apologies: Why Civilization Depends on the Strength of Men* (2022). He believes that it was man's "risk-taking, adventurous natures, strength and initiative" that made civilization and then modern life possible. This included "restless masculine activity" and masculine camaraderie, or the ability of men to form honor-and-duty bound hierarchical groups that serve common purposes. But Esolen is primarily concerned with human male creativity and status today in our feminist culture, not the origins of civilization, and not Western man per se.[70]

---

that *our* ways are 'universal.'" He admits indeed: "offhand, I cannot think of many researchers who haven't tacitly adopted some dubious (Western) universalist assumptions. I certainly have. We will all have to change our perspective." Perhaps if he had read Henrich's book before writing *From Bacteria to Bach and Back*, he would have avoided the universalist assumption that thinking about thinking is a universal cultural reality. It is unlikely, however; on the contrary, what he seems to imply in the review is that Westerners have "dubious universalist assumptions" and that to overcome this we must embrace multiculturalism even more!

[70] Dennett momentarily raises this question, writing about "the glaring fact that all the candidates . . . in my pantheon of great minds are men" (2017, 23). He tries to explain this huge discrepancy by mentioning "dozens of reliably detectable differences of neuroanatomy, hormonal balance, and other physiological signs, and their genetic sources." But eventually he backs off and accepts

Paglia offers a deeper, even if still impressionistic, Jungian interpretation that draws on Erich Neumann's classic *The Great Mother* (1951). She dares to go beyond current academic men by suggesting that European males, though not explicitly, were the major creators of high culture, the ones who have "taken us to the stars" with their "Apollonian rationality."[71] *Sexual Personae* is essentially about the creativity of western life and thought. I believe that, behind this discrepancy—between Paglia's declaratory statements about male creativity and her implied awareness that it was specifically Western men who produced an Apollonian rationality—lies a lack of differentiation between the generic civilizations created by males around the world (who never fully affirmed their masculine otherness against the unconscious Uroboric power of the Great Mother) and the ancient Greek civilization created by Indo-European males (who fully crystallized and detached their masculine consciousness from the "feminine" unconscious). But before we come to Indo-European males, we must address the importance of maleness as such in the emergence of consciousness and cultural development, since males in the non-West were also responsible for almost all cultural development in their lands. Paglia's intellectual struggle, we need to keep in mind, was directly against the feminist refusal to accept biological differences between the sexes, rather than to make an argument about the higher creativity of Western males.

Nietzsche and Neumann are among the most influential sources in Paglia's thought. Apollonian rationality represents the "light" of consciousness, associated with males, conceptual clarity, control over sexual impulses, moderation in the expression of one's impulses and appetitive drives, and cultural progress. "The cold light of [the male] intellect," its drive for "naming and classifying," must be imposed by men against the Dionysian, which is dark and chthonic, associated with females, with wild/chaotic nature, unconstrained sexual pleasure, and effeminacy. In all tribal cultures, women were identified with nature, "femaleness was honored as an immanent principle of fertility." But civilized life, urbanization, and commerce required the suppression of the violent, unconscious, subterranean hostility, and repetitive cycles of nature. "All cultural achievement is a projection," she writes, and only men "are anatomically destined to be projectors."[72] They are

---

the feminist argument that "the explanation for this is obvious: for millennia, very few women ever got a chance to develop their talents." (329) He avoids asking why, despite decades of "equity" in opportunities between the sexes, new ideas in science and many other fields keep coming from males.

[71] Paglia, 1990.

[72] Ibid, 17.

"genetically condemned to a perpetual pattern of linearity, focus, aim, directness." "Men are in a constant state of sexual anxiety, living on the pins and needles of their hormones. In sex as in life they are driven beyond. . . . They wander the earth seeking satisfaction, craving and despising, never content. . . . They must quest, pursue, court, or seize."[73]

Women have conceptualized less in history not because men have kept them from doing so but because women do not need to conceptualize in order to exist. Female anatomy is closer to nature, absorbed by the cycles of nature. Women do "not dream of transcendental or historical escape from natural cycles, since she is that cycle." Artistic creativity has been spurred on by this struggle between the Apollonian personality of "the west's absolutist ego structure" and the Dionysian fusion of male and female, between the orderly world of scientific classifications and the primal forces of sexual nature. Although "there is neither person, thought, thing, nor art in the brutal chthonian," and although it was the west's Apollonian individuation that produced its greatness, this greatness was not a product of peaceful and calmed ratiocination; the male struggle for individuation and creativity has always come along with "phallic aggression" and sexual anxiety.

Men were able to liberate their consciousness from the chthonian darkness of primal times, and create civilized life through their rationalism, but the energy of nature, the "chaos of the libido," remains. The struggle for the affirmation of masculine consciousness against the power of female nature remains a reality for each new generation of growing boys. As spectacular as the glory of "male civilization" has been ("which has lifted women with it"), and however much nature has been conceptualized and managed by males, and the primal sexual drives socialized into conventional marriages, we are delusional to think that nature can be nurtured out of existence. "Nature has a master agenda we can only dimly know."[74]

Notwithstanding Greek and Roman classicism, "clarity, order, proportion, balance," and the fact that the sky-cult "kept nature in her place," the pagans did not try to suppress sexual nature; they sought to give it form and promote beauty. "Apollonian high glamour," under the influence of the Egyptians, was aimed at fighting off the impersonal facelessness of primitive sex and the formlessness of the fecund female body. Christianity tried to defeat this pagan beautification of female sexuality, but it failed; and while "Western civilization has profited

---

[73] Ibid, 19.
[74] Ibid, 1.

enormously from the sublimation Christianity forced on sex,"[75] paganism survived in western art, "in the thousand forms of sex, art, and now the modern media." This has been a spur to western creativity along with the never-to-be defeated power of nature's chaos. The greatness of western civilization has entailed a constant struggle of Apollonian man against nature and the permanence of the unconscious.

Erich Neumann on the Emancipation of Male Ego Consciousness From the "Great Mother"

It is not Neumann's *The Great Mother* that is most valuable for us to understand male consciousness, but his demanding study *The Origins and History of Consciousness*, originally published in German in 1949. Paglia only references his *Great Mother*, and while she acknowledges the influence of Neumann's thought in general in a 2006 article, this article is descriptive. By all appearances, no one has ever discussed *The Origins and History of Consciousness* (1973) in attempting to understand the nature of Western Civilization. This interpretation of this book will be different from standard psychological interpretations of it, which lack an interest in history. This book is a profound attempt to outline the archetypal stages in the development of consciousness, with its implied argument that Western men brought this development to its highest level.

For Neumann, "consciousness, as such, is masculine even in women, just as the unconscious is feminine in men."[76] The development of consciousness and civilization entails the detachment of the male ego from the unconscious world of fertility goddesses. In using the term "ego consciousness," Neumann had in mind Carl Jung's identification of the component of the psyche that is responsible for decision-making. Being ego-conscious means that one has self-awareness of one's identity as a separate being in charge of one's thoughts, capable of distinguishing the inner and the outer world, in contrast to that part of the personality that is driven by unconscious primal forces.

In the foreword to this book, Jung praised Neumann for arriving "at conclusions and insights which are among the most important" in the field of depth psychology. The subject of study of this field, in Neumann's words, is how the

---

[75] Ibid, 25.
[76] Neumann, 1973, 42.

"collective unconscious reveals itself to the conscious mind in images." The collective unconscious is expressed through archetypes, which are universal thought-
forms or mental images that influenced an individual's feelings and actions. He
believes that the consciousness of individuals in each generation passes through
the same developmental stages that mark the development of human consciousness in history. The relation prehistoric humans have with their surroundings is
very similar to that of young infants who remain undifferentiated from their
mother. Similarly to children, who can't differentiate their egos, primitives are "at
the mercy of instincts, impulses, and reactions deriving from the world of the
body" and the "participation mystique."[77] As Jung observed:

> The further we go back into history, the more we see personality disap-
> pearing beneath the wrappings of collectivity. And if we go right back to
> primitive psychology, we find absolutely no trace of the concept of an in-
> dividual. Instead of individuality we find only collective relationship or
> what Lévy-Bruhl calls *participation mystique.*[78]

In using the term "participation mystique," Lévy-Bruhl had in mind your typical
hunting and gathering and simple agrarian societies, before the onset of civilizations, when individuals could barely distinguish themselves from the collective or
kinship consciousness of their tribe.

   While it is not necessary for us to go "step by step" over Neumann's very complex account of the evolution of ego-consciousness, we must start with the "uroboros" stage before we think about the meaning of *participation mystique.* The
uroboros is an archetypal symbol for the "earliest dawn," representing the

---

[77] Ibid, 110.

[78] This passage comes from Jung, 1921/1971. It is cited by Farhad Dalal in a 1988 article with the
title "Jung: A Racist." The aim of this article is to disqualify Jung as a serious thinker on the
grounds the "entire fabric of Jung's psychological theory" was permeated by racism in his hier-
archic ranking of the peoples of the world according to their degree of conscious differentiation.
Dalal misses altogether Jung's critique of modern Western individualism, the illusion that the
modern "solitary" individual who has broken with all tradition and sense of participation within
a larger whole is "the culmination of the history of mankind, the fulfilment and end-product of
countless centuries" (1933, 199). The *participation mystique* of primitives continues to inhabit
modern men, except that it now exists in the unconscious world of the psyche. It is delusional of
modern men to believe that they can tear themselves completely away from their unconscious
drives, or that "on the basis of widespread knowledge of the unconscious and its ways" they can
"effectively suppress" their primeval drives and live a life of full conscious clarity and understanding of each other's motivations in a state of material comfort (205).

"roundness," "the egg," "self-sufficiency," "the original unity," of humans in the womb. It is a circular symbol that depicts a snake or dragon devouring its own tail, and is used in cultures to represent the eternal cycle of mother nature "which circles in itself," and remains forever "unchanging and without history." It is an "evolutionary stage which can be 'recollected' in the psychic structure of every human being," "the immemorial experience of mankind that every new born creature comes from a womb."[79]

The uroboros is the phase of an "infantile ego consciousness which, although no longer entirely embryonic, and already possess[ing] an existence of its own . . . is still . . . marked by the predominance of the maternal side of the uroboros." This dawn is not a historical stage, the "natural state" of the noble savage Rousseau imagined, but an infantile ego consciousness, when the infant has zero awareness of its own reality and "differentness," completely absorbed in its union with the mother. However, it refers to the primordial depths of the unconscious stages in the evolution of humans, which every individual "re-experiences in the growth of childhood," its emergence from the womb, while "the world shelters and nourishes it," and he "scarcely wills and acts at all."[80]

The uroboros is followed by the intermediary stages of the World Creation, the Great Mother, the Separation of the World Parents, and then a sequence of stages coming after the Birth of the Hero. The notion that cultures were once under the spell of The Great Mother does not entail the argument that hunting and gathering and early farming societies were ones in which positions of authority were primarily held by women. Rather, one might take it to mean that before the rise of sky gods and the Olympian gods of ancient Greece, societies venerated the earth and its ancillary goddesses of fertility because they were in awe of the primal, self-creating force of nature, identifying the cyclic fertility of the earth and women's reproduction, and thus seeing the mother as the great maternal figure of nature. It was through the mother that men came into existence. The association of the primal mother with the underworld, defined as chthonic, and with the kingdom of the dead, came from the idea that all natural things including plants die for the regeneration of new living things necessary for the continuation of society.

But as men began to plow the earth, to subjugate Mother Earth with their created tools and to establish some control over the cycles of fertility, they started to dilute the hegemony of the primal mothers. Neumann is not definitive about this

---

[79] Neumann, 1973, 13.
[80] Ibid, 14.

with his Jungian expressions, but we can infer it. However, prior to the Birth of the Hero, the male ego barely manages to differentiate itself from the enveloping power of Mother Nature; the ego remains in an "inchoate state," without a conscious distinction between I and You, inside and outside, or between men and things, "group and group consciousness are dominant." Before the Hero we must continue to talk about *participation mystique*, when the individual within a tribal group lacks an individualized identity and is capable only of a minimal degree of volition and activity, without the experience of being something other than a part of the kinship group. All in all, primitive man, before the Heroic Age, can't disentangle himself "from its fusion with nature and the group," but instead tends to project his inner psychic content to natural objects. He remains "at the mercy of the instincts, impulses, sensations, and reactions deriving from the world of the body." The ego, at this point in time, is "undeveloped and still embedded in nature."[81]

Consciousness entails a marking off of oneself from the surrounding context: "I am not that" instead of "that art thou." Consciousness takes a major step when men experience the "masculine" character of their consciousness as peculiarly their own and the "feminine" unconscious as something alien to them. The "Birth of the Hero" is central to Neumann's argument. The hero is a character that emerges with the formation of male groups. "The male group is the birthplace not only of consciousness and of the 'higher masculinity,' but of individuality and the hero."[82] These groups include, in their inception, hunting and fighting bands, and a variety of other male societies seen throughout history: secret societies, war bands, cults—all relatively autonomous from the rest of the tribal kinship network and norms. While tribal families tend to live "huddled together in caves, houses, and villages, which have the effect of strengthening the *participation mystique*," hunting or masculine groups have a "propensity to roam," are "necessarily mobile and enterprising." Neumann surmises that it is "in the situation of constant danger" in which these male groups find themselves, that their consciousness awakens away from the slumber and haziness, comfort and security of childhood and their persisting attachment to the Great Mother.[83]

It is within these groups, with their rites of initiation, that young men learn "to master their unconscious impulses and childish fears," to overcome the body and

---

[81] Ibid, 109–110.
[82] Ibid, 144.
[83] Ibid, 138–140.

the "inertia of the unconscious"—by "fighting against tiredness," enduring hunger and pain. They strengthen their will to power, which is a "strengthening of consciousness." Through initiation and heroic deeds that test their virility and the stability of the ego, males "are reborn as children of the spirit rather than of the mother; they are sons of heaven, not just of the earth." In "triumphing over its pains, fears, and lusts the ego gains an elementary experience of its manly spirituality."[84]

One should not assume, however, that with hunting bands per se we get the "heroic age" celebrated in Homeric writings and other mythologies across the ancient world. While the signs of ego consciousness are witnessed among hunters "in early primitive society, it is nevertheless certain that the further back we go in human history, the rarer individuality becomes and the more undeveloped it is."[85] All hunting and gathering societies, before "big man" chiefdoms or civilizations (and before the uniquely aristocratic and individuated Indo-Europeans) are characterized by "an anonymous collectivity," by the experience of the "oneness of life," what Lévy-Bruhl called participation mystique. Although Neumann's book is not a historical work but a history of consciousness based on Jungian psychology as projected in universal myths, archetypes, and primordial images, we can gather that when he writes about "the hero myth" he has in mind the heroic myths behind the founding of literate civilizations.

The hero is the "higher man," who ceases to be overwhelmed by the Great Mother archetype, but starts to discriminate, divide, and classify the wealth of images, qualities, and symbols of the primal archetypes; no longer in fear of hideous creatures, the underworld of uroboric spirits and demons, he has achieved enough ego stability and individuation to begin creating a more anthropomorphic world of sky gods that are more human in their qualities and more familiar, which entails a correlation between heaven and masculinity and the creation of patriarchal-sky gods standing above the earthly fertility goddesses. Civilizations, we can infer from Neumann, are created by these new men—the chiefs, medicine men, or divine kings—who make themselves "the responsible center of the cosmos" and announce that on them "depends the rising of the sun, the fertility of the crops." These "individuated" men are "the source of all taboos, laws, and institutions that are destined to break the dominance of the uroboric Great Mother."[86]

---

[84] Ibid, 310.

[85] Ibid, 269.

[86] Ibid, 147.

Now, in writing about the "hero myth" as a cross-cultural phenomenon, Neumann does not consider whether some cultures during the mythical age of heroes may have been more obsessed with heroism, or whether there were more opportunities for individual heroism in some cultural settings, and thus for a more advanced "marking off of the ego from the anonymous collective." Yet, Neumann knows that one does not find everywhere in the world's cultures "all the stages of conscious development," and that the rise of ego-consciousness is strictly a phenomenon brought about by men trying to demonstrate their heroic (super maleness) by overcoming the demands of the body and the fear of death, and making their male ego the headquarters of decision-making. He knows, too, that the emancipation of the ego reached its highest levels in the West and that "the evolution of consciousness as a form of creative evolution is the peculiar achievement of Western man."[87]

> The creative character of consciousness is the central feature of the cultural canon of the West. In Western culture, and partly also in the Far East, we can follow the continuous, though often fitful, development of consciousness over the last ten thousand years.[88]

He indeed says that, with the development of modern science, the West attempted the complete emancipation of the male ego "from the power of the unconscious."

> The correlation of consciousness with masculinity culminates in the development of [Western] science [which] breaks up the original character of the world . . . the world becomes objective, a scientific construction of the mind.[89]

What if the struggle to subdue the primal feminine took on a more intensive form, through the creation of a thoroughly male, heroic culture, which is willfully and completely isolated from the world of women, in the European world? Neumann never poses this question; rather, in the degree to which he accepts the universality of the myth of the hero, he draws no differences between European and non-European hero myths. He commingles multiple stories, preferring to focus on their

---

[87] Ibid, xviii.
[88] Ibid, xviii–xix.
[89] Ibid, 340–41.

common archetypal meaning. While he uses the word "psychological stages" in the subtitle, there are no clear historical references and demarcations in regards to these stages. While he is aware of the continued existence of "stationary cultures . . . where . . . the earliest stages of man's psychology predominate," in stark contrast to the full development of ego consciousness in the West, he does not consider the implications of this dramatic contrast in the development of consciousness for a theory that is about the uniqueness of male consciousness.

It is worth pointing out here that, while Paglia does not write about Indo-Europeans, she is aware that ancient Greek civilization was more infused with masculine sky gods and more creative than any other ancient culture. She observes that Eastern cultures "retained the ancient meanings of femaleness long after the West renounced them." She notes as well that "the last major Western society to worship female powers was Minoan Crete," and that a Mycenaean warrior culture with a "sky cult" replaced Minoan culture and lay the foundations for ancient classical Greece. (It should be noted here that Mycenae was founded by Indo-European invaders who superimposed themselves on natives who venerated the earth and goddesses of fertility). She also observes that "compliance" with nature was the norm in the East, as opposed to Western "confrontation." The "sky-cult and earth-cult" were harmonized in Egypt.[90] In "Egyptian culture [there] was a fusion of the conceptual with the chthonian,"[91] whereas in Greek culture there was a split, with the sky gods in a position of dominance. Only Western man refused to reconcile with nature, however impossible it is to escape nature. The "Greek gods live on a peak touching the sky," and have "a higher human beauty." "Greece, unlike Egypt, never worshipped beast gods."[92]

The Struggle of Men to Become Men and the "Differentiation" of Consciousness

Before we move to consider the more individuated and heightened nature of the heroic male struggle for manhood among Indo-Europeans, and the higher beauty of Greek Olympian gods, we should say more about the psychology of maleness in general. For animals, women, and slavish men, nothing is at stake

---

[90] Paglia, 1990, 72.
[91] Ibid, 61–62.
[92] Ibid, 72.

beyond self-preservation and being an attractive being-for-another, which concerns the sexual eros between male and female. But for men as men, their self-worth, and thus sense of selfhood, is worthless without strife and without the honor that comes from being recognized as men by honorable men. In enduring bodily hardships and risking their life for peer approval, men prove that they can transcend their "girly" motherly dependence and naturally-inclined "effeminate" desire for comforting pleasure.

Because we inhabit a very safe society in which this struggle has been pacified, and because academic males don't spend much time with other men but are surrounded by feminist females who teach them that manly virtues are "toxic," or are trained to look up to the government for social advancement and approval, they are bound to be highly skeptical, with a degree of animosity, at the suggestion that there might be a connection between the perennial struggle of men to be recognized as men and the origins of selfhood. It is also the case that academics are inclined to view consciousness as a strictly mental capacity made possible by either the neurological structure or "cognitive fluidity" of the brain, or as an achievement of cognitive competences. Our view is the opposite: the primordial origins of selfhood lie in the least civilized aspect of human nature—the questing and violent struggle of men to become men.

There is a biological starting point to the emergence of consciousness, a necessary biological precondition, which consists in the fact that a man is not born a man, but must become a man. Throughout history, across all cultures, men became men only by proving their masculinity in risky contests with the surrounding environment and with other adversarial men. It is this struggle to become a man in the eyes of other men that sets the preconditions for the differentiation of the male ego from the enveloping womblike environment. But this precondition and embryonic differentiation cannot be seen as the first cultural sign of an emerging human personality; it is only a necessary precondition, a very important one, in making us realize that we must avoid thinking that consciousness automatically emerges with the biologically evolution of *Homo sapiens*, or that it can be grasped in terms of the mere use of language, or the beginnings of writing and civilization.

This is not mere speculation. While the vast majority of academic books on masculinity are about "patriarchal oppression," male violence against women, and "toxic masculinity," there is now a literature showing that manhood does not come naturally to men as they mature. Rather, the attainment of manhood has entailed throughout history, across cultures, arduous struggles, "self-mastery, self-denial, self-sacrifice," and conscious acknowledgment by other men of one's manhood. There is also a well-established literature showing that hunting was almost an exclusively male activity and that hunting played a crucial role in the evolution of the Homo genus and the cognitive expansion of the brain. Some of the best books covering these subjects include: Lionel Tiger, *Men in Groups* (1969), David Gilmore, *Manhood in the Making: Cultural Concepts of Masculinity* (1990), Jack Donovan, *The Way of Men* (2012), Walter J. Ong, *Fighting for Life: Contest, Sexuality, and Consciousness* (1981), Robert Ardrey, *The Hunting Hypothesis* (1976); and the previously referenced book by Anthony Esolen, *No Apologies: Why Civilization Depends on the Strength of Men.*

David Gilmore's *Manhood in the Making* effectively shows that across almost all cultures in history, both past and present, the state of being a "real man" was "a prize to be won or wrested through struggle." It would take too long to go over the many vivid examples of manhood validation Gilmore offers. What follows is the gist of his argument expressed as explicitly as possible. The manhood ideal is not biologically given in toto, but is constructed through struggle, not only in the context of survival, but through the conscious approval of other men. "Real manhood is different from simple anatomical maleness," for achieving manhood "is not a natural condition that comes about spontaneously through biological maturation, but rather is a precarious state that boys must win against powerful odds."[93] Boys or young men have always been expected to demonstrate their capacity to become men through painful rituals, ceremonies, actions, or risky contests. They have been expected to show contempt or remain stoic, without complaining or showing fear, in the face of pain and danger, and in the face of struggles with other men, never backing down. Men who failed to demonstrate their manhood were deemed unmanly, effeminate, emasculated. Women may have been called "unladylike" if they didn't meet cultural standards of femininity; however, becoming a "real lady" or a "real mother" never entailed "win-or-lose contests dramatically played out on the public stage."

While both boys and girls have been expected to go through what Freudians call "separation-individuation" from the mother as they mature in physical mobility (walking, speaking, attending to their bodily needs), the overcoming of the primal unity with the mother requires of boys the creation of a whole new gender away from the original symbiotic unity with the female-mother, to prove that he is not just a good boy, no longer enveloped by a dominating female figure, but,

---

[93] Gilmore, 1990, 11.

rather, that he is good at being a man who is no longer in need of motherly comforts and fearful of the dangers posed by other males and the environment at large. Being good at being a man is not about being a "good man" who performs kind acts for others, but, as Donovan explains, it is about showing to other men that you have self-mastery over your emotions (including your appetitive drives for pleasure and security), strength, courage and honor. The womanhood of girls develops more naturally in that it does not require a contest, a painful initiation, hazing, or a long and often threatening apprenticeship. Manhood can't develop on its own naturally without bravery and stamina, toughness, imperviousness to danger and pain, and decisive action, which are the exact opposite of the ideal female traits.[94] In other words, male selfhood is created through the deliberate demonstration that, as a real man, one is greater than one's mere biological existence and inclination for motherly tranquility.[95]

Of the books listed above, the virtue of Walter Ong's book, *Fighting for Life: Contest, Sexuality, and Consciousness*, is that it explicitly connects the struggle of men to become real men with the onset of consciousness. Perhaps this should not surprise us once we learn that Ong is best known for his 1982 work *Orality and Literacy: The Technologizing of the Word*, which explains that the transition from orality to writing and literacy allowed for the organization of the constituents of oratory into a scientific art, that is, a sequentially ordered body of explanation characterized by *self-reflection*. We will return to this idea in Chapter III, though by way of Eric Havelock's 1963 book *Preface to Plato*, which influenced Ong, with its claim that the beginnings of Greek "self-reflective" philosophy should be attributed to the restructuring of thought brought about by writing. In *Fighting for Life*, Ong suggests that there was a prior stage in the emergence of self-reflection linked to the male struggle for recognition as a real man. This obsessive need for validation through risky contests or acts of endurance fostered a masculine interiority, which is required for a concept of self to become a possibility in a world in

---

[94] Paglia, in another publication, *Sex, Art, and American Culture: Essays* (1992, 82), puts it succinctly: "A woman simply is, but a man must become. Masculinity is risky and elusive. It is achieved by a revolt from women, and it is confirmed only by other men."

[95] Interestingly enough, despite Gilmore's argument that this struggle for manhood is cross-cultural, he suggests in passing that this struggle may have been more intense in ancient Greece with its "agonistic view of life [witnessed in] . . . the restless heroism of the Homeric sagas . . . in Achilles' willingness to trade a long, uneventful life for a brief one filled with honor and glory." "In the flourishing Athens of the fifth century B.C., male life seems to have been an unremitting struggle for personal aggrandizement, for 'fame' and 'honor'" (37).

which all living beings are otherwise fixated and consumed by fertility and survival.

The starting point of Ong's argument is that while the "need for the adversative is common" to both male and female in the animal kingdom, "adversativeness is a larger element in the lives of males than of females."

> Females can also be highly competitive. But their competitiveness seldom if ever shows in the conspicuous, all-out, one-to-one ritual or ceremonial contest found among conspecific males, such as the intensive, protracted battles of stags or rams or of male Siamese fighting fish.[96]

Ong spends much of the book showing how men and women are crucially different in their agonistic behavior and how males developed an identity apart from their surroundings, a consciousness of themselves as beings with their own goals and identity, because of their absolute need to set themselves against their early boyhood identification with the feminine in order to become real men in the biological sense.

Some passages will follow here in sequence, because Ong provides a most insightful assessment of the role of masculinity in the development of consciousness. (It should be said right away that Ong is a Westerner and that his analysis of the intense need of males to prove their manhood, as I will show later, is heavily permeated by the unique historical experience of males in the West).

> The young male is very feminine in significant ways, and necessarily so, because of his earliest maternal environment. After initial identification with the feminine, the boy must grow away from 'the feminine identification that resulted from his first encounter with his mother's female body [sex] and feminine qualities.' . . .
>
> The human male is beset with the psychological as well as physical problems of proving his masculinity, which means in effect proving he is not female. . . . Though they may resist acknowledging the fact openly, human males find themselves in stress situations not only because of their biological insecurity but also because psychologically they must set themselves off from a backdrop of femininity that has not had to establish itself but is simply there, a given. As a boy, the young human male most 'prove

---

[96] Ong, 1981, 51.

himself a man,' differentiate himself from this given ambiance in which he finds himself. He must prove he is not a 'sissy' (sister, girl). Anatomical differences do not suffice, since the fact is that all boys started out in the feminine world. How are they to be psychologically sure, consciously or unconsciously, that they have ever left that world, that they have really achieved the differentiation that it is every male's business to achieve? They must cut girls out of their lives, scorn feminine sources of comfort and safety, do things that they hope their mothers and sisters cannot do. They have 'to fight it'—'it' being anything that seems easy. They must discover or invent risks. Accusations of 'effeminacy' normally strike the male heart with terror: you have not had the strength to become yourself. . . .

But why the predilection of males for fighting other males in particular? [F]or the only adversary who can enable one to establish male identity is another male. . . . [H]e must face the threat of masculinity within himself by facing it in others like himself. To be a man, the male must be able to face insecurity, for that is what maleness implies—existence in an environment that is both needed and hostile. . . .

All environment is enveloping, womblike. The male craves freedom, and for many males the symbolic independence of all environment which one establishes by setting up as a loner, with occasional participation in a bonded gang of loners, is the ultimate accomplishment and happiness. . . .

Masculinity in this sense means becoming something different, separation from origins, a certain kind of getting away, abstraction, transcendence. Hence, as has been seen, the haunting male insecurity: born of women, how can I be sure that I am not what I came from, that I am not a woman, too? I have to do something difficult, something that only a man can do, to prove that I am not. Born to be different from my source of life, I must live with stress and must invent stress to assure myself that I can perform. . . .

Masculinity is differentiation here, too, differentiation from one's own unconscious, which is antecedent to one's consciousness. Consciousness arises out of the unconscious by differentiation and thus has a masculine quality."[97]

---

[97] Ibid, 65, 70, 78, 82, 112–3, 115.

What makes Ong's study all the more relevant is that almost all the examples he draws on to demonstrate how the "adversativeness" of males found deep expression in the literature, religion, sports, science and logic produced by humans are Western. This is so apparent that Ong himself admits from the beginning of his book that the obsession with "polemic, hostility, confrontation tactics, clashes of personalities, competition, games" and "other adversative manifestations" is indeed to be found mostly among Europeans from ancient Greek times.[98]

> But the Greeks seem to have made more careful use of adversativeness than did other cultures, both as an analytical tool and as an operational intellectual procedure.... By contrast, Chinese culture minimized dispute, thought of rhetoric as serving propriety and harmony, downplayed individual difference in favor of conformity.[99]

---

[98] Let it be said here that European men invented almost all the athletic sports known in history, including the Olympics. The Greeks invented: Pentathlon, Discus, Javelin, Wrestling, Boxing (introduced as a sport in the seventh century BC, at which point boxers' hands and forearms were bound with soft leather thongs for protection), Equestrian Events, Gymnastics (as a form of exercise for both men and women that combined physical coordination, strength, and dexterity).

The English invented: Cricket (1787), Rugby (1871), Golf (1502, with the first eighteen-hole course constructed in 1764), Tennis (in 1873), Badminton (1887), Table Tennis (1880), Bobsleigh (1890), Curling (1541), Soccer (the English codified the first uniform rules for the sport, which made tripping opponents and touching the ball with the hands forbidden), Swimming (competitive swimming was first introduced in the early 1800s in Britain, and by 1837 six indoor pools with diving boards had been built in London).

The Americans invented: Volleyball (William Morgan invented volleyball in 1895, Massachusetts, YMCA), Football (it came into its own in 1879 with rules instituted by Walter Camp, a player/coach at Yale University), Baseball (Alexander Cartwright of New York invented the baseball field as we know it in 1845), Softball (in 1887, by George Hancock, a reporter for the Chicago Board of Trade), Basketball (the first formal rules for basketball were devised, along with iron hoops and a hammock-style basket, in 1893, and James Naismith wrote the sport's original 13 rules in 1891, Springfield, Massachusetts).

France invented: Fencing (sword fighting focused on strategy and form, and rules, were adopted first by French in the 1700s, including a practice sword, known as the foil, for training, and the first fencing masks), Cycling (the first documented cycling race was a 1,200-meter race held in 1868, Paris).

Canada invented: Hockey (the rules of modern ice hockey were created by Canadian James Creighton). See David Levinson, Karen Christensen, *Encyclopedia of World Sport: From Ancient Times to the Present* (1999), and Gary Belsky, Neil Fine, *On the Origins of Sports: The Early History and Original Rules of Everybody's Favorite Games* (2016).

[99] Ibid, 21–22.

We will be examining China's conformity, its "embedded consciousness," in Chapter V. The experts Ong relies on highlight Western culture for its "adversativeness." This fact strains Ong's thesis that adversativeness in human cultures generally can be understood in terms of human male nature. Ong is correct that a purely biological approach which reduces human behavior to mere survival cannot say anything about how this adversativeness fostered a disposition to value an immaterial thing such as honor over the otherwise powerful instincts for comfort and security. But Ong leaves hanging the crucial question as to why European culture, in its literature, art, logic, and rhetoric, has exhibited this polemical impulse to a far higher degree. He knows, too, that in Western culture one detects a "greater and greater interiorization of consciousness through history noted by Hegel," the development of the concept of the person and the "I." But he says next to nothing about this "interiorization" and never asks: why the West?

The "Hunting Hypothesis" and Men in Groups

Robert Ardrey's *The Hunting Hypothesis: A Personal Conclusion Concerning the Evolutionary Nature of Man* (1976) is another book on masculinity that merits serious consideration. This was the first concerted effort to show that hunting was an almost exclusively male activity and that the "qualities that we regard as uniquely human" were selected by nature during the 99 percent period of our history when hunting and meat eating became an important component of the diet of our *Homo* genus. The thesis of this book stands in stark contrast to the sanitized, over intellectualized image of evolution we have seen in the evolutionary accounts examined above, which are singularly focused on increasing cognitive abilities, as if evolution was a process aiming to create nerdy academic men.

Males were suited for hunting due to their larger stature, strength, and propensity for risk taking. "Human preadaptation" to hunting "involved three qualities without which there could never have been human beings: bipedal locomotion, free hands, and weapons."[100] These three qualities resulted in a dramatic enlargement of the brain of the Homo genus that emerged from the vegetarian genus that we call today *Australopithecus*. Hunting demanded our *Homo* ancestors "to carry a weapon [which] demanded free hands. To free our hands, a degree of

---

[100] Ardre, 1976, 40.

posture and bipedal movement, however awkward, became a necessity."[101] The
gathering of wild plants on its own, with its association with a small brain, would
have inhibited the evolutionary development of many other human qualities we
admire: "courage . . . willingness to dare, to persevere, to respond to challenge by
attack rather than escape . . . the capacity to take risks . . . cooperation, responsibility, self-sacrifice, loyalty."[102] Ardrey attributes the evolution of the "adventure-
some inclinations" of humans, the "exploratory" spirit that led them to pioneer
"the great world, Pacific to Atlantic, Indian Ocean shores to Artic desolation," to
the hunting way of life.[103]

Ardrey knew that in the liberal West there would be a reluctance among anthropologists to accept a hypothesis that went directly against their "Rousseau-
esque image of primal innocence and primal goodness" with early humans "happily, healthily chewing mongongo nuts."[104] Indeed, no sooner was his book released, the anthropologist Ashley Montagu, born Israel Ehrenberg, asked fourteen
scientists to refute Ardrey (and Konrad Lorenz[105]) in two volumes.[106] Montagu
was a very influential man, one of ten scientists invited to serve on a UNESCO
"Committee of Experts on Race Problems" responsible for a series of *Statements
on Race* to propagate the idea that race is not a valid biological concept. He was
also the author of numerous books and articles promoting the idea that humans
are inherently good, and that with a progressive education children would be able
to unleash their egalitarian potential. What may be less known is that he was the
author of *The Natural Superiority of Women*, published in 1952, claiming there
was solid scientific evidence supporting the conclusion that the female brain was
more highly developed and capable of thinking more soundly and intuitively than
the male brain. In a fifth edition published in 1999, Montagu added that there was
"much new information bearing on the natural superiority of women," in confirmation of "the conclusions reached in this book." One of the conclusions was that

---

[101] Ibid, 43.

[102] Ibid, 67–69.

[103] Ibid, 153–154.

[104] Ibid, 60.

[105] Konrad Lorenz is best known for his equally controversial book, *On Aggression*, originally
written in German, translated into English in 1966. Montagu despised the thesis of this book that
both "beast and man," in the words of Lorenz, shared the same instinct for aggression "against
members of the same species" (1966, 3).

[106] The book *Man and Aggression* (1973), edited by Ashley Montagu, the first book I reviewed as
a college student, is a collection of articles arguing against Lorenz and Ardrey, portraying them
as "genetic determinists" even though they don't deny the role of culture.

American culture should be reconstructed in such a way that the male values of physical aggression and acquisition of material goods, would be replaced by values reflecting the true spirit of humanity of the female brain. We may indeed say that this goal has been partly fulfilled across the West, accounting for why White academic men seem so reluctant to write positively about men and about their own history.

Still, Ardrey's thesis would eventually come to be accepted among many experts (see for example Speth, 2010), even if social science academics, and masses of feminists in academia, have been ideologically inclined to prefer the thesis that the gathering of wild plants by "both mother and grandmother,"[107] was equally if not more important, or that women were also important hunters.[108] Nevertheless, the evidence supporting Ardrey's thesis, not Montagu's, has increased in precision and factuality. In 2014, *Scientific American* published an article by Kate Wong, "How Hunting Made Us Human" summarizing some of the latest findings. It is worth bringing forth the highlights of this article for how it frames the evolution of the brain in terms of a human/male activity, rather than as a process of selection carried out by a "natural" world on its own, as we saw above in the case of LeDoux and others. The key ideas include:

- Many of the characteristics that set us apart from our closest living relatives, the great apes (from our ability to run long distances to our oversize brain) evolved in part as adaptations to hunting.
- The lineage that includes our genus, *Homo*, took a radically different road as hunting brought increasing consumption of animal protein and fat.
- With higher activity levels, as hunters, compared with their predecessors, hominins needed a way to avoid overheating. . . . The loss of fur and the selection of special glands in the skin that promote sweating helped our ancestors keep cool while chasing animals. With this built-in cooling system, the evolution of which was well under way by the

---

[107] Holmes, 2003.

[108] A recent article arguing that there is "evidence that females hunted (and went to war) throughout the *Homo sapiens* lineage" by Anderson A et al. (2023). The mainstream media is full of articles insisting that women were hunters no less than men, with a recent one in *The New York Times* entitled: "Move Over, Men: Women were Hunters, Too" (August 1, 2023). The research on the predominant role of males in hunting remains very solid, see Hill (1982), Domínguez-Rodrigo (2002), Speth (2010).

time of *Homo ergaster* 1.6 million years ago, humans became excellent long-distance runners.

- Traits that permitted high-speed throwing evolved: a flexible waist, a less twisted upper arm bone and a shoulder socket that faces out to the side rather than upward, as it does in apes. A better throwing arm afforded *Homo* improved access to animal foods rich in calories while allowing hominins to drive off predators that tried to attack them or steal their kills.

- For decades experts have debated whether early *Homo* hunted or scavenged. The earliest unequivocal evidence of hunting … was just 400,000 years old. But over the past few years compelling evidence of much earlier hunting has emerged, as early as 1.8 million years ago.

- These evolutionary changes established a feedback loop in which access to high protein food fueled brain growth, which led to the invention of technologies that permitted our ancestors to obtain even more meat (as well as high-quality plant foods), which in turn powered further expansion of the brain. As a result, between two million and 200,000 years ago, brain size increased from roughly 600 cubic centimeters on average in the earliest representatives of *Homo* to around 1,300 cubic centimeters in *Homo sapiens*.[109]

When we get to Lionel Tiger's thoroughly researched book, *Men in Groups*, the emphasis is on the evolutionary basis of the cross-cultural regularity of male bonds and groups. Throughout history, up to contemporary times, there has been a close relationship between maleness, hunting, politics, territory, work, and play. Men "court" men, and validate themselves in terms of the judgements of other men in their groups. Male groups, with their commitment to hunting, war, defense, hierarchy, exploratory activities, and their emphasis on loyalty, honor and respect, have fundamentally shaped the psychology of men. What I wish to draw attention to, although this is a marginally stated observation in this book, is that bonding in male groups, including hunting groups, has been invariably related to "achieved status," rather than to "ascribed status." "A male will not bond with just any member of his ethnic, religious, familial, or social class group; he will bond

---

[109] Wong, 2014.

with particular individuals because he has certain . . . standards."[110]

Tiger offers examples of a wide variety of male groups, secret societies, associations, and clubs, in which membership was "voluntary" and the "the process of male bond selection" was relatively independent of kinship ranking or one's established status in society, sometimes consisting, in the case of hunting and warbands, of young men aspiring for recognition, and thus for an achieved status. The intention of the initiation of young men into these male groups, with "its attendant physical pain and isolation from parents," was to "sever family-of-origin ties" and to demonstrate to the youngster that his family was no longer his sole protector; the brotherhood was. Underplaying kinship or family ties in exchange for ties with the brotherhood was part of the process of male-bond selection.

This means that male hunting groups, within which our genus *Homo* acquired many of its human-like traits, may have been the first human group to exhibit proto-voluntary, merit-based characteristics, wherein members were judged for their masculine abilities: courage, honor, strength, loyalty, and self-mastery. This is an important observation to keep in mind when we examine in Chapter VII Joseph Henrich's thesis in *The WEIRDest People* that the West began to diverge from the rest of the world's cultures in a modernizing direction when the Catholic Church dismantled kinship networks and opened the door to the creation of voluntary associations, such as chartered towns, guilds, universities, monasteries, and business corporations. It is also important to the argument on the uniqueness of the *Männerbund* or the *kóryos* among Indo-European peoples, a term which in Proto-Indo-European language stands for "detachment, war party," a "brotherhood of warriors" consisting of unmarried young males with a unique tradition of heroic poetry associated with the expansion of Indo-European peoples across most of Eurasia and Europe.[111] This will lead us straight into the question: why

---

[110] Tiger, 1969, 20. It is interesting that Max Weber's observations about kin groups included men organized on the basis of what he called "fictitious kinship" consisting of fighting men who were related by blood in a certain way but organized in separate dwellings by a charismatic leader as a sort of club where men lived, made weapons, and organized their military and hunting expeditions (Collins, 1990). This military group existed loosely and intermittently as a group of men who would call upon one another for blood revenge, not fixed entirely by family ties, broken up and rebuilt when a new charismatic leader brought together a new coalition of followers, with its members tracing themselves back to a "heroic" ancestor rather than a family ancestor. These "brotherhoods" would surround themselves with fear-inspiring artifacts such as masks and hideous emblems, and maintain secrecy against outsiders, especially women, who were forbidden to enter under violent penalties. Weber may have had in mind different types of male groups, including Indo-Europeans warrior groups, which we will describe soon.
[111] Ringe, 2006.

were European men responsible for the full development of consciousness, the "discovery of the mind," in the words of Bruno Snell, and for almost all the accomplishments in history? However, before we get to the Indo-European aristocratic culture, let us ascertain that Europeans at large are members of a distinct Caucasoid/European race.

The Evolution of the European Race

Kevin MacDonald, in *Individualism and the Western Liberal Tradition*, does an excellent job summarizing the latest research on population movements into prehistoric Europe to argue that contemporary Europeans were the products of three distinct population genetic movements. These populations were:

- A "primordial population" arriving in Europe about 45,000 years ago, which MacDonald calls "Western hunter-gatherers (WHGs)," and which developed a unique culture of egalitarian individualism in the northwest areas of Europe.[112] I will add that these people are associated with the "Upper Paleolithic revolution" that Mithen says brought about the rise of cognitive fluidity.
- A population of Early Farmers (EFs) arriving from Anatolia about 8000/9000 years ago, slowly spreading their farming lifestyle across the Mediterranean, into Greece, Sardinia, Italy, Spain, Portugal, and the Balkans, and having the greatest genetic effect on the WHG population in the southern areas of Europe.
- A population of Indo-Europeans (IEs) migrating from the Pontic-Steppes beginning around 4500 years ago, creating the Yamnaya culture, the first IE culture to spread across the entire Pontic-Caspian region, and settling into the lower Danube region (3300–2500 BC), to be followed by the Corded Ware (3000 BC—2350 BC), and the Bell-Beaker cultures (2800–1800). The greatest genetic impact of the Yamnaya and Corded Ware peoples was on central Europe and some regions in the north, with less impact in the east and south. I would include the genetic and cultural impact of the Mycenaean peoples who "Indo-Europeanized" Greece in the second millennium BC.[113]

---

[112] We will return in Chapter VII to MacDonald's argument that from its very origins among hunting and gathering peoples in northern Europe (and he includes Indo-Europeans), Western culture was characterized by "weak" kinship networks, and individualistic tendencies.

[113] I will return shortly to the culture of these Indo-European peoples in the next section below. A paper published in 2021 reaffirms that European ancestral peoples consist of three

Do not believe the Western media: it has been contriving headlines and half-baked arguments about how Europeans were an amalgam of Africans, "Near Eastern migrants," and "mysterious" Yamnaya people originally from Siberia who "shared distant kinship with Native Americans."[114]

First, the Upper Paleolithic peoples who started settling in Europe some 45,000 years ago, coming from Africa via the Near East, were not Europeans, that's true, but a people closely descended from the *Homo sapiens* who migrated out of Africa some 50,000 (or 60,000 years ago), carrying in their genes only a fraction of the African genetic diversity, which set them on a different evolutionary trajectory as they inhabited and reproduced under very different environmental pressures in Europe relatively isolated.

From a Darwinian perspective, the question that should matter is not whether the original inhabitants of Europe were "European" in physiology, but when and how these primordial inhabitants *became* European. Darwinism teaches us that breeding populations that are geographically apart for a long time in different environments with different selective pressures will experience an accumulation of genetic differences between them, through natural selection, genetic drift, and mutations. These Upper Paleolithic peoples eventually replaced the "original" Neanderthals, which by 200,000/250,000 years ago had evolved from *Homo heidelbergensis*, becoming extinct roughly 5,000 years after the Upper Paleolithic peoples came. It has been estimated that Neanderthals contributed about 2–4 percent of the DNA of present-day Europeans. We should not be surprised that the early Upper Paleolithic inhabitants of Europe were darker, and that lighter skin, including eyes and hair, were later evolutionary acquisitions. The cultural Marxist view that human genetic evolution somehow came to a halt after *Homo sapiens*

---

populations: "The transition from the Late Neolithic to the Bronze Age has witnessed important population and societal changes in western Europe. These include massive genomic contributions of pastoralist herders originating from the Pontic-Caspian steppes into local populations, resulting from complex interactions between collapsing hunter-gatherers and expanding farmers of Anatolian ancestry" (Seguin-Orlando A et al, 2021).

[114] The *National Geographic Magazine* (August 2019) states: "Europe . . . has been a melting pot since the Ice Age. Europeans living today, in whatever country, are a varying mix of ancient bloodlines hailing from Africa, the Middle East, and the Russian steppe." The ideological aim of these articles, as with every other similarly worded article, is to compel Europeans to view current immigration replacement numbers as a normal state of affairs, while warning readers that to question this in favor of the idea that Europeans are a race in their own right is to be "inspired by Nazism." Not just the mainstream media, but scientists themselves, are deceitfully speaking about the "mysterious" Yamnaya and the Anatolian farmers as evidence that Europe has always been a racially "diverse" continent (Gibbons, 2017; Callaway, 2014).

migrated out of Africa, as Stephen Jay Gould and Richard Lewontin have argued, and as the entire establishment today continues to insist, has been proven false.

About 8,000 years ago, the descendants of this early Upper Paleolithic peoples had already been selected for light-skin and even blue eyes in the northern areas of Europe, though some argue that it was not until about 5,800 years ago that light-skin genes, as well as genes for blue eyes and blonde hair, started to show up at a high frequency. Other studies show that only as farming was adopted by the pre-historic peoples of Britain and Scandinavia did they start to exhibit a European racial look, because the new grain diet from farming lacked vitamin D, and so lighter skin was selected as a more efficient way to synthesize vitamin D from the sun. According to Sandra Wilde et. al, "strong selection favoring lighter skin, hair, and eye has been operating in European populations over the last 5000 years."[115]

Second, with regards to the Near Eastern farmers, it has been argued that they carried genes for light skin, and that, "as they interbred with the indigenous hunter-gatherers . . . their light-skin genes swept through Europe, so that central and southern Europeans also began to have lighter skin."[116] A similar conclusion was reached by another study, namely, that the Near Eastern migrants who colonized Europe around 9,000 years ago, by "island hopping across the Southern European coast" as well as moving through Thrace and the Balkans, were indeed carriers of lighter skin and blond hair.[117]

Third, in the case of the Indo-Europeans (I-Es), while "proto-Indo-European genes for light skin pigmentation were relatively infrequent . . . compared to contemporary Ukrainians," as MacDonald observes, there was selection for white skin and other European physical traits as the I-Es "spread north" into Europe. MacDonald describes the I-Es from the Pontic Steppes that migrated into Europe as "white-skinned, brown eyed peoples."[118] Recent studies have confirmed that: a) "skin lightening happened as late as 5000 years ago [in Europe] through immigration of lighter pigmented populations from western Anatolia and the Russian steppes," with the two genes most closely identified with lighter skin in modern Europeans originating in both the Near East and the Caucasus about 22,000 to

---

[115] Wilde et al., 2014.

[116] Gibbons, 2015.

[117] Paschou et al., 2014.

[118] MacDonald, 2019, 15–16, 24. From Allentoft et al., 2015: "Our findings are consistent with the hypothesized spread of Indo-European languages during the Early Bronze Age. We also demonstrate that light skin pigmentation in Europeans was already present at high frequency in the Bronze Age."

28,000 years ago;[119] and b) that a later wave of lighter-skinned populations across Europe is associated with the Yamnaya culture and the Indo-European migrations generally. Moreover, it needs to be emphasized that the I-Es were not a "mysterious" people who came from outside Europe, but a people native to this continent. The official geographical definition of the continent of Europe is consistent with the cultural history of this continent in comprising European Russia, the Pontic Steppes located north of the Black and Caspian seas, and present-day Ukraine, the original homelands of the I-Es.

Finally, there is strong genetic evidence showing that once a European race emerged out of the three populations MacDonald highlights, Europe did not experience any major genetic mixing from non-European immigrant races. We learn this from Jean Manco's *Ancestral Journeys: The Peopling of Europe from the First Venturers to the Vikings*. This book draws on the recent ability of geneticists to trace ancestry and human migrations by studying two types of DNA, mtDNA, which traces direct chains of descent from mother to maternal grandmother, and Y-DNA, which traces descent from father to paternal grandfather. Using this technique, it investigates the peopling of Europe from the first Europeans all the way to the Viking era. Even as Manco plays up politically correct tropes about multiple "migrants" moving into Europe, most of the "invaders" and "migrants" she mentions came from within Europe's boundaries, with the ones coming from outside, according to the studies she cites, barely having any genetic impact, which is why she can't help concluding that there is a "high degree of genetic similarity among Europeans."

Who Were the Indo-Europeans?

The "hunting spirit" we saw throughout the prehistory of man was followed historically by the Neolithic revolution, the domestication of animals and plants, starting about 10,000 years ago—a transformation that eventually led to the rise of collectivist-despotic chiefdoms and civilizations across the non-Western world, where only the paramount chiefs and kings were free and the upper classes consisted of subservient court officials and governors, for whom obedience and deference, not daring, adventure, and individual heroism, were the principal virtues. As we will see in Chapter III, there were two basic types of chiefdoms emerging in the post-Neolithic agrarian world: the "group-oriented" chiefdoms of the non-

---

[119] Hanel and Carlberg, 2020.

European world and the "individualizing" chiefdoms of the Indo-European world.[120] In the former there was greater emphasis on centralizing-collective activities aimed at integrating the population in the performance of irrigation agriculture and the building of temples and monumental architecture at the behest of paramount chiefs increasingly taking on a divine character, leading to the emergence of the despotic civilizations of Mesopotamia, Egypt, the Indus Valley, China, and the Americas.

In contrast, in the individualizing chiefdoms created by Indo-Europeans in the Pontic Steppes and Yamanaya settlements (3300–2500 BC) in south-eastern Europe, there was greater emphasis on the personal status and prestige of ruling aristocracies, less communal and public construction, and a highly mobile pastoral economy driven by wheeled vehicles, horse-riding, and animal husbandry. Among the Corded Ware people (3000–2500 BC) in central and northeastern Europe, brought into existence by the westward expansion of the Yamnaya, as well as among the Bell-Beaker peoples (2800–1800 BC), in north-western Europe, descendants of Corded Ware migrations, this way of life now came in the form of a mixed farming-pastoral economy. In these individualizing chiefdoms, the aristocratic chief with his retinue of warriors was the focus of economic activity, and the units of production were not communistic estates but free-hold farmsteads.

As a result, pre-historical Indo-Europeans and their descendants sustained the hunting male bond of prehistorical times at a higher and more intense degree than other peoples. They also reflected in full the mythological age of the heroes. Europeans would go on to create aristocratic civilizations, with Mycenae being the first one, with republican institutions, after the age of individualizing chiefdoms, in which authority was vested in an assembly of nobles where everyone was seen as equal in dignity and in privilege to voice their views and participate in governance. These nobles, as I shall explain below, would partake in a culture that cultivated the first heroic epics in history, and the first personalities with an incipient introspective consciousness.

Who were the Indo-Europeans? This is a question I examined at length in *Uniqueness of Western Civilization*. I accepted the "Kurgan Hypothesis" proposed most eloquently by Marija Gimbutas, and further substantiated by the research of J. P. Mallory and David W. Anthony. At the time I wrote *Uniqueness*, not everyone was convinced, despite very strong archeological and linguistic evidence, that Indo-Europeans migrated out of their steppe homeland into south-eastern

---

[120] Kristiansen, 1991.

Europe (Yamanaya), and that their descendants created the Corded Ware and Bell Beaker horizons. But it has now been conclusively established, on the basis of new genetic evidence, first published in 2015, that "a large part of the genetic ancestry in modern Europeans" came from Indo-Europeans.

The Yamnaya culture migrated out of their steppe homeland eastward to the Altai Mountains and westward into south-eastern Europe between 3000 and 2500 BC, playing a key role in the spread of its language through a "massive migration."[121] New genetic studies demonstrate that populations associated with the Corded Ware and the Bell Beaker cultures, as well as the Sintashta (located in southern Urals, dated to the period c. 2200–1750 BC) and Andronovo (in southern Urals and central Siberia, 2000–1150 BC) cultures derived most of their genetic ancestry from the Yamnaya, and closely related populations.[122] Corded Ware and Bell Beaker "culture individuals exhibit stronger genetic links with Yamnaya culture individuals than individuals associated with earlier Neolithic cultures in Europe."[123] The Corded Ware culture was the product of a massive migration into central Europe of Yamnaya peoples, and the Bell Beaker culture descended from a massive migration by Corded Ware peoples organized into war bands.[124]

The term "Indo-European migrations," accordingly, is now used in reference not only to the migrations of Proto-Indo-European speakers, the Yamnaya, but also in reference to subsequent migrations of the descendants of these speakers of derived I-E languages.[125] The success of these migrations explains how I-E languages came to be spoken across a large area of Eurasia, and beyond in the Indian subcontinent and Iranian plateau, all the way to Atlantic Europe, and, in the course of time, by way of further conquests and migrations, across the Western world today. From this linguistic perspective alone, we can see that I-Es were a most successful expansionary people, with about 46 percent of the world's current population speaking one their derived languages as a first language, which is the highest proportion of any language family in the world.

To comprehend this incredible success, however, we must go beyond a linguistic definition of Indo-Europeans. The Yamnaya represented a "new, higher-

---

[121] Haak et al., 2015; Lazaridis et al., 2015; Anthony, 2023.

[122] As Reich (2018) writes: "There is now compelling evidence that the spread of the Yamnaya archaeological culture was the vector that also spread all the Indo-European languages spoken today."

[123] Bourgeois and Kroon, 2023.

[124] Mallory, 2023.

[125] Anthony, 2007; Anthony and Ringe, 2015.

mobility way of life in the steppes," the first people to invent "nomadic pastoralism."[126] They introduced wagon transport, ox-drawn wheeled vehicles, after 3500 BC, with the ability to transport tents, water, fuel, and food. They also introduced horseback riding for rapid travel, herd control, and warfare. Horseback riding was "already a common activity for some Yamnaya individuals as early as 3000 BC."[127] This was a revolutionary development providing a highly effective means of moving large herds, scouting for pastures, trading and raiding. It has been estimated that horse-riding allowed for the management of herds three times the size of a pedestrian herder using the same amount of labor. However, due to "lack of specialized gear and a comparably short breeding and training history, early horses were probably hard to handle."[128] The first fully modern genetic horses, like the ones we see today, were visible around 2200 to 2100 BC. All in all, this nomadic pastoral lifestyle included fierce competition for grazing rights, constant alertness in the defense of one's portable wealth, and an expansionist disposition in a world where competing herdsmen were motivated to seek new pastures, as well as tempted to take the movable wealth of their neighbors.

The pastoralism of I-Es is also associated with a "secondary products" revolution—which is about making the most of animal husbandry, eating dairy products and meat, and engaging in large-scale herding.[129] The Yamnaya "regularly consumed dairy products" such as hard cheese and yogurt. The superior nutritional diet of I-Es explains why their physical anthropology was more masculine than the farming peoples they conquered, with estimations that males were on average "taller and more robust" (over ten centimeters taller) than the Neolithic European farmers and Near Eastern peoples, who had very little meat and milk in their diet.[130]

While these traits are now recognized as part of the cultural package of I-Es, experts are at a loss as to the nature of their aristocratic/heroic ethos. They acknowledge their warlike nature, but take it as a given that there were no fundamental differences between the I-E aristocracies and your typical elites in other cultures. My view is that I-Es were a new type of post-Neolithic warrior people never seen before in history in that some men, not just the chieftain or the king, were free to strive for personal heroism. This definition of "aristocratic" goes

---

[126] Anthony, 2023.
[127] Trautmann et al., 2023.
[128] Ibid.
[129] Pronk, 2021.
[130] Anthony, 2023.

against its identification with countless other landowning or wealthy classes across the agrarian world living off the surplus produced by slaves or peasants while behaving subserviently in relation to the ruler. Here we define as "aristo-cratic" a state in which the ruler, the king, or the commander-in-chief is not an autocrat who treats the upper classes as unequal servants, but is a peer who exists in a spirit of equality with men who are deemed to be of the same noble class. The Romans had a term for this in reference to their republican government, which afforded the consuls or the two chief magistrates of the Roman Republic, elected by the senatorial patrician/aristocratic class, executive kingly powers without de-priving thereby the senate's privileges and rights: *primus inter pares*, first among equals.[131] This republican ideal, to be contrasted in the last chapter to current lib-eral principles of equal liberty for all humans, played a large role in shaping West-ern political institutions throughout ancient, medieval, and modern times.

Humans in general are capable of courage and great deeds, but the opportunity to achieve individual renown became increasingly difficult and rare as non-West-ern cultures moved towards centralized state governments, in which the King, the Pharaoh, the Emperor, or the Sultan came to be seen as the only decision-making individuals, treating their societies as royal extensions, empowering their favorite court officials, governors, and eunuchs, selecting them and assigning them spe-cific tasks. True warrior societies are those in which there is a class of men-at-arms who recognize the liberty and nobility of each other even when there is a recog-nized leader. The despotic nature of non-Western civilizations was symbolized in the pervasive practice of prostration and kowtowing. Vittorio Cotesta's *Kings into Gods: How Prostration Shaped Eurasian Civilizations* shows that, while prostra-tion as a bow or inclination was common in ancient Greece and Republican Rome, and as a solemn religious gesture of respect for the gods, full prostration, or kow-towing, in an excessively subservient manner, kneeling and sometimes bowing as low as to have one's head touching the ground, was common among members of the official upper classes in the Mongolian civilization during the Middle Ages, the Hindu and Chinese civilizations, and the Mughal civilization. This was the case also among "collectivist" chiefdoms around the world. In ancient Greek lit-erature, the act of kneeling observed among Persians was seen as a humiliating custom unacceptable to men who valued their nobility and liberty.[132]

---

[131] Wirszubski, 1968.

[132] As Wittfogel observes in his classic work, *Oriental Despotism* (1957), prostration is a "charac-teristic" of Eastern (including American) civilizations as it is "uncharacteristic of classical antiq-uity and the European Middle Ages" (152). In Inca Peru, the highest members of the state

The Indo-European "Brotherhood of Warriors"

This aristocratic egalitarian spirit was embodied in a dramatically intense fashion in the institution of the *männerbund,* a German word that specifically refers to a "band of men," which may be used interchangeably with the Greek word *kóryos*. Because the concept of the *männerbund* was developed in the early twentieth century by German philologists and scholars of comparative mythology who came to be associated with German *Völkisch* movements in the 1900s–1920s, which subsequently influenced Nazi ideology, it was discredited or studied in a very subdued fashion after WWII, as a mere arcane custom among many other mysterious ritualistic groups of the mythological history of cultures. Recent research, however, has established that the *kóryos*, which is the preferred term used today, was a fundamental custom across the IE world and the societies that were Indo-Europeanized, lasting through the medieval era in Europe.[133] This term has descendant cognates in Baltic, Celtic, Germanic, Sanskrit, Scandinavian, ancient Greek, and other European languages, reflecting the migration of IEs into these lands. The consensus today is that the *kóryos* played a key role in the expansion of I-Es across most of western Eurasia. Warrior bands were sent first in raiding parties to set up settlements and start the colonization of new lands, and thus laid the groundwork for the future migration of whole tribes.[134]

These "bands of brothers" were composed of adolescent or unmarried young males, from aristocratic families, operating in partial autonomy from tribal-kinship normative ties, initiated by either older males or a leader chosen on the merits of his martial abilities and memorable deeds. The relation between the chief and his followers was personal and contractual: the followers would pledge to serve

---

approached their ruler with their backs bent as if carrying a tribute. In Pharaonic Egypt, representatives of the king are shown crawling, kissing and sniffing the king's scent. In India, everyone was obliged and expected to touch and smell the feet of superiors as a symbol of unquestioning servility, flattery and sycophancy. In China, kowtowing, in a state of supplication, was expected by all subordinates, including knocking one's head to the floor. The highest Confucian "gentlemen" were regularly sentenced to be castrated. In contrast, when Alexander the Great started acting like a typical Persian despot, and insinuated to his elite Macedonian companions that they should prostrate before him, they laughingly derided this expectation as a "humiliating custom," asking Alexander: "do you really propose to force the Greeks, who love their liberty more than anything else in the world, to prostrate themselves before you?" See Arrian's *The Campaigns of Alexander* (1971, 221).

[133] Mallory and Adams, 2006.

[134] Anthony and Ringe, 2015, 214; Kristiansen et al., 2017, 339.

and die if necessary for the leader by oaths of loyalty in which they would promise to assist him while the leader would promise to reward them from successful raids. Joining these war bands was seen as a rite of passage into manhood before young men were fully integrated into their tribes as rightful members of the aristocratic elite. It is estimated that the initiation phase commenced during adolescence, sometime between twelve/thirteen to eighteen/nineteen years of age, and that it may have lasted from several months to a few years.[135] As they matured, they were sent away without possessions other than their weapons to live in the wild, hunting and raiding foreign lands. One's status and reputation among warriors was openly determined by one's actual deeds and/or the number of followers or clients one could attract—rather than by one's prescribed kinship ties and family ranking. What every warrior wanted above all else was to be renowned among his peers, to stand out as an individual: as Hippolochos, in the *Iliad*, tells his son Glaukos when he is about to go fight the Trojans: "to be always among the bravest, and hold [his] head above others."

Indo-Europeans Were a World-Historical People

It is important to contextualize the institution of the *männerbund* in terms of the world-historical position of Indo-European societies so that we can distinguish it appropriately from primitive hunting groups and other military groups in the non-Western world. In hunting and gathering societies, and simple agrarian villages, the men, notwithstanding the formation of hunting groups, had a very weak, almost imperceptible sense of self-hood, other than some degree of differentiation from their childhood state and from females. As Carl Jung inferred, among hunter-gatherers "we find absolutely no trace of the concept of an individual; instead of individuality we find only collective relationships or what Lévy-Bruhl calls *participation mystique*."[136] That is, we find little differentiation between individual men, undeveloped personalities, for these societies, despite their hunting groups, were still in awe of the powers of fertility goddesses, with extremely strong kinship norms and identities. With the "secondary products" revolution, and the coming of the Bronze Age, which succeeds the Neolithic and Copper Ages, Indo-European cultures during the Yamnaya period were sufficiently

---

[135] Mallory, 2006, 93; Kristiansen et al., 2017, 339; Anthony and Brown, 2019, 111.
[136] Jung, 1971.

advance to rise above the *participation mystique* of primitive peoples, while avoiding the despotism and the slavish, anonymous life of peasant farmers bent over tilling the soil, as was the case across non-Western chiefdoms and civilizations.

While I-Es also spread eastwards across the steppes as far as the Tarim Basin in present day Xinjiang, China, and southwards into present day Iran and northern India, their impact on China was not as deep; and although they did successfully conquer Persia and India, they would eventually be absorbed and "orientalized" by these advanced civilizations. The I-Es would give India its national epic, the *Mahabharata*, with its depictions of the feats of the early warlike I-Es, who herded cattle and fought from horse-drawn chariots, but as Beckwith observes, "the local peoples of India heavily influenced" these newcomers, "who mixed with them in every way conceivable, producing a hybrid culture."[137] By the late Vedic period (after 1000 BC) the power of the aristocratic assembly started to be replaced by a new kind of politics centered on the chief priest, the courtiers and palace officials.[138] The I-Es who migrated into the Anatolian highlands during the second millennium were also eventually assimilated to the native Hatti culture, "growing up learning Hatti customs and language."[139]

In stark contrast, the I-Es who migrated into the Greek mainland superimpose themselves culturally on the backward inhabitants, creating the first Indo-European civilization: Mycenae. The Mycenaean warriors, with their aristocratic polities, comprised the background to archaic and classical Greece. The Macedonians who conquered Greece rejuvenated the martial spirit of the Greek world after the debilitating Peloponnesian war, conquering Persia and creating the intellectual harvest of the Hellenistic world.[140] Indo-Europeans also developed a civilization in the Italian peninsula: Rome. They founded an aristocratic republic, preserved the legacy of Greece, and cultivated their own Latin tradition. Despite the eventual decline of Imperial Rome, the dynamic spirit of the West was sustained several times over thanks to the infusion of new waves of "barbarian" descendants of prehistorical Indo-Europeans, particularly Celtic and Germanic peoples.

There have been, of course, many other intensive warlike peoples—Aztecs and Iroquois, Zulus and Māori—but they were outside the main theater of world history, and their class structure, religious beliefs and cultural values were not aristocratic. The Pontic-Caspian regions out of which Indo-Europeans came, a stretch

---

[137] Beckwith, 2009.
[138] Kulke and Rothermund, 1995.
[139] Beckwith, 2009.
[140] Schofield, 2007.

of grassland that extends for 7000 kilometers and averages 500 miles in depth, may be described as the highway of world history, serving as a corridor for horsemen-pastoralists throughout history: Cimmerians, Scythians, Sarmatians, Avars, Huns, Magyars, Turks, and Mongols. The Pontic steppe is actually part of what is known as the "Great European Plain" which stretches without interruption for over 2,400 miles from the Urals to the Atlantic; and since the Ural Mountains are no real barriers, this plain is therefore connected to the entire extension of the steppe that stretches to China. The pastoral peoples inhabiting this highway exhibited a higher disposition for warfare than non-pastoral cultures. This is commonly acknowledged by historians.[141] They had to learn to be aggressive, stay aggressive, or be threatened by conquest and the constant movement and migration of pastoral tribes.

It is no accident that this area produced the greatest warriors in history. The Huns, the Avars, the Magyars, the Mongols, and the Turks were highly mobile horse-mounted nomads who expanded across the steppes from Asia to Europe. These nomads, however, came much later into a world that was already dominated culturally by Asiatic despotic civilizations. The relationship between these nomads and their advanced neighbors, from ancient times to the modern era, was one of symbiosis, conflict, trade, and conquest, but never dominion and cultural colonization.[142] Rather, "the ongoing contact between steppe and sown [i.e., settled agricultural societies] in Eurasia deeply affected the nomads themselves: their economy, political institutions, religious life, expression and methods of warfare."[143] In time, these nomads would be defeated by the Europeans and Russians.

While the Mongols would create a lasting empire, by the time the Mongolic/Turkic tribes experienced the leadership of Temujin (1165–1227), the Mongolian steppe world was far from the earlier "blood relationship between equals," but was instead dominated by a single supra-tribe known as the All Mongol State, which regrouped old tribal lines into an army based on a decimal system, a process aided by a bureaucracy staffed in large measure by educated elites obtained from the literate conquered civilizations.[144] The Turkic warrior class would eventually be transformed into "mamluks," not free men but slaves purchased to become loyal Muslim fighters for the personal use of a despotic Sultan; even if they were

---

[141] Keegan, 1994.
[142] Duchesne, 2017b.
[143] Amitai and Michal Biran, 2005.
[144] May, 2012; Morgan, 1986.

trained with a code that emphasized courage, horsemanship and other warrior skills, they were not true peers but servants.[145]

Heroic Poetry and the Thymotic Spirit of Indo-European Aristocrats

Indo-Europeans produced a heroic poetry that reflected their unique aristocratic lifestyle, which was deeply connected to the deeds of past members of war bands living on their own masculine/noble values outside the norms of society. In *How to Kill a Dragon*, Calvert Watkins follows the continuum of poetic formulae in I-E languages, showing that the myth of a divine hero who slays a dragon or overcomes adversaries recurs in various guises throughout the I-E poetic tradition over millennia, including Old and Middle Iranian holy books, Greek epic, Celtic and Germanic sagas, down to Armenian oral folk epics of the last century. This formula was a central part of the symbolic culture of speakers of the Proto-Indo-European languages. Poetry was a moral necessity for Indo-European society, where the poet could confer on patrons what they and their culture valued above all else: imperishable fame.

While there were other tales, Mongolian and Turkic, about the great deeds of men, we need to be aware of the following key distinctions. First, the I-E epic and heroic tradition precedes any other tradition by some thousands of years, going back to prehistoric times, and lasting through the medieval era.[146] Second, I-E poetry exhibits a keener grasp and rendition of the fundamentally tragic character of life, a truly aristocratic confidence in the face of destiny, the inevitability of hardship and hubris, but without falling into a pessimistic fatalism and without a sense of "bitterness at the harshness and unfairness of life."[147] The opportunity for adventure and heroism in the face of harshness and struggle are "matters for thankfulness."

Third, I-E epics show both a collective and individual inspiration, unlike non-Indo-European epics, which show characters functioning only as representations of their kinship communities. In some I-E sagas there is a clear author's stance, unlike the anonymous sagas of the East. The individuality, the rights of authorship, the poet's awareness of himself as creator, were acknowledged in many

---

[145] Waterson, 2006; Watkins, 1995.
[146] Watkins, 1995.
[147] Gunther, 2001.

ancient and medieval sagas. Fourth, only in I-E poetry, which extends beyond prehistorical times through to the ancient era and the Middle Ages in Europe, do we
find men with identifiable names, some degree of personality-differentiation,
sometimes consciously dialoguing with themselves, with private grudges and private frustrations, as exemplified in countless mythologies, sagas, and poems, in
the *Iliad, Beowulf, The Song of Roland, The Lesson of the High One, Edda,* and *The
Wasting Sickness of Cú Chulainn.*[148]

We will explore the *Iliad* in some detail in the next chapter to argue that in this
poem we find textual evidence for the beginnings of an interiorized concept of
selfhood. The European "I"—famously associated with Descartes's announcement "I think, therefore I am"—makes an embryonic appearance in the persona
of the aristocratic I-E warrior. We shall rely on Hegel/Kojève for the idea that man
starts to become truly self-conscious only to the extent that he actively engages in
a fight where he risks his life "for something that does not exist really"—that is,
"solely 'for glory' for the sake of his 'vanity' alone (which by this risk, ceases to be
'vain' and becomes a specifically human value of honor.") Man becomes self-conscious of "his humanity only by negating himself as animal," in his willingness to
risk his life, and thus negating his biological fear of death, for the sake of being
esteemed by another human being. It is in the status of "being-for-self" or self-
assertiveness (rather than in the attitude of "being-for-another" or deference) that
man first acquires a sense of selfhood.

In the risking of life, man first discovers or reaches a consciousness of his human self, because it is through this act that man negates his "objective-or-thingish
mode-of-existence," showing that he is not bound by "any determinate existence."[149] This is why "Man" must fight, for it is only through action and the risk
of life that consciousness of oneself as an independent being that is not merely
dominated by the dictates of nature comes to light. In the willingness to fight it
becomes clear that Man is not a "given-thing," does not exist in a purely passive

---

[148] As Henry Osborn Taylor (1919, 138–68) notes about the Icelandic *Saga of Egil*, the personal
life and character of the hero, Egil, is identified in detail: "As a child he was moody, intractable,
and dangerous . . . there was no great love between him and his father." The characters in these
tales are not totally stereo-typified heroes, ideal replicas without personalities, attributes and
flaws. "While the Saga-folk include no cowards or men of petty manners, there is still great diversity of character among them. Some are lazy and some industrious, some quarrelsome and
some good-natured, some dangerous, some forbearing, gloomy or cheerful, open-minded or biased, shrewd or stupid, generous or avaricious."

[149] The quoted words in this paragraph come from Alexander Kojève, Introduction to the Reading of Hegel: Lectures on the Phenomenology of Spirit (1999).

way, but is a being that creates himself by conscious action. One's willingness to assert one's "being-for-self" is the precondition for a life that is freely willed by one's intentions and goals.[150]

The desire for superior recognition, what the Greeks called "megalothymia," is the only desire that is quintessentially immaterial in that it is about gaining respect from one's peers. Of course, at this point in history the subjective side of man manifested itself only in the form of emotional self-assertiveness, through the pride and the haughtiness of free warriors. Men could still not differentiate the three parts of the soul Plato would later identify in *The Republic*: 1) an appetitive part that drives humans to survive and reproduce; 2) a "spirited" or *thymotic* part that drives humans (aristocrats, in our view) to stand for themselves, their honor and seek renown and respect from their peers; and 3) a rational part that allows humans to calculate the best ways to survive and reproduce, as well as be aware that they are beings with a faculty called the "mind" that is singularly rational and cognitively capable of drawing boundaries between the three parts of the soul.

The characters of Indo-European poetry, the Homeric heroes of the *Iliad*, tended to place the mind, *nous*, within the breast, conflating it with the *thymotic* part, while other times they tended to equate *thymos* with the "psyche" because of its association with intense desires and emotions, such as anger—not just any anger, but a special kind of anger activated when a man's honor was violated or when he failed to live up to his code of honor. The Greeks believed that it was man's sense of pride and dignity that drove him to seek recognition from others, to be the bravest, to prefer honor over pleasure and security. A man with a high *thymos* desires prestige for its own sake. Plato, in *The Republic*, calls *thymos* "the ambitious part [of the soul] and that which is covetous of honor." This is what makes this emotion so different, immaterial and "spirited," as contrasted to the "base" emotions associated with the appetitive drives.

This confounding of *thymos* with *nous* suggests to me that it was not the cognitive part of the brain, passively thinking, without desires, that brought about a feeling of selfhood; it was, rather, the thymotic part of the soul that initiated a feeling of selfhood. As the Greeks went on to create a civilization, a more urbane existence, a *polis* in which different clans agreed to a broader sense of identity based on equality of citizenship beyond the clannish aristocratic identities of the

---

[150] For a fuller textual analysis of Kojève's *Introduction to the Reading of Hegel: Lectures on the Phenomenology of Spirit* (1999), and of Hegel's ideas about the aristocratic "fight to the death for pure prestige," see *The Uniqueness of Western Civilization* (2011).

past, they came to emphasize a new virtue, *sophrosyne*, which encouraged the cultivation of a well-balanced character, capable of temperance, prudence, decorum and self-control.[151]

This ideal of moderation emerges after the dark age, in the archaic period of the *Iliad*, and then to a higher degree in the *Odyssey*, when we first witness, in literature, some degree of introspective control over the thymotic part of the soul by aristocrats—as expressed by Homer and after. The *Iliad* acknowledges many of the superior qualities of Achilles as the best warrior, brave and relentless in his pursuit of glory, but Homer also describes him as being unable to control his thymos, stubborn and mindless, consumed by anger and overweening pride. The first two lines of the *Iliad* read: "Sing, Goddess, of the rage of Peleus' son Achilles/the accursed rage that brought great suffering to the Achaeans." There is indeed in this work by Homer a self-awareness that man's *thymos* needs to be properly harnessed by thought or reason, if it is to be properly channeled into civilized behavior, and that doing so requires self-control through the introspective faculty of the mind, even though there is as yet no clear distinction between *thymos* and *nous*, as there would be among the Presocratics.

---

[151] North, 1966.

II

The Literary Origins of Introspection and Selfhood in the Iliad, and Its Further Development in the Odyssey, and After

The genuine aristocrat is the one who has an interior life.

– Nicolás Gómez Dávila

The Greatness of the *Iliad*

The *Iliad*, a poem composed sometime between 725 and 675 BC by a man named Homer, is the first extant work of Western literature. It is acknowledged by many, in the words of William Cullen Bryant, "to be the greatest production of poetic genius that the world had seen."[152] The names most often listed in the hierarchies of poetic genius I have seen are Homer, Virgil, Shakespeare, Dante, and Milton. The American poet and critic Ezra Pound once said that if there is a man for whom you can nearly get "all of poetry" it is Homer. For Tolstoy, when one compares Shakespeare with Homer, "the infinite distance separating true poetry from its imitation emerges with special vividness." The eighteenth-century English poet, Alexander Pope, whose translation of the *Iliad* Bryant read with "avidity," believed it was Homer's "invention" that made him "the greatest of poets." It

---

[152] Bryant was an American romantic poet who completed a translation of the *Iliad* in 1869. The cited words are from his Translator's Preface from a new edition of his translation published by Imperium Press, 2019, to which I contributed a Foreword, upon which this chapter partly draws.

is "invention," he said, "that distinguishes all great geniuses: the utmost stretch of human study, learning, and industry."

> Whatever praises may be given to works of judgment, there is not even a single beauty in them to which the invention must not contribute. . . . It is to the strength of this amazing invention we are to attribute that une-qualled fire and rapture which is so forcible in Homer, that no man of a true poetical spirit is master of himself while he reads him. What he writes is of the most animated nature imaginable; everything moves, everything lives, and is put in action. If a council be called, or a battle fought, you are not coldly informed of what was said or done as from a third person; the reader is hurried out of himself by the force of the poet's imagination, and turns in one place to a hearer, in another to a spectator. . . . This fire is dis-cerned in Virgil, but discerned as through a glass, reflected from Homer, more shining than fierce, but everywhere equal and constant: in Lucan and Statius it bursts out in sudden, short, and interrupted flashes: In Milton it glows like a furnace kept up to an uncommon ardour by the force of art: in Shakespeare it strikes before we are aware, like an accidental fire from heaven: but in Homer, and in him only, it burns everywhere clearly and everywhere irresistibly. [153]

Speaking personally, as a historian and a sociologist, rather than a translator or a poet, what was most surprising about Homer's *Iliad*, in comparison to the major writings which preceded him, songs or recitations of various kinds, including the celebrated epic of Gilgamesh, from civilizations in Mesopotamia, from the "eter-nal" Egyptian world of the Pharaohs, and from Asia generally, is the presence of vivid characters with identifiable personalities, capable of some degree of intro-spection and deliberation. The variety of personalities, of men who can be distin-guished from each other because they exhibit a certain capacity for free individu-ality, is also what Alexander Pope means by Homer's inventiveness as a poet:

> We come now to the characters of his persons; and here we shall find no author has ever drawn so many, with so visible and surprising a variety, or given us such lively and affecting impressions of them. Everyone has some-thing so singularly his own, that no painter could have distinguished them

---

[153] Pope, 1943, v–vi.

more by their features, than the poet has by their manners. Nothing can be more exact than the distinctions he has observed in the different degrees of virtues and vices. The single quality of courage is wonderfully diversified in the several characters of the *Iliad*. That of Achilles is furious and intractable; that of Diomede forward, yet listening to advice, and subject to command; that of Ajax is heavy and self-confiding; of Hector, active and vigilant: the courage of Agamemnon is inspirited by love of empire and ambition; that of Menelaus mixed with softness and tenderness for his people: we find in Idomeneus a plain direct soldier; in Sarpedon a gallant and generous one.[154]

We should not assume, however, that Homer was an artist who invented personalities out of his peculiar genius. When we refer to "Homer" we are not talking about an isolated creator but about a man who captured in the highest poetic form the aristocratic spirit of the ancient Greeks and of Indo-Europeans generally. The *Iliad* is the first literary expression of European selfhood. What we witness in the *Iliad* are characters who are relatively more conscious in exhibiting a slight degree of internal dialogue and responsibility, even if their interior selves are still heavily typified in acting according to the wishes of gods without explicitly declaring "Know thyself," as the Greeks would do during the sixth century BC, the age of the Presocratics. Western consciousness (or individualism) is not a one-time affair, something that emerges in complete form during one historical period; rather, it is a slow, grinding process with many identifiable historical moments, emergent qualities, and variety of expressions depending on the subject one is examining—art, literature, science, philosophy, or law. The *Iliad* is just the beginning of Western consciousness, and beginnings are always the hardest and most important to understand.

It is said that Homer's *Iliad* and *Odyssey* "exist to be translated." The *Iliad* has been translated into English countless times since the first translation in 1581, more than forty in the nineteenth century, another thirty in the twentieth, and sixteen so far in the twenty-first century.[155] Homer has been studied, annotated, and interpreted since antiquity. Not even experts can show command of the vast

---

[154] Pope, 1943, viii.

[155] For these numbers I am relying on Adam Nicolson (2015), and Ian Johnston, "Published English Translations of Homer's Iliad and Odyssey," posted on an online site that is "periodically updated" listing publications of complete English translations of the *Iliad* and *Odyssey*: http://johnstoniatexts.x10host.com/homer/homertranslations.html.

number of studies written over the centuries. They prefer to study limited periods, such as "eighteenth-century notions of the early Greek epic."[156] But while Sir John L. Myres was complaining in the 1930s that "it is not easy to say anything new about Homer,"[157] the number of "new" interpretations actually accelerated after WWII. In my estimation the most fruitful interpretations are contained in Bruno Snell's *The Discovery of the Mind: The Greek Origins of European Thought (1960),* Julian Jaynes's *The Origins of Consciousness in the Breakdown of the Bicameral Mind* (1976), and Keld Zeruneith's *The Wooden Horse: The Liberation of the Western Mind, From Odysseus to Socrates* (2007).

Snell, Jaynes, and Zeruneith

These three books, all based on a close textual analysis of primary textual sources, contain far more than an interpretation of the *Iliad.* Snell (1896–1986) was a German classical philologist, not an evolutionary psychologist or a philosopher of consciousness. His book is an attempt to demonstrate that the ancient Greeks did more than write excellent literary works and philosophical treatises; they actually "discovered the mind" as a faculty in its own right, and the individual as an agent with subjective interiority capable of differentiating human-generated thoughts from the world of gods, with their mandates and interventions, from bodily appetitive drives, and from "spirited" passions, making possible thereby a rational construction of reality. His study begins with "Homer's View of Man" and "The Olympian Gods," from which point it covers lyric poetry, tragedy, pre-Socratic thought, and early Greek ethics through to the discovery of *humanitas* and its impact on Western thought. It is implicit in Snell's book that the "discovery of the intellect" was "a historical growth," rather than a product of natural selection on its own. The coming into existence of the intellect is not merely about "recognizing another man" (viii). As Marc Hauser observes, animals already have "a mental tool for recognizing others, distinguishing males from females, young from old, and kin from non-kin."[158] What Snell means by "discovery of the intellect" is the recognition of one's self, one's mind, as the agency of thinking. "This

---

[156] Simonsuuri, 1979.

[157] Myres, 1958, 1. Myres' book, *Homer and His Critics,* was constructed from research and writings he completed in the 1930s.

[158] Hauser, 2000, 113.

intellect . . . comes into the world . . . in the course of history."[159] And it emerges when the ancient Greeks attain an awareness of their inner mental states as part of their selves.

Jaynes (1927–1997) was a psychologist who spent years studying the roots and nature of consciousness in animals and humans following the prevailing evolutionary assumptions starting to dominate this field in the second half of the twentieth century, eventually reaching the conclusion that, while natural selection played a role in the beginnings, consciousness was chiefly a cultural construction. He defined consciousness as a capacity to introspect upon one's sensations and thoughts, and argued, accordingly, that we can only speak of consciousness when we are able to identify the emergence of "a self that is responsible and can debate within itself."[160]

He placed the origin of this self sometime around 1400–600 BC, while insisting that consciousness did not arrive in one shot in complete form, but is actually still emerging in our times, as witnessed by the rise of studies about its origins. He warned, however, against the arrogance of scientists who presume that their methodologies hold the key to discovering "the Final Answer, the One Truth, the Single Cause"[161] of the nature of consciousness. He was critical of behaviorists for pretending they had "solved the problem of consciousness" by denying its reality. He was also critical of evolutionary psychologists for confusing consciousness with mere perception or awareness of sensory phenomena, and of cognitive psychologists for identifying consciousness with cognition defined in terms of the neural or computational processes observed and analyzed by scientists from a third person perspective. He insisted that true consciousness entailed a conscious act of thinking about one's mental states, reflective awareness of one's act of thinking, as contrasted to mere external observation.

Although Jaynes' book received reviews in major scientific journals, and a "Julian Jaynes Society" was actually founded in 1997 that is still operating, organizing conferences and publishing about his ideas, his work is mostly ignored by scientists today. His claim that consciousness was not chiefly a product of natural selection, or amenable to external observation, seemed out of line at a time, in the 1970s, when evolutionary psychology was just taking off with precise experimental and laboratory studies, along with the coming explosion in artificial

---

[159] Snell, 1960, xi.
[160] Jaynes, 1976, 79.
[161] Ibid, 443.

intelligence and cognitive science. His interdisciplinary approach, drawing not only from the sciences but primarily from "literary" fields, ancient myths, legends, historical accounts, poems, music, prophets, and studies of hypnosis and schizophrenia, gave his work a New Age quality mistrusted by "serious" scientists.

Yet, interestingly enough, Jaynes' argument that consciousness entails more than perceptual awareness of the external world, an awareness of one's awareness of the world, is consistent with LeDoux's argument that there is true awareness when perceptual "first order" information is conceptually re-represented by the prefrontal cortex of humans with its novel evolutionary features. A key difference between their approaches, besides LeDoux's reliance on the latest findings about the evolutionary structure of the brain, is that LeDoux assumes, as we saw in Chapter I, that the biological-neurological possibility of higher order thinking produced by natural selection tens of thousands of years ago automatically produced humans as aware of their consciousness as we are today. He projects the mental states of Western/modern individuals today to prehistorical humans who did not even have a written language. What makes *The Origins of Consciousness* an invaluable work to this day, despite major advances in our knowledge of the evolution of the brain and its workings, is precisely that it broke with the standard view that consciousness is strictly a matter for psychologists and scientists to understand, arguing instead that consciousness has been "built, formed, shaped" by cultural development in the course of human historical time.[162]

Zeruneith tell us that *The Wooden Horse* took him ten years to write and that he has been interested in classical culture since school days. He is the recipient of Denmark's highest literary honor, the Gyldendal Prize. The book has been praised by prominent classicists for its "profound exploration of ancient mythmaking" and as an "extraordinary book" that traces the "primal structures" of Greek consciousness. The method that Zeruneith uses is also textual analysis, though its focus is on ancient works rather than modern scholars. The thesis he advances is that with the character Odysseus "there are clear tendencies toward true introspection" and that in Homer's *Odyssey* we witness "for the first time . . . a human being thinking discursively . . . separating action from awareness, internal and external, which until then had been a unity."[163]

This thesis is very much in line with the inquiries of Snell and Jaynes, which he acknowledges in footnotes. The more important influence on Zeruneith,

---

[162] Ibid, 281.
[163] Zeruneith, 29, 15.

however, is that of Neumann's book, *The Origins and History of Consciousness*. He draws on Neumann's argument (though he never stops to analyze this work apart from a long footnote) that the liberation of consciousness required the separation of the male ego from its primeval absorption by maternal chthonic gods.[164] The difference is that for Zeruneith the full liberation from the Great Mother, the "repression of the original fertility gods," and the instauration of Olympian gods, was a revolution initiated by Homer and Hesiod. Zeruneith's mind is totally focused on ancient Greece, not any prior historical period.

The Wooden Horse is never mentioned outside the tiny world of classicists. Specialized neuropsychologists and philosophers of the mind would not be interested in it even if they knew about it. Classicists, as it is, think of it as an "imaginative, highly idiosyncratic" book with no wider implications beyond arcane debates about Greek mythology and poetry. That's how academia operates today, each to his own specialization. No one wants to connect arguments across disciplinary fields. The scholars involved with the "great divergence" or "the rise of the West" have no acquaintance with any of the books discussed thus far, nor with most of the books and subjects to be discussed in the next chapters. This is unfortunate, for Zeruneith's book reinforces, through a very studious textual analysis of ancient texts, the ideas of Jaynes, Snell, and Neumann.

Now, it may seem odd to praise these authors, since their central argument on the origins of consciousness contradict my view that Homer is the first writer in whom we find emerging signs of human deliberation and recognizable personalities. Snell writes:

> Homer does not know genuine personal decisions; even where a hero is shown pondering two alternatives the intervention of the gods plays the key role. . . . Mental and spiritual acts are due to the impact of external factors, and man is the open target of a great many forces which impinge on him, and penetrate his very core.[165]

---

[164] I read Neumann before Zeruneith. I came across Zeruneith by accident, upon seeing his book in a "for sale" pile of books.
[165] Snell, 20.

Jaynes writes:

> The characters of the *Iliad* do not sit down and think out what to do. They
> have no conscious minds such as we say we have, and certainly no intro-
> spection. It is impossible for us with our subjectivity to appreciate what it
> was like. When Agamemnon, king of men, robs Achilles of his mistress, it
> is a god that grasps Achilles by his yellow hair and warns him not to strike
> Agamemnon. . . . Iliadic men have no will of their own and certainly no
> notion of free will. . . . Iliadic man . . . had no awareness of his awareness
> of the world, no internal mind-space to introspect upon.[166]

Zeruneith writes:

> The difference between the *Iliad* and the *Odyssey* [is that of] entailing a
> development in the complexity of human consciousness, which the *Odys-
> sey* represents through its protagonist.[167]

These three scholars are nevertheless invaluable in arguing that the origins of a
self, in the words of Jaynes, "that is responsible and can debate within itself . . . is
the product of culture," even if they believe that this self was a product of post-
Iliadic Greece.[168] They all recognize, albeit in their various ways of accentuation,
that "from approximately 750 to 359 BC" a "new age and a new awareness," to use
the words of Zeruneith, establishes itself in the world, when "Western civilization"
witnesses "a capacity for reflection that can distinguish subject from object and
imagine what makes people act—and how."[169]

Let's start with Snell. Once his book moves past Homer, it is a most penetrat-
ing illumination of how "human thinking undergoes a radical change" characterized by the onset of "self-knowledge in the spirit of the Delphic motto: 'Know thyself.'"[170] *The Discovery of the Mind* tells us that starting in the archaic period of
Greek history, between 650 and 500 BC, we encounter lyrical poets "conscious of
their individuality" writing poetry expressing "inwardly felt emotions" and thus

---

[166] Jaynes, 70–75.
[167] Zeruneith, 22.
[168] Jaynes, 79.
[169] Zeruneith, 28.
[170] Snell, 207, 213.

showing "a more precise appreciation of the self."[171] Lyric poets "announce their own names; they speak about themselves and become recognizable as personalities."[172] Whereas in the Iliad "the truth that men have various goals is not yet clearly stated," in the poet Archilochus we read that "each man has his heart cheered in his own way."[173] Sappho distinguishes "her own aesthetic judgement from the values of others," and values "inwardly felt" emotions over the standardized expressed in the *Iliad* in which every character shows the same feelings of admiration for "parades of horse, soldiers, and ships."

In Homer "the emotions do not spring spontaneously from within man, but are bestowed on him by the gods."[174] But in Archilochus and Sappho, love is described as a privately-felt feeling. Of her beloved daughter Kleis, Sappho writes: "I would not exchange all the Lydian lands for her"—as contrasted to the customary morality of the *Iliad,* where nothing seems to be more valuable than for individuals to express their commitment to the pursuit of military grandeur, or follow a life-path as if it were their fate, "which leaves no alternative but to recognize the operation of a universal force."[175]

During the fifth century BC, we see a more dramatic contrast between Homer's men, who "act with perfect assurance," without knowing "what it means to be burdened with scruples or doubts," and the "tragedies of Aeschylus" where "the agent, conscious of his individual freedom of choice, makes himself personally answerable for his actions." In Greek tragedy, "for the first time in history man begins to look at himself as the maker of his own decisions." With Euripides we see a "radical critique" which deprives the gods of their unquestioned power over what is justice; "the fond ideals of religious tradition are unmasked and demolished so that a truer justice may be discovered" based on "personal feeling of what is right."[176]

In Euripides' *Medea,* for the first time in history, there is a "genuine monologue" in which Medea is portrayed deliberating over "the conflicting impulses of her heart," including what "reason" is telling her, without "the demands and warnings of some supernatural authority giving her guidance."[177] In Euripides'

---

[171] Ibid, 44–48.
[172] Ibid, 44.
[173] Ibid, 47.
[174] Ibid, 52.
[175] Ibid, 61.
[176] Ibid, 123–25.
[177] Ibid, 126.

character Iphigenia, we have moral decisions that do not "flow from the prestige of the State or the gods, nor from the pious honoring of ancient injunctions, but from the simplicity of her heart, chaste and untarnished in a confused and sense-less world."[178]

While the tragedians portrayed man in a state of conflicting impulses, some-times driven by their passions or their purely personal sense of what is right, Soc-rates begins a thorough investigation into the nature of virtue in response to the tragic hero who ponders over what is the right course of action when facing con-flicting moral expectations, be they from the gods, myths, society, or the passions. The answer Socrates gave is that men must "place their passions and impulses completely under the control of the understanding."[179]

Only those actions which are established by the reasoning mind can be said to be truly voluntary, rather than products of uncontrolled impulses emanating from the body or the "spirited" (passionate) part of the soul. The ideal of *sophrosyne* became a major topic in Plato: the idea that only through the attainment of self-control and temperance could men act freely, not by suppressing altogether their desire for honor, but by allowing the faculty of reason to be the arbiter, establish-ing thereby the "proper functioning of the emotions."

A very important argument in Snell is that it is only in the Greek language that we can trace the origins of a language that made possible the rise of theoretic thought. It was the Greeks who invented the definite article, which points to the ability to think abstractly. "All other languages . . . have borrowed or translated or got their [scientific] terms" from without. It was the definite article (such words as "the") that permitted the development of abstract concepts from an adjective or a verb, as well as formulate the idea of a horse beyond a concrete or particular horse. However, while the definite article is already present in Homer, the evolu-tion of the definite article is only "a seed for the growth of scientific concepts." In Homer, the phrase "the horse" is "never the concept of a horse, but always a par-ticular horse." The substantiation of the verb or the adjective is also required in order to describe non-physical facts.

The use of abstract concepts in Heraclitus points to the emergence of this ab-stract language, of someone who speaks in terms of "the act of thinking, the uni-versal, and the *logos*," which "do not refer to a unique or personal object . . . or

---

[178] Ibid, 131.
[179] Ibid, 182.

comprise a number of concrete objects."[180] Essentially, what we start witnessing among the Presocratics is a conceptual ability to distinguish the physical from the non-physical, to talk in terms of "the water" and "the cold," which is indispensable for the rise of true philosophic thought.

The flaw in Snell is that he never explains why the Greeks discovered the mind and why they became conscious agents capable of delimiting the role of gods, distinguishing their thoughts from the physical world, and producing thereby universal concepts, a system of logic and abstract scientific terms, to go about grasping the forces that underlie the multiple particularities we experience through the senses. He seems to imply that poets, literary writers, and philosophers somehow managed, through their sheer personal artistic and philosophical creativity, to bring about the liberation of the mind. Snell, moreover, views the achievements of the Greeks as the achievements of humans generally. He belonged to a post-World War II generation uncomfortable with differences between ethnic groups, compelled to think in terms of the "human species" rather than the "European species." He could not really think of the Greeks as a people that were on a fundamentally different historical-cultural path.

We can sense this in Snell's interpretation of the Greek invention of "humanitas," which he takes to mean that the Greeks were reminding us that "each and every human being has his own share of dignity and of freedom,"[181] confounding the Greek idea that the humanity of man is recognizable only in the degree to which he strives for the highest within himself, with the post-WWII human rights idea that all humans are equally born with inherent rights. There is no doubt that, in speaking of *humanitas*, the Greeks were rising above their ethnic/cultural particularities and norms, to think about humans in general. But, at this point in Western history, the term *humanitas* meant something very different from the modern idea that humans, as such, are in possession of inherent "natural rights" which must be recognized by the state as their birthright.

Humanitas was, for the ancient Greeks, an ideal that only a few men could attain through a long arduous life dedicated to the cultivation of their highest and noblest potentialities. It may be more accurate to say that the Greeks were ethnocentrically projecting their obsession with aristocratic excellence to humans across all cultures. This reluctance to identify the Greeks as very different, in their attainment of selfhood, combined with the ever-growing influence of the

---

[180] Ibid, 227–232.
[181] Ibid, 263.

Darwinian claim that all humans developed a uniform and ready-made conscious equipment in the pursuit of survival strategies, has made it very difficult for scholars to give a proper account of the development of consciousness in the West.

Jaynes, too, despite his argument that the *Iliad* is devoid of characters who are "conscious of their consciousness," recognizes that the ancient Greeks, particularly during the sixth century, exhibited a very high level of self-awareness. But the first signs of selfhood, in his view, are detectable in Mesopotamia "towards the end of the second millennium BC." Before this time, humans were dominated by a "bicameral mind." We don't need to get into the neuroscience underlying the term "bicameral" to understand Jaynes' meaning, which is a state of being in which humans are ruled by the voices of gods, customary mandates, mythical stories, and rigid theocratic norms. This does not mean that humans could not perform a whole range of practical tasks with full sensory awareness. Consciousness of consciousness, Jaynes explains, is not necessary for everyday thinking. We perform all sorts of practical tasks, drive cars, mop the floor, clean the garage, without being conscious of the performance of these activities. We are conscious when we are aware of our awareness.

A bicameral mind is a mind that does not consciously think about its own thinking, for it lacks "an interior self," as the self is barely differentiated, even if there is already a degree of male differentiation from the fertility cult of the Great Mother. It is a mind that is undifferentiated from the collective norms of the tribe or the despotic rule of the Pharaoh, the preserver of the God-given order responsible for his people's economic and spiritual welfare.

Jaynes offers an explanation of how consciousness began but not a persuasive one. He says that it began sometime around 1400–600 B.C., when men were compelled by the chaos of wars, catastrophes, and national migrations induced by overpopulation, and by the widespread use of writing, to question their bicameral mentality and to voice their own internally generated thoughts.[182] Jaynes emphasizes how the development of writing in the second millennium, combined with the weakening and collapse of theocratic empires, coupled with the intermingling of peoples from different nations with different beliefs, weakened the "auditory" power of the gods and the rigid norms of one's society, opening the door thereby for some reflective distancing from customary beliefs.

Jaynes has in mind not the writing first invented in Mesopotamia around 3500–3000 BC, as an inventory device, a way of recording the collection of taxes

---

[182] Jaynes, 204–222.

and God-commanded events. He excludes the legal texts of Hammurabi composed during 1755–1750 BC as being "behavioristic, commanding, and without greeting." He means the writing found in the "narratization of epics" in which an "I" of ourselves "doing this or that," and thus making "decisions on the basis of imagined outcomes" makes an appearance.[183] He explains that human introspection and self-visualization first emerged through the making of metaphors and analogies, metaphors of "me" and of "analog I." Humans came to experience consciousness of themselves as generators of their own thoughts only when they had developed a language sophisticated enough to produce metaphors and analogical models, that is, figures of speech containing an implied comparison of two things that are not the same. Literary critics today agree that the use of metaphors bespeaks of humans who can think and converse unconventionally about abstract and subjective experiences, for metaphors are about extending our reasoning to encompass different realms of reality—emotional, philosophical, and naturalistic.

But as Jaynes admits, what he presents by way of historical examples of this metaphorical thinking in Mesopotamia are a "few suggestions."[184] He finds historical chronicles after 1300 BC, with a "metaphor of time as a space that could be regionalized such that events and persons can be located therein, giving that sense of past, present, and future in which narratization is possible."[185] Events are "arranged systematically according to the yearly campaigns," with "statements of motive, criticisms of courses of action, appraisals of character ... political changes, campaign strategies, historical notes on particular regions," beyond the mere listing of plain actions by the king. In his judgement, this "spatialization of time" amounted to the "invention of history."

I disagree. The invention of proper historical writing was a Greek achievement, as I will argue extensively in Chapter X. By the time of Polybius (200–118 BC), we have an ecumenical or universal historian in considerable awareness that understanding one's place in time requires a historical grasp of "the whole of the inhabited world" and of the causes of historical change, the how, why, who, what, where, and when of things, including the recording of events with accuracy through the use of profuse references. Jaynes is nevertheless correct that we should not take the invention of historical writing for granted: "How strange it seems to think of the idea of history having to be invented!"[186] Placing one's actions within

---

[183] Ibid, 63.
[184] Ibid, 216.
[185] Ibid, 250.
[186] Ibid, 251.

a narrative of past, present, and possible future developments, testifies to a high level of self-awareness. A historical consciousness was less a product of natural selection than of cultural development. *Homo sapiens* lacked a historical consciousness before the emergence of advanced civilizations. If we agree with Le-Doux (and Brown and Lau) that "high order consciousness" is about being able to see "your self in the present moment in relation to your past and future . . . about experiences you have had, [with] a sense of continuity with your personal past [recollecting memories] to project into possible personal futures [wondering what you might do in an hypothetical future],"[187] then the invention of history by He-rodotus and Thucydides may surely be designated as the beginnings of a high level of "autonoetic consciousness and narration" beyond one's personal life.

Jaynes also refers to the seventh century rendering of the *Epic of Gilgamesh* as an instance of the emergence of "subjective thinking" in the way it "brings out the subjective sadness in the heart of Gilgamesh" at the loss of his friend, citing these words: "Why is thy heart so sad, and why are thy features so distorted? Why is there woe in your heart?" But that is all he offers to make the claim that this poem is calling upon readers to "imagine the interior 'space' and analog 'I' of the hero."[188] We will question this interpretation of Gilgamesh below. But, first, Jaynes's choice of the *Iliad* as a key example of the bicameral mind is perplexing considering that the *Iliad* was the most sophisticated example in the "narratization of epics" in ancient times, a poem written towards the end of the very period Jaynes said the bicameral mind broke down.

However, we should not ignore some important qualifications made by Jaynes. He admits there are signs of the breakdown of the bicameral mind in the *Iliad*, citing the famous statement by Achilles against Agamemnon: "Hateful to me as the gates of Hades is the man who hides one thing in his heart and speaks another"—as an "indication of subjective consciousness."[189] He cites the words in which both Agenor and Hector exclaim "the same astonished words"—"But wherefore does my life say this to me?"—as clear intimations of introspection. In the end, however, Jaynes concludes that these were exceptional expressions possibly added later after Homer.

One has to ask: if Greek literature after the *Iliad*, as Jaynes says, "very quickly became a literature of consciousness," and if "we may regard the *Iliad* as standing

---

[187] Brown et al., 2019.
[188] Jaynes, 253.
[189] Ibid, 82.

at the great turning of the times," the breakdown of the bicameral mind, would it not be more reasonable to suppose that the *Iliad* was a transitional work in which certain bicameral aspects co-existed alongside a newly emerging subjective consciousness? Why does Jaynes insist that the *Iliad* must be seen "as a window back into those unsubjective times when every kingdom was in essence a theocracy"?[190] Why not as a window into an emerging metaphorical mentality?

More questions are begged by Jaynes's sudden statement that in Homer's *Odyssey* there is a sharp distancing from the bicameral mentality of the *Iliad* "toward subjective consciousness . . . increasing use of spatial interiority and personification . . . a new mentality."[191] He justifies this sharp break by suggesting that the *Odyssey* was possibly the work of a poet writing "at least a century later. The consensus today, however, is that these two books were authored by the same person we call "Homer," despite the fact that, as Zeruneith says, "no one knows and no one will ever know who Homer was."[192]

The *Iliad* is already critical of Achilles lack of sober-mindedness, his inability to restrain his anger and control his thymos, admired though he was for being the greatest fighter. The *Iliad* also contains, in the portrayal of characters, as I will try to demonstrate further below, introspective monologues and signs of selfhood. The society depicted in the *Iliad* was not, as Jaynes says, "quite similar to the contemporary divinely ruled kingdoms of Mesopotamia."[193] The *Iliad* grew out of a prototypical Indo-European aristocratic society, Mycenae, in which the king was first among equals. Mycenaeans are the first people in history to have created a civilization, not just a chiefdom, in which "some men," rather than only the king, were free to deliberate over major issues affecting the group and free to aspire for heroic greatness. The *Iliad* is packed with metaphors and analogies, and with identifiable personalities with differentiated psychological dispositions.

In the case of Zeruneith, we have an extremely detailed textual study of the *Odyssey* totaling 273 pages (in small print) representing half of *The Wooden Horse*. We can barely do justice to the breadth of Zeruneith's learning about Homer other than to emphasize that he judges the *Odyssey* to be "the very first example of anything resembling introspection." Odysseus is "the master of eloquence" and "inner monologue." With his second book, we meet in Homer "a tendency toward rationality that breaks through in the philosophers [Presocratics] and is fully

---

[190] Ibid, 83.
[191] Ibid, 276.
[192] Zeruneith, 32.
[193] Jaynes, 80.

revealed in Socrates/Plato in whom we can finally say that the body and soul are completely separate." The mental life we encounter in the *Odyssey* is,

> still partially interwoven in the spirit of myth in a subject-object relationship that is alien to us, [but] Homer's presentation has passed beyond the non-reflective state of language in which human beings expressed themselves holophrastically without separating nouns and verbs –and, consequently, without causal relationships and differentiation, between the subject and its surrounding world.[194]

Whereas characters in the *Iliad* are portrayed as if they are not responsible for their actions, or their actions are seen to be brought about through the intervention of gods from without, Odysseus' motives for action come from within. The *Odyssey* manifests a deeper understanding of psychology and personal morality, with characters conscious of how their own desires for food, wine, power, and sex are what drives them to act in certain ways, not alien forces, thus accepting their "responsibility" for their behavior.[195]

In a chapter, "The Lyrical Sense of Self," Zeruneith maintains, similarly to Snell, that Archilochus' disassociation from "the heroic-aristocratic view of the world," from the obsession with attaining military fame, marked a "breach with inherited conventions" towards "emphasizing the value of inner human qualities," and judging "people individually."[196] This internalization by Archilochus allows him to know himself. Sappho, too, "by channeling the desire and pain brought about by passion, looks into herself in an extreme subjectivization of emotional life."[197] This self-insight points to a recognition that there is a boundary between inner and outer, without which cognition of the nature of things is impossible. In Presocratic thought, "self-insight also becomes an investigation into universal laws."[198]

In our next chapter we will return to this idea. Another important feature of Zeruneith's book is the observation that "in the *Iliad* we encounter a thoroughly male, heroic culture, which is completely isolated in its own heroic norms from the world of women." He clearly draws on Neumann (and reminds us of Paglia)

---

[194] Zeruneith, 52–53.
[195] Ibid, 116.
[196] Ibid, 300–303.
[197] Ibid, 310.
[198] Ibid, 317.

when he writes that "if man is to realize himself completely, he must not only differentiate himself from the primal feminine but reconquer the feminine in a higher form by confronting and integrating what is repressed in the most frightening form of the mother goddess."[199] The cult of the mother represents a "dark" and "faceless" world, in which the emphasis of the so-called Venuses is on the "fertility of their sexual markers: bulging and over-dimensional buttocks, breasts, hips and thighs."[200] This is a contourless, undifferentiated world, without selfhood and inner intelligence, dominated by primeval nature, which overwhelms and engulfs the consciousness of men.

Zeruneith astutely tells us that the Indo-Europeans who conquered Greece with their sky gods began a process of patriarchization, while retaining their "veneration of the earth and its ancillary gods of fertility . . . side by side."[201] It was with Homer's "invention of the Olympic gods" that we see, for the first time in human history, a full attempt to "reconquer the feminine," "to repress the cult of the Great Mother," not to eliminate the fertility gods altogether, but to subdue them to the patriarchal authority of the Olympian gods living in heaven and associated with light, the quintessential symbol of consciousness, and with the heroic lifestyle of the aristocracy. In other words, Zeruneith suggests, in a way that Neumann does not, that the full differentiation of the male ego is attained in a period around 850–700 BC, the age of Hesiod and Homer. The Olympian gods were developed "intellectually." We will return to this key subject later on.[202]

Iliad Reflects European *Thymos*, Not "Human Nature"

The academic position, as it now stands, is that the Iliad is a work that conveys profound, eternal human truths. Take Bernard Knox's introduction to Robert Fagles' 1990 translation of the *Iliad*. This otherwise learned introduction abounds in statements that seek to portray the *Iliad* as a poem written by and for humanity. Everyone after WWII was expected to write with a view to improving the "human

---

[199] Ibid, 99.

[200] Ibid, 91.

[201] Ibid, 87.

[202] Snell, too, observes that, while decisions are indeed shaped by the gods, the Olympian gods "carry the graceful stamp of an aristocratic society . . . when a god associates with a man, he elevates him, and makes him free, strong, courageous, certain of himself . . . far removed from the mysteries of chthonic darkness and ecstasy" (23–42).

condition," and the *Iliad*, or so we are told, contains moral messages by and for humanity. Here are some passages from this introduction:

> The *Iliad* accepts violence as a permanent factor in *human life* and accepts it without sentimentality, for it is just as sentimental to pretend that war does not have its monstrous ugliness as it is to deny that is has its own strange and fatal beauty.
>
> The tragic course of Achilles' rage, his final recognition of *human values*—this is the guiding theme of the poem, and it is developed against a background of violence and death. But the grim progress of the war is interrupted by scenes which remind us that the brutality of war, though an integral part of *human life*, is not the whole of it. . . .
>
> These two poles of the *human condition*, war and peace, with their corresponding aspects of *human nature*, the destructive and creative, are implicit in every situation and statement of the poem.[203]

This is confounding because the violence of the *Iliad* can only be fully comprehended in the context of a culture dominated by free aristocrats, because the values of the *Iliad* are not "human values" but European aristocratic values, because there is no tragic literature outside the West, because the *Iliad* points to the beginning of literary characters with a sense of selfhood, and because in the West the destructive and creative are not two corresponding aspects of human nature, but are instead inextricably dependent upon each other. Destructive warfare is the activity where ancient Greeks, before the full discovery of the mind, realized their potential for the highest. It was through their pursuit of heroic deeds that Europeans first achieved their individuality and started a process in which Europeans began to overcome the dark world of mysterious forces and unquestioned norms enveloping the subjective consciousness of humans. It is not just that war "releases essential creative instincts . . . heightens man's sense of life, his joy in his humanness, his sense of beauty in the world, and his love and respect for his fellow man."[204] It is that warfare carried out by aristocratic men was the primordial foundation for the emergence of consciousness and the cultural efflorescence of ancient Greece. It is very misleading to talk about "human values" and "fellow man" when the *Iliad* was singularly a product of a particular culture.

---

[203] Knox, 1990, emphasis mine.
[204] Johnston, 1988.

What makes this all the more intractable is that, in the same vein as the Iliad has been portrayed as a work that speaks about "the human condition," the literature of the non-Western world has been increasingly interpreted as if it were part of the same set of cultural values that made the West. Perhaps the best way to start bringing home how different the first book of Western civilization, the *Iliad*, is from all prior works produced by the surrounding bicameral civilizations, is to compare it to the Epic of Gilgamesh, seen as the greatest literary work produced in the East, and the "first heroic epic."

The *Epic of Gilgamesh* Is Not a Heroic Tragedy

The story of Gilgamesh is not a heroic tragedy because the world this story grew from was not aristocratic.[205] The upper classes of the Near Eastern world were not free; sovereignty in these states belonged to either god-kings or kings considered the viceroys of the gods. Yet, in our multicultural universities where "diversity" programs are the order of the day, the current trend has been that Gilgamesh is an epic with "striking similarities" to the *Iliad* and to other Western poems such as *Beowulf*. A known expert on Homer, Jasper Griffin, in a long review of Stephen Mitchell's *Gilgamesh: A New English Version*, states that the heroic themes of the *Iliad* were predated by over a thousand years in "an extraordinary epic poem" known as Gilgamesh.[206] Similarly, N. K. Sandars, in an earlier English translation of this epic, informs us that the king Gilgamesh is "the first tragic hero."

I cannot agree with these classicists. We can agree with Walter Burkert's sensible enough point that in both the Homeric poems and Gilgamesh we have "epic" narratives which employ long verses repeated indefinitely, dealing with gods, sons of gods, and great men from the past. Both epics, we can also agree, employ similar traits of style, standard epithets, formulaic verses, repetition of verses, and typical scenes. Up to a point, Burkert may be right at least on the surface, that the central characters in Gilgamesh and in Homer's epics are warriors who perform great deeds. But the differences, I would suggest, are far more striking than the resemblances.

---

[205] This section, and the following two sections, draw on sections from *The Uniqueness of Western Civilization* (2011).

[206] Griffin, 2006.

To start with, the "hero" Gilgamesh appears, from the very beginning, as a typical Eastern ruler who claims to have achieved all the great things for his society, and no one else has any achievements to their names. The only other fighting man in this epic is Enkidu, a wild man who lacks nobility. Unlike the *Iliad*, which consists of battle scenes constructed largely out of individual encounters designed to enhance the specific deeds of singular heroes, there are no individuals with identifiable biographies in Gilgamesh. The ruler, a king of Uruk or Erech, a city of Mesopotamia, first appears as a despot, in contradistinction to the ideal ruler who should be a shepherd of the city; and, although it is the case that this was an ideal that motivated Eastern rulers to show concern for righteousness, consider the following acts attributed to Gilgamesh in the opening scenes, which clearly give him a tyrannical touch: "his lust leaves no virgin to her lover, neither the warrior's daughter nor the wife of the noble."[207]

As this passage suggests, even the daughters of warriors and the wives of nobles were not safe from the whims and appetites of kings. In stark contrast, Agamemnon, King of Mycenae, appears in the opening pages of the *Iliad* facing the fury and insubordination of his most important vassal, Achilles, with all his followers, for having offended his honor in taking a girl Achilles had earned as a prize from his army. Although Achilles is "the best of the Achaeans," the performer of "the greatest deeds of martial valor," the *Iliad* devotes long sketches to the personal ancestries of other aristocrats including, for example, Diomedes in Book 5, Patroklus in Book 16, and Menelaus in Book 17. Even warriors who are not major figures are identified by name, their parents, wife, and children, and their homelands.

In Homer's vision of the Mycenaean past, Agamemnon is surrounded by free, prideful men who are always deliberating and debating their actions rather than subserviently following the commands of an autocratic king. The king Agamemnon, writes Martin Nilsson, "was no Pharaoh nor was he a king by divine right like the Hellenistic kings and the late Roman Emperors."[208] The right to attend the popular assembly was restricted to those who risked their lives in battle. The chiefs were the representatives of their contingents and spoke in their name. Freedom of speech was inherent at the assembly. Much of the *Iliad* consists of speeches by aristocratic warriors arguing over strategies, and debating the king's proposals over the conduct of the war. The *Iliad* is abundant in the creation of "some two

---

[207] Sandars, 1981, 62.
[208] Nilsson, 1968, 233.

dozen finely individualized major characters" in addition to numerous minor figures. No single autocrat made all the decisions and boasted about his deeds without challengers.[209]

Now, to be sure, the relation of the *Iliad* to historical reality has long been a
matter of scholarly interest. A few scholars have claimed that what Homer really
mirrors is his own contemporary world of the eighth century BC, while others
have argued that his epics call back the world of "Dark Age" Greece around 1050–
900 BC. The stronger consensus is that Homer's poems reflect the central cultural
values of the Mycenaean Age of about 1400–1100 BC. There are a variety of elements in his epics representing different periods regarding the types of weapons,
shields, and metals mentioned in the poems. But the social structures and values
are still drawn primarily from the world of late aristocratic Mycenae.[210]

Oswyn Murray thinks that Mycenaean states were rather similar to the "oriental despotisms" of Mesopotamia and Egypt.[211] He may be correct that the warrior people who founded Mycenae came to be influenced by the centralized palace
economies of the Near East. I tend to favor the view that the political structure of
the Greek mainland during the second millennium was one of autonomous "feudal" warlords surrounded by aristocratic retainers under the nominal overlordship of Mycenae. The king was the overlord or the *wanax* of other lords. Mycenaean records do refer to a class called *hepetai* or "followers" who formed the
court circle, but these were also identified as the "companions" of the king. There
are references as well to warriors called *telestai*, or men of telos, who were similarly
wealthy aristocrats, masters of parcels of land which they had obtained in return
for military undertakings with the king.[212]

With the collapse of Mycenaean culture around 1100 BC, and the destruction
of Mycenae and the administrators who managed the centralizing palaces of the
overlord, the distinction between the overlord and the vassal noble chieftains disappeared, and instead of a political order centered around an overlord-monarch,

---

[209] Actually, as M. L. West observes: "A king may himself be a hero, but in most cases the roles
are distinct. The outstanding hero—one may think of Achilles, Hector, Jason, Heracles, Arjuna,
Beowulf, Cu Chulainn, Lancelot—is usually not identified with the king. The king is remembered
for kingly virtues such as justice, prosperity, liberality or his lack of them." A hero in Indo-European poetry was "generally a man of supreme physical strength and endurance allied to moral
qualities such as fearlessness, determination, and a propensity for plunging into dangerous and
daunting enterprises" (2007, 411).

[210] Luce, 1975; Chadwick, 2005, 180–86.

[211] Murray, 1980, 18.

[212] Luce, 1975, 79–80; Robinson, 1983, 12–18; Chadwick, 2005, 72; Arnheim, 1977, 15–17.

one finds in Greece many decentralized petty chiefdoms.[213] This may explain why in Homer's poems—to the degree that they partly reflect the preceding Dark Age—the king Agamemnon is portrayed as having very limited powers. Be that as it may, in Homer's time, which is known as the Archaic Age (roughly between 800 and 500 BC), aristocrats expected kings to consult a council consisting of the heads of the noble families. "Debate within the council or before the people was the basis of decision-making."[214]

The crucial difference comes down to the absence of personal tragedy in Gilgamesh. We can't talk of heroism and tragedy when there is only one ruler with the chance to claim fame without peers to challenge him, question his deeds, and put him to the test. Burkert equates Gilgamesh's longing for immortality with the Homeric heroes' longing for "imperishable glory."[215] It is true that Gilgamesh longs for eternity, and on his journey, at the last moment, he finds a secret herb that promises the gift of eternal youth; but then a snake, a reptile, takes the herb as he is asleep, and so he fails to achieve eternity. The suggestion seems to be that even the king's destiny is ultimately decided by arbitrary (bicameral) forces or accidental events. Where is the heroism in a situation in which a snake decides the outcome? The message that death is the lot of mankind is decided by a snake. Moreover, while Gilgamesh is a hero who "wishes to make for himself a name" and in his journey defeats the giant monster Humbaba, it is noteworthy that what he yearns for is everlasting life, weeping bitterly when the snake steals the herb; which is, again, in direct contrast to the pursuit of personal immortality by Homer's Mycenaean warriors, who sought above all else, above comfort and life itself, to be renowned for glorious deeds. Indeed, whereas Gilgamesh yearned for everlasting life, the Greek heroes consciously rejected a long life without memorable deeds for a short life with immortal deeds. The contrast could not be greater.[216]

Sandars defines the tragic in Gilgamesh as "the conflict between the desires of the god and the destiny of man."[217] Griffin concludes with these words of wisdom:

---

[213] Ehrenberg, 1964, 17–20; Arnheim, 38–9.

[214] Oswyn, 58.

[215] Burkert, 2004, 27.

[216] Although Samuel Kramer (1959, 203) tries to mirror Gilgamesh as the "first heroic epic," he acknowledges that in comparison to the "written epics of the three Indo-European Heroic Ages" (the Greek, Indian, and Teutonic) "there is little characterization and psychological penetration in the Sumerian material. The heroes tend to be broad types, more or less undifferentiated, rather than highly personalized individuals."

[217] Sandars, 21.

"the highest nobility and the deepest truth are inseparable, in the end, from fail-ure—however heroic—from defeat, and from death." Griffin would have us be-lieve that Gilgamesh and the *Iliad* are in the end inseparable. There is a tragic ele-ment in both: no matter what their heroes accomplish, the same end awaits them, namely defeat and death. Burkert thinks that the main message of both epics is the ethos of the mortality of humans in contrast to the enduring life of gods. Again, I disagree. The gods of Mesopotamia were mysterious forces in the sight of which men felt fear and trepidation; they were gods lacking human traits yet in control of human destiny, responsible for the precariousness of life, military defeats, epi-demics, floods and droughts.[218]

This was not so with the Greeks and their gods. Their gods were human-like in their desires and looks, lacking in terror and mystery. The Olympians were quite differentiated in their personalities, identified with a specific human-per-sonal attribute. For all the tragic fate that awaited Achilles and the many other heroes, it was not a fate brought on by snakes stealing herbs, but a self-chosen fate by proud men who knew that men who yearn for greatness will be invaded by passions which appear as impersonal forces, sometimes as gods, which take over the individual in directions beyond their control. Yes, there is a common theme or atmosphere of fatalism and gloom in the *Iliad*, a keen awareness that those who strive for achievement in war pursue a course whose characteristic end is a short-lived life. But there is also a spirit of overweening confidence in man's capacity to strive, in the midst of moments of fear and doubt, against the most difficult ob-stacles.

Griffin writes that "there is no happy ending" in Gilgamesh just as in the *Iliad* (and the *Song of Roland* and other heroic sagas of the West). I would say that the ending of Gilgamesh seems to be that the ways of men are unchangeable, and that it is not for men to ever comprehend the ultimate meaning of life, the unfathom-able ways of the gods; all humans, the master and the servant, are the same before the destinies decided by mysterious gods. This same Sumerian outlook remains in all the other versions of Gilgamesh from Babylonian to Assyrian times. In con-trast, in the *Iliad*, as Katherine King writes, "it is only because death in its myriad forms is inescapable that it behooves a man to attempt to win honor, to win the right to have the tangible good things of life—ranking, place, rich meat, choice wine, and a good farmland—and to be looked upon to as the gods one cannot

---

[218] Muller, 1961.

be."[219] Humans are mortal; they are not gods, but they can win honor, good farm-land for their families, and a good name, which lives on after their death.

Greek heroes sometimes asked for visible signs of divine support—signs which cannot be willed by human effort to show up at the desired time, but which might nevertheless happen by a happy coincidence. In the *Iliad* there are gods behind every event; what happens between humans down on earth appears to be planned and brought forth by gods located on a higher, exalted plane. But when the gods present themselves to the aristocrats to deliver their wishes, they do so in a way that does not reduce them to a state of fright and feebleness. The gods of the *Iliad* are Olympian, the creation of men who have freed themselves from the cult of the Great Mother. They do not speak to their gods in a state of prostration with their faces touching the dirt, wailing, lamenting, pleading, and confessing their inher-ent failings, as would remain common among non-Europeans.

The gods of the underworld, to be sure, are still there among Homeric Greeks, such as Acheron, the god of the river and lake of pain, who ferried the souls of the dead across its dark waters, but they are no longer in total command of the minds of men; some have been humanized, such as the god Hades, king of the under-world, who defended the right of the dead to due burial. The Olympian goddesses, such as Demeter, who had connections with the underworld, are civilized, as the *Grain-Mother*, instead of *Earth-Mother,* in charge of the earth's rich bounty, asso-ciated with farming, health, birth, and marriage. The Olympian gods speak as if they were speaking to aristocratic peers, "with chivalrous courtesy," offering their advice, telling them it is better to follow the gods, if they wish, while the heroes communicate and react to the gods without losing their freedom and honor. As Snell writes:

> Throughout his poems Homer has his gods appear in such a manner that they do not force man into the dust; on the contrary, he elevates him, and makes him free, strong, courageous, certain of himself.[220]

---

[219] King, 1978, 5–7.
[220] Snell, 32.

Plato's Unified Self

The evolution of a rational self has been debated under various headings, including "the evolution of the concept of the Greek psyche," "the early Greek concept of the soul," the Socratic ideal "know thyself," and "Plato's Self-Mastery." I will examine this complex discussion as it relates to the unique evolution of a Western self increasingly aware of the distinction between personal agency (or acting under one's initiative) and extraneous forces (or acting under the influence of gods and bodily organs or processes). I will begin with Charles Taylor's major philosophical work, *Sources of the Self*. This book, as the subtitle indicates, is mostly on *The Making of the Modern Identity*. I am concerned here with the origins of consciousness and individual identity in a literary work, the *Iliad*, and will focus on that part of Taylor's book. According to Taylor, it was Plato who developed the idea of a "self-collected" character capable of ordering and controlling his extraneous appetites and emotions. He did so by articulating a concept of a "unified self" consisting of three parts—bodily appetites, emotions, and reason—of which reason was master of appetites and emotions.[221] As Plato explained it in his *Republic,* this tripartite self was said to be unified to the extent that reason was performing its proper virtue, namely wisdom. The emotional part (or "spirited" element) was guided by reason in the performance of its virtues of courage and fortitude. The appetitive part was performing its functions in a manner consistent with the virtue of temperance.

Taylor informs us that Plato's concept of the self was not "modern" in that its ultimate criterion as to what constituted a self was defined as an order that was seen as outside us—in the Good or the Forms—rather than within us. It was Augustine who later introduced the inside/outside dichotomy and bequeathed to the West "the inwardness of radical reflexivity."[222] This insight eventually led to the development of the Kantian idea that humans are truly free only when they come to legislate for themselves the normative ordering they wish to follow. Nevertheless, without Plato's concept of the "unified self" as a necessary means by which to come to terms with the proper cultivation of one's self-mastery, "the modern notion of interiority could never have developed."[223]

---

[221] Taylor, 1991, 115–126.
[222] Ibid, 131.
[223] Ibid, 120.

Taylor draws a sharp contrast between Plato's moral doctrine of self-mastery and Homer's concept of the self. He explains that in the modern West we take it for granted that "our thoughts, ideas, or feelings are 'within' us, while the objects in the world these mental states reflect on are 'without.'"[224] This way of localizing ourselves inside ourselves is so bound up with our modern ways of growing up as singular personalities (with our own projects and inner life experiences) that we now think of this as natural. He clarifies that, on one basic level, humans at all times and places have had a sense that there is person A and person B to whom different physical attributes, actions, and momentary expressions can be attributed.

Alongside this basic perception, there is, however, a newer and uniquely Western sense of agency that had its origins in ancient Greece. Plato represents the paradigmatic expression of the distinction between what is inside and what is outside a person. But this was not the way the self was viewed in Homeric times. Drawing on the commentaries of Snell and Richard Onians on the *Iliad* and the *Odyssey*, Taylor notes the absence in these epics of words that could be translated in a way that clearly designated the thoughts, psyche, feelings, and bodily sensations of each character. The meanings of these words portray characters with a fragmented and quasi-independent self. They lack a clear sense of the mental, emotional, and bodily components of their selves. The word psyche, for instance, rather than designating the site of thinking and feeling, appears to designate a life force that enters the body and flees from it at death through the mouth.

Taylor makes reference to Snell's observation that Homeric heroes were driven to perform impressive deeds by a surge of energy and manic enthusiasm. This energy and enthusiasm were thought to be infused into them by gods. He compares these heroes to berserkers in "primitive" Scandinavian and early Celtic cultures; they too were filled by a kind of raging madness on the battlefield—a psychic state ostensibly incompatible with the reflective and self-collected stance Plato envisioned as the ideal person in *The Republic*.

In other words, according to Taylor, in the Homeric epics, and in the berserker cultures of Europe, there were no fully integrated, autonomous agents or heroic characters capable of clearly distinguishing for themselves what was inside and what was outside. He reads Plato's philosophy as an effort to subordinate the warrior-citizen morality of strength, courage, and glory—which grew out of the berserker barbarian past—to a philosophical morality of dispassionate deliberation.

---

[224] Ibid, 111.

The part of the soul dealing with desire (thymos), which Plato associated with the warrior function, was thus relegated to a subordinate function in his Republic, secondary to the part of the soul dealing with reason, which he associated with the ruler function.

Taylor distinguishes, albeit broadly, between a Platonic (or Western-to-become-Modern view) of the self and a traditional view which prevailed everywhere else, including berserker/Homeric warrior cultures. He refers, in this context, to Geertz's anthropological reports from Java (Bali). Geertz pointed to the absence in the language of Balinese people of words drawing a clear distinction between individual and group actions, between what was inside and outside the individual. He pointed to the way Balinese culture did not think of individuals as isolated, detachable beings, but as persons whose individualities were inextricably connected to the community and its way of life.

Insofar as Taylor's argument explains that a notion of the self is not given naturally to us, and that introspection is a Western achievement alone, I agree. But his reading of the *Iliad* is flawed. Homeric man was already showing signs of selfhood. Let's go directly to Geertz's argument, which Taylor barely touches upon, in order to highlight the contrast between Geertz's Balinese subjects and Homeric warriors. Geertz's familiar essay is entitled "'From the Native's Point of View': On the Nature of Anthropological Understanding." The central passage of this article, on the "Javanese sense of what a person is," is the following:

> The "inside"/"outside" words, *batin* and *lair* . . . refer on the one hand to the felt realm of human experience and on the other to the observed realm of human behavior. . . . *Batin*, the "inside" word, does not refer to a separate seat of encapsulated spirituality detached or detachable from the body, or indeed to a bounded unit at all, but to the emotional life of human beings taken generally. It consists of the fuzzy, shifting flow of subjective feeling perceived directly in all its phenomenological immediacy but considered to be, at its roots at least, identical across all individuals, whose individuality it thus effaces. And similarly, *lair*, the "outside" word, has nothing to do with the body as an object, even an experienced object. Rather, it refers to that part of human life which, in our culture, strict behaviorists limit themselves to studying–external actions, movements, postures,

speech–again conceived as in its essence invariant from one individual to
the next.[225]

In contrast to modern Western individuals, Balinese men (and Geertz makes similar observations about other Near Eastern places) "do not float as bounded psychic entities, detached from their backgrounds and singularly named. . . . [T]heir
identity is an attribute they borrow from their setting."

Similarly, it has been a common perception that Homeric men, as well as Indo-
European barbarians, understood themselves to be members of a close-knit
group. As Aaron Gurevich has observed about the characters portrayed in Scandinavian Sagas, the "mental categories used are those of the unit, the individuals'
own group: they look at themselves from outside as it were, through the eyes of
society."[226] M.I. Finley has also written, regarding Homer's society, that its "basic
values . . . were given, predetermined and so were a man's place in the society and
the privileges and duties that followed from his status."[227] Every individual had a
given role and status within a well-defined cultural order. A warrior was thus expected to perform the role of a warrior, to show excellence in the performance of
the martial virtues.

Alasdair Macintyre, in his highly celebrated book, *After Virtue* (originally published in 1981), follows Finley's idea that in Homeric society, as in other heroic
societies like Iceland or Ireland, every individual acted "within a well-defined and
highly determinate system of roles and statuses." He says that "it is only within
their framework of rules and precepts that they [the characters of the *Iliad*] are
able to frame purposes at all." He contrasts this "traditional" world of prescribed
roles to the modern "capacity to detach oneself from any particular standpoint or
point of view, to step backwards, as it were, and view and judge that standpoint or
point of view from the outside."[228]

It is also the case that Snell and Onians, as Taylor points out, have argued that
Homeric man constantly felt himself decisively influenced by gods and passions
beyond his control. The Homeric self was likewise seen as fragmented, determined by the flux and fusion of inside and outside forces. Their bodily parts are
not just physical but act as agents charged with an overflowing energy. Man was
undifferentiated. The *nous* is mentioned in contexts that relate to intellectual

---

[225] Geertz, 1974.
[226] Gurevich, 1995, 53.
[227] Finley, 1954, 134.
[228] MacIntyre, 2003, 121–130.

functions—thinking—but at the same time one can hardly speak of Homeric individuals as having a separate faculty of thought, since *nous* is also mentioned in contexts whereby men are emotionally roused to action. "*Nous* is not mere intellect; it is dynamic . . . and emotional."[229] Yet *thymos* is also a term used mainly in reference to emotional issues; in numerous passages in the *Iliad* it is the seat of joy, pleasure, love, etc., but in others it is the organ of knowledge.[230] Mental acts like thinking, desiring, and feeling are ascribed to physical organs. Onians writes that the organ of mind in Homer is in the lungs; the mind or the "stuff of consciousness" is identical with breath.[231] The psyche is a word used to characterize the soul, and something that is the prize of battle, which is risked and saved in battle, but it is also a word used to denote the breath of life which departs through the mouth.[232]

The Beginnings of Selfhood in the *Iliad*

Thus, according to Snell and Onians, Homeric vocabulary showed an absence of awareness of a unitary self. Therefore, it would seem to follow (contrary to the argument in this book) that the notion of the "I" as seat of self-consciousness cannot be attributed to Indo-European/Homeric heroes. There are several reasons why these observations are only half the story.

First, the interpretation that is now commonly associated with the name of Snell has not gone unchallenged. For example, Jan Bremmer, in his book *The Early Greek Concept of the Soul*, believes that Homeric heroes are frequently portrayed using the personal pronoun, saying "I wish" or "I thought," which consequently suggests that they "must have had a general sense of psychic coherence and, at least, an imperfect notion of the unity of the personality." He also thinks that Snell ignored Homer's focus on individually named heroes, as well as the

---

[229] Onians, 83.

[230] Snell, 13.

[231] Onians, 32–3, 51–2

[232] Snell, 9. It should be re-stated that Snell, similarly to Jaynes, does not say outright that the *Iliad* is devoid of "human intellection." "The heroes of the Iliad, however, no longer feel that they are the playthings of irrational forces; they acknowledge their Olympian gods who constitute a well-ordered and meaningful world" (22). "It would be absurd to suppose that Apollo or Athena could have regarded the intellect as their enemy" (39). "Homer's myths reveal two features which anticipate the subsequent enlightenment. . . . They encourage self-knowledge in the spirit of the Delphic motto: 'Know thyself,' and thus they extol measure, order, and moderation" (207).

numerous heroes who defy the norms of gods and men, such as Ajax and Achilles. One should not be surprised by Bremmer's qualification that "in Homer's time the individual did not yet know of the will as an ethical factor, nor did he distinguish between what was inside and outside himself as we do."[233] Nevertheless, Bremmer believes that in Homer there was already a tendency to dematerialize mental attributes or words. He notes that psyche has mostly a non-physical mode of existence, that *nous* is "never conceived as something material," and that thymos is, "above all, the source of emotions."[234]

Secondly, as Malcolm Schofield has pointed out, the *Iliad* was structured around deliberation and clashes of views, about what course of action should be taken in any given circumstance, and about what values should be followed. While there is no question that in Homer's time one's class or status carried strong normative requirements, and that, in this respect, decisions cannot be seen as autonomous acts of self-legislation, but must be interpreted in reference to status-based considerations, the existence of debate and disagreement is a notorious feature of Homer's epics. Finley exaggerates when he writes that the obligation to abide by the norms associated by one's status "were not subject to analysis or debate ... [but] left only the narrowest margin for the exercise of what we should call judgment."[235] It is best to think there was an aristocratic code that celebrated competition for great deeds by free men with characters that would not submit to despotic rulers or to impersonal collective norms.

Expanding on Schofield, Christopher Gill examines four deliberative monologues in Homer's epics in which chieftains are clearly seen to face dilemmas over the proper course of action they should take, reasoning through alternative possibilities rather than acting as if their choices were settled definitely by the requirements of their status. He questions the assumption that status-based values such as *aristeuein* ("to be best" or "to win honor") were rigid codes which settled dilemmas unquestionably. He shows how four chieftains in the *Iliad* and *Odyssey*, including three major ones, Hector, Odysseus, and Menelaus, faced comparable dilemmas yet reached "different conclusions by different reasoning."[236] Although none of these characters disowns the "thick values" associated with their status, Gill's conclusion, after carefully examining each monologue, is that there was a

---

[233] Bremmer, 1983, 66–7.
[234] Ibid, 54, 57.
[235] Cited in Schofield, 1986, 6–31.
[236] Gill, 1996, 71.

kind of self-conscious agent involved in determining what "being best" meant in different situations.[237]

Gill also detects, particularly in the case of Hector's monologue regarding what course of action to take in his role as Troy's defender, and in response to alternative choices offered to him by members of his household, a "psychological agent who acts on the basis of reasons and reasoning." It is worth quoting this passage for the support it gives to the argument on the birth of selfhood:

> The self involved is also an ethical agent whose reasons and reasoning are informed by the action-guiding beliefs of his community and by his engagement with his social role. It is this kind of 'self' of which Hector's monologue shows 'consciousness,' and whose 'responsibility' is acknowledged. This kind of self-consciousness is displayed partly by the significant use of internalized dialogue. It is also displayed by other distinctive features. . . . One is the use of the deliberative formula, 'that would be much better.'"[238]

Finally, it is strange that the same Jaynes who says that in trying to understand the origins of consciousness we should pay attention to the use of metaphors in ancient writings, does not have a word to say about the continuous use of metaphors in the *Iliad*. I will only bring up a simple point in what is a very complicated topic in need of further analysis. According to Jaynes, "understanding a thing is to arrive at a metaphor for that thing by substituting something more familiar to us."[239] Drawing a connection or a comparison with something that is familiar to us is what allows us, and what shows to others, understanding of what we are speaking about. We use metaphors to try to convey to others what we are thinking, what's in our minds, which is an act of introspection, of inventing a subjective mind space inside our own heads, metaphorically seeing something by describing it in words familiar to us. When we imagine ourselves doing this or that heroic action, and making decisions on the basis of imagined outcomes, we are imagining ourselves behaving in an imagined world. We are seeing the reality we are describing, or ourselves moving about in our imagination "by way of analogy, by way of constructing an analog space with an analog 'I' that can observe that space, and move metaphorically in it."[240]

---

[237] Ibid, 70–93.
[238] Ibid, 85–6.
[239] Jaynes, 52.
[240] Ibid, 65.

Now, if Jaynes does not bring up a single metaphor from the *Iliad*, Snell dedicates many pages to the use of metaphors, but rather than framing this discussion in relation to the origins of consciousness, he gets into an intricate discussion of how Greek thought, as we outlined above, moved from Homeric analogies and metaphorical phrases "to the analogies of science and philosophy." He says that in Homer "the mind is understood by analogy with the physical organs and their function."[241] The motions of the soul are metaphorically described or made familiar by analogy with animal life. The hero rushes upon the enemy as a lion rushes upon the herd. A man who walks like a lion has a very healthy thymotic impulse, strength and courage.

Yet, from what we have said above, there is some degree of introspection in the *Iliad* in which heroes do seem to deliberate about what is the proper course of action to take, whether he ought to do this or that. While it is true that the scenes of reflection and resolution are stereotypical, and gods intervene to help bring about the choice, we do sense an "I" that imagines different outcomes as a result of different choices. Achilles imagines himself dying as a young man in a blaze of glory or living a long and obscure life. All the heroes come to the same fatal decision and the decision in this sense seems predetermined. Nevertheless, this is a culture in which men have decided to strive for heroism and immortality rather than give way to the appetitive instinct for comfort, or to the fear of death. It is not that they have fatalistically chosen a short life, but that they understand that violence and a shorter life are an inescapable part of a heroic life in their world.

A Full History of the European Discovery of the
Inner Self Remains to Be Written

One of the drawbacks in Snell, Zeruneith, and to a lesser extent in Jaynes, is the supposition that consciousness emerges in full in ancient Greece. "Socrates completes," says Zeruneith, "what Odysseus begins: ensuring that men learn to know themselves and take responsibility for their actions."[242] This tendency is common among specialized academics, as each seeks to demonstrate that one historical period, the one they are familiar with, is the one in which individualism or selfhood really emerged. We need to connect the dots, connect the ideas of the

---

[241] Snell, 198.
[242] Zeruneith, 278.

abundant scholarship already present about the West, so we can get a complete picture.[243]

Various other authors have identified particular points in time when they thought the individual, or the inner self, was discovered. Jacob Burckhardt, in his book *The Civilization of the Renaissance in Italy*, published in 1860, saw among Italians of this period a people "who have emerged from the half-conscious life of the race and become themselves individuals." In the Middle Ages, "man was conscious of himself only as a member of a race, people, party, family, or corporation. . . . In Italy this veil first melted into air . . . man became a spirited individual, and recognized himself as such."[244] He detected this individualism in the self-assertion of powerful public personalities freed from external frameworks of traditional authority, as well as in individuals preferring self-expression as private citizens.

Colin Morris challenges Burckhardt in his book *The Discovery of the Individual, 1020–1200*, published in 1972. In the Middle Ages he already detects, under the heavy influence of Greco-Roman civilization, a strong emphasis on the "value of the individual" and the expression of "personal convictions" along with a new emphasis on "intentionality." It began with Christianity, with its implicit attribution of a "sense of individual identity" among believers moved by "a God who has called each man by name."[245] Christianity takes seriously the inner convictions of the individual believer. The first inklings of this awareness of one's interiority were visible in the Roman era; for example, Morris finds, around the first century BC, lyrical poetry "freed from the conventional ethics" of the day, personally expressive. He finds historians Sallust and Suetonius reflecting about the motives and personalities of statesmen, "although they were still inclined to see them as types rather than as fully formed personalities."[246] He also detects in Seneca's letters a concern "with self-examination and the pursuit of disciplined virtue." But it is among the Christian writers of the early Middle Ages that he detects an intense passion and expression of inner feelings. Saint Augustine's *Confessions*, Morris says, is "the first autobiography ever written," "a product of Christian experience and reflection." "The *Confessions* . . . lay at the root of a good deal of medieval

---

[243] As Max Weber recognized, "the term individualism embraces the utmost heterogeneity of meanings." What Weber hoped for—a "thorough, historically oriented, conceptual analysis [of individualism]"—has yet to be accomplished (in Lukes, 1971).

[244] Burckhardt, 1958, 143.

[245] Morris, 1987, 10.

[246] Ibid, 14.

autobiography, and helped to establish the sense of importance of each individ-ual's experiences within the purposes of God."[247] The *Consolation of Philosophy* by Boethius is a form of rational self-examination, "a personal work" in which Boethius declares that he composed it "while I was mutely pondering within my-self and recording my sorrowful complaints with my pen."

But it is in the period 1050–1200 that Morris observes a "widespread desire for self-expression" and a growing awareness of the importance of intention. Peter Abelard, who authored a book in 1135 with the title *Ethics: or, Know yourself,* in-sisted that a man could not be called a sinner except in light of the intentions mo-tivating his actions. John Salisbury wrote in 1159: "Who is more contemptible than he who scorns a knowledge of himself?" "Self-knowledge," Morris argues, "was one of the dominant themes of the age." It was the path to God. Another component connected with the "growth of a keen self-awareness" among Europe-ans was an interest in the ideal of friendship. Discussions of friendship can be found in Plato, Aristotle, Cicero, and others, but only "the twelfth century has been called the century of friendship." The letter was the most salient vehicle for declarations of friendship. We have great collections of the correspondence of many educated individuals of this age. Friendship in the Middle Ages came to mean honesty about oneself, and the importance of accepting a friend as he is rather than as a type. Here is Saint Bernard (1120s) writing to a friend:

> You could reach me if you but considered what I am; and you can reach
> me still whenever you wish, if you are content to find me as I am and not
> as you wish me to be. I cannot think what else you see in me besides what
> I am, what it is you are chasing which is not me.[248]

This was also the century of courtly love, where lovers in the stories of Chrétien de Troyes "indulge in lengthy self-questioning about the nature of their feeling for each other."[249] While the cult of friendship was taken up primarily by members of the monastic orders and celibate intellectuals, and passionate love was regarded as sinful by the Church, and marriages among the upper classes were generally undertaken for political and social reasons, courtly love, the desire to serve and adore the beloved, was singularly a novelty of the lay aristocracy, or, more

---

[247] Ibid, 17.
[248] Morris, 103.
[249] Ibid, 76.

accurately, troubadours under the patronage of wealthy noblemen or women, who traveled extensively singing their love poems. It was a poetry of desire, devotion and adoration; and while it was a longing for a married woman, hidden love, adulterous and dominated by physical desire, it was not about actual adulterous affairs, but a celebration of the virtues of fidelity for the unavailable beloved, joy, and courtesy. One could say that the center of interest was not the mistress, "but one's own self, the thoughts inspired by the passions aroused, by the distant beloved."[250]

Courtly love was a discovery of the intensively personal nature of love, a focus on the inner experience of love, concerned with self-analysis of the nature of sexual longing and the joy involved in the sensations and sentiments associated with love. Chrétien de Troyes, who was more than a troubadour, as the major poet of his age, is said to have been the first exponent in human history of romantic love, and of marrying for love. His stories offer psychological insights of the thoughts and emotions of lovers, and the "differing qualities of people's minds . . . and their varied attitudes to love"—for instance, the contrast of a shy love with an obsessive, adulterous passion. He saw how in the "affairs of love" the power of the heart surpasses "the expectations of custom." "I will do as my heart wills."

We will return to the Middle Ages, particularly in Chapter VII, when we examine the how the Catholic authorities demolished kinship polygamous networks and promoted monogamous nuclear families, and Europeans went on to create civic associations freed from kinship-based norms. Larry Siedentop's powerfully argued book, *Inventing the Individual: The Origins of Western Liberalism*, reinforces Morris' thesis, but with a singular focus on Christianity as the foundation upon which individualism came to dominate the Western world. The central characters are St. Paul and St. Agustine; it is in them that we witness the "discovery of human freedom" through their emphasis on the inner conscience of believers, and the idea that the act of faith is a personal act, which encouraged Europeans, Siedentop argues, to think and choose, and to become self-conscious of their equality as rational beings with free will. The book is indeed a sweeping history of individualism in tracing its emergence from ancient times through to the Enlightenment era. We will return to this important book in Chapter XI when we examine the roots of modern liberalism.

Victor Davis Hanson, for his part, is convinced that the core Western values of consensual government, civil liberties, citizen armies, private property,

---

[250] Ibid, 119.

separation between religious and political authority, owe a great deal to the emergence in Greece between 700 and 300 BC of an autonomous group of independent farmers for the first time in history. This is also a very important piece of the puzzle we will get back to in Chapter VII. There are other interpretations of the origins of Western individualism which emphasize the modern era. For example, some believe that we must wait for the Reformation to finally see the full articulation of the principle of freedom of individual conscience—the priesthood of all believers—in opposition to an authoritarian Catholic hierarchy.[251] And there are others who identify the Enlightenment with "man's release from his self-incurred immaturity . . . the inability to use one's understanding without the guidance of another," as Kant wrote in 1784. Only in his time did Kant see a self-critical stand against dogmatism, against the habit of taking for granted beliefs without first subjecting its assumptions to a critique.

The development of the concept of selfhood, or individualism, can also be traced, as we shall elaborate in later chapters, within the history of each cultural sphere, within literature, painting, philosophy, historical writing, legal and political theory. A history of sculpture alone, for example, would have to acknowledge both the amazing breakthrough of the Greeks in the discovery of foreshortening and in the seizing, towards the end of the fourth century BC, of "the individual character of a physiognomy," a style that would be advanced by the Roman realistic portraiture of private individuals "in which every line, crease, wrinkle, and even blemish was ruthlessly recorded."[252] In the sphere of literature, the subject of Chapter IX, we have Ian Watt's argument, in *The Rise of the Novel: Studies in Defoe, Richardson and Fielding,* that the novel of the eighteenth century was a new literary genre which gave primacy to the concrete, personal inwardness of characters, away from the presentation of general human types based on the established literature of the past.

It is very hard indeed to establish when something new emerges in the West, for this civilization has always been in a state of continuous discontinuity. Peter Holbrook's book, *Shakespeare's Individualism,* makes a solid case that Shakespeare, in the age of Elizabethan England, was the first to show a commitment "to fundamentally modern values: freedom, individuality, self-realization, authenticity" in his portrayal of characters with a self-assured "I," or as expressed in a line

---

[251] Headley, 1987.
[252] Osier, 2016, 40.

from act 1, scene 3, of Shakespeare's play, *Hamlet*: "To thine own self be true."[253] It is important, nevertheless, to keep track of the subtle differences that exist between one epoch and another, rather than coalescing everything into one amorphous narrative about Western selfhood or individualism emerging in complete form in one period, or being always a characteristic of the West without drawing differences between Greek, Roman, medieval Christian, Renaissance, Reformation, Romantic, Enlightenment, and post-World War II European individualisms.

Hegel is the one thinker who saw a developing dynamic in Western history towards increasing levels of self-consciousness and selfhood. The basic truth of Hegel's *Phenomenology of Spirit* (1807), as I argued in *Uniqueness*, is that the West is the only civilization in which "freedom" and "reason" have progressed over the course of history. The Western spirit cannot be comprehended as a substance, a state of being, Confucian, Hindu, Talmudic, Buddhist, as other civilizations can to a reasonable degree. The West can only be apprehended as a restless spirit in a continuous state of creativity and deeper apprehension of history and increasing self-awareness. Yet, despite a growing body of scholarly work on Hegel since the 1970s, no one has applied his philosophy towards the understanding of the history of the *Western* spirit, but have instead assumed that he was writing about "the phenomenology of *human* consciousness."[254]

This current work is Hegelian in this respect.[255] There are many scholarly works about the history of Western individualism and Western selfhood, to be

---

[253] Holbrook, 2013.

[254] If you ask Hegelian scholars in a straightforward way whether the *Phenomenology* is really about the cognitive experience of European peoples, they would agree. Hegelian scholars also believe that Hegel's philosophy recounts the development of self-consciousness, and that it does demonstrate that humans became fully self-conscious of the character of their own thoughts only in post-Enlightenment times. However, if you then ask these scholars whether this means that only Europeans achieved self-consciousness, they will immediately find ways to insist that Hegel's philosophy should not be read as an account of the European spirit. But since it is obvious that it is, they will have no choice but to conclude that, insofar as it is, it is Eurocentric and therefore a flawed philosophical account. I am actually noticing more and more admirers of Hegel (see, for example, Terry Pinkard's *Does History Make Sense? Hegel on the Historical Shapes of Justice*, published in 2017), emphasizing the limitations of Hegel's philosophy due to his "Eurocentrism," condemning his observations about the lack of self-consciousness among Indians and Chinese peoples, though they don't have a single argument showing that outside the West there was any "self-consciousness" as they themselves define this Hegelian term.

[255] The Hegelian perspective I am offering applies to the "rise of the West" account, and not to the current ethnocidal path of the West, which is more in line, loosely speaking, with Nietzsche and Heidegger, and with other thinkers, as we shall see in Chapters X and XI. On the whole, this

discussed here, and about the nature, or lack thereof, of individualism in the non-Western world. But no one has apprehended these works in their connected totality within a historical dynamic from the prehistorical Indo-Europeans to our current times.[256]

---

book draws on numerous authors and scholarly sources, including other major thinkers, and can't be categorized as belonging to any one or two schools of thought.

[256] Marcel Mauss, an anthropologist, wrote a short article in the 1930s consciously recognizing that Western selfhood is not only "a rather peculiar idea within the context of the world's cultures," but a notion that developed historically over time. The title of the article is "A category of the human mind: the notion of person; the notion of self" (Mauss, 1997). Mauss observes that the category of self" was a "recent" category, an "aberration" in history. It was only India, outside the West, due to the influence of Indo-Europeans, that one sees some "notion of the individual, of his consciousness," the "creation of the 'I.'" In India, the word "*aham*" equals 'I.' This word is "the same Indo-European word as 'ego.'" However, "in contrast to Hindus and the Chinese, the Romans, or perhaps rather the Latins, seem to be the people who in part established the notion of 'person' *personne*." Only with the coming of Roman law do we have "the right to the persona . . . established." The slave is excluded from it, he has no 'personality,' but all Roman citizens are legally identified as persons with a capacity to be individually responsible for their actions and to engage in legal contracts as individuals. The Stoics added a "voluntarist and personal ethics," which enriched "the Roman notion of the person." Christianity added a "metaphysical foundation" to the notion of the person. Man as man was now seen as substantially a "*persona—substantia rationalis individua*."

But this was not the end of Western individualism: Mauss continues: "The notion of the 'person' (personne) was still to undergo a further transformation to become what it has become over less than one and a half centuries, the 'category of "self"' (moi). Far from existing as the primordial innate idea, clearly engraved since Adam in the innermost depths of our being, it continues here slowly, and almost right up to our own time, to be built upon, to be made clearer and more specific, becoming identified with self-knowledge and the psychological consciousness."

Mauss says next to nothing about the history of the self after Christianity, during the Middle Ages, the Renaissance, and the Reformation, but it is worth quoting another paragraph about how German idealist philosophers were the ones "who finally gave the answer that every act of consciousness was an act of the 'self' (moi), the one who founded all science and all action on the 'self' (moi), was Fichte. Kant had already made of the individual consciousness the sacred character of the human person, the condition for Practical Reason. It was Fichte who made of it as well the category of the 'self' (moi), the condition of consciousness and of science, of Pure Reason."

This remains, however, a sketchy article. Mauss felt confident in making this dramatic contrast likely after years of studying non-Western cultures. Scholars today would dismiss this article for its "ignorance" of advanced non-Western civilizations. Many would ask: Wasn't the Axial Age between 700 and 200 BC a world historical epoch characterized by the "simultaneous" emergence across the civilizations of India, Israel, Mesopotamia, Persia, Greece and China of rational "reflexivity," the onset of self-consciousness and the postulation of "transcendental" universal moral philosophies that would shape the history of these civilization for their entire subsequent histories? We will address the Axial thesis next.

III

AXIAL AGE VERSUS PRESOCRATIC DISCOVERY OF *LOGOS*

The Chinese had never believed in the existence of a sovereign and independent faculty of reason.

– Jacques Gernet

Ideological Origins of the Axial Age

From the nineteenth century through the 1960s and '70s, World History books were quite fair in their assessments of the varying accomplishments of civilizations. This fairness included paying more attention to the achievements of Europeans, particularly after the European discovery of the Americas, the consolidation of Newtonian science, and the spread of Western-created industrial technology. From the 1960s on, however, historians began to embrace the multicultural idea that all the peoples of the earth deserved equal attention and that it was "ethnocentric" to prioritize European history. How can Europeans be portrayed as the primary players in modern world history if all the races of the world are equal, and the task of liberal-minded academics is to nurture cultural harmony, overcome the belligerence exemplified in World War II, and produce "global citizens" in an interconnected world? But an obvious difficulty confronted this feeling: how can a new history of all humans—"universal" in this respect—be constructed in light of the clear pre-eminence of Europeans in all the fields of knowledge and technological innovations?

It soon became apparent that the key was to do away with the idea that the West was an exceptional civilization with its own unique path, the celebrated "Greek Miracle," the Roman rational legal system, the medieval invention of universities and mechanical clocks, the Renaissance invention of perspective painting, the discovery and mapping of the globe, the Copernican-Galilean breakthrough, and the Industrial Revolution. The focus should be on the way the peoples of the world were connected as human beings with the same biological nature inhabiting the same Earth in a constant state of interaction. The time for this new perspective seemed ripe. In the political climate of the mid-and late 1960s the West was at the center of everything that seemed wrong in the world: the threat of nuclear destruction, the prolonged Vietnam War, the pollution inflicted by the affluent lifestyle of Europeans. The West looked like an old empire opposed to a newly emerging global reality: the rise of pan-Arabic and pan-African identities, the "liberation movements" in Latin America, the Black civil rights movement, the feminist struggle against patriarchy, etc.

Not to be underestimated, this was the time when a highly influential school of thought, Dependency Theory, emerged, arguing that the reason Europeans modernized, in the first place, was that they stole the resources of other civilizations, enslaved their inhabitants, and enriched themselves through unfair trade practices. The West, it was argued, only managed to surpass other cultures, starting in the 1500s, by positioning itself, through dishonesty, duplicity, and violence, at the center of the world economy. Millions of students were indeed instructed that the capitalist West, in the words of Karl Marx, had progressed to become master of the world "dripping from head to foot, from every pore, with blood and dirt."[257] Old dead White males should no longer be praised for launching the

---

[257] From Karl Marx's *Capital*, Volume 1, Chapter 31, "On the Genesis of the Industrial Capitalist." Much attention has been directed at the role of the Frankfurt School, but a powerful case can be made that accusing Western countries of enriching themselves by impoverishing the non-Western peoples has been a very emotionally influential argument fueling much of "White guilt" to this day. The ultimate source of this idea lies in Marx, but the one person who formulated it into a highly accessible theory, capped by a very catchy phrase, "development of underdevelopment," was the German Jew A. G. Frank. His books are still mandatory reading in sociology of development and the politics of developing societies. Frank has also come to be known as a father of multicultural world history, with the publication of *ReOrient: Global Economy in the Asian Age* (1998). Even more influential, however, has been American Jew Immanuel Wallerstein, whose multivolume books on the "modern world system," penned in the 1970s, catapulted him

modern world, but should be held guilty for holding back the development of other civilizations and creating a world capitalist system that held down the "peripheral" Third World.

Accordingly, the West as the vanguard of world history, articulated since the Enlightenment, was rejected by the late 1970s, and eventually replaced by "world history."[258] Students would now have to learn that all humans were similarly capable, creators of different but equally worthwhile cultures, with a common origin in Africa, migrating to the rest of the world, occupying different ecological settings and creating "richly diverse" cultures, interacting with each other through trade, wars, empires, and migrations, and thus making world history together.[259] But the aim of these equalizers was hardly that Europeans were creatively involved with other civilizations; it was that they were morally and economically responsible for the "underdevelopment" of civilizations that were once more advanced than the Germanic "barbarians" of the Middle Ages—while insisting simultaneously that non-Europeans were the originators or co-participators of every great epoch in Europe's history.

But before this great fabrication was imposed on unsuspecting students, a preparatory, though by no means identical, idea had been articulated by a German named Karl Jaspers: the notion that in ancient times, roughly between 800 and 200 BC, the major civilizations of the Old World experienced, more or less at the same time, a "spiritual process" characterized by a common set of religious, psychological, and philosophical inquiries about what it means to be specifically human. This idea was composed in the now classic book, *The Origin and Goal of History*, originally published in 1949. The argument was that humanity, at this point in history, came to pose universal questions about the meaning of life with similar answers. Europeans did not carve out their own peculiar path. Rather, all humans had developed a common cultural outlook at more or less the same time, an outlook that was to shape their histories along similar trajectories, with the West rising in recent times due to a combination of unusual circumstances.

---

onto the global academic stage, assiduously followed by numerous pupils across the world. Wallerstein is likewise seen as a "founding father" of world history.

[258] The teaching of Western civilization has virtually disappeared from American colleges, with only two percent of them offering this course as a requirement. This abolition is detailed by Glenn Ricketts, Peter Wood, Stephen Balch, and Ashley Torne, "The Vanishing West, 1964–2010: The Disappearance of Western Civilization from the American Undergraduate Curriculum" (2011).

[259] Bentley, 1993; Christian, 2005.

The Goal of Jaspers' Axial Age

Jaspers, estimated as a highly gifted German philosopher, argued in *The Origin and Goal of History*, published four years after the end of World War II, that Western culture was not singularly gifted with transcendental ideas that influenced mankind generally and the course of history universally; other major civilizations had espoused outlooks about humanity together with moral precepts with universal content. Jaspers believed that this ability was "empirically" made possible by the occurrence of a fundamental "spiritual" change between 800 and 200 BC, which gave "rise to a common frame of historical self-comprehension for all peoples—for the West, for Asia, and for all men on earth, without regard to particular articles of faith."[260]

Believing that these spiritual changes occurred "simultaneously" across the world, Jaspers called it the "Axial Period." It is worth quoting in full Jasper's identification of the main protagonists of this period:

> The most extraordinary events are concentrated in this period. Confucius and Lao-tse were living in China, all the schools of Chinese philosophy came into being, including those of Mo-ti, Chuang-tse, Lieh-tsu and a host of others; India produced the Upanishads and Buddha and, like China, ran the whole gamut of philosophical possibilities down to skepticism, to materialism, sophism and nihilism; in Iran Zarathustra taught a challenging view of the world as a struggle between good and evil; in Palestine the prophets made their appearance, from Elijah, by way of Isaiah and Jeremiah to Deutero-Isaiah; Greece witnessed the appearance of Homer, of the Philosophers—Parmenides, Heraclitus and Plato—of the tragedians, Thucydides and Archimedes. Everything implied by these names developed during these few centuries almost simultaneously in China, India, and the West, without any one of these regions knowing of the others.

Jaspers used certain amorphous philosophical phrases to indicate what was spiritually novel about this Axial age: "man becomes conscious of Being as a whole. . . . He asks radical questions. . . . By consciously recognizing the limits he sets himself

---

[260] Jaspers, 1965, 1.

the highest goals. He experiences absoluteness in the face of self hood."[261] But in some instances, Jaspers offered more concrete sentences: "hitherto unconsciously accepted ideas, customs and conditions were subjected to examination, questioned and liquidated." Essentially, in this Axial Age, the age of myths came to an end. "The Greek, Indian and Chinese philosophers were unmythical in their decisive insights, as were the prophets [of the Bible] in their ideas of God."[262]

A number of religious figures, philosophers and prophets came to rely more on their own judgments, visions, and reasoning powers: *logos* was set against mythos. Humans were now willing to rely on their rationality to make sense of the cosmos, to draw a clearer contrast between the inner world of consciousness, refection, and the outer of accepted norms and beliefs, subject and object, spirit and matter. Combined with this spiritual awakening, came the idea of a transcendental One God as the basis of a new ethics against unreal demons, and as the locus for determining what was morally right for all.

It is not that the philosophical outlooks of these civilizations were identical, but that they exhibited similar breakthroughs in posing universal questions about the human condition: What is the ultimate source of all things? What is our relation to the universe? What is the Good? What are human beings? Prior cultures were more particularized, tribal, polytheistic, and devoid of self-awareness regarding the universal characteristics of human existence. From the Axial Age onward, "world history receives the only structure and unity that has endured—at least until our own time." The central aim of Jaspers' book was to drive home the notion that the different faiths and races of the world were once running along parallel lines of spiritual development, and that we should draw on this common spiritual source to avoid the calamity of another World War. The fact that these civilizations had reached a common spiritual point of development, without any direct influences between them, was likely, in his view, the "manifestation of some profound common element, the one primal source of humanity."[263] We humans have much in common, despite our differences.

Jaspers took the Axial Age personally, as a German in the aftermath of the Second World War. He lamented the fact that Axial Age civilizations, from their common trajectory, ceased to follow "parallel movements close to each other" after 200 BC, and instead began to "diverge" and "finally became deeply estranged

---

[261] Ibid, 2.
[262] Ibid, 3.
[263] Ibid, 12.

from one another."[264] The Nazi experience was, in his estimation, an extreme case of such divergence. It should be noted that Jaspers, whose wife was Jewish, was the author of a much-discussed 1947 book, *The Question of German Guilt*, in which he extended culpability to Germany as a whole, indeed, to every German, even those who were not members of the Nazi party. A passage from this book, cited in a 1997 BBC documentary, "The Nazis—A Warning from History," reads:

> That which has happened is a warning. To forget it is guilt. It must be con-
> tinually remembered. It was possible for this to happen, and it remains
> possible for it to happen again at any minute. Only in knowledge can it be
> prevented.

Jaspers saw the behavior of Germany as testimony of what happens when an otherwise modern culture decides to go its own way rather than coalesce with the world. Germans had strayed from "human history" by envisioning themselves as a special people with a unique destiny for greatness.

Axial Age proponents hoped that by making humans aware of themselves as beings with a profound spiritual unity, it would nurture a sense of human solidarity. This call for a common history would indeed coalesce with similar arguments about the "imaginary inventions of nations," the "social construction of races," and the idea that we are all primordially alike as *Homo sapiens*.[265] It was also the beginning of an effort to instill in European natives the belief that they were citizens of "propositional nations," and since these propositions could be held in common by all humans, they were citizens of the world—and all inhabitants of the world were potential citizens of their nations. "Germanness," in the words of Jürgen Habermas, a keen admirer of Jaspers, would "no longer be based on ethnicity, but founded on citizenship."[266]

---

[264] Ibid, 54.

[265] The promotion of the idea that European nations were always meant to be "civic," against any notion of ethnic national identity, was initiated and popularized by Jewish scholars: namely, Hans Kohn, Karl Deutsch, Ernest Gellner, and Eric Hobsbawm. See my essay: "The Greek-Roman Invention of Civic Identity versus the Current Demotion of European Ethnicity" (2015).

[266] An interesting figure drawn to the Axial Age idea was Hannah Arendt, a student of Jaspers. She obtained a copy of *The Origin and Goal of History* as she was completing her widely acclaimed book *The Origins of Totalitarianism* (1951). It is quite revealing that, in a short essay titled "Hannah Arendt's Jewish Identity," Elisabeth Young-Bruehl (2010) traces the roots of Arendt's cosmopolitanism to the role of the Jews of Palestine as one of the Axial Age peoples. Together with Jaspers, Arendt came to share the project of thinking about what kind of history was

The inquiries Jaspers started would indeed mushroom beyond his expectations, in a climate of continuous hostility to "Western-centric" views. While Jaspers had limited the "common history" to the period 800–200 BC, a growing number of historians would announce that the cultural and economic trajectories of Europe and Asia were "surprisingly similar" up until a sudden "accidental" divergence occurred around 1750–1830.[267] Felipe Fernandez-Armesto, celebrated by the mainstream media as an elite-level world historian, would insist that the thinkers of the Axial Age "anticipated and influenced the way we think now." Whereas Jaspers did acknowledge divergent paths after this age, with the West following a "special" path, Fernandez-Armesto would argue that the West was no different from other civilizations; every place was similarly "anticipated and influenced" by "the common content of the minds" of the Axial thinkers. In the many centuries after this age, the West "added so little to it."[268]

The Axial Age, Fernandez-Armesto would add, was not restricted to Eurasia; it was a worldwide story "because of the way axial-age thinking later spread and shaped thoughts and feelings in every clime and continent." The other areas were co-participants as members of trade networks, as colonial areas, or simply as members of the same species that had migrated out of Africa. World history is a

---

needed for facing the events of the war and the Holocaust, and for considering how the world might be after the war. The needed history should not be national or for a national purpose, but for humankind. Arendt agreed with Jaspers, Young-Bruehl writes, that the way for Westerners to overcome "the ill effects of their own prejudices and technological progress, which had made the worldwide war possible," was to open up to the world and think in a "cosmopolitan way about the future of humanity."

In light of her Jewish identity, as one of the Axial peoples victimized by German and European prejudices, Arendt further developed the arguments of Jaspers by invoking the cosmopolitanism exhibited by the Jews in the Axial Age, both as an "antidote to tribalist Jewish thinking" and to European ethno-nationalism. Young-Bruehl continues: "It is Arendt's Jewish identity—not just the identity she asserted in defending herself as a Jew when attacked as one, but more deeply her connection to the Axial Age prophetic tradition—that made her the cosmopolitan she was." But what kind of history writing does cosmopolitan thinking require, given that civilizations, according to Jasper, diverged in their cultural development after the Axial Age? For Arendt, this was beside the point; she was not a historian preoccupied with actual documentation. Her goal was to create a new state of mind among Europeans in the way they viewed themselves in relation to the world. She called upon Europeans to "enlarge" their minds and include the experiences and views of other cultures in their thinking; to overcome their ethnocentric prejudices and nurture a sense of the human condition and what is common to all mankind; how they are culturally shaped both by their particular conditions and the conditions and experiences shared by all humans on the planet.

[267] Pomeranz, 2000; Goldstone, 2008; Frank, 1998.

[268] Fernandez-Armesto, 2007, 159, 187.

wonderful tapestry of cultures working together, with the exception of the West, a civilization that sought to act as if it was ahead of other cultures, ignoring and undermining their accomplishments.[269]

Jaspers, at least in his book *The Origin and Goal of History*, did not go this far, but actually retracted, in later chapters, the general statements he made in the introduction about the Axial Age being a common spiritual experience across the planet, acknowledging the obvious: "[I]t was not a universal occurrence. . . . There were the great peoples of the ancient civilizations, who lived before and even concurrently with the Axial breakthrough, but had no part in it."

He further noted that the Egyptian and Babylonian peoples "remained what they had been earlier . . . destitute of that quality of refection which transformed mankind," even though they interacted with the Axial cultures.[270]

As it is, Jaspers admitted that after the Axial Age, the respective civilizations traversed very different spiritual pathways, which begs the question as to why they would cease to exhibit parallel developments despite increasing interaction. Perhaps even more important was his recognition that there was a "specific quality" to the West in the way it exhibited "far more dramatic fresh starts," whereas "in Asia, on the other hand, a constant situation persists; it modifies its manifestations, it founders in catastrophes and re-establishes itself on the one and only basis as that which is constantly the same."[271]

In the end, Jaspers could not avoid the ultimate historical question about why the West followed such a diametrically different path: "[I]f science and technology were created in the West, we are faced with the question: Why did this happen in the West and not in the other two great cultural zones?"[272]

The answer he offered was essentially similar to Hegel's heavily Eurocentric perspective about the unique pre-occupation of Europeans with freedom and reason. He actually delimited the veracity of the Axial thesis with the observation that only the ancient Greeks came to know political liberty, in contrast to the universal despotism of the East, and that "in contrast to the East, Greek rationality contain[ed] a strain of consistency that laid the foundations of mathematics and

---

[269] Fernandez-Armesto portrays Axial thinkers outside Greece as saintly, lofty and exalted sages, while ignoring most of the Greek thinkers and referring to Plato as a "member of an Athenian gang of rich aristocrats" who idealized "harsh, reactionary, and illiberal" states, "militarism," "regimentation," "rigid class structure," and "selective breeding of superior human beings" (2007, 52).

[270] Jaspers, 51–52.

[271] Ibid, 53–54.

[272] Ibid, 61–62.

perfected formal logic." He indeed drew many insightful contrasts between the West and the rest: "Tragedy is known only to the West." While other Axial cultures spoke of mankind in general, in the West this universal ambition regarding the place of man in the cosmos and the good life did not "coagulate into a dogmatic fixity." In the West "human nature reaches a height that is certainly not shared by all and to which ... hardly anyone ascends." What's so dramatically different is "the perpetual disquiet of the West, its continual dissatisfaction, its inability to be content with any sort of fulfillment."[273] This is clearly the language of Spengler's "Faustian Soul."

The Axial Age Thesis Today

Nonetheless, the substantial qualifications Jaspers made to his thesis would not matter in the end; no one quotes these "Eurocentric" passages. Only what he said about the Axial Age would find expression in the comparative study of civilizations and world history—in conscious opposition, as Peter Wagner happily affirmed, to "self-congratulatory" claims by Europeans about their "superior mode of societal rationalization." Scholars needed to "move beyond the opposition between a rationalizing Occident and other civilizations that lacked this potential" as a "means of broadening the debate about modernity, of making it less Eurocentric."[274] It was really in the 1980s that the Axial Age idea spread, in no small part through the work of Shmuel N. Eisenstadt.[275] He insisted that the classical theories of modernization, which prevailed in the 1950s and 1960s, with their focus on the Western industrial experience as a model for the rest of the world, were fundamentally wrong in ignoring the "multiple modernities" occurring outside the West with deep roots in the Axial Age.[276] Among his key publications are two sizable edited texts with articles from major Axial scholars: *The Origins and Diversity of Axial Age Civilizations* (1986), and *Axial Civilizations and World History* (2005), co-edited with Johann Arnason and Björn Wittrock.

---

[273] Ibid, 63–64.

[274] Wagner, 2004, 90–91, 101. Wagner recognizes that the Axial Age idea arrived "in its most forceful expression after the end of Nazism and the Second World War" (90).

[275] Robert N. Bellah writes that Eisenstadt, an Israeli sociologist, "has done more than anyone to make the axial age central for comparative historical sociology" (2011, 271).

[276] See Eisenstadt, "Multiple Modernities" (2000). According to Google Scholar, this article, published in *Daedalus*, has been cited over 3,000 times.

Reading these sources and others, including Robert Bellah and Hans Joas' *The Axial Age and Its Consequences*, we can say that the ideas Jaspers began have now been codified into three basic claims:

1) There was an increasing "reflexivity" involving the ability of humans to use their reason to examine their own thoughts and motives. Customary norms which had been taken for granted were subjected to examination, questioned and liquidated. Religious figures, philosophers, and prophets came to rely more on their own judgments, visions, and reasoning powers: *logos* was set against mythos.

2) There was an increasing awareness of historical time, what happened in the past, what was happening in the present, and what could happen in the future. This historicity involved a new capacity by humanity to reflect consciously about their own temporal location and to conceptualize future historical changes through their own agency—their own conscious actions. Humans became aware of themselves as makers of their own history.

3) There was an increasing capacity to transcend the immediately given world, to make a distinction between the mundane world of daily survival, and a transcendental world of ideals. This transcendentalism involved the formulation of universal ideals for humanity—in opposition to the conventional political orderings and particularized norms of one's society or kinship group.

The Axial Age thesis can be challenged with a simple question: why was it that this age was followed throughout the East by centuries of dogmatic fixation, stagnation, and religious traditionalism, whereas the ancient Greeks would engender a Western civilization characterized by continuous increases in reflexivity, historicity, and transcendentalism, starting with the Hellenistic period (323–31 BC), which is contiguous with the Axial Age? This period added about two centuries of Greek creativity, producing not just the new philosophical outlooks of hedonism, cynicism, and stoicism, but what many consider to be the first true scientists and greatest mathematicians ever: Eudoxos, Eratosthenes, Euclid, Hipparchus, Ptolemy and Archimedes, among others.

We will examine these mathematicians in the next chapter, including the origins of formal operational thinking in Aristotle and the Hellenistic Greeks. The focus of this chapter will be on the Presocratics of the sixth and fifth centuries BC, the ideas of Thales, Anaximenes, Anaximander, Empedocles, Xenophanes, Heraclitus, Parmenides, Zeno, and others, before the age of Socrates, Plato, and

Aristotle. It will be shown that they already exhibited clear signs of second-order thinking, or thinking about thinking itself, what Julian Jaynes calls consciousness of consciousness.

While proponents of this idea may think it chic and cosmopolitan to believe that everyone in the Axial Age was asking ponderous questions about the nature of reality, the divine, and the proper form of government, in reality, only the Presocratics had started to argue rationally about these questions, and only they managed to think universally about the nature of things and rise above ideas based on mere assertions or religious authority, without thinking of general explanations for the causes of things. We will go over some of the Presocratic arguments in the last section of this chapter to illustrate this point. The Presocratics, suffice it to say now, were the originators of the uniquely Western idea that there is a *logos* in the universe, a pattern, a structure underlying the natural world. They were the first to identify a faculty within the human soul, *nous*, which allows humans to offer arguments about the *logos* of the world and to speak or use words in a reasoned way about the way the world and humans are structured, and the way humans should live in accordance with this rational order.

The Israelites, the Indians, the Chinese, and possibly the Persians did experience the first inklings of historical consciousness, reflexivity, and transcendental moral precepts beyond the conventions of their time. In the degree to which this was the case, I will defend the Axial Age idea. But we will see that even by the criteria of the proponents of the Axial Age, non-Western religious and philosophical figures did not exhibit any true second-order thinking. Second order thinking presupposes more than thinking about what is the proper way to behave or be a gentleman, how meditation and good behavior are the ways to achieve enlightenment, or the mere pronouncement of commandments against murder, theft, adultery, and false swearing. It presupposes rational justification for one's claims, giving reasons and formulating incontrovertible arguments (either deductive demonstrations or the gathering of evidence) in support of an idea, action, or theory, with the aim of persuading others who are free to contest your arguments.

Basic Argument of *Religion in Human Evolution*

Many of the following sections in this chapter will be framed in terms of Robert N. Bellah's book, *Religion in Human Evolution: From the Paleolithic to the Axial Age*. This book really takes the Axial Age thesis to a new level of scholarship in its comprehensiveness, ambitiousness, and exhaustive reliance on the existing literature.[277] Against Bellah's defense of this Age, I will acknowledge that the concept of an Axial Age has substantial merits—so long as we appreciate the higher intellectual breakthrough of ancient Greece.

Religion in Human Evolution: From the Paleolithic to the Axial Age is a highly referenced book of 608 small print pages with over one hundred pages of notes; it took Bellah twelve years to write it. Because this sweeping book frames the Axial Age within the evolutionary history of living beings and the cultural history of societies from hunting and gathering, through to simple and complex chiefdoms, to the first "archaic" civilizations, before getting into an exhaustive analysis of the Axial Age, it crystallizes well what was different about the "theoretic" cultures of India, China, Israel, and Greece in contrast to prior non-reflective periods.

Bellah acknowledges the factuality of "new emergent capacities" in the course of human history against the notion that the cultural abilities of humans have remained the same from the onset of *Homo sapiens*, and against the Darwinian claim that our cultural ways of behaving and thinking were set in stone by the processes of natural selection. He believes that human cultural development was instead a product of the emergence of "relaxed fields" wherein humans were relatively autonomous from the pressures of natural selection and the struggle for existence—that is, relatively free to cultivate art, rituals, myths, and eventually "reflexive" philosophies with transcendental principles, relatively autonomous from tribal mandates, about the best forms of government and the nature of goodness as such—ideals which came to constitute conditions for the cultural evolution of humans beyond natural selective pressures.

Reviewers of this book have failed to connect Bellah's focus on play and "relaxed fields" of cultural activity with his argument about the origins of transcendentalism during the Axial Age and the construction of societies based on "reflexive" values relatively freed from evolutionary pressures, economic interests, and tribal-kinship norms. Bellah relies on Merlin Donald's influential 1991 book, *Origins of the Modern Mind: Three Stages in the Evolution of Culture and Cognition*. Before early humans emerged, according to Donald, we can only identify an "episodic consciousness" among primates, an ability to perceive the immediate

---

[277] In addition to numerous reviews in journals and the mainstream press, this book was the subject of a symposium in *Religion, Brain and Behavior* 2, no. 3 (2012), with six commentaries and a reply by Bellah. The book was also a New York Times Book Review Editor's Choice, an ABC Australia Best Book on Religion and Ethics of the Year, and received a Distinguished Book Award from the American Sociological Association.

significance of events without any long-term memory of those events and their significance in the far future.[278] Humans evolved beyond primates by developing, over the course of history, gestural, linguistic, and then written storage and thought structures, thereby constructing in succession what Donald calls mimetic, mythic, and theoretic cultures. The mimetic stage was achieved by early hominids or homo erectus (starting about 1.8 million years ago); the mythic stage was first achieved by *Homo sapiens* (starting about 500,000 years ago). The theoretic stage, which Donald actually dates (though he is not always decisive) to the ancient Greeks, culminated in modernity with its external symbolic universe, formal computerized systems of knowledge, advanced science, and massive external AI storage of information.

Bellah embraces Donald's central contention that the evolution of human consciousness, particularly since the emergence of the mythic stage, has been driven primarily by culture, or the interaction of culture and the evolving brain, not natural selective pressures alone. He agrees with Donald that culture is a product of consciousness, and that without consciousness we can't have cultural development. My argument is that Europeans far superseded others in their cultural development with the attainment of second-order thinking, or a true theoretic consciousness, and that Europeans attained a higher degree of relative autonomy from biologically-determined norms and traditional conventions.

Bellah follows Donald closely in describing the contrasting characteristics of mimetic and mythic culture, but has a different take on what exactly a theoretic culture entails and where it emerged among the world's civilizations. Mimetic culture, which he says began with homo erectus some 1–2 million years ago, consists in the ability to "use our bodies to enact past and future events as well as gesture for communication," including perhaps the use of dance, music, and the beginnings of some linguistic capacities. While mimetic communication is more elaborate than anything found among primates, and may have involved sung communication, "musilanguage," and led to ritual, it lacked language communication, which is necessary for the construction of mythical narratives.

Mythic culture, which Bellah says emerged between 250,000 and 100,000 years ago, with the emergence of *Homo sapiens*, involves a new capacity for narrative and storytelling combined with the use of full grammatical language. With mythic

---

[278] Donald offers a succinct analysis of his three stages in relation to the Axial Age in his entry, "An Evolutionary Approach to Culture: Implication for the Study of the Axial Age," in Bellah and Joas (2012).

culture, humans learned to think beyond the present, and tell stories with past, present, and future tenses, rather than be locked within the consciousness of the moment. Although the mythic mind, in Donald's view, is not theoretic, it is "impelled by a deep drive for conceptual clarification." With this new cognitive capacity, writes Donald, "the mind has expanded its reach beyond the episodic perception of events, beyond the mimetic reconstruction of episodes, to a comprehensive modeling of the entire human universe."[279]

Now, for Bellah, the emergence of theoretic culture is what the Axial Age is about. Yet, for Donald, a theoretic culture really emerged in ancient Greece, and it required a fully alphabetic writing system, and more than the mathematics and calendar-based astronomy witnessed, for example, in Babylonia. It involved a capacity for second-order thinking—that is, thinking about thinking, which he believes is evident in the geometrical proofs the Greeks offered.[280] Second-order thinking also involves a transcendental capacity to stand back and look beyond the accepted world views in the name of ideas based on reflexive argumentation. While Bellah quietly acknowledges a few times that strict second order thinking may have been lacking in some Axial civilizations, his overall argument is that Axial civilizations developed theoretic thinking. "The beginnings of science, of a critical view of the world, of knowledge for its own sake, can be found in all the axial civilizations."[281]

In the end, however, it is not science, theoretical mathematics, philosophical treatises about the nature of the universe, or about how to reason properly, that Bellah finds in Axial Age civilizations, apart from Greece. Indeed, because he can't find true second order thinking in non-Western civilizations, he focuses only on the formulation of "universal" ethical concepts above old kinship norms and rituals. He hangs his thesis on the claim that Axial thinkers outside Greece also took a "critical, reflective questioning" of the old mythical stories simply because they wrote books containing transcendental morals for a better future.

---

[279] Bellah, 2011, 134.
[280] Donald writes (2012, 70) "with the possible exception of China . . . it is debatable whether the claims of true Theoretic Culture existed anywhere but [Axial] Greece."
[281] Bellah, 595.

Who is Robert N. Bellah?

Bellah died two years after the publication of *Religion in Human Evolution* at the age of eighty-six. He was an American sociologist and the Elliott Professor of Sociology at the University of California, Berkeley. A White man, he converted to the Episcopalian faith and was married to a Jewish woman. He was a serious scholar, the most widely read sociologist of religion, best known for his now classic essay, "Civil Religion in America" published in 1967, and the best-seller *Habits of the Heart*, written with four additional authors.[282] But Bellah remains a prototypical progressive academic without cultural backbone, sheepishly welcoming the day the United States becomes majority non-White. In an interview he gave in Germany in 2012, right after Obama was re-elected, he identified the Republicans as "old White males" who will likely never win an election again because immigrants are replacing Whites.[283]

I have been accused of bringing politics into topics that should be judged strictly according to scholarly criteria. The reality is that academic research for the last few decades has been driven by the unchallenged or implicit supposition that the West is morally responsible for the problems of the world, for poverty in the Third World, for holding nonwhites back, and for creating societies founded on "White supremacist" prejudices. Blindly accepting these suppositions, and the mandate that our universities should be committed to diversity and equity, violates the principle of critical thinking to which academics should be committed. The fundamental flaws in *Religion in Human Evolution*, I would even argue, are a result of Bellah's rejection of the possibility that Western peoples attained far more "new developments."

Bellah actually suggests in the closing paragraphs of his book that the European "invention of racism" has been responsible for a lack of progress in the actualization of Axial Age ideals in the West! The "racist" creation of European empires, he says, "calls not only for apology, but for reparations for those who are still suffering from the results of what we have done."[284] He then brings up multiculturalism and calls for a "dialogue across differences" as a way of fulfilling Axial ideals. Bellah may not have lived to see it, but the call for including Mesopotamia

---

[282] Bellah, 2007.
[283] DAI Heidelberg, 2012, *Interview Robert N. Bellah - DAI Heidelberg 12.11.2012*. YouTube. https://www.youtube.com/watch?v=_1VMtcuvhQ8.
[284] Bellah, 599.

and Egypt, and even "the souls of black folks" into the Axial Age, is driven by this same ideology of multiculturalism.[285] If one were to follow multiculturalism and the moral standards of Bellah to their logical conclusion, we would have to eliminate the very idea of an Axial Age for privileging just a handful of civilizations, as Bellah himself would be considered guilty of doing.

"New Capacities" Under Conditions of "Relaxed Selection"

Religion in Human Evolution has been called a work of extraordinary ambition, and it is. After prefatory remarks, it opens with the Big Bang some 13.5 billion years ago, gradually taking us to the Axial Age, as the culminating point in the development of new capacities. Bellah gets into the novel features of the first unicellular organisms, prokaryotes, their "incalculable contribution to other forms of life" in creating an oxygen-rich atmosphere and recycling nutrients, and the continuing role of such bacterial organisms in aiding digestion. He outlines how eukaryotes "represent a significant increase not only in size but in complexity compared to prokaryotes," in having an internal nucleus with DNA , and leading to the evolution of the three major divisions of multicellular organisms: fungi, plants, and animals.[286] When he reaches warm-blooded mammals, he directs particular attention to the development of parental care, "a capacity that correlates with several other developments that have enormous potentiality" in making possible "increasing intelligence, sociability and the ability to understand the feelings of others."[287]

With this emphasis on parental care we start seeing Bellah's particular way of framing Donald's theoretic culture as referring merely to the ability of humans to empathize with others beyond everyday contests for survival, mating, and status. This is not an idiosyncratic take on Bellah's part, but expresses a preoccupation in the current Western world with encouraging empathetic inclinations among children and young adults so they learn to care for the plight of strangers, including millions of anonymous immigrants.[288] He contends that parental care, nurturance

---

[285] Boy, 2015.

[286] Bellah, 59–60.

[287] Ibid, 68.

[288] Daniel Coleman's *New York Times* bestseller, *Social Intelligence: The New Science of Human Relationships* (2006), insinuates that Europeans should suppress the "dark side" of their social intelligence, the Machiavellian "psychopathology" of calculating and promoting their in-group

and emotional care, although adaptive in origins, had the unintended consequence of new possibilities and new behaviors, such as play, cooperative breeding, and family life, which made possible advanced empathy among humans, which cannot be seen as merely adaptive, but points to the relaxation of natural selection pressures, with the result that other ends—culturally chosen ends and eventually transcendental moral values—come to influence the evolution of humans. He argues, thusly, that it was through their parental caring experience and emotional attachments that humans developed a capacity to become self-aware—aware of their own feelings, perceptions, and thoughts in relation to the feelings and thoughts of others. According to Bellah, this capacity foreshadowed the eventual ability of Axial thinkers to envision ideal polities beyond the immediately given world of political hierarchies and conventions.

From here Bellah goes on to argue that rituals are the cultural activity, in mimetic and mythic forms, in which a sense of moral equality was first exhibited among humans in all societies before the philosophical reflections of the Axial Age. Tribal members would experience a sense of communal solidarity temporarily freed from the hierarchies of family lineages during ritual ceremonies. However, once Bellah takes us beyond simple horticultural societies into complex chiefdoms, he has difficulties showing how these egalitarian impulses continued. The chief and other lineage heads, he admits, were "obsessed by a thirst for prestige and power, and a hunger for land, and ready to resort to violence to secure their ends."[289] But Bellah still senses an egalitarian atmosphere in these chiefdoms in the redistribution of goods by chiefs, and in the temporary suspension of hierarchical rules and the instinct to dominate during orgiastic ceremonies involving dancing, ritual bathing, and drinking.

Archaic Civilizations Lacked Reflexive/Transcendental Thinking

He next focuses on the archaic (not-yet Axial) civilizations of ancient Mesopotamia, ancient Egypt, and Shang/Western Zhou China. Even though archaic civilizations were trending towards inequality, divination of rulers, and subjection of the commoners, we see some proto-Axial tendencies. Archaic civilizations were

---

interests, in the name of a more "civilized" and "altruistic" intelligence that would make them empathetic towards immigrant outgroups.

[289] Bellah, 189.

characterized by monumental architecture, wide networks of trade, some form of writing, cities, intensive agriculture, a centralized bureaucracy, and rulers with an exalted status reaching divinity or close to it. Kinship by itself was no longer the basic principle governing the relationship between the state and the commoners. Religion now co-existed with an exalted and distant form of kinship. Kin relations obviously still played a role in the close-knit families out of which the ruling officials emerged, and within the extended families prevalent everywhere, but "something new in the religious realm appears in archaic societies: gods and the worship of gods," with kings having a singular relation to the gods, or frequently considered to be gods themselves.[290] Yet, at this point in historical time, obligations and prohibitions had little to do with universal ideals of morality. The orders of Mesopotamian kings came about "without discussion, without protest, without criticism, in a perfect and fatalistic submission."[291] The pharaoh in Egypt was seen as the incarnation of the god Huru, with his commandments accepted accordingly.

The invention of writing in these archaic civilizations, he explains, should not be equated with a "literacy revolution." In Mesopotamia, writing was used mostly for administrative purposes and the enactment of bureaucratic orders; repetitions of myths or hymns were the norm in the literary texts; these civilizations "remained largely oral cultures throughout their history."[292] In Egypt, too, texts were limited to administrative matters and temple ritual. The Middle Kingdom period (2040–1650 BC) sees some "wisdom" texts, hymns and tales imparting moral advice, as well as royal inscriptions about order, justice, and truth, but their language was restricted to the finite interests and customs of Egypt, without aiming at the construction of universal principles for humans as such. The notion that there was a deep unity between God and king precluded the idea of a God standing above the king with independently enacted moral commandments with a universal import.

In the New Kingdom (1550–1070 BC) a writing that seems to involve conscious reflection on religion emerges, but there was no theoretic discourse; the thinking remained mythical, although, according to Bellah, it was bordering on theoretical reflection. The centrality of the king in "every dimension of religious practice" (performance of cult, construction and maintenance of temples, responsibility for maintenance of the cosmic order), precluded any real discourse, as

---

[290] Ibid, 212.
[291] Ibid, 223.
[292] Ibid, 226.

would happen in Axial times, when a group of itinerant intellectuals would carry a persistent assault on the culture of ritual and myth, while searching for more universal answers about the meaning of life and the best forms of government.

The state in Shang China was essentially an extension of the ruler's court, in unison with lineages from members of the court. While it had bureaucratic attributes, a variety of appointed civil and military officers under the king, such positions were mere extensions of the patrimonial rule of the king. In fact, lineage was so pervasive in Shang China that ancestor worship was the central practice of religion, leaving a "permanent legacy for all later Chinese culture." It was difficult to create solidarity among all classes and regions, because even though archaic societies were territorially extensive and included millions of unrelated inhabitants, the rulers were a close-knit group connected by kinship ties without universal values connecting them to the people. No moral philosophy or texts were put forward from which to criticize unjust rulers based on notions about a universal God, a Mandate of Heaven, or the best form of government for humans as such.

Definition of "Axial Thought"

The concept of an Axial Age has historical merits. The period between 800 and 200 BC saw major intellectual developments in various parts of the Old World that came to shape the subsequent historical paths of millions of humans—the rise of Confucianism, Hinduism, Buddhism, Judaism, and Greek philosophy. But academics can't hide the fact that the Axial Age includes a very select group. The continents of North America, South America, Africa, and Australia saw no Axial revolution. Some academics, including Jaspers, include Zoroastrian Persia, but Bellah and many others include only Israel, Greece, China, and India.[293]

---

[293] There is growing pressure to include Egypt on the strength of Jan Assmann's contribution (2005), "Axial 'Breakthroughs' and Semantic 'Relocations' in Ancient Egypt and Israel." I am not persuaded by Assmann's grandiloquent claim that the Egyptian invention of the judgment of the dead was a pathbreaking idea in human history. Apart from being one of the first peoples to create a civilization, which involved the generic use of plows, intense irrigation works, a writing system, pottery, glassmaking and metalworking, the Egyptian contribution to mathematics and geometry was practical and elementary, without a single contribution to philosophy, political theory, literature, music, law, or theoretical science. After the Bronze or Archaic Age, Egyptian culture remained stagnant until it was shaken by the Hellenistic Greeks, and even then, only the Greeks in Alexandria made contributions in the sciences.

Bellah claims to be following Merlin Donald in saying that "the axial age breakthrough involved the emergence of theoretic culture."[294] He makes a distinction between first-order theory, which involves practical arithmetic and the beginnings of algebra in Babylonia; and second-order theory which involves explaining how one's rational exposition is possible, as well as explaining the grounds for thinking that one's exposition is true. In short, second-order thinking entails, in Bellah's own words, thinking about thinking. But in the end, Bellah makes the mere presence of first-order thinking a sufficient condition for Axial status outside Greece. In contrast, Donald, in a subsequent book, *A Mind So Rare: The Evolution of Human Consciousness*, published in 2001, is stricter in his assessment that a theoretic stage, or second-order thinking, emerged in ancient Greece only, where written texts "became reflective instruments, in which thought itself could be exposed to systematic analysis."[295] He understands, moreover, that "particularly in Western culture, we have placed consciousness and conscious experience on a pedestal." The religious and intellectual traditions of the West are unique in emphasizing "the development of awareness in the individual mind," as is particularly the case in the Socratic notion of the examined life—that is, a life made conscious by the habit of constant reflection."[296]

Sometimes Bellah realizes he is not following Donald's definition, but sometimes he seems unsure what the term "theoretic culture" means. What Bellah wants above all else is an Axial Age in which "new prophets" emerged: Confucius, Buddha, the Hebrew prophets, and the Greek philosophers, who called for a remaking of the world order on the basis of transcendental-egalitarian values.[297] But,

---

[294] Bellah, 273.

[295] Donald, 2001, 307.

[296] Ibid, 14.

[297] Without emphasizing "egalitarian values," Eisenstadt elevates the "transcendentalism" of the Axial Age above any other novelty. He writes that Axial religious figures were responsible for creating a basic tension between otherworldly religious values and the mundane world of everyday politics. These transcendental values were critical reflections about the injustices of the old kinship order, a longing for a new ordering of social life. The flaw in this elevation of religious transcendentalism into the supreme contribution of Axial times is that in ancient Greece there was no clear religious distinction between a transcendental religious sphere and a mundane sphere of politics. My sense is that Eisenstadt, who is Jewish, was mostly concerned with giving tiny ancient Israel a grand civilizational status akin to other ancient civilizations in the East, and the Axial Age concept of transcendentalism was the way to this enhanced status. Bellah tries to retain Eisenstadt's concept of transcendentalism without excluding Greece by recasting Greek philosophers as religious-mystical figures, as I will argue below. See "Introduction: History, Theory and Interpretation" by Arnason, Eisenstadt, and Wittrock (2005).

on its own, criticizing the existing order does not necessarily imply the presence of second-order thinking.

Axial Israel

Right from the start, Bellah has to admit that "thinking about thinking was not an Israelite concern." He insists that ancient Israel was Axial because it "clearly meets the standard for . . . preoccupation with and criticism of text, and the conscious evaluation of alternative grounds for religious and ethical practices" (283).[298] Israelites, beginning in the eighth century BC, articulated a new covenant between God and humans over and above the relationship between king and subjects. While the Israelites continue to be subordinated to worldly rulers, Yahweh is not subordinate to any earthly ruler, and the ultimate moral obligation of the Israelites is to God.

I have no difficulties accepting Bellah's view that the Israelites attempted real argumentation in making their case for a new covenant, "however unsystematic in presentation."[299] There is some form of first-order argumentation in the claim that a covenant with God supersedes kings, and that God is in the Word, and that if people abide by the Word they will be in right relation to God, regardless of what's going on in the world of men. The Israelites did articulate reasons why Yahweh is the only God there is, and they did conceive argumentatively a transcendent God as the ultimate moral legislator above any state power. But second-order thinking is a different matter, and involves a conscious awareness of the procedures one is using to make a distinction between true and false statements. It also means awareness of a faculty of reasoning that makes up its own criteria for truth and is not dependent on any external mythology, godly authority, or self-interested inclinations. This is not to say that the Israelite idea of a covenant was not a new vision radically different from the old mythical conceptions between ruler and ruled.

---

[298] Bellah, 283.
[299] Ibid, 314.

Axial China

Bellah opens this chapter with the words that axial China was "as stunningly innovative as the ancient Greeks."[300] He follows Heiner Roetz's thesis in *Confucian Ethics of the Axial Age* that ancient China was already showing signs of "post-conventional" moral reasoning, which Europe reached only in the Enlightenment era, merely on the textual basis of such flimsy Chinese phrases as: "society is men treating each other as men." We are supposed to believe that phrases like this were "almost Kantian," almost the same as Kant's *Critique of Practical Reason*, which directly examines the nature and scope of human reason as it relates to human moral judgements. Roet's argument on the post-conventional morality of Confucianism and Daoism will be addressed in chapter five, which deals with the embedded consciousness of the Chinese. Suffice it to say for now that Bellah is way off: just because the Chinese wrote about the "humaneness" of the gentleman, and about the cultivation of one's entire person—aesthetic and moral sensibilities, posture and comportment—as a model of how officials of the state should strive to become, it does not mean the concept of humaneness was articulated through second-order thinking. Bellah senses this, and deals with this problem by lowering the Axial Age standards for China, as he did for Israel.

First, it is strange that the same China that cultivated a human ethics allegedly characterized by a "remarkable lack of ethnocentrism," with a Mandate from Heaven calling upon the Chinese "to love all the people, and without distinctions," at the same time never abandoned a concern, in his words, "with ancestors, and so with lineage."[301] In all societies that move beyond the tribal stage, beyond chiefdoms, there is a decline in the significance of hereditary lineages, and China did create a state open to merit based on a rigorous examination process. But, as Bellah recognized in his assessment of archaic China:

> [T]he Shang emphasis on lineage left a permanent legacy for all later Chinese culture, of which the Confucian emphasis on kin relationships was an expression. Ancestor worship, so central in Shang cult, has continued at the domestic level to this day.[302]

---

[300] Ibid, 400.
[301] Ibid, 422, 429–430.
[302] Ibid, 250.

Confucius "inaugurated the Axial Age," we are told. Yet, Bellah can't deny that ritual is at the center of the thought of Confucius, and that the highest ethical term in Confucian thought, Ren, refers to the good-feeling gentlemen experience when being altruistic. This term is "not theoretical. . . . It is performative, enactive, mimetic, though it gives rise to thought."[303] He can't deny that the *Analects* "is an aphoristic book, at best anecdotal. [It is] . . . not a systematic work. . . . [It] does not ever develop systematic connections between its key terms."[304] While he mentions Mozi's "relentless logic," he can't deny that "formal logic never became central in Chinese thought."[305] He can barely demonstrate that Confucianism set up a transcendent normative standard with which to judge existing reality, because he can't deny that "Confucianism became something like an official ideology,"[306] and that all Chinese thinkers demanded that each rank of society observed "its own appropriate rituals," and that the ritual order was intended to reinforce the social hierarchy.[307] The Daoists did criticize the Confucian order, but only in the name of the "natural" way in which children behave. Daoist texts, he admits, "move from insight to insight rather than through systematic reflection."[308] In short, the only way Bellah manages to make a case for Axial China is by lowering the standard considerably for what Axial thought means compared to that set for ancient Greece. The standard is set even lower for India.

Axial India

There is no evidence for writing in India before the third century BC, and yet Bellah claims there was an Axial breakthrough in the late Vedic period with the Upanishads, a collection of ideas that were probably conceived between 800 and 500 BC, and passed down orally before they were put into writing much later, and interpolated and expanded over time; no one really knows who the authors were. Late Vedic society of about the sixth century BC sees the first cities in the Ganges,

---

[303] Ibid, 412.
[304] Ibid, 416.
[305] Ibid, 412.
[306] Ibid, 426.
[307] Ibid, 472.
[308] As Hans-Georg Moeller also understands, in the central text of Daoism, the *Laozi*, ideas are expressed in a "fragmentary manner," the topics "are not arranged according to a specific pattern, there are no analytical steps taken to solve any explicit philosophical problem, there is no particular order of logical conclusions, no chain of arguments" (2006, 3).

irrigation agriculture, considerable population densities, and networks of trade, combined with a shift from a society linked by kinship to a society of differentiated roles cutting across tribal boundaries. Bellah deduces a breakthrough in India from the fact that the ideas of the Upanishads, in their written version, were conveyed in dialogue form, involving "a tradition of questioning and debate." Bellah also cites older hymns from the Rig Veda, which he claims have "some continuity" with the Upanishads in asking big metaphysical questions, such as:

> Who really knows? Who will here proclaim it? Whence was it produced? Whence this creation? The gods came afterwards, with the creation of this universe. Who then knows whence it has arisen? Whence this creation has arisen—perhaps it formed itself, or perhaps it did not—the one who looks down on it, in the highest heaven, only he knows—or perhaps he does not know. [309]

Another supposed breakthrough is that the "lively discussions" depicted in the Upanishads were "not limited by caste or gender barriers," although Bellah can't deny that these barriers would not be crossed later in all subsequent Indian history until very recently. He notes as well an "incipient level of abstraction that moves beyond narrative into conceptual thinking;" "theory begins to emerge in the Upanishads." But he has to admit that "it does not do so by way of systematic reasoning. . . . It is revealed in metaphors." [310] He tries to argue that teaching about the identity of brahman and atman is "absolutely universal in content," citing an expert explaining what makes these ideas universal:

> The true self is not the individual self, but rather the identity that one shares with everything else. There is no true distinction among living beings, for they all emerge from being and retreat to it. All things animate and inanimate, are united in being, because they are all transformations of being. [311]

There is indeed universal content in these expressions, insofar as they speak about being as such, not about any particular being, and about the individual self as such.

---

[309] Bellah, 511.
[310] Ibid, 513.
[311] Ibid.

These expressions may be said to exhibit the beginnings in India of thinking about the absolute; however, not as a definite conception, but as an indeterminate and abstract conception, since we are not told anything concrete about the way being unites the particular within the individual self, but only that they are all transformations of being. Admittedly, it can also be said of the earliest Pre-Socratic ventures into the ultimate source of all things that they dealt with very abstract, indeterminate concepts devoid of concrete differentiation. Anaximander wrote about how the processes of change we see in the world are expressions of a universal, undefinable, limitless, divine Nature. He did this in writing, but Bellah excludes him from the Axial Age.

Moreover, with Heraclitus we have someone who does not obliterate the self within an undifferentiated universal being, but argues that the *logos* of human speech can express the *logos* which lies in the nature of things; speech (*logos*) is a manifestation of the *logos* of the universe; the *logos* of the universe discloses itself in human speech. In its deepest nature, the mind is *logos*; it has the capacity for apprehending the regularity and patterns of things. The mind is rational and therefore it can grasp the rational order of the cosmos through its rational speech. While Heraclitus did not have a concept of subjective freedom, Greeks were moving in this direction in creating institutions in which Greek male citizens were equally free and capable of participating in politics.

By contrast, Indian philosophy would never rise above the early abstractions of the Upanishads. As Hegel argued, the notion of brahman would fail to reconcile the universal, the absolute, with the finite or individual. The concept of brahman would always subsume all finite things, including the self, which would remain incapable of ever understanding the nature, the rationale, of the brahman. The independent self in India would indeed be obliterated in substance, in the indefinite oneness of a Being that would remain aloof and beyond reason.[312]

Bellah has to admit that the concept of dharma in the Bhagavad Gita, generally accepted to be a second-century BC text, which prescribes the right way of living in terms of duties and rituals, does not speak about humans in general, but about the way of life appropriate for members of each caste. "This discussion of dharma

---

[312] See Gino Signoracci's 2017 dissertation, "Hegel on Indian Philosophy: Spinozism, Romanticism, Eurocentrism." This is a thorough study, but its argument that Hegel was not fair to India's contribution to philosophy seems to be simply that it is "Eurocentric." I see "Eurocentrism" as the inevitable result of the higher level of philosophical reflection found in European philosophy in its encounter with lower levels of reflection.

leads inevitably to the vexed problem of caste."[313] Bellah is not happy dealing with the issue of caste, "because of its pejorative implications." He is afraid he will be "liable to the accusation of Orientalism." But he can't deny that caste "remained basic to Indian social organization until recent times."[314] So how does one square this observation with the idea that India made a breakthrough into a universal ethics?

At this point, Bellah's mind turns mushy, as he goes on to write that there was a breakthrough in religious thought while the "premises of society remained non-axial." Even though he believes the actual society remained non-axial, he insists he can't be charged with viewing "'Oriental societies as inegalitarian." As a politically correct, dutiful person, Bellah describes Chinese civilization as "profoundly egalitarian," and is "convinced that Islamic societies were also profoundly egalitarian." However, he then adds that he is not describing these societies in actuality, but referring to their ideologies. No society, after all, has been egalitarian since primitive times. Meanwhile, he warns his students that the United States has been "one of the most oppressive societies in history in its treatment of people both within and without."[315] Bellah downplays the fact that the most sacred and important text of Indian philosophy, the Bhagavad Gita, which supposedly advocated an egalitarian ethics, was in fact suffused with the notion of caste.

Many Westerners looking for meaning in their confused lives love to praise the Bhagavad Gita. Stephen Mitchell, in his new translation, acts as if he was one of the "blessed ones" writing about "the inconceivable depths of reality" of the Gita. Reading his translation, he says, is "a matter of the gravest urgency," a "battle for authenticity, the life and death of the soul . . . the struggle against greed, and ignorance, against ingrained selfishness." The Gita "presents some of the most important truths of human existence." Mitchell is impressed by the "tolerance and inclusiveness" he finds in the Gita. But he knows that "however powerful its thinking, its intention is not to be a treatise but a psalm,"—a hymn or poetic song. It is not a philosophical work. "The inconceivable depths of reality" it pronounces are unthinkable and do not require one to grasp them mentally.[316] From its nebulous-sounding phrases, meanings and conclusions can be generated with ease and without explanation.

---

[313] Bellah, 521.
[314] Ibid, 523.
[315] Ibid, 524.
[316] From Stephen Mitchell's introduction to his translation of Bhagavad Gita (2000), 13–30.

In the end, Bellah's case for India leaves us with the claim that Buddhism certainly "completed the axial transition."[317] He cites an author who says that it is the "man who practices Buddhist precepts to their utmost who has the highest status," not the man who is born a Brahmin. Within Buddhism, dharma is "available to all people, regardless of status or ethnicity."[318] But in what ways is Buddhism a product of systematic thought engaged with second order thinking? This criterion is relegated to the margins. What matters is that Buddhism engendered communities that attempted to exist as parallel societies, as alternative ways of life characterized by "ethical universalism," independently of criteria of kinship and lineage. Dharma, the truth told by Buddhism, was about good behavior towards slaves and servants, obedience to parents, generosity to friends and relatives, abstention from killing living beings.

Is that all there is to the Axial Age?

Axial Greece

Revealingly enough, when it comes to the one Axial case where one witnesses the "discovery of the mind," Bellah writes (from the opening page) that "being Eurocentric or Western-centric" is no longer acceptable. The "extreme enthusiasm" of older days for this civilization "has been countered with serious debunking." Greece will be treated "as just one of four axial cases."[319] But, in truth, Bellah treats Greece as a special case by applying Donald's criteria for a "theoretic culture" in a far more stringent manner.[320] He recognizes that Anaximander's account of the origins of the cosmos,

---

[317] Bellah, 531.

[318] Ibid, 537.

[319] Ibid, 324.

[320] I should mention here that Bellah cites Yehuda Elkana's article "The emergence of second-order thinking in classical Greece" (1986), which argues, similarly to Donald, that the Axial Age breakthrough of classical Greece was all about the "emergence of second-order thinking." Bellah, however, treats Elkana's views pretty much the same way he treats Donald's: he refuses to apply his criteria to eastern Axial civilizations, lowering the standards, while applying an even stricter standard than they do to ancient Greece. Elkana sees geometrical proofs as a "second-order idea par excellence" because this way of thinking seeks systematic justification for its claims, "a way to [rationally] convince the student rather than to supply the truth." However, Elkana does not include the Presocratics as second-order thinkers on the grounds that they spoke of "transcendental entities," such as the entity of a higher mind, *nous*, in a dogmatic fashion, as rigid statements about the ultimate nature of reality, without thinking reflexively about alternatives to their

appears to be both naturalistic and rational: everything is explained by impersonal forces, not only the origination of the universe, but the workings of the heavenly bodies, the weather and other natural phenomena. The Olympian gods are nowhere to be mentioned.[321]

Yet he can't help adding that "Greek science, by rejecting experiment, never amounted to much,"[322] thus imposing the strict criteria of modern experimental research to keep the Greeks down to the level of other Axial cultures, in the course of which he exhibits willful ignorance of the impressive observations Aristotle made in zoology, followed by the Hellenistic period from 320 BC to AD 230, which historians now recognize as a watershed moment, with science finally becoming preoccupied with experimentation and technical innovation. This period, which witnessed "an explosion of objective knowledge about the external world,"[323] included the empirical investigations in harmonics by Aristoxenus and Ptolemy, the scientific work in geography of Eratosthenes, Strabo, and Ptolemy, the incredible mathematics of Archimedes, which anticipated modern calculus by applying the concept of the infinitely small and the method of exhaustion to derive geometrical theorems, not to mention many other names. We will see indeed, in the next chapter, that Greek mathematics alone was theoretically more sophisticated than the mathematics of all the other Axial civilizations throughout their histories.

   Bellah admits that when Parmenides defined "the form of argument that could lead to truth," he was engaged in "thinking about thinking . . . giving a method . . . for finding the truth."[324] He insists, however, without offering any analysis, that only with the arrival of Plato and Aristotle do we see a breakthrough into theoretic thinking. Yet he has nothing to say about this breakthrough other than to say that Plato was the first to distinguish between myth and *logos*, and to ask rhetorically

---

claims. (I will defend the Presocratics as second-order thinkers later). The *polis*, he believes, encouraged second order thinking in giving speech and free debate a political power replacing brute force. In the *polis*, political ideas were subjected to debate and public criticism; politics was no longer a matter of ritualistic words or formulaic statements. The Sophists, too, introduced second-order thinking with their argumentative skills and their rhetorical ability to engage "opposing arguments." Herodotus' awareness that each culture possesses its own norms and modes of behavior was also an example of second-order thinking in anthropology.

[321] Ibid, 367.

[322] Ibid, 324.

[323] Russo, 2004.

[324] Bellah, 379.

whether Aristotle was the first "who reflected on the meaning of our representations in just about every field of knowledge."[325] In the end, the impression he wants to impart is that these two thinkers were interested in *theoria* as contemplation, from which point he likens them to the Daoists and Buddhists. Rather than saying a word about the first truly systematic act of thinking about thinking that is contained in Aristotle's logical works, he appeals to the worn-out phrase that "the European philosophical tradition is a series of footnotes to Plato."[326]

To his credit, he recognizes that Greece was not a typical Asiatic despotic polity even before the rise of democratic rule, but a society in which aristocratic warriors voiced their own views, and in which heroic prowess and eloquence in debate was the basis of leadership. "Nobles . . . viewed themselves as equals and resisted domination by any particular family. They competed for excellence and virtually created the culture of athletics as we know it today."[327]

But Bellah does not know what to make of this, how to connect this to the unique aristocratic nature of archaic Mycenaean Greece, other than to state that the "*polis* is a unique Greek institution." He does not link the aristocratic culture of Indo-Europeans and Mycenaeans to the rise of the polis. He brings up G. E. R. Lloyd's argument that the Greeks of the classical age, unlike the Chinese, never sought ancient authority for their arguments, but were always trying to outdo and criticize their teachers with original lines of inquiry. He notes this in passing only, and forgets that this culture of open debate was pervasive in Greece, manifested in the invention of competitive sports, the heated debates in assemblies open to all adult male citizens, and the competitions to have one's play performed in the theatre.

Indo-European "Individualizing" Chiefdoms
Versus Non-European "Group-Oriented" Chiefdoms

This failure to see a connection between the aristocratic culture of the Mycenaeans and the city-state politics of classical Greece flows directly out of Bellah's assumption that complex chiefdoms and archaic civilizations were alike in their class structures and that all "aristocracies" were mere exploiters of commoners. In contrast, the term "aristocratic" is used here in reference to a political order in

---

[325] Ibid, 365.
[326] Ibid, 582.
[327] Ibid, 335.

which the ruler was first among equals, and in which the prevailing ethos was that of "being-for-self," or self-assertiveness and defiance in the face of despotism and in the open pursuit of heroic deeds. The despotic archaic civilizations of the non-Western world were preceded by "group-oriented" chiefdoms, whereas the archaic civilization of Mycenae was preceded by the "individualizing" chiefdoms that prevailed in the Indo-European world. As we learn from the research of Kristian Kristiansen (1991) and Timothy Earle's 1997 comparative study, *How Chiefs Came to Power*, centralizing-collective activities aimed at integrating the population in the performance of irrigation agriculture, and the building of temples and monumental architecture at the behest of paramount chiefs who increasingly took on a divine character.

Individualizing chiefdoms, on the other hand, emphasized the personal status and prestige of ruling aristocracies, with the aristocratic chief and his retinue of warriors constituting the focus of economic activity, and the units of production being individual farmsteads rather than communal estates. Individualizing chiefdoms were dominated by "wealth finance" or prestige goods economies, whereas collective chiefdoms were dominated by staple finance and tributary systems. Staple chiefdoms were regulated by vertical relations of production and exchange, in the sense that chiefly authorities obtained their sources of income by extracting staple goods from the commoners to finance public works, to pay the personnel attached to the chief, and to trade with other chiefdoms. Prestige chiefdoms, by contrast, were characterized by horizontal relations whereby aristocrats obtained their income by controlling exchange networks, supplies of prestige goods, and decentralized units of rain-fed farming communities.

The rise of complex chiefdoms in Europe starting around 1500 BC was linked to an ideological and military complex of aristocratic warriors in control of long-distance elite exchange in prestige goods that spread from the Mycenaean area through central Europe and Scandinavia. The agrarian system of these chiefdoms was based on husbandry of free grazing herds and rotating fields in an open landscape. Prestige goods were used as political currency to reward followers and enhance one's status. The ethos of individual heroism was the engine behind the prestige goods economy, since the status of the chiefs was individually associated with the pursuit of prestige in warfare. The acquisition of prestige objects was not the means to acquire status. Rather, the possession of luxurious weapons and personal items symbolized that one had achieved high status in warfare.

The aristocratic ethos of companionship and equality is the most important trait of individualizing chiefdoms. Despite increased hierarchization, individual warriors were able to attract a retinue of followers through sheer personal initiative. The chiefs sought to attract followers and win the loyalty of lesser aristocratic warriors by giving gifts. The formation of voluntary war bands held together by oaths, camaraderie, and a common self-interest was a characteristic of these chiefdoms. One's status and rank as a noble were still openly determined by one's heroic deeds and by the number of followers and clients one could afford. Despite the principle of loyalty and companionship, there was always competition for power, and endless personal rivalries. This was not a rigid structure in which men lost their individuality and vitality, as was the case in staple chiefdoms.

What Kristiansen and Earle do not tell us, but is crucially important to understand, is that citizen-warrior states and republican governments emerged only out of prior individualizing chiefdoms. In group-oriented chiefdoms, however, authority became increasingly concentrated in the hands of one supreme chief from whom wealth and power were seen to flow vertically to the majority at the bottom, as well as to the few aristocrats under the subservience of the supreme despotic chief. While paramount chiefs faced competition from upstarts seeking to upstage them, and while status enhancement through the performance of deeds was still a factor in social mobility, the opportunity to achieve renown and prestige was increasingly difficult and rare as non-Western chiefdoms became centralized. It is prominently among the individualizing chiefdoms of Indo-Europeans that one finds true tales of individual heroism, and stories about the meetings, games, and feasting of chieftains, clients, and warriors. None of the staple chiefdoms produced a heroic epic literature.

This aristocratic spirit continued in the more advanced archaic civilizations of Europe, such as Mycenae during the second millennium. The political structure of Mycenaean Greece was one of autonomous feudal warlords surrounded by aristocratic retainers under the nominal overlordship of the city of Mycenae. For Bellah, however, Mycenae was just another archaic civilization, to which he pays no particular attention other than to identify it (erroneously) as "Eastern." Homer's poems reflect the central aristocratic values of the Mycenaean age. While the leader was now a king, rather than a chief of a tribal society, he did not have despotic powers, but ruled together with feudal warlords who were identified as the "companions" of the king. The *Iliad* captures this aristocratic relationship when it has Agamemnon, King of Mycenae, surrounded by free, prideful men who are always deliberating and debating their actions, rather than subserviently following the commands of an autocratic king. Agamemnon was no pharaoh ruling by divine right. There were councils where aristocrats could voice their differences with the king, which was the original ground for the rise of city-states in Greece and republican forms of government thereafter.

Arete and the "Relaxed Field" of Indo-European Aristocratic Men

Bellah is on to something, a very important aspect of cultural evolution, when he identifies the emergence of "relaxed fields" of human activity, and then connects the Axial Age breakthrough with the emergence of a theoretic culture advocating universal values relatively freed from older hierarchies and Darwinian power politics. Bellah astutely interprets, within a grand historical narrative, the ritual practices of cultures, the dancing, feasting, music, and "sense of moral equality that the ritual generates," as moments of relaxed play."[328] He identifies "relaxed fields" in chiefdoms during those ritual times when all the people "devote themselves to feasting, mockery, obscene and satirical singing, and, above all, to dancing," including the "violation of rules of deference to superiors." When he reaches the Axial Age, he looks at the social criticism entailed in the universal egalitarian ethics articulated by Axial Age philosophers as expressions of "relaxed fields" of cultural creativity. He writes:

> I did not shy away from the fact that natural selection is the primary mechanism of evolution, biological and cultural, but I was concerned with the emergence of "relaxed fields" in animal play and human culture, where the struggle for existence or the survival of the fittest did not have full sway, where ethical standards and free activity could arise, forms that in many cases did turn out to be selected, as they had survival value, though they arose in contexts where the good was internal to the practice, not for any external end.[329]

Evolutionary psychologists are very good at explaining "cultural universals"—answering why certain cultural practices, patterns, traits, or institutions are common to all cultures, and the ways in which these practices and norms conform to the imperatives of survival and the struggle for power and sexual reproduction. But a Darwinian approach falls short when it comes to the understanding of the highest

---

[328] Ibid, 570.
[329] Ibid, 600.

expressions of these cultural universals, not their common, basic levels. While evolutionary theorists can write about the adaptive functions of dance, music, and philosophy, they don't have explanations for the origins of European ballet, the unparalleled history of its choreographic notation, its associations with theatre, opera, and classical music, the incredible variety of classical musical compositions, variety of philosophies, or architectural and painting styles in Western history. Bellah has a point that Axial thought contains an element of "relaxed play" in envisioning improved worlds in which Darwinian pressures are suspended in an imaginary world of non-violence, social justice, plentiful harvests, and peaceful contemplation of the divine.

But there is a fundamental flaw in Bellah's conception of "relaxed fields" of cultural activity in the assumption that humans exhibit their highest talents and best ideas, artistic, and philosophical expressions, in the articulation of mothering, egalitarian, and empathetic ideals. In the realm of Darwinian necessity, humans can express incredible feats of perseverance, physical prowess, and talents that bespeak greatness. Just because the mothering side of life is essential for building strong bonds within families, we can't look to the feminine side of life to explain the vitality and striving for high recognition required to achieve greatness. One is reminded of Camille Paglia's blunt statement that "if civilization had been left in female hands, we would still be living in grass huts."[330] Kant is likely correct that without the "unsocial sociability" of humans, their "self-interest, ambition, and vainglory," humans would have lacked the drive to create great art, architecture, glorious empires, new scientific explanations, and countless other great accomplishments.

The "unsocial sociability" of humans is primarily a male attribute, which assumed a more intense expression among Indo-European speakers as a result of their aristocratic lifestyle, in affording individual warriors the opportunity to strive for personal prestige, in a state of "being-for-self," or self-assertiveness, which is rooted in the thymotic part of the soul, and which entailed indeed a willful relaxation from the appetitive instincts. The demand for recognition and self-worth, as Nietzsche elucidated, is inherently aristocratic and inegalitarian, in that this demand involves a striving for superior recognition among aristocratic peers. Every human wants some form of recognition, but most humans throughout history either did not have the chance to strive for high ideals, or were satisfied with being the same as others. The desire to be superior is known in ancient Greek

---

[330] Paglia, 1990, 38.

language as "megalothymia," which is a desire by prideful aristocrats for something more than mere material well-being or being accepted by others as one in many. The aristocratic warrior is willing to negate his biological urge for life for the sake of a recognition by his peers that is nonmaterial, but entails acquisition of respect and honor.

It is not that IEs acted against selective pressures, but that they created a cultural field of action that was for the love of glory over the immediate attachment to life. Darwinian dynamics are always at play since humans are bodily creatures, and the strategies they pursue must have positive evolutionary consequences—the Indo-Europeans, after all, conquered a vast area in Europe and Asia. But humans are not imprisoned to one cultural strategy; varying cultural options are available in the struggle for life; humans are "flexible strategizers"[331] and, in the case of Indo-Europeans, they opted for an aristocratic lifestyle in the environment of the Pontic steppes, which intensified the thymotic or the "spirited" part of the soul. The "megalothymia" of aristocratic warriors differentiated the male ego, promoted liberation from chthonic gods and the creation of sky gods closer to light and consciousness, away from the dark underworld of the fertility goddess. This attitude is not conceptual. It is not theoretic, but it does lead to selfhood, as we explained in the last chapter. The attitude of the individual who risks his life for prestige is that of "being-for-self" or self-assertiveness, which is rooted in the thymotic part of the soul. We can say, then, that the field of relaxation from Darwinian pressures achieved among Indo-Europeans took on the form of a "struggle to the death for pure prestige," to use Hegel's language, over and against the mundane desire for personal self-preservation and comfort.

We should not assume, however, that the moment there is relaxation from the necessities of life, or the moment we witness the beginnings of a sense of selfhood and personality among the Homeric Greeks, there was bound to be theoretic or second-order thinking. So how and why did the ancient Greeks start to develop a theoretic consciousness after the *Iliad*? The consensus has been that it began with the Presocratics during the Archaic Age, which began around 750 BC, following the Dark Age, which was the period after the end of the Mycenaean civilization, around 1100 BC. This period is associated with the re-emergence of sustained contact with Mesopotamian, Egyptian, and Persian civilizations, with the rise of city states with their new concept of civic virtue and the idea that equal

---

[331] The phrase "flexible strategizers" is used by Richard Alexander in *Darwinism and Human Affairs* (1979).

membership and legal status in the city-state should be more important than the old tribal/clannish identities of Homeric heroes. This age is also associated with a new style of warfare, dominated by hoplite independent farmers, rather than aristocrats, who pushed for democratic representation in the *polis*, and with the origins of the Greek alphabet. For these reasons, scholars have been inclined to find the roots of theoretic thinking in these new institutions or in alphabetic literacy.

There is no denying that without these changes, without the Greeks inhabiting a world of advanced civilizations, from which they learned much, while developing their own institutions, citizenship politics, independent farmers, hoplite warfare, and the alphabet, the Greeks would not have gone beyond the brawling, coarse, unrefined aristocratic lifestyle that Homer started to criticize in his depiction of Achilles' gruesome treatment of Hector's dead body, and his preference for Odysseus' higher capacity for introspection and self-control over his impulses. *Arete*, which refers to "excellence" of any kind, was the central idea in the development of Greek culture. With the spread of a more urbane, civilized, and literary lifestyle in the Archaic age, Greeks began to broaden this ideal beyond its traditional association with physical prowess, martial valor, and honor. In *Uniqueness*, I traced the way this ideal came to denote not only mastery over one's appetitive drives in the pursuit of glory, but also mastery over the thymotic part of the soul, in a civilized and literary direction, leading eventually to its association, above all other activities, with a contemplative theoretic life in Plato and Aristotle. The moderation that Apollo preached—"nothing in excess," and "know thyself—was an attempt to sublimate the aristocratic Will to Power of martial men, not by pacifying them, but by encouraging them to use their seeing mind (*nous*) to control the excesses of the emotive mind (thymos), mitigating its ferocity and reckless bloodlust. The ideal of excellence retained its power, but now it came to be associated as well with high cultural pursuits, with each artist and intellectual driven by a desire to outdo their predecessors or contemporaries in originality and fame.

However, in emphasizing how the *polis* and an urban lifestyle were behind the rise of a "theoretic" culture, we should not lose sight of what needs to be explained, which is the rise of self-consciousness. The immediate explanation for this was not a new technology of communication, a cosmopolitan life in Miletus where the first Presocratics were located, however important these factors were to the whole historical dynamic; it was the continued evolution of self-awareness from the prior stages discussed in the prior two chapters, the differentiation of the male ego from the Great Mother, the aristocratic culture of Indo-Europeans and Mycenaeans, and the onset of selfhood among Homeric Greeks. We should avoid speaking of a "transition from myth to logic," or the "rise of rationality," or a mere "theoretic" mind, as if we are trying to establish the origins of a new cognitive ability. What we are trying to understand is the further intensification of self-consciousness during the Archaic Age.

Hegel: Philosophy Begins "When Thinking Turns in Upon Itself"

Hegel is the one philosopher who apprehended best that archaic Greece witnessed, with the Presocratics, the origins of a true philosophical consciousness. In his *Introduction to the Lectures on the History of Philosophy*, Hegel qualifies Aristotle's observation that humans start to philosophize "when the necessities of life have been met" with the argument that philosophy is possible only when thinking has "vanished" "everything foreign to itself and the spirit is absolutely free," no longer "mixed up with much that is particular and sensuous," "free from all natural determinants," "the heart, our impulses, feelings," and free from "fear" of theocratic and despotic rulers.[332]

> Philosophy's history begins where thought comes into existence in its freedom, where it tears itself free from its immersion in nature, from its unity with nature, when it constitutes itself in its own eyes, when thinking turns in upon itself and is at home with itself.[333]

This separation of "theoretic" consciousness from what is not-conscious first began in ancient Greece. While "the spirit does arise" in the East, it arises intermixed with nature; "the Indians and Egyptians, for example, had in animals their consciousness of the divine. Moreover, they had this consciousness in the sun, the stars." Hegel continues:

> On the one hand there are natural powers and forces which are personified and worshipped by Eastern peoples; on the other hand, inasmuch as consciousness rises above nature to an infinite being, the chief thing is fear of this power, with the result that the individual knows himself as only accidental in the face of this power.

---

[332] Hegel, 1805/2003, 55–56, 63, 80, 163, 169.
[333] Ibid, 164.

When they do not fear these natural powers, and the spirit crystallizes itself to a higher degree, it is a spirit characterized by "the emptiest abstraction, pure negativity, nothingness—the sublimity of abandoning everything concrete." This was the case among Indian mystics who spent "years in expiations . . . mortifying every pain . . . contemplating the tip of their nose without locating in this exercise any thoughts or interest in consciousness but simply persisting in this inmost abstraction, this perfect emptiness, this stillness of death."[334]

The "emergence of philosophy implies the consciousness of freedom," persons who are capable of thinking about thinking, and desiring institutions in which they are recognized as such, away from despotic rule. This state of mind is reflected in the civic culture of the Greek city-states. The Greeks were the first to establish a self-relation wherein the self confronted its own thinking as an object of thought, rather than allowing something external—things without reason—to dictate its thinking. It is thought that produces the universal concepts by which nature is comprehended, and these universals do not arise from any outside source but, from thinking itself.

The world of material things is always subject to external necessities and causal relationships; on the other hand, consciousness has the potential to decide what is the essence of things, what is the universal in the particular, and to legislate for itself its own cognitive criteria for what constitutes truth and what are moral actions, and thus become the source of itself rather than a product of something alien. It was in ancient Greece that thought—consciousness—started to exhibit this potentiality to make itself explicitly the object of its own reflections and its own activity. Philosophy as defined by Hegel did not emerge in other Axial civilizations.

Hegel writes that "in development nothing emerges but what was there originally in germ or in-itself."[335] He agrees with Aristotle that all things are continually striving to express their potentialities, to make explicit what is implicitly highest in them. The essence of consciousness is to make consciousness explicit to itself, to reach self-consciousness. The seed for man's aspiration to freedom and the seed for man's apprehension of himself as the only being that can become aware of his capacity to self-determine are already there inside man as such, insofar as man is a being with the capacity for consciousness. But Hegel knows that this implicit

---

[334] Ibid, 167, 36, 170.
[335] Ibid, 72.

capacity only started to become explicit and actual with the ancient Greeks. It never manifested itself anywhere else.

Logos

The Presocratics invented a style of thinking capable of producing knowledge and truthfulness.[336] Once this style was inaugurated, there was no end to the ideas Europeans could produce continuously beyond the Axial Age. The faculty of reason is the generator of knowledge, and the more reason is freed from extra-rational constraints—able to rely on its own internally generated principles, axioms, and inferential dynamic—it will inevitably produce novel ideas about nature, man, and society, since there is an infinite number of things to be discovered and learned about. Novel facts engender empirical progress, corroborate existing ideas or call for new explanations. In philosophy generally, reliance on open debate, through reason's own criteria, for and against, thesis and antithesis, through blind alleys and aimless meanderings, produces new ideas and ways of observing reality.

There is a key word, which is sometimes defined to mean "the word," which captures the essence of the Presocratic Revolution—*logos*. There is much ambiguity about the meaning of this word due to successive appropriations, misappropriations and disputations, going back to ancient times,[337] but the core meaning of *logos* is that there is a ratio, a principle, a proportion, a measure in the world that can be accounted for by human reason through the use of words, explanations, and arguments. Humans can be cogitators of this *logos*, so long as they engage in reasoned, balanced, proportionate debate, in a way that is commensurate with the order of the world. *Logos* means to argue with words, not "word" as used in grammar, but in the sense of giving an account through speech, through discourse—that is, to offer reasons and truth-claims through the use of arguments.

The Presocratics were no longer satisfied with the taken-for-granted beliefs of their times, asking, for example, "why should we believe mythical stories about the origins of the universe." "Do you have good reasons to believe them?" Thales offered reasons about the underlying nature of all things: water must be the primeval stuff, since water is essential for the nourishment of all things living and it is the only naturally occurring substance that can change from solid to liquid to

---

[336] Barnes, 1982; Kirk and Raven, 1983.
[337] Schiappa, 2003; Hillar, 2012.

gas. But Anaximander then went on to question Thales, countering that, if we are to find the original source of all things, there must be something that itself has no beginning, which he called the "infinite" or the "Boundless." The Boundless "encompasses all things," and "steers all things." It is not water but the Boundless that is the ultimate source. But how does the Boundless engender the many individual things we experience in the world? Anaximander offered an answer to this question, unsatisfied with simply stating, in Lao-Tzu's fashion, "Tao is empty but inexhaustible, bottomless, the ancestor of all."[338] He argued that the Boundless generates the many through its own vortex motion, which results in the lightest objects moving up and the heavy ones down, leading to the ordered arrangement we see around us of fiery stars, airy sky, watery clouds, and earthly objects. Xenophanes, for his part, explicitly challenged the notion that the gods had "revealed all things from the beginning to mortals," and the poets' claim to divine revelation; humans must look for themselves what is true "by seeking," by asking questions: How much can we know? How can we know it? This is epistemology, a branch of philosophy uniquely European. It involves thinking about what distinguishes justified belief from mere opinion; it is the study of knowing, of what it means to have knowledge—*logos*.

Heraclitus in particular uses the term *logos* to refer to the in-built patterns of change he discerned in the world. Things become through opposing forces and conflict; everything is in a state of continuous becoming, driven by a *logos* wherein everything that exists results from the opposition of forces, and this is the way things must be—justice—since all things presuppose their opposite; there can be no light without darkness. This endless movement is the basic principle, the *logos*, the ground of all things. Only the few can apprehend it:

> This *logos* holds always but humans always prove unable to understand it, both before hearing it and when they have first heard it. For though all things come to be in accordance with this *logos*, humans are like the inexperienced when they experience such words and deeds as I set out, distinguishing each in accordance with its nature and saying how it is.[339]

---

[338] From Sam Hamill's *Tao Te Ching: A New Translation* (2005, 6).
[339] Cited in Johnstone, 2014.

Strife and opposition are not evil, but part of the order of things. One can apprehend this pattern not with eyes and ears, but by looking within oneself, one's mind, and discovering therein the *logos*, which is the truth, and which is common to all things. As Heraclitus once said: "I thought for myself."

But Parmenides, known for his insistence that one must go wherever reasoning takes you, even if it contradicts the senses, came to the conclusion that there can be no becoming, no change, no beginnings or endings, since something that is, cannot cease to be, for that would mean that there is always a point at which it is passing into what it is not, and what is not cannot be thought, for it is nothing; therefore, all things that exist must be "all at once, one and continuous." The ultimate is present in all things, and it is one, eternal, and indivisible. This led Zeno to propose his famous paradoxes, which we will examine in another chapter, revolving around the idea that motion is impossible because it contains the contradiction that something is and is not simultaneously.

To apprehend the "theoretic" culture of Axial Greece, we need to focus on the Greek discovery of *logos*. There is a large literature on the Presocratic invention of philosophical reasoning completely ignored by Bellah. One need not be an expert in the writings of the Presocratics to be confident in making this argument. What follows below is a historiographical-textual attempt in support of this argument by way of an examination of four relatively recent books, namely, André Laks, *The Concept of Presocratic Philosophy: Its Origin, Development, and Significance* (2006 in French, 2018 in English); Maria Michela Sassi, *The Beginnings of Philosophy in Greece* (2009 in Italian, 2018 in English); Christopher Lyle Johnstone, *Listening to Logos: Speech and the Coming of Wisdom in Ancient Greece* (2009); and Constantine J. Vamvacas, *The Founders of Western Thought: The Presocratics* (2001 in Greek, 2009 in English). We will conclude with an old classic, Eric Havelock's *Preface to Plato*, which will be re-read as a study of the birth of self-consciousness, rather than as a mere study of the rise of a literate, alphabetic culture over an oral culture, or a defense of Plato's attack on the poetic tradition. The interpretation of these texts, identifying agreements and disagreements, is guided by many other readings about and by the Presocratics, some of which will be referenced here and in other chapters.

It is worth starting with Laks' book, for it is itself a historiographical survey of "the various senses in which Presocratic philosophers [were] considered Presocratic" from ancient to contemporary times. For a long time, beginning with Aristotle and Diogenes Laertius (third century AD, author of a biography of Greek philosophers, *Lives and Opinions of Eminent Philosophers*), the Presocratics were viewed as "natural philosophers" who conducted inquiries into nature—the "principle" or "substrate" in Aristotle's words—"of which all beings are made," the way in which the universe and the Earth were formed, including the study of specialized topics such as the distance and size of the heavenly bodies, the luminosity of the Moon, the causes of earthquakes, and the origins of living things. They were seen as the "first ones to philosophize" about the nature of things. Nietzsche criticized this "Aristotelian" interpretation and focused instead on the "tragic" element in early Greek culture and the power of myths, while Heidegger reinterpreted Presocratic writings not as inquiries into the nature of things, but as inquiries into man's relationship-of-Being towards the world.

In the twentieth century, as academics came to have misgivings about placing Western civilization on a higher cultural footing than other cultures, and as progressivism came to be identified with a critique of "European-centered assumptions," particularly in the wake of the disastrous two World Wars, we begin to witness a reluctance on the part of some academics to identify the Presocratics as the originators of philosophical reason. Members of what is known today as the Frankfurt School, Max Horkheimer and Theodor Adorno, went as far as to blame the Presocratics for initiating the false illusion that reason could be disinterested and purely concerned with the pursuit of truth. It was, rather, a will to dominate nature, not superior to mythological accounts, but a myth itself, a totalitarian myth seeking to displace other forms of thinking. Anthropologists welcomed this critique, "by showing either that rationality is at work in myth itself or that there are other rationalities besides Western rationality."[340]

Laks brings up studies about the "Orientalizing" aspects of Greek culture, borrowings from the Near East, briefly mentioning Jaspers' thesis about similar breakthroughs elsewhere in the world from mythology to rationality during the Axial Age period between 800 and 200 BC. He also pays particular attention to J. P. Vernant's central book, *The Origins of Greek Thought*, and its claim that there was no "Greek miracle" in the sense that Greek reason did not arise suddenly out of some innate Greek genius, but was a product of the democratizing political atmosphere within the city-states, which encouraged debate and a form of rationality that was then extended to the study of nature. Laks wants to defend the older Aristotelian interpretation, but in a way that acknowledges more recent interpretations, making his book a rather weak (never elaborated) defense of the "new rationality" of the Presocratics. He spends a chapter lauding Ernest Cassirer's

---

[340] Laks, 2018, 37.

early twentieth-century writings on the Greeks, but what may make this short book, just over 100 pages, worthy for our purposes is that it closes with a Hegelian passage from Cassirer that fits directly with the view we are advocating here: "Greek philosophy can be characterized to a certain extent as the first manifestation of the act of thinking itself: as a thought that in the midst of its pure movement gives to itself its content and its firm configuration." Laks leaves this great passage hanging without explanation. What does it mean for thought to give itself its own content?

Maria Sassi's book is a more decisive defense of the Aristotelian interpretation. The Presocratics were responsible for the birth of philosophy, the cultivation of a "rationalistic" approach to the study of nature, and "the elaboration of a critical stance toward received opinions."[341] She gives serious attention to the revisionists, and acknowledges early influences from the Near East and the continued presence of magic, mythological motifs, and soteriological aspirations among the Greeks, while explaining, nevertheless, how Presocratic thought "represents a truly new contribution to the understanding of the nature of things . . . an epochal break from the structure of the mythological cosmogonies."[342] Rather than emphasizing the link between Greek philosophy and the rise of the city-states, Sassi pays attention to the role of prose writing during the second half of the fifth century in expressing and solidifying rational argumentation. She objects to the way an "anti-classicistic trend has become mandatory" in an academic setting "obsessed with the need to push as far back as possible the infancy of philosophy, to the point of causing philosophy to 'disappear' into myth."[343] She mentions the indebtedness of archaic Greece to the Semitic East, "from technology to medicine to mythology," but insists that after the Homeric Age "*logos* gains more and more importance as the designation of speech that does not depend on tradition but only needs to be evaluated with respect to its internal organization . . . in the context of argumentative strategies."[344]

Aristotle was correct in identifying the Presocratics as the first philosophers of nature in their search for the principle of things, and something ultimate beneath the sensory variations we observe in nature, without appealing to any divine force. Already in Hesiod (700 BC), Sassi tells us, we have the first author in history "to talk about himself in the first person" rather than anonymously, as was the case in

---

[341] Sassi, 2018, xiv.
[342] Ibid, xv–xvi.
[343] Ibid, 14–15.
[344] Ibid, 19.

the Near East. This is an important observation Sassi makes, though, without explaining why writing in the first person was such a significant attribute of Greek
originality. Speaking in the first person, using your name to signal that you are the
author (authority) of your ideas, was an expression of the Presocratic liberation of
the self from external controls and obfuscations. Hesiod is just the beginning; he
was still inhabiting a world of myths, but, as Sassi tells us, he was the first to compose a systematic genealogy of the gods, "an organizational system for the gods'
respective spheres of influence . . . exhibiting unprecedented, encyclopedic ambition, with the aim of presenting his own arrangement as the *right one*" (emphasis
original).[345] Hesiod wants to know, in his words, "how in the beginning the gods,
the earth and the rivers were born, and the boundless sea seething with its swell,
and the bright stars and the broad sky above." There is "a logic in this [Hesiod's]
cosmogony. Rather than the product of a mytho-poetic process, it appears to be
the result of a series of systematic choices stemming from an original reflection."[346]

   This movement away from mytho-poetic explanations is intensified in subsequent Pre-Socratic writers, beginning with Thales' use of a common noun, *water*,
rather than a mythic name, to identify the ultimate source of all things. Anaximander (610–546 BC), writing some forty years after his teacher Thales, would
try to locate in a precise sequence the increasing distance of the Moon, the Sun,
and the stars, from the Earth. Anaximander wrote about heavenly bodies as impersonal forces without any anthropomorphic traits, using a language "keen on
processes of abstraction and conceptualization."[347] Even in political thinking, one
finds in the works of Solon an emphasis on human responsibility for one's misfortune and a denial of intentionality on the part of gods.

   Around 500 BC we have Heraclitus describing the universe as a *kosmos*, an
orderly arrangement characterized by regularity without divine influences. Sassi
notes the "pointedly polemical character" of Heraclitus' writing and, indeed, how
each Presocratic thinker, from Heraclitus on, proposed a new theory in self-conscious refutation of preceding theories, engaging in second-order questions as to
why their theoretical approaches were superior to previous assessments. This self-
conscious knowledge bespeaks of thinkers who were increasingly aware that
knowledge flows out of their own knowing minds in competition with other

---

[345] Ibid, 32–33.
[346] Ibid, 36.
[347] Ibid, 41.

rationalizing minds. Sassi cites Heraclitus' proclamation, "I went in search of my-self," in order "to stress that he extrapolated the contents of *logos* from an isolated and highly personal reflection."[348]

Sassi could have said more about how Heraclitus connected his conception that there is a rational order in the world, a *logos*, with the idea that the *logos* is present within the inner self in the degree to which the psyche is self-conscious of being the source of knowledge. The *logos* can only be revealed to humans who know that their minds are the agency through which the rationality of the world can be revealed. In order to achieve knowledge, the individual must be self-conscious of his psyche as the repository of knowledge, as the only vehicle through which the *logos* of the world can be understood. By looking "within themselves," inside their thinking minds, humans can reveal the *logos* that is outside them.

Sassi contrasts as well the "conservation" role of writing in the Near East, which remained religious and was "composed anonymously within a circle of priests and then copied for centuries without any conceptual changes," to the writing of the Greeks, which was open to everyone.[349] She estimates that about thirty percent of male citizens in the *polis* were able to read and write. The Greeks adopted prose writing in the last decades of the fifth century in their "search for directness and unambiguousness" and their preference for truths freed from the "restraints of prosody," and in contradistinction to the texts of Mesopotamia with their "revelations of a preestablished traditional" worldview immune "from authorial interventions."[350] Herodotus' *Histories* was the "first extended prose narrative of Greek literature," followed by Zeno, Melissus, the Pythagoreans, Anaxagoras, Leucippus, and Democritus. This was a prose "rich in elaborate syntactical structures in unison with a linguistic inquiry that prefers precision over metaphors and evocative expressions."[351]

The Greeks knew they had a mind intended for thought. This found expression in their determination to stand out as singular authors relying on their own minds, as testified in their increasing use of "I" when formulating a new argument. Herodotus used the first person 1,087 times in *The Histories*, to show his authorial presence in his understanding of the Persian wars, "accompanied by a growing focus on methodological questions, such as the role of empirical observation and

---

[348] Ibid, 73.
[349] Ibid, 75.
[350] Ibid, 142.
[351] Ibid, 171.

the evaluation of symptoms/testimonies as proof of an argument."[352] This increasing self-reflectedness was not happening outside the Greek world.

Sassi knows there is a relationship between the redefinition of the psyche as the source of reasoning and the pursuit of truth, the emphasis on authorial responsibility, the emergence of prose writing, and the description of the nature of things through the use of increasingly abstract concepts. But she never says in a clear-cut manner that the essential achievement of the Presocratics that made possible their magnificent creativity in multiple fields, and that laid the grounds for Socrates and those who followed, was their discovery that knowledge ultimately comes from the faculty of the mind and the awareness of the thinking self as the agent that can decide what it means to know.

Only one-third of Christopher Johnstone's book, *Listening to Logos: Speech and the Coming of Wisdom in Ancient Greece* is about the Presocratics; nevertheless, he offers a tighter account of the relationship between the invention of alphabetic writing, the appearance of prose composition, the discovery of the mind, the rise of a consciousness "rooted in a distinction between the knower and the known," and the idea that the psyche of man, "in its deepest nature," is *logos*. He also brings out in a slightly more acute way the seminal ideas of Eric Havelock. In the end, however, Johnstone's conclusion about the exact contribution of the Presocratics is similar to Sassi's. The Presocratics, he writes, offered a new understanding of the world "from a purely mythopoetic view to include a naturalistic/philosophical orientation."[353] This conclusion is flawed in giving the impression that the Presocratics merely originated a rational and critical approach to the study of nature that would culminate in modern science. But Johnstone does have a keener sense, though he never says it directly, about the Presocratic discovery of the faculty of the mind as the only authorial agency that can be trusted in the pursuit of truth.

He explains well that mythical accounts as such are not irrational insofar as they are efforts to make sense of the world, to give meaning and order "to the variety and variability in what happens around us and of apprehending the causes behind events." A myth is a story, "a narrative that enables a people—a tribe, a clan, a culture—to make sense of the mysterious," how things came into being, where we come from, and who our original ancestors are. Myths allow individuals and groups to fit into the order of things, to find a moral ground for action, and a

---

[352] Ibid, 173.
[353] Johnstone, 2009, 2.

means to pass from one generation to another the most fundamental truths of a people. Using Jean Piaget's theory, to be examined in the next chapter, we can say that myths are accounts by a people who don't have the cognitive capacity to engage in formal operational thinking, which entails an ability to understand abstract principles which have no physical reference and to think in terms of hypothetical "what-if" type situations, though they do have a capacity to engage in concrete operational thinking in their daily survival strategies. If we identify rationality with formal thinking and the ability to offer explanations of natural events without appealing to, or appeasing, gods and demons, then the Presocratics were the first to rely on rational concepts.

But this Piagetian emphasis on formal rationality, that is, on cognition per se, rather than awareness of the thinking self, does not hit the spot. Mythological people are unable to understand the real causes behind events precisely because they lack consciousness of their consciousness and have no concept of an "I" in separation from the world around them. They are overwhelmed by multifarious forces within and without, feelings and instincts, noises and natural events, storms and hurricanes, the darkness of the forests, the vastness of the sea and the sky, all intermingled with their dreams, fears, emotions, and appetites. Johnstone deserves praise, nevertheless, for incorporating Julian Jaynes' view about the inability of the Homeric Greeks to identify the *logos* within them, their own minds as the locus of the "I" in distinction from what lies outside the self. He also cites Bruno Snell's estimation that "in Homer every new turn of events is engineered by the gods . . . For human initiative has no source of its own."[354]

Classicists today don't even know Jaynes; and the few who know Snell may be inclined to believe that their hyper-specialized research about minor subjects stands above his "dated" ideas. Johnstone should also be credited for attempting to incorporate Havelock's ideas. In my estimation, as I will argue below, Havelock's book, *Preface to Plato*, published in 1963, should be read alongside Jaynes, Snell, and Zeruneith, in identifying the emergence of self-conscious personalities as the central breakthrough of the Greeks. Unfortunately, Havelock directed attention away from this insight by attributing the origins of Greek self-consciousness to the rise of a new "technology of communication," or the "invention of alphabetic writing" per se. Every time Havelock's name comes up, it is about his "theory" that alphabetic writing engendered a different mental attitude, or, in the words of Johnstone, about how the transition from an oral to a literate culture

---

[354] Ibid, 20.

"induce[d] a form of consciousness rooted in a distinction between the knower and the known."[355] My argument, on the other hand, is that alphabetic writing, the fact that Greek prose came to be "characterized by unparalleled lucidity," to cite Vamvacas, "precision, suppleness, and aesthetic dexterity,"[356] was itself a manifestation of the growing interiority of the Greeks.

Johnstone's account is thus limited in its focus on alphabetic writing as such, which leads him to ponder about other "conditions . . . that incubated the seeds of Western scientific and philosophical thought." He brings up the city of Miletus, from which the first Presocratics came, as a location at the "crossroads for east and west." He says that exposure in this city "to a wide variety of mythic traditions and to alternative ways of understanding" somehow produced, in the words of an academic he cites, "a breakthrough in man's thinking, a shift toward rationalism."[357] Academics love this stuff about diverse cities creating "cultural enrichment." They never care to ask why the far older cosmopolitan cities of the Near East, Babylonian, Assyrian, and Persian empires failed to produce any rationalism, and why Europeans are always the ones responsible for new ideas.

For all this, Johnstone appreciates how original the Greeks were; how their speech was no longer characterized by ritualistic formulas, but was based on critical reflection; and how they developed a language capable of the abstraction that is necessary for analytical and rational accounts. Anaximander was the "first Greek to produce a written account of the workings of nature,"[358] a language which still contained mythopoetic images, but which also spoke of impersonal forces governing the universe. Subsequently, the Presocratics would produce "more abstract conceptualizations." Heraclitus would find a *logos*, unity, and harmony beneath the apparent multiplicity evinced by the senses, coupled with the realization that fire, not water or earth, was responsible for the changes we observe, the unstable and dynamic side of natural processes, which are likewise ordered by the measures of a *logos*. Parmenides rationalized reality even more in claiming that Being itself is what is logically possible, and that the *logos* of the soul is the instrument by which we can grasp the truth of Being. All in all, Johnstone merits attention for his awareness of the "psychological side" in the Presocratic revolution, the way the Greek thinker "was rid of interference from the gods in his/her inner life, and was therefore free to develop a sense of self-directedness. . . .

---

[355] Ibid, 39.
[356] Vamvacas, 2009, 7.
[357] Johnstone, 38.
[358] Ibid, 47.

The move toward subjectivity and agency is an important departure from the Homeric mind, marking the origin of the Western concept of self-hood as autonomous and morally responsible."[359]

Constantine J. Vamvacas's book, *The Founders of Western Thought: The Presocratics*, published as Volume 257 of the *Boston Studies in the Philosophy of Science*, has a textbook-like quality, with a chapter dedicated to each of the major Presocratics. There is one passage in which Vamvacas brings up directly the realization of self-consciousness by the Greeks: "[T]he Greek of the Homeric period did not feel independent, and thus did not consider himself responsible for his actions and feelings. He attributed everything to the gods, and he even lacked the realization that he himself could be the cause of his decisions and feelings."[360] But this passage stands alone. He does not refer to Jaynes and Havelock. He cites Snell a few times, but not in regards to his central argument about the Greek discovery of the mind. The main figure in Vamvacas' study is Karl Popper, who argued that the Presocratics "created the rational or scientific attitude, and with it our Western civilization, the only civilization which is based upon science." Those who think that the rise of Galilean-Newtonian science is the defining attribute separating the West from the rest will be drawn to Popper's interpretation. My view, on the contrary, is that the continuous creativity of Europeans in all the spheres of life since ancient times has been a result of their growing realization that inside them there is a mind (soul or psyche) capable of being the seat of autonomous reflection and artistic creativity.

Vamvacas finds Jaspers' argument that there were breakthroughs in civilizations outside Greece limited in its inability to appreciate the Greek scientific spirit. The Chinese were concerned with practical-ethical questions about "proper human relations," and the Axial writings of India remained within the ambit of religious longings about the meaning of life. Only the Greeks sought to understand the "ultimate reality hidden beneath the phenomenal world of sense-experience."[361] It was the Greeks who first wrote about the universal laws of nature, about an underlying reality beneath sensory experiences, explainable through the proper use of deductive and inductive methods, a mathematical order in the natural world ultimately made of atomic particles, characterized by symmetry and proportion.

---

[359] Ibid, 80.
[360] Vamvacas, 9.
[361] Ibid, 249.

Vamvacas makes the very important point that "Presocratic philosophy is not the culmination of a sudden awakening of the Greek spirit. It is the culminating result of a long development and maturation of the Greek mind."[362] He says little, however, about this long development, apart from noticing that Hesiod's *Theogony* goes beyond standard mythological accounts in placing the gods "in a consistent, complete, ordered system," posing questions about the beginning of the world, and communicating an interest in truths. Vamvacas refers briefly to the "awakening of the personality of the Greek" in early lyric poetry—the fact that such poets as Archilochus, Simonides, and Sappho (writing in the seventh century after Homer, and before the Presocratics) expressed their own personal values. But not much else is said. Snell still remains the go-to source for the argument that Greek lyric poets were the first ones to separate the individual self from prescribed expressions and norms.

Vamvacas is nevertheless an excellent source for a comprehensive argument about the scientific orientation of the Presocratics. He states that, during the Presocratic era, "for the first time the human mind focuses on the truth."[363] He does not explain the connection between the discovery of the mind and the pursuit of truth, but it is implicit in his overall argument that there can be no truth-seeking without an inner awareness of the faculty of reason—the only faculty that can legislate for itself principles, concepts, and theories, because, as Aristotle would put it later on, it is the only faculty that is "able to think itself."

Eric Havelock's *Preface to Plato*, published in 1963, is part of the older school of thought about Greek uniqueness. It is a defense of Plato's attack on the oral Homeric tradition and a study of the rise of a literate culture in Greece. But there is more to it than that: it inhabits indeed a similar interpretative world as found in chapter two in Jaynes, Snell, and Zeruneith, in its emphasis on self-consciousness. This is not, however, how Havelock frames his study, and this is why the full implications of his book have not been fully absorbed. But the standard interpretation is not inconsistent with the view that Havelock was not solely concerned with the emergence of alphabetic writing and Platonic rationalism, but with the onset of self-consciousness and inner freedom, and its connection to the rise of an abstract and theoretical language with a different syntax away from the oral Homeric tradition with its formulaic rhythms, visual imagery, and memorialized thoughts.

---

[362] Ibid, 19.
[363] Ibid, 20.

Without forcing my own interpretation onto Havelock, we can say that his thesis is that the invention of the Greek alphabet, in contrast to all previous systems of communication, including the Phoenician, brought about a revolution from a Homeric state of being, in which Greeks could not differentiate a man's breath from his mind, and were thus devoid of self-consciousness, to a Platonic state of mind, in which they came to develop a conception of their personalities as autonomous agents no longer absorbed within an oral tradition and a poetic language incapable of abstract thinking. What is most illuminating in Havelock is the emphasis on the Greek discovery of the psyche as the seat of self-consciousness and the separation of the knower from the known. But it is hard to accept the claim that the introduction of alphabetic writing was the one factor that brought about this revolution.

Havelock writes about how "the alphabet proved so much more effective and powerful an instrument for the preservation of fluent communication than any syllabary had been."[364] Oral cultures are preoccupied with "formulaic directives" and the transmission of immemorial norms through incantation and repetition. In oral poetry, the utterance is immediate, mnemonic, surviving only in memory and recitation, accepted without inviting inquiring minds to think for themselves. The alphabet, by contrast, encourages a form of consciousness in which pronouns are used, "both personal and reflexive . . . in new syntactical contexts . . . as objects of verbs of cognition, or placed in antithesis to the 'body' . . . in which the 'ego' was thought as residing."[365] The "I" as the authorial agent of his own ideas becomes the norm, together with prose writing without any metrical (or rhyming) structure but aiming at analytical precision and open argumentation. Havelock also points out that the written word exists independently of the subject, outside the reader, and can be studied, underlined, and analyzed—not merely memorized and recited as sacred oral tales, but as accounts which can be subjected to endless questioning.

But while alphabetic writing eventually became an indispensable means of communicating truths (during the fourth century BC), beyond poetic recitations about the norms to be valued in a community, "there are clear signs in Homer himself that the Greek mind would one day reach out in search of a different kind of experience" beyond poetic recitation. It is not necessary to reiterate that Homer was a transitional figure; it should suffice now to point out Havelock's recognition

---

[364] Havelock, 1963, 137.
[365] Ibid, 198.

that alphabetic writing barely existed before Euripides, by which time the Presocratics had already achieved so much. Havelock knows this: "the Presocratics themselves were essentially oral thinkers . . . but they were trying to devise a vocabulary and syntax for a new future, when thought should be expressed in categories organized in a syntax suitable to abstract statement." [366]

The gradual emergence of personalities capable of introspection, already evident in the *Iliad*, and certainly in the emerging abstract thought of the Presocratics, is what precipitated the widespread use of alphabetic writing. I disagree with the cause-effect relationship Havelock identifies in this key passage:

> One is entitled to ask . . . given the immemorial grip of the oral method of preserving group tradition, how a self-consciousness could ever have been created. . . . The fundamental answer must lie in the changing technology of communication. [367]

This tendency to identify alphabetic writing as an independent variable has led Havelock's interpreters to view *Preface to Plato* as an argument about the importance of alphabetic writing. No one has paid much attention to Havelock's qualifications: "In fact it is probably more accurate to say that while the discovery [of the psyche as the seat of self-consciousness] was affirmed and exploited by Socrates, it was the slow creation of many minds among his predecessors and contemporaries. One thinks particularly of Heraclitus and Democritus." [368]

Once we look past the idea of alphabetic writing as an independent variable that somehow came onto the scene as a "new technology of communication," pushing the Greeks into philosophical reflection, we may be able to appreciate how insightful *Preface to Plato* remains. There is more to this book than what is outlined above. The following passages are worth citing in that they demonstrate Havelock's realization that what was witnessed in ancient Greece was the arrival at self-consciousness for the first time in history.

> Homeric man . . . was part of all he had seen and heard and remembered. His job was not to form individual and unique convictions but to retain tenaciously a precious hoard of exemplars. These were constantly present

---

[366] Ibid, x.
[367] Ibid, 208.
[368] Ibid, 197–8.

with him in his acoustic reflexes and also visually imagined before his mind's eye. His mental condition, though not his character, was one of passivity, of surrender, and a surrender accomplished through the lavish employment of the emotions and of the motor reflexes. . . .

The speech of men who have remained in the Greek sense 'musical' and have surrendered themselves to the spell of the tradition, cannot frame words to express the conviction that 'I' am one thing and the tradition is another; that 'I' can stand apart from the tradition and examine it; that 'I' can and should break the spell of its hypnotic force; and that 'I' should divert some at least of my mental powers away from memorisation and direct them instead into channels of critical inquiry and analysis.

This amounts to accepting the premise that there is a 'me,' a 'self,' a 'soul,' a consciousness which is self-governing and which discovers the reason for action in itself rather than in imitation of the poetic experience.

It was his [Plato's] self-imposed task, building to be sure on the work of predecessors, to establish two main postulates: that of the personality which thinks and knows, and that of a body of knowledge which is thought and known. To do this he had to destroy the immemorial habit of self-identification with the oral tradition. For this had merged the personality with the tradition, and made a self-conscious separation from it impossible. . . .

So it is that the long sleep of man is interrupted and his self-consciousness, separating itself from the lazy play of endless saga-series of events, begins to think and to be thought of, 'itself of itself,' and as it thinks and is thought, man in his new inner isolation confronts the phenomenon of his own autonomous personality and accepts it.[369]

The major weakness in current interpretations of the "great divergence" or "the rise of the West" is their incredibly limited time scale and one-dimensional disciplinary approach. Most of the contenders in this debate invariably assume that the West only began to follow a different historical path as it was moving towards the industrial revolution sometime during the 1700s or early 1800s. The field is dominated by economic historians who pay attention to the cultural history of the West only if they can detect a direct connection between such a history (the rise of Galilean-Newtonian science) and the history of industrial innovations. By the

---

[369] Ibid, 199–201, 210.

same token, many excellent studies, such as Havelock's *Preface to Plato,* are not recognized as having direct relevance to the uniqueness of the West. Scholars today like to paint themselves as "multi-disciplinary" for bringing into their analyses of the industrial revolution, or the Reformation, or the Enlightenment, for example, studies accomplished by academics from different disciplinary fields. Yet the focus of their attention remains on one period of time and on one transformation—economic, religious, technological, or political. Understanding the trajectory of the West requires not only a long-term perspective but an appreciation of changes and divergences in all spheres of life—in mathematics, philosophy, psychology, warfare, politics, and in culture generally—from every single disciplinary perspective. In the next chapter we will bring the never-before discussed relevance of Jean Piaget's research on child psychology to this debate.

IV

A Piagetian Interpretation of the
Rise of the West and the Superlative
Mathematics of the Ancient Greeks

Lack of historical sense is the family failing of all philosophers; many, without being aware of it, even take the most recent manifestation of man . . . as the fixed form from which one has to start out. They will not learn that man has become, that the faculty of cognition has become. . . . What is needed from now on is historical philosophizing.

– Nietzsche, *Human, All Too Human*

The Argument

Jean Piaget is widely recognized as the greatest child psychologist of the twentieth century.[370] Unlike many other influential figures, Piaget's discoveries have withstood the test of time. His argument that human cognition develops stage by stage, from sensorimotor, through preoperational and concrete operations, to formal operations, is generally endorsed in psychology and sociology texts as a "remarkably fruitful" model.[371] Aspects of his theory have been revised and supplemented by new insights. One important criticism is that his fixed sequence of clear-cut stages does not always apprehend the overlapping and uneven process in the development of cognition. But even the strongest critics admit that his

---

[370] Hunt, 2007.
[371] Ginsburg and Opper, 1988.

observations accurately show that substantial differences do exist between the cognitive processes (linguistic development, mental representations of concrete objects, logical reasoning) of children and adults.

What the general public does not know—and what the mainstream academic world is suppressing—is that many years of cross-cultural empirical research by Piaget and his followers have demonstrated that the stages of mental development of children and adolescents reflect the stages of cognitive evolution humankind has gone through from primitive, ancient, and medieval, to modern societies. The cognitive processes of humanity have not always been the same, but have improved over time. The civilizations of the world can be ranked according to the level of cognitive development of their populations. The peoples of the world differ not only in the content of their values, religious beliefs, and ways of classifying things; they differ in the cognitive processes they employ, their capacity to understand, for example, the relation between objects and concepts, their awareness of objective time, their ability to draw inferences from data and to project these inferences into the hypothetical realm of the future. Most humans throughout history have been "childlike" in their cognitive capacities; they have not been able, for example, to recognize contradictions between belief and experience, or to conceive multiple causes for individual events. Europe began to produce adolescents capable of reaching the final stage of Piagetian development, labeled "formal operational reasoning," before any other continent.[372]

This neglected aspect of Piaget's theoretical work will be addressed in this chapter together with an effort to demonstrate that the superior achievement of Greek mathematics over non-Western civilizations can be attributed to its second-order thinking, or its thinking about mathematical thinking. Numerous answers have been formulated about why the West became the most powerful civilization, the harbinger of modernity, and the culture with the most prodigious creators. The sociologist Georg W. Oesterdiekhoff, author of twelve books in German, deserves much credit for being the first to employ the insights of Piaget to explain the rise of the West. This section will examine and affirm Oesterdiekhoff's Piagetian argument that the development of a capacity for formal operational thinking among Europeans was a decisive factor in the rise of modern science, enlightenment, industrialism, and democracy in the West.[373] The originality of this Piagetian argument is that it goes beyond the standard emphasis on the rise

---

[372] Oesterdiekhoff, 2014.

[373] We will be relying on articles Oesterdiekhoff has published in English journals in recent years.

of modern Galilean and Newtonian science and how this science was necessary to the making of the industrial revolution, in terms of external and preceding "cultural" changes, without examining the comparative mental states of difference peoples.[374] The Piagetian argument focuses, rather uniquely, on the rise of a "new man" with psychogenetic capacities—psychological processes, personality, and behaviors—for formal operational reasoning.

A number of disagreements with Oesterdiekhoff's theory must be mentioned, however. First, in trying to answer how this new man with formal operational capacities emerged, he falls back on the rather banal explanation that the rise of literacy combined with modern schooling was behind the cognitive growth propelling the rise of the West. One is left wondering who were the new men who promoted a new type of education with an emphasis on rational reasoning? Why did Chinese, Indian, and Middle Eastern civilizations fail to develop these educational facilities, given their deeper roots in civilization-producing abilities dating back a few thousand years before ancient Greece? Oesterdiekhoff insists that formal operational thinking was first really visible in modern Europe. But how do we explain the incredible mathematical accomplishments of ancient Greece, the way it laid the groundwork for modern mathematics? How do we account for the institutionalization of a rational curriculum in medieval universities with its emphasis on astronomy, mathematics, logic, optics, and natural philosophy? How do we explain the rise of nominalism in the Middle Ages with its new awareness of the distinction between the knower and what is known? And how do we account for the emergence of a new ability to think in terms of abstract universal time and what Don LePan calls a "new sense of expectancy" into the "hypothetical realm of the future"? This chapter will address these questions.

The higher cognitive abilities of Europeans should be traced back to the appearance of "new humans"—a phrase Oesterdiekhoff uses—in ancient Greek times, who discovered that they have a mind separate from their bodily functions, a mind which is located in the physical cranium but invisible and immaterial, as the seat of thinking, and thus of knowledge, capable of making itself "a possible object of thought to itself," as Aristotle said in his book, *On the Soul*.[375] This

---

[374] For an excellent study that examines numerous contributions about the significance of modern science, see Floris Cohen, *The Scientific Revolution: Historiographical Inquiry* (1994).

[375] From Richard McKeon's 1941 edition of *The Basic Works of Aristotle*, which contains in full Aristotle's *On the Soul*; these words come from Book III: Ch. 4. Thomas Aquinas would write similarly that "truth is known by the mind according as the mind reflects on its act, not only as

discovery of the mind was the precondition for Aristotle's clear ability to engage in formal operational thinking. The standard argument that Europeans acquired this cognitive capacity by "learning" logic or getting "educated" seems to be flawed. The rise of this stage of reasoning entailed thinking about thinking, and eventually the development of rules for proper thinking, without contradictions and faulty inferences. Connected to this was a strong sense of awareness about one's inner faculty of reasoning and how this faculty can self-impose upon itself proper rules for reasoning, as well as a clear apprehension that there is a distinction between the thinking "I" and the external world, in contradistinction to the widespread belief among humans that the mental experiences in their heads constitutes a oneness with nature.

Focusing on the Greek awareness of the existence of thought as a distinct phenomenon within a Piagetian theoretical framework may be seen as farfetched and out of touch with what Piaget meant by formal operational thinking. I don't think it is. As C.R. Hallpike explains in his highly regarded book, *Foundations of Primitive Thought*, Piaget considers that the key effective tests for the mastery of the notion of thought and the elimination of conceptual realism [the notion that our thoughts are part of the things they denote] are the understanding that: a) thought is a process in the head which is invisible and immaterial; b) names and words are quite distinct from their referents and are conventional in origin; and c) dreams are located in the head.[376]

Formal operational thinking inherently entails thinking about the processes of reasoning, which presupposes an awareness of the cognitive processes of the mind, grasping self-evident or axiomatic truths and deducing theorems from these axioms, with a clear distinction between what is truthful, based on self-legislated rational criteria, which presupposes a consciousness of the "I" as the agent that establishes what is truthful and what is not.

This flaw in Oesterdiekhoff is combined with another flaw, which can be attributed directly to Piaget: the assumption that any baby from Africa, Asia, or the Yukon, can advance to the stage of formal operational thinking, at its most

---

knowing its act but also as knowing the relation of conformity between the act and the thing. . . . [T]he mind knows truth according as it reflects on itself" (cited in Copleston, 1963, 47).

[376] Hallpike, 1979, 385. While Hallpike's book was ignored and rejected by anthropologists for challenging their orthodoxy that no substantial differences exist in the cognitive processes of peoples, and for condemning anthropologists for promoting this egalitarian idea "without any empirically based theory of learning and thinking" (vii), his rigorous book has quietly remained a standard book among scholars trying to understand the development of human cognition in history.

sophisticated levels, as long as they are beneficiaries of a cognitively modern educational environment. He believes that the developmental paradigm of Piaget applies universally across the world, and that it is only a matter of time before all the cultures and nations converge in their cognitive development. He takes it as a given that the spread of modern education, and the attainment of higher Piagetian stages, will bring an equalization of IQ levels across the world. While the subject of IQ differences among the races of the world is an area outside my expertise, it does seem that acceptance of the Flynn effect—the fact that modernization has been associated with increases in average IQs—does not preclude the perseverance of biologically ingrained gaps in IQ scores between different racial groups despite similar levels of modernization. Furthermore, operational thinking, at its highest and more original levels, entails a high degree of self-consciousness and individual creativity.

On the other hand, we should not think of the origins of formal reasoning as if it were a product of a higher cognitive ability or the result of a higher IQ in and of itself. The mathematical achievements of the Greeks were superior to the combined achievements of all the Axial and post-Axial civilizations of the non-Western world, not necessarily because the Greeks were more intelligent than other Axial peoples, or superior in their arithmetical calculations and problem-solving abilities, but because of their attainment of a higher degree of self-consciousness. Indian, Chinese, and Islamic civilizations attained a high level of cognitive proficiency in arithmetical calculations, what might be called algorithmic thinking, which involves problem-solving by breaking down complex problems into smaller, more manageable parts, and then solving those parts one at a time.[377] They applied this approach to a wide range of problems, entailing complex algebraic equations. The difference with Greek mathematics was a higher awareness of the thinking involved in mathematics.

The axiomatic method that Euclid systematized in geometry would have been impossible without a self-conscious mind capable of identifying or differentiating undefined terms and axioms, and capable of adjudicating what it takes to be *self-evident* propositions, and the basis upon which the mind can then deduce theorems as incontrovertible mathematical statements. Second-order thinking requires a sense that the self is the agency of thinking and therefore the agency that decides how to arrive at truthful statements. This operational/self-legislating style of reasoning was evident in what Reviel Netz identifies as the "routine use of

---

[377] Joseph, 2000.

imagination in Greek mathematical writings," that is, the ability of mathematicians to imagine a purely hypothetical world, "let X be," a virtual presence, "as if it were on equal footing with the real."[378] This requires a purely hypothetical realm constructed by the mind.

Suppression of Piaget's Cross-Cultural Findings

Before I write about Oesterdiekhoff's important contribution, it is worth to point out, yet again, how our current climate of liberal pluralism, the idea that all cultures should be recognized as equally valuable, stands behind the suppression of Piaget's cross-cultural findings, which is why we rarely hear a word about it. Critics interpreted the lack of formal reasoning among adolescents in many non-Western societies as evidence that his theory was limited and lacking in universal evidence, rather than as further confirmation that his theory of child development, first developed through extensive research on children in the West, could not be automatically applied outside the West. Because many critics erroneously assumed that Piaget's theory must be about how all children naturally mature into higher levels of cognition, they took this lack of cognitive development in pre-modern cultures as a demonstration that different cultural contexts engender different modes of cognitive development and content. While it has been observed that in primitive cultures—hunting and gathering and simple agrarian villages— healthy humans will necessarily develop sensorimotor skills, language, memory, and imagination, and that in agrarian civilizations with writing and cities, they will become less egocentric and start to work things in their heads through the use of symbols, Piaget explained that the level of formal operations is not biologically inevitable, but requires a particularly modern intellectual atmosphere. His cross-cultural studies made it evident that the ability to reach the stage of formal operations depended on the degree to which a society had developed culturally and psychologically, rather than on a predetermined biological maturation process.

It can be argued indeed that Piagetian cross-cultural studies laid the groundwork for an account of the cognitive psychological development of humankind in world history from hunting and gathering societies through agrarian societies to modern societies. Piagetian research pointed towards a grand theory covering the cognitive experience of peoples throughout history, from primitive peoples with

---

[378] Netz, 2009.

a preoperational mind, to agrarian peoples with a concrete operational mind, to modern peoples with a formal operational mind. Oesterdiekhoff observes that "thousands of empirical studies across all continents and social milieus, from the 1930s to the present" have been conducted demonstrating that the nations of the world in the course of history can be identified as preoperational (which is the stage of children from their second to their sixth or seventh year of life), concrete operational (which is the stage from ages seven until twelve), and formal operational (which is the stage of cognition from age twelve onward).[379]

Adults living in a modern culture are more rational (and intelligent) than adults living in pre-modern cultures. For example, according to studies conducted in the 1960s and 1970s, even educated adults living in Papua New Guinea did not reach the formal stage. Australian Aborigines who were still living a traditional lifestyle barely developed beyond a preoperational stage in their adult years. Without a population that has mentally developed to the level of formal operations, which entails a capacity to think about abstract relationships and symbols without concrete forms, a capacity to grasp syllogistic reasoning, comprehend algebra, formulate hypotheses, there can be no modernization.

However, despite all the studies confirming Piaget's powerful theory, from about 1975/1980 a wave of ideological attacks was launched across the Western academic world against any notion that the peoples of the earth could be ranked in terms of their cognitive development. According to Oesterdiekhoff, nearly all child psychologists of the first two generations of developmental psychology "knew about the similarities between children and pre-modern man," but "due to anti-colonialism, student revolt, and damaged self-esteem of the West in consequence of the World Wars this theory as the mainstream spirit of Western sciences and public opinion declined gradually." As another author observed in 1989, "any suggestion that the cognitive processes of the older child might possess any similarities to the cognitive processes of some primitive human cultures is regarded as being beneath contempt."[380]

---

[379] Oesterdiekhoff, 2015, 85.
[380] LePan, 1989, 7.

Georg W. Oesterdiekhoff's Ranking of Cultures

I came across Oesterdiekhoff's research after a long search through Piagetian theory. It was an interesting question, what Piaget's stage theory might have to say about the cognitive development of peoples in history. But only sources of Piaget as a cognitive psychologist of children, not as a grand theorist of the cognitive development of humanity, were to be found—until coming across Oesterdiekhoff's many publications, which draw on pre-1975 Piagetian research and current research. This research, as Oesterdiekhoff notes, "no longer belong[s] to the center of attention and research interests. Most social scientists have never heard about these researchers and have only a very scanty knowledge of them."[381] This is an unavoidable scholarly atmosphere in a liberal world where all cultures are deemed to have the same human rights. It is why it is so hard for Western academics nowadays to explain the "great divergence."

Oesterdiekhoff is very blunt and ambitious in his arguments, convinced that Piagetian theory is "capable of explaining, better than previous approaches, the history of humankind from prehistory through ancient to modern societies, the history of economy, society, culture, religion, philosophy, sciences, morals, and everyday life."[382] The rise of formal operational thinking among Europeans was the decisive factor behind Galilean/Newtonian science, the enlightenment, and the industrial revolution. India, China, Japan, and the Middle East did not start the industrial revolution due to "their inability to evolve the stage of formal operations."[383]

Primitive and pre-modern peoples are at the preoperational and concrete operational stages of cognition, and so they cannot be described as having a similar rational disposition as modern peoples. Primitive adults share basic aspects of the preoperational thinking of modern children no more mature than eight years old. Adults in premodern civilizations share the concrete operational thinking of six-to twelve-year-old modern children. Modern children and premodern adults share the same mechanisms and basic understandings of physical dimensions such as length, volume, time, space, weight, area, and geometric qualities. Both groups share the animistic understanding of nature and regard stones, mountains,

---

[381] Oesterdiekhoff, 2014, 280.

[382] Oesterdiekhoff, 2016, 304.

[383] Oesterdiekhoff, 2014b, 375.

woods, stars, rivers, winds, clouds, and storms as living beings, their movements and appearances as expressions of their will, intentions, and commitment. Premodern humans often manifest the animistic tendencies of modern children before their sixth year. Fetishism and the animistic religion of premodern humans reside in children's mentality before concrete operational stage. The biggest parts of ancient religions are based on children's psychology and animism before the sixth year of life.[384]

It is not that adults in primitive and premodern cultures are similar to modern children in their emotional development, experience, and ability to survive in a hostile environment. The reasoning abilities of adults in pre-modern cultures are restricted to what they apprehend at the perceptual level, and bound up with the sensory appearances of the world, barely transcending appearances and context-bound experiences through the development of hypothetical reasoning. As Lucien Lévy-Bruhl (1857–1939) had already observed in *Primitive Mentality* (1923), among his many other studies, the primitive mind is devoid of abstract concepts, analytical reasoning, and logical consistency. Lévy-Bruhl never denied, as is commonly propagated by academics, the obvious ability of primitives to be "acute reasoners" in their survival skills, their "wonderful memory" and "great powers of observation." His thesis was that "the entire mental habit" of primitives ruled out "abstract thought," the ability "to inquire into causal connections" beyond noticing simple sensory relationships. "Nearly all that happens is referred . . . to the influence of mystic or occult powers, such as wizards, ghosts, spirits."[385] In the minds of primitives, the objective-visible world is not distinguished from the subjective-invisible world; dreams, divination, incantations, sacrifices, and omens, not inferential reasoning and objective causal relations, are the phantasmagorical doors through which primitives get access to the intentions and plans of the unseen spirits they believe control natural events.

> The visible world and the unseen world are but one, and the events occurring in the visible world depend at all times upon forces which are not seen. . . . A man succumbs to some organic disease, or to snake-bite; he is crushed to death by the fall of a tree, or devoured by a tiger or crocodile: to the primitive mind, his death is due neither to disease nor to snake-venom; it is not the tree or the wild beast or reptile that has killed him. If he has

---

[384] Oesterdiekhoff, 2016, 301; 2012, 470–78.
[385] Lévy-Bruhl, 2018, 24, 27, 90.

perished, it is undoubtedly because a wizard had "doomed" and "delivered him over." Both tree and animal are but instruments, and in default of the one, the other would have carried out the sentence. They were, as one might say, interchangeable, at the will of the unseen power employing them.[386]

One must have some reservations, however, about the extent to which the rise of operational thinking on its own can explain the uniqueness of Western history, but in agreement with Oesterdiekhoff, without adolescents reaching the stage of formal operational thinking, there can be no modernization. The study of the geographical, economic, or cultural factors that led to the rise of science and the industrial revolution are not the only factors we should be focusing on. The rise of a "new man" with psychogenetic capacities for formal operational reasoning needs direct attention.

Cultural Relativism

First, though, it seems odd that for Oesterdiekhoff, two seemingly diametrical outlooks, "cultural relativism and universality of rationality," were responsible for the discrediting of Piagetian cross-cultural theory.[387] He does not explain what he means by universality of rationality. We get a sense that by cultural relativism he means the rejection of unreserved confidence in the superiority of Western scientific rationality. Social scientists after WWII did become increasingly ambivalent about setting up Western formal thinking as a benchmark to judge the cognitive

---

[386] Ibid, 438. Lucien Lévy-Bruhl's *Primitive Mentality*, originally published in 1923, is essentially an ethnographic account of the mystic beliefs of primitive peoples. It quotes numerous graphic descriptions by educated Europeans who lived among primitives. Lévy-Bruhl's work was eventually dismissed as anthropology and ethnography came to be occupied by followers of Franz Boas and Margaret Mead. Hallpike's book, *The Foundations of Primitive Thought* (1979), should be seen as an attempt to resurrect, on the basis of a solid theoretical framework and extensive scholarship, the line of inquiry begun by Lévy-Bruhl. It is difficult to understand why Hallpike retains, however, the standard claim that Lévy-Bruhl was wrong in saying that primitive thought was "illogical" or "irrational." Lévy-Bruhl clearly states that primitives were necessarily practical, capable of "reasoning" about their immediate needs. "There is no type of community, however inferior, in which some inventions, some process of industry or art, some manufacture may not be found to wonder at" (443). His point is that primitive thought did not rise to abstractions and logical formulas.

[387] Oesterdiekhoff, 2014, 281.

processes and values of other cultures, even though the non-Western world was happily embracing the benefits of Western science and technology.

The pathological state to which this relativism has affected Western thinking can be witnessed right inside the otherwise hyper-scientific field of cognitive psychology today. Take the very well-known 2016 textbook, *Cognitive Psychology*, by IBM Professor of Psychology at Yale University, Robert Sternberg: it approaches every subject in a totally scientific and neutral manner—except the subject of intelligence, at which point this text immediately embraces a relativist outlook, informing students that intelligence is "inextricably linked to culture" and that it is impossible to determine whether members of "the Kpelle tribe in Africa" have less intelligent concepts than a PhD cognitive psychologist in the West. Intelligence is "something that a culture creates to define the nature of adaptive performance in that culture and to account for why some people perform better than others on the tasks that the culture happens to value." It is "so difficult," the text continues, to "come up with a test that everyone would consider culture-fair—equally appropriate and fair for members of all cultures." "If members of different cultures have different ideas of what it means to be intelligent, then the very behaviors that may be considered intelligent in one culture may be considered unintelligent in another."[388]

This textbook pays detailed attention to the scientific achievements of Piaget, but portrays him as someone who investigated the "internal maturation processes" of children as such, without considering his cross-cultural findings. Pretending that such findings do not exist, the book goes on to criticize Piaget for ignoring "evidence of environmental [cultural] influences on children's performance."[389] This is not to suggest that cultural relativism has taken over Western sciences in the way it has the humanities, sociology, history, and philosophy. But this relativism is being effectively used by scientists against any overt presumption by Western scientists that their knowledge is "superior" to the knowledge of African tribes and Indigenous peoples.[390]

---

[388] Stenberg, 2003, 503–04.

[389] Ibid, 456.

[390] Frances Widdowson, for example, was fired from her tenured academic position at Mount Royal University, Canada, December 2021, after woke faculty filed vexatious complaints against her researched-based claim that "indigenous knowledge" lacks the appropriate self-critical standards to produce critically-based scholarship about ecological issues.

Cultural Universals

Oesterdiekhoff does not define "universality of rationality," but we can gather from the literature he uses that he is referring to other anthropologists who argue that the "actual structures of thought, cognitive processes, are the same in all cultures."[391] This is the position of those who believe that humans qua humans are rational beings, and that what differentiates peoples across time and place are the religious, aesthetic, and moral content of the values and ways of classifying things in nature. Primitive, Islamic, and Confucian peoples, it is argued, were quite rational in the way they went about surviving in the natural world, making tools, building cultures, and enforcing customs that were adaptive to their social settings and environments. They did not develop science because they had different priorities and beliefs, or were less obsessed with mastering nature and increasing production.

The anthropologist Claude Levi Strauss, and the sociologist Emile Durkheim, were the first to argue that the primitive mind is "logical in the same sense and same fashion as ours," and that the only difference lies in the classification systems and thought content.[392] George Murdock and Donald Brown, in more recent times, came up with the term "cultural universals" (or "human universals") to refer to patterns, institutions, customs, and beliefs that occur universally in all cultures.[393] These universals demonstrated that cultures differ a lot less than one might be led to conjecture from their different levels of technological knowhow. Murdock and Brown pointed to strong similarities in the gender roles of cultures, the common presence of the incest taboo, similarities in their religious and healing rituals, mythologies, marriage rules, use of language, art, dance, and music.

This idea about the universality of rationality and "cultural universals" was subsequently elaborated in a more Darwinian direction by evolutionary psychologists. Evolutionary psychology is generally associated with "right wing" thinking, in contrast to cultural relativism, which is associated with "left wing" thinking. Evolutionary psychologists like E. O. Wilson and Steven Pinker hold that these

---

[391] Hallpike, 1979, 3.
[392] Le Pan, 309.
[393] Brown, 1991.

cultural universals are naturally selected, biologically inherited behaviors.[394] Likewise, rationality is a naturally inherited disposition among all humans, though they don't say that the levels of knowledge across cultures are the same. Humans are rational in the way they go about surviving and co-existing with other humans. These universals were selected for their adaptive enhancement. Some additional cultural universals are bodily adornment, calendars, cooperative labor, cosmology, courtship, divination, division of labor, food taboos, funeral rites, gift-giving, greetings, hospitality, inheritance rules, penal sanctions, puberty customs, residence rules, and status differentiation.

Most evolutionary psychologists are convinced that the existence of cultural universals amount to a refutation of the currently "fashionable" notion that all human behaviors, including gender differences, are culturally determined. But if the West is very similar to other cultures, why did modern science and liberal democratic values develop in this civilization? Since evolutionary psychologists search for general explanations, the notion of cultural universals meets this criterion, whereas the idea that Europeans exhibited unique cultural behaviors and inclinations does not. For this reason, evolutionary psychologists, with the exception of Kevin MacDonald, as we shall see in Chapter VII, have ignored this question, or reduced Western uniqueness to a concatenation of historical factors, or to just another survival strategy. They have pointed to how modern science has been assimilated by multiple cultures, from which point they have argued that science is not culturally exceptional to the West, but a universal method that produces universal truths for humanity.

Piagetian Universalism and IQ Convergence

Piagetian theory is also universalist in maintaining that the developmental psychology of Piaget "explains the psyche and mind of the whole human race," and in believing that the cultures of the world are now reaching the stage of formal operational thinking.[395] The West merely initiated formal reasoning. This cognitive convergence is happening across all the realms of social life, because changes in the cognitive structures of humans bring simultaneous changes in the way we

---

[394] Wilson used this argument effectively in his popular book, *On Human Nature: Twenty-Fifth Anniversary Edition, With a New Preface* (2004), to push the idea that human nature was not constructed differently in different cultures, but exhibited very similar behavioral patterns.
[395] Oesterdiekhoff, 2016, 308.

think about politics and institutional arrangements. The more rational we become, the more we postulate enlightened conceptualizations of government in
opposition to authoritarian forms. Drawing on the extension of Piagetian theory
to explain the moral development of humans (initiated by Piaget and elaborated
by Lawrence Kohlberg), Oesterdiekhoff writes that once humans reach stage four,
they start to grasp "that rule legitimacy should follow only from a correct rule
installation, that is, from the choices of the players involved."

> Thus, they regard only rules correctly chosen as obliging rules. Only dem-
> ocratic choices install legitimate rules. Youth on the formal stage surmount
> therefore the holy understanding of rules by the democratic understand-
> ing. They replace an authoritarian understanding of rules, laws, and cus-
> toms by a democratic one. Thus, they invent democracy in consequence of
> their cognitive maturation.[396]

The emergence of the adolescent stage of formal operations gave birth not only to
the new sciences after 1650, but also to philosophers such as Locke, Montesquieu
and Rousseau, who formulated the principles of constitutional government, representative institutions, and religious tolerance. Extensive cross-cultural research
has shown that "children do not understand tolerance for deviating ideas, liberty
rights for individuals, rights of individuals against government and authority, and
democratic legitimacy of governments and authorities." They are much like the
adults of premodern societies, or current backward Islamic peoples, who take
"laws and customs as unchangeable, eternal, and divine, made by god and not
modifiable by human wishes or choices."[397]

This argument may seem similar to Francis Fukuyama's thesis that modernizing humans across the world are agreeing that liberal-democratic values best satisfy the longing humans have for a state that recognizes the right of humans to
pursue their own happiness within a constitutional state based on equal rules. The
difference—a crucial one—is that for Fukuyama, the rise of democracy came from
the articulation and propagation of new ideas, whereas for Oesterdiekhoff, psychogenetic maturation is a precondition of democratic rule. Adults who were
raised in a premodern culture, and have a concrete operational mind, can "never
surmount" this stage, no matter how many books they read about the merits of

---

[396] Oesterdiekhoff, 2015, 88, 93.
[397] Ibid, 90.

liberal democracy. These adults will lack the appropriate ontogenetic development required for a democratic mind.

> The absence of stimuli and forces of modern culture during early childhood in premodern cultures prevents later psychological development from going beyond certain stages. . . . Unused developmental opportunities in youth stop the development of the nervous system, thus preventing psychological advantages in later life. This explains why education and enlightenment, persuasion and media programs could not draw adult premodern people out of their adherence to magic, animism, ordeal praxis, ancestor worship, totemism, shamanism, and belief in witches. Such people, moving in adulthood to modern milieus, cannot surmount their anthropological structures and their deepest emotions and convictions.[398]

Moreover, with the attainment of higher Piagetian stages comes higher IQ levels. Psychogenetic differences, not biological genetic differences, are the decisive factor. "All pre-modern peoples stood on intelligence levels of 50 to 70 [IQ points] or on preoperational or concrete operational levels, no matter from what race, culture or continent they have come." He insists that,

> not only the Western nations, but all modernizing nations have raised their scores. The rises in stage progression and IQ scores express the greatest intelligence transformations ever in the history of humankind and stem solely from changes in culture and education. When Africans, Japanese, Chinese and Brazilians have raised their intelligence so dramatically, where is the evidence for huge genetic influences? Huge genetic influences might be assumed if Europeans had always had higher intelligence and if Africans, Indians, Arabs and Vietnamese had been unable to raise their intelligence to levels superior to that of Europeans 100 years ago. But Latin Americans and Arabs today do have higher IQ scores than Europeans had 100 years ago. . . . Where is the leeway for genetic influences to affect national intelligence differences?[399]

---

[398] Oesterdiekhoff, 2016, 306–07.
[399] Oesterdiekhoff, 2014b, 377.

What about the substantive gap in IQ scores still remaining between American Blacks and American Whites, despite the Flynn effect and similar levels of education and income?[400] Not that we should dismiss Oesterdiekhoff's point that it is very hard to attribute the remarkable increases in IQ identified over the last century to evolutionary-induced increases in levels of heritable intelligence alone. The argument that all modernizing nations have raised their IQ scores, and that operational thinking has been central to this modernization, should be part of the explanation. By the same token, one is left wondering how valid the observation is that "Latin Americans and Arabs today do have higher IQ scores than Europeans had 100 years ago," when 100 years ago Europeans were at the forefront of science and industrial innovations, whereas Latin Americans and Arabs today still lack originality in the sciences. I will return later to this complex discussion.

Formal Reasoning Is Not a Cultural Universal

Only the stage of formal operations cannot be said to be endogenously generated, inevitable and biologically primary. The abilities associated with the first two stages (e.g., control over motor actions, walking, mental representation of external stimuli, verbal communication, ability to manipulate concepts), have been acquired universally by humans since prehistoric times. In this sense they can be called "biologically primary" qualities that children across cultures accomplish at the ages and in the sequence more or less predicted by Piaget. They are universal abilities built into human nature, ready to unfold with little educational socialization. While the concrete-operational abilities of stage three (e.g., the "ability to conserve," or to know that the same quantity of a liquid remains when the liquid is poured into a differently shaped container) are either lacking in primitive cultures, or emerge at later ages in children than they do in modern cultures, these abilities may also be described as biologically primary insofar as they have emerged in all advanced agrarian civilizations. It is also the case that in modern societies all individuals with a primary education acquire concrete operational abilities. The abilities required in the first three stages can thus be identified as culturally universal.

Only stage four cannot be said to be endogenously generated. The skills associated with this stage (inductive logic, hypothesis testing, reasoning about

---

[400] Sailer, 2016.

proportions, combinations, probabilities, and correlations) are not cognitive skills bound to emerge in all literate civilizations. They are highly specific skills that a significant proportion of the population even in modern Western cultures fail to acquire.[401] There is abundant evidence that normally intelligent college students with a long background in education have difficulties distinguishing between the form and content of a syllogism as well as other types of formal operational skills. The abilities required in formal operational thinking are better described as biologically secondary abilities. Oesterdiekhoff acknowledges that "only when human beings are exposed to forces and stimuli typical of modern socialization and culture do they progress further and develop the adolescent stage of formal operations."[402]

But, as critics of Piaget have observed, even in modern societies where children inhabit a rationalized environment and adolescents are taught algebra and a variety of formal operational skills, many students with a reasonable IQ find it difficult to think this way. According to P. Dasen's 1994 research, only one-third of adults ever reach the formal operational stage. Some evolutionary psychologists have thus disagreed with the idea that this stage is bound to unfold among most humans as long as they get a modern education. We should make a distinction between the biologically primary abilities of the first three stages and the biologically secondary abilities of stage four. To take it a step further, the performance of intellectual works at the highest levels of stage four requires more than modern socialization and a high IQ: it requires as well a cultural setting populated by individuals with a high behavioral aptitude for personal creativity and imagination to explore the unknown. The highest levels of cognition are not arrived at by learning the current path with utmost precision. Original scientists are aware that major breakthroughs—say, marriage of relativity and quantum theory, random matrix theory—entail a mind that expands through the use of the imagination into the unknown, an individual willing to contemplate never seen realities, a will daring to break free from known paths into new continents. But how did "new humans" with a behavioral inclination for independent thinking emerge out of a pre-modern world with a seemingly lower average IQ than today's, and devoid of modern education?[403]

---

[401] Ginsburg and Opper, 1988, 203–04.

[402] Oesterdiekhoff, 2016, 307.

[403] Michael Woodley and A.J. Figueredo (2014) correctly fault Oesterdiekhoff for ignoring evolutionary-genetic forces, but, while these two authors write about the integrated role of "culture-gene" forces, they view culture only in terms of how it works as an environment for the selection

Our concern here is with the origins of formal operational thinking, which seems to be a by-product of the higher degree of individuation and personal introspection among Europeans.

Western Versus Chinese Thought

Some may say this individualism can't possibly be a requirement for formal thinking in our current age, when scientific reasoning and modern educational institutions have spread around the world. Granted, it is not easy to apprehend this individualism in the fields of logic and science, which have been formalized and institutionalized in many nations, unlike other attributes that go by the phrase "stuff White people like," such as a peculiar love of nature, bird watching, enjoyment of multiple hobbies, love of animals, and high creativity in the arts,

---

of genes. They see the rise of IQ intelligence as the one factor that brought about Western modernity. In other words, culture is important to them only in the degree to which it acted as a setting for the selection of genes promoting intelligence. One can agree with their endorsement of the argument by Cochran and Harpending (2009) that the rise of agriculture created a new set of cultural opportunities for reproductive success, leading to selection of new genes.

Likewise, one can agree with their endorsement of Gregory Clark's argument in *Farewell to Alms: A Brief Economic History of the World* (2007) that the industrial evolution was made possible by the higher survival rate of children of the British upper classes and the consequent spread of genes for industriousness and intelligence. It sounds reasonable enough for Woodley and Figueredo to say that "genes and culture were both co-evolving in a direction consistent with increasing levels of general intelligence throughout the entire period that Clark describes, culminating in the industrial revolution of the nineteenth century" (347). But they overextend the co-evolution of genes and culture during the modern period Clark describes into a general and unsubstantiated statement about how the rise of intelligence explains on its own "many of the intellectual trends in the history of Western civilization."

The West is packed with intellectual trends, including the rise of modern science, the Italian Renaissance, the twelfth century Renaissance, the Printing Revolution, the Roman invention of rational law, the "Greek Miracle." It seems outlandish to think that this long sequence of intellectual revolutions and novelties was due to a "process of accelerated culture-gene co-evolution," a process of continuously rising general intelligence. As it is, they are aware that the Chinese, "despite enjoying a genetic advantage in general intelligence over Western populations," remained a stagnant culture with minimal novelties after medieval times. Their fallback claim that the ecological setting of China produced "conformist" genes together with higher intelligence hardly persuades. My view is that we need to look at other behavioral and psychological dispositions among Europeans, of which individualism is the key. Nevertheless, Woodley and Figueredo do make a very good case for the dysgenic effects of our contemporary affluence, thus questioning Oesterdiekhoff's assumption that rising levels of formal operational thinking and modernity are automatically guaranteed to sustain higher levels of intelligence.

literature, and humanities. It can't be denied, however, that the highest quality scientific research is still happening in Western nations,[404] and that high IQ East Asians continue to lack individual creativity. According to Lawrence Mead, Chinese-American students retain their "quiet and submissive" state of mind, "repeating what teachers say on their tests and papers, rather than making personal arguments." "Even successful Asian immigrants . . . are less individualistic than the American norm . . . they tend to adjust to the expectations around them. . . . In school and then college, they expect to be rewarded for repeating what teachers tell them."[405]

It may be that it is only a matter of time before East Asians start exhibiting high levels of creativity in formal thinking. This is not the view, however, of a well-known article, "Culture and Systems of Thought: Holistic Versus Analytic Cognition," about how Asians and Westerners think very differently.[406] The authors counter the claim that Piaget's theory can be universalized to all modern humans, arguing that "fairly marked differences in knowledge about and use of inferential rules exist among educated adults." They first contrast the ancient ways of thought of the Greeks and the Chinese, and then provide data contrasting current ways of thinking in the West and China. Their research shows that,

> to a remarkable extent, the social and cognitive differences that scholars have reported about ancient China and Greece find their counterparts among contemporary people. Moreover, these are not mere parameter differences, but in many cases differences that are quantitively very large and even qualitatively different.

East Asian thought tends "to be holistic," taking account of the "entire field," making "little use of categories and formal logic." East Asians take contradictions as

---

[404] See Nature Index, 2018.

[405] Mead, 2019, 233. Amazingly, Mead refers to a *New York Times Education* article (November 6, 2011) which estimates that "90 percent of Chinese applicants to American universities submit false recommendations, 70 percent do not write their own personal essays, 50 percent have forged high school transcripts, and 10 percent claim academic awards and other honors that they did not receive" (262).

[406] Nisbett et al., 2001, 290–293. This co-authored article has been cited thousands of times. Nisbett would go on to write *The Geography of Thought: How Asians and Westerners Think Differently . . . And Why* (2003), with the general argument that "human cognition is not everywhere the same" and that Asians and Westerners "have maintained very different systems of thought for thousands of years," and that these differences can be measured (xvi).

part of the nature of things, and instead of trying to reach a precise definition, a point of certainty, they look for "multiple perspectives, searching for the 'Middle Way' between opposing propositions." In contrast, "Westerners are more analytic," using rules, including formal logic, to differentiate objects and thereby explain and "predict its behavior."

This article, however, can only take us so far with its PC insinuations about how "holistic" Asian cultures are and how cold-blooded and narrow-minded Westerners are. The difference, as I will explain in detail in the next chapter, is that the Chinese mind is embedded in its cultural surroundings—the norms, rules, and habits of the society, which educated Chinese follow without critical reflection, and so their reasoning has less individual autonomy from the "entire field." It is not that the Chinese have, as Nisbett wishes us to believe, a broader, more comprehensive outlook. The "multiple perspectives" they express are an expression of the multiple norms, circumstances, and bodily impressions surrounding them and unconsciously coalesced with their reasoning. Their minds have remained lodged in the world, trapped to their surroundings and their millennial customs. The East Asian self is determined by the flux and fusion of inside and outside forces. Their minds have not been fully differentiated from the world around; the qualities of self and person, as known in the West, are not present in Chinese civilization.

In contrast, it is not only that the ancient Greeks "developed a sense of personal agency," as the authors of this paper recognize; it is directly that since ancient times, Westerners have been aware that each individual has a mind that is the seat of knowledge, which can be differentiated from bodily appetites, subjective emotions, and external objects.

Searching for a fixed, supra-temporal ground, an objective method, requires a self capable of identifying itself apart from everything that is outside itself, an awareness of the individual self as the locus of reasoning, and the only agent capable of postulating axioms and developing methodologies that draw a distinction between knowing and believing, thought and object, mind and body. Only Westerners came to apprehend reason as the one faculty that can be conscious of its own actions, and thus understand the nature and role of other forces and surrounding circumstances.

Origins of Western Operational Thinking

Why did Europeans reach the fourth stage of formal operations long before any other peoples in the world? When pressed in an exchange about the causes of the emergence of stage four, Oesterdiekhoff responded that,

> schooling and other cultural factors must have been more elaborated in early modern Europe than in Asia, antiquity, and medieval times. The trigger to arouse the evolution of formal operations would have been especially the systems of education.

He added:

> Admittedly, this begs the question about the causes of this alleged fact and necessitates yet another level of causal explanation. . . . I rather prefer cultural explanations and think about the possible relevance of the advantages of the Greek/Roman alphabet or Aristotelian logic, phenomena fostering the use of abstraction and logic.[407]

This is as far as Oesterdiekhoff goes explaining why the ancient Greeks reached the fourth stage first. He prefers to jump right into the modern era, the seventeenth century, as the century in which formal operational thinking really emerged, from which point he then identifies "the rise of formal operations, the cognitive maturation of people" in itself as the cause of the rise of modern Europe. He insists that his Piagetian theory "is crucially a causal theory of modernity."[408] But no explanation is provided as to the original causes of the rise of formal operational thinking.

If Oesterdiekhoff's point is that, without a population in which the children have ontogenetically developed a capacity for formal operations, you can't have adults engage in formal operational thinking, then we can agree that this ontogenetic development is a precondition for a modern society. But we still need an explanation of the rise of "new humans." Does he mean that the Greek/Roman alphabet and Aristotelian logic already contained the seeds of formal reasoning?

---

[407] Oesterdiekhoff, 2014b, 373–4.
[408] Ibid, 375.

The alphabet is indeed the most abstract symbolic system of writing in which both consonants and vowels are represented.[409] Can it be denied that Aristotle's theory of the syllogism is at the level of stage four, considering that this theory teaches that we can abstract altogether from the concrete content of an argument and judge its merits solely in terms of how the terms are formally or logically connected to each other?

Oesterdiekhoff says that the Ionian or Pre-Socratic philosophers of the sixth century BC were the first to establish the concrete operational stage and, in the same vein, implies that Aristotle's philosophy did not rise above this concrete stage. "Aristotle's physics strongly resembles the animistic physics of children aged 10 before they establish the mechanistic world view." "The formal operational stage comes into being predominantly with Descartes in the seventeenth century."[410] We can agree that it "comes into being predominantly" in this century, but if we also agree that this stage has "many sub-stages" (as Oesterdiekhoff points out), why can't we identify Aristotle's extensive writings on logic, induction and deduction, affirmations and contradictions, syllogisms and modalities, definitions and essences, species, genus, differentia, and the categories, as the beginnings of stage four?

Oesterdiekhoff knows he needs some origins, and admits he is caught in a chicken-egg dilemma. He writes about "a positive feedback loop" in the interrelationship between "the knowledge taught in schools and universities" in modern Europe, and the rise of formal reasoning. But instead of "finding the causes for the emergence of formal reasoning in Europe some centuries ago," he prefers to say that the "highest stage, the stage of formal operations, directly accounts for the rise of modern sciences." Or more bluntly: "The rise of formal operations in the Western world after 1700 is the single cause of the rise of the sciences, industrialism, enlightenment, humanism, and democracy."[411]

---

[409] Henri-Jean Martin says that with the Greek alphabet "writing reached a new stage. Unlike purely consonantal systems, the Greek alphabet attempted to break down spoken discourse into sounds, the indivisible atoms of speech. . . . The question arises whether this new and totally analytical form of writing engendered new forms of thought. . . . Thus geometry was invented, a discipline in which figures and arguments have equal weight. . . . Anaximander dared draw the inhabited earth, and he created the geographical map, an exercise requiring a high degree of schematization. Hippocratic medicine developed, inspiring a number of treatises composed for written publication and authors who relied on writing to lend accuracy and pertinence to their descriptions of illnesses" (1994, 35–6).

[410] Oesterdiekhoff, 2016, 304.

[411] Oesterdiekhoff, 2014, 269, 287.

This may be understandable since Oesterdiekhoff is not a historian. He has made a very important contribution to the "rise of the West" debate, explaining the direct relevance of Piaget's theory of cognitive development. None of the participants in this debate talk about cognitive development, but assume that humans throughout history (since we became *Homo sapiens* in Africa) are equally rational. Oesterdiekhoff wants to fit Western history within a stage theory of developmental psychology in which ancient/medieval times are clearly demarcated from modern operational stages. "The kernel of Enlightenment philosophy is the surpassing of childlike mental states, of the world of fairy tales, magic, and superstition, as it prevailed in the pre-modern world." He qualifies this estimation a bit when he writes that "formal operations . . . evolved in the intellectual elite of early modern Europe and slowly spread to other milieus."[412] But his pervading message is that it was only during the 1700s, or even "after the 1700s," that Europeans came to reach the operational stage. There is no reason to disagree if he means that only the 1700s and after saw sufficient numbers of Europeans maturing into the last stage, making possible a full-scale industrial revolution. But we still need an explanation of the origins of his "new humans."

It is understandable that many will be tempted to point to social and educational forces as the causes of this initial cognitive transition to operational thinking. They will argue that as literacy was mastered, and as institutes of learning were established, and arithmetic, reading, and other subjects were taught, a major shift occurred in human mental activity. This emphasis on the educational environment is a view often attributed to the Soviet psychologist A.R. Luria (1902–1977). From this claim, it takes but one step to the identification of the social and economic mode of production as the underlying factor of this cognitive revolution, thus combining Piaget with Marx's historical materialism. Ancient Greeks developed operational thinking in the new milieu of urban life, growing trade in the Mediterranean, and money exchanges. The flaw in this standard explanation, one that Robert Bellah sympathizes with, is that these new economic ways were present in greater abundance in the older and larger civilizations of Mesopotamia and elsewhere. These commercial and urban activities could be performed effectively with concrete operational habits of thinking.

---

[412] Ibid, 292–95.

Hellenistic Greeks

It is hard to deny, in light of our prior arguments about the Presocratics, that the first signs of abstract thinking were evident in Greek culture around the sixth century BC. Once we get to Aristotelian logic, which would continue to dominate right through the consolidation of Newtonian science and beyond, with Kant still believing in the late 1700s that Aristotle had discovered everything there was to know about logic, it is impossible to deny formal operational thinking in Greece. Beyond Aristotle, what many forget is that the development of Greek thinking did not end with the Axial Age period of 700–200 BC, as it did for all other Axial civilizations, but continued through what has been identified as the "Hellenistic Age," which covers the period between the death of Alexander the Great in 323 BC and the conquest of Egypt by Rome in 30 BC. Oesterdiekhoff seems aware of Hellenistic science when he writes that "Roman intellectuals no longer understood the superior contributions of the Hellenistic scholars."[413] But he says no more, even though Hellenistic scholars lived during what is known as the golden age of Greek science. This is the subject of Lucio Russo's *The Forgotten Revolution: How Science Was Born in 300 BC and Why It Had to Be Reborn*. This era saw, for the first time, the institutionalization of scientific research in the Museum and Library at Alexandria, which contained 500,000+ papyrus scrolls, and funded 100 scientists and literary scholars. The harvest of this era included the conics of Apollonius, the trigonometry of Hipparchus, the hydrostatics and the science of weight of Archimedes, the heliocentric proposal of Aristarchus, the calculations to determine the circumference of the earth of Eratosthenes, among other major accomplishments.[414]

We will examine below the contribution of Greek mathematics both before the Hellenistic age and after, to argue that it surpassed the achievements of all the other non-Western civilizations combined during and after the Axial Age. It is

---

[413] Ibid, 281.

[414] These accomplishments are well recognized today, even if we agree with some reviewers (Rowan-Robinson, 2004) that Russo exaggerates in claiming that the breakthroughs of Copernicus, Kepler, Galileo and others were due to their possession of the writings of these Hellenistic thinkers, given that a considerable proportion of their writings were lost, or unknown to them. Russo also exaggerates when he says that they had a fully developed heliocentric theory, and that they discovered the inverse square law of gravitation. Nevertheless, Russo's ideas are part of a well-established consensus that the Hellenistic period was the golden age of Greek science and mathematics; see Jones and Taub (2018); Luce (1988); and von Staden (1975).

hard to understand why Oesterdiekhoff would insist that the hypothetic-deductive form of thinking was not intrinsic to Euclid's *Elements*—the way in which circles, right angles, parallel lines are explicitly defined in terms of a few fundamental abstract entities, such as points, lines, and planes, on the basis of which many other propositions (theorems) are deduced. Newton, be it remembered, was still using Euclidean proofs in *Principia*.[415]

While the Romans did not make major contributions in mathematics and theoretical science, it should be noted that Claudius Ptolemy, in the second century AD, while living under Roman rule in Alexandria, wrote highly technical manuals on astronomy and cartography. The *Almagest*, which postulates a geocentric model, employs pure geometric concepts combined with very accurate observations of the orbits of planets. It postulates epicycles, eccentric circles, and equant points, with the latter being imaginary points in space from which uniform circular motion is measured. Attention should be paid as well to the "formal-rational" codification and classification of Roman civil law into four main divisions: the law of inheritance, the law of persons, the law of things, and the law of obligations, with each of these subdivided into a variety of kinds of laws, with rational methods specifying how to arrive at the formulation of particular rules. The rules upon which legal decisions were based came to be presented in categories headed by definitions. The most general rules within each of these categories were the principles from which more specific rules were derived. This ordering was in line with a formal operational mode of reasoning insomuch as the rules were presented without reference to the factual settings in which they were developed, and the terminology used in these rules was abstract.[416]

This effort at a rationally consistent system of law was refined and developed through the first centuries AD, culminating in what is known as Justinian's Code, 527 to 565, which served as the foundation of the "Papal Revolution" of the years

---

[415] In a recent study, Ronald Henss (2024) cites the ancient Greek historian Diodorus Siculus, who lived in the first century BC: "The Egyptians are intelligent, but in a way that is different from other peoples. They are adept at the exact sciences and geometry, but they are not as capable in abstract reasoning as the Greeks." Henss adds: "This statement is quite extraordinary. It appears as if Diodorus distinguishes between concrete-operational and formal-operative thinking in the sense of Jean Piaget. Only a few centuries before, at the time of Socrates and Plato, such a statement would not have been possible, because formal-operative thinking did not exist yet. The beginnings were with Aristotle and after a short flare-up among the Hellenists, it disappeared again until it started its triumphal course in the process of modernization in the western world."

[416] Stein, 1999.

1050 to 1150, associated with the rise of Canon Law. This Papal Revolution, by separating the Church's corporate autonomy (its right to exercise legal authority within its own domain), and by analyzing and synthesizing all authoritative statements concerning the nature of law, the various sources of law, and the definitions and relationships between different kinds of laws, and encouraging whole new types of laws, created a modern legal system.[417]

Medieval Europeans

Oesterdiekhoff acknowledges in passing that ancient Greece saw "seminal forms of democracy . . . for a certain period," a form of state which actually entails, in his view, the fourth stage of cognitive development. If Greek democracy was short-lived, what about the Roman republican form of government, and the impact it had on the modern Constitution of the United States?[418] We can also mention the representative parliaments and estates of medieval Europe.[419] To be sure, ancient Greece and Rome, and the Middle Ages, were far from the formal operational attainment of modern Europe (even if we draw attention to the continuation of witchcraft and magic in Enlightenment Europe). It is telling, however, that according to Charles Radding's 1985 book, *A World Made by Men: Cognition and Society, 400–1200,* new lines of formal operational reasoning were "well established by 1100" in some European circles. I say "telling" because this book (one of only two to do so) directly employs Piaget's theory to make sense of Europe's intellectual history. Oesterdiekhoff references this work without paying attention to its argument. From a Europe that employed ordeals of boiling water and glowing iron to decide innocence and guilt, and that "looked for direction" to divinely inspired pronouncements from superiors, kings, abbots, or the ancients, and that was rarely concerned with human intention, we see, after 1100, a growing number of theologians insisting that humans must employ their God-given reasoning powers to determine the truth. Whereas the way theological disputes were settled before 1100 was "by citing authority," "it was even increasingly the case [after 1100] that the very authority of a text's author might be denied or disregarded."[420]

---

[417] Berman, 1983.
[418] Hammer, 2015; Sellers, 1994.
[419] Myers, 1975.
[420] Radding, 1985, 204.

Using "one's own judgment" was encouraged, combined with the study of logic as "the science of distinguishing true and false arguments."

Although Radding is not definitive and barely elaborates key points, he understands that this increase in logical cognition entailed a new awareness of the distinction between the knower and what is known, between the I and the not-I. Medievalists actually went ahead of the ancient Greeks. For Plato, an idea existed and was correct if its origins were outside the mind, in the world of immaterial and perfect forms, which he differentiated from the untrue world of physical things. Perfect ideas were independent of the human mind, outside space and time, immutable. These ideas were not the products of human cognition. While the only way the human mind could apprehend these ideas was through intense training in geometrical (formal) reasoning, the aim was to reach a world of godlike forms to which the human mind was subservient.

While Aristotle transformed Plato's forms into the "essences" of individual things, he believed that universal words existed in individual objects, or that abstract concepts could be equated with the essences of things. It is not that Aristotle did not perceive any dividing line between the supernatural, the world of dreams, and the natural; it is that he was a conceptual realist who believed that the contents of consciousness really existed as the essences of particular objects. As much as ancient and medieval philosophers would agree that "truth is known by the mind," in the words of Aquinas, "according as the mind reflects on ... itself,"[421] they believed that the truth apprehended by humans was that of a natural order created by a divine power. For Aquinas, "all things are perfectly ordered through natural law," and natural law "is a participation in eternal law," and "natural law suffices for ordering all human affairs."[422]

Medieval nominalists, however, showed a deeper grasp of the relationships between the mind and the external world by abandoning the notion that Forms (or Ideas preconceived by a divine being) represent true reality, the source of the mind's ideas. They argue instead that general concepts are mere names, neither the essences of things nor forms standing outside the material world. Only particular objects existed, and the role of the mind was to make true statements about the world of particular things, even though ideas are not things, but mental tools originated by men. Nominalism represented a higher level of awareness of the role the human mind plays in cognition, and of the distinction between the knower

---

[421] Cited in Copleston, 1963, 47.
[422] Aquinas, 1998, 621.

and the world outside. While Plato distinguished reason from the world of sensory phenomena, including natural desires, and, in so doing, identified the faculty of reasoning in its own right, he viewed human (intellectual) activity as dependent or subservient to a world of perfect and purely immaterial forms existing independently of the mind. Moreover, among medieval philosophers we find (in Peter Abelard, for example) a greater emphasis on intention, the view that the intention of humans should be considered in determining the moral worth of an action. Human action should not be attributed to supernatural powers or evil forces entering into human bodies and directing it. Humans have a capacity to think through different courses of action, and for this reason human actions cannot be understood without a consideration of human intentions. Nominalism would eventually culminate in the philosophy of natural rights and the German idealist principle that true self-consciousness is attained when the human mind realizes that there is no natural order other than the order the human mind brings to the world.

If Radding is not explicit about these intellectual changes between ancient and medieval thinkers, he does touch on some additional key points, such as the emerging "idea of nature as a system of necessary forces" in the late medieval times, in opposition to the early medieval idea about miraculous events, as well as the "treatment of velocity itself as a quantity . . . comparing motion that follows differently shaped paths," in the work of Gerard of Brussels in the early 1200s.[423] However, a better example of formal operational concepts would be Nicole Oresme's (1320–82) depiction of uniformly accelerated motion, which was not about motion in the real world, but an effort to explain how motion increases uniformly over time in a totally abstract way.[424] This view anticipated Galileo's law of falling bodies. Among other examples Radding brings to elucidate this medieval shift to formal operational thinking is the observation that by the reign of Henry II (1133–89), the idea had taken root that consultation of members of the upper classes should be the norm in the workings of the monarchy,[425] as well as the legal idea that mental competence should be a prerequisite in deciding criminal behavior.

Finally, there were about thirty-four universities across Europe by the end of the fourteenth century enjoying the privileges of a corporation with the right to a neutral space of free inquiry, along with a curriculum, as Edward Grant has

---

[423] Radding, 249.
[424] Babb, 2005.
[425] Bisson, 1973.

carefully documented, "overwhelmingly oriented toward analytical subjects." As I will further elucidate in another chapter, universities with the legal right to regulate their own affairs independently of customary law, kinship ties, or religious and state authorities, were a unique creation of Europe. These universities tended to have four faculties (arts, theology, law, and medicine), with the program of the arts consisting of the three verbal disciplines of grammar, rhetoric, and logic (the trivium or threefold way to wisdom) and the four mathematical disciplines of arithmetic, geometry, astronomy, and music (the quadrivium). While medieval teachers were prohibited from reaching ultimate truths that were contrary to revealed truth, natural philosophers were free to pursue knowledge about the universe "in a remarkably secular and rationalistic manner with little interference from the Church and its theologians."[426] Indeed, medieval theologians, by applying logical techniques to theological questions, cultivated a religion like none before: a systematized and rationalized Christian faith.[427]

The Birth of Expectation in the Early Modern Era

Don LePan's book, *The Cognitive Revolution in Western Culture* agrees with Radding that "there is considerable evidence of at least the beginnings of changes in the cognitive processes occurring among the educated elite in the twelfth century."[428] But he believes that new cognitive processes began to spread in the early Modern period (or the Renaissance) when Europeans developed the capacity of "expectancy," which he defines as "the ability to form specific notions as to what is likely to happen in a given situation." It is around this sense of expectancy, LePan says, that most of the cognitive processes Piaget identifies with the fourth stage are clearly evident. This sense of expectancy involves a "rational assessment of probabilities," evaluating "disparate pieces of information" within a chain of events and circumstances as to whether something is likely to transpire in the

---

[426] Grant, 2001, 15.

[427] It is important to emphasize that we are not merely saying that medieval intellectuals used their rational faculties (for, as we pointed out earlier, humans have always been rational in the way they go about survival and creating the tools thereof); we are speaking about "the self-conscious, explicit use of reason," as Grant often says, though he does not elaborate. This explicit use of reason is only possible, as I have argued at length in prior chapters, when humans become conscious of themselves as unique possessors of a faculty called the "mind" capable of reasoning.

[428] LePan, 45.

future or not, drawing inferences from this information, and projecting "these inferences into the hypothetical realm of the future." Before this capacity developed, the sense of future expectation that humans had was of a predetermined sort, or accidental and beyond reason, in which an outcome was believed to happen "regardless of the intervening chain of events," and without an objective assessment of human intentions and events about how the future event would likely happen.[429]

This sense of expectancy involved the emergence of an ability to think in terms of abstract universal time, as contrasted to the commonly held notion of pre-modern peoples that "time moves at variable speeds, depending on the nature and quality of the events."[430] Among primitives, the recounting of past events, or history, is merely an aggregation of disconnected anecdotes, lacking a sense of chronology, and causal relationships as well as a clear grammatical distinction between words referring to past events or to present events. The past is conceived similarly to the present. While early Christian historians did have a sense of chronology, a universal history where all events were framed within a temporal sequence, they did not have a framework of abstract and objective time. They were more interested in detecting the plan of God rather than in understanding how humans with intentions made their own history.

Because pre-modern peoples lack a framework of abstract and objective time, the "when" of an event is merely about before or after other events, and not about the length of time elapsed between it and other events. Premodern peoples are also incapable of distinguishing between travelling the same distance and travelling at the same speed. They lack the habit of thinking of velocity as a quantity distinct from those of distance and time. Without a temporal conception wherein one can think of causes as anterior to the effect, it is not possible to consider historical events in terms of causal relations within a sequence of past, present, and future events.

For these reasons, premodern peoples were unable to think in terms of expectations of a hypothetical future, in terms of multiple chains of causation, and the ways in which these causes, sometimes happening simultaneously in different places, may bring about a future effect. LePan is particularly keen in showing that William Shakespeare's originality was a result of his ability to create complex plots which gave the audience "a continual sense of anticipation . . . by drawing them

---

[429] Ibid, 74–75, 79.
[430] Ibid, 100.

into [an] unfolding pattern of connections with the past and the future of the story."[431] The curiosity of a premodern audience is restricted to what will happen next within a sequence of episodes in which the reader or audience is confident about what is likely to happen, or what the final outcome will be, and in which there is, therefore, no sense of anticipation as to whether it will happen, no concern to envisage other hypothetical possibilities or situations, no weighing of causes and intentions against each other, and no judgment of what the probable outcome of the future will be.

As to what brought this new sense of expectation and the spread of the habits of thought associated with stage four, LePan is inclined to follow A. R Luria's argument that the causes of cognitive change are due to social and educational factors. He is rather vague; as society changes, literacy is mastered, the level of education increases, the cognitive processes change. Which came first: new cognitive processes, new ways of educating children, or new "underlying economic changes"? They "reinforced each other," answers LePan. He carefully distances himself from any claim that Europeans were genetically wired for higher levels of cognition. Even though he rejects the establishment idea that "all peoples think with exactly the same thought processes," he believes that all humans are equally capable of reaching this stage. Without realizing that Piaget laid the groundwork for Kohlberg's moral stages, he insists there is no "direct correlation between degrees of rationality and degrees of moral goodness."[432] The book ends with a strange postscript about how he has been living with his wife in rural Zimbabwe for the last two years. He wishes the primitive and the modern mind could coexist with each other, praises the "cultural vitality" of this African country, and then concludes with the expectation that "if something like a new Shakespeare is to emerge, it will be from the valleys of the Niger or the Zambezi."[433] The subtitle of *The Cognitive Revolution in Western Culture* is *Volume I The Birth of Expectation*. He did not write a second volume.

---

[431] Ibid, 175.
[432] Ibid, 15.
[433] Ibid, 307.

Formal Operational Reasoning Presupposes Onset of Self-Consciousness

We can agree with Oesterdiekhoff that the faster cognitive maturation of European peoples "is the decisive phenomenon" in need of an explanation. We disagree with him and LePan, however, that the origins of formal operational habits lie in the creation of educational institutions teaching this way of thinking. This presupposes the prior existence of formal thinkers. How come these thinkers originated only in ancient Greece? The issue is not, however, why logic emerged in Greece, as if we are merely talking about the emergence of a cognitive capacity. We need to step outside the world of logic, or formal operations, to understand why one small ancient civilization would generate a logic that would prevail in Europe right into the 1800s, whereas an advanced modern China, with a long tradition of rigorous education in the ancient classics, and an economy that was definitely more advanced in the modern era than that of ancient Greece, would not even produce a rudimentary logic.

In explaining the development of the fourth stage, we should start by focusing on the rise of individuals with an awareness of their own identity as knowers, with a relatively strong sense of selfhood and mind-consciousness. The Greeks did not have a higher IQ than the modern Chinese, nor did they develop the cognitive tool of logic because they lived in a cosmopolitan world, or were educated in better schools, or had democratic institutions where they were encouraged to debate. The Piagetian C.R. Hallpike realizes correctly, though he does not belabor this point, that stage four could not have originated without "awareness of the cognitive aspects of the mind," or an "awareness of the processes of reasoning," of the distinction between what is a product of human thinking and what is a result of our passions, the difference between reasoning and believing, between the acts of the mind and the acts of the body.[434] He notes that among the Homeric Greeks this awareness was undeveloped; thinking was described as "speaking" and located sometimes in the heart and sometimes in the lungs. The soul was not neatly divided into the three parts that Plato would divide it later on. Only when the Presocratic Greeks, with their latent sense of selfhood, came to discover the mind as the seat of thinking and knowledge, would they start an intellectual process that culminated in Aristotle's logic.

---

[434] Hallpike, 384–88.

Oesterdiekhoff identifies Descartes as the first thinker to offer a systematic methodology for the pursuit of knowledge based strictly on formal operational principles. He does not tell us that Descartes, revealing enough, is also known as the first modern philosopher for having postulated self-consciousness as the first principle of his formal-deductive philosophy. The only secure ground for his formal operations, Descartes argued, after all, was his certainty that he was a thinking being, despite doubting everything else. Everything could be subjected to doubt except his awareness that his own mind is the one authority capable of deciding what is true knowledge, not the external senses and not any external authority.[435]

This is what starts emerging in ancient Greece, although their self-consciousness was undeveloped, or, as Hegel would put it, still immersed in the collectively accepted values of the city-state, in that Greek citizens experienced their selfhood only as members of city-states and never as private individuals with a conscience of their own. This explains why Socrates was put to death, although, as Hegel saw him, he was the first individual with an emerging moral conscience—a conscience that appealed, nevertheless, to extra-human moral principles believed to be ordained by the natural order of things as apprehended by the mind, rather than as developed and justified by human reason itself. The ancient Greeks did not value the privacy of the individual, and did not have a modern theory of natural rights pertaining to each individual. We will address modern liberal individualism in Chapter XI. My point now is that Piaget's fourth stage, in its modern form, would have been impossible without the onset of self-consciousness.

The theoretical mathematics of the Greeks outperformed the mathematics of all other Axial civilizations combined because its hypothetic-deductive nature testified to its higher degree of reflexivity, in contrast to the practical, trial-and-error reasoning of non-Westerners. Non-Western mathematics justified its validity by

---

[435] Descartes could not have been clearer when he wrote "The first was never to accept anything for true which I did not clearly know to be such; that is to say, carefully to avoid precipitancy and prejudice, and to comprise nothing more in my judgment than what was presented to my mind so clearly and distinctly as to exclude all ground of doubt." *Discourse on the Method and Meditations* (2008, 21). It is worth citing Hegel's treatment of Descartes in his *History of Philosophy*: "Actually, we now first come to the philosophy of the modern world, and we begin this with Descartes. With him we truly enter upon an independent philosophy, which knows that it emerges independently out of reason. . . . Here, we may say, we are at home, and like the mariner after a long voyage over the tempestuous seas, we can finally call out, 'Land!' In this new period the essential principle is that of thought, which proceeds solely from itself. . . . The universal principle is now to grasp the inner sphere as such, and to set aside the claims of dead externality and authority; the latter is to be viewed as out of place here." See *Hegel's Lectures on the History of Philosophy, Volume 3: Medieval and Modern Philosophy* (1837/1995, 217).

induction and analogy, or approximate inferences based on observation and calculations, rather than on the basis of self-evident premises, with a mental awareness that its conclusions can only be valid if they are inferred deductively from its
premises. This capacity for geometrical deductions and rational proofs was not a
mere cognitive skill, but an achievement of the higher degree of selfhood and self-
consciousness of the Greeks.

Ancient Greek Mathematics Surpass
Mathematics of Non-Western Civilizations

Morris Kline, in his comprehensive 1972 history, *Mathematical Thought from
Ancient to Modern Times*, believes that "in the history of mathematics the Greeks
are the supreme event" and "one of the great problems of the history of civilization
is how to account for the brilliance and creativity of the ancient Greeks."[436] Yet
Greek mathematics is usually left unmentioned in "rise of the West" debates, even
though it had a direct, indispensable role in the rise of modern industrial civilization, and even though Sir Thomas Heath may be right that "of all the manifestations of the Greek genius, none is more impressive and even awe-inspiring than
that which is revealed by the history of Greek mathematics."[437] We know that
mathematics is characterized by rigorous reasoning and precise quantitative calculation, and that it has real-world applications in physics, biology, epidemiology,
engineering, chemistry, technologies, computer science, social sciences, and finance. But mathematics is not a mere adjunct to the sciences and technology, a
"cognitive tool-kit" to conduct calculations. Mathematicians have conceived
many ideas decades before anyone foresaw their possible applications to science.
Without the geometry of Bernhard Riemann, invented in 1854, and other mathematical ideas, the general theory of relativity could not have been articulated. "The
revolution in modern physics which began with the work of W. Heisenberg and
P. Dirac in 1925," Eric Temple Bell explains in *Mathematics: Queen and Servant
of Science*, "could never have started without the necessary mathematics of matri-
ces invented by Cayley in 1858, and elaborated by a small army of mathematicians
from then to the present time."[438]

---

[436] Kline, 1972, 24.
[437] Heath, 1921, 2.
[438] Bell, 1951, 1–2.

The Greeks constructed an entire geometrical system known as Euclidean geometry, the study of plane and solid figures, about the nature of reality, on the
basis of axioms and theorems, without physical evidence, through hypothetical
judgements ("let X be"), such that if you entertain one thought, you must go on
and entertain a second, all without making a judgement about the real, but constituting an operation of the mind, or taking place in thought only, but which subsequently found verification and application in the development of modern physics. They achieved this because they were conscious enough to reflect about the
nature of mathematical thinking. They were the first people to realize that the universe expresses itself naturally in the language of mathematics, and that mathematical truths have a validity that transcends the limits of time and space. This
realization persuaded Plato that mathematics comprehends a reality that exists
independently of human beings, and that mathematicians can apprehend this
eternal reality through the sheer power of their hypothetical deductive reasoning.
One does not have to be a Platonist who believes that mathematical truths exist
eternally and independently of material reality, however, to agree with Adam
Smith that mathematical terms express "the most abstract ideas which the human
mind is capable of forming,"[439] and that it was the Greeks who first conceived a
mathematics based on rigorous proofs, which subsequently found full experimental applications in Galilean and Newtonian science.

Since prehistoric times, humans have formulated conceptions of number and
geometrical forms in creative art. There is ancient evidence for the invention of
the abstract concept of number—that is, the realization that three sheep, three
fingers, and three days share a common property of "threeness"—as well as for
the idea of a one-to-one correspondence between the objects of one collection and
those of another, including counting an ordered sequence of symbols, such as
knots on a cord, basic addition, subtraction, multiplication, and division. But the
fact remains, most of the cultures of the world made zero contributions to mathematics defined as a specific field of knowledge, entailing a system of numeration,
with a variety of arithmetical calculations with whole numbers and fractions, the
solution of linear equations, and the mensuration of simple areas and volumes.
We only have the Egyptians, Babylonians, Chinese, Indians, and Islamic peoples
to compare to the Greeks.

---

[439] As cited in Struik, 1948, 3.

"Multicultural Mathematics"

We must once again take an ideological detour. The mathematical achievements of the Greeks, and of modern Europeans who grounded themselves on their achievements, is deeply unsettling to the current effort of the West to become a multicultural place where the diverse races, cultures, and religions of the world are expected to be co-equals in talent and in the very making of this civilization. The current *zeitgeist* holds that mathematics has been a "global effort . . . spanning . . . multiple cultures," or that the achievements of modern Europeans "involved an extensive exchange of ideas among individuals around the world."[440] "Multicultural mathematics," as one can easily see by googling these words, is now an educational staple in the West. The co-authored book, *Multicultural Mathematics: Teaching Mathematics From A Global Perspective*, published in 1991, explicitly states that the "customs, heritage, history, and other aesthetic aspects" of non-European immigrants must be incorporated as "essential components" of "an effective educational program."[441] The key academic text is *The Crest Of The Peacock: Non-European Roots of Mathematics*, by George Gheverghese Joseph, professor at University of Manchester. First published in 1991, reprinted three times by Penguin, republished by Princeton Press in 2000, with a third edition released in 2011, this book has been cited about a thousand times, with great reviews in prestigious journals. It claims that Europeans scholars have distorted and devalued non-European contributions as "part of the rationale for subjugation and dominance." Only two sources are referenced to back this claim: a book published in 1908 by Rouse Ball, and a book by Morris Kline, *Mathematics in Western Culture*, originally published in 1953. The latter book in particular is faulted for ignoring "a considerable body of research pointing to development of mathematics in Mesopotamia, Egypt, China, pre-Columbian America, India, and the Arab world that had come to light [by the time Kline wrote his book]."[442]

Joseph proposes a "new model" of the history of mathematics, in which multiple cultures are shown to have played equally significant roles with "cross-

---

[440] Hosch, 2010.

[441] The authors of this book are David Nelson, George Gheverghese Joseph, and Julian Williams. Other recent titles are: *Mathematics for Equity: A Framework for Successful Practice* (2014), and *Multicultural Curriculum: Transformation in Science, Technology, Engineering, and Mathematics* (2018).

[442] Joseph, 2000, 4–5.

fertilization between different mathematical traditions" happening at various times. He flaunts his model as complex, cosmopolitan, and nuanced—superior to the simplistic, linear, one sided, parochial, Eurocentric model. The fact remains, however, that both the old and the new research contradict and invalidate these claims.

First, most of the books Joseph relies upon to construct his new model are authored by Europeans themselves.

Second, the book by Rouse Ball is actually quite cognizant of the contribution of non-Europeans. The title is, *A Short Account of The History of Mathematics*, and it begins with four sections on "Knowledge of the science of numbers possessed by Egyptians and Phoenicians," and "Greek indebtedness to Egyptians and Phoenicians." Ball's point is that theoretical-deductive mathematics originated with the Greeks.

Third, Joseph complains about the "neglect of Arab contribution to . . . mathematics," without telling his readers that Rouse Ball's book includes two long chapters with the titles "The Mathematics of the Arabs" and "Introduction of Arabian Works into Europe, 1150–1450," in which he affirms original contributions: "From this rapid sketch it will be seen that the work of the Arabs . . . in arithmetic, algebra, and trigonometry was of a high order of excellence."[443] Why would Joseph, in what is otherwise a solid book in its effort to bring out the best in non-western mathematics, distort the scholarly contribution of Rouse Ball in this manner? Because academics are committed to multiculturalism, and this ideology allows one to distort the truth, for the sake of promoting cultural equality and fighting "White racism."

Fourth, regarding Kline's book, Joseph leaves out the fact that it is specifically about Western mathematics: "The object of this book is to advance the thesis that mathematics has been a major cultural force in Western civilization."[444]

Fifth, why did Joseph ignore so many books published after the 1950s, such as Carl Boyer's 1968 *A History of Mathematics*? This book has chapters dedicated to Egypt, Mesopotamia, China and India, and a chapter with the title, "The Arabic Hegemony." Why did he ignore Kline's subsequent 1972 book, *Mathematical Thought from Ancient to Modern Times*, possibly the most authoritative historical

---

[443] Ball, 1893. This is actually not a "short account"; the "unabridged and unaltered republication of the author's last revision, the fourth edition which appeared in 1908," was 522 pages long. The most recent edition published in 2020 by Maven Books is 459 pages. I am using a version located in the Internet Archive, the 1893 edition. https://archive.org/details/117770582.
[444] Kline, 1978, vii.

survey published so far, which opens with chapters on Mesopotamian and Egyptian mathematics, with an additional chapter on "the Hindus and Arabs?" Every book I have read has chapters on non-Europeans. We can go back to D.E. Smith's two-volume work, *History of Mathematics*, originally published in 1923, to find two opening chapters on non-European contributions, and one chapter plus half of another on "Oriental" mathematics, along with separate sections on Oriental contributions inside all the chapters about European contributions. Smith actually co-authored a 1914 book with the title *A History of Japanese Mathematics*.

The basic arguments that D. E Smith presented in *History of Mathematics* are still valid. He offered an opening chapter on Egypt, Mesopotamia, China, and India, as "pioneers in mathematical development before 1000 BC." Then chapters on the contributions of the Classical and the Hellenistic Greeks, from 600 BC to AD 400. We are informed that during the "five centuries from AD 500 to 1000 . . . Europe was intellectually dormant," while "there were four or five mathematicians of prominence in India,"[445] and furthermore, that China saw the greatest accomplishments during the five centuries from AD 1000 to 1500. While Smith may have neglected Muslim contributors, believing that they were "transmitters of learning rather than creators," he did offer sections on the "greatest mathematicians" during the Islamic ascendancy from the eight' to the fourteenth century. After 1200–1400, Smith's focus shifted back to the Europeans, because from this point on the original ideas came from them alone.

Greeks Compared to Egyptians, Babylonians, and Chinese

The indubitable reality is that, if you look past politicized books on "multicultural mathematics," the scholarly consensus coming from the best books on the history of mathematics for over a century now is that the Greeks, as Kline says in *History of Western Mathematics*, initiated a mathematics that "differed radically from that which preceded them."[446] Dirk Struik's 1948 edition of *A Concise History of Mathematics* acknowledges that Babylonian math "rose to a far higher level than Egyptian . . . in its computational technique,"[447] while arguing that "nowhere" in Babylonian mathematics "do we find any attempt at what we call a

---

[445] Smith, 1958, 152.
[446] Kline, 1978, 24.
[447] Struik, 1948, 23.

demonstration. No argumentation was presented, but only the prescription of certain rules"). William Berlinghoff and Fernando Gouvêa follow a similarly developmental interpretation in *Math Through the Ages: A Gentle History for Teachers*. This book, keep in mind, was published by The Mathematical Association of America, which is attuned to the multicultural sensitivities of teachers and students. They point out that, while the Egyptians "could solve simple linear equations ... [and] knew how to compute or approximate the areas and volumes of several geometric shapes," Babylonian mathematics was superior in making "use of extensive tables of products, reciprocals, conversion coefficients, and other constants," and in solving "a wide range of problems that we would describe as leading to quadratic equations." However, with the Babylonians, "the ideas behind the methods for solving quadratic equations were probably based on 'cut-and-paste geometry' [and] Babylonian geometry was devoted mainly to measurement. . . . The Greek mathematicians were unique in putting logical reasoning and proof at the center of the subject."[448]

Stuart Hollingdale, in his 1989 biographical book, *Makers of Mathematics*, agrees that "the concept of proof [in Babylonia] is conspicuous by its absence; and there is no clear distinction between exact and approximate results."[449] Carl Boyer's text, *A History of Mathematics*, a revised 1989 version co-authored by Uta Merzbach, is unequivocal in its assessment that "pre-Hellenic peoples had no concept of proof, nor any feeling of the need for proof . . . there are no explicit statements from the pre-Hellenic period that would indicate a felt need for proofs or a concern for questions of logical principles."[450]

But what about the Chinese with their long history, past ancient times, and their greatest mathematicians who lived during the Song Era (960–1279)? "Chinese mathematical works . . . are in the spirit of the Babylonians rather than the Greeks. They consist of collections of specific problems and present a curious mixture of the primitive and the sophisticated," concludes Hollingdale. In the course of their long history, the Chinese eventually became "more advanced than the Babylonians in that they gave general rules, often with formal proofs," and excellent mathematicians "flourished during the twelfth, thirteenth and fourteenth centuries," when the Europeans were experiencing their "long interlude" in the Middle Ages merely rediscovering the Greek works.[451] Nevertheless, as Joseph

---

[448] Berlinghoff and Gouvêa, 2015, 9–15.
[449] Hollingdale, 1989, 11.
[450] Boyer, 1989, 47.
[451] Hollingdale, 93–4.

Needham points out, Chinese algebra was "utilitarian" and "concrete," "devoted to the [practical] problems ruling officials had to solve." Unlike "the predilection of Greek science and mathematics for the abstract, the deductive and the pure over the concrete," Chinese mathematics lacked "the idea of rigorous proof" but inhabited "a mental outlook which avoided the development of formal logic . . . and which allowed associative or organic thinking to dominate."[452]

Boyer and Merzbach agree that the ancient Chinese were "repeating the old custom of the Babylonians and Egyptians of compiling sets of specific problems," in contrast to the Greeks of this period who were "composing logically ordered and systematically expository treatises." Zhu Shijie (1249–1314) was "the last and greatest of the Song mathematicians," but he was a lone, wandering scholar, about whom little is known. Shijie was author of two treatises, of which the first, *Introduction to Mathematical Studies* (*Suanxue qimeng*), was a "relatively elementary work . . . lost until it reappeared in the nineteenth century." His greater work, *Jade Mirror of the Four Origins* (*Siyuan yujian*), which also "disappeared in the eighteenth century, to be rediscovered In the next century," represents "the peak in the development of Chinese algebra, for it deals with simultaneous equations and with equations of degrees as high as fourteenth."[453] We will see below, however, that symbolic algebra was a product of early modern Europe, and that Greek mathematics was directly responsible for the development of modern mathematics. This is the reason Morris Kline's text, *Mathematical Thought from Ancient to Modern Times*, ignores Chinese mathematics in preference for the contributions of Hindu and Arabic mathematics to modern Europe.

Forerunners of Modern Mathematics

While reasonable people will have no problems agreeing that Greek mathematics stood far above Egyptian and Babylonian accomplishments, many will find the additional claim that in ancient times the Greeks were already more accomplished than the combined civilizations of China, India, and Islam to be an exaggeration bordering on historical falsification. How could a small population in ancient Greece accomplish more than civilizations that lasted thousands of years, with China and India practicing mathematics after ancient Greece was gone, and

---

[452] Needham, 1995, 62–64.
[453] Boyer, 222, 229–230.

Islam appearing to stand on the shoulders of Greek achievements? The most popular argument taught to students today, which prevails online, even though it is not supported by serious scholarly research, is that Hindu and Islamic mathematicians nurtured the rise of modern European mathematics. Here's what "the World's #1 Online Encyclopedia" says:

> Through contact with other cultures, and especially the absorption of Arab ideas and innovations, European learning in fields such as mathematics was able to go beyond the work of ancient scholars. New fields of study unknown to the Greeks were opened, leading to such developments as the calculus of Newton (1642–1727) and Leibniz (1646–1716), which would revolutionize both mathematics and science.[454]

The impression they want to convey seems reasonable enough: ancient Greek mathematics came before Indian (AD 200–1200) and Islamic mathematics (AD 700–1400), with the latter "picking up the best from Greek and Indian mathematics and developing it further." The best historical scholarship shows, however, that the modern development of analytic geometry, infinitesimal calculus, and the theory of functions, was substantially based on ancient Greek mathematics. This scholarship acknowledges that the modern West owes a debt to 1) "Islamic scholars who collected, preserved, and translated the Greek mathematical texts"[455]; and 2) the Hindu "creation of the decimal positional number system that is universally used today," that is, separate symbols for the numbers one to nine, negative numbers, and the notation for a missing position, i.e. a zero symbol.[456]

What about the argument that, while the Greeks originated deductive geometry, the Hindus and Muslims added substantially new ideas to arithmetic leading to the rise of modern symbolic algebra and to trigonometry? Muhammad ibn Musa al-Khwarizmi (780–850) is thus eulogized as the "father of algebra," offering "the first" systematic solution of linear and quadratic equations. Wikipedia informs impressionable students, in a long entry, that he is "the first person to treat algebra as an independent discipline."[457] Furthermore, Al-Biruni (973–1050), we are told, was among those "who laid the foundation for modern trigonometry,"

---

[454] "Overview: Mathematics 700–1449," 2019.
[455] Hollingdale, 101.
[456] Ibid, 101; Kline, 1972, 183–197.
[457] "Al-Khwarizmi," 2024.

which allowed Muslims to take Greek geometry to higher heights, since trigonometry studies relationships between side lengths and angles of triangles.[458]

In response, we need to be aware that ancient Greek mathematics extended
from 600 BC to AD 500, which equals about 1100 years of history. It is commonly
assumed that Greece's greatness was restricted to the "Classical" period of the fifth
and fourth centuries BC—the age of Socrates, Plato, Aristotle, Aeschylus, Sophocles, Euripides, Hippocrates, Herodotus, Thucydides, the defeat of the Persians,
the rise of Athens, the birth of democratic citizenship, and so on. People forget
the Hellenistic period between the death of Alexander the Great in 323 BC and
the rise of Augustus in Rome in 31 BC, and the fact that Greek high culture remained dominant through Roman times. The Classical Period is known as the
"Golden Age"—but not in mathematics. The golden age of Greek science was during the Hellenistic era, and, within this era, the golden age of mathematics was
from about 300 BC to 200 BC, the time of the three greatest mathematicians: Euclid, Archimedes, and Apollonius. There were many other great mathematicians
before and after this age. The birth of mathematics in Greece is generally identified
with Thales (623–545 BC), about whom Aristotle said: "To Thales . . . the primary
question was not 'What do we know, but How do we know it.'" Among the things
he is said to have proven is that "the pairs of vertical angles formed by two intersecting lines are equal." The next great figure is Pythagoras (580–500 BC), who
founded a very influential school, the first to classify numbers: real numbers, rational and irrational, integers, rational fractions, algebraic irrational numbers, and
transcendental numbers.

The list of mathematicians and their achievements is too long: Archytas (b.
428 BC), Hippasus (400 BC), Hippias (b. 460), Hippocrates of Chios (430, not to
be confused with the "father of medicine"), Zeno of Elea (450), Anaxagoras (428),
Democritus (460), and the greatest of the Classical Period, Eudoxus (b. 408 BC),
known as the father of mathematical astronomy, and the first to formulate the
method of exhaustion, which some see as a precursor to the methods of calculus.
Menaechmus (380–320 BC) is known for his discovery of conic sections and his
solution to the long-standing problem of doubling the cube using the parabola
and hyperbola. These men wrote books, some of which have been lost, though we
have commentaries on them and some of the titles; for example, Democritus
wrote: *On Numbers, On Geometry, On Tangencies, On Mappings* and *On Irration-
als.*

---

[458] Ali Abdullah Al-Daffa, 2015.

After the "golden age" of Euclid, Archimedes, and Apollonius, we have more greats: Aristarchus (310–230 BC), who wrote *On the Sizes and Distances of the Sun and Moon*; Eratosthenes, remembered for his almost accurate measurement of the Earth; Hipparchus (b. 180 BC), the father of trigonometry; Menelaus (AD 100); Ptolemy (AD 100–170), the founder of Cartography and Geography, and author of the famous *Almagest*. Heron (AD 62) is best known for his important formula for determining the area of a triangle based on its side lengths. We could go on with Diophantus (b. AD 200), author of a series of books called *Arithmetica*, which is seen as the "highest point of Alexandrian algebra," with its "most striking feature" being the solution of indeterminate algebraic equations.[459] The last of the greats is Pappus (b. AD 290), known for his *Collection* (c. 340), and his hexagon theorem in projective geometry, the full significance of which "was not realized until the seventeenth century."[460]

It is the "golden age" that needs emphasis. Archimedes (b. 287 BC) is consistently "ranked with Newton and Gauss as one of the supreme mathematical geniuses of all time."[461] Suffice it to list his writings that are preserved in full: *On the Equilibrium of Plane Figures, Quadrature of the Parabola, On the Sphere of the Cylinder, On Spirals, On Conoids and Spheroid, On Floating Bodies, The Measurement of the Circle, The Sand Reckoner*, and *The Method*. The *Conics* by Apollonius is known as a "masterpiece" containing 487 propositions proven by the "rigorous deductive methods characteristic of the Greek masters."[462] Before I address the role of Hindu and Muslim algebra, I will close with a few words about Euclid. His book, *The Elements*, has been "by far the most influential work ever written," matched only by the Bible. Copernicus, Galileo, Kepler and Newton all built their theories on the basis of Euclidean geometry. *The Elements*, which Bertrand Russell said was "one of the best books ever written," compiles, organizes, and reworks many of the mathematical concepts of Euclid's predecessors into a consistent whole. Its deductive method has been the most important procedure used by Westerners for demonstrating scientific certitude until the seventeenth century.

No book in the non-west provided such a self-conscious presentation of what it means for a statement to be "known to be true." It states that there must be some set of statements, called axioms, that are assumed to be true intuitively, from which point one can derive other basic statements or theorems. Some have said

---

[459] Kline, 1972, 138–43.

[460] Hollingdale, 90.

[461] Ibid, 64.

[462] Ibid, 57.

that a book entitled, *Aryabhatiya*, written in AD 499 by the Indian mathematician Aryabhata, is "somewhat akin to that of Euclid's *Elements*" in that both are "summaries of earlier developments, compiled by a single author." But as Boyer and Merbach point out: "There are, however, more striking differences than similarities, between the two works. *The Elements* is a well-ordered synthesis of pure mathematics with a high degree of abstraction, a clear logical structure, and an obvious pedagogical inclination; the *Aryabhatiya* is a brief descriptive work."[463]

Now, it is true that it was in the field of geometry, not arithmetic, that the Greeks constructed their Euclidean deductive method. In Greek arithmetic operations, which did include algebra, there is no "explicit deductive structure." These are the words of Morris Kline, whom it is worth quoting at length on this question, both by virtue of the clarity of his ideas, and because as a non-expert, we will rely on his authoritative knowledge.

> The work of Heron, Nichomachus, and Diophantus, and of Archimedes as far as his arithmetic is concerned, reads like the procedural texts of Egyptians and Babylonians, which tell us how to do things. The deductive, orderly proof of Euclid, Apollonius, and of Archimedes' geometry is gone. The problems are inductive in spirit, in that they show methods for concrete problems that presumably apply to general classes whose extent is not specified.[464]

Kline, however, is less impressed by the achievements of Indians and Muslims in arithmetic: "The high period [of Indian mathematics] may be roughly dated from about AD 200 to 1200."

> Hindu mathematics became significant only after it was influenced by Greek achievements.... The geometry of the Hindus was certainly Greek.... Geometry during this period showed no notable advances.... They did have a special gift for arithmetic." They gave "rules for the multiplication, division, and square roots of irrational expressions.... They used abbreviations of words and a few symbols to describe operations.... The Hindus recognized that quadratic equations have two roots and included negative roots as well as irrational roots.... In indeterminate

---

[463] Boyer, 237.
[464] Kline, 1972, 144.

equations the Hindus advanced beyond Diophantus. . . . In trigonometry the Hindus made a few advances.

However,

> the Hindus were less sophisticated than the Greeks in that they failed to see the logical difficulties involved in the concept of irrational numbers. Their interest in calculation caused them to overlook philosophical distinctions, or distinctions based on principles that in Greek thought were fundamental.[465]

Moreover, by about 1200:

> [S]cientific activity in India declined and progress in mathematics ceased. . . . It is fairly certain that the Hindus did not appreciate the significance of their own contributions. The few good ideas they had, such as separate symbols for numbers 1 to 9, the conversion to base 10, and negative numbers, were introduced casually with no realization that they were valuable innovations.

Regarding Islamic mathematics, Kline has this to say: "The cultural resources available to the Arabs were considerable. They invited Hindu scientists to settle in Baghdad." Fundamentally:

> [What] the Arabs possessed was Greek knowledge. . . . In arithmetic the Arabs took one step backward . . . they rejected negative numbers. . . . To algebra the Arabs contributed first of all the name. The word "algebra" comes from a book written in 830.

They did not invent algebra: their algebra is "founded on Hindu and also Babylonian and Greek influences. . . . Arabic geometry was influenced mainly by Euclid, Archimedes, and Heron." In conclusion:

---

[465] Kline, 1972, 183–90.

The Arabs made no significant advance in mathematics. What they did was absorb Greek and Hindu mathematics, preserve it, and, ultimately, transmit it to Europe.

This view is corroborated by the authors cited thus far. For example, Berlinghoff and Gouvêa say of Indian mathematics that "the main thing that is mostly missing from their texts is any explanation of how their methods and results were found. They did not give proofs or derivations."[466] Boyer and Merzbach highlight the accomplishments of Brahmagupta (598–668 CE) for being the first to "give a general solution of the linear Diophantine equation," and add that "the trigonometry of the sine function came presumably from India." Overall, however, in the estimation of Boyer and Merzbach, there was a "lack of nice distinction on the part of Hindu mathematicians between exact and inexact results." In their view, indeed, "analytic geometry and calculus had Greek rather than Indian roots, and European algebra came from Islamic countries rather than India."[467] Kline, for his part, insists that in trigonometry the Hindus made only "a few minor advances."[468] According to Hollingdale, the period of Arab pre-eminence between the ninth and eleventh centuries, only "saw many useful—but not outstanding—advances in algebra, number theory, trigonometry, optics, and, to a lesser extent, geometry."[469]

When all is said, for all the contributions made by Indians and Muslims, it would be Europeans in the modern era, on the direct strength of what the Greeks had accomplished, who would transform arithmetic/algebra into proper sciences by introducing symbolism and making "extensive and impressive contributions to the theory of numbers," and thus learning to justify algebraic reasoning by viewing algebra as an extension of logic in treating quantity, and by reversing the dependence of algebra on geometry, and indeed using algebra to help solve geometric constructions problems. When the Greco-Roman world ended in the sixth century, and Islam took the Mediterranean world, only a small part of the Greek mathematical corpus was known in Europe—until the eleventh century, when scholars from Europe went to Islamic Spain to translate into Latin the works that Muslim scholars had preserved and commented upon. For some time, until about 1400, European mathematics benefitted from this Islamic legacy with its adoption of Hindu numerals. Through the twelfth and thirteenth centuries, Kline writes,

---

[466] Berlinghoff and Gouvêa, 28.
[467] Boyer, 245–50.
[468] Kline, 1972, 189.
[469] Hollingdale, 101.

Europeans "energetically sought out copies of the Greek works, their Arabic versions, and texts written by Arabs," while contributing their own translations of Greek works into Latin rather than relying on translations that had passed through Arabic translations.

We should not forget, however, that this absorption of Islamic mathematics occurred within an emerging rationalist Christian framework, the "Renaissance of the 12th Century,"[470] which included the invention of universities with a "rational" curriculum and a continuous sequence of scholastic philosophers (Hannam, 2009). To mention only a few names: Roger (not Francis) Bacon (1220–1292) is identified as beginning experimental science, and for writing about the importance of mathematics to all science;[471] and Jean Buridan and Nicholas Oresme are both acknowledged for their demonstration that "the effective velocity in uniformly difform motion was the average of the initial and final velocities." It is even said that Oresme anticipated Descartes coordinate geometry, with "contributions towards the development of the concept of graphing functions and approaches to investigating infinite series."[472]

This broader rationalist atmosphere, together with the rise of universities, was absent in the Islamic world, despite its admiration for Aristotle. Only Christians would seek to provide logical proofs for the existence of God. Spectacles and mechanical clocks were both invented in thirteenth-century Europe. Romanesque and Gothic architecture required more practical geometry than the architecture of other civilizations. For the sake of modesty, however, let us say that, up until about 1500, European mathematicians, "with their algebraic emphasis, derived more inspiration from Arabic and medieval mathematics than from the much richer inheritance of Classical Greece."[473] It still remains the case that the European breakthrough into modern mathematics that came in the 1600s was primarily grounded in Greek mathematics.

Before this breakthrough there was Leonardo Pisa, also known as Fibonacci (1175–1250), identified as "the most creative mathematician of the medieval Christian world," who followed Islamic mathematicians "in using words rather than symbols and in basing the algebra on arithmetical methods." His 1225 work, *De practica geometrie*, however, was based on Euclid's book. Nicolas Chuquet's 1484 *Le Triparty en la science des nombres* explained the Hindu-Arabic number

---

[470] Haskins, 1972.
[471] Clegg, 2003.
[472] Babb, 2005.
[473] Hollingdale, 107.

system and how to perform arithmetic with this system. This treatise was novel, however, in devising an exponential notation where the power of the unknown was indicated by an exponent, and in presenting an algebraic notation with an isolated negative number, though he viewed negative numbers as absurd. Girolamo Cardono astonished the mathematical world by giving algebraic solutions to both cubic and quartic equations in his 1545 book, *Ars magna*.

After other prominent names, the most significant transition to modern mathematics came with the introduction of a fully symbolic algebra by François Viète [Franciscus Vieta] (1540–1603). Because Hindus and Muslims had placed their practical arithmetical calculations in the forefront of their mathematics, and had elevated algebra on an arithmetic rather than a geometric basis, and because the European transition to modern mathematics took place in arithmetic and algebra, it is commonly believed that Hindu and Islamic mathematics laid the groundwork for Vieta's transition to algebraic symbolism, and subsequent developments in analytic geometry, calculus, and functions. This is not the case. Vieta's book, *In artem analyticem isagoge* [*Introduction to the Art of Analysis*] (1591), was part of his "program of rediscovering the method of analysis used by the ancient Greek mathematicians," as Erik Gregersen recognizes in *The Britannica Guide to the History of Mathematics*.[474] His algebra had a firm Greek geometrical foundation. "His aim was to uncover and restore the algebraic relationships that were, he believed, hidden behind the geometrical presentations of the Greek masters."[475]

Vieta saw his new symbolic algebraic method "as an advancement over the ancient method, a view he arrived at by comparing the geometric analysis contained in Book VII of Pappus's *Collection*, with the arithmetic analysis of Diophantus's *Arithmetica*."[476] Despite the attempt of the *Britannica Guide* to portray mathematics as a "global effort ... spanning ... multiple cultures," it can't hide the actual truth. Once this *Guide* hits the modern era, not a single non-European is mentioned ,since none participated in modern mathematics.

Vieta was the first to use algebraic symbols or letters deliberately and systematically, not only to represent unknown quantities, but also as general coefficients. "The Arabs had not advanced one iota in symbolic notation." The "turning point in the history of algebra" came with Vieta.[477]

---

[474] Gregersen, 2011, 96.
[475] Hollingdale, 120.
[476] Gregersen, 96.
[477] Dantzig, 1956, 85–7.

Before him, in Europe, letters had been used for the unknown, and the first abbreviations used from the 1400s on were p for plus and m for minus; the = was introduced in 1557 by Robert Recorde. These changes in notation, the use of special words and number symbols, were essentially abbreviations of normal words. In fact, prior to Vieta, it was only Diophantus (AD 200) who had consciously introduced symbolism to make algebraic writing more compact and efficient. Vieta's education was overwhelmingly based on the writings of the ancient Greeks—Apollonius, Archimedes, Pappus, Diophantus; and the works of European mathematicians such as Cardano, Tartaglia, and Stevin. After Vieta, his analytic algebra was applied to the study of curves by his French countrymen Fermat and Descartes, who were also motivated by the same goal of applying new algebraic techniques to Greek geometry, leading to the development of analytic geometry. Vieta actually drew a conceptual line between his new symbolic algebra and arithmetic, calling the former a true algebra, with the potential to become a universal science. In other words, the arithmetic algebra of the Hindus and Muslims was not, in his estimation, truly algebraic.

This transition to modern mathematics was founded primarily on the Greek achievement, not as a mere intellectual exercise, but in response to the newly emerging scientific world of the Renaissance era, the age of exploration, and the rise of Copernican astronomy. Copernicus's heliocentric system, and Kepler's (1571–1630) three planetary laws, were based on the Platonic belief that the universe was ordered according to a mathematical plan, and that the truths of nature could be revealed in mathematical laws and geometrical terms—ideas that were absent in both the Islamic and the Hindu world. Renaissance perspective painting, the realistic depiction of scenes on canvas by incorporating three-dimensions, relative distances, size, and positions of objects, was likewise based on a thorough study of Euclidean geometry.

The European cartographic revolution, about which we will write in Chapter VI, was intimately connected to Greek mathematics; Gerardus Mercator's (1512–94) map solved the problem of projecting figures from a sphere onto a flat surface. The advantage deductive geometry had over practical arithmetic, trial and error, or reasoning by induction and analogy, is that its validity came from the logical derivation of conclusions from self-evident premises, rather than from approximate inferences based on observations restricted to a time and place. Even if we were to argue that deductive mathematics is merely a conventional language that Westerners imposed upon the world, rather than an accurate revelation of the structure of the universe, the success of Euclidean mathematical models lay precisely in mimicking or predicting the behavior of physical bodies. In the ideal world of abstraction that Galileo created, without resistance or friction, in which physical bodies were reduced to geometrical forms, perfectly smooth bodies moving on a perfect plane, the principles of Euclidean geometry held. As Galileo famously declared in 1623 in *The Assayer*: "the grand book of the universe . . . cannot be understood unless one first learns to comprehend the language and to read the alphabet in which it is composed . . . the language of mathematics." It was the Greeks who discovered the language of nature.

"Let X Be"

When we compare the Greeks to everyone else, the following conclusion seems inescapable: the Greeks were the first to derive mathematical concepts from pure reasoning alone, with little reference to the external world—that is, the first to think about numbers and operations abstractly, as products of the rational powers of man, and to realize that geometry is concerned not with physical objects, but with points, lines, triangles, squares, as objects of pure reason. They invented deductive reasoning, a method wherein reason proposes self-evident premises or axioms from which it deduces theorems in a rigorously consistent (and self-conscious) manner. Although ancient Greek mathematics (600 BC–AD 600) came before Indian (AD 200–1200) and Islamic mathematics (AD 700–1400), with the latter allegedly "picking up the best from Greek and Indian mathematics and developing it further"—in truth the modern European development of analytic geometry, infinitesimal calculus, and the theory of functions, was substantially based on the accomplishments of the ancient Greeks. Isaac Newton acknowledged the importance of Euclidean geometry in his articulation of his presentation of his laws of motion in the form of two mathematical theorems: "it's the glory of geometry that from so few principles . . . it can accomplish so much."[478]

Reviel Netz finds the "systematic use made of the ability to imagine a virtual presence, and to refer to this virtual presence as if it were on equal footing with the real" to be the "chief characteristic" of Greek mathematics.[479] The Greeks made continual use of the hypothetical phrase "let X be" in their construction of "a universe based wholly on the imaginary." This phrase, habitual to us today, "can

---

[478] As cited in Garrison, 1987, 609.
[479] Netz, 2009, 19.

hardly even be translated into most other languages!" When the Greeks asserted such phrases as "let the point be the center of the circle," they were not asserting that the point *is* the center of the circle, but that it is possible to make this claim for the sake of argument. In contrast, "the statements and commands of non-Western mathematics" appear through "personal imperatives and indicatives;" "not as Greek theoretical statements of possibility, but rather as concrete acts and directions."[480]

There is an issue, however, with the way Netz, currently the major specialist in Greek mathematics,[481] frames this routine use of purely hypothetical statements as a product of Greece's "free-for-all" intellectual atmosphere. He reaches the awkward conclusion that in this world of "radical thought experiments"—such as "how should one live: in a democracy or an aristocracy?"—the Greeks invented this imaginary world as a way of allowing themselves "the possibility of expressing incontrovertible truths" without necessarily committing themselves to any claim about the nature of reality, and avoiding thereby, in this polemical culture, refutations from others.[482] It makes a lot more sense, firstly, to see this polemical culture as the product of the aristocratic culture of individual striving for renown, and of a people that were relatively freed from polities based on kinship norms, and thus capable of thinking about alternative political orders, democratic versus aristocratic rule; and, secondly, to see the hypothetical-deductive mind of the Greeks as the product of a people becoming conscious of their consciousness, and thus capable of postulating imaginary worlds freed from immediate practical problems. We will address in Chapter VII the relative liberation of the ancient Greeks and Romans from kinship identities in their creation of polities based on citizenship.

---

[480] Ibid, 19–22, 40–42.
[481] He is the author of *The Shaping of Deduction in Greek Mathematics: A Study in Cognitive History* (1999), and *A New History of Greek Mathematics* (2022), among other works.
[482] Netz, 49–50.

V

THE TRANSCENDENTAL CONSCIOUSNESS OF EUROPEANS STANDS ABOVE THE EMBEDDED CONSCIOUSNESS OF THE CHINESE

Chinese reasoning is radically situated and cannot be interpreted as residing in a transcendental self.

– David Hall and Roger Ames

The Debate

China is the only civilization that academics have been able to compare (with some justification) with the West in its level of intellectual sophistication. Not a single scholarly study comes to mind that makes a realistic case about how the peoples of the Kingdom of Aksum, the Songhai Empire, the Aztecs, the Polynesians, or even Indians, were as significant in their intellectual achievements as the Europeans.[483] Only in the case of China do we find historians writing about its "great flowerings of intellectual life" with the same comparative assurance as they have written about the West. The intellectual achievements of different civilizations, not just their economic and technological achievements, should matter in our comparative historical assessments. The human brain is the "most

---

[483] I deal briefly with Indian philosophy in Chapter VI, and India's complete lack of historical writing in Chapter XI.

complicated object in the known universe."[484] The greatest ideas this brain has produced should be taken with the utmost seriousness.

There are two major schools of thought about China's intellectual history, which we may identify as the universalist and the neo-pragmatic schools. The universalist school maintains that during the Axial Age, China had already "gone through an epoch of early enlightenment" in the articulation of "transcendental" ideas about "human dignity, equality and autonomy . . . no less than in the Occident."[485] By "transcendental," this school means that the Chinese had formulated universal ideas for humanity based on rationally validated principles. It means also that China regularly produced intellectuals who challenged the conventions of their time and proposed new outlooks about the nature of reality and political life. The neo-pragmatic school, in contrast, maintains that the Chinese abstained from the "naïve Western supposition" that intellectuals could transcend the social context from which they emerged. Early on in their history, Chinese intellectuals came to the pragmatic realization—well before Western pragmatism and hermeneutics in the nineteenth and twentieth centuries—that all thinking is "embedded" in a time and a place.[486]

These two schools of thought, the academic establishment currently believes, constitute a very strong negation of the old "Eurocentric arrogance" about Europe's intellectual superiority. This Eurocentric view is sometimes identified as the "Hegelian-Weberian" school. This school argues that Chinese thought barely experienced any fundamental modification in its outlook after the rise of Confucianism, Daoism, and Legalism in ancient times—other than in the "refinement and more detailed articulation" of these perspectives. It argues that the West experienced a far richer sequence of intellectual novelties, combined with a universal scientific methodology that the rest of the world came to accept eventually, in alignment with liberal-democratic principles, equality of rights for all men beyond kinship ties, and religious beliefs. The Hegelian-Weberian school argues that Chinese intellectuals barely produced any universalist notions about the nature of reality, or social and political institutions, but remained guided by a purely utilitarian attitude to nature, ritualistic thinking, and "unreflected" customs and traditions.

---

[484] Kaku, 2014
[485] Roetz, 1993, 5–6.
[486] Hall and Ames, 1998.

The argument in this chapter is that the old Hegelian-Weberian interpretation of Chinese culture remains valid in its essentials. It goes without saying that the research and knowledge we have of Chinese history today is superior to what was available to G. W. F. Hegel (1770–1832) and Max Weber (1864–1920). We will see, however, that the verdict of the best up-to-date historical scholarship, if you look past its ostensible statements about "the great flowerings of Chinese intellectual life," merely qualifies the broad emphasis of the Hegelian-Weberian view. As Frederick Mote, a highly respected contemporary sinologist, put it, every major philosophical outlook in China's history occurred "within a revitalized Confucianism"—notwithstanding the role of Daoism and Buddhism.[487] Our defense of the Hegelian-Weberian interpretation is strictly in regards to the lack of substantive intellectual novelties in China after the ancient era, the lack of reflective thinking beyond the conventional norms of the time, and the absence of transcendental concepts.

We will add to the Hegelian-Weberian school the idea that it was precisely the transcendental capacity of Western thinkers to reason in terms of universal concepts independent of context that gave them the pragmatic or hermeneutic ability to understand the ways in which knowledge-claims are culturally embedded. The West's transcendental capacity did not spring out of the "human mind" as such, but out of its unique sense of self and search for the truth by relying on reason-based judgements. The Chinese mind was embedded in its particular traditions and historical contexts, without being self-aware of this, because the Chinese mind lacked a transcendental capacity. The transcendental capacity of Europeans did not emerge without historical conditions, outside a particular context, but was a capacity developed over time, with deep roots in Western history. On the other hand, the Chinese mind has been perennially embedded within its social surroundings in a rather habitual and unreflective manner. In a final section in this chapter, we will argue that Europeans were responsible, amazingly so, for the conceptualization of all the paradoxes of the mind, because of their ability to think in formal operational terms, in contrast to the Chinese examination of paradoxes, which exhibited a mind that was still context-dependent, barely able to rise above the concrete operational level of thinking.

---

[487] Mote, 1999.

The Chinese as Universalists: Heiner Roetz's Critique of Hegel

I will start with the school that sees a China following a universalist path of intellectual development similar in quality to the Western path. Various scholars have been arguing over the past decades that in China we see many "Western" or "modern" ways of thinking. But most of these works, as I have debated at length in prior publications, have remained focused on the economic, technological, practical-scientific, and institutional aspects of China's "modernity," rather than its intellectual history.[488] The one academic who has focused directly on the question of whether China nurtured a transcendental way of thinking, with an argument set directly in opposition to the Hegelian-Weberian thesis, backed by appropriate references and primary readings, is Heiner Roetz, professor for Chinese History and Philosophy at the Ruhr-University Bochum in Germany, in his 1993 book, *Confucian Ethics of the Axial Age.*[489] This book contends that from the Axial Age (800–200 BC) onward one can detect in China "an epoch of early enlightenment in the sense of a reflective disassociation from everything hitherto valid, and of a breakthrough towards 'postconventional,' detached thinking."[490]

---

[488] Referring to the "revisionist" historians and sociologists I evaluated *in The Uniqueness of Western Civilization* (2011) and *Faustian Man in a Multicultural Age* (Arktos, 2017): A.G. Frank, *Re-Orient: Global Economy in the Asian Age* (1998); Jack Goldstone, *Why Europe? The Rise of the West in World History, 1500–1850* (2009); John M. Hobson, *The Eastern Origins of Western Civilization* (2004); Prasannan Parthasarathi, *Why Europe Grew Rich and Asia Did Not: Global Economic Divergence* (2011); Kenneth Pomeranz, *The Great Divergence: China, Europe and the Making of the Modern World Economy* (2000). This "revisionist" school can be categorized within the universalist school, though with the major qualification that these authors barely engage with the intellectual histories of these two civilizations. In the realm of thought, we can mention the book by Fung Yu-Lan, *A Short History of Chinese Philosophy* (1948), which points to anticipations or similarities in Chinese "rationalism," "nominalism," and "hedonism," including a Chinese "theory of relativity." But this book, to be brought up again in the next chapter, is a descriptive survey that does not take on the "Hegelian-Weberian" school. The famous work of Joseph Needham on the technology and science of China, to which I will return in the next chapters, does not make the claim that Chinese philosophy was transcendental, or that China's overall philosophical outlook was on a par with that of the West.

[489] Perhaps Benjamin Schwartz's *The World of Thought in Ancient China* (1985) might be seen in the same lineage as Roetz's book, in light of its argument that Chinese thought is very similar to Western thought. However, Schwartz's book is not directly set up against the Hegelian-Weberian school; it simply follows Karl Jaspers' Axial Age argument examined in Chapter III.

[490] Roetz, 6.

Roetz objects to Hegel's use of the term *Sittlichkeit* (which essentially means "ethical behavior grounded in custom and tradition and developed through habit and imitation")[491] to describe Chinese ethical behavior. Hegel believed that Chinese ethics remained "embedded in the unquestioned habits of the community." Roetz counters that the Chinese had reached the level of *Moralität* (another Hegelian term to designate ethical behavior grounded in rationally-approved principles, rather than unquestionably accepted norms). Roetz rejects Hegel's placement of China at the "unreflected" beginning of world history, in which Chinese individuals, in Hegel's words, had "no self-cognizance at all in antithesis to the Substantial. . . . In China the Universal Will immediately commands what the Individual is to do, and the latter complies and obeys with proportionate renunciation of reflection and personal independence."[492]

In using the term "unreflected substantiality" in reference to China, Hegel meant that this mind called upon rulers to follow "the Way" as the natural order of the universe, without subjectivity or reflective thought. It took "the Way" as a naturally given substance, and its attitude toward the laws and institutions was not a self-conscious one based on rationally mandated criteria. Likewise, Chinese thinkers spoke of the Mandate of Heaven in very vague terms, without elaboration, as some sort of ethereal thing that could be discerned spontaneously or immediately without the need for critical reasoning. The Chinese, for Hegel, never differentiated the mind as a distinctive faculty, but instead confounded the mind with the "heart" or with unreflected substances. In this respect, the Chinese mind remained submerged in the world, absorbed by nature and unquestioned conventions.[493]

Roetz claims that the Chinese mind did separate itself from the surrounding world, from bodily attributes and personal inclinations, becoming conscious of itself and taking an independent standpoint against the everyday world of magic, rituals, and habits of thought. To counter Hegel, Roetz brings up Karl Jaspers' theory of the Axial Age. He acknowledges in passing that "a great number of cultures [did] not take part" in the Axial Age, but he never clarifies whether China was the one Axial Age civilization that nurtured an "early enlightenment," or whether this was a phenomenon among all Axial Age cultures. The implication

---

[491] See Philip J. Kain (2005, 89); there are no indications that Roetz is that familiar with the current scholarship on Hegel.

[492] Roetz, 7.

[493] Hegel's view on Chinese thought can be found in *The Philosophy of History* (1837/1956), and *Introduction to the Lectures on the History of Philosophy* (1805/2003).

seems to be that China was unique in forging universalist moral concepts. In any case, Roetz brings up Lawrence Kohlberg's well-known stages of moral reasoning to frame his argument that ancient China, as the West would do in modern times, reached the highest level of moral reasoning, "the universal ethical principle." Roetz sets for himself a hard task, since Kohlberg's theory very distinctly says that the highest stage only came with modern Kantian philosophy, when the mind came to legislate for itself principles with a universal intent applicable to all men. For Kohlberg, only in countries with liberal oriented institutions do we observe a socializing atmosphere wherein citizens can be seen to mature morally from the first stages of punishment and obedience orientation, through the stage of satisfying one's immediate needs, to the conventional stage of law and order, family and state loyalty, through to the social contract orientation, and to the post-conventional, universal-principled orientation. Kohlberg believed that the final "post-conventional" stage was first reached by modern Europeans.[494]

There are, evidently, enormous problems with Roetz's claim that ancient China in the Axial Age had already reached the highest stage of moral reasoning. For Hegel, Axial Age Greece was still a culture heavily embedded within extra-rational norms, even though he observed a process of separation from nature in the philosophies of the Presocratics, the beginnings of a concept of self, and signs of subjective distancing from the conventions of the time in the person of Socrates. The Greeks lacked a fully articulated concept of moral self-determination. Socrates represented defiance against the gods, but he did not argue that humans have a "natural right" to disagree and to oppose the consensus of the city-state, the common will of the *polis*. It was only in the modern era, during the Enlightenment of the eighteenth century, that Hegel saw the stage of *Moralität*, or, in Kohlberg's language, the post-conventional stage. Roetz has to make the most of ancient China because the moral reasoning during this era was never superseded in later centuries. He admits in passing that China experienced "the intellectually most fruitful epoch of her history" during the Axial Age.[495] Confucianism became the orthodoxy during the Han dynasty (202 BC–AD 220), with no major original ideas emerging thereafter.

---

[494] Kohlberg, 1971. Roetz surely knows this about Kohlberg's theory, about which he elaborates at length. He cites Habermas, who also relied on Kohlberg's stages for his theory of moral progression, and distinctly identified the post-conventional stage with the modern West. See the chapter "Moral Development and Ego Identity" in Jürgen Habermas, *Communication and the Evolution of Society* (1979).

[495] Roetz, 47.

Trying to argue that Axial China had already reached the highest levels of moral reasoning strains Roetz's otherwise serious scholarly effort beyond repair. It should be clarified that Kohlberg's highest stage is akin to the Hegelian concept of *Moralität*, which refers to the stage of moral reasoning embodied in Kant's categorical imperative, where the individual arrives at moral maxims singularly through the use of reason, irrespective of feelings, personal interests, or the conventions of the time, and in which the relation of the subject to the world is that of a relation of "ought-to-be," or a relation in which the subject imposes its own rationally constructed categorical principles upon society. Kant sought a moral law that could be universalized, coming up with the imperative: "Act only according to that maxim whereby you can at the same time will that it should become a universal law."[496]

But Hegel correctly criticized this categorical law as a purely formal and subjectivist statement in its presumption that the determination of what is right can be a pure act of willing by an abstract agent, rather than the achievement of a concrete people. The philosophy of Kant should be seen as a highly educated expression of the self-knowledge of the European community in the late 1700s. The self-legislating individual could not have sprung out of Kant's isolated mind, but was constructed out of a historically specific ethical community with a high level of transcendental reflection embodied in the emerging institutions of the modern compassionate family, the modern contractual market, and the modern constitutional state.[497]

Moral principles generated out of the inner reflection of thinkers unaware of the embedded character of their reasoning are always deficient and one-sided in that, on their own, they are willful expressions that cannot but suffer from the elevation of the moral will of particular individuals above the will of the community, the spirit of a people. For Hegel, only by exercising one's conscience in concert with the ethical life of the community, which includes reflective institutions, laws, and customs, can the moral will of individuals be permeated with both objectivity and subjectivity. The world to which Kant owed his education was coeval with the French Revolution of 1789, and this revolution, its limited early non-

---

[496] This famous line comes from Immanuel Kant, *Grounding for the Metaphysics of Morals* (1993, 30).

[497] Hegel's critique of Kant's moral philosophy has been the subject of countless books and articles; suffice it to mention here, in addition to Philip Kain's book cited earlier, Terry Pinkard's *Hegel's Phenomenology: The Sociality of Reason* (1996), and Allen Wood's *Hegel's Ethical Thought* (1990).

Jacobin phase, institutionalized the Enlightenment discourse of moral autonomy, and cultivated a public sphere in which moral norms and political decisions were open to discussion. This Hegelian synthesis of *Moralität* and *Sittlichkeit* means that the norms of the post-Enlightenment era, the state and its institutions, already embodied the self-consciousness of citizens, and thus could no longer be seen as unreflected, coercive norms alien to individuals, since individuals are critically involved with the institutions of their society. They are no longer inhabiting a community based on a normative system lacking in reason-giving accounts. The authority of the norms comes from their being grounded in principles validated by citizens exercising their rational faculties in communication with others, rather than grounded in the particularistic interests of powerful individuals or, as we will discuss in Chapter VII, in kinship-based norms.

Roetz's Thesis

Essential to Roetz's case is the claim that Confucianism and Daoism were in confrontation with the given world in their affirmation of the ideal qualities of the Way—the governing principle of the cosmic and social order—and the "golden past," when the social order was thought to be in perfect harmony with the Way or the Mandate of Heaven. Roetz compiles many sayings by Chinese intellectuals which apparently constituted public indictments (based on universal principles) against the political order and the behavior of state officials, starting with the "Collected Sayings" (or *Lunyu*) of Confucius, which express "an ideal which contrasts with the reality of the time."[498] He cites passages with words such as these: "There are many rulers in the world, but only few of them are humane." "Nothing is better than to make Heaven the norm."[499]

Roetz believes that, even though Confucianism became the orthodoxy of the state, this school was "far from advocating unconditional obedience." Filial piety, a respectful and obliging attitude towards the elders of the family, and dutiful performance of one's ascribed role, were not blindly expected without considering the inner moral attitude of both subordinates and superiors. While Confucians were "far from formulating any alternative to monarchy," they tried to "make change unnecessary by humanizing the existing system as far as possible and

---

[498] Roetz, 49.
[499] Ibid, 57.

putting strong moral obligations on the powerful."[500] It is not the ruler, he continues, who determines what is the ideal, but the Dao, and the "Confucian concept of the Dao, like the Daoist one, often refers to something not realized in the given world." While Roetz acknowledges that the Chinese never developed a republican conception of government, and that their ideals "projected back to a Golden Age," he believes the concept of the Dao, in itself, was "the most important cipher of the postconventional perspective of classical Chinese philosophy."[501]

Mengzi (Mencius) (372–289 BC), Roetz tells us, argued that a ruler is legitimate only insofar as he devotes himself "to the service of the moral possibilities which every human is endowed with by his very nature."[502] Mengzi already conceptualized the modern Western principle of natural rights when he said that rulers must not disregard the "innate good nature conferred to man by Heaven."[503] In Xunzi, or Xun Kuang (310–235 BC), Roetz detects a social contract theory akin to Thomas Hobbes in the argument that hierarchical orders are necessary because this is how the general interest of all men can be satisfied, since a society without different roles and orders would collapse into chaos, leaving men at the mercy of violence, without security and livelihood. Mengzi, in giving precedence to the Dao over duty, was implying that "man . . . can in principle choose his way freely" because he is capable of judging the existing order from a detached standing and "of suspending his very interest in self-preservation" by doing what is humane rather than what those in power may prefer.[504] He cites Xunzi: "The heart is free and unrestricted in its choices," as a clear expression of the Chinese belief that the mind was free to choose and reject according to its own standards.[505]

The Chinese ideas of justice and of humaneness—in contrast to the conventional norms of filial loyalty and obedience—are "postconventional in that they do not refer to what is due to the role, but to the organization of the society as a whole."[506] "Humaneness is an extension of the natural compassion which every man will feel in view of the hardship and misfortune of others."[507] Roetz believes that "humaneness represents a basic moral intuition" which transcends any specific cultural norm. The Chinese principle of fairness—the Golden Rule—is also

---

[500] Ibid, 74–5.
[501] Ibid, 80–81.
[502] Ibid, 78–9.
[503] Ibid, 85.
[504] Ibid, 154.
[505] Ibid, 160.
[506] Ibid, 118.
[507] Ibid, 131.

grounded "in a region beyond social and historical values in a timeless formal rationale." The Confucian Golden Rule—if I treat the other well, the other will treat
me well too—should "hardly be understood in terms of group morality" for it
speaks "in favor of universalism" in the way that it calls upon everyone to put
themselves in the place of others, including "barbarians."[508] He cites Lao Tzu, the
founder of Daoism: "Humaneness means to love others from one's innermost
heart. When a humane person rejoices in the happiness of others and cannot en-
dure misery, then this comes from an uncontrollable emotion."[509]

These kinds of expressions about the meaning of humaneness, Roetz says, take
"no account of context, status, casuistry, and tradition, and represent the abstraction of the 'other' as a being of equal dignity like myself." They are the declarations
of "the self-reflected ego ... and thus comprise the elements of autonomy and
freedom."[510]

Insofar as Confucianism advocated "self-respect, self-strengthening, and self-
examination," the Chinese held an ideal of individuals standing up against social
injustices out of their own moral convictions without being "absorbed by the social environment." Confucius says:

> A scholar sets his heart on the Dao. But he who is ashamed of poor food
> and poor clothes does not deserve to speak with him. To live on coarse
> food and water, and to have the bent arm for a neck support—joy is also
> in this. But wealth and high position, attained by unjust means, for me are
> like passing clouds.[511]

It was Xunzi's view, moreover, that inner conviction through "inner examination," rather than "any external criterion," should be the ultimate ground of one's
moral behavior. Mengzi, too, teaches that "to regard compliance as correct behavior is the way of wives and concubines." He who dwells in humaneness "strides
his way alone ... cannot be led to dissipation by wealth and high position, led
astray by poverty and mean conditions, and bent by authority and power."[512]

Against Max Weber's argument that Confucianism was a mere ethics of accommodation which "intentionally left people in their personal relations as

---

[508] Ibid, 135–38.
[509] Ibid, 144.
[510] Ibid, 148.
[511] Ibid, 161–62.
[512] Ibid, 172.

naturally grown or given by relations of subordination," Roetz brings up the ideals contained in the principle of Heaven—benevolence, trustworthiness, justice. These ideals, he thinks, resembled the Western Augustinian teaching of "two kingdoms," the kingdom of God and the kingdom of Man, with the former in a constant state of tension with the latter, representing a critical impulse against unjust authority. Mengzi, like Augustine, sets up an idealized concept of human nature "against the brutal politics of his time." His claim that human nature is inherently good represented a "challenge to the political institutions" to recognize this goodness and avoid treating humans as evil creatures in need of coercive disciplinary measures.[513]

There is a rationalist mind at work in Xunzi's argument that we cannot dispense with sage kings, propriety, and state order because human nature is evil. "Reason is the true pivot of Xunzi's philosophy," in that it distinguishes the rational utility of the state from the natural inclinations of humans to do evil. Xunzi explains the necessity of strong institutions by following through the implications of human evil without a social order. Nature on its own generates chaos; humans agree to create institutions for reasons of social utility, because without a state order, without rules of propriety and hierarchical structures, humans would be in a state of constant quarrelling. He writes:

> Quarrel leads into chaos, and chaos into misery. The early kings hated this chaos. They therefore established propriety and justice, in order to set up a division [of roles between men], meet their desires, and supply their demand.[514]

Xunzi's legitimation of the state was thus based on rationalistic-utilitarian principles similar to the contract-based social theories produced by modern Europeans. Xunzi's arguments attribute "reasonable deliberation" to humans as such in their calculated utilitarian decision to be governed by a state.[515]

But it is really in Mo Di's "utilitarianism" (or Mozi, founder of the Mohist school, 480–397 BC) that Roetz detects a fully developed rational theory of "the authoritarian state." The Mandate of Heaven is for humans to build an authoritarian state, not because such a state is sanctified by tradition, but because it is the

---

[513] Ibid, 198.
[514] Ibid, 224.
[515] Ibid, 269.

only state that is consistent with the self-interest of humans to prefer order over the chaos of nature where there is no generally agreed upon distinction between right and wrong. Just as in Hobbes' theory of the Leviathan state, it is human self-interest to enter into an agreement to live under an authoritarian state. Mo Di was "an uncompromising universalist" in proposing a general theory of the origins of the state that applied to all men including "barbarians." His thought is character-ized by a far more radical detachment from tradition than Confucius's Golden Rule, for it sets up pure rational self-interest against "all established customs" and a "criterion of validity" for the existence of the state anchored on human reason. He is "the first thinker of the Chinese Axial Age to recognize the necessity of giv-ing detailed arguments for one's position," making him "the most important pre-cursor of Chinese logic."[516]

Roetz classifies "Daoist Naturalism" as "an enlightened postconventional per-spective" for its "critique of the given order" from the perspective of "an ideal pri-mordial state" in which men were as pure as infants in their closeness to nature, uncorrupted by civilization. The ideal is that of man acting spontaneously and unconsciously in a good way, as an innocent child, without any guidance from conventional norms. Roetz detects in the Daoists the "carefree existence" exem-plified in Kohlberg's early post-conventional stage, the phase of youthful protest characterized by a radical rejection of conventionalism. While the Daoists did not formulate or develop a discourse with a universal principled orientation, their nat-uralism "undoubtedly contains the idea of universality" since it renounces the use of all living things as a means to a social end, and acknowledges the right of every living being to express its natural destination.[517]

I am not persuaded by any of these arguments. Hegel was essentially correct in his assessment that the *Sittlichkeit*, the ethical life of China, was characterized by "unreflected substantiality." In China, it was not humans reasoning for them-selves who were in charge of moral norms, but substances lacking in precision, such as the Mandate of Heaven and the Dao, commanding individuals what to do. It can be argued, to be sure, that the high civilizations of the Axial Age, including China, with their strong centralized order and monopolized jurisdiction, literacy, division of labor, education, and public law, did engender quasi-universal values that stood above the "group morality" of clans, kinship ties, the principles of re-venge, and redress in accordance with the *lex taliones* (an eye for an eye). It can

---

[516] Ibid, 242–43.
[517] Ibid, 255.

also be argued that the Axial Age civilizations, with their centralization of many tribal groupings under one legal authority, and the breakdown of the old localized religions, gods, and mythologies, did produce new religions and philosophies seemingly speaking for man in general with a new set of moral ideals (in Confucianism, Daoism, the Hebrew Bible, and Hinduism) that could be contrasted against the everyday comportment of rulers and the immoral realities of the time.

But Roetz is not merely arguing that Axial China promulgated principles functionally relevant for a sizable agrarian civilization beyond the particular norms of tribal units. He is arguing that China promulgated "post-conventional" ethical principles with a universal intent based on rationally approved criteria. He has a downgraded and ultimately flawed understanding of the transcendental mind of Europeans. Just because the Chinese mind conceived the notion of a Mandate of Heaven or the Dao as the substance and activity of the Universe, above and beyond the time and space of any particular culture, and the legislator of universal morals, it does not mean they were in possession of a transcendental mind. They were advocating unconditional obedience to an external power or ideal being in relation to which their minds were lacking in self-determination. Hegel does not deny that non-Western peoples had a concept of a universal substance existing outside this world; his claim is that this conception of a substance remained "unreflected" because it was taken to be true over and above the ultimate authority of human reason.

Now, it is true, as we saw briefly in the previous chapter, that before the modern era, we find a Platonic reliance on Ideas or Forms existing outside the human mind, which persists through the medieval concept of Natural Law. But there was already a crucial difference between the Chinese concept of "the Way" or the Mandate of Heaven and the Western concept of Forms or Natural Law—in that the Europeans did emphasize the importance of rational deliberation, *logos*, and rigorous proof. Europeans before the modern era were also far less tied to kinship-based norms, having already developed concepts of citizenship beyond tribal identities and a whole range of civic associations based on voluntary contractual norms, as we shall explain further in Chapter VII.

Roetz tends to confound the idealization of conventions in relation to the everyday behavior of self-interested individuals, with post-conventional transcendental principles. He does not realize that conventions are not easy to follow, but stand as ideals which selfish humans have a hard time living up to. The Confucian statement that "there are many teachers in the world, but only a few of them are humane" should not be taken to be a contrast between a transcendental ideal and the normative conventions of the time, but should be taken to be a statement about the inability of most Confucians to live up to the accepted values of Confucianism, an ideology which, as Roetz could not deny, became an ossified orthodoxy for centuries after the Axial Age. If Roetz wants to tell us that Confucianism and Daoism were less particularistic philosophies that broke away from the transmitted customs of pre-Axial China (forgetting for the moment that these two philosophies never looked forward to an ideal future but to a pre-existing past), then he is making a plain enough argument. But what he aims to say is that Confucianism was heavily loaded with post-conventional ideals close to what Hegel meant by *Moralität*—and he is wrong about this.

We will see below that much of what Weber says remains valid, particularly his assessment that Confucianism was characterized by a this-worldly orientation sustained by a bureaucratic elite with vested interests in their offices, an elite preoccupied with the maintenance of order and the preservation of traditional rituals, rather than the transformation of reality according to ideals determined by a transcendental mind. But first we will raise some objections about Roetz's effort to show that Chinese political theory was as advanced as Western political thinking.

Thomas Hobbes

Roetz admits that in Confucius and his pupils "elaborate argumentation and giving reasons are missing."[518] Mo Di, apparently, is the first and only thinker "to recognize the necessity of giving detailed arguments for one's position;" and yet, in the end, Roetz admits that Mo Di too does not build his case for an authoritarian state from the perspective of free contractual individuals deliberating about universal principles, but from the perspective of what he deems to be the self-interest of humans for order rather than chaos.[519] It is true that Roetz refers primarily to Hobbes' contractual theory, not John Locke's natural rights theory, and that Hobbes does appeal to self-interest or self-preservation as the ultimate reason for individuals foregoing their natural freedoms in the brutish state of nature, in the name of a Leviathan that would ensure order and longevity. There is a world of difference, however, between Mo Di and Hobbes.

---

[518] Ibid, 47.
[519] Ibid, 242–3.

The Chinese produced some geometrical calculations and showed some inter-est in spatial ordering, but there was no deductive geometrical thinking in China, whereas Hobbes began his incredible intellectual journey towards a science of pol-itics with a thorough study of Euclid's *Elements*. Remember, as argued in the pre-vious chapters, Chinese mathematics lacked the idea of rigorous proof. Euclid im-pressed upon Hobbes the possibility that one could construct a rigorous argument about politics by building up one's line of reasoning on the basis of very simple, self-evident propositions. Hobbes also absorbed Galileo's law of inertia, from which point he came up with the idea that motion was the natural state of men, and that to develop a science of politics, one would have to consider man as one kind of body in motion. Humans were self-moving creatures consisting of sense organs, muscles, imagination, memory, and reason, driven by the impulse to avoid death and to give satisfaction to their physiological appetite for bodily pleasures, riches, and power, with a rational capacity to deliberate about the best means to gratify their appetites. But since the desire or the strength of appetites differed among men, different men exhibited different levels of inclination for pleasure and power. Since every man was impelled to seek some resources and power, and some more than others, there would always be a competitive struggle for riches and power; everyone, including those men with a moderate desire, would be caught up in a perpetual and restless desire to satisfy their appetites.

It was from these two postulates, that every man shuns death, and that men are naturally engaged in an incessant struggle for power, that Hobbes rigorously reasoned that men would live in a state of perpetual conflict in a state of nature in which there was no common authority to restrain this struggle and penalize those who engaged in violent dispossession of others. Only their fear of death persuaded men, who were capable of reasoning about their interest for self-preservation, to agree to give up their natural right to pursue power as they pleased, and make a contract with a supreme authority delegated with powers to ensure the peaceful pursuit of men's desires.[520]

There is a world of difference conceptually between observing that men prefer order over chaos, and employing a method that relies on both inductive generali-zations about the behavior of men, and on self-evident premises for the deduction of a full-fledged theory about the necessity of an authoritarian state. Hobbes knew

---

[520] Thomas Hobbes, *The Leviathan* (1985). I benefited from the excellent introduction to the Pen-guin edition of this book by C.B. Macpherson. Hobbes' deep knowledge of modern science is well documented in Adams (2023).

what Aristotle had already explained in his logic: that the premises of a science ought to be self-evident, and that a deductive argument cannot convey more information than is implied in the premises, if the conclusions derived from the premises are to be as self-evident as the premises themselves. Hobbes' argument was not without flaws. He uses the words "appetites," "power," "riches," and "pursuit of honor" interchangeably. While a reasonable argument can be made for the conflation of the first three words, the pursuit of honor, as we learn from Plato's *Republic*, is not about the satisfaction of a bodily appetite or pleasurable acquisition of riches, but about the "spirited" side of the soul and its desire for respect and honor as a man and as a member of a group.

Max Weber: A Defense

Mengzi's argument that humans are naturally good is not equivalent to the Western concept of natural rights. It is a stretch to extrapolate from Mengzi's argument that humans are born with goodness in their hearts, to the argument that humans are endowed with natural rights which the state should not violate. Europeans developed a theory of natural rights only in the modern era, out of the Roman-Medieval concept of natural law. The Chinese barely had a concept of natural law. In the Western medieval tradition, natural law stood for the idea that humans have a rational faculty, which allows them to comprehend the laws of nature, implanted in them by the divine, insofar as they were created in the image of God. From Roman times, Europeans were of the view that their laws could be justified if they were ultimately, in the words of Cicero, in "agreement with nature," "of universal application, unchanging and everlasting," "valid for all nations and all times," "commanding us to do what is right, forbidding us to do what is wrong."[521] This idea of natural law presupposed the idea that humans were endowed with a rational faculty that allowed them to explain this natural order.

Some sinologists have argued (Roetz does not cite these sources) that concepts of natural law can be found in Chinese thought, as "a fighting weapon in Man's struggle against the tyranny of unlimited power and authority."[522] For Shih, certain Chinese words "possess some of the meanings of the Western concepts of Natural Law" insofar as one finds in Chinese thought appeals "to the authority of

---

[521] Lloyd, 1979.
[522] Shih, 1953.

an imagined and quite freely idealized antiquity, the Golden Age of the ancient sage-rulers," or appeals "to the Way of Heaven or Nature, which is the Law of Nature."[523] More recently, Norman Ho has argued that only the "Ming dynasty Confucian philosopher Wang Yangming's (1472–1529) philosophical system can be understood as a coherent natural law theory."[524] But both arguments by Shih and Ho cannot but be identified as flawed if we abide strictly to the meaning of natural law in the Western tradition.

First, in the case of Ho, he can only identify a "coherent" concept of natural law in one isolated thinker, rather than in a long line of thinkers, as we find in the West from Roman to medieval times. Second, Ho says that it is in the reference of Yangming to the "heart-mind" that we find a principle of natural law that is "discoverable via reason," but, as I will explain soon below, the term "heart-mind" points to the fact that the Chinese never clearly differentiated the faculty of the mind from other bodily organs, but remain rather Homeric, in this respect, through history. Third, it is a big stretch for Shih and Ho to claim that vague notions about "the Mandate of Heaven" or Yangming's use of the word "Pure Knowing," are equivalent to the long treatises of Aristotle on the nature of reasoning, or to Aquinas's long explanation of the meaning of natural law. For Aquinas, natural law referred to the God-given ability of humans to understand the nature of things, and how to legislate just laws, through "the light" of the rational powers given to them by God. As we shall see soon, Confucian thought in general, as well as Yangming's thought, all remained within the Chinese "embedded" tradition of thinking, without reason ever identified as a separate faculty in its own right, and as the "light" that comprehends the laws of nature and society.[525] Chinese law relied instead on such Confucian terms as "propriety, politeness," which appeal to traditional modes of behavior. Roetz does not engage with these debates, but prefers to cite vaporous expressions in this or that Chinese thinker about how they "remind" him of the Western principle of natural rights, going as far as to cite

---

[523] Ibid, 123.

[524] Ho, 2017.

[525] Aquinas argued that other than certain truths that God has revealed to us, such as the revelation that Jesus is the Son of God, which are beyond the capacity of reason to comprehend, and thus depend on faith, humans were granted with a natural ability to reason about the first principles and causes, and to strive thereby towards knowledge of the divine. The natural sciences can only develop through the use of our capacity to reason and on the basis of sensory observations.

ancient Chinese sayings "reminiscent" of John Rawls' twentieth century theory of justice.[526]

Weber recognized that in certain respects, the political order in China operated according to rational bureaucratic principles, in the hierarchy of offices and in the formal equality of opportunity built into its system of examinations, which were open to everyone and organized in a very strict sequence, starting at the local level all the way to the court of the Emperor, with the candidates examined according to the same standards. But Weber called China's bureaucracy "traditional" in the degree to which it was not based on specialized knowledge, or no technical qualifications were required for particular offices. The exams tested the ability of the candidates to know the classics by heart, acquire a polished literary style, learn how to write in excellent calligraphy, as well as master the rules of polite behavior. In the words of Weber's still valid assessment, "the Chinese examinations did not test any special skills, as do our modern national and bureaucratic examinations regulations for jurists, medical doctors, or technicians."[527]

Moreover, as Weber also observed, in China "the fetters of the kinship group were never shattered."[528] The Chinese masses were not composed of individuals but of kinship clans, and these clans exhibited a very high degree of "collective solidarity"[529] where "filial piety" was strictly mandated, from the children all the way up to the high patron of the family tree. Although Confucianism called upon office holders to be "humane" as rulers within a bureaucratic hierarchy, these ethical principles, duties of honesty and fair treatment, were hardly conceptualized and hardly exhibited in practice as impersonal principles, beyond one's kinship network. Every office holder and every resident of a town was inextricably tied to an extended family network. So, although the offices were open to everyone, the most prominent families were in control of these offices, since the kinship network was crucial for the funding of the education of sons, and this meant that the most prominent families could gain control over the distribution of offices, and thus gain access to the income generated by these offices and the administrative services afforded to the office-holder. Kinship ties, not rational-bureaucratic principles, ran deep into the state, coupled with a Confucian doctrine that taught that

---

[526] Roetz,115, 269. We will discuss Rawls' liberal pluralism at length in Chapter XI.

[527] Weber, 1951, 121.

[528] As cited in Bendix, 1977, 100.

[529] This wording comes from Talcott Parsons, the foremost American sociologist of the first half of the twentieth century, before he was dethroned by Marxists and feminists; see Talcott Parsons (1968, 542).

the interests of the family, filial piety, and ancestor worship were crucial to the stability of social relations. This reality explains the pervasiveness of nepotism and favoritism in China to this day.

It is hard to envision exactly how China could have produced experts in jurisprudence and rational law when, in Weber's words:

> Chinese philosophy itself did not have a speculative, systematic character, as Hellenistic philosophy had. . . . Chinese philosophy did not have a rational-formalist character, as occidental jurisprudence has. . . . Chinese philosophy did not give birth to scholasticism because it was not professionally engaged in logic. . . . The very concept of logic remained absolutely alien to Chinese philosophy, which was bound to script, was not dialectical, and remained oriented to purely practical problems.[530]

Chinese thinkers never sought any metaphysical foundations for their claims. For Confucians and Daoists, human society should be a microcosm of the order they saw in "Heaven," but they never sought to explain the nature of "Heaven"—why it was orderly, how it operated, by what rules, under whose guidance, and how exactly it was connected to human society. The Chinese were, and still are, a strikingly utilitarian people, interested in this world, not in any world beyond. Confucianism consisted of social ethical precepts about how to behave in this world in a way that would ensure the harmonious functioning of society. As Talcott Parsons put it, "the rationalism of Confucian ethic . . . was a rationalism of this world . . . nothing to do with transcendental things. . . . Chinese society placed an unquestioned value on the good things of this world, above all wealth, long life and a good name."[531]

As it is, for all his talk about Chinese transcendentalism, Roetz confesses towards the end of his book that Chinese ideals were merely intended to "safeguard" the "conventional ethos" of the existing order, "not to be played off against" it, a view close to Weber's own assessment.[532] Weber also observed that the Confucian ideal about the perfectibility of the gentleman was not about remaking the world, but about sustaining the ideal qualities of the governing principle of the cosmic order and the golden past. Weber thus wrote about how,

---

[530] Weber, 1951, 121–127.

[531] Parsons, 1968, 548.

[532] Roetz, 123.

the conventionally educated man will participate in the old ceremonies with due and edifying respect. He controls all his activities, physical gestures, and movements as well with politeness and with grace in accordance with the status mores and the commands of propriety, a basic concept of Confucianism. . . . 'Cultivated man' . . . is a man who is both inwardly and in relation to society harmonically attuned and poised in all social situations. . . . The corresponding individual ideal was the elaboration of the self as a universal and harmoniously balanced personality. . . . For the Confucian ideal man, the gentleman, 'grace and dignity' were expressed in fulfilling traditional obligations.

Roetz can't deny that "Confucianism accepts the given world," and that the principle of humaneness was intended to "moderate" the failures of office holders to live according to the conventional ethos of Confucianism.

Confucianism cannot really take its leave of the world of subordination and inequality. Wherever necessary, it restrains the ruling powers, but it hardly disputes their position which invites abuse. This means that the potential of its postconventional, egalitarian, moral side does not really win out over the conventional side which basically accepts the given structures as they have always been. . . . This potential is hardly employed to bring about structural change, but primarily to make the given world more human and prevent the necessary fulfilment of customary duties from its degeneration into opportunism and corruption. [533]

In recent decades sinologists have been desperately trying to discredit Weber's *Religion of China* (originally published 1915). But a book refuting the essential observations of Weber remains to be found, including his observation that Chinese thought tended to be static, always revolving around the same classics, and always using the same concepts. One can say that Weber was somewhat uncharitable when he observed that "no entirely independent thinker has appeared" since "Chinese philosophy . . . was developed . . . during Antiquity . . . or since the unification [of China], at about the beginning of the Christian era."[534] But no book so

---

[533] Weber, 1951, 156, 228, 277, 279.
[534] Ibid, 152. Paraphrasing Weber rather than quoting lines in their exact ordering.

far, including Roetz's, as we have seen above, can point to any major conceptual revolutions in China in opposition to the ancient Confucian classics.

Frederick Mote

For a chapter I wrote on Weber in *Uniqueness,* I read a substantial amount of Weber's works and secondary sources, but I did not read *Religion of China*, although I cited John Love's observation in "Max Weber's Orient" that "a considerable body of contemporary literature gives support to Weber's argument and indeed furthers it."[535] Having now studied *Religion of China*, I can't emphasize enough how relevant and insightful this book remains. In *Uniqueness* I brought to bear a number of scholars who, on the one hand, claimed (ostensibly) that Chinese thought was dynamic and innovative, but, on the other hand, ended up acknowledging that Chinese thought, aside from some refinements and disputations over interpretation of concepts, remained canonical from its inception in ancient times right into the twentieth century. I noted how Frederick Mote opened his 1989 book, *Intellectual Foundations of China*, with celebratory statements about the "vitality" of China's culture, only to later emphasize "the unbroken thread" of China's philosophical history, and the fact that ancient Chinese thought "developed . . . without any fundamental modification other than its refinement and more detailed articulation."[536]

I also brought attention to the way Jacques Gernet, in his authoritative work, *A History of Chinese Civilization*, told his readers that Chinese cultural life between 1650 and 1800 was characterized by "openness of mind and intellectual curiosity" as opposed to "conformism"—without coming up with a single thinker in this period who was not singularly preoccupied with the classics, commenting on them, debating, or re-evaluating past interpretations. Nowhere in Gernet's book, or, for that matter, in any book I have read, do we get a sense that China after the Axial Age witnessed intellectuals with the originality of Descartes, Hobbes, Kepler, Harvey, Huygens, Buffon, or Newton. The one book I would like to address now is Frederick Mote's *Imperial China, 900–1800*, a comprehensive study of about 1107 pages. This is a crucial source for a number of reasons. First, it is the most commanding book written on the history of China for the medieval and

---

[535] Love, 2000, 179.
[536] Duchesne, 2011, 288.

modern epochs. Second, Mote is eager to showcase the "extraordinary" periods of "flowering of thought and learning" China saw at various points during this long epoch. Third, and conversely, he actually ends up arguing that every single variation in Chinese thought (by "the utilitarians, the idealists, the rationalists") occurred "within a revitalized Confucianism."[537]

What comes across from Mote's book is that the main lines of inquiry in the intellectual history of China consisted of three or perhaps four key phases "in the development of Confucianism." After the ancient establishment of the Confucian school, Daoism, and Legalism (which is really a variation within Confucianism), we have to wait until the Song era to witness the rise of "Neo-Confucianism" led principally by Lu Xiangshan (1139–1191) and Zhu Xi (1130–1200). Daoism and the Indian philosophy of Buddhism were undoubtedly playing a role, but the concern of the major thinkers was invariably about how to employ Confucian thought to either integrate or counter certain insights from these unofficial currents.

Lu Xiangshan was the most influential exponent of what is known as the idealist School of the Mind within Confucianism. Although he was formally opposed to Buddhism, some detect in this idealist variation the Buddhist emphasis on the importance of the subjective awareness of the mind in the apprehension of reality. One of the major sayings of Xiangshan was: "The universe is my mind and my mind is the universe."[538] However, it was the School of Principle led by Zhu Xi, with its emphasis on "the learning of principle," the acceptance of the Way as the ultimate reality, rather than the subjective mind as the ultimate reality, which came to dominate Chinese thought until the end of the imperial era. Zhu Xi is the one held responsible for the foundation of Neo-Confucianism, the most significant outlook in China's history after Confucianism. For this reason, Mote designates Zhu Xi as "the most influential figure in Chinese intellectual history after Confucius himself." Zhu Xi "reaffirmed the ancient Chinese cosmological system shared by all the indigenous schools of thought." His main scholarly work consisted in grouping "together four books: the *Analects* of Confucius, the Mencius, and two chapters called *The Great Learning* and *The Doctrine of the Mean*, taken from the Han period compilation as the Book of Rites." These books became known as *The Four Books*, "the foundation of Chinese thought thereafter."

Zhu Xi's fastidiousness about the classics reflected his conviction that the ideas to be accepted in China "all had to have a textual basis in the Confucian canon."

[537] Mote, 1999, 119, 929.
[538] Ibid, 339.

This solidification of the canon would allow for a clearer identification of those extraneous elements in Chinese thinking that were original to Daoist and Buddhist thought, rather than original to Confucian thought. A century after Zhu Xi's death in 1200, "his editings of the Confucian classics," writes Mote, "were officially designated the standard for the civil service examinations; they remained so through successive dynasties and successive eras of cultural growth, until the abolition of the civil service examination in 1905."[539]

But Mote can't help playing up to multicultural expectations, writing later in his book that the sixteenth century witnessed a "profoundly transforming change in the realm of thought" in the writings of Wang Yangming (whom we just met above) and his followers.[540] Yet when we read his argument carefully, we find that Yangming's novelty consisted in elaborating and affirming the idealist School of the Mind, which had been neglected after the complete consolidation of Zhu Xi's School of Principles. Some may say that in Yangming's writings about the importance of utilizing one's mind in apprehending the good, the importance of personal involvement in life's duties, and his emphasis on gaining self-awareness about one's obligations as a gentleman, we have an introspective-transcendentalist outlook.

Mote cites Yangming's phrase, "Search within your own mind," and then says that Yangming enunciated the idea that knowledge is "innate to the mind," which may lead some to think that he was some sort of Cartesian before Descartes. But the use of Western terms, "idealist," "rationalist," "mind," and "innate," create more confusion than clarification. There is nothing comparable in Chinese history to the *Discourse on Method* or the *Meditations on First Philosophy* by Descartes, which were thoroughly deductive works with sustained arguments building upon each other with analytical precision, rather than intuitive statements. A well-known insight of Yangming is: "The faculty of innate knowledge is to know good and evil."[541] But there is no explanation why this is so; and, as Mote adds later, the Chinese concept of "mind" included the "heart." What Yangming did, as Mote admits, was to "re-orient Neo-Confucian thought" in a more authentic direction, closer to the ancient philosophy of Mencius, who was known for his idealistic conception of human nature within Confucianism. Yangming wanted Confucian scholars and officials to be sincere in their actions, to fully commit their

---

[539] Ibid, 340–43.
[540] Ibid, 654.
[541] Ibid, 676–683.

minds to the observance of the good, rather than looking to their bureaucracy positions as a mere means to gain wealth, following rules and rituals without sincere feelings for the "good" of their local communities.

Finally, Mote writes about "a late flowering of thought and learning" in the eighteenth century "that changed the character of Neo-Confucian thought." This movement has been called "evidential research" and even "empirical research" and "inductive method." Yet, again, when one actually reads Mote's argument, it becomes clear that there was nothing "inductive" and nothing really new about this movement. The "evidential research" movement was simply a "philological" call for a careful exegetical reading of Confucian texts "employed" in "Han times" (206 BC–AD 220). The members of this movement, in Mote's words, believed that "Han learning stood first of all for the systematic examination of texts, and for rigorous demonstration of meaning utilizing inductive reasoning." Its argument was that the validity of one's ideas depended on the degree to which one could demonstrate that one's ideas were based on a careful reading of the classic texts, which involved "delving into etymology and semantics."[542]

It is amazing that some scholars have pointed to this "evidential research" as evidence of a scientific method in China comparable to Galilean and Newtonian science.[543] Kai-wing Chow seems to be accurate in his depiction of this movement in late imperial China as entailing the "rise of Classicism, ritualism, and purism." Chow believes that this evidential (k'ao-cheng) movement was really a response to the threatened position of the Chinese gentry, an effort to restore an elite culture considerably weakened by the commercialization of Chinese society during Ming times. The philological scholarship was a subsidiary component of a broader socio-cultural movement by a class seeking to preserve its status. This movement rejected the Ming Neo-Confucian School of the Mind, with its appeal to the innate capacities of the common people, and instead stressed the distinction between the elite gentry and the commoners. "Filial devotion, loyalty to the monarch, and wifely fidelity"—these were their mottoes combined with "punctilious observance

---

[542] Ibid, 928, 931–34.

[543] Ian Morris, in his highly touted book, *Why the West Rules—For Now: The Patterns of History, and What They Reveal About the Future* (2010) gushes over this movement with the outrageous estimation that it "paralleled Western Europe's scientific revolution." In a review essay (2011b) I reviewed the many ridiculous claims this book makes about the West's place in world history, and about China's intellectual history and the Islamic world.

of hierarchical relationship, and the exaltation of the ritual authority of the Classics."[544]

A Note on Transcendentalism

One can't break with "unreflected substantiality" without reason being aware of itself as that through which all claims must be ascertained. Roetz uses words from Benjamin Schwartz to define transcendence as "a kind of standing back and looking beyond, a kind of critical, reflective questioning of the actual and a new vision of what lies beyond."[545] But this definition is inadequate. If this "reflective" questioning is based on authoritative precepts which have not been grounded through reason by humans who are consciously aware that these precepts are reason's own creations, then we can't talk about transcendence. German idealists Kant, Fichte, Schelling, and Hegel, were at the forefront writing about the "self-grounding" of reason as a form of transcendentalism, wherein thought comprehends itself as the ultimate point of validity, and one explains therein why one prefers certain values and precepts over others, as opposed to relying on external givens (revelation, the Dao, the Mandate of Heaven, poetic inspiration).

What Hegel observed about Chinese thought is not that it was devoid of utilitarian reasoning and Confucian-conventional ideals, but that its thinkers were still absorbed within their natural and social worlds, and their values and notions of truthfulness were premised upon some pre-constituted order. Chinese thinkers remained in a state of tutelage following customs, rituals, and mysterious forces in heaven, rather than adopting maxims by means of rational deliberation. Weber did not write about the self-grounding of reason, nor did he say that China was "substantively irrational," but rather that "Confucian rationalism meant rational adjustment to the world," not rational mastery of the world. "The power of *logos*, of defining and reasoning, has not been accessible to the Chinese." Chinese "intellectual tools remained in the form of parables, reminding us of the means of expression of Indian chieftains rather than of rational argumentation."[546]

Logos comes from a verb meaning "to speak" and refers to the words that a speaker uses to back up a claim in a disputation. *Logos* means "rationale" or

---

[544] Chow, 1994, 3, 227.
[545] Roetz, 273.
[546] Weber, 1951, 248, 125, 127.

"argument." Much of what Chinese philosophers have said are assertions, not arguments. Aristotle was the highest point of Greek *logos* in his systematic efforts to explain what standards must be employed to decide what knowledge is. Knowledge is giving a reason, giving an account of why we believe what we believe, offering premises for a conclusion, defining the basic terms making up our statements. But it is more than that, or so one learns from the German idealist tradition. By the time we get to Kant, we have a philosopher realizing that the "I think" is the agent that accompanies all the experiences and representations of the mind and that there is nothing underneath or below the "I think" determining what is to be believed, since all representations (substances, premises, faith, received traditions) obtain their authority through the thinking "I."

The categories of Kant's philosophy (i.e., unity, plurality, quantity, quality, cause and effect, necessity and contingency) are transcendental because they cannot be perceived but are presupposed by reason independently of experience; they are reason's own creatures. Kant, however, thought that the categories could not be extended beyond the limits of possible experience, and that we could not, therefore, know things-in-themselves, the ultimate nature of things, or God, the soul, ultimate causes, not even the transcendental subject could be known, since it is not itself an object of sensory experience, but is something presupposed by the fact that all the representations of the thinking "I" cannot but be the representations of a thinking "I" conscious of its mental experiences.

But this means that Kant left us with something that is accessible only to thinking, which cannot be defined as an external object in charge of thinking, since it is beyond experience and a creation of the mind. It is the mind that gives itself its criteria for thinking about things, and in thinking about this, the European mind came to grasp itself as the ultimate authoritative agent. This was not the traditional, pre-critical rationalism of Spinoza and Leibniz, since Kant denied that the categories produced by the thinking subject could reveal the nature of reality as such. Kant also argued that freedom could only be attributed to humans, since only they can act according to principles uncaused by anything other than their own self-legislating reasons, against the urging of the senses and received traditions. Only a human being can freely act on what ought to be done. From Hegel we learn, beyond Kant, that this was a historical achievement, not a philosophical discovery of the human mind per se. It was in-and-through the actual historical practices of modern Europeans, of giving and asking for reasons, without taking anything for granted, without relying on things beyond reason, that we see the emergence of self-authorizing subjects. It was not the human mind as such that came to this realization, but a community of individuals at a particular point in the history of Europe.[547]

The Embedded Chinese Mind

But there is another school which says that the Chinese mind was superior to the Western mind, on the grounds that this mind, long before the Western mind, came to the realization that thinking inevitably occurs within a context, and that only a naïve culture would assume that it could live outside itself, or transcend the culturally-specific context from which all thinking emerges. The idea that all knowledge is "contextual" is very dominant in the West today, and for this reason this school has had a wider appeal than the "universalist" school. Among the publications which have made this case, the most comprehensive is *Thinking from the Han: Self, Truth, and Transcendence in Chinese and Western Culture*, by David L. Hall and Roger T. Ames. This book effectively draws a fundamental contrast between the "transcendentalism" of European thinkers and the "embeddedness" of Chinese thinkers. It is not surprising that the authors (Ames won the Confucius Culture Award in 2013) side with the Chinese. Fighting "Eurocentrism" and downplaying Europeans are official policies in our universities. I would like to reverse this argument with the claim that our ability to understand other cultures presupposes a transcendental self that is capable of identifying and reflecting upon its own thinking, without being swallowed up by a contextual setting.

The advocates of cross-cultural dialogue, anthropologists generally, and the multicultural West, think that understanding other cultures entails adopting the other culture's perspective, putting oneself inside the shoes of the other inhabitants, by bracketing one's own particular perspective. Westerners, they insist, must let go of their own cultural presuppositions, their individualistic and rationalistic outlooks, if they are to grasp the perspective of the Other. The Western worldview

---

[547] This schematic statement will hardly convince those who are justifiably skeptical of idealism. I bring up German idealism and Hegel throughout this book. Chapter VI includes a long section evaluating the philosophical contributions of the civilizations of the world. This brief statement benefited from a reading of Immanuel Kant's *Prolegomena to Any Future Metaphysics* (1950) and Hegel's *Philosophy of Mind* (2007). To get a sense of Kant's place within European philosophy, see the very readable and studious biography of Manfred Kuehn, *Kant: A Biography* (2001). I would also recommend Anthony Kenny's *The Rise of Modern Philosophy, Volume 3 of A New History of Western Philosophy* (2006).

is only one among many, and using this perspective is bound to obfuscate matters, resulting in the imposition of one's concepts upon the "Other."

Cultural relativists have failed to understand that the West developed appropriate disciplines (ethnography, anthropology) and methodologies (pragmatism, historicism, hermeneutics) to understand other cultures and other historical epochs, because only the West produced a transcendental mind able to stand outside its own cultural norms, to understand how it is bounded by a particular context. In this respect, insofar as Western thinkers learned to define the nature of the mind, separate it from all other externalities, they were able to stand above any limiting context, and thus demonstrate the unconditional character of their judgments.

The inhabitants of advanced civilizations such as China and India did exhibit, during the Axial Age, inklings of a reflective mode of thinking, a mode of critiquing their rulers and norms on the basis of higher moral principles. But the Confucian and Daoist stance, as well as the Indian Buddhist and Hindu beliefs, were stalled in their development, eventually degenerating into mere custom and acceptance of what was asserted by the ancients. Academics today, however, are instructing their students that Westerners must become more like the cultural beings of other civilizations, and embrace the outlooks of the East, where the thinking self is inescapably embedded to a social context, obedient and complaint.

The authors of *Thinking from the Han* thus tell us that we must overcome the Western notion of the individual abstracted from any context if we are to understand the uniqueness of Chinese culture, with its notion of the self "embedded within a ceaseless process of social, cultural, and natural changes," in which self and society are never disjointed from each other, but are always seen as "mutually entailing and interdependent correlatives."[548] They don't realize that only the Western transcendental ego could have generated the ideas and methodologies necessary to apprehend Chinese ways, which is why Westerners, as we shall see in later chapters, mapped the location of China on world maps and wrote proper historical accounts of this civilization, dating with precision its dynasties, major events, and overall historical pattern—whereas the Chinese did not become self-conscious of the ways in which their selves have been embedded within a ceaseless process of powers and forces outside them, because they failed to differentiate the thinking mind from its surroundings.

---

[548] Hall and Ames, 27.

Transcendental West Invented Pragmatic Method and Hermeneutics

Hall and Ames have dedicated their lives to the understanding of Chinese culture. They believe there are no "universally human, culturally neutral grounds to which we can appeal as a basis of comparison of particular cultures," since any account will necessarily "presuppose something of the theoretical stance of the tradition from which the analysis and evaluation begins."[549] Only a "pragmatic method" provides us with an escape from the Western arrogance of a "disembedded" or detached "I" capable of adjudicating over different traditions. According to them, we must reject the Western effort to reach a universal account of moral rationality, and call instead for morals that are consciously embedded in historically grounded social practices. We should rely on pragmatic thinkers such as George Herbert Mead, John Dewey, and Richard Rorty, for an appropriate vocabulary for understanding how the self is socially constituted. This pragmatism, they argue, fits right in with the Chinese perspective that the person can never be identified in abstraction from the social roles that define and constitute the person. Mead was correct in writing that "the unity of the self is constituted by the unity of the entire relational pattern of social behavior and experience in which the individual is implicated." Mead's notion of the self "as a field of social relations constituting and constituted by the person is fundamental to our understanding of Chinese conceptions of self-hood."[550]

Besides pragmatism, Hall and Ames mention hermeneutics and poststructuralism as forms of thinking that allow us to overcome the "dualistic thinking" of the West, with its separation of mind and matter, self and society, and its pretensions to a view that is objectively valid, stable, and directly meaningful, through an independent subject that is somehow able to produce truths above any historically specific conditions. But don't these two academics realize that pragmatism, hermeneutics, and poststructuralism are Western products? They acknowledge this in a low-key way, stating that these schools of thought arose late in Western history; and yet their argument is that Westerners have been unable to understand Chinese thinking, because they have relied on dualistic ways of thinking. They believe that their pragmatic and "historicist" method is the best way to apprehend the meanings of Chinese words and writings, against Western-centric readings,

---

[549] Ibid, xii.
[550] Cited in Hall and Ames, 42–43.

which judge other cultures in terms of such Western concepts as "mind," "self," "transcendence," "person," "subject," "object," which lack corresponding terms in the Chinese language, or have very different meanings within Chinese culture. So, implicitly, without wanting to draw attention to the irony of it all, and perhaps without even recognizing it, Hall and Ames rely on Western schools of thought to criticize Western-centric readings of Chinese culture.

What Hall and Ames have done is not incidental, but a powerful dogma in academia today. Academics believe they have deconstructed Western thinking, the scientific idea that we can formulate concepts that capture the essence of reality, what is real and substantial behind the appearances, and the Western idea that we can produce concepts about the best political society for humans generally. The reviews of this book praise the efforts of the authors to think about China through Chinese ways of thinking, rather than through Western concepts. Yet, when we examine the schools of thought these academics have relied upon, pragmatism, hermeneutics, postmodernism—all of them grew inside the West.

The very academics who say that we need to contextualize our thinking, because it is impossible to have a view from nowhere, fail to contextualize the particular historical roots of their way of thinking. The bibliography of *Thinking from the Han* lists about 260 sources, of which only thirty-six are from Chinese authors; and if we do not count the obvious use of primary Chinese sources or authors, such as Confucius and Mencius, there are only twelve books listed by contemporaneous Chinese academics. We are dealing here with an outstanding lapse in interpretative self-awareness that is pervasive in current academia. It is not that they have relied mostly on Western sources, but, more importantly, that the knowledge, ideas, concepts, and methodologies which taught these Western academics to think from the perspective of the Han people were originated by Europeans.

What makes this so culturally bizarre is that Hall and Ames argue that if we think through Chinese ways of thinking, we will learn that it was the Chinese who produced pragmatic and hermeneutical ways of thinking. Before Westerners even had a clue, apparently, the Chinese were already saying that individuals are "radically situated as persons-in-context, inhering in a world defined by specific social, cultural, and natural conditions."[551] The Chinese, we are supposed to believe, were always aware that it is not possible to draw an artificial divide between subject and object, individual and society, mind and matter, and that only the invention of a

---

[551] Ibid, 264.

pragmatic method by Europeans in the nineteenth century finally allowed them to see how profoundly ahead the Chinese were in their pragmatic and hermeneutical thinking since ancient times.

What Hall and Ames fail to realize is that the Chinese have never self-consciously thought of the way knowledge is context-bound, the way the "consciousness," "will," "desires," and "ideas" of individuals are culturally situated. The Chinese mind has always been context-bound without being aware of it, because it has been unable to stand back from its surroundings, the conventions of its Chinese context, to reflect upon the ways it has been culturally situated.[552] The Western mind was able to develop methodologies to understand texts from different eras and different cultures, because this is the only culture that learned how to draw ontological distinctions between mind and matter, individual and society, the three parts of the soul, and so on. In the course of this development, this mind eventually developed particular sciences—physics, chemistry, biology, botany, sociology, economics, et cetera—to explain different aspects of reality, newly emerging properties, while also realizing that the concept of "man in general" is limited by historically determinate factors.

Pragmatism Presupposes a Transcendental Mind

The prior ability of Whites to discover the distinctiveness of the faculty of the mind eventually made possible the pragmatic turn, the development of hermeneutics. This transcendental capacity to detach oneself from one's personal experience is not an aptitude that can be understood outside a uniquely Western context. The beginnings of this transcendental capacity are to be found in ancient

---

[552] In Etienne Balazs's words, China was "roused to a new self-awareness" and the Chinese learned to "discover their own country"—their historical, geographical and intellectual placement in the world—only after it was impacted by the more advanced culture of the West (1964, 5). Balazs's book, *Chinese Civilization and Bureaucracy*, is one of many currently "outdated" Eurocentric books for claiming that the Chinese state had "complete control over all activities of social life.... Trade, mining, building, ritual, music, schools, in fact the whole of public life and a great deal of private life as well" (17). I am sure some have been equally irritated by Balazs's view that, even though Hegel overplayed the "immobility" of China, "Hegel was right" about the "unchanging character of Chinese social structure, and in this he is singularly in accord with the opinion of almost all historians of China" (15). At the same time, Balazs does not detract from emphasizing the more advanced economy of China through the Middle Ages, citing Marco Polo's well-known observations about the incredible size and commercial activity of Chinese cities, in contrast to the quieter and smaller cities of Europe.

Greece when the mind was identified as a distinctive faculty in distinction from everything else, and when Greek philosophers began to reflect self-consciously about the inner and the outer world, the rational and the irrational, weaker and stronger arguments. Through a long historical course, Westerners also came to understand the limitations of reason and the ways in which thinking is always embedded, with Kant claiming that there are things that lie beyond reason, things-in-themselves, and thus implicitly saying that reason is aware of its limits, and Hegel then arguing that insofar as reason can think about its limits, it is able to think outside its limits.

Just because one learns to contextualize the transcendental mind, it does not follow that this mind is an illusion, for this mind did seek to rise, in a self-conscious manner, above personal biases and conventions, and it did come up with universal principles in both the sciences and ethics. It is also a fact that this mind came up with a variety of pragmatic methodologies to understand other cultures in their own terms. The understanding of other peoples from their own perspective presupposes indeed a mind that can transcend its own context and look at the "other" from a more neutral perspective. The ability of Hall and Ames to provide us with insights about the Chinese mind is a result of a Western education that taught them how to stand above their own prejudices in order to bring out the Chinese ways of thinking. The aim of this chapter is to identify the multicultural Western prejudices of Hall and Ames, so we can have a more objective and accurate assessment of Chinese thought.

Hall and Ames acknowledge that "one of the most striking features of Chinese intellectual culture from the perspective of the Western interpreter is the absence of transcendence in the articulation of its spiritual, moral, and political sensibilities."[553] For this reason, Hall and Ames criticize scholars who have applied Western transcendent concepts to interpret such Chinese terms as "Heaven" and "the Way." The Chinese concept of a cosmic order, they argue, cannot be conceived as a transcendent ruler, since the Confucian concept of "Heaven" or the Daoist concept of "the Way," are "this-worldly," referring to the world as a whole, not outside spirits who created the universe, but indwelling within nature and man. Since the natural and the human are continuous in Chinese thinking, it is misleading to apply Western dualistic concepts such as mind and matter, man and society, God and Nature. In China, they argue, there is no rational "view from nowhere." The thinking subject is always embedded within the world he is interpreting, and so

---

[553] Hall and Ames, 189.

he cannot know the "objective truth."[554] Hall and Ames believe that this Chinese outlook is "more liberating and friendly."

The first obvious dilemma in this account is that all the sciences developed by Europeans have been assimilated by non-Europeans. This shows that there is a universalizability in the sciences of the West, a transcendental aspect, even if we reject the idea that the sciences can ever apprehend the ultimate nature of things, and even if we notice that Europeans are really the ones who are conducting most of the research about way things are the way they are, rather than merely using science to make things. The second obvious dilemma is that Europeans were the ones who developed self-conscious philosophies examining the ways in which thinking is contextualized.

Saying that all knowledge is historically situated, the expression of a particular people, is not enough. If all knowledge is contextual, then all knowledge claims are equally valid. We have to ask why the West developed all the theories about how knowledge is context-bound, and why the West produced all the modern sciences. Self-conscious cultural relativism—a relativism in which subjects are not completely absorbed by their culturally specific world views—presupposes a subject that has come to a transcendental understanding of the relativistic views of other cultures, and is thus able to understand its own relativism, and in this way transcend it, and understand that it is the measure of all other cultures. The key to this transcendental standpoint is no longer a belief in a God standing outside as creator of the universe, or a belief in unchanging essences determining what there is, or a belief that reason can come up with moral principles for all cultures. Whenever we talk about a transcendental being uncaused by anything other than itself, or about natural rights inhering in all humans outside time and outside any social order, or about natural (transcendent) laws regulating the universe, we are inescapably talking about a historically situated European human who is positing these transcendental ideas. There can be no proper comparative cultural assessments without a conscious acknowledgment of a European transcendental self that is aware of its presuppositions, aware that its consciousness—not any Natural Law, not any God—is the ultimate adjudicator of knowledge.

Hall and Ames would have us believe that the Chinese never set out to find ultimate principles or ultimate causes upon which all else depends ontologically because they always knew that such endeavors were bound to fail, since it is beyond humans to know what is ultimate without presupposing some anterior

---

[554] Ibid, 247.

principle or cause. It would be more accurate to say that the Chinese did not care to explain the why of things, the root of things, but took the world as it was given to their senses and intuitions; they did not concern themselves either with offering criteria as to what makes an argument weaker or stronger. And that's why they did not develop a logic and a metaphysics about the causes of things and the essence of things. The Mohist school discussed valid inference and the conditions of correct conclusions but it was mostly about rhetorical analogies.[555]

From the Piagetian perspective we examined in the previous chapter, we can say that the Chinese mind did not rise above the concrete operational stage—that is, above the third stage in Piaget's theory of cognitive development. While the Chinese mind showed signs of formal operational thinking in some of its mathematical operations and rationalization of state bureaucracy, it did so only at an elementary level. In stark contrast to Hobbes, who employed analytical reasoning in order to reach generalizations about the nature of political power, the ideas espoused in *The Analects* of Confucius, for example, are tied to actual historical times and personalities. As Burton Watson notes:

> In the *Analects*, therefore, the reader will find no lengthy discussions of terminology or expositions of ideas. Instead, moral and political concepts are presented in terms of particular individuals, the teacher Confucius and the disciple or other persons with whom he is conversing and the particular circumstances under discussion.[556]

Like the concrete operational mind, the Confucian mind was limited to thought concerning things that were available to immediate perception about past virtuous rulers; it did not seek to reach general rules, or understand cause-effect relations detached from particular contexts. The writings of Confucius consist of aphorisms advising future rulers and officials how the ideal gentleman should comport himself if he is to meet the established conventions set in the past, the roles and rituals the ideal gentleman must follow in order to rule properly according to the Way.

Hall and Ames portray the Western concept of self as being based on the misleading supposition that an individual by himself can know who he is without any

---

[555] Weber was not far off the mark when he observed about Chinese thought generally: "Puns, euphemisms, allusions to classical quotations, and refined and purely literary intellectuality were considered the conversational ideal of the genteel man." *Religion of China*, 132.

[556] Watson, 2007, 7.

relationships with other humans in a state of complete isolation. They argue that, in contrast to the "detached" self of the West, "in the Chinese model . . . the self is contextual," and always entails a "shared consciousness of one's roles and relationships." In China, "one is self-conscious, not in the sense of being able to isolate and objectify one's essential self, but in the sense of being aware of oneself as a locus of observation by others."[557] They rely on George Herbert Mead's concept of the "I" and the "me" to illuminate what the Chinese sense of self is. For Mead, while the "I" is the active, creative agency, the "me" is the socialized aspect of the person. In Mead the "I" only acts within the context of the "me." The "me" refers to what the "I" has internalized from society. But what stands out here is the constant reliance of Hall and Ames on Western thinkers to explain the Chinese mind. We can all agree with Mead that we can't talk about the "I" outside a Western social context, that the "I" of Western thought presupposes the unique historical experience of Europeans.

Moreover, Mead can't deny that he was socialized by a transcendental culture in which the inner "I" was aware of the outer social context, insomuch as the "I" had managed to differentiate itself from the not-I, and thus identify what was specific about the thinking "I" in contradistinction to everything outside it, while eventually elucidating the many ways in which this "I" does not emerge out of thin air, but out of a particular culture. The Chinese person, however, has always been embedded within society, unable to separate the "I" analytically as an entity that is capable of thinking about what is outside. Without Westerners teaching Hall and Ames about how the self is embedded, they would not have been able to understand the Chinese conception of selfhood, because Chinese thinkers have never explained what this conception is.[558]

Hall and Ames agree with the sinologist Jacques Gernet that the Chinese language does not have correlates for the words of "mind" and "rationality." Gernet is right that the Chinese never conceived "of a sovereign and independent faculty of reason." Whenever the Chinese wrote about the act of thinking, or the act of knowing what is proper behavior, they thought of the heart as well. Truth was "set in one's heart." What this seems to imply is that the Chinese never identified the

---

[557] Hall and Ames, 26.

[558] As Weber noted: "The very word 'liberty' was foreign to the language" (1951, 147). Confucian scholars were hardly aristocratic in their predilection for kowtowing. Here is Etienne Balazs's assessment: "Even the highest officials were, as individuals, at the mercy of the absolute and despotic state, and were liable to disappear suddenly from view. Any one of them might be minister one day, and consigned to a dungeon the next" (6).

mind as the purely cognitive side of humans, and as the faculty that allows humans to think rationally, without allowing extra-mental forces to interfere.[559] But instead of reaching this conclusion, Hall and Ames instruct us to admire the way "thinking and feeling are not separate" in Chinese thought, "but occur together as the concrete human expression of the resolutely contextualized 'heart-mind.'" They point to the Chinese terms of *zhi*, *li*, and *xin*, as radically situated terms, which integrate "the human world and its natural, social, and cultural environments."[560] Academics love this stuff about feelings and the integration of humans to their environment. But if one's reasoning is radically situated, and if a culture does not have a word for reason, but something that translates as "heart-mind," then we are talking about a culture in which the mind has no identity of its own, but is subsumed by the enveloping world of feelings and natural forces. No wonder the Chinese did not develop any of the sciences, since the development of clearly identifiable fields of knowledge requires a mind that makes analytical distinctions and demarcations in the real world, even though all things are interrelated.

According to Hall and Ames, the Chinese express a higher form of individual uniqueness in their rituals than Europeans.

> Ritual practices . . . have a significant creative dimension since what distinguishes ritual from rule or principle as a source of order is that ritual practices not only inform the participant of what is proper, they are also performed by them. They are formal structures that, to be efficacious, must be personalized to accommodate the uniqueness and the quality of each participant. In this sense, ritual actions are a pliant body of codes for registering, developing, and displaying one's own sense of importance. . . . [T]he creative product is the consequence of the play between one's personal uniqueness and some continuing historical structure or aesthetic convention. New cultural models are continually emerging as qualitatively achieved persons who personalize formal ritual practices, write commentary on some canonical text, or create some particular variation on a conventional example of calligraphy or a painting prized by the tradition. . . . What is most fundamentally and significantly human in the Confucian

---

[559] Hans-Georg Moeller (2006, 38) argues that the Chinese Daoist term *xin* was used in reference to both "heart" and "mind," and that the heart "was taken to be the location of consciousness."
[560] Hall and Ames, 30, 32.

tradition are the seemingly indeterminate possibilities for growth, cultivation, and refinement.[561]

Hall and Ames know about the "centrality of ritual" in Confucian culture, and they acknowledge that rituals bespeak of a very traditional or fixed way of thinking and behaving. They also know that rituals are intended to enforce conformity. Their point that rituals can be beautifully performed, and that there is a bit of room for individuals to express themselves through the performance of rituals, is all well and good. But the effort to portray the Chinese as a highly creative people, unique in their ritualistic behaviors in ways more profound than Western individuals, is dubious. Further, there is ample historical evidence supporting Max Weber's observation that this civilization remained highly ritualistic through the modern era.

Kai-Wing Chow, cited earlier, shows that "the major intellectual trend in China from the seventeenth through the early nineteenth century was Confucian ritualism." Contrary to the claims of revisionist historians that China was following its own path to modernity, science and enlightenment, we see instead a prolonged effort by the ruling elites at "rediscovering the authentic rituals of the sages," coupled with "the core values of Confucian orthodoxy." The aim of this "rediscovery of the 'original' or 'pure' Confucian norms and language" was to fight the perceived moral laxity, "corruption of local officials and rapacity of clerks" during the last years of the decaying "late Ming" order.[562] Keep in mind that in this same period Europe saw the full consolidation of Newtonian science, a revolution in the sciences of chemistry, cartography, and geology, as we will explain in the next chapter, and a full-scale industrial revolution.[563]

---

[561] Ibid, 32–24.

[562] Chow, 1–9.

[563] For all the efforts of sinologists to portray China as a civilization progressing as much as the West, in the end they tend to recognize that China's development stalled right when the West took off after 1500. This is true even of Joseph Needham's famous multivolume work, *Science and Civilisation in China* (1954–1984). Notwithstanding his argument about Chinese originality in the invention of the magnetic compass, the clock, paper, the printing press, and other inventions, his conclusion is that China remained "traditionally" attached to its "feudal" institutions. We will discuss in the next chapters Needham's assessment of Chinese contributions to the sciences. Similarly, John King Fairbank's excellent survey, *China: A New History* (1992) shows how China continued to experience extensive growth after 1600—but "without development," that is, without real novelties in production, without modern technology, and without modern institutional arrangements. In this respect, these authors remained implicitly Weberian, even if they didn't directly endorse his sociological interpretation or mention his name.

Hall and Ames tell their students that the wonderful Chinese people make no "invidious distinctions" between things, the mental and the natural, the intellect and the emotions. The Chinese establish no "hierarchies" among things. Without "invidious distinctions," however, nothing in the natural world would have been classified, and no proper scientific study of nature would have been possible. The "bottomless complexity of particulars" Hall and Ames celebrate amounts to leaving the world as it is without trying to understand it, passively accepting one's ignorance. They claim that the "nonassertive action, and objectless desire" of the Chinese "enrich the world by allowing the process to unfold spontaneously on its own terms," but this simply means the Chinese don't subject the world to investigations.[564] It does not mean that they have allowed nature to be itself: throughout history the Chinese have been the biggest destroyers of the environment and the biggest exterminators of living forms.[565]

Amazingly, these two academics tell us that Western culture is "single-ordered," "fixed and permanent," whereas Chinese culture "guarantees novelty and uniqueness" and "variety of perspectives." If so, why did China's intellectual life barely change beyond the ancient outlooks of Confucianism, Daoism, Mohism, and Legalism? Why was the West responsible for all the technological novelties of the world after 1500s? Why were all the sciences in human history singularly developed by Europeans: geology, geography, chemistry, philosophy, paleontology, economics, archaeology, history—all of them? This is the subject of our next chapter.[566]

---

[564] Hall and Ames, 57.

[565] Mark Elvin's carefully documented work, *The Retreat of Elephants: An Environmental History of China* (2006) argues that environmental decimation has been a continuous reality in China since ancient times.

[566] Hall and Ames tell us that "the reason the biological sciences never developed in China as they did in the West is that the Westerner, encountering a strange plant or animal will ask 'How may I classify this' while the Chinese will immediately ask 'How may this be cooked'? . . . For the Chinese, knowledge is not abstract, but concrete; it is not representational, but performative and participatory" (104). We will point indeed in a later chapter that Europeans classified all things: plants, minerals, animals, solar systems and galaxies. This notion that knowledge should be "performative and participatory" is currently taking over academia. The rioters who destroyed monuments and painted graffiti everywhere during the summer of 2020 are being celebrated as "intellectual performers." Will we reach a time when students will be able to get PhDs purely by engaging in activism, howling about their feelings, and trashing the historical memorials of European greatness?

The West Conceptualized All Paradoxes of the Mind

That Europeans conceptualized all the paradoxes in history, with a minimal contribution by the Chinese, testifies to a major contrast in the intellectual trajectories of civilizations. As R. M. Sainsbury writes, "paradoxes are fun," but "unlike puzzles and teasers, which are also fun, paradoxes raise serious problems." Sainsbury defines a paradox as "an apparently unacceptable conclusion derived by apparently acceptable reasoning from apparently acceptable premises."[567] Patrick Hughes and George Brecht tell us that paradoxical propositions may be described as: *self-referential*, in which the statement refers to itself; *contradictory*, in which the statement is false and true at the same time; and *circular*, in which the statement is characterized by a vicious circle, or infinite regress.

Some believe that most paradoxes, whether they are semantic, set-theoretic, or epistemic, share the same underlying self-referential structure.[568] Consider the famous Liar's paradox: "This sentence is false." Trying to determine whether this sentence is true or false leads to a contradiction. If we conclude that the sentence is true, then it cannot be true. If we agree that the sentence is false, then the sentence is true. Either answer leads to a contradiction, or a vicious circle. This paradox is self-referential in that the sentence is talking directly about itself.

What makes the Liar's paradox more than a witty remark or a sophism is that both of the two contradictory conclusions were obtained by seemingly rigorous reasoning based on apparently sound premises. However, paradoxes come in different degrees of difficulty; some paradoxes, Sainsbury says, are "weak or shallow," based on unfounded suppositions, faulty reasoning, or ostensibly vague wording. The famous Barber paradox, he thinks, is "not very deep." This paradox asks who shaves the barber if the barber shaves all and only those villagers who do not shave themselves. This paradox makes the supposition that such a barber exists, even though such a barber or such a village does not exist.

The Western mind came up with many paradoxes for which they attempted solutions, because this mind has a peculiar inclination to seek the truth according to its own self-legislated rational capacities, rather than in acquiescence to kinship norms or theocratic mandates. It is a most dynamic mind that came up with three fundamental laws of proper reasoning: *the law of contradiction*, which states that

---

[567] Sainsbury, 1995, 1.
[568] Bolander, 2017.

a proposition cannot be both true and false; *the law of excluded middle*, which states that for every proposition, either this proposition or its negation is true; and *the law of identity*, which states that each thing is identical with itself. For the Western mind, if a claim is logically inconsistent, in violation of these laws, then the claim or the reasoning behind it must be rejected.

Europeans took Zeno's paradoxes seriously, for they seem to suggest that one could reach a logically unacceptable conclusion on the basis of sound reasoning from apparently sound premises.[569] They wondered whether these paradoxes revealed deficiencies in the way we reason, calling for improvements in our reasoning powers, a better system of logic, and a more precise usage of language. For example, Russell's paradox (conceived in 1901) of a set that includes all and only those sets that do not contain themselves as members, encouraged or was itself part of an investigation into the realm of the foundations of logic and the philosophy of mathematics, which revealed errors in classical logic that were instrumental in the development of modern logic and set theory. With this new logic, and the insights of physics and contemporary mathematics, many paradoxes have found a solution.

Reasoning Through the Contradictory Character of Reality

We would be mistaken, however, to assume that all European thinkers came to view paradoxes as mere expressions of faulty reasoning calling for a more logically perfect language, in which equivocation could not arise because all the ambiguity of everyday words was removed. Without denying the classic laws of logic, and agreeing that sentences cannot admit of self-nullifying contradictions, some Europeans came to the view that the nature of reality is contradictory, and that the human mind is limited in its capacity to offer rationally consistent answers about the ultimate questions of the universe and life. Heraclitus came to the conclusion that reality was inherently contradictory, and thus paradoxical. Other European thinkers encountered complex riddles, conundrums, and puzzles for which they believed there were no rationally justified solutions. The ultimate questions of reality were inherently unanswerable or beyond rational solution or dogmatic certainty. Sextus Empiricus (AD 160–210) believed that all belief

---

[569] Huggett, 2019.

systems were ultimately grounded in dogmatic premises or criteria, for which any attempt at their justification inevitably led to an infinite regress.

Roy Sorensen's 2003 *A Brief History of the Paradox: Philosophy and the Labyrinths of the Mind* is the best book in the English language about the many great European thinkers who have grappled for millennia with the most puzzling philosophical conundrums. Kant famously presented the four "antinomies of pure reason" as demonstrations of reason's inability to reach completeness on the most fundamental questions of the universe. He believed one could give equally justified answers for: the thesis that the universe has no beginning, and the antithesis that the universe has a beginning; the thesis that every composite substance in the world is made up of simples, and the antithesis that no composite substance in the world is made up of simples; the thesis that there is freedom in the world, and the antithesis that everything is ruled by necessity; the thesis that a necessary being is either part or cause of the world, and the antithesis that a necessary being is neither part nor cause of the world.

The rational inclination of the European mind should not be equated with arrogance. Kant believed that reason could come up with two impeccably solid arguments against the infinity of the past and against the idea that the past has a finite beginning, by rigorously showing how each of these positions leads to an equally absurd conclusion, and how each position is no less justified than the other. The thesis that there is no beginning, or an infinite past, leads to the absurd conclusion that we had to wait an infinite time to get to the present, and since we are living in the present, it follows that the past is finite with a beginning in time. But the antithesis that there is a beginning leads to the befuddling conclusion that there must have been a preceding time in which there was no world and no time, which leads to the conclusion that the past is infinite.

For Hegel, however, the very recognition by the mind that there are limits beyond which reason can't provide answers is a demonstration that cognition understands its limits, and, in this respect, is capable of going beyond those limits, by realizing that the coexistence of opposites is inherent to the nature of reality: an antinomy is not, therefore, an imperfection or defect of the mind, but a demonstration that every determination in the actual concrete world is a unity of opposing contradictions. Hegel's dialectical logic was an attempt to provide a new way of thinking through the contradictory nature of things. "Identity is merely the determination of the simple immediate, of dead being; but contradiction is the root of all movement and vitality; it is only insofar as something has a contradiction within it that it moves, has an urge and activity."[570]

While many contemporary logicians believe that Zeno's paradoxes have been solved by transfinite arithmetic, originated by Georg Cantor in the late 1800s, and that there are logically consistent ways to "solve" all paradoxes, some have come to the neo-Hegelian view known as "dialetheism," which proposes that some paradoxical inconsistencies or contradictions can be accepted without incoherence, in the sense that both "A" and "not-A" can both be true.[571] Dialetheism is associated with the development of a "paraconsistent logic" to deal with sentences in which both its affirmation and its negation are true.

Lower Degree of Sophistication of Chinese Paradoxes

The only other civilization to have articulated and debated paradoxes is China. During the Warring States period (479–221 BC), a group of scholars identified with the "School of Names" (*Míngjiā*) relished in the use of paradoxical and puzzling expressions, and in the discussion of the semantic relations between words and the world they pointed to. The intellectual culture of paradoxes in China, however, was fundamentally different from the West, in their degree of sophistication, the reaction of intellectuals to them, and the absence of philosophical reflections about the contradictory nature of the universe. The School of Names remained an isolated moment in China's intellectual history. The Confucians in control of intellectual discussions dismissed the paradoxical expressions of the School of Names as "bizarre expressions" that discouraged young minds from the proper use of language and the obligation of educated gentlemen to promote "ritual propriety and righteousness."

With the exception of brief texts attributed to Gōngsūn Lóng, very little first-hand knowledge of the figures associated with this School survived. What we know about Chinese paradoxes is mostly based on the *Xunzi*, which is an ancient Chinese collection of philosophical writings attributed to Xunzi (Xun Kuang), a third-century BC philosopher associated with the Confucian tradition, who condemned paradoxical expressions as "frivolous."[572] While members of the Mohist School (479–221 BC) summarized many of the paradoxes of the School of Names,

---

[570] Cited in Smith, 1991, 198.
[571] Priest, Graham, Berto, and Weber, 2023.
[572] Goldin, 2018.

they did so only to offer counter-arguments against what they perceived to be sophistic ideas inconsistent with the commonsense use of language.

The current academic Chen Bo makes a strong effort to show that the School of Names reached the same level of logical sophistication and use of abstract universals as the ancient Greeks, or at least "comparable to Greek civilization to some extent." But while Chen sometimes even tries to show that some Chinese paradoxes exhibited the abstract "concepts of class, kind, and membership" found in Russell's paradox about classes discovered in 1901, in the end Chen barely shows that Chinese paradoxes reached the same degree of abstraction as Zeno's famous paradoxes. He basically acknowledges this in his decision to define paradoxes in "quite a broad way, almost including all the fallacies, sophisms, puzzles, riddles, and paradoxes [which were] quite influential" in China. As Chris Fraser recognizes, there are expressions categorized as "paradoxes" that are best described as mere philosophical statements about the nature of reality, such as: "The ultimately great has no outside, call it the Great One. The ultimately small has no inside, call it the Small One." Or, "Universally care for the myriad things. Heaven and earth are one body."

Chen confounds his otherwise good analysis of Chinese paradoxes when he tries to argue that the mere utterance by Chinese philosophers of statements about whether "there is really an external world independently of us," or "do we really know the states of external things," or "do we really know other minds and their states"—actually constitute paradoxes, rather than basic epistemological and ontological questions. Chen is on stronger ground showing that the following Chinese paradoxes are "quite close to Zeno's paradoxes of motion and infinity":

"A wheel does not touch the ground."

"The shadow of a flying bird has never moved."

"A one-foot stick has taken away half of its length every day, it will still not be exhausted after ten thousand generations."

For example, the third resembles Zeno's dichotomy paradox. This Chinese paradox says that a finite-long stick can be cut into infinitely many sections since half of the length of the stick will remain no matter how many times you cut it. Zeno's dichotomy paradox states that you will never reach a finite destination no matter how fast and how long you run since any given distance that you try to cover will consist of infinitely divisible distances.

Chen admits, however, that from the Chinese version of this paradox we can only get the concept of infinite divisibility, not the concept that all motion is an illusion. Chris Fraser correctly points out that another Chinese paradox—"The barbed arrow at its swiftest, there is time when it neither moves nor stops"—which has been likened to Zeno's paradox of the arrow, is actually different in that the Chinese arrow is neither in motion nor at rest, whereas Zeno's arrow is at rest in every instant of time and does not move. Zeno invented his paradoxes in order to demonstrate, through rigorous reasoning that any kind of change was impossible, and that reality was indivisible, despite appearances to the contrary.

Fraser further notes that the "steps in the reasoning" behind the articulation of Chinese paradoxes are almost entirely based on second-hand accounts by critics of the Schools of Names, in which the reasoning about their meaning "remains confusing and the justification for them murky." While we know Zeno's paradoxes second-hand through Aristotle's writings, we do so through the highly rigorous logical mind of Aristotle. Rather than dismissing them as sophistic, Aristotle tried to find a solution to Zeno's paradoxes. Zeno's paradoxes raised serious philosophical problems in the Western tradition because they were seen to be based on sound reasoning and thus to constitute a challenge to the claims of reason about its ability to understand the nature of things. The solutions offered in contemporary times have come from mathematics, modern logic, and physics.

Moreover, whereas Europeans would come up with numerous paradoxes, some of which came to be associated with crises in European thought and with revolutionary advances in logic, in China the tradition of the School of Names dissipated, never to be improved upon. Thus, the paradoxes remained rather simple; basically, their prevailing theme, as Fraser notes, was that the distinctions we observe in the world are "not inherently fixed but relative to a standpoint" or scale. For example, take the paradox "The sky is as low as earth, mountains are level with marches." It simply says that by the scale of the Great One, the difference between the height of the sky and earth, mountains and marches, are insignificant. Another so-called paradox—"Eggs have feathers"—merely states that potential feathers are already possessed by the egg.

The most discussed Chinese paradox is one attributed to Gōngsūn Lóng that simply states: "The white horse is not [a] horse" (*báimǎ fēi mǎ*). An entire discourse developed around this paradox. The Mohist School in particular sought to counter it with the commonsense idea that words do represent or signify things, and that language should be used to communicate by appealing to commonly shared use of language, for distinguishing similar and different kinds of things. Yet, interesting as this discourse was in generating sophisticated semantic discussions, this statement seems to lack a true paradoxical nature. It seems to be a semantic claim that insofar as the terms "white horses" and "horses" denote distinct features about horses, it follows that white horses and horses cannot be equated. Critics argue that it is simply a statement that refuses to distinguish the true claim that the term "white horse" is not identical with "horse," from the false claim that the less general term "white horse" is not part of the more general term "horse."

Chen Bo tries to argue that Chinese paradoxes use abstract universals, terms that can be instantiated or exemplified by many particular things, much like the ancient Greeks and Europeans in the modern era. The academic Fung Yu Lan claims that the Chinese terms *mǎ* (horse) and *bái* (white) are used to designate abstract concepts—"horseness" and "whiteness." But Chad Hansen believes that the grammatical structure of the ancient Chinese language was such that it lacked abstract entities, such as ideas and concepts. Chinese nouns are "mass nouns," or nouns without a plural form, which do not inflect for abstraction and plurality. It seems that the best way to understand why the Chinese were unable to conceive paradoxes with a high degree of sophistication is that the Chinese mind remained embedded in its linguistic and social context, and barely reached what Jean Piaget identified as the "formal operational stage of cognition."

VI

EUROPEANS DEVELOPED ALL THE
DISCIPLINARY FIELDS OF KNOWLEDGE

Ignorance is the curse of God; knowledge is the wing wherewith we fly to heaven.

– William Shakespeare

Synopsis of Human Accomplishments in World History

The greatest divergence between Europe and the other civilizations may be that European men originated and developed all the disciplinary fields of knowledge taught in our universities: archaeology, botany, economics, sociology, anthropology, history, biology, chemistry, genetics, physics, geology, philosophy, geography—all of them, including theology.[573] This is a claim you are not allowed

---

[573] This can be ascertained through a reading of the histories of disciplines; see, for example: Gabriel Gohau, *A History of Geology* (1991); Joseph Schumpeter, *A History of Economic Analysis* (1955); Paul Bahn, *The History of Archaeology: An Introduction* (2014); Marvin Harris, *The Rise of Anthropological Theory* (1971); John Burrow, *A History of Histories: Epics, Chronicles, Romances and Inquiries from Herodotus and Thucydides to the Twentieth Century* (2009); Robert P. Multhauf, *The Origins of Chemistry* (1967); Margarita Bowen, *Empiricism and Geographical Thought from Francis Bacon to Alexander von Humboldt* (1981); Martin Rudwick, *The Meaning of Fossils: Episodes in the History of Palaeontology* (2008); Eric Osborn, *Tertullian, First Theologian of the West* (1997); Stephen Mason, *A History of the Sciences* (1967); John Gribbin, *The Scientists: A History of Science Told Through the Lives of Its Greatest Inventors* (2002); J. H. Abraham, *Origins*

to make in the universities that teach these disciplines. The official university mission of "inclusiveness, diversity, and equity" prohibits it. We are indeed in the midst of one of the most paradoxical phenomena ever witnessed: the very civilization that insisted more than any other that truthfulness requires impartial reasoning and a "weight of evidence approach" is now fabricating facts to fit with an ideological agenda. Why?

This is a question we will address in the last two chapters. Suffice it to state now that the multicultural view that members of all cultures deserve the same respect and equal rights, and that humans across the world have an "inviolable human right" to get citizenship in Western nations, are rooted in the West's supreme political ideology of liberal pluralism. Multiculturalism is not an ideological aberration one can easily explain as a "march through the institutions by cultural Marxists"; it is a deeply embedded expression of the emancipatory project of Western liberalism itself.

Demonstrating that non-Western cultures did not develop any formal disciplinary fields should not surprise us. Most of the cultures of the world, for one, never became civilizations on their own initiative. The first Western civilization was Mycenae in the second millennium BC. Before that time, the West was behind the first civilizations in the Near East. The regions of Mesopotamia and Egypt are known as the "cradle of human civilization," the site where writing, calendars, simple arithmetic, metallurgy, sailing ships, the plough, and legal codes originated. Many conclude from this that non-Europeans were the "founders" of the West. But, as we saw in Chapter III, the Axial Age was the peak level of intellectual development for most non-Western civilizations. With the arrival of iron technologies in the Near East in the late second and early first millennium BC (the evidence supports an Anatolian origin "for extractive iron metallurgy in the early second millennium BC"),[574] these civilizations experienced renewed economic growth, but once this technology spread, they would achieve mere extensive growth, that is, quantitative increases in labour, capital and land, using the same technologies, with minimal increases in labor productivity.

Persia, starting with the Indo-European ruler Cyrus the Great around 550 BC, created an empire unprecedented in scale ruled by an efficient network of inspectors. It also participated in the Axial Age (800–200 BC) breakaway from

---

and Growth of Sociology (1973); Ernst Mayr, The Growth of Biological Thought: Diversity, Evolution, and Inheritance (1985).
[574] Erb-Satullo, 2019.

particularistic myths and gods, with its original conception of a monotheistic religion, Zoroastrianism, one universal and transcendental God. But thereafter Persia lost its vitality except for the influence of Hellenistic culture via Alexander the Great's conquest. Islamic civilization experienced a "golden age" from about AD 800 to 1200. China was quite creative up until the end of the Song dynasty (960–1279), inventing water clocks, paper, rudimentary gunpowder technology, simple magnetic compasses, spinning wheels, huge sailing ships, movable types, and iron furnaces that smelted ore with coke, while achieving continuous increases in land productivity.[575] But this creativity, other than the continuation of its perennial demographic colonization of foreign lands, ceased during the Ming (1368–1644) and the Qing dynasties (1644–1912), which only saw mere extensions, not innovations, in the existing technologies. China saw no new ideas, but mere refinements and recombinations, after the intellectual traditions of Confucianism, Legalism, and Daoism were set down during the Axial Age (700–200 BC). India and Israel were Axial Age participants with their respective Hinduism/Buddhism/Jainism and Hebrew religions. But, again, after these Axial Age breakthroughs, these two cultures remained preservers of old traditions.

Only Western Civilization would exhibit a continuous sequence of novelties, a high number of renaissances, sustained creativity in science and technology after 1500, heterodoxies in Christianity followed by a world-shaking Reformation, along with the discovery and mapping of the world, ongoing sequences of new philosophical outlooks, and artistic and architectural styles. It all began with the Indo-European origination of the secondary products revolution, co-invention of wheel vehicles, riding of horses, and invention of chariots, conquest of the Old World, the emancipation of the male ego from the cult of fertility goddesses, the creation of patriarchal sky gods, the beginnings of selfhood based on individual heroism, and the inauguration of a new style of republican aristocratic rule.

For all the talk about multicultural equity, the only competitor to the West in achievements is China—in a few endeavors. It is really in their agricultural techniques, and their ability to sustain prolonged increases in land productivity, rooted in the nature of wet rice farming, that the Chinese managed to be ahead of the West, in economic terms, before the modern era.[576] The unsurpassed surpluses they obtained in agriculture, which require intense labor inputs, allowed the

---

[575] In *Uniqueness* I try to counter in great detail all the major claims of the "revisionist" multicultural historians who argue that, as late as the 1750s, Asia/China remained more advanced that Europe.

[576] Braudel, 1981; Duchesne, 2011.

Chinese to achieve the highest gross national outputs, to build huge cities, canals, and irrigation systems, as well as originate the technologies listed above, although without much improvements thereof. Since ancient Greek times the West has been far more creative in most intellectual and artistic fields, including theoretical science and geometry, and in a number of technologies, surpassing China with ever increasing momentum after 1200 in mechanical clocks, printing press, navigation technology, labor productivity, and other fields.

The University: European Institution Par Excellence

Our focus in this chapter will be on the disciplinary fields of geology and chemistry, cartography and geography, and philosophy. Since these fields of knowledge would come to be formalized in universities, let's start with the origins of the university.[577]

The existing consensus among the remaining serious scholars in our universities is that the "university" was invented in medieval Christian Europe.[578] The first university was Bologna, founded in 1088, followed by Oxford in 1096. By the end of the fourteenth century, in 1400, there were about thirty-four universities across Europe; in 1500 there were sixty-six, and none outside.[579] In 1789, the year of the French Revolution, there were about 143 universities in Europe, with only one university outside in Turkey. The original Latin word *universitas* designated any corporation (from the Latin *corpus, corporis*—a body) intentionally created by a group of individuals, be they guilds by craftsmen, associations by merchants, or municipal communes by town residents—to regulate their own affairs and security, independently of customary law, kinship ties, or religious and state authorities. While corporations were invariably self-organized and not originated by the state, the university was said to exist when it was authorized to act as a single entity ("born out of statute") by an official document or edict from the Pope or a Bull from the Emperor. Corporations were self-governed in that their members participated in specifying the rules that regulated their activities; power was shared and leaders could be held accountable for their actions.

Gradually, the word *universitas* came to be associated with the term *studium*

---

[577] We will discuss other fields of knowledge in Chapter IX, and the field of history in Chapter X.
[578] Moore, 2019; Pedersen, 1997.
[579] Verger, 2003, 57, 62–65.

generale, which referred to any institution (at the beginning of the thirteenth century) that "attracted students from all parts of Europe, not merely those of a particular country or district," and where at least one of the higher faculties of theology, law, or medicine was taught by a plurality of masters. In the course of the fourteenth century, as Rashdall carefully explains in his classic work, *The Universities of Europe in the Middle Ages*, first published in 1895, the term "*universitas*" became a mere synonym for *studium generale*," with numerous communities of students and teachers in charge of higher learning enjoying the privilege to conduct their own affairs, make their own rules for curriculum, and receive students from across Europe.[580]

It is no accident that only Europe saw the rise of corporate bodies. In the rest of the world, outside Europe, kinship groups were in charge of governing the lives of extended family members, providing security, rules of inheritance and marriage, and choice of occupation. Kinship groups were governed by customary norms, by authoritarian chiefs, or by religious authorities. The situation in medieval Christian Europe was radically different as a result of the serious weakening of kinship polygamous groups by the Catholic Church starting in the early Middle Ages. As Joseph Henrich explains in *The Weirdest People in the World*, the medieval Church sanctioned monogamous marriages against polygamy and concubinage, and it restricted marriages among individuals of the same blood (consanguineous marriages). It also encouraged marriages based on voluntary choice or consent. By the eleventh century the nuclear family was predominant in Europe. These changes freed Europeans from kinship ties and norms, leading them to form new voluntary, civic-based corporations to cooperate economically, solve conflicts, and secure a livelihood with individuals from wider circles of life.

The reconstitution of medieval Europe away from kinship institutions in favor of voluntarily created institutions, such as urban communes, guilds, diocese of bishops, monasteries, and universities, came along with the rise of new systems of law based on universal principles. During the tenth and eleventh centuries, as the Church went about imposing monogamous and nuclear families, Europe underwent a legal revolution that conceded corporate rights for self-government to the Christian church and a variety of associations and groups to make contracts, to enact their own ordinances and statutes, "to own property, to sue and be sued, and to have legal representation before the king's court."[581] Manors, cities, and

---

[580] Rashdall, 2010, 6, 8.
[581] Huff, 1993, 119–138.

merchant associations, among others, enacted whole new systems of law, including manorial law, urban law, canon law, and merchant law.[582]

Such legislative, executive, and juridical powers were not a possibility in Islamic societies where polygamy and cousin marriages remained a powerful means for consolidating the power of kinship groups, and where there was no legal separation between the sacred and the secular, no texts or rules to define and limit the jurisdictional powers of the courts, and no legal conception freed from the customary normative world of kinship groups. China never evolved a conception of law that recognized the right of corporate bodies, including cities, capable of composing and promulgating new laws independently of the state or the bonds of kinship.

It is within the context of the Catholic breakdown of kinship groups, the consolidation of nuclear monogamous families, and the legal revolution of the eleventh century, that we should apprehend the unique invention of universities in medieval Europe. In conferring legal recognition and liberties to the universities, the kings of France, England, and Spain, and later Portugal, Austria, Bohemia, Poland, and Hungary, as well as dukes and princes, expected their universities to provide them with effectively trained lawyers and Roman legal principles to consolidate their expanding powers against the centrifugal forces of the old feudal landed classes.

Similarly, the popes that endowed associations of teachers and students with the title and privileges of a university did so in awareness that the teaching of theology and Roman law, with its natural law principles, was an effective means of making Catholicism a rationally intelligible and unified doctrine to counter the diverse and mutually contradictory beliefs of heterodox religious orders. Both the papacy and the monarchies of Europe sought to recruit educated persons who could serve as staff for their offices. From the thirteenth century onward, the majority of popes had attended university and were increasingly surrounded by learned cardinals. Likewise, the cities recognized the advantage of having a partnership with universities that brought them prestige, and provided them with trained lawyers who could handle difficult legal problems in the conduct of businesses, and the articulation of the newly emerging fields of merchant law, contract law, and maritime law. Municipal authorities recognized the corporate right of students and teachers (many of whom were foreigners in need of rights they did not enjoy in the cities) to conduct their own affairs as members of autonomous

---

[582] Berman, 1984.

universities, as well as certain privileges such as exemption from tolls and taxes, and the fixing of maximal rents.

It would be a mistake, however, to view the recognition by monarchs and popes of the corporate status of universities as driven solely by their self-interests. The desire for knowledge, and the ethos of common Christian values transcending national boundaries, were very strong in medieval Europe. This was a time of Christian belief in a rational world order created by God that was accessible to human reason and education. This belief cultivated an interest in scholarly research, going back to the establishment of Christian cathedral schools and monastic schools in the early Middle Ages, in which monks dedicated themselves to the preservation and transmission of Greek-Roman high culture. At the same time, the Christian understanding of man as a creature fallen into sin, and thus as an imperfect being, encouraged the norms of intellectual criticism and collegial cooperation, and the norms of "modesty, reverence and self-criticism" as the image of the ideal scholar.[583] As Frederick I Barbarossa said in 1155 in his justification for the granting of academic liberties: "it is by learning that the world is illuminated and the lives of subjects are shaped towards obedience to God."[584]

The medieval ideal was that the university was a universal community of masters and students, open to everyone interested in the higher faculties of knowledge, as well as being at the service of the public interest to the benefit of the whole Christian world, without being hampered by national or regional borders. In the thirteenth century, *universitas* came to mean the totality of the branches of knowledge, the whole community of learners, in classical Latin. University teachers came to acquire the status of a group which transcended local and disciplinary boundaries in possession of a universally accepted corpus of knowledge. The fact that this one institution spread over the entire world, with the bachelor's degree, the master's degree, and the doctorate adopted in the most culturally diverse nations of the world, points to its universality.

European civilization originated this universal institution. No other society conferred the privileges of a corporation to institutions of higher learning. Medieval Christian Europe was the first civilization to "institutionalize reason" within self-governing universities offering a curriculum "overwhelmingly oriented toward analytical subjects."[585] The universities tended to have four faculties (arts,

---

[583] Rüegg, 2003, 33.
[584] Cited in Rüegg, 14.
[585] Grant, 2001.

theology, law, and medicine), with the most important being the arts faculty, which had the largest numbers of students, and the theology faculty. The program of the arts consisted of the three verbal disciplines of grammar, rhetoric, and logic (the trivium, or threefold way to wisdom) and the four mathematical disciplines of arithmetic, geometry, astronomy, and music (the quadrivium).

This interpretation of the origins of universities was widely accepted in academia. But the pressures of multiculturalism are leading some academics to argue that Muslims should be given precedent for the origins of universities. They are demanding that the University of al-Qarawiyyin be identified as the "first university," although this place was designated as a "university" only in 1963, and was originally founded as a mosque in 859.[586] Other academics are claiming that Al-Azhar University, which was also founded as a mosque in 970–972, should be designated as "the second oldest university in the world." They maintain that Islamic centers of learning originated the practice of organizing foreign students into associations, and the idea of universal validity of the qualification for teaching based on the title of the *baccalarius*. But according to Rüegg, "the term *baccalarius* could not be an Islamic import of the twelfth century because it was already in use in the ninth century as the Latin designation of a preparatory or auxiliary status in a variety of social careers."

Even the Islamicist George Makdisi, despite finding some general affinities between Islamic centers of learning and European universities, has concluded that "the university is a twelfth century product of the West both in its corporate structure and in the privileges it received from Pope and King."[587] Makdisi himself cautions that "in studying an institution which is foreign and remote in point of time, as is the case of the medieval madrasa, one runs the . . . risk of attributing to it characteristics borrowed from one's own [Western] institutions. . . . The most unwarranted of these [comparisons] is the one which makes the 'madrasa' a 'university.'"[588] The madrasa was not a high degree-awarding institution, but a "college of Islamic law" lacking corporate status and a rationalistic curriculum, supported by an endowment or charitable trust, that is a waqf, which consisted of a building or plot of land, for Muslim religious or charitable purposes.

---

[586] Esposito, 2003.
[587] Cited in Rüegg, 8.
[588] Makdisi,1970.

The Invention of Chemistry

You will recall, from chapter one, Steven Mithen's strange argument that Upper Paleolithic peoples exhibited a higher level of cognitive fluidity than Westerners today because they saw all the domains of life, individuals, society, and environment, as one world. One can be all for criticizing the hyperspecialized cognition of academics today, their inability to see anything in the forest except a few leaves and branches. But as pointed out against Mithen, the differentiation of cognitive fields is itself an expression of increasing awareness that nature and society are not an undifferentiated blob, but are characterized by different (emergent) levels of reality, with different qualities, modes of behavior and ontologies.[589] The sociologist Herbert Spencer first theorized that all the things throughout the universe develop from a simple, undifferentiated homogeneity, to a complex, differentiated heterogeneity, at the same time as they evolve increasing integration of the differentiated parts. What is less known is that Spencer extended this idea to account for the emergence of individual professions in modern Europe, each dealing with one aspect of reality.[590] Professional specialization entails identifying different parts of reality and developing specific disciplines to deal with these different parts. A field of knowledge can only acquire a disciplinary status in the degree to which it identifies its subject of knowledge and develops specific concepts, methodologies, and techniques for it. There was a time when all knowledge was identified with mythical stories, prophets, medicine men, traditions, and then philosophy. Each discipline came about by separating itself from this prior domination by one "politico-ecclesiastical" agency, as Spencer put it, or by differentiating itself from its prior conjunction with another discipline, as economics did in the 1700s, separating itself from "political-economy" (as was conceived by mercantilists) and from "ethics" (as was the case in medieval "economics"). This separation

---

[589] The idea that reality is organised into different levels of complexity which involve different sets of emergent properties and laws, characterized by distinctive behaviors and taxonomies, which are the subject matter of the various branches of the sciences (physics, chemistry, geology, biology, psychology, sociology), is known as emergent materialism. The German philosopher Nicolai Hartmann (1952), whom I read with enthusiasm as an undergraduate, believing that he offered a solution to Cartesian dualism with his argument that reality consists of different levels with their own ontologies, is seen as one of the key founders of this idea. This idea gained prominence among materialists who rejected "reductionism." It was re-interpreted as "critical realism" by the Marxist Roy Bhaskar.

[590] Offer, 2019.

does not preclude the combination of different fields of knowledge to gain further insights into reality.

Chemistry is a relatively young field, becoming a science between the seventeenth and eighteenth centuries. It was then that it became a science and a discipline in its own right with "its own concepts, its own techniques, and its own applicability."[591] Whereas sixteenth-century physics (mechanics/astronomy) was a "highly organized, mathematically sophisticated, theoretical science,"[592] with a long line of great scientists going back to ancient times and the Renaissance, backed by figures like Euclid, Archimedes, Ptolemy, and Copernicus, modern chemists were preceded by alchemists, druggists, iatrochemists, and sorcerers.[593] It was only during Robert Boyle's (1627–91) generation that chemistry started to become conscious of its own distinctive field of study, with its own specialized concepts.[594]

Some believe that chemistry came into the light only when the investigation of gases proceeded rapidly in the hands of Henry Cavendish (1731–1810), the theologian Joseph Priestley (1733–1804) and Carl Scheele (1742–1786),[595] when chemists came to see that air was an active ingredient in chemical reactions ,and not the only sort of gas; when Joseph Black showed in the 1750s that "fixed air" (CO_2) was distinguishable from normal air, and when Antoine Lavoisier's oxygen theory of combustion was confirmed in 1772 in his book, *Traité élémentaire de chimie*. This was the first modern chemical textbook with a new nomenclature, in which precise terms came to identify the nature of the substances, with hydrogen, for example, replacing the vague term "inflammable air," and oxygen replacing Priestley's "eminently respirable air." It was then, some argue, that a new scientific paradigm emerged in the study of matter deserving the name of chemistry. Today we can say that chemistry is the science that studies the properties and behavior of matter, or the way the atoms and molecules that make up the ultimate elements of nature interact and adopt new combinations to create compounds.

We should be mistrustful, then, of headlines about "Chemistry in the Ancient World" or "Alchemy and the Birth of Chemical Science," as books on the history of chemistry, or chemistry books for high school students, are increasingly doing

---

[591] Hall, 1960, 303.
[592] Rossi, 2000, 139.
[593] Mason, 1962.
[594] Butterfield, 1965.
[595] Kuhn, 1970.

to be more "inclusive."[596] The science of chemistry was developed by Europeans. This does not mean that researchers in mineralogy, pharmacology, and alchemy did not play a significant role in the eventual development of chemistry. A.R. Hall, in his classic book, *The Scientific Revolution, 1500–1800: the Formation of the Modern Scientific Attitude* (first published in 1954), goes too far claiming that "it is almost useless to look to them [the alchemists] for the beginnings of a chemical attitude."[597] It is true that alchemists had no criteria for distinguishing factual knowledge "from the products of their own extravagant imaginations," and believed they were searching for the ultimate elixir, an alchemical substance capable of turning base metals like mercury into gold, or affording immortality to humans. Everywhere in their writings there were invisible forces, vital agents, mysterious spirits inside matter.

Yet, in fairness, alchemists did explore and greatly expand our knowledge of substances and their reactions, including the Islamic alchemist Jabir ibn Hayyan (721–815), who identified two elements, sulfur and mercury, and synthesized ammonium chloride. It may be an exaggeration to say that Paracelsus (1493–1541), a Swiss physician, took alchemy "on the road to becoming chemistry," but he did forge a new field, iatrochemistry, which endeavored to unite medicine with chemistry; and he offered descriptions of the properties of mercury, zinc, cobalt, potassium, and other metals.[598] The nobleman from Brussels, Jan Baptist van Helmont (1580–1644), despite his belief in vital animistic forces in matter, developed iatrochemistry in a more quantitative direction, adopted the theory of void space, and advanced an explanation of digestion as the action of acid as an agent in the transformation of foods.

Hall is far more sympathetic to the "empirical knowledge of the phenomena of chemistry" rooted in glass-making, the metallurgical industry of smelting and refining of metals, the pharmacological preparation of medicaments, and the discovery of alcohol, including the differentiation of saltpeter from soda (which made gunpowder possible)—knowledge which emanated from a Hellenistic tradition centered in Alexandria, and from India, China, and the Islamic peoples. The mineralogical and pharmacological knowledge of the Chinese, as Joseph Needham has documented, was considerable, their distinction between saltpeter, alum, and their knowhow in tanning, dyeing, painting, and firework-making, but

---

[596] Levy, 2007.
[597] Hall, 1960, 307.
[598] Multhauf, 1967.

this scattered knowledge was descriptive and for practical uses, unguided by any scientific principles.[599] It would also be a mistake to say that the origins of chemistry are to be found in the ancient Greek idea that everything on earth was made up of four foundational elements (earth, water, fire, and air), or that indivisible particles "generate all composite things."

Perhaps the best candidate to represent the beginnings of the science of chemistry is the Anglo-Irish Robert Boyle. Boyle, a devout Anglican who sponsored missionary activities and wrote theological treatises, was a prominent figure in the articulation of the modern science of mechanics, with its idea that natural phenomena operated according to mechanical laws. He actually sought to integrate chemistry with physics as the two sciences that are seeking to explain the properties of matter. His 1661 book *The Sceptical Chymist* attacked the ancient doctrine of the four elements, proposed a clear definition of element as a "perfectly unmingled body, which not being made of other bodies . . . are the ingredients of which . . . mixt bodies are immediately compounded"—which anticipated the modern theory of molecules and atoms. He is known for his famous "Boyle's law," which states that there is an inverse relationship between pressure and volume of gas, and for promoting the idea that air played a vital part in combustion. From this point on, there is a consensus among historians that the following names were critical in the consolidation of the science of chemistry: G. E. Stahl, Cavendish, Priestly, Black, and Lavoisier.

Once Lavoisier, who was raised in a pious Catholic family, set chemistry on a firm scientific footing, and established a good working definition of an element as a substance that cannot be broken into more fundamental constituents, it was a matter of time before new elements would be discovered. Don't believe the incredibly deceptive Wikipedia claims about how the elements of gold, iron, copper, lead, silver, and tin were discovered in the ancient Middle East and Africa.[600] These metals were used but not *consciously* discovered as chemical "elements." It was only as the science of chemistry came into its own, with a self-awareness of its distinctive field of knowledge, that elements came to be progressively discovered. Phosphorus in 1669, cobalt in 1735, nickel in 1751, magnesium in 1755, hydrogen

---

[599] Throughout this chapter, the references to Needham are based on the three-volume abridgement, *The Shorter Science and Civilisation in China,* by Colin A. Ronan, drawn from Needham's monumental fifteen-volume work, *Science and Civilisation in China* (Cambridge University Press, 1954–1984). The section on mineralogical knowledge is contained in volume 2 of *The Shorter Science and Civilisation* (1997, 306–324).

[600] "Periodic table," 2023.

in 1766, oxygen in 1771, nitrogen in 1772—by European names.

The big question in chemistry soon became how to classify the elements. This effort led to the development of the Periodic Table, one of the greatest scientific accomplishments in human history. John Dalton, teacher at a Quaker boarding school, played a crucial role in the classification of elements with the publication of his 1808 book, *A New System of Chemical Philosophy*, with its observations that the atoms of different elements differed in size, weight, and number per unit volume, and that when two elements combined to form a compound each atom of the first element united with one atom of the second element in a series of whole numbers. The studies by Swede Jakob Berzelius (1779–1848) and the Belgian Jean Stas (1813–91) on the atomic weights of the elements, and the law of isomorphism, which allowed Berzelius to determine the formulae of many salts and the atomic weights of their constituent elements, were also important steps in the classification of the elements in a scientifically accurate way.

The making of the Periodic Table included an all-European cast, consisting of Johann Wolfgang Döbereiner, John Newlands, Lothar Meyer, and Dimitri Mendeleev. Newlands showed how if the elements were listed in order of atomic weight, each element shared properties with those eight and sixteen places later. The German Lothar Meyer also noted the sequences of similar chemical and physical properties repeated at periodic intervals. The Russian Mendeleev is the one immortalized for drawing up the Periodic Table in 1869, spelling out systematically how the characteristics of the elements recur at a periodic interval as a function of their atomic weight. Meyer had produced a similar, if less systematic, version of the Table in 1868, but it was Mendeleev who applied himself to the elaboration and defense of his Table, predicting the properties of five unknown elements and what their compounds would be, even before their discovery.

Today the periodic table outlines each element's electron configuration, the atomic number of the element, and the chemical properties of the element. Many great chemists would come in the late nineteenth and early twentieth century. Sometimes it is difficult to distinguish chemists from physicists. Ernest Rutherford, for example, was awarded the Nobel Prize for chemistry in 1908 "for his investigations into the disintegration of the elements, and the chemistry of radioactive substances," even though he was a physicist who believed that his main contribution was in the pioneering of the nuclear structure of the atom. Marie Curie, on the other hand, a highly gifted chemist, was awarded a Nobel Prize in physics in 1903 for her work on radioactivity.

I could go on listing great chemists by naming Nobel Prize winners during the twentieth century. Most of the names are European, though Jews do start winning prizes during the 1970s, a high number in the 1980s, and some afterwards, along with some non-Europeans. Nevertheless the basic fact stands: Europeans (or Westerners, if you prefer) originated the science of chemistry, pioneered all the fundamental ideas, from the seventeenth until the twentieth century, created the research centers and university departments that would transform chemistry into an institutionalized field with thousands of scholars and researchers, working less as individuals than as members of research teams funded in the millions, and making new contributions, but relatively minor, and none in the macro scale of the pioneers listed above.

The Invention of Geology and the European Discovery of Time

Geology, a seemingly innocuous field concerned with the study of rocks and minerals, is the field responsible for the discovery of time. European geologists were the first to realize that the Earth had a history, that it came to be in the course of time, and that humans could discover this history by studying the rock strata and fossils of the Earth's crust. Don't confuse the measurement of time, which began with the invention of sundials in ancient Egypt, with the discovery of time. Neither calendar nor chronology was worked out with the intention of discovering the Earth's time.

Every mythical account of the origins of the world postulated that the Earth was either formed through an initial "moment of creation," or that it was part of an "eternal order" embedded in a "cyclical cosmos." Newtonian physics had nothing to say about the development of nature, but assumed that once God created the universe it had remained the same. The task of the scientist was to understand the "universal laws of nature at work" that ordered the repetitive movements of the world and its parts. God, in Newton's words, was "like a watchmaker" who may occasionally tinker with the motions of the planets "to ensure that it continued operating in good working order," but scientists essentially dealt with the world as it had been set in motion by God. The reigning consensus prior to 1750 accepted the Biblical narrative that the Earth was 6,000 years old. The notion that natural objects were formed over the course of millions of years was inconceivable—until the science of geology came into its own in the 1800s.[601]

While evidence was accumulating about strange rocks with fossilized marine shells found inland in stratified layers, these anomalies were explained within the Creation-story and the accepted time-scale. Robert Hooke (1635–1703) reasoned that the Earth had a history characterized by earthquakes, floods, deluges, eruptions, which had altered the earth and its living organisms, but this history, he insisted, was explainable within the Biblical narrative. Thomas Burnet (1635–1715) argued in *Telluris Theoria Sacra* that the Earth was hollow, with most of the water inside until Noah's Flood, at which time mountains and oceans appeared, as the sun's rays dried up the Earth and the crust was split open into continental land masses.

John Woodward in his *Essay Towards a Natural History of the Earth* (1695) argued that the "whole Terrestrial Globe was taken all to Pieces, and dissolved at the Deluge." The existence of fossilized remains confirmed the Mosaic Flood as described in the Bible. New rock strata came to be formed, after the Flood, by a process of sedimentation, with the remains of animals and plants relegated to the deepest strata. This emphasis on the action of water through the Flood in the formation of fossilized rock strata came to be known as the "Neptunist" view of the Earth's history. Other geologists like John Ray advocated the "Vulcanist" view that the mountains and dry land had been raised above the oceans by the internal fires of the Earth at the command of God.

While the Neptunist view tended to sit comfortably with the Flood cataclysmic narrative and the view that it was possible to explain the appearance of rocks, fish, animals, and man, in the order presented in the Book of Genesis, the Vulcanist view became associated with a more gradual process occurring over a longer time scale. John Whitehurst, in a daring book published in 1778, *Inquiry into the Original State and Formation of the Earth*, argued that the geological record suggested a much older history of the Earth than the Noachian Flood. The Italian Giovanne Arduino (1714–1795) even denied the Flood and contended that the rock strata of the earth, which he classified with the names Primitive, Secondary and Tertiary, also pointed to a much older Earth.[602]

The beginning of the idea of an older Earth, however, is associated with Georges Louis Leclerc (the legendary Comte de Buffon), who was less a geologist than a historian of nature and *encyclopédiste*. Buffon hypothesized that the Earth

---

[601] Rossi, 2001.
[602] Gohau, 1991.

originated from a collision of a comet and the sun, much earlier than the Biblical six-thousand-year account. He suggested this argument in his multivolume work, *Histoire naturelle, générale et particulière* (1749–1788), and in his 1774 *Introduction to the History of Minerals*, although it was in his 1778 *The Epochs of Nature* in which he formulated in explicit terms the idea that "the surface of the Earth has taken different forms in succession; even the heavens have changed, and all the objects in the physical world are, like those of the moral world, caught up in a continual process of successive variations."[603] He inferred the age of the Earth experimentally by heating a small metallic globe and measuring the rate at which it cooled, which yielded an estimate of 75,000 years old.

While scriptural geologists attracted to the Neptunist view, such as Alexander Catcott in his *Treatise on the Deluge* (1768), would try to defend the Genesis account of a recent Creation by arguing that a global Flood could account for the geological record, the growing scientific temperament in Europe pushed the Neptunist view in a more secularized direction. The German geologist Abraham Werner (1749–1817) thus proposed that in the beginning the Earth was covered by a primeval ocean, which gradually receded to its present location, depositing by a process of crystallization and chemical precipitation almost all the rocks and minerals in the Earth's crust over the course of about one million years. In his estimation, heat was not an important initial geological force; volcanic heat from the interior of the earth was a late and a secondary rock-forming agency after the main strata had been consolidated through slow sedimentation. In the spirit of science, Werner devised a comprehensive color scheme for the description and classification of rock strata according to their mineral content and age. His Neptunist theory, however, could not account for the disappearance of the original ocean after the strata had been formed.

John Playfair, a Scottish clergyman, popularized Hutton's ideas in his *Illustrations of the Huttonian Theory of the Earth* (1802) and defended Hutton against the charge of atheism by arguing that uniformitarian geological processes were like Newton's laws of regular planetary motion. Hutton's theory, however, was not widely accepted by a British geological world unwilling to break altogether with the Biblical narrative. Meanwhile, the French Georges Cuvier, known as the "founding father of paleontology," countered uniformitarianism with another geological hypothesis called "catastrophism," which argued that the geological features of the earth, along with the history of life, could be explained by catastrophic

---

[603] Toulmin and Goodfield, 1982, 145.

events, not a single catastrophe, but several, causing the extinction of many species of animals and resulting in the sharp lines of demarcation between the successive strata and the presence of distinctive fossil remains in each layer of rock.

But soon a new perspective known as "uniformitarianism" came on the horizon thanks to the Scot James Hutton (1726–1797), identified by some as the first student of the earth who may properly be called a geologist. In his 1788 *The Theory of the Earth, or an Investigation of the Laws observable in the Composition, Dissolution, and Restoration of Land upon the Globe*, he provided a rigorous explanation, grounded in scientifically acceptable principles and based on the existing geological data, why the age of the Earth was indefinitely long.[604] The same geological forces that are seen to be in operation in our present-day, he argued, should be used to explain the past geological formation of the Earth. "The past history of our globe," in his words, "must be explained by what can be seen to be happening now. . . . No powers are to be employed that are not natural to the globe, no action to be admitted except those of which we know the principle."

The powers of nature act uniformly through time, rather than suddenly through cataclysms. This is the uniformitarian principle. While stressing the internal heat of the Earth, he did not neglect the geological effects of water, observing two sorts of rocks in the Earth's crust, one of aqueous origin and the other of igneous origin. The intense internal heat of the Earth was responsible for uplifting mountains to form land masses, bending and stilting strata, where they would then be subjected to erosion, re-deposition, and volcanism, and these processes acted over a very long-time scale.

In time, however, the uniformitarian school gained the upper hand, particularly after Charles Lyell published his celebrated three volume work, *Principles of Geology* (1830–33), which synthesized thirty years of geological discoveries in favor of Hutton's uniformitarian theory. Although Lyell did not argue in favor of the transmutation of species, some in the geological community felt ill at ease with the notion that the succession of fossils in the rock strata pointed in the direction of the evolutionary succession of species. The Anglican priest Adam Sedgwick (1785–1873), notwithstanding his proposal of the Cambrian and Devonian period of the geological timescale, thought that a uniformitarian history of the earth could be harmonized with the Bible, though he never explained how, other than objecting to the evolution of new species. It was not until Charles Darwin's theory

---

[604] Mortenson, 2007.

of evolution (1859) was widely accepted that Lyell's theory ceased to be widely opposed. [605]

We often hear that Darwin obtained the idea of the mechanism of evolution from Thomas Malthus's famous essay on population. We rarely hear that it was Lyell's theory, in Darwin's own words, that led him to the theory of evolution itself. Once the Biblical time barrier on the history of the Earth was broken by geologists, a historical revolution was precipitated in biology, leading to Darwin's theory of natural selection about how species form and change over time. The current geological consensus today is that the Earth's history is a slow, gradual process, punctuated by occasional natural catastrophic events.

Every participant in these debates was a European. The rest of the world was oblivious about this revolution in geology, as it was about Newtonian science, and the amazing revelation that the Earth's history was very old and could be explained with the powers of the human mind.

Chinese "Geology"

Be on guard about the multicultural claim that geology began in ancient China. Colin Ronan's three volume abridgment of Needham's exhaustive work on Chinese science offers a section with the title "The sciences of the earth: Geology and related sciences," arguing that long before the "largely modern, post-Renaissance science" of geology emerged in the West, the Chinese in the eleventh century already "understood those conceptions which, when stated by James Hutton in 1802, were to be the foundation of modern geology." [606] However, no actual Chinese treatises on geology are brought up by Needham, for none existed. What we get instead are isolated passages from various Chinese "masters" which supposedly amounted to explanations of the "origin of mountains, uplifting, erosion, and sedimentary deposition." Here is one passage from Shen Kua written "about the year 1070" supposedly explaining "how the earth formed as a deposit from the water":

Now I myself have noticed that Yen-Tang Shan is different from other mountains. All its lofty peaks are precipitous, abrupt, sharp and strange;

[605] Gillispie, 1973, 300.
[606] Needham, 1997, 290, 292–93.

its huge cliffs, 300 metres high, are different from what one finds in other places. . . . Considering the reasons for this I think that the mountain torrents have rushed down, carrying away all sand and earth, thus leaving the hard rocks standing alone.

This is followed by another passage where Shen Kua explains the origins of "uplifted strata": "Naturally mud and silt will be carried eastwards by these streams year after year, and in this way the substance of the whole continent must have been laid down."

Needham provides pictorial representations of fossil animals along with descriptive passages to show that the Chinese anticipated modern European geology. He mentions "the most famous text" on the origins of the earth, namely, the "Collected Works of Master Chu Hsi" (1130–1200):

I have seen mountain conchs and oyster shells, often embedded in rocks. These rocks in ancient times were earth or mud, and the conchs and oysters lived in water. Subsequently everything that was at the bottom came to be at the top, and what was originally soft became solid and hard. One should meditate deeply on such matters, for these facts can be verified.

These are the best passages provided by Needham. They are intelligent descriptions for their time, but nowhere near a science of geology. Isolated descriptions, without principles and without a theory, do not constitute a science. Geology became a science in the West in the wake of the Galilean-Newtonian science of mechanics, the theory of universal gravitation, the theory of the circulation of the blood, along with the consolidation of the science of chemistry, botany, paleontology, and evolutionary biology.

The Chinese believed that the Earth was flat until the Jesuits taught them otherwise in the seventeenth century.[607] None of the geologists Needham mentions wrote a treatise that can be classified as "geological" in dealing with the origins of

---

[607] Couprie, 2018. Some Western academics have tried to find a spherical conception in China, but to no avail. As C. Cullen argues (2009, 107): "Chinese thought on the form of the earth remained unchanged from early times until the first contacts with modern science through the medium of Jesuit missionaries in the seventeenth century...While the heavens were variously described as being like an umbrella covering the earth, or like a sphere surrounding it, or as being without substance while the heavenly bodies float freely, the earth was at all times flat, although perhaps bulging up slightly."

the Earth. If the Chinese were so advanced in their geological reflections back in ancient times, anticipating Hutton, how come no further insights came out of China in the next thousand years? After Hutton, Europeans would develop techniques to date the rock strata of the Earth, as well as a variety of methods to understand the Earth's structure and evolution, including field work, rock description, geophysical techniques, chemical analysis, physical experiments, and numerical modelling.

The Treatises of Theophrastus, Agricola, and Steno

As it is, the ancient Greeks were already writing treatises that were more theoretical in their geological insights than the descriptive passages of the Chinese.[608] Theophrastus (372–287 BC) in his treatise *On Stones*, classified rocks and gems based on their behavior when heated, grouping minerals by common properties, and writing about the fossilized remains of organic life. The Wikipedia page on Shen Kuo (1031–1095) portrays him as a scientist in all the fields of human knowledge:

> He was a mathematician, astronomer, antiquarian, meteorologist, geologist, entomologist, anatomist, climatologist, zoologist, botanist, pharmacologist, medical scientist, agronomist, archeologist, ethnographer, cartographer, geographer, geophysicist, metallurgist, mineralogist, encyclopedist, military general, diplomat, hydraulic engineer, inventor, economist, academy chancellor, finance minister, governmental state inspector, philosopher, art critic, poet, and musician.[609]

Clearly, the multicultural establishment has lowered the criteria of what constitutes a science in their eagerness to be inclusive, yet they can barely hang on to China as a viable intellectual competitor. The etymology of all the sciences is European, because Europeans originated all the sciences, and so is the idea of *logos*, of making an argument through reasoned discourse, on the basis of explicitly stated principles.

---

[608] Gohau, 1991
[609] "Shen Kuo," 2023.

The etymology of geology tells us that the root of this word is very recent; only in 1795 do we find explicit statements about geology as a "science of the past and present condition of the Earth's crust," from Modern Latin *geologia* "the study of the earth."[610] German *Geologie* is attested in 1785. The word-forming element meaning "the Earth" comes from the Greek term *geo-*, and the word-forming element meaning "discourse, treatise, doctrine, theory, science" comes from the Greek term *-logia*.

The Chinese did not write a single treatise on geology because they lacked a notion of writing theoretical scientific works.

Whereas Shen Kuo left us with no scientific treatises, we have two surviving botanical works by Theophrastus, *Enquiry into Plants* and *On the Causes of Plants*, which are recognized as the first systemization of the botanical world, with plants classified according to their modes of generation, their localities, their sizes, and their practical uses. Before Hutton, we have the German Georgius Agricola (1494–1555), who wrote full treatises, including *De Natura Fossileum*, *De Ortu et Causis Subteraneum*, and *De Re Metallica*, where he attempted to explain the existence of mountains, volcanoes, and earthquakes, recognized the power of wind and water as an erosive force, associated the hot interior of the Earth with volcanoes and earthquakes, and put together a classification system of the mineral kingdom. *De Re Metallica* remained the standard textbook on mining and metallurgy for over two hundred years. Herbert Hoover, a mining engineer before he became U.S. President, translated *De Re Metallica* into English in 1912, believing that Agricola was "the first to found any of the natural sciences upon research and observation, as opposed to previous fruitless speculation."[611] If anyone deserves to be celebrated for making an essential contribution to the beginnings of the science of geology, it is Agricola.

Then we have the Danish Nicholas Steno (1638–1686), who went beyond mere description to formulate path breaking geological principles in an actual treatise, *Dissertationis prodromus*, published in 1669. This treatise is acknowledged today for establishing, on the basis of inductive reasoning, four of the foundational principles of the science of stratigraphy: the law of superposition, the principle of original horizontality, the principle of lateral continuity, and the principle of crosscutting relationships.[612]

---

[610] See the Online Etymology Dictionary: https://www.etymonline.com/word/geology.

[611] Cited in Keating, 2017.

[612] Hamblin, 1978.

The Earth Is 4.54 Billion Years Old

I left other names from this account of the discovery of geological time, such as William Smith, who published three works from 1815 to 1817, gave geology a descriptive methodology for assigning relative ages to the various strata of the Earth, and provided the first geological map of England and Wales. After the 1830s, geology became a professional vocation, with many names making important contributions and reaching ever more accurate estimations of the Earth's age with the assistance of European physicists and chemists.

In 1896, radioactive isotopes were discovered by the French physicist Henri Becquerel showing that heat from their decay pointed to an Earth hundreds of millions of years old. Between 1903 and 1906, the renowned New Zealand physicist Ernest Rutherford (1871–1937) determined that isotopes could be used to date rocks. By the 1930s, through the efforts of Arthur Holmes, the age of the earth had expanded to about 2 billion years. In 1946, Willard Libby proposed an innovative method, radiocarbon dating, which allowed for the dating of organic materials by measuring their content of carbon-14. This method provided objective age estimates for carbon-based objects that originated from living organisms. The "radiocarbon revolution" finally allowed Europeans to reach the conclusion that the Earth was 4.54 billion years old.

The Invention of Cartography (and Geography)

A supremely high proportion of the greatest cartographers in history—reaching one hundred percent after 1400—were Western. While China did have a tradition of map-making, and did originate the rectangular grid system, most of its maps were lost, and a flat earth conception was at the basis of its cartography, whereas a spherical earth was at the basis of Western cartography from its origins in ancient Greece. Needham makes the case that after the great ancient Greek cartographer named Ptolemy (100–178), scientific cartography "was unknown to Europeans" until about 1400 when they rediscovered Ptolemy's writings, whereas the Chinese developed their own "scientific" tradition steadily from ancient times until they started copying the West after the arrival of the Jesuits.[613] He has to

---

[613] Needham, 1997, 252–3.

acknowledge, however, that the Chinese had no conception of the determination of the size and curvature of the earth, and that a flat earth conception underpinned Chinese cartography.

He persuasively identifies Pei Hsiu, or Pei Xiu, (224–271), as "the father of scientific cartography in China" for his grid way of "depicting the correct relations between the various parts of the map," and for, to use the words of Chen Cheng-siang, his "method of fixing the lengths of derived distances from right-angled

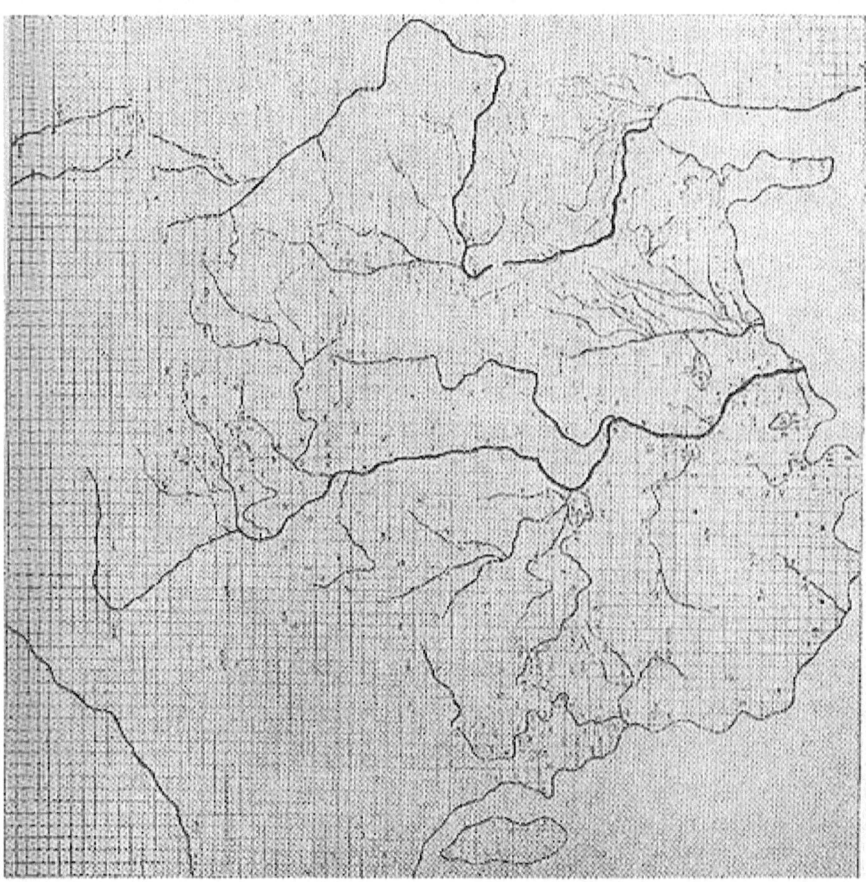

The Yu Ji Tu map, the most remarkable cartographic work of its age in any culture, carved in stone in AD 1137 but probably dating from before AD 1100 (from Chavannes). The scale of the grid is 100 li to the division. The costal outline in relatively firm and the precision of the network of the river systems extraordinary. The size of the original, which is now in the Pei Lin Museum at Sian, is about 3 square feet. The name of the geographer is not known.

triangles."[614] Needham and Cheng-siang bring up many other cartographers, and allude to many cartographic books and maps. But many of these books and maps were lost, so they rely instead on references to these maps and cartographers in other publications that seem to be bureaucratic reports. Reading the 1978 article by Chen Cheng-siang, "The historical development of cartography in China," I get the impression that improvements after Pei Xiu consisted in more precise grids, a greater quantity of maps with "a greater variety of alien lands and of frontier areas," though many of the maps are heavily pictorial in their drawings of mountains, rivers, irrigation projects, cities, and palaces. The culmination of Chinese cartography may be seen in the famous "Yu Ji Tu map" of AD 1137, which is quite remarkable.

It is hard to accept without some qualifications Needham's judgment that China cultivated a "scientific" tradition in cartography when it had no conception of the sphericity of the earth, no determination of the size of the earth, no coherent and systematic integration of geography and cartography, no idea how crucial it is to have a conception, in the words of Ptolemy, of the "known habitable earth as a unit in itself" to draw maps to scale, and no systematic integration of astronomy and cartography and how important astronomical measurements of latitudes and longitudes are for finding unknown distances.

Greek Cartography

Claudius Ptolemy (AD 100–170) was the greatest cartographer in history before Gerardus Mercator came along in the sixteenth century. He was the culmination of a tradition of Greek cartography (combined with geography, astronomy and mathematics) going back to Hecataeus (550–476 BC), Pytheas of Massalia (350–306 BC), Eratosthenes (276–196 BC), and Hipparchus (190–120 BC).[615] In the book *Journey Round the World by Hecataeus*, based on his extensive travels ending at the Atlantic coast of Morocco following the coast of the Mediterranean and Black Sea, and in his "World Map," one sees a mapping ambition to look outward beyond one's place of birth in order to grasp the totality of the earth's geography—notwithstanding its complete lack of a grid.

---

[614] Cheng-siang, 1978, 103.
[615] Whitfield, 1998.

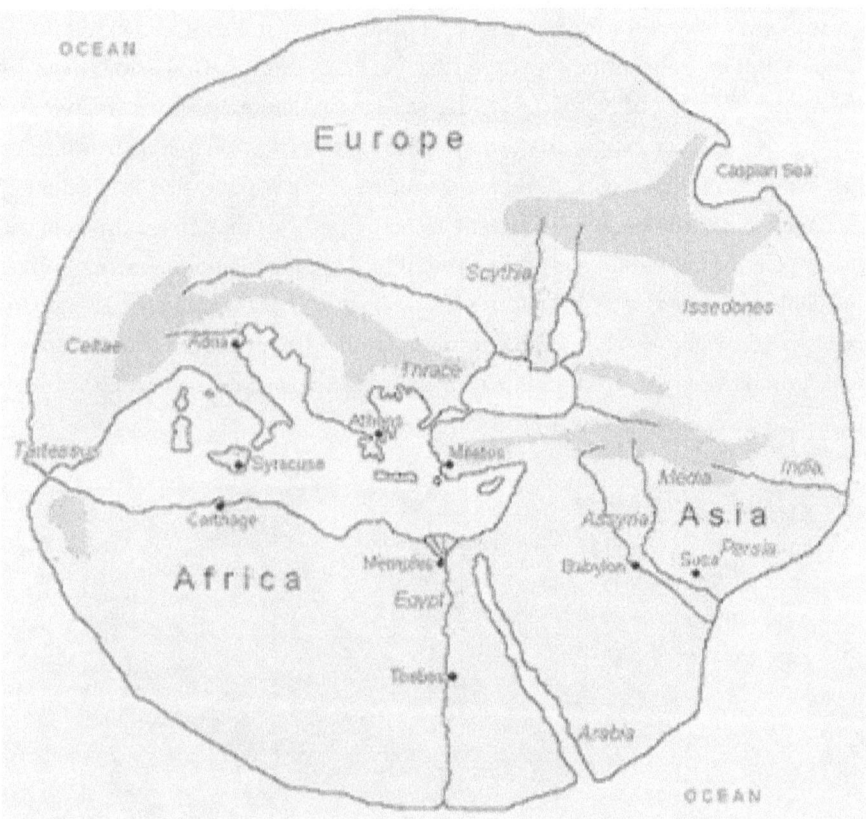

World map of Hecataeus.

This worldly view is enhanced in Pytheas's book, *On the Ocean*, which recounts an amazing journey (ca. 310 BC) northward to Brittany across the Channel into Cornwall, through the Baltic Sea, the coast of Norway, and even Iceland. While the Chinese retained their flat conception of the earth until the Jesuits taught them otherwise, way back in ancient times, Eratosthenes (276–185 BC) contextualized the location of Europe in relation to the Atlantic and the North Sea, and calculated the spherical size of the earth within 5 percent of its true measure.

Then came Hipparchus, "the first to use the grade grid, and to insist that the map must be based only upon exact measurements of latitude and longitude," to determine latitude from stellar measurements, rather than solar altitude, and to determine longitude by timings of lunar eclipses, rather than dead reckoning. Hipparchus also listed latitudes for several tens of localities and improved

Eratosthenes' values for the latitudes of Athens, Sicily, and southern extremity of India.[616] But the consensus seems to be that Claudius Ptolemy (c. 85–165) deserves the honor of "father of cartography." He was first to define the subject matter and explain that the key task of the cartographer is "to survey the whole world in its just proportions;" that is, to draw maps to scale.[617] He realized that the "extent of our habitable earth from east to west . . . is much greater than its extent from the north pole to the south." He was interested in mapping the whole earth, not just the habitable part, and to fit the earth into the scheme of the universe. He said, in fact, that cartography should be contrasted with what he called "chorography," which merely consists in describing or mapping a region or district. Can we say that Chinese cartography was indeed chorography?

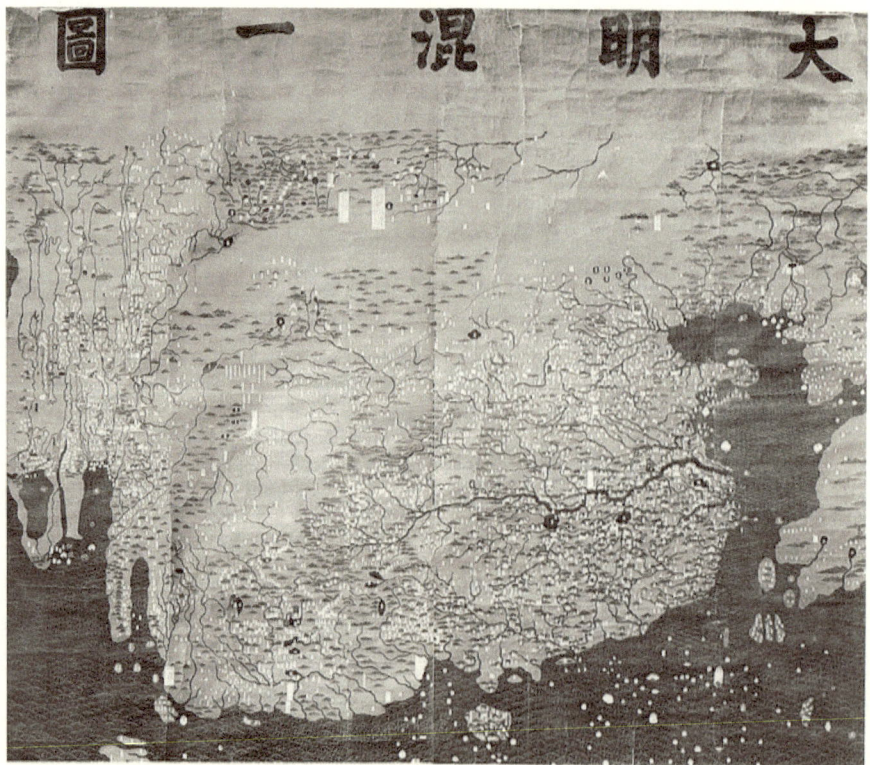

The Da Ming Hun Yi Tu map (ca. 1390). This is the only surviving Chinese world map created sometime during the Ming dynasty (1368–1644), over a thousand years after Ptolemy, possibly at the same time as Mercator's map.

---

[616] Shcheglov, 2005.
[617] Hubner, 2000.

Ptolemy insisted (following in the footsteps of Hipparchus) that astronomy and mathematics were indispensable disciplines in the task of mapping the earth as accurately as the heavens had been charted. He was interested in the relationships between the earth and the sun, and the earth and the moon. His treatise *Analemma* was a mathematical description of a sphere projected on a plane, and a method for specifying the location of the sun. His work *Planisphœrium* described a sphere projected on the equator, with the eye envisioned at the pole. His *Almagest* lay down the foundation of trigonometry, and set forth his famous geocentric view of the universe. His *Geographike hyphegesis* was, in his words, "the geographical guide to the making of maps," both of the whole inhabited world and of the Roman provinces, including the necessary topographic lists, and captions for the maps, and the nature of the materials and expertise mapmakers require. Ptolemy was well aware that he knew about only a quarter of the globe. This treatise was not superseded until the sixteenth century.[618]

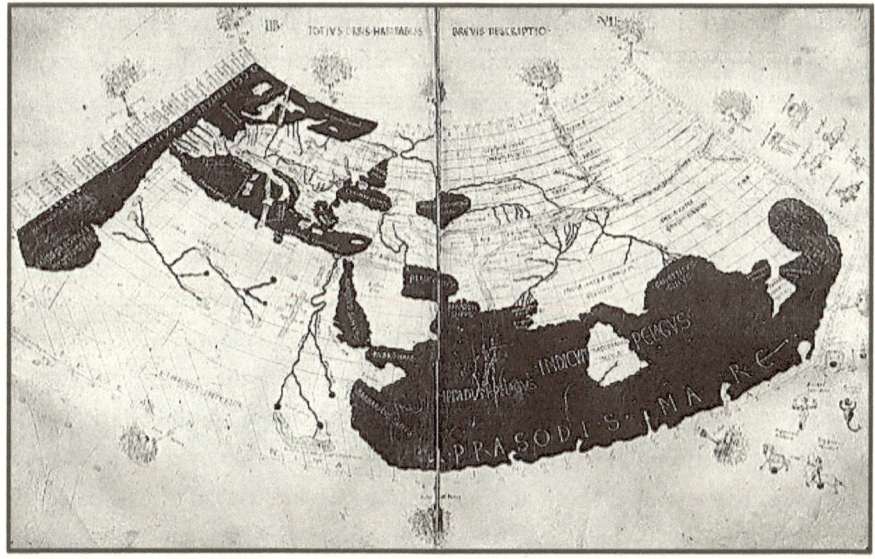

Florentine map, ca. 1450–1475, based on Ptolemy's projection.

---

[618] Hubner, 2000.

The Age of Discovery

Needham tells us that China steadily developed its scientific map-making tradition over the course of its history as the European map-making tradition "degenerated" after Ptolemy into "religious cosmography." This is true: Ptolemy's maps provided a more realistic and accurate cartographic view of the world than the so-called medieval *mappa mundi*, which were pictorial in showing coastal details, images of mountains, towns and provinces, as well as figures and stories from the Bible and classical mythology. On the other hand, Chinese cartography, as I noted above, did not really improve upon what Yu Ji Tu accomplished in his AD 1137 map. Its "flat earth" perspective persisted.

Meanwhile, the marvelous European age of discovery would begin in the fifteenth century, preceded by the world-historical travels of Marco Polo (1254–1324), which found expression in the Catalan Atlas of 1375, a synthesis of medieval *mappa mundi* and the travel literature of the time, showing compass-lines, and a rather accurate delineation of the Mediterranean.[619] The fourteenth century also saw the emergence of the mariner's compass, which made it possible to determine from the location of a ship any coastal feature, harbor, or island. We should acknowledge the Islamic contribution of the cartographer al-Idrisi, who produced a large planispheric silver relief map that was original in not portraying the Indian Ocean in a landlocked way, and in offering a more precise knowledge of China's eastern coast. But Islamic geography would go no further.

The first real turning point leading directly to the sixteenth century cartographic revolution was the fifteenth century Portuguese planned discovery and mapping, under the leadership of Henry the Navigator, of the African West coast down to the southern tip of Africa, rounding this massive continent and finally uncovering the full extent of this "Terra incognita" or "unknown land." A mere two years after Diaz had sailed around the Cape, Henricus Martellus created his World Map of 1490, which showed both the whole of Africa generally and the specific locations of numerous places across the African west coast, detailing the step-by-step advancement of the Portuguese.[620]

Similarly, a few years after the discoveries of Columbus, Juan de la Casa produced the first world map in 1500 to include the New World. And in 1507

---

[619] Larner, 1999.
[620] Edson, 2007; Brotton, 2014.

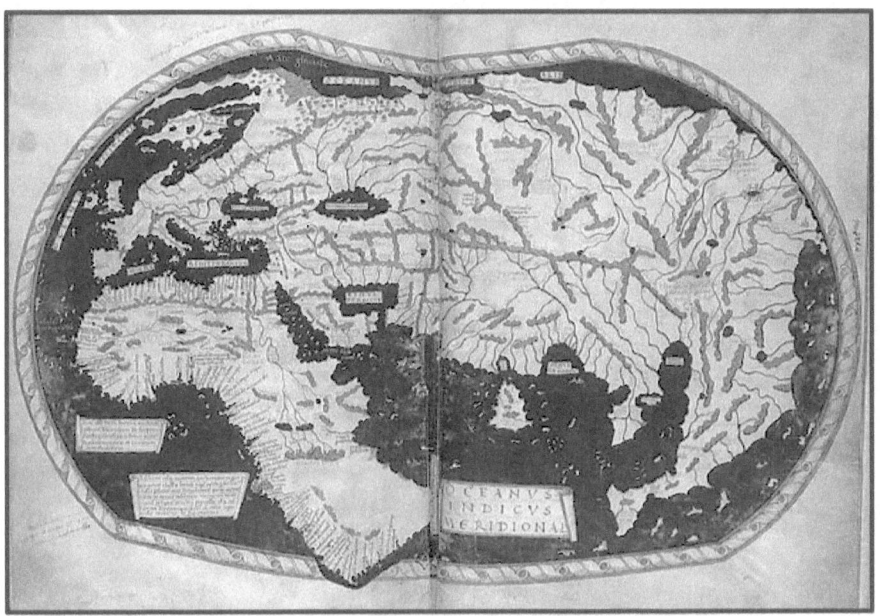

Martellus world map, ca. 1489.

Martin Waldseemüller produced his *Universalis cosmographia*, identified as the first map to use the name "America" in honor of the Italian explorer Amerigo Vespucci. Waldseemüller was also the first to map South America as a continent separate from Asia, the first to create a printed wall map of Europe, the first to emphasize the scientific importance of surveying, and to use a forerunner to the theodolite, which he called the *polimetrum*, an optical instrument for measuring angles.

There were other European cartographers, but none as great as Gerardus Mercator, who solved the perennial problem of how to translate the spherical Earth into the flatness of a map.[621] What Mercator realized, among other things beyond my expertise, is that to create a proper projection of the globe onto a flat surface "the spacing of the parallels of latitude would have to be made progressively larger away from the equator toward the poles" and that "the spreading of the parallels would have to be in exactly the same proportion as the spreading of the

---

[621] Crane, 2003. In his book, *Mercator, The Who Mapped the Planet*, Crane portrays Mercator as the greatest cartographer of his age, not as a lone genius, but as man belonging to one of the most vibrant intellectual centuries of Europe's history, the sixteenth century, "Age of Discovery", which saw a true cartographic revolution backed by many other mapmakers and a growing body of empirically-based sources.

meridians."[622] Mercator was not a lone soldier; in 1570 Abraham Ortelius, though not a cartographer himself, published the first edition of *Theatrum orbis terrarum*, which incorporated seventy maps created by many cartographers.

Waldseemüller map (1507). The first map to include the name "America."

The Mercator world map (1587).

---

[622] Wilford, 1981, 73–86.

Mapping in the Age of Modern Science

Once the age of discoveries intersected with the rise of modern science and the development of geodesy, which began as a surveying technique to determine with accuracy positions on Earth, which involved the invention of accurate measuring instruments and the development of new mathematical techniques, all of which happened in Europe, it stands to reason that all subsequent cartographers in history would be European. Some of the surveying tools and techniques which allowed for detailed hydrographic surveying of sea shores and islands, the topography of lands, heights of hills and mountains, included the general use of the plane table for establishing and recording angles; the method of triangulation to determine distance of remote objects without going there; angle, distance, and elevation-measuring instruments ... and John Harrison's (1693–1776) 'longitude' clock, which finally solved the problem of determining longitude at sea.

It is said that the Cassini family were the first to start mapping the interior of France, with César-François Cassini (1714–84) being the most illustrious in the utilization of new surveying tools, such as triangulation and establishing that the Earth was flattened at the poles, and in the production of an accurate map of France.

James Cook (1728–1779) is best known as one of the greatest explorers ever, for his three voyages between 1768 and 1779 in the Pacific Ocean, reaching the southeastern coast of Australia for the first time in history, circumnavigating New Zealand, crossing the Antarctic Circle three times, and exploring the Northwest Passage all the way to the Bering Strait. He embodied the Faustian spirit of exploration in its purest form, driven solely by a will to explore, without economic self-interest or missionary zeal, confessing to an ambition which "leads me not only farther than any man has been before me, but as far as I think it possible for man to go."[623]

What many don't know is that Cook was also one of the greatest cartographers in history. His voyages were models of reconnaissance mapping. He produced the first hydrographic surveys of the coast of Newfoundland based on precise triangulation. He discovered New Zealand and mapped its entire coastline using the sextant, which measures the angular distance between two visible objects. He surveyed and mapped South Georgia. In his search of the Northwest Passage, he

---

[623] Cited in Wilford, 1981, 174.

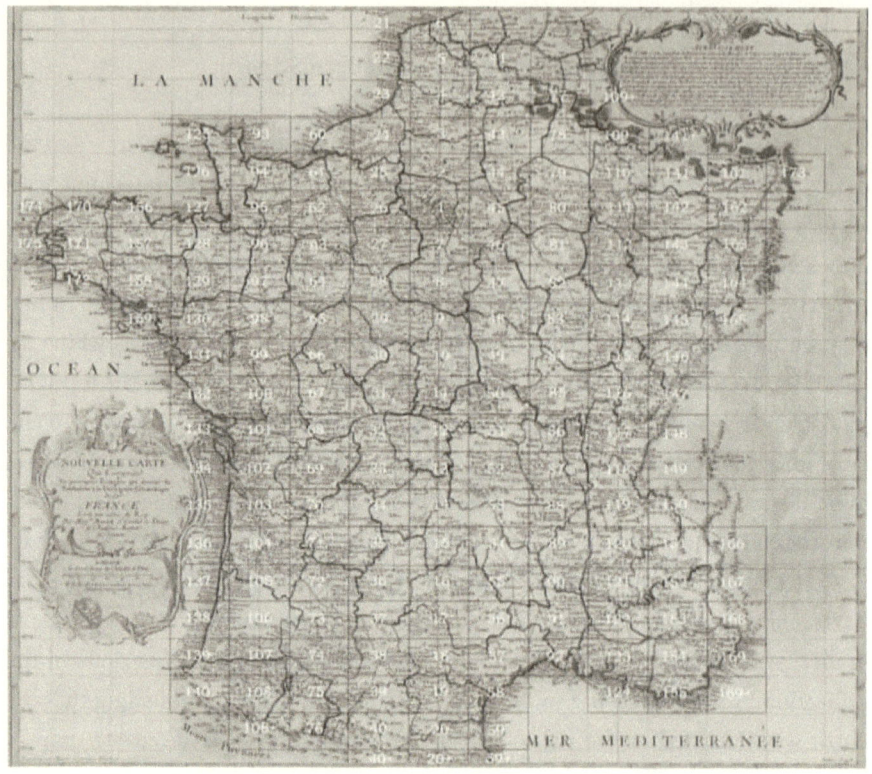

Cassini's map of France (1744).

mapped the coast all the way to the Bering Strait. This is a kernel of what this man accomplished. Today he is disdained as a "colonizer" who did not discover anything because natives were already there—even though Cook exhibited "an entirely new civilized attitude towards the natives of the lands."[624]

There are too many great European cartographers to suppress. Francis Beaufort produced in 1792 the first map of Ireland, as the great hydrographer of his generation. He instructed map-making explorers that "the height of all headlands, isolated hills, and remarkable peaks should be trigonometrically determined. . . . The nature of the shore, whether high cliff, low rock, or flat beach . . . the material of the beach, mud, sand, gravel or stones."[625] I won't say anything about the men who started mapping the interior of India, and only a few words about the ones who began land surveying and mapping the United States. One has to start with

---

[624] Hough, 1995, 2.
[625] Wilford, 159.

Lewis and Clark, who conducted one of the most renowned journeys in history, crossing the uncharted American West from August 1803 to September 1806, reporting in detail about the geography and wildlife, and producing about 140 maps of the area. They were followed by John Charles Frémont (1813–90), the first presidential Republican candidate, mapping the country between Missouri and the Rocky Mountains, Oregon and Upper California, and the "still and solitary grandeur" of the Great Salt Lake. Then there was Almon Harris Thompson, the mapper of Colorado through the Grand Canyon, southern Utah, part of Arizona, who produced topographical maps to illustrate rivers, canyons, and mountains, all with a geological perspective.

Mappers of the Bottom of the Ocean and the Universe

For all this, it has been estimated that in 1885 less than one-ninth of the land surface of the earth had been surveyed—which should not surprise us, since the rest of the world remained asleep, without much cartography other than the knowledge percolating from the West. In 1884, the West encouraged the world to adopt the Greenwich meridian, dividing the Earth into the Eastern and the Western hemisphere, along an imaginary line of 0° longitude, establishing an International Date Line between one day and the next.

With the merger of the Western technologies of aviation and the camera, including aerial photogrammetry, cartography was revolutionized yet again, leading them to the rapid mapping of the globe through the twentieth century. From this point on, we are no longer speaking of trailblazers as much as institutionalized cartographers assisted by scientists sitting on desks, who would go on to develop newer technologies, automation techniques, electronic distance-measuring instruments, inertial navigation systems, high resolution radars, remote sensing, and computers—revealing great geographic details at long distances. These technologies allowed radar imagery to be converted into maps of impenetrable regions like the Amazon, including geologic and seismic mapping of the earth beneath.

They also began to map the mountains, chasms, and plains beneath the oceans, with the use of deep-sea echo sounders, magnetometers, and underwater sonars. And the universe. Europeans had begun mapping the moon back in the seventeenth century, with the lunar cartographer Johannes Hevelius producing his famous Map of the Moon in 1647. Today, hundreds of teams of scientists are working with complex technologies, such as the Hubble and Spitzer Space Telescopes, mapping everything from the far reaches of the universe to the most infinitesi-mally small particles within it. This Faustian drive for mastery of the unknown has now produced (as of 2010), based on the ground-based telescopes of the 2MASS Redshift Survey, 3D images of 43,000 galaxies.[626]

The West Produced Far the Greatest Number of Original Philosophers

It could be that the most important historical question that points to a monu-mental contrast between the West and the rest is the following: why did Western civilization produce all the greatest philosophers in history? If we agree that phi-losophy, at least until the first half of the nineteenth century, covered every branch of knowledge and dealt with ultimate questions about the nature of reality and the meaning of life, being and becoming, why there is anything rather than nothing, what is good and evil, what is the difference between knowledge and opinion, then it follows that identifying the nationality of the greatest philosophers may be a most revealing factum in our evaluation of the comparative achievements of civi-lizations. One does not have to agree with Aristotle that the "highest good" is the pursuit of wisdom to take seriously his claim that, if "all men by nature desire to have knowledge," and if the highest form of knowledge is expressed by philoso-phers, because, as Heraclitus said, "they are inquirers into many things," then it can be reasonably stated that the civilization that produced the greatest philoso-phers is the civilization that achieved the highest.

When scholarly histories of philosophy began to be written after the mid-1750s, that is, histories based on a relatively comprehensive study of the sources, it was agreed that true philosophy began in sixth century BC in Greece, when a group of men known as the Pre-Socratics introduced a new way of inquiring for the "causes and principles" of the natural world, grounded on rational judgements rather than on legends, myths, or gods responsible for the happenings of the world. They generally agreed with Aristotle's confident claim that Thales of Mile-tus (623–545 BC) is the first known "inquirer into nature" who can be distin-guished from earlier poetical "myth-makers" such as Hesiod and Homer.

It is not only that histories of philosophy began their accounts with ancient Greece. These histories were almost entirely, if not completely, about the contri-butions of Western philosophers in the conviction that philosophy as a venture

---

[626] Rooney, 2017.

that relies on reasoned arguments for its truth claims—even in philosophers like David Hume who believed that "reason is the Slave of the passions"—is a uniquely Western achievement. G. W. F. Hegel's *Lectures on the History of Philosophy* (1837/1995), which were given to students, and recently published by University of Nebraska Press in three volumes, devote a brief opening section on "Oriental Philosophy," and thereafter the three volumes are entirely dedicated to European thinkers, starting with Thales. As Hegel writes at the beginnings of *Lectures*:

[Western philosophy] shows us a succession of noble minds, a gallery of heroes of thought, who, by the power of Reason, have penetrated into the being of things, of nature and of spirit, into the Being of God, and have won for us by their labors the highest treasure, the treasure of reasoned knowledge.

This conviction that philosophy was almost entirely a Western phenomenon was held by historians of philosophy from every school of thought until recently. The neo-Kantian Wilhelm Windelband, believing that philosophy concerns the "independent and self-conscious work of intelligence which seeks knowledge methodically for its own sake," began his two-volume classic, *A History of Philosophy*, published in 1892, with the ancient Greeks, without mentioning a single non-Western philosopher.[627] Windelband believed that "the history of philosophy is the process in which European humanity has embodied in scientific conceptions its views of the world and its judgments of life."[628]

The historicist and existentialist Julián Marías, in his *Historia de la Filosofía* (1941), which went through countless editions, and was translated into English, also starts with the Pre-Socratics, and ends with José Ortega y Gasset (1883–1955), without a word about a non-Western thinker—even though he says that "philosophy is a way of life," which seems to fit with the "Eastern" tradition of seeing philosophy in terms of an inner or spiritual religious quest. The difference is that Marías thinks that philosophy is also about knowledge that "justifies itself [and] constantly demonstrates and proves its validity." Therefore, philosophy is a way of life "that consists precisely of living according to a certain knowledge; therefore, this way of life postulates and requires this certain knowledge. It is this knowledge which determines the meaning of the philosophic life." Of course, the word

---

[627] Windelband, 1958, 23.
[628] Ibid, 9.

"knowledge" is also used in Eastern philosophies, but Marías agrees with the standard Western view that it was with the Pre-Socratics that "a completely new human attitude" emerged: a theoretic instead of a mythical attitude. The "mythic man" is enveloped by the surrounding world, living in a world of things he can't differentiate in terms of their properties and contrast to the thinking self. In contrast, the "theorizing" philosopher differentiates the knowing self: "instead of being among the things, he is opposite them, alienated from them, and thus things acquire a meaning of their own which previously they did not have."[629]

The liberal-minded Will Durant, in his popular 1926 book, *The Story of Philosophy: The Lives and Opinions of the Greater Philosophers*, profiles only Western philosophers. In a "Preface to the Second Edition," written in 1962, we see the first inklings of multiculturalism, however, as Durant faults his book for leaving out "Chinese and Hindu philosophy," even though he adds that Chinese philosophers were "averse to epistemology" or to inquiries into the nature of knowledge and how it is acquired. The analytical-empiricist philosopher Bertrand Russell, in his widely-known 1945 book, *History of Western Philosophy*, which was cited as one of the books that won him the Nobel Prize for Literature in 1950, took it for granted that the history of philosophy should be about Western philosophers. Philosophy began with the Pre-Socratics, because it is only then that we see speculations on the nature of things with "appeals to human reason rather than to authority, whether that of tradition or that of revelation."[630] He offered a chapter on "Mohammedan Culture and Philosophy," only to the extent that Muslims wrote commentaries on Aristotle. The Catholic philosopher, Frederick Copleston, in his magisterial work, *A History of Philosophy*, published in nine volumes between 1946 and 1975, began with Greece and stayed in Europe right to the end, including a volume on Russian philosophy.

This Western-centric attitude was unquestioned until recent times. It was the typical perspective of texts for university students. Konstantin Kolenda's 1974 *Philosophy's Journey: A Historical Introduction*, says that it was the ancient Greeks who "were able to think through to new, unorthodox questions." "Mythical accounts about gods and about the world . . . do not necessarily concern themselves with the question of truth. Myth is something that is told and need not call for critical scrutiny, examination, justification."[631] It is not only that the ancient

---

[629] Marías, 1967, 1–4.
[630] Russell, 1974, 13.
[631] Kolenda, 1974, 5.

Greeks posed critical questions—"Is there some substance or some basic stuff out of which everything is made?"—but that their answers consisted of reasoned arguments. Not a single Eastern philosopher is included in Kolenda's book.

In 1991, Norman Melchert published *The Great Conversation: A Historical Introduction to Philosophy*, in which he tells students the value of philosophy is that it teaches you "to believe for good reasons." Opinions are as good as the reasons behind them. "That's what philosophy is,": teaching students how to think "clearly and rationally."[632] Every philosopher in Melchert's "great conversation" is Western. But didn't Nietzsche say the "will to power" lies behind the grandiose claims of reason? And didn't Heidegger deny reason's ability to reveal the nature of being? Both Melchert and Kolenda include these two great philosophers for their originality and immense impact on contemporary thought. We can add that these thinkers did not rely on mandates and conventions, educated in a world of myths and fables. The Nietzschean argument that behind the claims of philosophical reason lay a primitive unconscious will to power, archetypes inherited from the past long before any rational consciousness, was articulated in the context of an education in the rationalist tradition of the West. Heidegger attempted to access being (*Sein*) by means of a rigorous phenomenological analysis of human existence in respect to its temporal and historical character, conducting meticulous exegeses of philosophical texts from the Pre-Socratics onwards through the writings of medieval and modern philosophers.

The Great Philosophers, a 1987 BBC television series presented by Bryan Magee, which was made available in a book of the same name, only discusses Western philosophers in its fifteen episodes, beginning with Socrates and ending with Bertrand Russell and Ludwig Wittgenstein. It is true that in recent decades there have been noticeable attempts accentuate the word "Western" in book titles, in order to make it clear that it is not a history of philosophy *per se*. *The Columbia History of Western Philosophy*, edited by Richard Popkin and published in 1999, explicitly states that the book "has assembled 63 leading scholars to forge a highly approachable chronological account of the development of Western philosophical traditions"—from Plato to Wittgenstein and from Aquinas to Heidegger. At the same time, it says that "the Columbia History significantly broadens the scope of Western philosophy" to reveal the influence of non-Western contributions. There is a chapter "dedicated to Jewish and Moslem philosophical development during the Middle Ages, focusing on the critical role of figures such as Averroës and

---

[632] Melchert, 1991, 10–11.

Moses Maimonides in introducing Christian thinkers to classical philosophy."[633] The book also acknowledges the influence of the Kabballah upon Spinoza, Leibniz, and Newton, and the influence of Moses Mendelssohn upon the work of Kant. Nevertheless, the focus remains entirely on the Western tradition; Muslims and Jews are included insomuch as they were shaped by this tradition and contributed to it.

The book *A New History of Western Philosophy*, which consists of four separate volumes published between 2004 and 2007, by the British philosopher and theologian Anthony Kenny, also focuses on those works in the Jewish and Islamic tradition that became important to the Western tradition. Surely if Popkin and Kenny really believed there were African, Aztec, or Eskimo philosophers, who had made philosophical contributions as significant as Aristotle, Descartes, or Locke, they would have included them. There have indeed been very strong pressures since about the 1990s for a more "inclusive" history of philosophy—in a Western world dedicated to multicultural immigration.

A recent, highly publicized book is *Taking Back Philosophy: A Multicultural Manifesto*, by Bryan Van Norden. It condemns American universities for "failing their students by refusing to teach the philosophical traditions of China, India, Africa, and other non-Western cultures." Without a background in Western philosophy other than reading a few books by members of the Frankfurt School, van Norden demands that Western philosophy be seen as merely one current among many equally gifted ones. In a much-commented 2016 *New York Times* article, co-authored with Jay Garfield, under the threatening title, "If Philosophy Won't Diversify, Let's Call It What It Really Is," he called upon universities "to look beyond the European canon in their own research and teaching." As if aware that he lacked reasoned arguments to back the claim that Inca philosophy was as profoundly significant, Van Norden embraced Herbert Marcuse's "repressive intolerance" idea in another 2018 *New York Times* article titled "The Ignorant Do Not Have a Right to an Audience." We should tolerate leftist views only, for "justice dictates that access be granted to opinions and people . . . [that] benefit the community"—that is, multicultural communities. Those who disagree with him, and believe that the Bantus did not produce great works of philosophy, are complicit with "nationalism" and "racism." In support of him, Patricia McGuire, the President of Trinity Washington University, was direct in stating that inclusiveness in philosophy had nothing to do with the quality of non-Western philosophy: "Let's

---

[633] The quoted words are from the Introduction authored by Popkin (1999).

face facts: there's a Muslim Mayor in London, signifying the fact that even those who revere All Things British need to catch up with the *now-settled reality of great diversity* in contemporary life. The canon of learning should reflect that, including Philosophy."[634]

These mounting pressures to avoid "racist" exclusions of non-Western philosophers clearly account for A.C. Grayling's decision in his otherwise serious 2019 book, *The History of Philosophy*, to include a "Part V: Indian, Chinese, Arabic-Persian, and African Philosophy." Grayling tries to argue that India, China, and the Arabic-Persian world developed schools of thought that discussed such perennial questions as what is truth, meaning, existence, and value—the truth, however, is that he has a hard time showing they did so in "intellectually rigorous ways." At most, using his own criteria of what constitutes philosophy (which excludes religion, casuistry, apologetics, or beliefs devoid of sound reasoning), he shows that there was an incipient philosophical tradition in India, China, and, due to the influence of Aristotle, in medieval Islamic civilization. He does not demonstrate that in these civilizations (again with the exception of Islamic Aristotelians) there were sustained inquiries "into the nature of knowledge and how it is acquired." While there were "inquiries into the nature of reality and existence" and into "what is good," there were no treatises on what constitutes valid and sound reasoning. Moreover, it is implicitly obvious that Grayling's account of these civilizations concerns an ancient or medieval period of creativity, consolidation of a few basic outlooks, followed by repetition or decline.

When it comes to "African philosophy," Grayling finds himself in a quandary of his own making: "are there philosophical schools of thought in Africa that are distinguishable from traditions, religions, folklore, mythology, poetry, art, and collections of maxims?" He can't avoid suggesting that Africa did not produce a philosophical tradition. Only "if one attaches an extended and very loose sense to the label 'philosophy'" is it possible to talk about African philosophy. But he cautions not to equate "denials of its existence" with "an implicit dismissal of Africa." "There is much to discover in Africa, for example the rich and deeply attractive concept of Ubuntu." This term stands for "kindness, goodness, generosity, compassion, caring." While these virtues are not unique to Ubuntu, "it is appropriate that as humankind itself came out of Africa, so one of the best ideas about how it can flourish—the idea of Ubuntu—should emanate from there too."[635] This is

---

[634] Cited in Tessier, 2016.
[635] Grayling, 2019, 575–81.

actually how this otherwise very intelligent history ends: with a childish call upon Whites to think about Ubuntu. There is an implication here that it is also important to practice Ubuntu towards the African migrants moving into Europe.

Who Are the Greatest Philosophers?

Below is a list of the fifty greatest philosophers, created on the basis of many years of reading philosophical texts and histories of philosophy. They are all Western. There are very strong reasons to exclude non-Western philosophers from this list. However, a second list follows of the next fifty greatest, which do include a reasonable number of non-Western thinkers—insomuch as they had a profound impact on their respective cultures, and did contribute the best philosophies outside the West. How were these two lists constructed? By trusting the authority of the histories of philosophy referenced above, including additional histories of both the West and the East to be cited below. Throughout my own student days, undergraduate and graduate, and as a professor, I read a sizable number of primary philosophical works, in combination with many secondary books and articles. My own philosophical views have influenced to some degree the choices of these lists, but, overall, I have relied on histories written by authors from a wide variety of perspectives—Kantian, Hegelian, materialist, phenomenological, empiricist, pragmatic, existentialist, analytical—and specialists in non-Western philosophies. I have also tried to bring out the best from ancient, medieval, modern, and contemporary periods.

First List

1. Abelard (1079–1142)
2. Anaximander (b. 610 BC)
3. Anselm (1033–1109)
4. Aquinas (1225–1274)
5. Aristotle (384–322 BC)
6. Augustine (354–430)
7. Bacon, Roger (1214–1292)
8. Bacon, Francis (1561–1626)
9. Bentham (1748–1832)
10. Berkeley (1685–1753)
11. Carnap (1891–1970)
12. Democritus (460–360 BC)
13. Deleuze (1925–1995)
14. Derrida (1930–2004)
15. Descartes (1596–1650)
16. Fichte (1762–1814)
17. Frege (1848–1925)
18. Hegel (1770–1831)
19. Heidegger (1889–1976)
20. Heraclitus (535–475 BC)

21. Hobbes (1588–1679)
22. Hume (1711–1776)
23. Husserl (1859–1938)
24. James (1842–1910)
25. Kant (1724–1804)
26. Leibniz (1646–1716)
27. Locke (1632–1704)
28. Marx (1818–83)
29. Mill (1806–73)
30. Nietzsche (1844–1900)
31. Ockham (1285–1347)
32. Parmenides (b. 501 BC)
33. Peirce (1839–1914)
34. Plato (428–348 BC)
35. Plotinus (204–270)
36. Pythagoras (570–495 BC)
37. Quine (1908–2000)
38. Rawls (1921–2002)
39. Reid (1710–1796)
40. Rousseau (1712–1778
41. Russell (1872–1970)
42. Sartre (1905–1980)
43. Schelling (1775–1854)
44. Schopenhauer (1788–1860)
45. Duns Scotus (1266–1308)
46. Socrates (470–399 BC)
47. Spinoza (1632–1677)
48. Wittgenstein (1889–1951)
49. Zeno of Lea (b. 489 BC)
50. Žižek (1949–)

It must be emphasized that this is not a comparison of the West against three or four other civilizational groups, but a competition of the West versus the rest. Aside from the Muslim, Chinese, and perhaps the Indian world, no other culture in the world—not the Mayas, not the Aztecs, not the Khmer Rouge Cambodians, not the Tibetans, not the Aksum civilization, not the Egyptians, not the Assyrians, not the Bantus, not the Babylonians, not the Japanese, not the Koreans—*no* other culture in the world produced any historically great philosopher. Let it be repeated: this is not a list based on arbitrary, idiosyncratic, purely personal, or politicized assumptions. It is based on solid, widely recognized histories of philosophy. Let's take a look at the second list, created for the purpose of finding a way to include non-Western thinkers, for the sake of argument.

Second List

1. Al-Farabi (870–950)
2. Alghazali (1058–1111)
3. Anaxagoras (500–428 BC)
4. Aurelius (21–180)
5. Averroes (1126–1198)
6. Bonaventura (1221–1274)
7. Bergson (1859–1941)
8. Böhme (1575–1624)
9. Boethius (AD 480—524)
10. Brentano (1838–1917)
11. Zhuang Zhou (369–286 BC)
12. Comte (1798–1857)
13. Confucius (551–479 BC)
14. Collingwood (1889–1943)

15. Davidson (1917–2003)	33. Lucretius (96–55 BC)
16. Dewey (1859–1952)	34. Luhmann (1927–1998)
17. Diderot (1713–84)	35. MacIntyre (1929–)
18. Dilthey (1833–1911)	36. Malebranche (1638–1715)
19. Dugin (1962–)	37. Mencius (372–289 BC)
20. Dummett (1925–2011)	38. Montaigne (1533–1592)
21. Epicurus (341–271 BC)	39. Mo Tzu (479–438 BC)
22. Erasmus (1469–1536)	40. Merleau–Ponty (1907–1961)
23. Evola (1898–1974)	41. Ricour (1913–2005)
24. Gadamer (1900–2002)	42. Rorty (1931–2007)
25. Grotius (1583–1645)	43. Schmitt (1888–1985)
26. Habermas (1929–)	44. Scruton (1944–2020)
27. Hempel (1905–1997	45. Seneca (4 BC–AD 65)
28. Herder (1744–1803)	46. Sextus Empiricus (ca. AD 200)
29. Hsun Tzu (Xunzi) (298–238 BC)	47. Spencer (1820–1903)
30. Kierkegaard (1813–1855)	48. Strauss (1899–1973)
31. Kojève (1902–1968)	49. Thales (624–548 BC)
32. Lao Tzu (604–532 BC)	50. Zhu Xi (Chu Hsi) (1130–1200)

If there is a bias in these lists, it is that philosophers of history (Spengler, Vico), philosophers of science (Kuhn, Nagel, Feyerabend), of mathematics (Hilbert, Lakatos), of language (Jakobson, Austin, Searle), of law (Pufendorf, Kelsen, Hart), of logic (Boole, Turing, Gödel), and social theorists (Montesquieu, Sorokin, Weber) were neglected, all of whom are no less philosophical than Chinese thinkers like Confucius.

The Score

The totals for the two lists combined are:

- Europeans 82.5 = 82.5 percent
- Jews 7.5 = 7.5 percent
- Chinese 7 = 7 percent
- Muslims 3 = 3 percent

If we add Jews to the European list, insofar as they were all educated in Europe, then the Western proportion is 90 percent. Augustine was a Berber according to

Gerald Bonner's authoritative biography *Augustine of Hippo:* "There is no reason to suppose that he was of any but Berber stock."[636] Augustine was thoroughly educated in the West. The top four philosophical nationalities are the ancient Greeks, the Germans, the English, and the French.

Indian and Chinese Philosophy

The fact that Indian philosophy can't be divorced from India's major religious traditions, or was never conceived as a separate intellectual pursuit, explains why Indian philosophers could not be included, great as they may have been as religious thinkers. Surendranath Dasgupta's impressive five-volume work, *A History of Indian Philosophy*, published between 1922 and 1955, is fundamentally about Buddhism, Jainism, "the six systems of Hindu thought," including the Bhagavad Gita, the "most revered of all the Hindu texts," the philosophy of Srikantha, which argues that the Shiva and the Brahman are one and the same, and Saiva philosophy, which posits "the soul's bondage within the fetters of existence." Sue Hamilton, an expert in Indian philosophy, acknowledges that "what Westerners call religion and philosophy are combined in India," and that its philosophies are "correctly referred to as soteriologies, or 'systems of salvation.'" The Indian philosophical tradition holds that "understanding reality has a profound effect on one's destiny." The attempt "to understand the nature of reality" is a "spiritual undertaking, an activity associated with a religious tradition." The aim of Indian philosophy was to escape from consciousness, to obliterate the thinking self, and every philosopher, or every philosophical outlook—Buddhism, Hinduism, Jainism, and Sikhism—were preoccupied with the notion of reincarnation, the process of birth and rebirth, the transmigration of souls and the "release" of the soul from that process.[637]

We know that a belief in rebirth/metempsychosis was held by Greek historical figures, such as Pythagoras, Socrates, and Plato. But as Russell qualifies, the very Pythagoreans who believed that the "soul was subject to a sequence of transmigrations . . . gave rise to a scientific and more especially a mathematical tradition . . . in spite of the mystical element arising from the orphic revival."[638] Sue

---

[636] Bonner, 2002, 36.
[637] Hamilton, 2001, 1, 7.
[638] Russel, 1974, 51–56.

Hamilton agrees, adding that while in Western medieval philosophy the existence of God was taken to be true as an article of faith, attempts were made to separate truths established by means of reason alone, and to even establish the existence of God by means of reason. In modern times, Kant, a devout Christian, would go further by insisting that "what one could know for certain was strictly limited to what could be ascertained by means of reasoning . . . one could never have certain knowledge about issues of faith." Nevertheless, Sue Hamilton, as is generally the case with Westerners who study Eastern thought, misleads readers with her view that Western philosophy "tends to be concerned with detailed and technical questions about kinds of logic and linguistic analysis"—whereas Indian philosophy is a "spiritual undertaking" about "big metaphysical questions" concerning the meaning of life and how to live one's life in order to have an effect on one's destiny.[639] Van Norden also criticizes the notion that the West discovered the "one universal method of rationality." Chinese philosophy has its own modes of reasoning and its own way of searching for the truth.

Let's leave aside the fact that both India and China have now embraced the scientific rationality of the West, apparently with the conviction that this rationality is universally useful. The Western philosophical tradition even contains the most reasoned critiques of the pretensions of reason in favor of alternative ways of finding meaning and making sense of the universe—intuitive, poetical, artistic, archetypal ways. The difference is that those philosophers who pointed to the limitations of reason would go on to develop alternative methodologies, or fully articulated philosophies, such as hermeneutics, phenomenology, and existentialism—by individuals well-educated in the Western rationalist and empiricist traditions. We will return to this point. Jacob Böhme, whom Hegel called "the first German philosopher," and is included in the second list above, had a major influence on Schelling, and German thinking in general, with his idea that an irrational force, the *Ungrund*, a groundless Will, was the primary fount of being, not reason.

Seven Chinese philosophers out of 100 is more than enough. In China there are five major philosophical traditions: Confucianism, Taoism, Legalism, the School of Names, the Mohists, and the Yin-Yang school. All these traditions emerged in ancient times, and thereafter, in what we called the "medieval" and "modern" eras, all we get are "neo" developments of these schools: "Neo-Confucianism" and "Neo-Taoism," or philosophers who combined aspects of the various schools to produce slightly different ideas. The highly respected sinologist,

---

[639] Hamilton, 8.

Frederick Mote, goes as far as to say that every major philosophical outlook in China's history occurred "within a revitalized Confucianism"—notwithstanding the role of Daoism and Buddhism. This is why only one philosopher that is not from ancient times was included, namely Zhu Xi (1130–1200). Xi is indeed seen as the philosopher who "exercised the greater influence on Chinese thought," except for Confucius, Mencius, Lao Tzu, and Hsun Tzu. He synthesized most currents within Chinese philosophy within a grand Neo-Confucian system, with his "most radical innovation" being the selection of "the Analects, the Book of Mencius, the Great Learning, and the Doctrine of the Mean . . . as the Four Books," commenting on them, and making them the orthodox foundation of the Chinese civil service examinations from 1313 to 1905.[640]

Including other Neo-Confucians in the list would have been the same as including notable European philosophers who followed in the footsteps of prior great philosophers, such as the so-called Cambridge Platonists:[641] Henry More (1614–1687), Ralph Cudworth (1617–1688), Benjamin Whichcote (1609–1683), Peter Sterry (1613–1672), John Smith (1618–1652), Nathaniel Culverwell (1619–1651), John Worthington (1618–1671), George Rust (d. 1670), Anne Conway (1630–1679), and John Norris (1657–1711). Including Neo-Taoists would have required including many gifted Cartesians: Antoine Arnauld, Balthasar Bekker, Tommaso Campailla, Johannes Clauberg, Michelangelo Fardella, Antoine Le Grand, Adriaan Heereboord, François Poullain de la Barre, Edmond Pourchot, Pierre-Sylvain Régis, Henricus Regius, Jacques Rohault, Christopher Wittich.

We may indeed ask: is Confucius really a philosopher? After all, Confucianism is a "doctrine of worldly social-mindedness," a guide for proper moral behavior for the scholar gentry class of China's despotic bureaucratic state, a doctrine that, in Needham's view, became a "cult, a religion, based on a kind of hero worship and borrowing from the cults of nature-deities and ancestor worship."[642] Confucius never asked questions about the ultimate nature of reality. The Confucian term "all under heaven" does not refer to the universe, the infinite, but is a term that denotes the geographical area associated with the political sovereignty of the emperor.

One could seriously argue that China produced individuals better described as writers of guidelines on how best to rule, to meditate, and contemplate nature,

---

[640] Chan, 1963, 588–90.
[641] See Hutton, 2023.
[642] Needham, 1997, 79.

combined with some allusions and illustrations about the "boundless" and about the ways of nature, without "elaborate reasoning and detailed argument." These last quoted words are from Fung Yu-Lan's *A Short History of Chinese Philosophy*. Fung Yu-Lan, after stating that China has a rich philosophical tradition with contributions in logic and metaphysics; and after clearly stating that a "philosopher must philosophize ... must think reflectively on life, and then express his thoughts systematically . . . [and offer] theories [that are] the products of reflective thinking," goes on to say:

> The fact is that Chinese philosophers were accustomed to express themselves in the form of aphorisms, apothegms, or allusions, and illustrations. The whole book of Lao-tzu consists of aphorisms, and most of the chapters of the Chuang-tzu are full of allusions and illustrations. This is very obvious. But even in writings such as those of Mencius and Hsun Tzu, when compared with the philosophical writings of the West, there are still too many aphorisms, allusions, and illustrations. Aphorisms must be very brief; allusions and illustrations must be disconnected.

This way of thinking, he continues. is "not articulate enough," though this "insufficiency" ("briefness and disconnectedness") is "compensated" by the "suggestiveness" of the allusions.[643] Fung Yu-Lan is right that this lack of "elaborate reasoning" is "obvious" to anyone who reads Chinese philosophers. One might even say that Chinese philosophy never rose above the pre-rational, mystical, poetic, or bureaucratic style of writing that prevailed in all cultures up until the ancient Greeks discovered the faculty of reasoning and came to realize that there is a mind that reasons capable of self-generating its own rules of reasoning in conscious distinction from extra-theoretical presuppositions.

This conscious differentiation of reason from its object, and appearance of free self-determination, reached its culmination in post-Kantian idealism, but it was Aristotle who did the most in ancient times to delineate what constitutes a proper philosophical statement about what there is and what constitutes a valid form of reasoning about why something is so. He invented formal logic, a precise language about reality, about what things can be said to be substances and the reasons why

---

[643] Fung Yu-Lan, 1948, 2, 11–12.

they are as they are.[644] He showed that true philosophical statements are composed of basic categories—substance, quantity, quality, relationship, place, time—which express the various ways in which being is, and that these statements can be formulated to be subject-predicate statements.[645]

At most, it might be argued that Chinese philosophers resemble Pre-Socratic philosophers. Aristotle criticized the Pre-Socratics for failing to fully articulate criteria for differentiating faulty arguments from good arguments. This is what he sought to provide with his formal logic and the syllogism. Chinese philosophical statements lack demonstrative reasoning and clearly-stated primary premises. In fairness to the Pre-Socratics, even though they did not invent syllogistic reasoning, they did discover *logos*, a rational order in the world, and *nous*, a rational faculty which humans can employ to seek the truth.

The words from Needham cited above about Confucianism come from *The Shorter Science and Civilisation in China: 1*. While Needham, still recognized as the most impressive scholar of Chinese culture, was not keen about Confucian philosophy, he wrote admiringly about the Taoists, Mohists, and Legalists, claiming that they made fundamental contributions to scientific knowledge, empiricism, and to a "mechanistic-naturalistic" conception of the world. Members of these schools rose above the "metaphysics" of philosophy. It seems to be the case that all the passages Needham brings up from Chinese philosophers are poetical, mystical, or alchemical statements. The founding text of Taoism written by Lao Tzu, *Tao Te Ching* (300 BC), consists of a string of impressionistic statements about "the Way" amounting to five thousand words. Needham claims that Lao Tzu wrote in a language similar to the proto-scientific language of the Pre-Socratics, citing the following:

The ways of men are conditioned by those of the earth, the ways of Earth by those of Heaven, the ways of Heaven by those of the Tao, and the Tao came into being by itself.[646]

---

[644] The encyclopedic *Handbook of the History of Logic*, which consists of eleven volumes (2004–2012), dedicates only two chapters of the first volume to the contributions of non-Western civilizations, namely, Indian and Arabic logic, with the rest of the volume covering Aristotelian logic, and every other volume singularly dedicated to Western logic. Hard as it may be to apprehend, the Chinese had no formal logic, and the so-called "Arabic" logic consists of commentaries on Aristotle's logic.

[645] McKeon, 1957.

[646] Needham, 90–91.

He cites many similarly worded passages from later Taoist texts, for example:

> All phenomena have their causes. If one does not know these causes, alt-
> hough one may happen to be right, it is as if one knew nothing, and in the
> end, one will be bewildered. . . . The fact that water leaves the mountains
> and runs to the sea is not due to any dislike of the mountains and love of
> the sea, but is the effect of height as such.[647]

But these statements are not "*mechanistic*" in outlook. They are not even at the
level of the Pre-Socratic search for naturalistic causes. The way Taoists write about
the Tao, the being that came to be by itself, lacks rigor; it is really a mystical way
of apprehending a oneness that is complete unto itself, which they describe in hazy
words and assert that "it is."

In contrast, when Parmenides wrote about "*the One*" he tried to deduce it from
prior statements. Parmenides contrasts the expression that *something is* to the expression that *something is not*. He then argues that saying that *something is not*
does not make sense since you cannot know what is not, and you can't even express it. He writes:

> There are only two ways of inquiry that can be thought of. The first,
> namely, that it is (and that it is impossible for it not to be), is the way of
> belief, for truth is its companion. The other way of inquiry, namely, that it
> is not (and cannot be), is a path that none can learn at all. For you cannot
> know what is not, nor can you express it.[648]

Having said this, Parmenides follows up with his main point that only that which
is can be thought about in a meaningful way, and only that which can be thought
about can be:

> It is the same thing that can be thought and that can be. What can be spo-
> ken and thought must be; for it is possible for it to be, but impossible for
> nothing to be. . . . One path only is left for us to speak of, namely, that it is.

---

[647] Ibid, 93.

[648] The following three quotes from Parmenides are taken from Barnes's exhaustive study, *The
Presocratic Philosophers* (1986), Chapters IX, X, XI.

From here he infers that what we can say about the One is that it is eternal, indivisible, unmoving—that is, uncreated and indestructible. He offers a rational reason for making this inference, saying that if we say that the One became, or came into existence, or will cease to exist, then this would be the same as saying that it was not before it became, and that it will not be after it ceases to be, which would amount to making expressions about things which are not, which is impossible, since you cannot know or say anything about what is not. Therefore:

> [The One is eternal], for how can "what is" be going to be in the future? Or how could it come into being? If it came into being, then it is not. Nor is it, if it is going to be in the future. Thus is becoming extinguished and passing away not to be heard of.

Should we even include any of the major members of the Legalist school? As Frederick Mote says:

> Legalism is not a movement in philosophy. It is not concerned with truth. It is not reflective thinking on the great individual and social problems of life. It does not seek the general principles under which all facts can be explained. It is a system of methods and principles for the operation of the state, and even the state is given only the barest of ideological foundations. Legalists were content to justify their system by the single comment: "It works."[649]

So, it looks like Hsun Tzu (298–238 BC), the founder of legalism, should be taken out from this list. If we include the Legalists, then we should include many other European political philosophers who were left out, starting with Machiavelli, Bodin, Cicero, Thoreau, Bakunin, Hooker, Calvin, Lenin, Harrington, Blackstone, Paine, Jefferson, Burke, Godwin, Constant, Madison, Gentile, Sorel, Oakeshott— to name just a few.

---

[649] Mote, 1989, 108.

VII

EUROPEANS HAVE ALWAYS BEEN "WEIRD": HOW WEAK IN-GROUP KINSHIP TIES AND REPUBLICAN CIVIC VALUES MAKE THEM THE LEAST BIOLOGICALLY BOUND PEOPLE

Most beautiful is the sight of those near and dear to us when our original kinship makes us of one mind.

– Epicurus

Kinship

Lewis Henry Morgan (1818–1881), an American descended from Welsh pioneers, remembered today as the founder of the discipline of anthropology, was the first scholar to argue that kinship was the fundamental institution regulating human relations and norms throughout much of history. He articulated this in a detailed 600 page-work titled *Systems of Consanguinity and Affinity of the Human Family*, first published in 1871. This book "created at a stroke what without exaggeration might be called the seminal concern of contemporary anthropology, the study of kinship."[650] Its basic argument was that the ties humans develop along kinship lines based on the principles of consanguinity (kinship by blood) and affinity (kinship by marriage) determine the way primitive societies are organized. I must admit that I never paid much attention to kinship until very recently. I was taught, as a university student, that Morgan's ideas had been "properly framed"

---

[650] Schweitzer, 1996, 543–46.

by his contemporaries Karl Marx and Friedrich Engels within their "scientific theory of historical materialism" with its emphasis on the way the material conditions
of life and the relations between classes shape the norms of society.

Friedrich Engels's well-known 1884 book, *The Origin of the Family, Private
Property and the State*, drew heavily on Morgan's work, including his subsequent
1877 book, *Ancient Society; or, Researches in the Lines of Human Progress from
Savagery, Through Barbarism to Civilization*. Marx wrote extensive notes about
Ancient Society, which Engels used for *The Origin of the Family*. As acknowledged
in the preface of this book, Engels "had reserved . . . the privilege of displaying the
results of Morgan's investigations in connection with [their] own materialist conception of history." *The Origin of the Family* was required reading when I was a
student, a foundational text of Marxist anthropology, the study of early societies,
and of feminist theory. Evelyn Reed credited Morgan, in an introduction to a new
1972 edition of *The Origin of the Family*, with the realization that the "key institutions of civilized society—the family, private property, and the state—were non-
existent in prehistoric life."

But instead of highlighting Morgan's crucial discovery of the institution of
kinship, Reed credited him with establishing that "procuring the necessities of
life" has been the most important activity throughout history. Having integrated
Morgan into the Marxist fold, Engels was credited with explaining the origins of
private property, and how societies became class-divided. He was also praised for
his argument that the development of civilization had come along with the imposition of sexual inequalities, and showing thereby that "male supremacy and female inferiority are integral features" of the "patriarchal class system" of all civilizations, including modern capitalism. The Victorian monogamous family was a
recent construct of capitalist society intended to ensure the transfer of property
along the male line. Overcoming this sexual inequality required the abolition of
the nuclear monogamous family and the restoration of the "matrilineal" and communal sexual lifestyle of primitive societies.

Morgan's concept of kinship was thus appropriated by Marxist feminists as a
weapon against the monogamous nuclear family. Among academic anthropologists, kinship would remain a valuable concept in the study of early societies only.
When the discipline of sociology emerged in the early 1800s, its goal was to understand the origins of modernity in the West and the nature of modern institutions. Sociologists did not find kin-based institutions in the Western societies they
studied, so they paid very little attention to kinship. The nuclear family was studied as a modern institution belonging within a wider society that was no longer

structured by kinship ties, clans and tribal relationships. Although Max Weber wrote about kin groups, all the key concepts in his studies were aimed principally at explaining the unique rationality of Western culture: rational-legal authority, bureaucracy, means-end rationality, capitalism, the Protestant Work Ethic, disenchantment of the world, the iron cage.

But even anthropologists, upon which Marxist thinking exerted a powerful influence, came to accept the materialist explanation that the values, religious beliefs, and customs of a society are "superstructural," and that a proper scientific study requires the study of economic factors, climatic conditions, and class relationships. The functionalist school in anthropology remained preoccupied with the idea that institutions exist ultimately to meet the physiological needs of humans for reproduction, food, and shelter, and that all institutions are equally important in their contribution to the survival of the whole social system. The influential cultural materialist school initiated by Marvin Harris in 1971 even chided Marxists for being insufficiently materialist in their excessive preoccupation with class relationships over "material realities" such as technological, environmental, and demographic factors. The recent arrival of Darwinism has entailed a greater preoccupation with the way environmental pressures select for the norms of society—with much less attention paid to the way kinship shapes these norms with a cultural dynamic of its own, not altogether reducible to natural selection.

Joseph Henrich's Novelty

Joseph Henrich's 2020 book, *The WEIRDest People in the World: How the West Became Psychologically Peculiar and Particularly Prosperous*, must be considered one of the most important studies about the perennial question of why the West became the first modern industrial civilization—precisely because of its focus on kinship and its insistence that this institution continued to exercise a fundamental influence on the basic values of societies, from hunting and gathering through to the advanced civilizations of the world, until the West finally "demolished" its kinship institutions in the Middle Ages. The thesis of this book is that the kinship-based in-group psychology dominating traditional societies was fundamentally altered in Europe into individualistic habits of thinking and behaving as the Catholic Church in the Middle Ages unintentionally transformed the psychology of Europeans in a direction that ignited the rise of liberal institutions and norms by prohibiting cousin and polygynous marriages and promoting

monogamous nuclear families. This release of Europeans from their kin-based relationships and obligations encouraged them to choose their spouses, social
friends, and associates, which opened the door to the creation of voluntary associations, chartered towns, guilds, universities, monasteries, and representative institutions. This new world socialized Europeans to extend their trust to anonymous strangers, to think in a less contextual way, and to judge objects and humans
in terms of universal principles and rules applicable on the basis of rationally-
based criteria.

This emphasis on the immemorial role of kinship institutions in the shaping
of human psychology, and how the psychology of Europeans was "rewired," differentiates Henrich from the standard approaches that have dominated this debate with their focus on the autonomous role of market relations, modern scientific and enlightenment ideas, the transition from feudalism to capitalism, exploitation of the Americas, or geographical "good luck." According to Henrich, kinship norms and the "scaling up" of kinship relationships have played a foundational role in shaping the mind and behavior of humans and directing the broad
patterns of history. Kinship has determined the survival and social identity of humans, status and obligations, sense of right and wrong, normative relationships
between family members, when and whom one should marry, where newlyweds
should find residence, who owns the land, and how property should be inherited.
The world humans have inhabited since their early *Homo-sapiens* days has been
one of intense kinship relationships characterized by a corresponding psychology
that was clannish, conformist, deferential, and highly context-sensitive, without
the ability to detach objects and persons from particular settings, and thus without
the ability to generate abstract concepts and think analytically.

Henrich is also different in arguing how the "demolition" of kinship ties, not
liberal ideas or growing commercialization, was the one factor that spurred the
rise of "new forms of urbanization and fueled impersonal commerce, from merchant guilds and charter towns to universities and transregional monastic orders,
that were governed by new and increasingly individualistic norms and laws."[651]
While the influence of blood ties continued to exert their natural influence, all in
all, a whole new institutional setting gradually emerged in medieval Europe based
on rational principles and centered on the intentions of individuals, with objectively defined rights, as members of institutions. Only Europe, Henrich explains,
would see the rise of self-governing cities guided by abstract constitutional

---

[651] Henrich, 23.

principles that welcomed individuals as individuals from many backgrounds regardless of tribal origins. Only Europe would witness the spread of impersonal markets in which one's reputation with strangers as a reliable dealer would come to depend on one's fairness and impartiality, rather than on one's personal kinship status. These changes would be accompanied and followed by the rise of rational systems of law, continuous technological innovations, and the emergence of Galilean and Newtonian science, and an industrial revolution that would put Europeans on top of the world.

It is hard for Westerners socialized in "WEIRD" (Western, Educated, Industrialized, Rich, and Democratic) societies, where families have been nuclearized and a wide network of other institutions have been created independently of kinship ties, to appreciate the cardinal importance of kinship, even as they appreciate how significant the family remains today in the ontogenetic development of humans. Westerners who write about the rise of modern industrial Europe prefer to talk about the role of ideas, Malthusian demographic pressures, modes of production, technological innovations, institutional changes, warfare, and religion. The books currently dominating "the Great Divergence" debate tend to downplay any substantial differences between the West and other civilizations. They argue that there were "surprising similarities" between the major civilizations as late as the 1750s, and that the West began to diverge as the Industrial Revolution took off.[652] Some books go back in time to the gunpowder revolution and Europe's military supremacy after the 1600s (Parker, 1998; Hoffman, 2015), or to the rise of modern science in the seventeenth century, or to the "unique" family structure of medieval Northwest Europe (Macfarlane, 1978).

However, Henrich goes beyond a strictly anthropological perspective by combining his ethnographic field studies with cognitive/cultural psychology and the most recent scholarship on the economic history of Europe. Years of intense ethnographic field studies of non-western peoples led him to question the prevailing assumption in Western psychology that the "patterns and dimensions of personality observed" among Americans and Europeans "represent the human pattern." While social scientists generally drew a distinction between traditional and modern norms, the implicit argument was that industrialization automatically strengthened naturally human dispositions for time thrift, love of choice, impersonal prosociality, analytical thinking, trust, and fairness towards strangers. These universal traits were believed to be found everywhere in the world, innate to the

---

[652] Frank, 1998; Pomeranz, 2000.

psychology of humans as humans. The reason for this major error in the under-standing of human psychology, according to Henrich, was that "most of what was known experimentally about human psychology and behavior was based on stud-ies with undergraduates from Western societies." Ninety-six percent of "experi-mental participants were drawn from northern Europe, North America, or Aus-tralia." There were studies done with participants from outside the West, but these relied heavily on highly Westernized "relationally mobile university students in urban centers."[653]

Another novel feature of *The WEIRDest People* is that it is packed with exper-imental surveys, figures, graphs, and tables, based on game theory, measuring the psychological differences between populations across the world, to counter the "massively biased samples" from the past that had been derived almost entirely from Western students. The types of experimental games, conducted by Henrich's research team and many other independent researchers, include the Dictator Game, Random Allocation Game, Public Goods Game, Impersonal Honesty Game, Ultimatum Game, and the Sharing Game. This experimental research is what led Henrich to conclude that there were two fundamental psychological pro-files in the world: the "WEIRD" profile of Westerners, and the non-WEIRD pro-file of kinship-based peoples.

Drawing as well on data from the World Values Survey, covering 75 contem-porary countries, persuaded Henrich that the greater the intensity of kinship, as measured particularly by degree of cousin marriage, the less trust individuals will have for "people they have just met, foreigners, and adherents of other religions." Moreover, "the higher the rate of cousin marriage in a country, the more willing managers were to give false testimony in court" to protect their ingroup members. "The executives from countries with stronger kin-based institutions hire more rel-atives into senior management." People from countries with intensive kinship rarely ever donate blood to strangers, they don't like to report crimes within their own ingroups, and they much prefer to dodge taxes. Henrich's book also compiles a substantial amount of evidence showing that Western peoples generally tend to be less in-group oriented, less tightly bound to traditional norms, more individu-alistic, less distrustful of strangers, highly inclined to believe in impartial notions of fairness, and more honest in their dealings with strangers.[654]

---

[653] Henrich, xii.
[654] Henrich, 21–30, 237–242.

Western peoples, to this day, are uniquely "WEIRD": they do trust foreigners a lot more than non-Western peoples; they do believe that Muslims and nonwhite immigrants generally are no different from them, as long as Westerners treat them with impartial fairness. One of the experiments mentioned by Henrich, the "Public Goods Game" (designed to measure whether individuals are willing to act "in the interests of their broader communities" by giving time, money, and effort to voting, donation of blood , joining the army, reporting crimes, following traffic laws, and paying taxes) distinctly showed that WEIRD individuals are far more inclined to act in the interests of the public good, whereas immigrants from kinship intensive cultures identify the public good with their own in-group.

Kevin MacDonald's Evolutionary-Genetic Approach

The only scholar who comes to mind who traces the divergence of the West to its monogamous families, individualism, and openness to the formation of contractual relationships with non-kin, is Kevin MacDonald. His insightfully original 2019 book, *Individualism and the Western Liberal Tradition*, is the first to argue that the "great divergence" is rooted in the contrasting kinship systems of the West and the rest. Although MacDonald does not examine the general patterns of historical evolution in terms of kinship networks, he explains the divergence in terms kinship systems, whether lines of descent were bilateral or patricentric, whether marriages were exogamous or endogamous, monogamous or polygamous, whether families were nuclear or extended, whether there was individual choice in marriage or arranged marriages, and whether individuals were inclined to establish relations outside their kinship group, with relatively weak ethnocentric tendencies, or whether they were seen as embedded to their kinship group, with relatively strong levels of ethnocentrism. There are, however, some crucial differences between the approaches of MacDonald and Henrich. While MacDonald recognizes the cultural role the Catholic Church played in the prohibition of polygamy and in the moral enforcement of monogamy, he employs an evolutionary psychological approach to argue that the individualism of Europeans was a genetically based behavior rooted in the weaker kinship institutions and norms of prehistorical hunting and gathering peoples of northern Europe, selected by the colder environmental pressures of this region.

Macdonald, to be clear, is not the first to attempt a "genetic" explanation for the different behavioral patterns of the races of the world. Philippe Rushton, among others we will meet below, is well known for his excellent research pointing to crucial differences in the racial profiles of Caucasoids, Africans, and Orientals, in brain size, intelligence, temperament, sexual behavior, and rates of fertility. MacDonald, however, is the only scholar to investigate the bio-evolutionary origins of Western individualism. He observes that all humans have common biological adaptations, but "differ in degree in adaptations" depending on environments. These differences in degree can generate "major differences" between cultures.

Under the "harsh evolutionary pressures of the Ice Age" in northern Europe, there would have been more pressures to live in small groups and in relative social isolation, rather than for the selection of "extended kinship networks and collectivist groups" competing in close proximity for resources. There were selective pressures for males to provision simple households or nuclear families characterized by monogamy, exogamy, and bilateral kinship, because the ecology and availability of resources could not have selected for large polygynous families.[655]

This was in contrast to Near Eastern regions, with their long fertile rivers supporting "large tribal groups based on extended kinship relations."[656] The strategy pursued by northern Europeans was quite successful, enabling them to develop complex hunting-gathering cultures during the Mesolithic era for a long time, 15,000 to 5,000 years ago, delaying the advance of farming, which was slowly spreading into central and northern Europe after Anatolian farmers settled in various parts of southern Europe starting some 8000 years ago.

Mesolithic cultures in Europe did consist of larger bands of hunter-gatherers due to their more efficient exploitation of resources and improved stone age tools, but lacking any "stable resource" that could be controlled by an extended lineage group, their residences remained seasonally occupied by relatively small families living in a state of egalitarian monogamy, and without one extended family superimposing itself over the others by controlling fertile and stable land areas. In northern Europe, MacDonald explains, tribes "were periodically forced to split up into smaller, more family-based groups." These smaller groups were forced to interact with related families and with "non-kin and strangers" also moving around from season to season. These interactions were not regulated by kinship norms but instead led to emphasis on "trust and maintaining a good reputation within

---

[655] MacDonald, 2019, 94–98.
[656] Ibid, 99.

the larger non-kinship-based group."[657] These evolutionary-selected behaviors characterized by small families, exogamous and monogamous marriages, and relations based on trust with outsiders, were the primordial ground out of which Western individualism emerged.

In the Near East, complex hunting-gathering societies soon evolved into agrarian chiefdoms controlled by lineage groups in charge of stable resources. We can add, as Jared Diamond observed, that since most of the animals and plants susceptible to domestication were found in the Near East, this abundance of resources encouraged or made it easier for kinship groups to coalesce together within one territory into huge tribal societies based on polygamous networks. Therefore, whereas monogamy and exogamy persisted in the West, in the East the tendency was for marrying relatives, even first cousins.

A central argument of MacDonald is likewise that insofar as northern Europeans evolved in the context of small families interacting with outsiders, and in the context of meritocratic Indo-European warbands, they were selected to think morally beyond their own kin group about how best to cooperate with strangers. Individuals who were untrustworthy in their relations with outsiders were shunned for the simple reason that maintaining one's reputation as honest was important for future dealings. In contrast, the larger kinship groups of the East restricted cooperation with outsiders, and thus felt less pressure to nurture moral principles that would extend beyond their group or that would involve altruistic attitudes towards outsiders. In the East, morality was defined mostly in terms of the needs of the in-group, but among northern Europeans, a tradition of universal moral thinking emerged. MacDonald hints as well that the northern environment of Europe resulted in the selection of traits for spatial and mechanical ability, a tendency toward analytical thinking, "thinking of oneself as independent" in contrast to the East, where thinking remained "linked to thinking of oneself as interdependent with other people."[658]

Another pillar in MacDonald's analysis that is completely absent in Henrich's study is that the Indo-Europeans who invaded the Balkans and then central Europe, starting in the fourth through to the third millennium, were also quite individualistic. Macdonald draws this argument from my book, *The Uniqueness of Western Civilization*, although he pays more attention to the ways that kinship was "de-emphasized" within the central Indo-European institution of the

---

[657] Ibid, 101–102.
[658] Ibid, 112.

Männerbund. These warrior bands were organized primarily for warfare, which was the main way aristocrats found a livelihood consistent with their status as warriors, opportunities to accumulate resources and followers, and a chance to attain heroic renown among peers. Membership in these war bands, MacDonald explains, was open to any aristocratic warrior willing to enter into a contractual agreement with the leader, with the greatest spoils and influence going to those who exhibited the greatest military talents. In other words, these war bands were open to individuals on the basis of talent, rather than "on the basis of closeness of kinship." The aristocratic character of Indo-European culture is also emphasized by MacDonald, as it is in *Uniqueness*: the leader, even when he was seen as a king, was "first among equals," with war bands commanded by men who gained their reputation through the performance of honorable deeds, proud of their freedom and unwilling to act in a subservient manner. MacDonald highlights, as part of the *Männerbund*, the "guest-host relationships (beyond kinship) where everyone had mutual obligations of hospitality," and where "outsiders could be incorporated as individuals with rights and protections.[659]

MacDonald could have clarified for readers unfamiliar with evolutionary theories of marriage and family that when he writes about "an aristocratic elite not bound by kinship," or about how ties between aristocrats "transcended the kinship group," he is not denying the importance of blood ties between extended I-E family members and extended I-E families grouped into clans. He observes that marriages occurred within clans, and that punishments and other disputes were decided in terms of kinship customs. The difference is that I-Es developed social ties above their kin relations that "tended to break down strong kinship bonds." While the strong kinship cultures of the East were characterized by arranged marriages within the extended family, and political-military ties were heavily infused by kin customary relations; among the Corded Ware culture that grew out of the Yamnaya (which we mentioned in our first chapter), one finds exogamy or marriage outside the extended family, or with females "non-local in origin," including the practice of monogamy. Exogamous marriages between I-E groupings, including the peoples they dominated, were a key component of their guest-host networks, and a means to pull together military alliances and integrate new talent.

Although some may argue that MacDonald does not have direct genetic evidence demonstrating that crucial elements of these "WEIRD" traits were selected

---

[659] Ibid, 29–44.

in hunting and gathering times,[660] he does bring up solid findings on the family structure of Europe showing a gradation in family relations, very early on in its history, from an "extreme individualism" in northwestern Europe, where the family was cut off from extended kinship networks, to a "moderate individualism" in central Europe, to a "moderate collectivism" in southern and eastern Europe.[661] It stands to reason that an evolutionary psychologist would want to dig further back in time to identify possible environmental conditions that may have selected for individualism, rather than assume, as Henrich does, that the psychology of humans across the planet was identical before the "demolition" of kinship networks in the medieval era by the Catholic Church. One major difference between Mac-Donald and Henrich, besides their respective biological and cultural approaches, is that while MacDonald understands that the individualism and weak ethnocentrism of the West was critical to the rise of the West in its ability to build efficient institutions with impartial rules, and conceptualize nature in scientific/analytical terms, he also recognizes that this lack of an in-group ethnic identity is currently a major weakness that threatens the very survival of the West, as its population naively welcomes millions of immigrants with strong ethnocentric traits exploiting for their own benefit the weak ingroup ties of Europeans. Henrich knows this contrast, but persists, as we shall soon see, in believing that Westerners can successfully assimilate millions and millions of immigrants to Western values. We will return to this argument by MacDonald in Chapter XI.

---

[660] The evolutionary psychologist Peter Frost (2020) cites and reinforces MacDonald's argument about the way the environment in northern Europe selected for weaker kinship ties, nuclearized monogamous families, late marriage, and a relatively high proportion of unmarried people. But Frost acknowledges that "as we go farther back in time, we have less data to work with"—for the period before the Church openly imposed its family program. The case for weaker kinship ties in northern Europe is, nevertheless, reasonably based on the principles of evolutionary theory. But it also stands to reason that, as chiefdoms emerged in northern/central Europe, among the Germanic tribes that brought Rome down and created the first medieval kingdoms, the tendency for polygamy would have increased among men with plentiful resources. There is historical evidence for widespread polygamy in this era, along with customary laws based on kinship. It is all relative, of course. The evidence also shows that prehistorical Indo-Europeans and Germanic peoples were more willing to extend interpersonal trust beyond close kin in the formation of contractual feudal relations.

[661] There is very solid research behind the different family systems of northern, eastern, and southern European regions, known by the term "the Hajnal line." See Hajnal (1965) and Kertzer and Barbagli (2001).

Cultural Learning

This chapter will examine many books in its careful examination of Henrich's book, because I believe that the focus of *The WEIRDEST People* on kinship, the fundamentally different psychology of Europeans, and on "cumulative cultural learning," are crucial to the understanding of the great divergence. However, among the many critical evaluations, and alternative lines of interpretation against Henrich's thesis, the key one will be that his emphasis on Europe's cultural learning barely captures the foundational difference between European and non-European cultures. My interpretative angle is different from both Henrich's and MacDonald's, in that I view the enforcement of monogamy and the creation of civic associations as an expression of the relatively higher degree of freedom Europeans enjoyed from the biological determinations of kinship ties, rather than its cause. European cultural behavior since ancient times has come under conditions of a higher level of "relaxed selection" (to use Bellah's term as examined in Chapter III). The creation of nuclear families should not be understood solely as a blind selective pressure imposed on Europeans by particular environments, or an "unintentional" decision by a Catholic Church, as Henrich says, seeking to expropriate kinship-held lands. It was partly a product of the realization, already in ancient Greece and Rome, that monogamy was both a morally and socially superior way of constructing broader identities based on civic membership (though without excluding ethnic identities) over clannish/tribal bonds based on polygamous-cousin marriage networks. Henrich knows that Europeans were unique in creating institutions based on rational grounds and individual choice, yet he reaches the rather inconsistent conclusion that European rational deliberation did not play any feedback role in the making of the very WEIRD psychology he identifies with free choice and rationality.

My emphasis on the consciousness of consciousness of Europeans, their higher sense of selfhood, introspection, and intentionality, does not abrogate the importance of natural selection, but simply affirms the emergent quality of these mental attributes. While recognizing the reasonableness of MacDonald's emphasis on the evolutionary selection of European individualist traits, I am more sympathetic to Henrich's "cultural" argument than MacDonald is. Among members of the dissident- or alt-right, Henrich's argument that the WEIRD psychology of Europeans was a product of cultural evolution, not genetic evolution, and that the psychology of humans can be altered through cultural changes, will indeed be seen as another version of "social constructionism." Darwinians prefer to talk about human nature, innate biological drives, and the evolutionary selection of different behavioral traits, including the selection of different degrees of mental aptitude.

Gregory Cochran and Henry C. Harpending attempted a gene-based evolutionary account, coupled with the effects of culture on genes as central to history. In his 2007 book, *Understanding Human History*, Michael Hart argued that differences in average intelligence between separate groups should be given priority in our efforts to understand the divergent patterns of civilizations. The origination of a modern technological culture required a population with a high level of intelligence. But while Hart offered a persuasive explanation about how, in the course of time, various physical differences arose between "human groups widely separated from each other geographically, with relatively little interbreeding between them," he could not explain why East Asians with their higher average intelligence were unable to create the first modern scientific civilization.[662] We will see below that MacDonald also encounters difficulties trying to explain why it was that ancient Greece would witness the origins of analytical thinking, universal moral philosophies, and monogamous families, despite the fact, as he recognizes, that ancient Greece had "moderate collectivist" kinship ties, unlike the more individualistic cultures of northern and central Europe.

Henrich can definitely be faulted for focusing almost singularly on "cumulative cultural learning" without allowing much influence to innate genetic factors, other than saying that humans were genetically selected to be cultural learners. He defines humans as a cultural species precisely because they "evolved genetically to learn adaptively in ways that calibrate our minds and behavior to the environment we encounter."[663] How different environmental settings may have exerted different selective pressures for different genetic traits upon different populations in the world, is not a question he addresses. From the position that humans have a common genetic stock, he moves on to explain why the psychology of Westerners has been so different for centuries. His approach is nevertheless different from standard cultural approaches in that it goes deeper into the brains and psychology of

---

[662] Conversely, while the geographical approach of Jared Diamond's *Guns, Germs, and Steel* (1997) was very good at explaining why the cultures of Eurasia got a head start in the development of complex civilizations, by showing that this area had most of the wild crops and wild animals that could be domesticated, and by showing that the east-west orientation of this area favored the diffusion of domesticated crops, animals, and knowledge, this approach failed to explain why the civilization of Europe within Eurasia moved past the Asian world after 1500.

[663] Henrich, 61–68.

Europeans to explain their divergent path. Humans can't be easily re-wired in a WEIRD direction with the mere introduction of new classroom lectures or the placement of children in new institutional settings. Living with or without kinship relations has deep ontogenetic effects in the neurological (though not genetic) wiring of the brain.[664] Beyond Henrich (and Daniel Dennett, Robert Bellah and others) I believe that, not only was human evolution "gradually de-Darwinized" with the emergence of human culture generally, but Europeans were the freest from Darwinian pressures early on in their history, simply because they were more conscious of their consciousness, making their cultural history (increasingly so in the modern era) a more foresighted and intentional affair, and therefor exhibiting higher levels of cultural creativity.

Scaling Up Kinship Networks

It is worth analyzing at length Henrich's concept of "scaling up kinship" for its novel insights in the cultural evolution of societies from simple to complex civilizations. For him, the concept of learning has to do primarily with the ways humans have learned to expand their ties of kinship beyond their immediate genetic relatives through the creation of broader kinship networks, the spread of "universalizing religious beliefs," and the creation by Europeans of WEIRD institutional associations with different self-reinforcing, culturally-learned, and interlocking beliefs, practices, and incentives. The fundamental factor driving history, the "secret" of successful peoples, has consisted in their ability to create widening networks of cooperation and solidarity.

"Intergroup competition," or the biological struggle for survival pervading all living beings and all societies, is what compelled or incentivized humans to create wider networks of cooperation beyond early small bands. "Violent conflict . . . among bands, clans, and tribes" has been "the most striking feature" of kinship-

---

[664] He offers revealing data showing that immigrants from intensive kinship backgrounds persist in their ingroup behaviors even when their income and education rise in the West. Immigrants "coming from places with more intensive kinship continue to care more about in-group loyalty and less about non-relational morality" (210). He observes that cousin marriage has actually increased "among immigrants to WEIRD societies such as Britain and Belgium," including among second generation immigrants, "compared to the home country" (546). Although Henrich does not address this issue, it can safely be said that from his perspective the clannishness of immigrants will start to decline in the third or future generations as WEIRD traits penetrate deeper into their psychology.

based societies. Those communities that failed to create wider networks of cooperation were liquidated or absorbed by those societies that managed to "scale up"
their networks of kinship cultural cooperation.[665] Yet, oddly enough, this concept
of "violent intergroup conflict" is left undeveloped. This is not an innocent absence. The social sciences in the West are dedicated to the "solution" of human
conflict by finding ways to enhance cooperation. Since World War II, this has
meant nurturing cooperation across the world through the invitation of diverse
races and cultures to overcome "xenophobic ethnic attachments."

Henrich, as we will see below, is committed to this project. This is an unspoken
ideological message in *The WEIRDest People* that reviewers have missed. Western
academics love the words "cooperation" and "solidarity," which explains in part
the great success of Henrich's prior book, *The Secret of Our Success: How Culture
Is Driving Human Evolution, Domesticating Our Species, and Making Us Smart*
(2015). Henrich is convinced that the "underlying processes" driving history forward have been the enhancement of cooperative strategies across groups and societies through the scaling up of kinship networks, from the relatively simple
bands of hunter-gatherers in Paleolithic times, to the vast empires of pre-modern
times, to the future creation of a global world of WEIRD multi-racial race-mixed
individuals with great possibilities for "residential mobility" anywhere they
choose—a perspective that stands in complete contrast to MacDonald's far more
realistic assessment.

So, what did humans do to create greater unity within their bands and between
bands, as well as wider networks of solidarity? Henrich's answer to this question
is one of the most original components of his book. Whereas prior explanations
on the dynamics of history have centered around the impact of external forces,
geographical and demographic pressures, or the role of ideas, without any analysis
of psychological profiles, Henrich focuses on the way humans have gone about
rearranging, extending, and intensifying the most basic institution of all: their
family ties (albeit under the pressure of intergroup competition).[666] It all started

---

[665] Henrich, 78–85.

[666] Mind you, in the last few years a number of economic historians have been exploring the role
of kinship and monogamous families in the divergent paths of the West and the East. Avner
Greif (2006) observed that "little attention has been given to the impact of the family structure
and its dynamics on institutions. This limits our ability to understand distinct institutional developments—and hence growth—in the past and present." Henrich draws on Greif's work, citing among other papers "Family structure, institutions, and growth: The origins and implications of Western corporations" (2006). In this paper Greif presents "the reasons for the decline
of kinship groups in medieval Europe and why the resulting nuclear family structure, along with

with the family, whom one could marry, how many wives one could have, where married couples could reside, and how descent should be traced. "Pair bonding" was naturally selected as a mating strategy because it permitted "males and females to team up to rear offspring." From this genetic starting point, marriage became a norm, and these marriage norms were gradually expanded to include rules aimed at constraining women's sexuality in order to increase the confidence of the husband and his family that her children were really his biological children. These marriage norms increased "paternity certainty," which firmed up the links between children and their fathers, as well as links with the in-laws. In-laws are not genetically related, but through marriage norms, humans have learned to think, for example, of the wife's brothers or the mother's sisters as part of the family, and to believe that we share genetic interests. These ties with in-laws were reinforced through social norms "involving gifts, rituals, and mutual obligations." Hunting and gathering bands have in fact consisted mostly of in-laws rather than blood relatives.

Humans were selected with an aversion to sex with siblings and parents because of the chances that the offspring will be unhealthy. From this evolved disposition, they came to "figure out" ways to extend this aversion beyond close relatives through incest taboos prohibiting sex with step-siblings, and prohibiting marriages with first, second, and even third cousins. This encouraged norms compelling parents to arrange marriages for their children with more distant kinfolk, which extended their social networks and solidarity in times of droughts, floods, and in the face of threatening enemies. Only those norms that enhanced success in competition with other groups would tend to survive and spread. "Psychologically-potent communal rituals" involving synchronic dances and rhythmic music were commonly used to enhance in-group solidarity, alleviate personal divisions, and induce members to collaborate in major public works.

With the "emergence of food production," intergroup competition was intensified, which encouraged new forms of cooperation, ritual bonds, and interpersonal relations within groups. As societies grew in size with agriculture, additional non-kin-based institutions were developed; however, these institutions were "built atop a deep foundation of kin-based institutions." Henrich observes, furthermore, that building societies based on cooperative relationships beyond a handful of family clans is very hard once the population exceeds a few hundred

---

other factors, led to ... intentionally created, voluntary, interest-based, and self-governed permanent associations" such as guilds, fraternities, universities, communes, and city-states.

people. Large villages of over a few hundred people (though this depends on the environment) tend to fracture into feuding clans. Anthropologists have thus been very interested in understanding why and how some societies managed to integrate large numbers of clans. The best strategy for "scaling up" kinship ties included the use of social norms regarding residence after marriage, inheritance and ownership, incest taboos, arranged marriages, broadening of gods and rituals across clans, and rituals. Arranged marriages, for example, involved using daughters for strategic alliances with other clans, which had the effect of extending blood lines between clans. Patrilocal residence had the effect of solidifying ties between the new couple's children and the father's children and other patrilineal relatives.

By focusing on kinship-based relationships, Henrich manages to find a very firm ground upon which to explain the entire movement of history from bands, to big man societies, to chiefdoms, to pre-modern states. Many theories have been offered to explain the rise of pre-modern states. Among the most famous explanations is the "hydraulic hypothesis" proposed by Karl Wittfogel in 1957, and the class-based explanation proposed by Marxists. Bruce Trigger believed that religious fear was the main reason an exploited majority was initially prepared to support a state system based on inequality. But perhaps the most respected argument nowadays is the circumscription theory proposed by Robert Carneiro in 2012. He argued that environmental constriction in the context of population growth intensified intergroup competition and warfare, and that this set of causal factors eventually led to the formation of centralized authorities to meet competitive pressures for scarce resources.

Henrich's focus is on how pre-modern states "were built on an underlying social and psychological foundation formed by intense kin-based institutions."[667] The consolidation of the ownership of rituals by the most powerful clans "has been one of the main ways in which some clans have set themselves above others." By excluding weaker clans from control of key rituals, the leaders of powerful chiefly clans could accumulate most of the rituals, and in this way spread their legitimacy and sacred authority. They could also attract more marriage offers from patrilineal clans seeking to link themselves directly through their daughters' children with the chiefly clan, and thus gain greater prestige for themselves. And because polygyny was a key norm of all pre-modern kinship-based societies, the chiefly clans could easily take multiple wives, and thus accumulate links with many other clans and reproduce faster. They could also wrap themselves with the

---

[667] Henrich, 112.

most powerful gods and give themselves a divine and superior status; and they could take ownership of the land "away from the clans of the commoners."

As chiefly clans evolved into fully stratified chiefdoms, new bureaucratic institutions gradually emerged in charge of collecting taxes, adjudicating disputes, conducting long-distance trade, gathering armies, and organizing the building of public works. While the relationships between the upper clans and the growing lower strata of the population were not directly based on kinship ties, the upper elite continued to rely directly on family connections to manage and control these bureaucratic institutions, just as the lower clans continued to be thoroughly based on kinship ties within their own localities. Early state religions, such as that of the kingdoms of Judah and Israel, and later the major world religions of Buddhism, Christianity and Islam, played a similar historical role in the way they successfully "scaled up" human cooperation among believers over and above (though not against) tribal ties. These religions, Henrich insists, were not WEIRD in their beliefs, including Christianity, but remained rooted in kinship institutions, though they did expand the field of cooperation beyond tribal lines.

The promotion of fellow-feelings for strangers was far less powerful in encouraging cooperation than the threat of punishment against those who violated the commandments of supernatural beings. Henrich provides experimental surveys showing that religious people are far more motivated by fear of punishment than empathy for strangers to follow the moral codes of their religions. Humans as cultural learners are inclined to accept and conform to those religious beliefs that have great rituals, including food taboos, sexual prohibitions, fasts, martyrs, daily prayers, and grace before meals, that enhance the credibility of the religion. Humans also gravitate towards prestigious or successful advocates of beliefs and rituals. Universalizing religions were able to create "super-tribes" of believers with a greater inclination to trust members of other clans with the same religious beliefs. But Henrich carefully notes that the broader cooperation and encompassing identity the universalizing religions encouraged among believers did not dispense with the old kinship ties. These universalizing religions, together with the civilizations they worked to sustain, were in fact built atop the old kinship systems. Only later in the Middle Ages would Christianity set out to demolish kinship ties and thus promote a truly WEIRD pan-tribal world of Christian believers, for whom shared beliefs alone functioned as their unifying identity, rather than shared tribal lineage.

The Catholic Church Intentionally Imposed Monogamy

The foundational core of Henrich's argument about how Europe "unintentionally" followed a divergent path that led to the industrial revolution is that "between about 400–1200 CE the intensive kin-based institutions of many European tribal populations were slowly degraded, dismantled, and eventually demolished by the . . . Roman Catholic Church."[668] It was only after this demolition that Europeans "began to form new voluntary associations based on shared interests or beliefs rather than on kinship or tribal affiliations." It was during the High Middle Ages that Europe began to witness "novel institutions such as charter towns, professional guilds, and universities." Pre-Catholic Europe was a normal culture without WEIRD institutions, where the social identities of individuals were determined by their position and role within their kin-based groups. Disputes were adjudicated on the basis of the customary norms of the kinship group, not impersonal legal principles. There was no concept of intentionality and free will. Kinship groups collectively owned the land, and even in those places where individual ownership existed, the kinfolk had inheritance rights. Marriages were arranged, and marriages with relatives were customary. Polygamy was accepted, and polygynous marriages were common for high-status men.

The Church dismantled Europe's clans and kindreds by using its moral authority, threatening excommunication, expanding the incest taboos, and imposing numerous prohibitions during the course of many centuries, until by about 1200 it managed not only to dissolve Europe's extended families, but to create in substitute for them a new pan-tribal Christian identity across much of Europe. It prohibited all marriages between both blood relatives and affinal or in-law kinfolk, sororate and levirate marriages, polygynous marriage, marriage to non-Christians, and arranged marriages, while requiring bride and groom to publicly consent to marriage, and it promoted individual ownership of land and inheritance by personal testaments against customary inheritance. All these prohibitions seriously undermined the authority of kinship groups, forcing people to reach out beyond their clans and localities to find marriage partners, releasing individuals from age-old kinship obligations and inherited interdependence, into new voluntary associations.

---

[668] Ibid, 189.

With individual ownership and the promulgation of the idea that wealthy individuals could bequest by testament their wealth to the poor (to be administered
by the Church), kinship groups lost much of their land to the Church. The idea
that charitable acts could ensure one's entry into heaven, along with the power of
priests to administer to the dying in preparation for the afterlife, encouraged many
wealthy landowners to give their wealth to the Church, as they were freed from
the duties of kinship inheritance. "By 900 CE," Henrich observes, "the Church
owned about a third of the cultivated land in western Europe."[669]

Henrich raises a crucial question at this point: "Why did the Church adopt
these incest prohibitions?" More precisely, why did the Church identify polygamy
and cousin marriage, including marriage with distant cousins, as immoral acts?
Why did it advocate for monogamous marriage as the only morally acceptable
relationship in the procreation of families? What reasons did it offer to justify
these supposedly never-seen interferences in the sexual behavior and family arrangements of humans in history? His preferred answer is that the Catholic
Church "unintentionally" abolished kinship groups and cousin marriage for the
wealth it stood to gain, and for its own peculiar "obsession" with controlling "people's sex lives." The "Catholic Church stumbled onto a collection of marriage and
family policies that demolished Europe's intensive kin-based institutions" in its
greedy pursuit of economic power.[670] To Henrich, there were no cognitively-based
moral reasons for the Church's decision to prohibit pederasty, concubinage, and
polygamy. The most crucial transformation in Western history was driven by
plain economic interests and peculiar sexual obsessions.

This is very odd in a book that seeks to emphasize cultural learning and the
eventual spread of intentionality, individual responsibility, and reason-based actions. Henrich believes that "in nearly all societies, individuals don't consciously
design the most important elements of their institutions and certainly don't understand how or why they work."[671] He says "nearly" without mentioning a society
that has consciously planned its institutions. It is his view, as we will see in a later
section, that WEIRD individuals are no more conscious than non-WEIRD people
in their creation of societies. But how can the Europeans, who began to talk about
"free will," invent logic and deductive reasoning, and articulate ideals and

---

[669] Ibid, 185.
[670] Ibid, 471.
[671] Ibid, 94.

pragmatic programs about how to build better states, going back to ancient times, in Plato's *Republic* and Aristotle's *Politics*, be deprived of any intentionality?

WEIRD Sexual Morality of Christianity From Its Beginnings

The historical record shows, however, that Europeans were already quite WEIRD in their family laws and practices in ancient Greek and Roman times, and that Christians had already articulated a "new sexual morality" favoring monogamous marriage before the Middle Ages. *The Western Case for Monogamy over Polygamy* by John Witte, which Henrich ignores, effectively shows that, from the fourth century BC, Greek philosophers, Plato, Aristotle, and Roman Stoics eulogized monogamous marriage as the proper way to create a family and raise children. Early Christians saw monogamy as the "most beneficial" form of union between a man and a woman for a society to prosper. For "nearly two millennia," Witte writes, Europeans treated "polygamy as a malum in se offense—something bad in itself"—because it "deprecates women," "fractures fidelity," "divides loyalty," "promotes rivalry," "foments lust," and "harms children."[672] Only Europeans, among all the peoples of the world, would extoll, in the words of Plutarch (AD 46–120), "the union for life between a man and a woman for the delights of love and the getting of children."[673] When Catholics set out to demolish polygamous kinship groups, they did so in awareness of the merits of monogamy for the raising of a family and the harmonious functioning of society. Europeans did not become WEIRD because they accidentally abolished polygamous kinship groups; they abolished polygamy because they were the first to emancipate their moral consciousness from norms dictated by their biological inclinations.

Henrich's claim that the "package of prohibitions" the Catholic Church implemented had "only tenuous (at best) roots in Christianity's sacred writings" is untenable. It was not rooted in Judaism; as Henrich observes, "Jewish law . . . permitted cousin marriage, polygynous marriage, and uncle-niece marriage."[674] Abundant evidence has been compiled and interpreted by Kyle Harper in his book, *From Shame to Sin: The Christian Transformation of Sexual Morality in Late Antiquity*, showing a "transition from a late classical to a Christian sexual morality

---

[672] Witte, 2015, 459.
[673] Ibid, 107.
[674] Henrich,176.

... a quantum leap to a new foundational logic of sexual ethics." Christians consciously preached against sexual activity outside marriage, including sex with minors, divorce, infanticide and abortion, on the grounds that these practices were harmful to the soul of humans, their families, and the social order.

While the early Roman Republic was a traditionally conservative farmer-warrior society in which monogamy was emphasized and the family was seen to consist of father, mother, and children in a state of "affectionate devotion," it can't be denied that, as Rome became an empire with millions of slaves supporting the ruling class, the moral character of Romans weakened, divorce became normal, the birth rate declined, and the pornographic exploitation of slaves, especially girls, women, and boys, became rampant in elite circles. As Harper observes, slave minors were "subjected to untrammeled sexual abuse."[675] It was quite common for wealthy men to own boy slaves for sexual usage right inside their households. It was against this late Roman decadence that Christians objected. They rejected the Roman notion that a man born free could have sex with slaves, prostitutes, and boys. Paul condemned same-sex relations and sexual activity outside of marriage as *porneia* ("fornication"). Harper does not get into polygamy, but it should be noted that late-antiquity Christians Paul, Justin Martyr, Irenaeus, and Tertullian, spoke against polygamy, without getting rich for it.[676]

The WEIRD Hellenistic roots of Christianity

It needs to be emphasized, however, that the Bible was not the original source for monogamous marriage. The Old Testament permitted polygamy, and the New Testament did not make any substantial calls for monogamy. The principle of monogamy came to Christianity through the Greek-Roman cultural ecumene, where monogamy had long been a culturally mandated institution. Christianity was from its very beginnings a WEIRD Hellenistic religion deeply infused with Greek reason and Roman legalistic modes of thinking. It was the only religion that originated and developed within a metaphysical framework consistent with a rationalistic understanding of the natural world and in an intellectual setting where freedom was the subject of much discussion.[677] The way Greek reason entered into

---

[675] Harper, 2015, 8, 26.

[676] Crossan and Reed, 2004; Witter, 2015.

[677] The rationalizing impulse that transformed early Christianity into a theology was the subject matter of Edwin Hatch's *The Influence of Greek Ideas on Christianity*. Christianity was

Christianity could be seen in the tendency to draw inferences from clearly stated definitions, to construct systems from these inferences, and to ascertain the validity of these inferences in terms of their logical consistency within those systems. From the middle of the third century BC the Greek philosophical language came to influence Judaism from the middle of the third century BC, long before the New Testament period.[678]

Christianity, too, was born inside the womb of Hellenism. The Greek language, rather than Hebrew, was the language through which the Christian faith spread. The first Christians were Hellenized Jews. All the books of the New Testament were written in Greek. The Gospel of St. John reinterpreted Jesus in Platonic terms, and non-Jews who became Christians were typically educated Greeks. The majority of Jews in the first Christian century were not living in Judea but in the *politeuma* of Alexandria, Antioch, and the Hellenistic *oikoumene* at large. Philo of Alexandria (20 BC–AD 50) played a significant role in this adaptation of Christianity to Hellenism. Convinced that the Scripture could be elucidated through the use of Greek philosophy and science, Philo started a theological tradition within Christianity by bringing together in a rich mixture the religious beliefs of the Septuagint, the Torah and Mosaic Law, and the Platonic and Stoic idea of a single rational law inherent in nature.[679] By the early second century, Christ had come to personify the *Logos*, the "Word" of the opening of St. John's Gospel. The four fathers of the Latin Church, St. Ambrose (340–397), St. Jerome (340–419), St. Augustine (354–430), and St. Gregory the Great (540–604), received a thorough classical education that taught them that God is a purposeful designer of the world who can be known through the things He has made. The Latin apologists, Tertullian, Minucius Felix (late second century), and Lactantius (250–326), came to Christianity from a classical professional background. Minucius

---

"profoundly modified by the habit of mind of those who accepted it. It was impossible for the Greeks, educated as they were with an education which penetrated their whole nature, to receive or retain Christianity in its primitive simplicity." Christianity became "no less a philosophy than a religion" (1895, 49)

[678] The foremost scholar on this topic is Martin Hengel, starting with this two-volume work, *Judaism and Hellenism: Studies in Their Encounter in Palestine During the Early Hellenistic Period* (1974). His basic finding was that Judaism was deeply influenced by Greek thought much earlier than commonly believed, at least by the third century BC; Greek words penetrated the Bible itself; the book of Daniel, for example, includes themes mediated by Hellenistic writings. Hengel's conclusion, however, was not that we should underestimate the religious differences between Judaism, Hellenized Judaism, and Hellenized Christianity.

[679] Chadwick, 2001.

deliberately borrowed the Greek literary style of the dialogue, together with the Roman use of legal rules of evidence, to persuade pagans that Christianity was consistent with the classical search for wisdom and goodness. Lactantius, known as the "Christian Cicero," told his readers that the Stoic notion of a cosmic rational order was consistent with the Christian idea of a benevolent Creator who rules the world providentially.[680]

Clement of Alexandria's (150–215) effort to write a regular and orderly treatise of Christian beliefs—a theology—has to be seen in this context as an effort to elevate the unreflecting faith of simple "Jesus believers" to a higher understanding by means of classical learning. The goal was not to elevate philosophy above faith, but to employ philosophy as a "preparatory discipline" to the study of Christianity and thus to the establishment of Christian faith as a WEIRD theology. Clement, who was very well-read in Platonic philosophy, argued that although faith was sufficient for salvation, it was consistent with Christian faith to educate and discipline one's mind to reach a higher, more coherent understanding of God. Origen, who succeeded Clement as head of the Catechetical School in Alexandria, took further this effort to construct a systematic body of truth on the basis of rigorous argumentation. His *On the First Principles* starts with the elements of faith of apostolic preaching and then goes on to maintain, as F. E. Peters words it, "that in many cases apostolic tradition did no more than announce that a thing is so, without explaining the how or the why."[681] Origen is said to have provided the "first Summa Theologica" in presenting all Christian beliefs in the manner of a dogma, a canon, a system of beliefs.[682]

---

[680] Colish, 1998, 10–15.

[681] Peters, 1970, 625.

[682] Jaeger, 1961; Miles, 2005. Additional works on how Judaism and Christianity were "Hellenized" include Miles (2005) and Jaeger (1961). There are many additional studies explaining how Christianity was substantially rationalized and transformed into the only "WEIRD" theological religion of the world before the Middle Ages. A drawback of Henrich's "experimental" approach is that it relies on the simple-minded opinions of contemporary individuals to reach judgments about the nature of Christianity, while ignoring the scholarly literature on the intellectual development of Christianity. While I can't claim to have read this work, the notion that Christianity was one of many other religions, rather than a highly theological doctrine, is decisively put to rest by the monumental five volume work of Jaroslav Jan Pelikan, *The Christian Tradition: A History of the Development of Doctrine: Volume 1: The Emergence of the Catholic Tradition 100–600, Volume 2: The Spirit of Eastern Christendom 600–1700, Volume 3: The Growth of Medieval Theology 600–1300, Volume 4: Reformation of Church and Dogma 1300– 1700, Volume 5: Christian Doctrine and Modern Culture since 1700* (University of Chicago Press, 1973–1990).

Henrich inadvertently slips out that "by roughly 200 BCE universalizing religions included [concepts] of free will . . . [and] moral universalism."[683] Don't we need humans with WEIRD psychologies to have concepts of free will and moral universalism? He identifies "free will" with the WEIRD "notion that individuals make their own choices and those choices matter," and he lists "moral universalism" as one of the key WEIRD traits. His point may be that universalizing religions contained some incipient ideas about free will and moral responsibility based on religious texts, rather than on customary obligations stemming from kinship ties. But while it can be argued, as we saw in chapter three, that during the Axial Age (800 to 200 BC) the high cultures of Israel, India, China, and possibly Persia, did articulate quasi-universal ideals for "humanity" in opposition to the tribalistic conventions of the day, the subsequent histories of these cultures where characterized by dogmatic fixation, stagnation, and religious traditionalism, whereas only the ancient Greeks would engage in what Merlin Donald calls "second-order theory" or "thinking about thinking," as is evident in their geometrical proofs, in Plato's incessant dialogical questioning of taken-for-granted conventions about what is truthful and what is rational, followed by Aristotle's articulation of a system of logic about how to think properly and consistently, without contradiction, on the basis of "self-evident" reason-based premises.

We don't have any textual evidence that any religion other than Christianity articulated ideas about free will and universal ideals on the basis of a systematic assimilation of the Greek philosophical heritage. The first proper articulation of the idea of free will can be found in the writings of the Hellenistic thinker Epicurus, who thought that it was possible for human decision or choice to exist outside a causal chain of determinism, and thus for humans to be responsible for their actions, and for praise and moral blame to be possible.[684] Larry Siedentop, in a tightly constructed 2015 book, *Inventing the Individual: The Origins of Western Liberalism*, to which we will return in Chapter XI in our effort to explain the nature of liberalism, argues that Christianity (in contrast to every other religion) was responsible for a WEIRD (to use Henrich's term) moral revolution in the first centuries AD before the Middle Ages. This revolution called for the moral equality of humans regardless of ancestry, and insisted that humans are intentional beings in possession of an inner conscience that should not be obligated by mandates imposed without reasons. Hellenized Christians were the first to elaborate

---

[683] Henrich, 146.
[684] Long and Sedley, 1987.

philosophically the concepts of person, conscience, truth, dignity, and liberty. Kyle Harper also makes a strong case that it was the early Christians who developed a "thoroughly libertarian view of free will, defined by the capacity to act in a certain way," in the same vein as they articulated a new family ethic.[685]

In the Roman world, people were in awe of the powers of fate and fascinated by astrology, but Christians came to emphasize the power of human freedom to transcend sexual appetites, and the possibility of redemption for all, including sinners. Christianity framed the Greco-Roman views on monogamy within a powerful new sexual morality backed by the sanctified authority of one God in charge of ultimate moral judgement. These early Christian ideas were gradually adopted and transmitted in the second and third centuries to Roman populations. Saint Ambrose (340–397) and Saint Jerome (347–420) insisted on the right of women who chose celibacy not to be forced into unwanted marriages, and on the need to judge women not by sex but by soul.[686] Christians were thus "unique" in sincerely believing that unrestrained sexuality and suppression of the free will were damaging to human relationships.

The Culturally-Mandated Monogamy of
Ancient Greece Over the Biology of Polygamy

Kevin MacDonald, in his 2021 review-essay of *The WEIRDEST People*, counters Henrich's argument that monogamy was not real in Greece because high status men "could also purchase sex slaves, take foreigners as concubines, and use numerous inexpensive brothels."[687] The essence of MacDonald's critique is that Solon introduced laws on marriage aimed at curbing "the power of the aristocracy by limiting the benefits to be gained by extra-marital sexual relationships." Solon's law made monogamy the only form of union between a man and woman that could engender legitimate children "with the possibility of inheritance." Solon's laws provided for "state-subsidized brothels staffed with cheap and therefore readily available female prostitutes," in order to alleviate the polygynous inclination of men. This fact does not negate the monogamous character of ancient Greece, since children born outside a monogamous marriage were not recognized

---

[685] Harper, 118.
[686] Colish, 1998, 16–24.
[687] MacDonald, 2021, 273.

as biological members of the household and were excluded from any inheritance. Prostitution and concubinage was "a substitute for polygyny by the wealthy."

Henrich is also off in his claim that Rome lacked monogamy. While Henrich acknowledges that "Roman law only recognized monogamous marriages" and that "early Roman law . . . prohibited close cousin marriage," he thinks the presence of "secondary wives and sex slaves" seriously limited this institution.[688] He fails to mention that in Roman law, monogamy was the only valid form of marriage that could produce legitimate children with inheritance rights. Henrich references articles by W. Scheidel, including "A peculiar institution? Greco-Roman Monogamy in a Global Context" (2009) in support of his claims. Perhaps he thought that Scheidel's observation that Greco-Roman monogamy "accommodated a variety of men's polygynous relationships outside the nuclear family" disqualified calling these cultures monogamous. But the conclusion Scheidel actually reaches is that Greeks and Romans regarded polygamy as a "barbarian custom or a mark of tyranny."[689] The thesis of another 2008 paper by Scheidel, also referenced by Henrich, reads: "Greek and Roman men were not allowed to be married to more than one wife at a time and not meant to cohabit with concubines during marriage, and not even rulers were exempt from these norms."

But why would the Greeks and Romans institute monogamy when polygyny is a naturally-selected institution consistent with the evolved psychologies of humans? Henrich offers an insightful analysis of the evolutionary selection of polygyny we can rely upon to start answering this question. Monogamous pair bonding does not exist among any species living in large groups like *Homo sapiens*. Our closest primate relatives are highly promiscuous and don't form pair bonds. While humans did evolve a psychological disposition for emotional pair bonding, and for men to invest in the children of their sexual partner, both males and females were naturally selected to favor polygynous marriage. This may seem odd because males and females evolved different mating strategies, with females limited in their reproduction to the number of children they could raise due to ovulation, gestation, and lactation. Males, however, can produce sperm over their lifetime and potentially have thousands of offspring. Males are very strongly inclined to favor multiple mates because this means greater reproduction and greater biological "fitness." Females can only have one pregnancy at a time. Having multiple sexual mates does not augment their reproductive success but harms it by creating

---

[688] Henrich, 163.
[689] Scheidel, 2009.

confusion and conflict among males over paternity, and minimizing their willingness for parental investment. Nevertheless, females do have their own particular
type of "polygyny bias." Females want to form a pair-bond with those males who
can best guarantee support for her during pregnancy and during the maturation
of the child. They want security and comfort. Therefore, they are psychologically
inclined to gravitate toward high-status men with resources. This means that in a
world where high-status men are always seeking and acquiring multiple wives,
and many low-status men are deprived of sexual mates, young females will have a
larger pool of males to choose husbands from than would be available in a society
where monogamy was the law. While she might prefer to be the singular wife of a
high-status man, rather than marrying a low-status man who can't provide security, a woman would be better-off being the wife of a married wealthy man in a
polygynous household with lots of resources and much to learn from older co-
wives.[690]

All the societies witnessed in history, except the WEIRD societies created by
Europeans, practiced polygamy as a naturally selected mating strategy that allowed for the transmission of the genes of the most biologically fit men. Most human societies throughout history have accepted polygynous marriage. Almost all
hunter-gatherer societies around the world, about 90 percent, "had some degree
of polygynous marriage."[691] The hunter-gatherer societies that were "monogamous" were so because resources were too scarce for some men to accumulate
extra resources to invest in additional wives, such as the hunter-gather culture of
northwestern Europe. In the primitive societies that were polygynous, Henrich
informs us, only about 14 percent of men and 22 percent of women were in polygynous marriages, because only men with the ability to acquire extra resources
had the means to support more than one wife. This does not mean that most men
were in monogamous relationships; many simply had a hard time finding partners.

Monogamy can only be said to exist, I would argue, when it is a consciously
culturally-mandated norm in opposition to high status men who are biologically
inclined for polygamous marriage. Once societies began to practice agriculture
and increasing inequalities between classes emerged, with some men appropriat-
ing large tracts of land worked by low-status peasants, the acquisition of multiple

---

[690] Henrich, 55–283. He forgets that a major downside of polygyny for women is the fractious
hostility which often occurs between co-wives.
[691] Ibid, 260.

wives by a few men intensified. Only 15 percent of agricultural societies in the Ethnographic Atlas are identified as monogamous. With the rise of complex chiefdoms and civilizations, it became customary for high-ranking men to have multiple wives, with some kings having a few elite wives and several thousand secondary wives. This is the way nature works.

So, again, we need to ask: Why would the ruling elite in ancient Greece promote monogamy?[692] Here we can continue to draw from Henrich some keen insights on the benefits of monogamy and the dysfunctional aspects of polygamy, so long as we keep in mind that he is talking about *current modern societies*, and that he does not attribute these insights to the Greeks and Romans, or to the Catholic Church. The main problem with polygynous marriages is that they "generate a large pool of low-status unmarried men with few prospects for marriage or even sex."[693] Large percentages of unmarried men are associated with high crime rates and general anti-social behavior. Polygynous men invest less in their offspring because they tend to have more children and because they dedicate more resources pursuing additional wives.

It has been shown, moreover, that "getting married and becoming a father lowers men's testosterone." The level of testosterone (T) influences men's psychology; men with lower T are less aggressive and more able to self-discipline their emotions and allow the prefrontal cortices of their brains a greater say over decision-making. Monogamy means that a higher proportion of men will have the opportunity of finding a spouse. Marriage suppresses T levels, which lowers the likelihood of property crimes, drug abuse, and violent aggression. Levels of T also "affect a person's assessment of the trustworthiness of strangers." Monogamous men are more inclined to trust strangers and to behave according to impartial principles. In polygynous societies, men's T levels decline slower with age because they remain on the marriage market. Studies have shown that marriage cuts the overall crime rate by about 35 percent.

For all these reasons, Henrich concludes that "monogamous marriage norms . . . create a range of social and psychological effects that give the societies that

---

[692] Henrich pays little attention to the scholarly literature portraying ancient Greece as a monogamous culture; see Lacy (1968) and Patterson (2001). Patterson makes a strong case that Greek society since archaic times was already rooted in monogamous households rather than clans, that in law courts the violation of marital relationships was categorized as a public danger and the adulterer as a sexual thief, and that monogamous family households were seen as integral to the sustenance of the city's civic identity and norms.

[693] Henrich, 256.

possess them a big edge in competition against other groups."[694] But Henrich employs this argument solely to explain why non-western societies eventually came to implement laws favoring monogamy. They did so under the competitive pressure of the incredibly successful Western world in the twentieth century. "Intergroup competition"—the competition of nation states for geopolitical power and survival as independent nations—motivated the non-Western world to copy Western secular institutions, not just monogamy, but rule of law, constitutions, elections, and scientific methodologies.[695]

While non-Western states did not get rid of all the kinship characteristics that underlay their age-old bureaucratic institutions, they did come to the realization (though Henrich does not quite say this) that favoring monogamy was a great way of limiting the deleterious effects of powerful polygynous clans continually contesting for power and obstructing the creation of a centralized modern-nation state. But when it comes to the origins of monogamy in the West, Henrich takes away any intentionality and rational decision-making from Europeans. This can be contrasted with MacDonald's view that monogamy was already present in ancient Greece and Rome, though I believe that the Greeks, not hunter-gatherers in northern Europe responding to environmental pressures or scarce resources, were the first to *consciously* mandate monogamy as an institution that enhanced the solidarity of city-state members. In all polygynous societies, as it is, one finds a majority of men with only one wife. The issue is: Why was Greece the first culture to prohibit polygyny among high-status men economically able to give satisfaction to their evolved disposition for polygamy? The ancient Greeks originated monogamy due to their understanding that the polygamous practices of aristocrats in charge of clan leaders was a major obstacle to the inducement of internal solidarity within the new WEIRD city-states they had created. They consciously opposed polygamy because it created a situation in which high-status men monopolized the bride market, expanded their clannish networks, deprived many men of marriage, and thus weakened the civic ties within the new city-states. What neither Henrich nor MacDonald stress is that the city-state was a totally new institutional arrangement, a new way of grouping humans on the basis of the reason-based concept of "citizen," in opposition to the traditional norm that membership depended on lineage and tribal origin.

---

[694] Ibid, 263.

[695] It should be noted that polygyny is still common in sub-Saharan Africa, and that African American men, more than any other racial group, often sire many children by different women.

Before the creation of city-states and the rise of family farms after 700 BC, aristocratic men, with their military retinues, clannish relationships, and large landholdings, were the main competitors for the allegiances of the local population. It was Solon (640–560 BC) who took the first legalistic steps to create a new civic identity centered around membership in the city-state of Athens, rather than away from the older clannish alliances that we read about in Homer's *Iliad*. Solon opposed the endless squabbles of aristocrats with their private retinues in the name of a new ideal of good order and harmony between men. He was against the kin-based ingroup norms of the aristocrats. Solon wanted a legal code applied equally to all male citizens. And he recognized the indispensable contribution to the harmony of the city state of non-aristocratic yet independent family farmers who worked incredibly hard to sustain the economic viability of the city-state. These free farmers, about which more will be said soon, were included as citizens.[696]

After Solon, Cleisthenes (b. late 570s BC) is said to have "dealt the fatal blow to Athenian tribalism by dissolving the traditional connections of clans entirely and creating in their place a remarkable system of 10 groupings that were artificial tribes."[697] These new groupings were called *demes*, and the members of these *demes* were identified as citizens regardless of kinship lineage. They were free, native-born males with the right to participate in the general assembly of the Athenian city-state and in local assemblies of each *deme*. The laws that these assemblies passed were not customary, but based on open discussion by Athenians as members of a political order relatively freed from tribal groupings. The ancient Greeks were indeed the first historical people to invent the abstract concept of citizenship, a (WEIRD) civic identity not dependent on birth, wealth, or tribal kinship, but based on laws common to all citizens.

By culturally mandating monogamy, and forcing high-status men to focus on their families as members of city-states rather than polygamous kin groups, the ancient Greeks created highly competitive societies. Henrich's argument about the indispensable role of the Church's family program would have carried a lot more weight if he had acknowledged the prior existence of monogamy in the Greco-Roman world ,while arguing that polygynous marriages were common among the wealthy leaders of the Germanic tribes that took Europe in the early Middle Ages, and that it was these kinship networks that the Church set out to

---

[696] Hanson, 1999.

[697] Rensberger and Farquhar, 1995.

abolish. Of course, this would have required an entirely new research project as to why the ancients were already monogamous.

The WEIRD Civic Republican Values of Greeks and Romans

One of the major drawbacks in Henrich's book is the complete lack of any mention of Greek civic values and Roman republican institutions. MacDonald analyzes very effectively how the aristocratic individualist ethos of Indo-Europeans shaped the course and structure of politics throughout the Roman Republican era. At the same time, he recognizes that, among Romans, despite their strong aristocratic individualist ethos, "there were also wider groupings" shaped by strong kinship ties, and that "cities developed when several of these larger groupings (tribes) came together and established common worship," and that Roman cities were not "associations of individuals," which is a modern phenomenon.[698] The Senate worked as a political body mediating the influence of extended families in politics, not by eliminating kinship patron-client relations, but minimizing their impact at the level of politics.

Another way to express this is that the Senate was a civic-political institution within which elected members (backed by their extended families and patron-client connections) acted in the name of Rome, even as they competed intensively with each other for the spoils of office. MacDonald observes as well that the Roman government would eventually be broadened to include representative bodies, tribunes, for non-aristocratic plebeians with wealth, towards a separation of powers, between the senate of the patricians and the tribunes of the plebs, along with two consuls selected from both patricians and plebians (after 367 BC). This meant, it must be added, that this government developed further "weird" traits in a populist direction. This was the case in both Greece and Rome, at the root of which stood the often neglected, and singularly unique trait, of a class of homesteading independent farmers with citizenship rights.

Let's start with Greece, the first civilization in history in which one finds a class of small-to-medium homestead farmers freed from wider kinship networks and from control by a despotic government. In the ancient civilizations of the Near East, and the later civilizations of India, China and the Americas, the ruler and his court of blood relatives, administrators, and provincial elites owned most of the

---

[698] MacDonald, 2019, 71.

land, huge estates, from which they extracted taxes and rents from slaves, serfs, indentured servants, or faceless peasants with tiny plots owned by clans. This is an argument Victor Davis Hanson makes in his studious, primary research-based 1999 book, *The Other Greeks: the Family Farm and the Agrarian Roots of Western Civilization*. Hanson argues that, roughly between 700 and 300 BC, Greece saw the emergence of "an autonomous group of independent farmers" never seen before in human history. These independent farmers "were most definitely not peasants" since they "had a title to their small farms, enjoyed political rights as full citizens, took on the defense of their communities," and were responsible for the "general Greek cultural characteristics of pragmatism, confidence in the middling classes, individualism, and self-reliance."[699]

While one third to one half of the adult male population in most city states never became independent farmers, independent farmers brought (at the beginning of the polis period) "a transformation in the mind, a radical change of attitude, as farmers learned to invest their efforts in the land in an entirely novel way." They also brought a new ideology of work derived from land ownership . . . an idea that manual labor, time spent on the soil, was both intrinsically ennobling [in contrast] to the well-known aristocratic dislike of manual labor and widespread presence of chattel slavery."[700] Having ownership and control over one's land encouraged individualism and free will in the sense that farmers were responsible for making their own decisions and initiating new methods of farming through trial-and-error.

The ideals of Solon, for moderation and justice between the extremes of wealth and poverty, in opposition to the excessive wealth and unrestrained behavior of power-hungry aristocrats prone to disrupt the unity of city-states, were connected to these farmers. To this end, Solon abolished debt slavery, and allowed those who had been sold abroad as slaves to return as free men, in order to secure the existence of a class of self-sufficient farmers as a political counter balance to the greed of big landowners. With the subsequent reforms of Cleisthenes and Pericles towards the inclusion of smallholders as citizens, fifth-century Athens became quite democratic, though not in the sense of universal suffrage and mass popular cultural values, but in the extent to which the state was open to participation by about one-third of the population, excluding slaves, women, and alien residents. Every decision had to be approved by a popular assembly; every judicial decision was

---

[699] Hanson, xiv.
[700] Ibid, 91.

subject to appeal to a popular court of some fifty-one citizens, and every official was subject to public scrutiny before taking office.

These citizen farmers were "new men" engaged in a new type of "hoplite warfare" (face-to-face battle of rank-and-file formations of infantrymen), in contrast to the Mycenaean aristocratic warriors who fought from chariots. This is not to detract from the reality that Athens remained a city ruled by a small elite of aristocratic families with the means, knowledge, and leisure to regulate the affairs of the state. But we can say that the extension of citizenship to wider segments of the farming population amounted to the extension of the aristocratic spirit of freedom, honor, and heroism, to farming men of talent.

Citizen-warrior farmers were likewise a central foundational pillar of Roman civic republicanism. As Maurice Muret put it: "the Roman citizen was originally a man given to working in the fields who took to arms when his territory of Latium or the city of Rome, seat of the royalty, was threatened."[701] The patricians we often associate with an exclusive aristocracy in control of an oligarchic senate, were actually in their origins men who worked the land and constituted the Roman army. These patricians were "aristocratic" in spirit, but for many centuries they were not men living off the labor of others, though they did have more land, and did hire laborers, and later used slave labor in their extended landholding as Rome defeated one rival after another and thereby accumulated land. The "austere crucible," to use Muret's apt phrase, in which the soul of the Roman patrician farmer-soldier was formed was a mixture of rural life and camp life. For many centuries during the Republican period, Romans believed that "a Roman citizen, no matter how poor he was, was honored if he lived on the land, cultivated his estate, raised a numerous family.[702]

Moreover, the Roman patrician aristocracy was open to talent. As early as the fifth century BC, the patricians granted the plebeians the right to annually elect their own leaders, the right to appeal to the people and hold plebiscites binding on the whole community, and the right to marry patricians. During the 300s, plebeians were successively allowed to become consuls, censors, praetors, pontiffs, and augurs; and, by 300, they had achieved substantial equality with the patricians, with both patricians and the upper plebeians becoming wealthy landowners.[703] The struggle between classes would henceforth be between the "*nobiles*"

---

[701] Muret, 2022, 34.

[702] Ibid, 37–8.

[703] Cornell, 2004.

consisting of large landowning and commercialized patricians and plebeians, and the poorer plebeian small holders. These *nobiles* were far removed from their former austere lives of patricians as farmers, though some would retain to the last days of the Republic the civic republican values that made Rome great in the first place.

We have heard about the most important contributions of Romans: their aqueducts; concrete; the most sophisticated system of roads in the ancient world; their arches, which allowed the weight of buildings to be evenly distributed along various supports in the construction of their bridges, monuments and buildings; the Julian Calendar; their systematic compilation of juristic writings, *corpus juris civilis*; their new types of surgical tools, along with the first field surgery units. But it may be that their greatest legacy was the republican form of government, characterized by a balance between monarchy, aristocracy, and democracy. An aristocratic class freed from a despotic ruler does not guarantee a republican government. In their primordial tendencies, aristocratic governments are oligarchic rather than republican, although republicanism presupposes the higher (senatorial) authority of a class of aristocrats. Roman aristocrats despised those among their ranks who elevated themselves above their peers to rule in the interests of the lower classes. Like the Greeks, they viewed aristocrats who attacked the privileges of their noble peers, and sought the popular support of plebeians, as tyrants. But, as the plebeians gained substantial equality in citizen rights through the 300s BC, a "democratic" element was added to the Roman government. This democratic element was controlled by the upper plebeians, not the lower landless plebs, which became a mob in the city of Rome. The monarchical element came in the annual election by the Senate of Consuls with extensive powers, often holding in wartime the highest military command.

The essential idea of this civic/republican form of freedom, articulated from Aristotle through to Cicero, was that man's essential nature was actualized through his participation in his public civic community. The highest virtues eulogized by Republican Rome were virility, strength, energy, self-control, patience in misfortune, impartiality, and sacrifice for the public good. However, citizens remained attached to their extended families; not only were they expected to participate in state-sponsored religious rituals and festivals, but each Roman family was expected to perform daily rituals honoring their ancestors and placating various gods. The patrician farmer was seen as a venerable paterfamilias, the high priest of his own household religion. These customs and rites sustained and reinforced Roman civic identity and greatness for centuries. The patricians saw themselves both as members of their extended families and clannish patron-client groups, and as members of the Roman republic. For a long time, they served their city as a matter of public service with patriotic devotion and without seeking to enrich themselves. "In war, the most affluent wished to fight in the front rank." Muret estimates that "of all the human societies of antiquity," the most devoted, honest, and competent functionaries of the state were the Romans of the Republican era.

This was not to last. As Rome grew rich from its successes and vast amounts of wealth started pouring in, masses of slaves were pushed into working the lands of the rich, while at the same time soldier-farmers were losing their farms from neglect after years of military service and from debt. A percentage of the upper classes became involved in commercial undertakings, acting as tax-farmers milking the provinces; the old Roman spirit of discipline, austerity, and virility slowly died away. The decline of the Roman character is a pervading theme of Roman historiography; already apparent in Cato the Elder (234–149 BC), author of *Origins*, of which only fragments survive, about the beginnings of Rome up until the victory over Macedonia in 168 BC. Cato eulogized the "Spartan" austerity and simplicity of the early men who built Rome, and lamented the effeminate influence of Greek learning. In the first century BC, Sallust (86–35 BC) saw the old Roman virtues of frugality and piety decline under the influence of luxury and Asiatic indulgences and taste. The empire certainly lasted a few more centuries until the fifth century AD, demonstrating the remaining greatness of Rome as it declined slowly. Nevertheless, the legacy of republican Roman practices, a topic to which we should return in Chapter XI, would exert a powerful influence on the political evolution of Western civilization.[704]

Having said this, we should avoid projecting onto the Greeks and Romans a modern sense of civic identity. The ancient Greeks retained a strong sense of being a people with shared bloodlines, a shared culture, language, mythology, ancestors, and traditional texts. This sense of ethnic identity, however, transcended old tribal kinship ties, with the Greeks envisioning themselves during the Persian wars as

---

[704] Sellers, 2006. Homestead family farms were a key component of European medieval agriculture, modern Europe, and the settler states of America, Canada, Australia and New Zealand. Only in Western history do we find the famous "yeomen" farmers who owned their own piece of land and, in the case of Greece and Rome, fought in citizen armies. The image of yeomen farmers as honest, hardworking, virtuous, and independent played a significant role in Western republican thought. The founding fathers of the United States, Thomas Jefferson and others, were of the view that the yeoman farmers were "the most valuable citizens," the one segment of the population that could be trusted to be committed to republican values, as contrasted to financiers, bankers and industrialists with their "cesspools of corruption" (Wood, 2002) in the cities.

part of a wider Panhellenic world in lieu of their common civic spirit, which they consciously contrasted to the "slavish" spirit of the Asians. As Lynette Mitchell observes, "there was in antiquity a sense of Panhellenism ... closely associated with Greek identity."[705] While this unity was ideological, rather than politically actual, weakened by endless quarrels between city-states, the Greeks (as Pericles noted in his famous "Funeral Oration") contrasted their citizen politics with the despotic government of the Persians.[706]

The aristocratic Romans did go on to create a more encompassing form of "weird" identity beyond the city-state. Unlike the Greeks, who restricted citizenship to free-born city inhabitants, the Romans extended their citizenship across the Italian peninsula after the Social War (91–88 BC), and across the Empire, when the entire free population of the Empire was granted citizenship in AD 212. However, I am less inclined than MacDonald to view the Roman extension of citizenship to non-Italians as a clear demonstration of their lack of ethnocentrism. Ethnicity remained a very important marker for ancient empires generally, no less important to their makeup than domination by social elites over a tax-paying peasantry or slave force. As Azar Gat has observed, "almost universally they were either overtly or tacitly the empires of a particular people or ethnos."[707] Gat neglects to mention that all the residents of Italy (except the Etruscans, whose status as an Indo-European people remains uncertain) were members of the European genetic family. Romans/Latins were so reluctant to grant citizenship to outsiders that it took a full-scale civil war, the Social War, for them to do so, even though Italians generally had long been fighting on their side, helping them create the empire. When citizenship was finally granted in AD 212 to the free population of the empire, outside the Italian peninsula, it came in graduated levels with

---

[705] Mitchell, 2007, xv–xviii.

[706] A strong argument can be made that the prevalence of despotism in the East was due to the prevalence of kinship ties in the running of governments, and the consequent inability of Eastern elites to think about higher forms of identity in the way the Greeks and Romans did. Eastern empires were highly nepotistic, with rulers using the state to expand their kinship networks, favoring relatives while behaving in a predatory way against rival ethnic-tribal groups, without a sense of city-state or national unity, and without the ability to generate loyalty among inhabitants or members belonging to other kinship groups. The historian Jacob Burckhardt (2007, 57) once observed about the Muslim caliphates that "despite an occasionally very lively feeling for one's home region which attaches to localities and customs, there is an utter lack of patriotism, i.e., enthusiasm for the totality of a people or a state (there is not even a word for 'patriotism')." Burckhardt does not say anything about kinship, but it seems reasonable to infer that the strong kinship ties that prevailed in the East made it very difficult to forge a common identity.

[707] Gat, 2011, 111.

promises of further rights with increased assimilation. Right until the end, not all citizens had the same rights, with Romans and Italians generally enjoying a higher status.

Moreover, as Gat recognizes, Romanization was largely successful in the Western half of the empire, in Italy, Gaul, and Iberia, all of which were Indo-European in ethnicity, whereas the Eastern Empire consisted of an upper Hellenistic crust combined with a mass of Mesopotamian, Egyptian, Judaic, Persian, and Assyrian peoples following their ancient ways, virtually untouched by Roman culture. This is the conclusion reached in Warwick Ball's book, *Rome in the East*. Roman rule in the regions of Syria, Jordan, and northern Iraq was "a story of the East more than of the West." Similarly, George Mousourakis writes of "a single nation and uniform culture" developing in the Italian Peninsula as a result of the extension of citizenship, or the Romanization of Italian residents. [708]

The Protestant Role, or Europeans Have Always Been the Most Highly Literate People in History

In Henrich's historical model, Protestantism plays a rather important role in heightening the emerging WEIRD traits of Europeans by encouraging the spread

---

[708] *The Historical and Institutional Context of Roman Law* (Ashgate, 2003). Among the long-standing peoples in the East the Romans conquered, it was the culture of the Greeks that drew their highest admiration. Roman literature, rhetoric, history, art, religion, education, architecture, and philosophy were as deeply influenced by the Greeks. The educated Romans were bilingual. This is the basis of Horace's famous statement: *Graecia capta ferum victorem cepit et artis-intulit agresti Latio.* "Greece, the captive, made her savage victor captive, and brought the arts into rustic Latium." This deep cultural connection was rooted in the common Indo-European aristocratic culture of the Greeks and Romans. The Greeks were connected with the Romans since Mycenaean times.

Cornell informs us that "Mycenaean finds in southern Italy are indeed impressive, and point to intensive contacts with the Aegean world in the Bronze Age" (40). The most important IE language in Italy was "spoken in the Greek colonies that were established around the coasts of southern Italy from the eighth century BC onwards" (43). "Recent archeological finds have increasingly demonstrated that the natives of central Italy were deeply influenced by Greek culture in the archaic period" between 580 and 490 BC (66). Indeed, "by the fifth century southern Italy was known as 'Great Greece.' . . . The arrival of the Greeks in Italy had a profound impact on the social, economic, and cultural life of the native peoples . . . especially on the formation of the aristocratic order" (87).

of literacy, which had deep effects on the neurological wiring of the brain.[709] He calls Protestantism "the WEIRDest religion" and estimates that it acted "like a booster shot for many of the WEIRD psychological patterns we have been examining throughout this book." He compiles experimental surveys showing that countries today "with Protestant majorities show even higher individualism, greater impersonal trust, and a stronger emphasis on creativity compared to majority Catholic countries."[710] Protestants are likewise "less tied to their families," less" tolerant of those who do not consistently follow the impartial rules, and more inclined to trust and interact with strangers.

Evidence also shows that Protestantism induces people to work longer hours than is the case with Catholicism. Of course, Protestantism did not spring suddenly onto the historical scene, but was anticipated by prior heterodox religious currents in the Middle Ages.[711] Luther's message spread fast because it "resonated deeply with important swaths" of a population that was already proto-WEIRD. The importance of Protestant literacy is high enough in Henrich's explanation that he dedicates a "Prelude," before Chapter 1, arguing that the Protestant spread of "high rates of literacy" brought about a fundamental alteration in the brains of Europeans. He cites research showing that the neurological wiring of the brain can be altered in a WEIRD analytical direction through the spread of literacy. In the development of reading skills, specialized areas of the brain are re-wired, "thickened," "altered," "broadened," and "improved." Without altering the "underlying genetic code," literacy "changes people's biology and psychology . . . their cognitive abilities in domains related to memory, visual processing, facial recognition, numerical exactness, and problem-solving." "Literacy thus provides an example of how culture can change people's biology, independent of any genetic differences."[712]

---

[709] Henrich allows for other factors to play a role in the cultivation of WEIRD tendencies. He provides surveys which point to some psychological differences "within China and India" based on differences in the intensity of kinship resulting from ecological differences in types of farming. These variations are "relatively small compared to the impact" of the Church in Europe, which "nearly annihilated Europe's clans, kindreds, cousin marriage, polygamy, and inheritance norms." He wonders whether the "regions of northern Europe" "may have faced somewhat less resistance" against the Church's family program, and indeed whether "the rain-fed, wheat growing regions of northern Europe" engendered weaker kin-based ties.

[710] Henrich, 418.

[711] Ozment, 1980.

[712] Henrich 3–7, 17.

It is interesting that when Henrich writes about literacy it is always about "high literacy rates" or "mass literate societies." He wants masses of people who can at least "read" a bit in order to talk about alterations in the brain and WEIRD profiles. He is not satisfied with a small elite of highly educated individuals who can also write excellent books. An industrial society requires mass literacy, but Europe did not need mass literacy to bring about the Renaissance in the fifteenth century and modern science in the sixteenth and seventeenth centuries. Literacy only began to spread in the sixteenth century, as Henrich observes. Before this century, "never more than 10 percent of any society's population could read, and usually the rates were much lower." Throughout the modern era, the most literate societies in the world were Protestant: the Netherlands, Britain, Sweden, and Germany. He supplies numbers showing that "literacy rates grew the fastest in countries where Protestantism was most deeply established."

He zooms in on Prussia to show that this was not a mere correlation: "counties with more Protestants had higher rates of literacy and more schools." This "pattern prevails . . . when the effects of urbanization and demographics are held constant." Why did Protestantism promote literacy? Henrich's answer, again, reveals a belief that bespeaks of someone who thinks that Christians (even the ones increasingly becoming WEIRD) could not possibly have acted intentionally and rationally in the promotion of literacy for its beneficial effects on the development of a Christian culture with individuals who legislate for themselves their own religious beliefs. He appears to be acknowledging this when he says that "embedded deep in Protestantism is the notion that individuals should develop a personal relationship with God and Jesus [and to] accomplish this both men and women need to read and interpret the sacred scriptures for themselves, and not rely primarily on the authority of supposed experts, priests, or institutional authorities like the Church."[713]

In the end, however, the impression he wants to convey is that the irrational search for eternal salvation had the unintended consequence of promoting literacy, altering the neurology of the brain in a more analytical direction, raising the intelligence of the general population, and thus fueling the industrial revolution. But if the "European populations at the close of the Middle Ages were so susceptible to the unusually individualistic character of Protestant beliefs" because they had already become "proto-Weird," why not argue that Protestants emphasized individual conscience as proto-intentional beings? Protestants were consciously

---

[713] Ibid, 7, 9.

for the liberation of the inwardness of individual believers from the unquestioned authority of priests, and for the use of one's own literate ability to read the Bible against externally imposed interpretations. This emphasis on the right of private judgement reflected an independent and critical spirit. Henrich views all religious peoples as if they were on the same level of cognition in their common irrational belief in "ghosts," "demons," "spirits," and "angels." This is why he has a hard time acknowledging WEIRD attributes of the very same religion he calls "the WEIRD-est."

There are additional flaws in his assessment of Protestantism. While Henrich is correct that we need "high rates of literacy" to operate an industrial economy, Europe did not need *mass* literacy to bring about modern science in the sixteenth and seventeenth centuries. He himself notes in passing that "only about 1 percent of the German-speaking population was ... literate" when Luther began the epoch-making Reformation. Henrich's criterion for what constitutes "literacy" is very low—namely, the mere ability to read. Why should we assume that a modern nation with mass literacy—say, Equatorial Guinea, where 95.3% of the population knows how to read and write—is inherently more capable of generating novel ideas than ancient Athens, or Renaissance Florence, or Shakespearean London, without mass literacy, but nevertheless enjoying a highly literate elite capable of reading and writing extensively? As it is, Henrich is not accurate when he says that before the sixteenth century the literacy rate was "never more than 10 percent of any society's population." One of the most thorough studies of literacy in ancient Greece concludes that "the great majority of Athenian citizens" in the fifth and fourth centuries BC could read and write.[714] These were male citizens, to be sure. Oswyn Murray says that in the period 750–650 BC "writing became widespread in Greece."[715] More conservative estimates tell us that in the ancient Greek-Roman world at large it was "very improbable" that the level of literacy "was above 10%, or 25%, or 50%." This same source says that in the major cities of the Hellenistic world the literacy rate was around 20 to 30 percent of the population.[716] This is relatively high considering that in Protestant England in the period 1580–1700, as noted in this conservative study, "far fewer than 20 percent of adults could read and write." Why not talk about alterations in the brain in reference to the highly literate male adult population of ancient Greece?

---

[714] Harvey, 1966.
[715] Murray, 1980.
[716] Harris, 1989.

Lack of attention to the high intellectual achievements of Europeans is a trademark of Henrich's book. He never ponders over the question why Aristotle, an ancient thinker from a supposedly kin-based culture, remained the most influential thinker through the entire medieval period, unsurpassed in his logical writings until the nineteenth century. Aristotle argued that truth can only arise if the mind frees itself from particular contexts and learns to provide reasons or philosophical explanations based on abstract-analytical categories (substance, quantity, quality, relationship, place, time, state) for why something is so. Aristotle called a "good syllogism" a statement that had nothing to do with a context but depended for its truth only on how the terms were formally related to each other.

The translations of Aristotle's *Categories* and *On Interpretation* had already been accomplished by Boethius in 510–2 before the alleged creation of WEIRD Europeans by the Catholic Church. Boethius transmitted to Europe, before the full recovery of Aristotle's work in the twelfth and thirteenth centuries, the analytical art of "classifying the objects external to the mind."[717] He taught how to think analytically with "the terms genus and species, differentia, property and accident, and to apply these conceptions in argument and discussion." Amazingly, Henrich mentions Aristotle only in passing to say that "the impact of a WEIRDer psychology" in science in the sixteenth century was evident in the realization that "the great ancient sages, like Aristotle, could be wrong."

This is very misleading. While Aristotle's ideas about motion were superseded, the geometry of Euclid, which systematically organized together everything that was known in the ancient Greek world, famously known for its axioms, definitions, and theorems, exercised an indispensable influence on the rationalistic methods of modern science. The geometry of Isaac Newton's *Principia Mathematica* was Euclidean. Newton called his famous laws of motion "axioms," and deduced his law of gravitation in the form of two mathematical theorems. Nor can we ignore the WEIRD contributions of the scientists of the Hellenistic era, not just Euclid's geometry (300 BC), but scientists such as Eratosthenes (276–195 BC), who measured the distance between the Sun and the Earth, and the size of the Earth quite accurately; and Archimedes (287–212 BC), who laid the foundations of hydrostatics and statics, and explained the principle of the lever; and Ptolemy, who introduced the WEIRD principles of Euclid to mapmaking, depicting with geometric consistency a curved surface (of the globe) on a flat surface (a map)

---

[717] Southern, 1953, 175–180.

using a gridwork of latitudes and longitudes, and thus laying the foundations for the science of cartography.[718]

Henrich's New Insights on the Industrial Divergence of Europe

Nevertheless, we can't overestimate the power of Henrich's focus on kinship institutions and norms, or his emphasis on the emergence of a new persona in the rise of the West. The concept of WEIRD individuals driving Europe's economic changes from the Middle Ages right into the industrial revolution is very enlightening. He seriously challenges the currently popular multiculturalist argument that, as late as 1750, China/Asia was more advanced economically than Europe, with its highly productive agriculture, its extensive international networks of trade, and larger urban centers. But what matters is not the size of urban centers and international trade networks per se, but whether these markets were based on principles of fairness and trust, impersonal forms of credit, insurance, and long-term agreements, rather than on "interpersonal relationships and kin-based institutions." Market networks in Asia and the Islamic world remained rooted in a "different cultural psychology and family organization." The Asian markets were ultimately controlled by large extended families, clan ties, and interpersonal agreements.

With the imposition of the Church's family program, Europeans were increasingly able to break away from kin-based relations and norms, choose their own business partners, move freely into newly created chartered towns with their professional guilds, and expand market networks with anonymous strangers across the world. Much has been made of Marco Polo's excitement over the larger urban centers in China, but Henrich effectively shows that the rate of urbanization in Europe was accelerating from 1000 to 1800, when the number of people living in cities of over 10,000 increased twenty times, whereas China's urbanization rate

---

[718] Russo, 2004. Henrich's observation that universities trained lawyers to think in a WEIRD manner "in the wake of the rediscovery of the Justinian Code of Roman civil law in the 11th century" can't explain why a Justinian Code written in sixth century Byzantium became so useful for the WEIRD development of voluntary associations in Europe. Since the Justinian Code was based on Roman law, the question is: How did Romans (with their supposedly non-WEIRD psychology) develop a legal system characterized by a high degree of logical consistency in the classification of different types of law, the definition of terms, the formulation of specific rules, and in the way questions and answers from jurists were systematically collected?

"remained relatively constant."[719] The freeing of individuals from kinship ties resulted in a sustained rise in residential and relational mobility across Europe. While the cities of Asia remained structured by kin-based relationships, the chartered towns of Europe were a new phenomenon in history, based on representative institutions and open to people from all walks of life.

Henrich provides data showing that those urban centers that were exposed to the Church's family program (due to the presence of nearby bishoprics) grew and developed representative forms of government faster. The inhabitants of these chartered towns—the merchants, artisans, and shopkeepers—were not "enmeshed in patrilineal, polygynous clans." Therefore, their success did not depend on kin-based connections, but on "their reputation for impartial honesty and fairness, and on their industriousness, patience, precision, and punctuality."[720] In kin-based cultures, the occupational choices of individuals are strongly set by families, clans, or ethnic groups. In the emerging WEIRD cultures of medieval Europe, where one finds an increasing number of individuals seeking to join voluntary associations, guilds, cities, apprenticeships, and business partnerships, individuals had to "sell themselves" by emphasizing their personal abilities and attributes. Personal family connections remained important, as they do today, but personal success was heavily dependent on one's reputation in a world of strangers. Having a reputation as a hard and reliable worker with the proper specialized talents, personality, and aptitudes to do the job became crucial.

The field of economic history has produced many excellent scholarly contributions on the factors that led Europe to become the first industrial civilization. But these studies have faced numerous quandaries and impasses on a wide variety of pertinent subjects. For example: why did Europeans become obsessed with punctuality in the Middle Ages, inventing mechanical clocks long before industrial capitalist businesses would impose their disciplinary pace of work and assembly line?[721] Why were so many Cistercian monasteries founded before 1300, long before the rise of the Protestant work ethic, emphasizing hard work and self-discipline?[722] Why did Western Europe see a steady decline in interest rates, below 5 percent in England and Holland before the Industrial Revolution, compared to

---

[719] Henrich, 309.

[720] Ibid, 317.

[721] Cipolla, 1967; Landes, 1983.

[722] On the Cistercian "entrepreneurial organization of capital," "rational cost accounting," and "inner-worldly asceticism" during the Middle Ages, see Randall Collins (1990).

the otherwise advanced economies of Asia, where rates tended to average between 25 and 50 percent?

The flaw in all prior answers, Henrich explains, lay in the assumption among economic historians that the psychology of economic actors throughout the world was fixed and generic. Rather than focusing on how low interest rates reflect a people's willingness to delay gratification, economic historians looked to a whole range of factors affecting the risk of lending, or at the ways new credit banks eased the lending of money. Similarly, when trying to explain the rapid spread of mechanical clocks, they looked at the demands of capitalism for punctuality, rather than at the underlying psychological importance WEIRD people attach to spending time productively and cultivating a reputation for punctuality and reliability. It was the emerging WEIRD psychology of Europeans that prompted them to create a new type of capitalism based on this new psychology. China had developed mechanical water clocks, but these remained mere "showpieces and curiosities," even though this civilization had widespread markets. When the true mechanical clocks from Europe arrived in the Islamic world, there was little interest in them in a culture in which occupations were set by family ties, reputations were dependent on one's adherence to kinship norms, and prayer times were based on the sun's position.

One of the other consequences of the spread of WEIRD traits is that Europeans began to work longer and harder. Contrary to popular notions and images, Third World peoples have always worked far less than WEIRD Westerners. For some time now, a number of studies have shown that there was an "industrious revolution" (before the industrial revolution), led by a middle class with the workweek lengthened by 40 percent in London from the 1650s to the 1750s (De Vries, 1994). After 1800, people were working about one thousand hours more per year, or about an extra nineteen hours per week. The common explanation is that demographic pressures were forcing people to work longer. Population was increasing steadily through the eighteenth century, but studies now show that when one compares diverse societies, the men who are involved in the commercial sector tended to increase their weekly work time on average by about five hours. Henrich thus recognizes the role that the spread of markets had on psychology; however, what was going on in Europe was deeper than having the opportunity to buy newly available commercial goods: tea, sugar, coffee, pepper, nutmeg, and rum. People were also working more intensively because they had a different personality, a greater inclination to postpone gratification, a more clock-time mindset, and a wish to cultivate a reputation for self-discipline and punctuality.

In a chapter titled "Escape Velocity," Henrich brings up the incredible "innovation-driven economic and military expansion ... of Europe after 1500."[723] Those who prioritize genes and IQ believe that rising intelligence in England during the modern era was the driving factor behind the innovations leading to the industrial revolution. Possibly the best book proposing this argument is Gregory Clark's *A Farewell to Alms*. It argues that in the years 1250–1800, "economic success translated powerfully into reproductive success, with the richest individuals having more than twice the number of surviving children at death as the poorest."[724] The result in the long run was that the more literate and intelligent members of British society "left twice as many children as the poorest." While in the past the ruling aristocratic class was "barely reproducing itself" because the death rates from its professional pursuit of warfare were too high, the rise of an urbane, mercantile, and professionally-minded elite, with many surviving children, brought about a new situation in which the kind of people who survived and succeeded the most were those with the "smarter" genes and the middle-class values of hard work, patience, literacy, and thrift.

This argument makes sense as far as it goes. But so does Henrich's argument that we should not assume that inventions by lone geniuses automatically translate into the "successful diffusion and implementation" of technologies and widespread innovations in the economy. Such geniuses are best seen as products of the "growth of Europe's collective brain," nourished by the spread of voluntary associations, charter cities, and universities, knowledge societies and widespread publications, monasteries and apprenticeships. Henrich provides solid evidence showing that "the larger the population of engaged minds, the faster the rate of cumulative cultural evolution."[725] The "larger the network of people learning or doing something, the more opportunities" there were for inventions and innovations/improvements in technology.

While this argument does not necessarily preclude Clark's emphasis on rising average intelligence in modern Britain, it does challenge more directly Edward Dutton and Bruce Charlton's thesis in *The Genius Famine* that geniuses were behind the industrial revolution in Europe.[726] Henrich goes over a number of key innovations—the printing press, steam engine, spinning mule, vulcanized rubber, and incandescent light bulb—to show that multiple people interconnected with

---

[723] Henrich, 433.
[724] Clark, 2007, 113.
[725] Henrich, 436.
[726] Dutton and Charlton, 2020.

each other were developing the ideas associated with these innovations. He does not identify them as "inventions," because these innovations were "just novel recombinations of existing ideas, techniques . . . a tool taken from one domain and applied in another." The collective brain of Europeans was expanding at an accelerating rate as individuals from all walks of life came together in voluntary associations "unconstrained by the bonds of kinship," with opportunities to become part of "sprawling networks of experts" in a wide variety of subjects and apprenticeships. Some of the salient points he makes are: The promotion of neolocal residence meant that newly married couples became head of their households at a young age, when people are "less risk-averse and less tied to tradition." Monasteries, which diffused throughout Christendom independently of kinship groups, "carried with them the latest crops, agricultural techniques, production methods, and industries." "The Cistercian Order, in particular, built a sprawling network of monastery factories that deployed the latest techniques for grinding wheat, casting iron, tanning hides, fulling cloth, and cultivating grapes."

The "growing urban centers of the Middle Ages" were open to "residential-mobile artisans and craftsmen." Cities expanded the collective brain of Europeans by bringing people with "different skills and areas of expertise to work on ideas and technologies together." Data show that "four out of five apprentices were not sons of their master" in medieval guilds from the Netherlands. In seventeenth-century London, "the percentage of artisans trained by nonrelatives ranged from 72 to 93 percent," whereas in India and China "almost all skilled artisans" were trained by a close family member. "More than three-quarters of the 4,000 masters" in Vienna in 1742 "had been born elsewhere."[727]

Evidence shows that "for each 10-fold increase in population size (from 10,000 to 100,000) there's 13 times more innovation," and it also shows that the collective brain of European nations expanded substantially from 1200 to 1900 as measured by the size of the urban areas and the interconnectedness of people.[728] The number of knowledge societies grew substantially after 1600, with analytically minded individuals networking through much of Europe via letters, books, pamphlets, technical manuals, and eventually scholarly journals and public libraries. The evidence shows a strong relationship between the number of knowledge societies in a region and the number of innovations. When talent was suppressed in one nation competing with another, say, the energetic and educated Protestant Huguenots in

---

[727] Henrich, 442–447.
[728] Ibid, 451.

France, another nation open to Protestantism would welcome them to join their voluntary associations.

End of Kinship Norms = Rise of Ideological
Struggles and Rise of WEIRD Nationalism

Henrich presumes throughout that the end of kinship-imposed norms brought an end to collectively-imposed norms, resulting in a world of non-conformist individuals freely seeking the best means to achieve the highest returns according to impartial criteria. It is beyond his cognitive radar how the abolition of traditional institutions opened up a new ideological world where individuals, classes, religious groups, including ethno-linguistic groups, would have the opportunity to push forth programs (including nationalism) regarding how their institutions and communities should be organized. The WEIRD modernization of Europe entailed the use of rational-impartial criteria wherein the validity of programs for reform came to be judged not only in terms of the economic interests and personal biases of the respective populations, but also in terms of the reason-based arguments and evidential content given in support of these programs. The serious weakening of the monarchical order in Europe with the Enlightenment and the French Revolution of 1789 opened up an intense ideological struggle by a wide variety of WEIRD groups over what moral values, future orientation, and interests should underlie Western institutions. Many historians have identified the post-French Revolution period as "The Age of Ideology," in reflection of the keen ideological struggles that ensued in the 1800s between liberalism, conservatism, nationalism, socialism, Marxism, proto-fascism, and other isms.[729]

---

[729] Schwarzmantel, 1997. According to Kenneth Minogue, with the end of the traditional order in post-revolutionary France, an aggressive ideological style of practicing politics took over "always in terms of oppression, followed by struggle and leading to emancipation." These are the words of Martyn P. Thompson in the Foreword of Minogue's book, *Alien Powers: The Pure Theory of Ideology* (ISI Books, 2008), who further says that "Marx was arguably the most thoughtful of all the innovators" in this ideological style, though there were many other advocates of different isms driven by the goal to emancipate humanity from the "shackles of false ideas by establishing and applying for the first time, a genuine 'science of ideas'" (x–xiii). Michael Oakeshott blamed this ideological style on modern rationalism's privileging of technical knowledge at the expense of traditional knowledge, authority, and prejudice. I tend to be a Hegelian in thinking we can judge the importance of hierarchy and White identity politics by the giving of reasons in their support through the social practice of open inquiry and critical argumentation.

This should be a main take-away insight of Henrich's book: ideological struggles are originally Western because they can only occur in societies where individuals can give reasons to a mass audience freed from tribal norms in support of their claims about how to construct a new social order. Because individuals come from many different backgrounds, with varying personalities, class interests, ethnic attachments, and historical memories, including moral visions about the future, which are heavily influenced by contextual factors, there will always be different ideological claims with their own built-in reasons and forms of argumentation. No ideology can claim to embody strictly impartial and universal principles for humanity.

Henrich tends to assume that increasing WEIRDness is about "building broader social networks" across the world beyond xenophobic and irrational nation-states, leading to a globalized world where individuals act strictly on the basis of scientific criteria in a cooperative and harmonious way, with intergroup competition becoming a contest between market agents seeking the most rational means to maximize returns that translate (via the support of a managerial elite) into increased general welfare. With the spread of affluent WEIRD states and harmonious "interfirm competition," he implies, the world will see an end to the still irrational ideological struggles of the post-French revolutionary era, with social scientists offering strictly impartial accounts based on coevolutionary genetic-cultural principles. He can't see that advocating for cultural nationalism (for civic liberal principles and for a collective attachment to a nation's heritage, folkways, and historical memories) can be done in a WEIRD way (along with the interests and biases that come along with all ideological programs), by giving reasons for its beneficial effects, and by offering scientific evidence about how diversity destroys social trust and social capital.[730] He can't see that it is possible to rationally

---

[730] The evidence that diversity reduces trust and participation in one's community while creating various social pathologies is now overwhelming. Despite the bias of academia for diversity, and the strong bias of research funding agencies, it keeps growing, though barely anyone talks about it, including Henrich, who prefers to repeat what he hears from mainstream narratives. While many are familiar with Robert D. Putnam's research on the downsides of diversity, most are unaware of recent studies showing that increasing cultural and racial diversity beyond a certain proportion of the population eventually brings more harm than benefits to the host population. Keep in mind that many of the following studies are ten to twenty years old, when immigrant diversity was just accelerating in Europe, and its downside was not as palpable: Costa and Kahn (2003); Delhey and Newton (2005); Dinesen and Sønderskov (2016); Dinesen, Schaeffer and Sønderskov (2020); Fieldhouse and Cutts (2010); Hooghe et al. (2009); Lancee and Dronkers (2011); Öberg, Oskarsson and Svensson (2011); Rice and Steele (2001); Ziller (2015).

justify the soundness of traditional family values, hierarchy, and limited demo-cratic rights, on the grounds that these values are healthy for the progression of societies and the raising of children.

Unfortunately, open argumentation in Western universities about the merits and demerits of immigrant diversity, or traditional family norms, is very difficult to conduct in an open, liberal manner. The officially declared mission of almost every university in the West, including Harvard (where Henrich works), is to pro-mote "diversity, inclusiveness, and equity"—as if the merits of these values were already proven beyond further thinking. It was likely within this ideological at-mosphere that Henrich decided (for the first time in his career) to publish a 2021 article extolling the benefits of mass immigration a few months after the publica-tion of The WEIRDest People.[731] This atmosphere may also explain why he side-steps how WEIRD Europeans were able to conceptualize themselves as members of nation-states in terms of broader identities, such as language, religion, common history, and ethnic ancestry—in the degree to which they were freed from kinship tribalism. The identification of the peoples of the world within clearly demarcated nation-states, in combination with liberal legal codes that recognize the equal rights of citizens, was indeed one of the greatest accomplishments of WEIRD Eu-ropeans. Without this identification, humans would have been forever bickering with each other along kinship and tribal lines. According to Steven Pinker's re-search, the rates of violence experienced by tribal and nonstate societies were much higher than they were after 1600, when nation-states were consolidated in Europe. Despite mass atrocities inflicted by nation-states in the twentieth century, the rates of violent death during this century, particularly after the 1950s, were clearly lower than at any previous time in history.[732]

Prior to the centralization of power by monarchs in the late medieval and early modern era, the authority to wage war, to tax the population, to administer and enforce the law, were personally owned, hereditary rights of a feudal class with patrimonial/tribal authority. Patrimonialism is a form of authority that retains as-pects of the old patriarchal kin-based rule centered on extended family lineages,

---

[731] He declared in a PBS interview that "Every time you turn up immigration you turn up inno-vation." https://www.pbs.org/video/who-are-weirdest-people-world-k5jlpb/. I suspect this was a calculated move to counter potential criticisms that he was a "Western cultural supremacist" in arguing that Europeans became affluent due to their personality traits for honesty, punctual-ity, lack of nepotism, and fairness, rather than the colonial exploitation of nonwhites, which is the standard explanation in academia.

[732] Pinker, 2011.

with the difference that it projects the rule of the patriarch onto a broader segment of the population atop kin-based relations. With the rise of absolutism in the seventeenth century, the ruler came to justify his right to complete sovereignty over a territory on the basis of divine and natural law, with kin-based norms playing a minimal role. It was argued that a sovereign ruler had a right to monopolize all power and justice away from private feudal families because that is the rational way by which God ordained all creation to be ordered, for the purpose of achieving the common good and the peaceful coexistence of people within a territory.

During the late eighteenth and nineteenth centuries, the idea came to prevail that the right of the government to rule comes from the people who inhabit the territorial state, and that a legitimate national state presupposes a territory that is made up of people who actually have a common ethnic lineage, as well as a culturally-constructed civic identity. While the formation of absolutist states and modern nation states had eliminated intra-group feudal warfare, it certainly did not eliminate inter-state competition and power struggles. But with the spread of the idea that the territories of a nation are justifiable only on the basis of common ethno-cultural identities and the representative consent of the governed, equality under the law and equal rights for all citizens, the notion of national self-determination spread, with the result that empires were dissolved, many new European nation-states were created by formerly suppressed ethnic minorities, and the League of Nations was born to ensure the self-determination and peaceful coexistence of peoples in Europe.

The reality of WWII, however, thoroughly discredited the idea of ethnic and cultural nationalism. Nationalism came to be seen instead as an ideology driven by "divisive" and "aggrandizing" ethnic interests, in opposition to the cardinal liberal principle that individual rights should constitute the foundation of nation-states. The persistence of disputes over the legitimate ethnic borders of European peoples, the determination of the highly powerful Germanic peoples to unify themselves within one nation-state, and particularly the attempts by the National Socialists to conquer lands of non-Germanic countries, resulted in the complete discrediting of ethnic nationalism, leading to the prevalence of the idea that Western nations should only have a civic-liberal identity.

For some time, up until the 1960s, immigration policies favored White immigrants, and it was commonly believed among the liberal-minded nations of the West that they could have both a civic-liberal and a broadly Christian and ethnic identity. But, as we will explain in Chapter XI, the progressive logic of liberalism, its fundamental belief that the full emancipation of the individual requires the elimination of all collective identities, would eventually undermine the notion of a strong cultural identity among European peoples. The notion that European nations were based on a particular ethnic group, and that immigration policies should respect this, came to be equated with "racial supremacy." Only minorities would be allowed to enjoy some degree of multicultural protections and celebrations to remedy past injustices. Even the idea of civic nationalism based on Western liberal values alone, without much emphasis on cultural heritage, would come to be discredited as "Western-centric."

Henrich wants us to believe that WEIRD Europeans never created ethnic nation-states with strong civic-liberal identities. We are supposed to believe that WEIRDness inevitably leads to the dissolution of national identities, a process of "residential mobility" across national borders, and a scaling-up involving global companies manned by WEIRD creatures from all over the world. He cannot fathom the possibility of nations exhibiting traits for fairness, rule of law, analytical thinking, and equality under the law, as well as a strong sense of national identity. He believes that social evolution requires the promotion of racial diversity across the West. Henrich ignores the role of culturally-constructed ethnic-liberal identities in the formation of nation-states. The terms "ethnic group" or "ethnicity" remained unexamined. He writes a lot about clans and tribes without addressing the ways in which ancestry, a common ethno-linguistic heritage, and similar cultural and religious symbols, played a role in the scaling-up process and the formation of larger national groups. This absence weakens his analysis of the types of groups Europeans created after their kinship networks were dissolved. We are supposed to think that, as individuals were freed from kinship ties, they went on to create voluntary associations based on impersonal norms without any sense of their broader ethno-cultural identities other than the new identities they forged with "strangers" as members of these associations.

The extensive research of Anthony Smith, the most prolific scholar on the origins of nation-states and nationalism, has confirmed that the modern states of Europe were more than the "imagined communities" or "invented traditions" that Hans Kohn, Eric Hobsbawm, and Benedict Anderson wrote about.[733] Nation-level infrastructures, official languages, centralized systems of taxation, national currencies, and unified laws were culturally constructed by elites seeking powerful territorial states with mass appeal on the basis of actual ancestral ties and territorial roots. As Smith argued in *The Ethnic Origins of Nations*, modern nations were

---

[733] Duchesne, 2015.

not created ex nihilo on the basis of modern techniques and civic values alone, but also on the basis of "myths, memories, symbols, embodied in customs and traditions" by "fairly homogeneous ethnicities."[734] The minorities that did not identify with the core ethnic group did so in reflection of their own distinctive sense of ancestry, language, and overall cultural identity.

Nevertheless, it can't be denied that Henrich's way of treating nation states reflects the current state of liberal thinking in the West. Liberalism has indeed culminated in the idea, which currently pervades every institution in the West, that states should not impose any collective identity upon their populations, not even a cultural identity, other than the identity that they have an equal right to choose their own cultural values in a state of mutual tolerance. Why and how liberalism came to this conclusion will be increasingly addressed in Chapters X and XI.

Europeans Are the True Cultural Species

The last chapter of Henrich's book is titled "The Dark Matter of History," a metaphor from the world of physics. Some physicists believe that dark matter accounts for approximately 85 percent of the matter in the universe, although they can't see this matter directly. They can only describe its nature on the basis of shadows attributed to it without observing its source. In using this term, he is implying that the WEIRD psychology of Westerners is the "dark matter" that lies beneath their unique historical trajectory. This psychology was undetected, or never uniquely attributed to Westerners as such, because social scientists were trained to believe that the psychological dispositions of the world's peoples were the same. But Henrich has now revealed for us the WEIRDness of Westerners, and has proposed how they came to acquire this psychology, which should raise the question: if he has brought so much light to the perennial subject of Western uniqueness, and if this psychology entails free will, intentionality, and reason-based institutional arrangements, why identify this psychology as the "dark matter that flows behind the scenes throughout history"? His implied answer is that Westerners have been unaware of their culturally-evolved WEIRD history until his book came out.

---

[734] Smith, 1991.

There is a fundamental difference in awareness about the origins and nature of one's society between non-WEIRD peoples who create institutions by following norms closely tied to the evolutionary imperatives of kinship, and WEIRD people who create voluntary institutions freely adjudicated by them on the basis of relatively impartial principles over and above the evolutionary mandates of kinship. Don't get distracted by Henrich's use of the words "culturally-mandated" when he writes about kin-based norms and practices, cousin marriage, patrilocal residence, and ancestor worship. These practices, to be sure, were culturally mandated and transmitted through learning from generation to generation, for humans don't act according to instincts alone. We should not underestimate, however, the contrast between kinship-based norms and the culturally-mandated norms of Western societies conceptualized in a state of relative mental independence from age-old customs and biologically-determined sexual impulses. The Western norm of monogamy, which stood in opposition to the genetic-biological predisposition of high-status males for polygynous marriages, was unnatural and strictly cultural. Henrich can thus be confusing when he writes about the "cultural learning" of the "human species" as such, in abeyance of his own thesis about the cultural WEIRDness of Whites. The influence of free deliberation and the role of reason in history increases in the degree to which humans have the opportunity to choose their own normative paths in life rather than being obligated to following customs set in stone without reflexivity.[735]

Insomuch as Europeans were the only people to become aware of the downside of kinship ties, by proposing new norms based on impartial criteria, and consciously creating nuclear families as superior over polygamous cousin marriages, and constructing thereby broader identities based on liberal citizenship with a strong sense of ethnic ancestry above clannish/tribal natural bonds, we can say that they were transcending, or, in the language that we saw Bellah using in Chapter III, acting under conditions of "relaxed selection." This is one of my main disagreements with MacDonald's attempt to trace European "weird" behaviors back

---

[735] As John Stuart Mill observed (1956, 71) "The human faculties of perception, judgement, discriminate feeling, mental activity, and even moral preference are exercised only in making a choice. He who does anything because it is the custom makes no choice. . . . If the grounds of an opinion are not conclusive to the person's own reason, his reason cannot be strengthened, but is likely to be weakened. . . . He who lets the world, or his own portion of it, choose his plan of life for him has no need of any other faculty than the ape-like one of imitation. He must use observation to see, reasoning and judgment to foresee, activity to gather materials for decision, discrimination to decide, and when he has decided, firmness and self-control to hold to his deliberate decision."

to evolutionary pressures. He is correct to insist that, as inherently biological beings, we cannot but pay attention to the genetic basis of human behaviors, including the individualistic behaviors of Europeans. But neither can we ignore the relatively higher degree of self-awareness among Europeans, and ability to pursue goals and ideals (music, art, and philosophies, as we will see in the next chapters) of their own choosing, even if these ideals, as MacDonald reminds us, cannot violate the laws of biological self-preservation. We can say that Europeans were unique in abolishing the blind determination of biologically-based customs over their social relationships.

Henrich knows that Europeans were unique in creating institutions based on rational grounds and individual choice. And yet he believes that European free rational deliberation did not play an autonomous role in the making of the very WEIRD West that is identified with free choice and rationality. The WEIRD rationality employed by Henrich to understand history is that of the third-person point of view we encountered in the first chapter, which is typical of the omniscient scientist, the neutral observer who understands the historical subjects he is explaining while the historical subjects don't know what they are doing, but behave essentially like inanimate objects, or sentient but unconscious beings without self-chosen purposes.

His claim that Enlightenment intellectuals "positing grand theories . . . about constitutional governments, liberty, natural rights, progress, rationality, and science" were not responsible for the making of the modern West makes a lot of sense.[736] The essential kernel of the ideas attributed to the Enlightenment were elaborated in the Middle Ages as these ideas became thinkable to a population that was becoming increasingly individualistic and WEIRD after the Church's demolition of the strong kin-based institutions of the Germanic tribes that had taken over Europe. The ideals of liberalism were formulated gradually, long before the Enlightenment era. "By 1200," as Henrich observes, there were incipient notions of natural rights "already in circulation," articulated by Catholic scholars and lawyers during the so-called "Papal Revolution" of the twelfth century. Urban centers with charters offering citizens "legal protections, tax exemptions, property rights, mutual insurance, and freedom from conscription" proliferated during the medieval era. Lawyers trained in universities enjoying corporate autonomy formulated principles for individuals in a world with growing occupational specializations,

---

[736] Henrich, 398.

and "increasingly focused on [individual] attributes, intentions, and dispositions."[737]

It is hard to envision how anyone living in a kinship group, where everyone is a member of a collective with a prescribed set of obligations, no matter how intelligent, would ever come up with the notion that individuals have "natural rights" as individuals. The notion that individuals have rights to life, liberty, and property would be unthinkable in societies where political power and privileges flow directly out of lineage ties, family descent, or the divine commands of religions rooted in kinship. It is likewise hard to envision how kin-based people would learn how to think analytically about properties like mass, electric charge, gravity, and geometrical points. Kinship-oriented people are deeply socialized to think in contextual terms about how objects fit within their overall world of interpersonal relations and in terms of the mythical/religious views sustaining these relationships. Liberal ideas with actual institutional consequences could have spread only when they favored an emerging world of individuals increasingly relying upon their own choices, interacting regularly with strangers in impersonal markets, and forming voluntary associations.

The question that needs answering is whether the Greek imposition of monogamy set them on their WEIRD rationalist history, or whether this cultural imposition was instead a product of a psychology that was already latently WEIRD. And if the Greeks were already latently WEIRD, why? We met earlier MacDonald's contention that the origins of monogamous families should be traced back to the "harsh evolutionary pressures of the Ice Age." This environment selected for smaller family groups dispersed across wider territories, as contrasted to the "extended kinship networks and collectivist groups" typical in the non-Western world. But MacDonald does not quite explain why monogamy was adopted in the southern environment of ancient Greece where, as he otherwise points out, the individualism he observed in northern Europe was "moderate." We should also draw a distinction between the adoption of monogamy to cope with scarce resources and evolutionary pressures, from the reason-based prohibition of polygamy in ancient Greece among high-status men. The latter is an act of a true "cultural species." It is not clear whether monogamy was invented prior to the ancient Greeks as a culturally mandated norm. It would be a mistake, in any case, to think that reason became self-authorizing, self-legislating, and self-grounding, as it has been claimed to have become in the Germanic world of Kant, Fichte, and Hegel,

---

[737] Ibid, 399.

the moment kinship relationships were weakened and monogamy was introduced in ancient Greece.

The Claims of Kinship Versus the Claims of Reason in Ancient Greece

The claims of kinship were still strong in ancient Greece. While different clans and tribes coalesced around city-states after the eighth century BC, tribal groups with their own names and ancestral ties were still common at the time of the first Presocratic philosophers. Notwithstanding the imposition of monogamy during the time of Solon (630–560 BC), before the rise of Socratic philosophy (470–399 BC), there were no philosophers making rational claims about moral standards over and above the traditional norms prescribed by particular city-states, even though we find attempts in the Presocratics to formulate universal concepts about nature—that *nous* governs the world, and that there is reason in the universe. Social practices and norms were accepted unreflectively as the way things were. Only with the consolidation of city-states, during the age of Socrates, do we see philosophical arguments about the universal meaning of friendship, courage, self-restraint, wisdom, and justice. We witness philosophers conceptualizing reason-based standards by which to question the values of one's community. Socrates and Plato spoke about human life as it ought to be. However, these new ideals could not achieve much influence yet. Socrates was put to death. The sophist's argument that a view from nowhere was impossible, that all value judgments were relative to a particular community, and that there is no justice as such, was dominant among members of the elite. It is a very complicated cultural history. The contextual thinking of the Sophists was itself a product of a culture transcending its particular context with a capacity to reflect upon, and thus distance itself from, its own contextual thinking.

In the tragic drama of Aeschylus (525–455 BC) and Sophocles (497–406 BC), there were two incomparable conceptions of the good: the moral imperatives of kinship loyalty, versus the moral imperatives of the city-state; and beyond the particularities of each city-state, the moral imperatives ascertained by reason as such. However, before the modern era, throughout the medieval era, reason still sought these imperatives in some cosmic order existing beyond time and outside subjective consciousness. Something outside man was in charge of dictating the moral precepts by which he should organize society. Only with the onset of the modern era, though with anticipations in the Christian principle of inner conscience, do we find an emphasis on the ultimate authority of thinking for oneself about what is to be decided as truthful, rather than appealing to some external cosmic order. Only in modern times do we find the principle, which begins with Descartes, that truth can only be ascertained by a subject who thinks freely and draws its truthfulness from within his own cognitive activity.

The ancient world and the medieval world were still far from this modern view. The ancient world remained caught between the moral imperative of kinship norms and the notion that reason could discover what was absolutely true through a process of intense education until one's mind learned to apprehend the nature of the cosmic moral order. In Aeschylus' *Oresteia* we have a conflict between the rules of kinship vendetta and the orderly procedures and laws of the city-state, between the barbaric furies and vengeance of clans and the civilized self-restraint and balanced judgment of the citizen. In Sophocles' *Antigone* we have a conflict between the stubborn determination of Antigone to follow the immemorial claims of kinship, which required her to perform proper burial rites for her dead brother, in defiance of the edicts of the city-state that she should not perform burial rites because he had been accused of committing treason against the laws of the city-state.

Yet, for all this, and in time, the claims of reason would grow considerably in ancient times. Starting with the consolidation of city-states and Solon's rule, and culminating in Plato and Aristotle, the Greeks would promote a whole new ideal of education, *paideia*, in which the emphasis was on what is best for the education of man as a man, what it means to be a good citizen, rather than what it means to perform one's kindred obligations, and what are the eternal standards of excellence, rather than what constitutes excellence for a particular people.[738]

Once the mind was discovered, and the highest intellects of the age began to rely on their reason, increasingly freed from the envelopment of nature and kin-based prescriptions, reason became an agent in its own right. Learning can be cumulative, so long as humans realize that the *logos* of the world can be revealed to those who know that their minds are the agents through which the rationality of the world can be grasped, which is possible only as humans become conscious of their consciousness. This started in ancient Greece, as we explained extensively in prior chapters, long before the Catholic Church imposed its family program. When the historian Herodotus recognized that each culture has its own norms and behaviors conforming to its own habitat, he was standing above the accepted

---

[738] Jaeger, 1986.

claims of his own culture, and thus taking a universal stand, even though he suggested there were no universal standards.[739] It was for Socrates and then Plato to search for absolute standards. Plato sought these standards in the mind's apprehension of an eternal cosmic order. Although the Greeks discovered the mind, they saw this mind as a particular, imperfect expression of a cosmic mind. They were not fully aware that the grounding of truth is possible only as self-consciousness, and that the mind—in a state of communication with other minds—is the only agent capable of determining the validity of truth-claims. This was the accomplishment of the modern age.

---

[739] Herodotus was one of the first ethnographers in history (Skinner, 2012). In fact, the stark contrast Henrich draws between the analytical mind of Europeans and the contextual or holistic mind of non-WEIRD people is misleading. Westerners, as we saw in Chapter V, were the first to consciously argue for the validity of contextual thinking, to develop self-conscious philosophies and methodologies for the investigation of how thinking is mediated by historical time and social context. The non-Western world was unconsciously contextual, enmeshed in their kinship groups and strong traditions.

VIII

PURSUIT OF THE HIGHEST, CONTINUOUS ORIGINALITY, AND EVENTUAL DECOMPOSITION OF SELF-AUTHORIZING EUROPEAN ARTISTS

Insist on yourself; never imitate.

– Ralph Waldo Emerson.

It is possible that the production of genius is reserved to a limited period of mankind's history.

– Nietzsche

When first envisioning the current book, my aim was to offer a more thorough demonstration and explanation of the higher achievements of Western civilization than I did in *Uniqueness* and *Faustian Man*. But witnessing how this civilization is clearly on an ethnocidal path could not but compel me to ask whether there is a connection between the creative nature of this civilization and its current ethnocidal path. We will address this connection directly in Chapter X and XI; however, in the current chapter, in which the subject is art, it is impossible to ignore Spengler's famous observation made in 1918 that the West needed to confront "the cold, hard facts of a late life. . . . Of great paintings or great music there can no longer be, for Western people, any question."[740] While the following chapter

---

[740] Spengler, 1980, 40.

will be essentially focused on the far higher levels of European accomplishment in music, furniture design, architecture, and painting, and on the reasons for this creativity, it will also suggest that the complete break from a premodern aesthetic, with its "dogmatic" acceptance of Classical-Christian ideals of perfection, towards a more self-assertive, freely creating artist who chooses his own standards, cannot be ignored in our attempts to understand this decline. The paradox is that one can identify this (increasingly) self-authorizing individual artist as the main agent behind Western creativity, particularly from the Renaissance through to the Romantic and the Impressionistic ages.

The higher consciousness and self-determination of individuals can be seen as the main agent driving the persisting originality of the West. Through the industrial and bourgeois revolutions, and through the first half of the nineteenth century, this "autonomous self," however, still had collective classical aesthetic ideals and relatively strong community ties. They were "grounded." With the complete disenchantment and desacralization of nature, brought about by the intensification of liberal capitalism, along with the bureaucratic standardization of social relations, and the seeming mastery of science over nature, individuals found themselves facing a collective void, while continually pressured to produce new forms of art, from within their own isolated egos, leading to the exploration, and eventual exhaustion, of all the possibilities in music, furniture-architectural design, and painting. In other words, this decline cannot be regarded as merely a product of lack of standards, but of the exhaustion of new original possibilities, coupled with the atomization of Europeans. This chapter consists of three major parts about music, furniture design, and painting, respectively. It is mainly in regards to painting, to be covered last, that we will address the subject of decline, waiting until Chapters X and XI to start offering a full theoretically oriented explanation that goes beyond art to cover the current ethnocidal path of Western nations.

European Striving for *Ars Perfecta* in Linear Time

In academia, music is regarded as a "cultural universal" or "human universal" found among all peoples in history. This view is attractive to academics who want to promote the idea of a "common humanity" in our globalizing world, multiculturalists who believe that it is "imperative" to teach about the equal value of all musical traditions in light of "the ethnic mix of peoples that now exists in most countries of the West," and evolutionary psychologists who believe that all humans are equally "hardwired for music."[741]

Various theories have been offered on the origins and role of music: 1) it evolved as an elaborate form of sexual selection, primarily to seduce potential mates; 2) as a "shared precursor" of language; 3) as a practical means to assist in organizing and motivating human work; 4) to encourage cooperation within one's community; 5) as a pleasant preoccupation or source of amusement, relaxation, and recuperation; 6) to express one's cultural identity and feel united with one's culture through social celebrations, such as weddings, funerals, religious processions, and ceremonial rites.

These explanations about the nature and origins of music have a major, disquieting flaw: they can't explain why Europeans were continuously creative in music for many centuries, responsible for the highest, most complex form of music—classical music—along with the invention of the most sophisticated musical instruments, and the articulation of all the treatises on music in matters related to pitch, notes, intervals, scale systems, tonality, modulation, and melody.[742] Classical music expresses the best that man has achieved in music. It is not that other cultures did not create great folk music, which is essential to a people's identity. It is that their music was performed by custom over countless generations, without exhibiting a continuous line of creative composers, each personally striving for higher levels of musical expression.

---

[741] Antweiler, 2018; Fletcher, 2004; Ravignani et al., 2017. Peter Fletcher says that his book, *World Musics in Context: A Comprehensive Survey of the World's Major Musical Cultures* (2004), "contains a wide-ranging survey of musics of the world in historical and social contexts, from ancient times to the present day"—but it is clear, by his own admission, that his book aims to "lead those who practice Western music towards a deeper understanding of the various musical traditions that contribute to the modern, multicultural environment . . . in the West," with its "ethnic mix of peoples." In this vein, while he happily accounts for the achievements of non-Western peoples without ideologically intrusive judgements, once he gets to "European musical styles" he can't help but write about "Europe's intellectual debt to earlier civilizations in Africa and Asia, which later made possible Europe's subsequent political and cultural colonialism." He is less interested in Europe's Post-Renaissance music than "the twin senses of cultural superiority and racial superiority that came to pervade the thought of post-Renaissance European music" (31–35).

[742] While this chapter relies on many other sources, particular mention should be made here of the over 1000-page textbook, *A History of Western Music*, by Peter Burkholder, Donald Jay Grout, and Claude Palisca, originally published in 1960, with a tenth edition published in 2019. This text, as good a textbook as one can get in any subject, can't be praised enough for its comprehensiveness and intricate details. It would not be surprising if many so-called "musicologists" in academia have not read this exhaustive study. The sixth edition is cited here.

Treatises on Music

From its beginnings in ancient Greece, we witness systematic treatises about the nature of music, outlining its terminology, note names, tetrachord names, conjunct and disjunct tetrachords, the meaning of *tonoi*, harmony, species of consonances, names of octave species, as well as efforts at a scientific theory of acoustics. While Pythagoras is generally considered to have initiated a theoretical study of acoustics, the 330 BC treatise *Elements of Harmony* by Aristoxenus is now regarded by many scholars as the first book to have argued that the nature of music is fundamentally different from the natural world, and that the laws of traditional mathematics by which the Pythagoreans explained natural phenomena could not explain the phenomena of music. Music merited a science of its own.

Musical space is incommensurable, Aristoxenus argued, and the elements of music are not isolated entities, but integral parts of an organic whole from which each part derives its meaning and position. Aristoxenus, according to Flora Levin, "accomplished something whose importance cannot be overstated: he freed the science of harmonics from the bonds of the Pythagorean theory of proportions, the numerical theory that is applicable only to commensurables."[743] The correct way to determine the size of intervals was not by numerical ratio, but by ear.

Other important Greek theorists of music with a predilection for rigorous thought, systemic definition and classification included Cleonides (c. 100s–200s BC), Ptolemy (AD 100–170) and Aristides Quintilianus (AD 35–100). Of these, only parts of the writings of Ptolemy, famous for his outstanding works in geography and astronomy, survive under the title *Harmonikon*. He followed the theoretical approach of the Pythagoreans, for basing musical intervals on mathematical ratios. Ptolemy also argued, with respect to *tonoi*, that the height of pitch was only one source in the variety and expression of music, along with the arrangement of intervals within a vocal register. Greek theory influenced all subsequent Western thinking on music.

In the Middle Ages, Boethius' *De institutione musica*, which described the Pythagorean unity of mathematics and music, and the Platonic concept of the relationship between music and society, was widely read; but the most significant theoretical contribution came from Guido of Arezzo (991/992–1033), on the strength of his invention of modern musical notation (or staff notation) that replaced

---

[743] Levin, 2009, 197.

neumatic notation. The staff enabled scribes to notate relative pitches precisely, and freed music from its dependence on oral transmission. Guido is also credited with the use of the "ut-re-mi-fa-sol-la" (do-re-mi-fa-so-la) mnemonic device, or memory device. Guido's treatise *Micrologus Guidonis de disciplina artis musicae* [*The Epitome of Guido on the Discipline of the Art of Music*] was highly regarded among the educated.

Another important figure was Franco of Cologne, who codified a system of notation in his 1280 *Ars cantus mensurabilis [Art of Measured Song]*, in which the relative time values of notes, ligatures, and rests were clearly laid out. This led to the revolutionary invention of polyphony, a type of musical texture consisting of two or more simultaneous lines of independent melody, as opposed to just one voice—an aspect of Western music not duplicated in any other culture. Then came Ars Nova through the writings of Johannes de Muris (1290–1355) and Philippe de Vitry (1291–1361). The former's treatise, *Notitia artis musicae [A Note on the Art of Music]* (1321), is credited with dramatically increasing the "fidelity with which a musical notation system could represent complex rhythmic patterns . . . modeled on the astronomical method for mathematically organizing time."[744] The latter's writings contain "a detailed account of the various uses and meanings of the coloured notes, and the introduction of additional durational symbols in the new notational system."[745]

Great Composers of the Middle Ages and Renaissance

All the greatest composers in history were Western. With the invention of the Ars Nova, we can start identifying great individual composers, beginning with the Frenchman Guillaume de Machaut (1300–77), who adapted poetic forms into polyphonic music, including not only the *motet*, which is based on a sacred text, but also secular song forms, such as the *lai*, based on short tales in French litera-ture, and the *formes fixes*, such as the *rondeau*, *virelai*, and *ballade*, into the musi-cal mainstream. Francesco Landini (1325–1397) was the foremost musician of the Trecento style, sometimes called the "Italian ars nova," known for his virtuosity on the portative organ, and for his compositions in the *ballata* form. Writers noted that "the sweetness of his melodies was such that hearts burst from their

---

[744] Arnsdorf, 2020.
[745] Britannica, 2023.

bosoms." He may have been the first composer to think of his music as striving for perfection, writing: "I am Music, and weeping I regret seeing intelligent people forsaking my sweet and perfect sounds for street music."[746]

The English would produce their own great composers, most notably John Dunstable (1390–1453), who developed a style, *la contenance angloise*, which was never heard before in music, using full triadic harmony, which refers to "a set of notes consisting of three notes built on successive intervals of a third." Along with harmonies with thirds and sixths, this time period also witnessed the Burgundian School of the 1400s, associated with a more rational control of consonance and dissonance.[747] A member, the composer and musical theorist Guillaume Dufay (1397–1474), was known for his masses, *motets, magnificats*, hymns, and *antiphons* within the area of sacred music, as well as secular music following the *formes fixes*. This School originated in the "cosmopolitan atmosphere" of the Burgundian court, which was very prestigious in this period, influencing musical centers across Europe.[748]

Creating a bridge beyond the Middle Ages, the Burgundian School paved the way for the Renaissance, which saw a rebirth of interest in the treatises of the Greek past. Franchinus Gaffurius' *Theorica musicae* [*Theory of Music*] (1492), *Practica musicae* [*Practice of Music*] (1496), and *De harmonia musicorum instrumentorum opus* [*A Work on the Harmony of Musical Instruments*] (1518), incorporated Greek ideas brought to Italy from Byzantium by Greek migrants. These were the most influential treatises of the late fifteenth and early sixteenth centuries. There were significant composers during the early Renaissance, particularly Johannes Ockeghem (1420–97), with his *Missa prolationum*, a "technical tour de force in which every movement is a double mensuration canon."[749]

The most renowned, and possibly the first in the pantheon of "greatest composers," is Josquin des Prez (1450/1455–1521), called the "father of musicians," who made extensive use of "motivic cells," easily recognizable melodic fragments which passed from voice to voice "in a contrapuntal texture"—a basic organizational principle in music practiced continuously from 1500 until today. This figure of the Renaissance distinctly aimed to raise music into an *ars perfecta*, that is, "a perfect art to which nothing can be added." Theorists such as Heinrich Glarean

---

[746] Gleason and Becke, 1981.

[747] Pen, 1992, 81.

[748] Grout, 1996.

[749] Ibid, 167.

and Gioseffo Zarlino agreed that his style represented perfection. For Martin Luther, Josquin des Prez was "the master of the notes."

The next giant in the pursuit of musical perfection was Adrian Willaert (1490–1562), the inventor of the antiphonal style (which involves two choirs in interaction, often singing alternate musical phrases) and an experimenter in chromaticism and rhythm.

Striving for Perfection

This striving for perfection through a long historical sequence by individuals from different generations, seeking to outdo the accomplishments of the past, points to a fundamental contrast between the models of beauty and achievement in the Western and the non-Western worlds. The impression one gets from the history of music in such civilizations as ancient Egypt, Mesopotamia, China, or Japan, is that of time standing still in a state of accepted perfection after a sequence of achievements. In the Western world, the history of music is heavily characterized by linear time and continuous novelties, if sometimes slow and interrupted, but always moving; whereas in the East, after some initial achievements, further changes are rare, as if perfection, believed to have been achieved, needed to be frozen in a world of cyclical time.

To understand the European linear conception of perfection, their consistent striving for higher forms, it might be useful to go back to the ancient Greek ideal of *arete*, a term that originally denoted excellence in the performance of heroic valor by individuated aristocratic Indo-European warriors. In pre-Homeric times, it signified the strength and skill of a warrior. It was his *arete* that ranked an aristocrat (*aristos* meaning "best," "noblest") above the commoners; and it was the attainment of heroic excellence that secured respect and honor among aristocratic peers. The word *aristeia* was used in epic stories for the single-handed adventures of the hero in his unceasing strife for superlative achievements over his peers. In its origins, *arete* was thus "closely bound up with the physical power" of warriors.[750] But starting with Homer, the word came to denote excellence in spiritual qualities. In the *Odyssey*, we witness a new type of heroic personality, Odysseus,

---

[750] Jaeger, 1973.

who rejects Achilles' brutal treatment of Hector's body, and shows self-awareness and self-control, inventiveness and craftiness.[751]

Thereafter *arete* came to denote all kinds of actions and spiritual qualities expressing the best in human abilities. But the ancient Greeks still had a cyclical conception of time, which found philosophical expression in Plato's idea that there are perfect Forms existing outside time, unchanging ideals that transcend time and space, and that humans require strenuous training and breeding to approximate these Forms. Nevertheless, the competitive aristocratic individualism of the ancient Greeks could not be contained, with subsequent philosophers before and after Plato proposing their own conceptions of truth and originating novel ideas, along with the development of geometrical thinking, prose writing, civic citizenship, a sequence of masterful writers from Aeschylus to Sophocles to Euripides, the development of ggraphy, musical theory, and much more.

This ideal of excellence had a profound influence on the development of Christianity as a European religion that aimed at raising humans to the highest demands of God. Unlike the gods of non-Western peoples, which asked for submission and fear, Christianity called upon Europeans to rise to the skies in search of perfection. This ideal was one of the most important contributions of Greek thought to Christianity, "to honor the Most High God," "to produce a well-sounding harmony to the glory of God" (in the words Bach would use later on). As the individualism of the West took off with the demolition of kinship ties, the promotion of nuclear monogamous families, the rise of voluntary associations and institutions based on legal contracts, a historicized linear conception of perfection developed; the idea that perfection lay in the future, rather than in some golden past, or in some Platonic Form frozen out of time.

Chinese Music

In contrast, no linear conception of perfection emerged in the non-western world, where kinship institutions prevailed and the individual was thus submerged within traditional collective norms and obligations. Artistic achievement in this world was measured in terms of the reenactment of past achievements, in some past golden age. The cultural and intellectual history of China was always characterized by a turning to the past, to restore the idealized society of earlier

---

[751] Zeruneith, 2007.

times, as admired by Confucius. The history of music in China (and the rest of the non-western world) is characterized by this traditionalism, coupled with stereotypification, and conformity to a general pattern or type. Once instruments of music had reached a reasonable level of efficiency, and once a level of expertise had been reached, these were passed on without any changes for hundreds of years.

Encyclopædia Britannica offers a long entry on the history of Chinese music, identifying it as one of "the most highly developed of all known musical systems."[752] This is true: as in many other endeavors, the Chinese musical tradition is relatively accomplished, with some degree of historical development. This *Britannica* entry, however, soon acknowledges that except for archeological records and a few surviving written sources, it is only from the Song dynasty (AD 960–1279) onwards "that there is information about the actual music itself." Ancient Chinese written sources provide "images of courtly parties, military parades, and folk festivals," but they do "not provide a single note of music." The Chinese theory of music, as expressed in the "Yueji" ("Record of Music") chapter of the *Liji* (*Book of Rites*) was about how "music is the harmony of heaven and earth while rites are the measurement of heaven and earth. Through harmony, all things are made known; through measure, all things are properly classified. Music comes from heaven; rites are shaped by earthly designs." This basic philosophical outlook would remain intact throughout China's history until Western influences came.

A tonal system was conceptualized to some degree in China. They created bamboo tuning pipes from which twelve pitches could be derived, and a "tonal vocabulary from which assorted scales—specific orderings of a limited number of pitches—can be extracted and reproduced on different pitch levels." Still, the Chinese never conceived a science of music as a separate field. This is implicitly acknowledged in the *Britannica* article:

> The five core tones of Chinese scales are sometimes connected with the five elements, or *wuxing* (earth, wood, metal, fire, and water), while the 12 pitches of the tonal system are connected by some writers with the months of the year, hours of the day, or phases of the moon. Music merited a science of its own.[753]

[752] Malm, 2021.
[753] Ibid.

They developed a system of classification of instruments; however, "this system was based upon the material used in the construction of the instruments, the eight being stone, earth (pottery), bamboo, metal, skin, silk, wood, and gourd." The classification system of the West was focused on the actual tonal range of the instruments:

- Higher-than-sopranino instruments: soprillo saxophone, piccolo
- Sopranino instruments: sopranino saxophone, treble flute
- Soprano instruments: concert flute, clarinet, violin, trumpet, oboe, soprano saxophone
- Alto instruments: alto flute, alto recorder, viola, French horn, natural horn, alto horn, alto clarinet, alto saxophone, English horn
- Tenor instruments: trombone, euphonium, tenor violin, tenor flute, tenor saxophone, tenor recorder, bass flute
- Baritone instruments: cello, baritone horn, bass clarinet, bassoon, baritone saxophone
- Bass instruments: bass recorder, bass oboe, bass tuba, bass saxophone, bass trombone
- Lower-than-bass instruments: contrabass tuba, double bass, contrabassoon, contrabass clarinet, contrabass saxophone, subcontrabass saxophone, tubax, octobass

The history of music in China through the medieval and modern eras consists of the effects of foreign instruments and ideas coming from the Persians, Arabs, Indians, and people from the Malay Peninsula, particularly during the Tang dynasty (600s–900s). After this era, starting with the Song dynasty (960–1279), one sees the consolidation of earlier intra-Chinese trends, a more national rather than international cultural atmosphere. The Chinese did not produce a single treatise of music that we can identify as theoretical, on matters related to pitch, notes, intervals, scale systems, tonality, modulation, and melody. *Britannica* says that "the official *Song shi* (1345; 'Song [Dynasty] History') contained 496 chapters, of which 17 deal directly with music, and musical events and people appear throughout the entire work." They also wrote manuals on how to play some instruments. However, these were descriptive works. The *Britannica* article does not mention one single Chinese composer. After all, China did not produce any classical music.

Revolutionary Epochs in Western Music

Europeans invented the opera. *Britannica* confounds Chinese musical theatre with "operas." True operas could not have emerged outside Europe, because opera is a drama that combines soliloquy (literary form of discourse in which a character talks to him/herself when alone or unaware of the presence of other characters), scenery, dialogue, continuous music inspired by literary ancient Greek tragedies and comedies, together with allegorical and pastoral interludes, with choruses and large instrumental ensembles—all without parallels outside Europe. As it is, *Britannica* admits that Chinese "operas . . . all tend to follow a tradition of using either standard complete pieces or stereotyped melodic styles (*banqiang* [musical text settings])."

It should be noted, moreover, that the literary form of tragedy does not exist outside Europe. Tragedy grew out of the singularly aristocratic warrior culture of Indo-Europeans, with its overriding obsession with heroic accomplishment. You need men with no other purpose than to achieve renown and immortality, which inevitably engenders characters with excessive pride, self-confidence, or hubris, which plunges heroes into actions that bring about their demise, unrealistic undertakings, excessive behaviors lacking in magnanimity, undue sufferings to others, and early death. Operas grew out of madrigals, and the madrigal originated from the three-to-four-voice frottola (1470–1530); from the unique interest of European composers in poetry (particularly pastoral poems about shepherds), and from the stylistic influence of the French *chanson*; and from the polyphony of the *motet*.

It is not inaccurate to use the title "Confucian China" from ancient times until Mao, or to say Islamic civilization from the beginnings until the present, or "Hindu India" from the beginnings until recently—but it is very inaccurate to say Platonic, Aristotelian, Stoic, Catholic, Protestant, Renaissance, Newtonian, Enlightenment, or Existentialist Europe. Europe sees a continuous history of grand epochs. These epochs, with varying titles depending on subject of study, can be found in all the realms of culture, painting, architecture, music, literature, and philosophy.

We can identify the Ancient, Medieval, Renaissance, and Reformation eras before the onset of the Baroque. There is no space here to list every major composer of "late Renaissance" Italy, England, and Germany, but mention should be made of John Dowland's (1562–1626) lute songs, and the increase in new forms of instrumental music and books about how to play instruments, of which the most influential was Michael Praetorius's *Syntagma Musicum* [*Encyclopedia of Music*] (1614–1619), an encyclopedic record of contemporary musical practices, with many illustrations of a wide variety of instruments, such as the harpsichord, trombone, pommer, bass viola—demonstrating the fact that Europeans would go on to create almost all of the most widely-used musical instruments in history.

The greats of the Reformation period included John Taverner (1490–1545), best-known for his masses based on a popular song called *The Westron Wynde*, and *Missa Gloria tibi Trinitas*, as well as the composers Christopher Tye, Thomas Tallis (1505–1585) and Robert Whyte (1538–1574). The greatest of them all, Giovanni da Palestrina (1525–94), who was called the "Prince of Music" and his compositions "the absolute perfection" of church style, composed over 105 masses, 68 offertories, 140 madrigals, over 300 motets, 72 hymns, 35 magnificats, and 11 litanies. He is remembered as a master of contrapuntal ingenuity; for his dynamic flow of music, not rigid or static; for the variety of form and type of his masses; for melodies that contain few leaps between notes; and for dissonances that are confined to suspensions, passing notes and weak beats.[754]

While the rest of the world would not yet see a treatise on music, Girolamo Mei (1519–1594) carried out a thorough investigation of every ancient work on music, writing a four book treatise, *De modis musicis antiquorum* [*Concerning Ancient Musical Styles*], soon followed by Galileo's father, Vincenzo Galilei's *Dialogo della musica antica et della moderna* [*Dialogue on Music Ancient and Modern*] (1581), where he used Mei's ideas to attack vocal counterpoint in Italian madrigal, arguing that delivering the emotional message of poetical texts required only a single melody with appropriate pitches and rhythms, rather than several voices simultaneously singing different melodies in different rhythms.

The Baroque

The next epoch is the Baroque between 1600 and 1750. Baroque originally meant "bizarre," "exaggerated," "grotesque," or "in bad taste," but it came to mean "flamboyant," "decorative," "bold," and denoting a juxtaposition of contrasting elements conveying dramatic tension. This period saw instrumental music become the equal of vocal music as Europeans learned how to make instruments

---

[754] Jackson, 2023; Grout, 1996.

with far higher expressive capacities, replacing the reserved sound of viols with the powerful and flexible tone of violins, better harpsichords, and originating orchestral music.

It is not easy to demarcate new epochs in Western history, for this is a continuously creative civilization in many interacting fields—music, painting, exploration, architecture, science, literature—with different dynamics, and therefore different yet mutually influential cultural motifs and reorientations. Some figures are considered "transitional" figures. Claudio Monteverdi (1567–1643) is one such transitional musician between the late Renaissance (since there was no Reformation in Italy) and the Baroque. The originality of Western cultural figures, moreover, never came out of the blue, but obtained its vitality from its rootedness in the European past, reinterpreting and readapting ancient Greek, Roman, and medieval Christian themes. [755]

Monteverdi's famous opera L'Orfeo (1607), for example, drew from the Orpheus of Greek mythology (as transmitted by Ovid and Virgil). Monteverdi's "Lamento d'Arianna" was based on the Greek Ariadne myth. Orpheus, in Monteverdi's adaptation, was a musician and renowned poet who descended into the Underworld of Hades to recover his lost wife Eurydice. Orpheus is allowed to go to his wife so long as he does not look at her, but, overcome with his love, he breaks the law of the underworld, looks at her, and loses her forever. Orpheus is a godlike figure in this heroic rescue mission, who experiences intense emotions in rapid succession: bravery, euphoria, and despondency. This adaptation was mediated by the personal experiences of Monteverdi: his intense grief and despair at the loss of his wife, combined with his chronic headaches and deteriorating eyesight. The cultural influence of Rome is evident in his trilogy, the operas Il ritorno d'Ulisse in patria (1640), L'incoronazione di Poppea (1643), and Le nozze d'Enea con Lavinia (1641) [now lost], inspired by a historical trajectory that moves through Troy, the birth of Rome to its decline, and forward to the foundation and glory of the Venetian Republic. Republican rule by proud aristocrats unwilling to submit to a despotic ruler is unique to the West, inspiring the American "res-publica." In the 1600s there were nineteen Orphean opera versions, and countless operas based on other mythologies about Venus, Adonis, Apollo, Daphne, Hercules, and Narcissus.

The invention of the Italian madrigal found its highest expression in Monteverdi, whose first five books of madrigals between 1587 and 1605 are esteemed as

---

[755] Schonberg, 2006, 1–18.

monuments in the history of the polyphonic madrigal. What made Monteverdi stand out among many other luminaries of his age (such as Henrich Isaac and Orlande de Lassus) was the way he established in his opera a complete unity between drama and music for the first time in history, a repertoire of textures and techniques "without parallels." While Italian opera was flourishing in every corner of Europe except France, France would soon build up its own opera tradition, through the emergence of French tragedy in the grand literary works of Corneille (1606–1684) and Jean Racine (1639–1699). To these dramatic works, opera added music, dance and spectacle, beginning with Italian-born Jean-Baptiste Lully (1632–1687), the national director of music as a member of Louis XIV's orchestra.[756]

This was merely the beginning of the Baroque achievement. The composers of this period constitute a veritable who's who list of innovators. Arcangelo Corelli (1653–1713) was the first to create basic violin technique on the newly invented violin; Domenico Scarlatti (1685–1757) wrote 555 harpsichord sonatas and made use of Italian, Portuguese, and Spanish dance rhythms; Henry Purcell (1659–1695), recognized as one of the greatest English composers, is still admired for his intricate harmonies, expressive melodies, and careful attention to detail. There is also Jean Philippe Rameau (1683–1764), known for his bold melodic lines and harmonies, *tragédie lyrique* opera, and for his *Traité de l'harmonie réduite à ses principes naturels* (*Treatise on Harmony reduced to its natural principles*), which sought to establish a "science" of music. In this age of Newtonian principles, deriving the principles of harmony from the laws of acoustics, it argued that the chord (a combination of three or more notes that are heard as if sounding simultaneously) was the primal element in music.

There were also the giants Vivaldi, Handel, and Bach. Antonio Vivaldi (1678–1741) wrote over five hundred concertos, of which 350 are for solo instrument and strings, such as violin, and the others for bassoon, cello, oboe, flute, viola, lute, or mandolin; as well as forty-six operas, and invented the ritornello form (recurrent musical section that alternates with different episodes of contrasting material). Georg Handel (1685–1759), sometimes identified as the first international composer, though in reality deeply rooted in Europe's cosmopolitan culture—born in Germany but becoming naturalized British—wrote for every musical genre, along with instrumental works for full orchestra, with the most significant known as Water Music, six concertos for woodwinds and strings, and twelve

---

[756] Grout, 1996.

Grand Concertos, and his masterpiece Messiah, judged as "the finest Composition of Musick that was ever heard."[757]

Johann Sebastian Bach (1685–1750) mastered the organ and harpsichord, and wrote over one thousand compositions in nearly every type of musical form, driven by a search for perfection, to "produce a well-sounding harmony to the glory of God." Bach assimilated all the music that had gone before him in his compulsive striving for *arete* in technique; what he absorbed, he shaped into his own endless variety of musical compositions. His music for the harpsichord and clavichord includes masterpieces in every genre: preludes, fantasies, and toccatas, and other pieces in fugal style, dance suites, as well as sonatas and capriccios, and concertos with orchestra. Bach was a Faustian man with passionate drives, measuring himself against other composers, hard to get along with, and a father of twenty children. Living in an age of mighty composers, it is said that he surpassed them in his harmonic intensity, the unexpected originality of the sounds, and his forging of new rules for the actualization of harmonic potentials. It is inaccurate to say that perfection is impossible. Europeans achieved it in many art forms, and would continue to do so in music, painting, and architecture through the 1800s.

The Classical Period

The eighteenth-century Enlightenment is often celebrated for giving birth to a cosmopolitan age in which the West embraced "universal values" for humanity's well-being against age-old customs and beliefs limited by ethno-national boundaries. Kant's famous 1795 essay, "Toward Perpetual Peace," is now seen in academia as a project for the transformation of millions of immigrants into "world citizens" of the West with the same universal rights. It does not matter that Kant was calling for a federation of republican states coexisting with each other in a state of hospitality, rather than in a state of open borders.

This Enlightenment project has prompted many dissidents to reject the very notion of cosmopolitanism. Yet cosmopolitanism is an inherent product of the European pursuit of the highest in human nature. European national elites have always borrowed from each other, even as they developed musical styles and philosophical outlooks with national characteristics. Bach is very German in a way that Vivaldi is not—though he absorbed into his works all the genres, styles, and

---

[757] Ibid; Schonberg, 2006.

forms of European music in his time and before. *Ars perfecta* should not be confused with the pursuit of one uniform model settled on at some point in history and then fixated into a state of unoriginal repetition thereafter. *Ars perfecta* allows for national authenticity of performance, intention, sound, and personal interpretation. Authentic works can be deeply rooted in a nation's history and personality, while also informed by cosmopolitan experience.

When we read the German flutist J. J. Quantz writing in 1752 that the ideal musical style would be "a style blending the good elements" of "different peoples," "more universal" rather than the style of a "particular nation"—we should interpret this as an expression of the reality that the language of classical music, which is singular to the "different peoples" of Europe (and should not be confused with a people's musical folklore) was cosmopolitan from its beginnings.[758] This is evident in the European preoccupation with a universal theory of harmonics, the nature of scale systems, pitch, and melodic composition. It is evident in the way Europeans went about earnestly creating, during and after the Baroque era, the most perfect instruments to achieve a maximum of musical flexibility between strong and soft, crescendo and decrescendo, with almost imperceptible shades: perfect violins, violas, violoncellos, flutes, oboes, bassoons, horns, and pianos. This strive for perfection was required to express and arouse all the shadings of human feeling as Europeans dug deeper into their interior selves to manifest in full their joys, afflictions, grandeur, rage, compassion, contemplation, and exaltation.

To be sure, the peoples of the world are "gifted with conscious rhythm." Man "cannot refrain from rhythmic movement, from dancing, stamping the ground, clapping his hands, slapping his abdomen, his chest, his legs, his buttocks." This rhythmic disposition, it is true, prompted all peoples to create musical instruments.[759] Primitives developed a variety of simple instruments: drums, flutes, trumpets, xylophones, and harps. These were "folk and ritual instruments"; but with the rise of civilizations in the Near East, India, and the Far East, we see a distinct class of musicians developing instruments with greater musicality and flexible intonation, enhancing the artistic expression of sounds. We see a greater variety of stringed instruments: new lutes and violins in Mesopotamia; in Egypt, vertical flutes with greater musical possibilities than the whistle flutes; and the complex double clarinet. Among Asiatic peoples, we see vertical and angular harps, lyres, lutes, oboes, and trumpets. Instruments in ancient China include the

---

[758] Cited in Grout, 443.
[759] Sachs, 1940, 26.

mouth organ, pan pipes, percussion instruments, and long zither; and in the medieval Far East we find the fiddle bow, flat lutes, resting bell, and hooked trumpet.
The *gamakas* are said to be the "life and soul" of Indian melody; the veena and the
fiddle sarinda with its fantastic shape are found in India.

But in the West, early on in history, we see both musical instruments and treatises on harmonics. It is really during the Renaissance that the West starts to out-
pace the rest of the world in the creation of more sophisticated and original musical instruments, including a *tabula universalis*, a classification of all wind and
stringed instruments in all their sizes and kinds, as well as numerous scientific
manuals on how to play them "according to the correct tablature."[760] By 1600, the
level of sophistication and variety in kinds of European instruments is the highest;
between 1750 and 1900 the quantity of timbres "increased astonishingly," along
with the quality of the sound of each instrument; for example, the harp was made
chromatic after being strictly diatonic for 5000 years; and under the pressure of
orchestration all instruments were developed to the "greatest possible technical
efficiency." The magnificent piano was invented and improved upon continuously.

It can be argued that with modern individualism—that is, the complete breaking out of individuals from kinship groups and norms—European music witnessed an intensification in the expression of personalities through music, leading
to more sophisticated, refined, and specialized musical instruments. in order to
express the wider range of personal feelings and experiences afforded by a liberal
culture. This culture propelled modern Europeans to breach the medieval limits
of the traditional order of consonance and dissonance, of regular and equable
rhythmic flow, to improvise chromaticism and tonalities, and create many styles
of monody, recitative, aria, madrigal, and the integration of theater and music for
dramatic expression. It can not be denied that modern Europeans did in fact originate a far greater variety of genres and instruments capable of bringing out the
complex emotional and psychological constitutions of Europeans into the light.

The cosmopolitanism of Europeans in their striving for novel ways of achieving perfection has misled historians into thinking that the language of music expressed in Monteverdi, Scarletti, Bach, Rameau, and Brahms was "global" and not
limited by civilizational and national boundaries. While they acknowledge that
each of these composers absorbed into his music their national traditions, they
insist upon the "internationalism" of the music of the Classical era, believing that

---

[760] Ibid, 300.

with Handel, Haydn, and Mozart we have "international composers." Handel (1685–1759), they tell us, borrowed, transcribed, adapted, and rearranged universally accepted practices in music. They hail Christopher Gluck (1714–84) as a "cosmopolite" who professed a new style of opera away from the particular embellishments and ornateness of Baroque opera towards the Classical (universal) ideals of purity and balance. They cite Gluck's own words about how he created "music suited to all nations, so as to abolish these ridiculous distinctions of national styles."[761] Mozart (1756–1791), they insist, was a cosmopolite who travelled extensively throughout Europe, becoming familiar with every kind of music written and heard, his work "a synthesis of national styles, a mirror that reflected the music of a whole age, illuminated by his own genius."[762] While Haydn (1732–1809) was localized in Vienna, they tell us that his music was an outgrowth of an increasingly cosmopolitan Europe.

What this "cosmopolitan" interpretation misses is that classical music, in its origins and development, was one hundred percent circumscribed to the continent of Europe; it had no connection with and no resonance outside Europe. When composers like Bach and Mozart absorbed all the genres, styles, and forms of music of their age, they were striving to express the highest potentialities in European music, rather than express "international music," as we understand that term today. Handel said that when he composed his Messiah he was guided by the perfect hand of God, driven by a state of pure spirituality, in tears, ignoring food and sleep. It was a common belief among European philosophers that God is the all-perfect being embodying the perfections of all beings within itself. Schelling (1775–1854) then suggested that the perfection of God existed only *in potentia*, and that it was only actualized through the human striving for the highest.[763]

---

[761] Cited in Grout, 466.

[762] Ibid, 510.

[763] This argument from Schelling is astutely summed up by Arthur Lovejoy in *The Great Chain of Being: A Study of the History of An Idea* (1936/1960, 317–26). Schelling's reasoning moved along these lines: why should God be identified with a transcendental *Logos* from the beginning, envisaged as a self-sufficient, absolutely perfect being, ab initio, only to create an imperfect world of lower unconscious beings, the imperfect flowing out of the perfect? In the beginning, he surmised, God was not yet realized, but came to be through his creation of nature, for God is itself a form of life subject to becoming. God was pure nothingness in the beginning, an undifferentiated dark ground. *Logos* existed only potentially, not actually, coming to be in the course of time, through nature and history. To believe that God existed in a state of perfection from the beginning, writes Schelling, "is difficult for many reasons, but first of all for the simple one that, if it were in actual possession of the highest perfection, it would have no reason (*Grund*) for the

Conservatives often lament the restless striving of Europeans. They wish the West had been collectivist like China or the Incas, without a linear conception of time, attached to an eternal golden age in the past, without seeking to overcome the resistance of things, without disruptive individualists full of energy and fire. Some dislike Beethoven. They prefer the continuous tonic dominant harmonies of the eighteenth century, even before Bach. Beethoven is seen as an admirer of France's 1789 revolutionary ideals of liberty, equality, and fraternity; the composer of the Eroica symphony dedicated to Napoleon, the conqueror who is blamed for ending Europe's monarchical order. Such has been the nature of European creativity.

Beethoven's music was an expression of his propulsive inner state of being, for whom the elegant, highly refined sense of Mozart was not enough; he needed to bend classic rules with unexpected metrical patterns to convey his sense of the conflict, transformation, and transcendence of his age. The *Eroica* (the Third Symphony) was very Western in its expression of the ideal of heroic greatness, which he saw in Napoleon, and which was built into this civilization since prehistorical Indo-European times. With Beethoven, the expression of inner feeling became more intense and personal, for European individuality had reached a higher level of inward reflection. His Sixth Symphony, "the Pastoral," is about his feelings aroused by delight in nature, apprehension of a storm approaching, awareness of the fury of the storm, and gratitude for the washed calm afterwards. He was drawn into his silent world of increasing deafness and solipsism, as he continued to compose. The great Romantic composer, Hector Berlioz, said that in the Sixth "the most unexplored depths of the soul reverberate."[764] Beethoven, a corpulent man who had a habit of spitting whenever he felt like it, a clumsy guy who could never dance, sullen and suspicious, without social graces, prone to rages, was nevertheless a man of immense inner strength, who once told a friend: "I don't want to know anything about your system of ethics. Strength is the morality of the man who stands out from the rest and it is mine."[765]

---

creation and production of so many other things, through which it—being incapable of attaining a higher degree of perfection—could only fall to a lower one" (in Lovejoy, 322).

[764] Cited in Grout, 551.

[765] Cited in Schonberg, 2006, 123.

The Romantic Epoch and the Efflorescence
of the Subjective Feelings of Europeans

Only Western history is characterized by a continuous sequence of discontinuous revolutionary epochs. New epochs tend to be morphologically present across many fields, from politics to science, painting to architecture, philosophy, and music—although each field sees movements and schools peculiar to itself. The romantic period in music runs roughly from 1830 to 1900; however, the variety of compositions is outstanding, with many characteristics of the preceding classical period persisting, and new nationalistic tendencies coalescing with it, along with new impressionistic tendencies.

This makes the West incredibly hard to understand. The word "Hindu" or "Talmudic" can define a people for centuries. Not the West. "Romanticism" alone is very difficult to grasp.[766] In literature, it spans a shorter period, from 1790 to 1850, displaced by "Realism," which does not appear in music. The different names associated with this movement bespeak of its intricacy: Joseph de Maistre, Rousseau, Stendhal, Goethe's *The Sorrows of Young Werther*, Chateaubriand, Coleridge, Blake, Herder, Byron, Wordsworth, Delacroix, Brontë's *Wuthering Heights*, Hölderlin, Novalis, Schlegel. In music one can choose Liszt, Schumann, Wagner, Mahler, Tchaikovsky, Weber—but Verdi, possibly Wagner, and the Russian Mussorgsky are best identified as nationalist composers. Brahms had little respect for most composers of his era, remaining a classicist.

Perhaps the best composer to convey the meaning of Romanticism in music is Hector Berlioz (1803–69). It is said that "after him, music would never be the same . . . he did it all by himself, impatiently brushing aside convention."[767] He departed from the convention of "four-squareness" in melody, the rigidity of rhythms, and formulaic harmonies, expressing his moods and attitudes to the world. Experts say that Berlioz broadened the definition of orchestration by allowing each instrument to create sounds not heard before. He also expanded the use of programmatic music to accentuate the emotional expressiveness of the music by recreating in sound the events and emotions portrayed in ancient classical legends, novels, poetry, and historical events. He was a deep admirer of Western history and literature: Homer, Virgil, Dante, Shakespeare, and Byron. What experts leave out is

---

[766] Barzun, 2000, 467–485.
[767] Schonberg, 160.

that the "intensity and expression of feeling" (to use the words of Liszt) in Romantic music was itself an expression of the amplification of the introspective consciousness of Europeans after the 1750s.

Whereas expression of feelings in the Baroque era had been confined to a few moods, each at a time, now music sought to express the complex shadings of human moods in the same breath. To express this subjectivism, this period saw the development to the greatest technical efficiency and musical effectiveness of all instruments, with the piano reshaped and enlarged to seven octaves with felt-covered hammers for both expressiveness and virtuosity. In the Romantic age, a need emerged for instruments that would go beyond the expression of a few general moods at a time, to make use of all possible timbres so as to express all the shadings of feelings, modulating from chord to chord. Romantic Europeans, rather than being in one emotional state, anger or fear, until moved by some stimulus to a different state, were in a constant state of psychological flux, with unpredictable turns.

Evolutionary theory is incapable of explaining the intense subjective expressiveness of modern Europeans, the virtuosity and continuous creativity one detects from Bach to Haydn, Mozart and Beethoven, and from the Classical composers to Schubert, the German Schumann, Chopin, Liszt, and Wagner. The transcendence of European high culture over evolutionary pressures is one of its defining features. It is very hard for simpler cultures to rise above these pressures, and so they are easier to explain in evolutionary terms. Schopenhauer once said that classical music "is entirely independent of the phenomenal world, ignores it altogether, could to a certain extent exist if there was no world at all." What he meant is that the history of European music does not obey evolutionary pressures, but is an immaterial realm of freedom where pure aesthetics reign supreme. This transcendence peaked in the Romantic era.

Evolutionary psychologists believe they can instruct us about the "biological basis of human culture." But they can only explain culture at its most basic level. They can tell us, rather boringly, that music is a "cultural universal." They can't explain the difference between Beethoven and Berlioz, and between them and traditional folk music. For this reason, evolutionary theories are inclined to ignore, if not trivialize, high cultural achievements in philosophy, art, and literature. Steven Pinker once said that "the value of [European] art is largely unrelated to aesthetics: a priceless masterpiece becomes worthless if found to be a forgery; soup cans and comic strips become high art when the art world says they are, and then command conspicuously wasteful prices."[768] They see high culture as "gratuitous but harmless decoration," without much import, as contrasted to what Marx called the real foundations of culture: eating, digestion, getting money, and satisfying one's appetitive drives.

The way to explain European cultural creativity is to recognize its greater freedom from evolutionary/materialistic pressures. European consciousness acquired the power to turn in upon itself, to take possession of itself, not merely to be conscious, but to be aware that its consciousness is uniquely its own, constituted as a center from which all other realities, the successive data of sensory experiences, the pressures of the world, are held together in what Kant called a "transcendental unity of apperception," which implies a unity of self, the discovery of the self as the agent of consciousness, doubling back upon itself, and thus rising to a new realm with its own autonomous inner life.

Age of Nationalism

It is invariable in regards to Western art and literature that scholars speak about their timeless universal themes depicting love, suffering, good and evil, deception, heroism—that are supposedly observable in all cultures of the world. They tell us that Shakespeare's plays, Jane Austen's *Pride and Prejudice*, and Mozart's symphonies, speak for "humanity." But they can't quite persuade themselves about the qualities that make these works "universal." What is it about Tolstoy's *War and Peace* that makes it a story of "history through human beings and human beings through history," considering the strong presence of Russian national feelings and characters?[769] German composers tend to be the ones identified with "cosmopolitanism." Is this because Germans are generally judged to be the best classical composers during the Baroque and Classical periods, and through the 1800s?

They certainly had the greatest influence upon the rest of Europe, as the Italians did during the Renaissance and the early Baroque. This explains why Giuseppe Verdi (1813–1903) called upon his countrymen to develop their own musical style and deplored German influence: "If the Germans, setting out from Bach and arriving at Wagner, write good German operas, well and good. But we

---

[768] Pinker, 2010, 126.
[769] Clifton Fadiman, 1942, XXIV.

descendants of Palestrina commit a musical crime to imitate Wagner. . . . We cannot compose like the Germans, or at least we ought not to; nor they like us."[770] Verdi is known as a nationalist. Yet he could not escape the cultural cosmopolitanism of Europe in his operatic adaptations of writers such as Schiller, Victor Hugo, Alexander Dumas, and Byron. And if his music is nationalistic, why is Verdi today considered a timeless composer with universal appeal? Frédéric Chopin (1810–49), with his mazurkas and polonaises, who is also known as "the first of the great nationalists," was born in Warsaw, not quite a cosmopolis. Yet Chopin's music is likewise seen as universal, not a mere reproduction of Polish folk melodies, although it is said that this folk tradition was part of his "racial subconscious." In his abilities, he transcended his nationality and time, making the piano a total instrument, "an instrument of infinite color"—remembered today as a "perfect virtuoso."[771] Does universality mean striving for perfection and the Most High, even as you are a nationalist wanting your European nation to strive for the same universal greatness as the Germans?

Richard Wagner said that all great art must be based on mythology, "the sagas and legends of past ages." Some say his music was not nationalist, for it was not rooted in German folk music, but on symbolic-mythological themes that comprise "the archetypes of the collective unconscious," which are common to human beings (and therefore universal).[772] Can one say that his superlative accomplishments, combined with his originality, are what make his music universal, a model of human achievement? We are told that "Wagner changed the rules of opera. His operas are 'through-composed'—there are no stops and starts for arias and duets. Singers ceased to be the stars around whom performances were centered. He made the orchestra, and thus the conductor, into a crucial protagonist."[773] But others have countered that Wagner's *Der Ring des Nibelungen* is based on particular Germanic mythologies, Teutonic gods, the heroic Wotan galloping in a storm, with a nationalist German agenda in opposition to "Semitic" cosmopolitan influences. Wagner's Wotan constituted a resurgence of German primeval Indo-European passions, the archetype of a particular people.

The rise of Russian classical music certainly came with a very strong nationalist impulse rooted in the use of folk music. Of the so-called "mighty five" Russian composers who developed a classical tradition, Mussorgsky is credited with true

---

[770] Cited in Schonberg, 287.
[771] Ibid, 204.
[772] Kovačev, 2009.
[773] Kettle, 2013.

masterpieces, though all he wanted was to express the soul of the Russian people. It has been noted that Pyotr Tchaikovsky's music, which came a generation after the "mighty five," contained a peculiarly Russian melody. However, while his early compositions quoted folk songs, his later music has been categorized as "more cosmopolitan," although Igor Stravinsky insisted that it remained "profoundly Russian." Antonín Dvořák (1841–1904), a peasant from Bohemia, said that his music expressed his love for his native motherland. But what made him a "genius" rather than a gifted provincial composer was precisely his ability to absorb folk influences, while finding ways to integrate them into the perfectionist-universal-transcendental impulse inherent in classical music. In varying degrees, the greats were all rooted in their nations, combined with some degree of Pan-Euro-peanism—the singular tradition of classical music in Europe.

Modernism

The last great composers of the late nineteenth and early twentieth centuries were: Tchaikovsky (d. 1893), Debussy (d. 1918), Stravinsky (1913, *The Rite of Spring*), Rachmaninoff (d. 1935), Bartók (d. 1945), and, for some experts, though not the general educated public, Schoenberg (born 1874) and Webern (d. 1945). For Spengler, the West of his time had reached the "winter of full civilization." Its vital forces were extinguished, its people were "traditionless ... religion-less, clever, unfruitful" city-dwellers "with no ties to community and soil." This obser-vation carries weight. While the above names belong in the list of great composers, it is hard to deny that with Schoenberg and Webern, original and highly gifted as they remained, classical music starts to lose something vital that may be traced to the effects that increasing urbanism, rootlessness, standardization, and abstract rationalism had upon European psychology.

The most original name above may be the impressionist Debussy, with his new concepts of light and color in music, intended to capture fleeting moods occa-sioned by the external world as perceived at a given time, such as a momentary impression of the sea or a moonlight. Debussy did not care for Brahms, Tchaikov-sky or Beethoven. His musical "impressions" had no major unifying theme, with tonality almost dissolved, or with timbre, rhythm, and color assigned the same importance as harmony and melody. *La Sacre du printemps* by the Russian Stra-vinsky "was a genuine explosion" with its "metrical shifting and shattering force, its near-total dissonance and breakaway from established canons of harmony and melody."[774] For Stravinsky, a Russian expatriate who embraced suburbia in America, music should not be about "expressing" anything except music, since music is primarily about form and logic, incapable of conveying anything other than broad emotions. Béla Bartók (1881–1945) is identified as a Hungarian nationalist who systematically incorporated old Magyar folk melodies. Yet, again, it would be a mistake to view Bartók as a folk musician in the same way that non-Western musicians are seen. Bartók's music remained classical through and through: Richard Strauss and Debussy strongly influenced his musical development, and his large-scale orchestral works were in the style of Brahms and Strauss.

Notwithstanding the extended influences of nationalism, neoclassicism, and the original impressionism of Debussy, the deeper current in twentieth century music may be categorized as modernist. Modernism found expression in all the arts, including literature and philosophy, and it arose from the globalization of industrialization, rootlessness, anomie, and the emerging industrial world, as well as new technologies and the standardization of life, skepticism about the meaning of life, the feeling of powerlessness in the face of massive urban growth, and the sense that everything had already been explored in music except "testing the limits of aesthetic construction," or "searching for new models in atonalism, polytonalism or other forms of altered tonality."[775] Arnold Schoenberg (who proclaimed his Jewishness after his music was labeled "degenerate" by German nationalists) was the major composer initiating modernist techniques, aimed at deconstructing the millennial concept of tonality, to convey "a prophetic message revealing a higher form of life toward which mankind evolves."[776] He coined the term "emancipation of dissonance" in treating dissonances like consonances and renouncing a tonal center. His greatest influence was after 1950.

His follower Anton Webern pushed the idea of "serial composition" in which no single tone was more significant than the other, for ephemeral, pointillistic sounds—abstract music, impersonal, music constructed like a precision instrument, based on mathematical relationships without substantial content. Edgard Varèse discarded every element of the past, employing new instruments to create new sounds, wails and shrieks, creating music without melody, harmony, or counterpoint. Steve Reich came up with a technique called "phase shifting" in which a single note or a pattern of notes was constantly repeated by tape machines at

---

[774] Schonberg, 551.

[775] Tarasti, 1979, 272.

[776] Schonberg, 669.

different speeds. National characteristics evaporated; every work sounded as if it had been created by the same abstract modern person, a nowhere man, void of a collective identity other than the identity of a culture which tells him that there is no pre-given ethnic, sexual, or national identity.

Heidegger once wrote that "everything essential and great originated from the fact that the human being had a homeland and was rooted in traditions."[777] This is half true. Through the modern era, up until the hyper-industrialization and hyper-individualism of the late 1800s, liberal Europeans were still sustained by Christianity, and countless towns rooted in history dotted the geographical landscape, filled with authentic folk sounds, foods, and sights from childhood. The nationalist composers drew their inspiration and creativity from the very marked differences that continued to prevail between the national cultures of Europe going back centuries, and from the prevalence of folk music and art. But as these collective identities dissolved, with increasing urbanization, or what Heidegger called "asphalt culture," Europeans were left with nothing much but the formal rationalism of classical notation. At the same time, it can be said that there was nothing left for Europeans to create: all the possibilities of music had been explored, or would soon be explored during the twentieth century. But what may be more disquieting is that when one searches for "decline of classical music," what comes up are articles about how "for the last 50 years" classical music has been losing its audience at an accelerated state. Among the answers provided by this, I side in part with the view that "people are increasingly made to feel guilt or shame for loving or teaching Bach, Beethoven or Wagner,"[778] except that I don't see this as a mere product of a cultural war, but as an enforced way of thinking to downplay a music that does not resonate with a Western world committed to racial diversity and equality.

The Sustained Creativity of European Furniture Design (and Architecture)

Standard histories of furniture emphasize the utilitarian and hierarchical nature of furniture, including changes in building techniques, while recognizing that furniture also provides a mirror into the aesthetic standards and cultural creativity of different societies in different times. Edward Lucie-Smith's 1979 *Furniture: A*

---

[777] Bambach, 2003, 12.
[778] Pace, 2021.

Concise History recognizes this, but adds that "furniture is related to the general development of society, and to the psychology of the individual."[779] But other than showing how a more urbane bourgeois life promoted modern attitudes towards furniture design—leading to a greater emphasis on comfort, away from the "stiff style" of the royal courts and aristocracies of Europe, and to new types of furniture constructed with industrial materials and technology—Lucie-Smith fails to apprehend how his emphasis on "the general development of society" is itself a unique product of the very European culture his book is almost entirely about.

Apart from dedicating half a chapter to "Ancient Egypt" and "Western Asia"—along with Greece and Rome—the next eight chapters of his book are singularly about Europe. Why? If pressed today, Lucie-Smith would likely apologize for his "Eurocentrism." He can be faulted, to be sure, for ignoring such major civilizations as China, Japan, and India. Yet even more recent books that try to meet multicultural standards dedicate most of their chapters to European furniture. Judith Miller's elegant 2010 book, *Furniture: World Styles from Classical to Contemporary*, which covers more than 3000 years of furniture design in over 500 pages, packed with illustrations, dedicates a few pages to ancient Egypt and ancient China, with a few additional pages to India, Japan, and China in the nineteenth century. Miller recognizes the aesthetics of furniture-making in these cultures, while implicitly noticing that once these civilizations created certain ideals in furniture design and decoration, these types remained in continuous use for centuries with only slight variations, until the West impacted them in the nineteenth century. She observes that the "golden age" of furniture production that was witnessed in the Ming era (1368–1644), with its ideal of "simple furniture with clean lines and sparse decoration limited to lattice work and relief carving," would "remain entrenched" through to the entire Qing era (1644–1912), except that furniture pieces became larger and heavier.[780]

One gets the impression that the authors of furniture histories, and the related subject of interior design, believe it is only natural to focus primarily on Europe—because the historical reality, the images, drawings, and documentary evidence we have, demonstrate that Europe saw a continuous sequence of changing styles. A proper aesthetic assessment of these styles requires separate chapters and explanations. The above authors don't seem to think they have to justify their implicit Eurocentrism. It comes naturally to them, on the strength of Europe's creativity.

---

[779] Lucie-Smith, 1979, 12.
[780] Miller, 24–5.

One of the best books on this subject, *History of Interior Design and Furniture: From Ancient Egypt to Nineteenth-Century Europe*, by Robbie G. Blakemore, opens with a chapter on Egypt, and then, without any hesitation, as a matter of fact and reasonableness, dedicates the next 400 pages singularly to European interior design of floors, walls, ceilings, chimneys, decorative materials, tables, chairs, windows, doors, beds, storage pieces, and stairways.

The same Eurocentric tendencies can be seen in the popular subject of architecture. *A World History of Architecture* by Michael Fazio, Marian Moffett, and Lawrence Wodehouse informs us that their book offers a "diverse sampling" of the world's architecture, with one chapter assigned to "The Beginnings of Architecture" in ancient Mesopotamia and Egypt, another chapter to "Ancient India and Southeast Asia," one to "China and Japan," one to "Islamic Architecture," and one to the Pre-Columbian Americas. Eleven chapters, however, are reserved exclusively for Europe or the West generally. Similarly, *Architecture: A World History* by Daniel Borden et al., is mostly a chronology about European architecture, once it covers the stereotypical models of ancient civilizations in the opening chapters.

But we can't underestimate the pressures of multicultural politics in the West, and the lucrative incentives provided to academics who follow the official university values of diversity and equity. Books are increasingly coming out that intentionally twist and obfuscate the history of architecture, so that the European legacy stands as one among many "equally sophisticated" legacies in Asia, Africa, and the Americas. This is what *A Global History of Architecture*, by Ching, Jarzombek, and Prakash is about. These authors "organized the book by time slots," according to a chronology dictated by the impact of "global events" on architecture, rather than by changing architectural styles. In this way, the authors happily give the same attention to multiple cultures in the modern era that were equally impacted by "global connections," regardless of whether any significantly new styles emerged. What matters, the authors declare, is to see architecture from a "global perspective" at all times, and the relationship of architecture to global events, including European imperialism and colonialism—"rather than viewing the history of architecture as driven by traditions and essences."[781] Very clever: emphasize European global imperialism in the modern era, its effects on the non-Western world, and thereby include this world in the modern era, and forget the reality that non-Western architecture was indeed driven by unchanging stylistic essences.

---

[781] Ching, Jarzombek, and Prakash, 2017, xii.

Let's cut to the chase. The one architect outside the West who can be named in a list of the one hundred greatest architects in history (before Western culture impacted the rest of the world in the twentieth century) is the Ottoman Mimar Sinan. The civilizations of the Mayans, Aztecs, and Incas saw "monumental" stone buildings, pyramids and temples, constructed at the behest of state officials, but these architectural attainments were a one-time affair in their originality, deserving only one chapter or section in a world history survey.

The architecture of Mesopotamia, Egypt, and Persia is more impressive, but not on the same aesthetic and geometrical level of harmony as the ancient Greek Parthenon of Athens, built in the mid-fifth century BC, the Doric Temple of Zeus at Olympia (460 BC), or the Temple of Poseidon at Sounion (440 BC). It is certainly below the level of proficiency and beauty attained by the ancient Romans. Once these ancient monuments were created, little originality followed thereafter: no new epochs in aesthetics, no major architects to identify. The same continuity we see in these civilizations in other fields—science, historical writing, philosophy, painting, mathematics, technology—is apparent in architecture.

What about Chinese architecture? It is worth quoting what Nancy Steinhardt, a well-known expert, tells us about architects in *Chinese Architecture: A History*:

Most of them were officials whose service at court included directing imperial-sponsored projects, perhaps occasionally even designing, and writing about construction. The classical Chinese language has no word for "architect," only one for a person who engages in the craft of building. Instead, from as early as written records can confirm, namely the final millennium BCE, in every branch of Chinese construction—public or private, imperial or vernacular, religious or secular—principles and standards established centuries earlier dictated building practices. The standards were sanctioned and guarded by the Chinese court, and the government was the sponsor of all major manuals that dealt with official architecture. Craftsmen were not required to be literate, only to follow prescribed modules and methods so as to ensure that court dictums were followed. The treatises expound a standardized system of construction that is enforced not just in the construction of imperial buildings and religious monuments, but in temples hidden in the mountains, houses, and shrines, and in paintings and relief sculpture of architecture through the ages.[782]

---

[782] Steinhardt, 2019, 1–7.

All the popular talk about "Chinese Garden Architecture," "Chinese Buddhist Architecture," "Chinese Taoist Architecture," or "Chinese Confucian Architecture," cannot hide the standardized, bureaucratic reality of China. As a huge country with many different ecosystems and historical settings, different stereo-typified styles emerged in different regions. I say "stereo-typified" because once these styles were established, they became ready-made models for hundreds of years.

Only Europe sees a "developmental" history. The one memorable "architectural treatise" from China was the *Yingzao Fashi*, published in 1103, during China's Song Dynasty. We are told that this work (titled "Treatise on Architectural Methods or State Building Standards") was written by Li Jie (1065–1110), the Directorate of Buildings and Construction.[783] He was a bureaucrat in charge of continuing the standardized pattern of construction, not an "architect" with the cultural opportunity to challenge existing aesthetic models. We learn from Xinian Fu, considered to be the world's leading historian of Chinese architecture today, that architecture as an academic discussion only entered China in the late 1930s, through the pioneering studies of Liang Sicheng (1901–1972), educated in the West and awarded an honorary doctoral degree in 1947 by Princeton University.[784]

The conclusion cannot be avoided that Europeans originated a continuous sequence of major architectural stylistic periods (within which there were other national styles), each deserving a chapter in a fair-minded world history.

- Classical (850 BC–AD 476)
- Romanesque (AD 900–1200)
- Gothic (1100s–1500s)
- Renaissance (1300s–1600s)
- Baroque (late 1500s–late 1600s)
- Rococo (1700–1760)
- Neoclassicism (1760–1830)
- Victorian-Eclecticism-Restoration (1815–1900)
- Art Nouveau (1890–1910)
- Art Deco (1915–1930)
- Modernism (early 1900s–1980s)

---

[783] Feng, 2012.
[784] Steinhardt, 2002.

Furniture Making and Interior Design

Let's get back to one of the main subjects of this chapter: furniture design and interior architecture. I am no expert on this subject, but drawing on my extensive research on Western civilization from a comparative historical perspective, including the many sources cited in this chapter, I will summarize the following four interconnected key traits about Western interior design and furniture:

- It exhibits the greatest variety within each kind of furniture; for example, in the variety of chairs, beds, and tables, including a variety of ceiling configurations (flat, coved, or vaulted, for example), chimney pieces, stairways, and spatial relationships.
- Its artistic inspiration, creativity, and originality were driven by a Faustian will for recognition on the part of the artists, pursuit of individual renown, and a desire to surpass prior accomplishments.
- Close to one hundred percent of pre-twentieth-century treatises (fully articulated arguments) on the principles of furniture-making, architecture, the geometric shapes and patterns of room/spaces, height and configuration of ceilings, internal arrangement of stairways, and chimneypieces, were written by Europeans.
- The Platonic striving for perfection, the highest in beauty, and the discovery of a "blueprint" of perfection, have been very powerful motivations, notwithstanding the pursuit by each individual artist of his own style, and the subsequent powerful influences of technology, new materials, and mass consumerism in the twentieth century.

The epoch of continuous creativity in interior design and furniture-making in Europe began in the Renaissance around the mid-fifteenth century.[785] The Greeks built some of the finest architectural monuments in history, such as temples, theatres, and stadia, with their sophisticated geometrical proportions, perfectly straight lines and harmonious spatial configurations. The Romans mastered the Greek arch and vault as well as the use of domes to cover large areas with no

---

[785] A good proportion of the details here covering the period up until the end of the 1800s, though not the interpretive scheme, benefitted from a very careful reading of Robbie G. Blakemore's excellent book, *History of Interior Design and Furniture: From Ancient Egypt to Nineteenth-Century Europe* (2005).

internal support. The Romanesque and Gothic periods in the Middle Ages were likewise very significant, but it was only in the modern era that Gothic motifs would come to play a role in furniture-making and interior design. There is, of course, a strong relationship between furniture/interior design and architecture. To this extent we must mention architectural accomplishments, insofar as they had a direct impact on the history of furniture-making and interior decoration of ceilings, floors, chimneys, and stairways.

Renaissance

Italy was the springboard for the Renaissance in furniture-making and architecture beginning in the 1400s. A critical factor was the "rediscovery" of the legacy of classical antiquity, including a treatise written by the Roman Marcus Vitrivius Pollio (80/70–15 BC), a multi-volume work entitled *De architectura*. This work was very influential in launching the Renaissance style, with its idea that buildings should have "strength," "utility," and "beauty" or perfect proportions. It inspired Battista Alberti (1404–72) to write the first architectural treatise of the Renaissance, emphasizing the layout of the interior of buildings. We are speaking about treatises—that is, not mere descriptive guidelines, but systematic, extensively argued discourses, in which the principles of a particular subject are discussed and explained. Alberti influenced the architect Filippo Brunelleschi (1377–1446), recognized for developing linear perspective in art and for designing buildings heavily dependent on mirrors and geometry, to express the highest perfection in Christian spirituality. Antonio Averlino's (1400–69) twenty-one-book treatise on architecture, and Sebastiano Serlio's illustrated book on architecture, published in 1537–75, were both influenced by Alberti. The foremost architect of the sixteenth century, Andrea Palladio (1508–80), author of *The Four Books of Architecture*, was particularly interested in conceptualizing the function of each part of the interior of buildings in terms of their geometric form, and delineating thereby a hierarchy wherein a larger interior order would override a lesser order: the divine and perfect world of faith over the earthly world of humans.

At the same time, the Renaissance was also permeated by a humanism focused on the earthly world of people, and on man as the highest form of creation. The Renaissance preoccupation with symmetry and horizontality, the idea that beauty was enhanced by calculating mathematical ratios, was indeed based on the measure, and actual potentiality, of the human body as a system of proportional relationships. The Renaissance employment of exact perspective to create optical illusion of three-dimensional spaces, depth, and distance, played a very significant role in the unprecedented variety of decorative treatment of walls that character-ized Italian interiors during the fifteenth and sixteenth centuries.

This period witnessed an unprecedented variety of wall decorations, ornately treated door refinement with classic elements, stop-fluted pilasters, pedestals, and entablature. Flat, vaulted, and coved ceilings were prevalent forms, with surfaces of every description. While chairs in the medieval period were rare status symbols, the Renaissance saw new types of chairs emerge, including the *sgabello*, an armless back stool, and the *cassapanca*, a multi-seat unit, which also served as a chest. The credenza, a cupboard with great variety in design, and dining tables (rectangular, long, and narrow) were also introduced. And since Europe is made up of distinc-tive national peoples, there would be a French Renaissance with its own variations, for example, in types of materials used for floors: stone, marble, tile, brick, and wood.

Chimney, Château de Fontainebleau.

The number and size of windows increased substantially in the early years of the French Renaissance, and highly ornamented chimney pieces (such as the one at Château de Fontainebleau) became the focal point of the room, with a wide variety of carved relief decorated panels and freestanding statues. The caquetoire chair was introduced around the mid-sixteenth century, a wooden chair with a tall, narrow paneled back attached to the trapezoid seat, along with storage pieces (buffet, armoire, dressoir, or a cupboard) becoming more architectural in the use of columns or pilasters carved with fluting.

The English version (1500–1660) of the Renaissance was influenced by German and Flemish pattern books, such as the 1577 book *Architectura* by Johannes de Vries, and the translation into English of a work by Sebastiano Serlio, done by Robert Peake and published in 1611 under the title *The First Book of Architecture*.[786] The English would soon write their own books: first a 1563 treatise by John Shute, entitled *Chief Groundes of Architecture*, which set down the requirements for the "perfecte architecte"; and then a 1624 practical building guide by Sir Henry Wooton, titled *Elements of Architecture*. New to the English Renaissance were the use of stairways as a processional route to the high great chamber, upholstered pieces of furniture, with further improvements in board and trestle dining tables, and a new gateleg table which allowed the drop leaf of the table to be raised, thereby enlarging the tabletop surface.

Baroque

Italy remained dominant in ceiling decoration during the Baroque period of 1600–1700, featuring a highly opulent, large-scale designing style, entailing incredibly intricate details, high contrasting colors, and elements of surprise through the use of light, curves over straight lines, painted and vaulted ceilings, columns, arches, niches, and fountains. The materials used were stucco, paint, and fresco. Also utilized was an illusionistic perspective through the use of *quadratura*, which dramatically extended the vertical dimensions of interior spaces. A new chair with lower backs was designed, with boldly treated curves and detailed carvings on the legs. The storage pieces included the cassone, the credenza, the

---

[786] None of these old books mentioned in this section regarding interior and furniture design are listed in the bibliography, as I make no claim to have read them, though I checked all of them online to read further about their content, in addition to what is contained in the secondary works cited.

armoire, the cabinet, and the chest of drawers characterized by intricate moldings, and sometimes flanked by marble columns.

The French Baroque of 1600–1715 found its most creative culmination in the reign of Louis XIV, with France becoming the major source of artistic inspiration to other countries in the late seventeenth and early eighteenth centuries. The most prominent architect was François Mansart (1598–1666), credited for works renowned for their high degree of refinement, subtlety, and elegance, as well as the encouragement of vistas through the use of the enfilade in the arrangement of rooms, vistas from the main suites to the landscaped garden, and vertical perspectives through the dramatic use of light and dark contrasts in the staircase. Jean Barbet's book *Livre d'architecture* (1632–41) and Jean Le Pautre's *Cheminées à la modern* (1661) were very influential in the design of highly complex, massive, and sculptural chimney pieces with a variety of motifs: swags, scrolls, cartouches, pilasters, entablatures, and pediments. The commode, a chest of drawers, was introduced, with some pieces ornamented with ebony veneer using marquetry of tortoiseshell and brass. André-Charles Boulle (1642–1732) was "the most remarkable of all French cabinetmakers."

The English Baroque was a modification of ideas from France and the Netherlands. The premier British architects were Sir Christopher Wren, Sir John Vanbrugh, William Talman, and Thomas Archer. A spectrum of wall surfaces was used, including wood paneling, mirrors, tapestries, textiles, leather, and paintings. After the chimney piece, the most decorated feature of a room was the ceiling, deeply compartmentalized. The most impressive houses used wrought or cast-iron balustrades for their stairways. The primary influence in the making of these stairways was the French smith Jean Tijou and his work *A New Book on Drawings* (1693). Increasing importance was attached to the drapery of beds (patterned velvets, silk damask, chintz, and brocade), absorbing most of the costs.

Rococo

France was the setting for the next major epoch in interior and furniture design, which came along with a new emphasis on relaxation and pleasure, with furniture becoming more comfortable, designed for conversation, and chairs more graceful, informal, and less stiff than in the age of Louis XIV. This was a reflection of both the Enlightened court aristocracy and the *nouveaux riche* financial bourgeoisie. Rococo was a highly ornate, theatrical, and over-the-top style developed

Boulle, commode.

King's staircase, Hampton Court Palace.

as a reaction to the strictness of Baroque. It was a flamboyant, freer, and more lighthearted style, with decorative elements that often emulated the look of shells, pebbles, flowers, birds, vines, and leaves.

The foremost French Rococo architects were Robert de Cotte (1656–1735) and Gilles-Marie Oppenhord (1672–1742), as well as the goldsmith and decorator Juste Aurele Meissonier (1695–1750), who published a book, entitled *Livre d'ornements*. Two types of chairs became common, the fauteuil and the bergère, with floral carving, tapestry upholstery, separate cushion, and with emphasis on informality. Many kinds of tables were introduced, some multifunctional, while others were for specific functions, such as gaming tables, work tables, serving tables, and coffee tables. Beds were of several types. In England, the style of the period 1715–1760 was Georgian rather than Rococo. The Georgian style is a unique combination of Classical and Baroque stylistic features. It is interesting that Lord Shaftesbury, one of the most important philosophers of his day who lived from 1671 to 1713, just before this style emerged in England, insisted that "a man of breeding and politeness is careful to form his judgments of arts and sciences upon the right models of perfection."[787]

The models of this time emphasized the architectural principles of classicism and the ideas articulated by Andrea Palladio, an expert on Roman architecture. Palladio saw perfection in the classical concept of harmonic proportion based on mathematical ratios. In 1715–1725, Colen Campbell published *Vitruvius Britannicus*, a survey of English Classical architecture of the seventeenth and early eighteenth centuries. Richard Boyle made a grand tour in 1714–15 through France, northern Italy and Rome, where he studied the works of Palladio. James Gibbs also visited Rome and Palladio's buildings, publishing in 1728 the *Book of Architecture and the Rules for Drawing the Several Parts of Architecture*. Gibb's influence is visible in the design of the White House, which employed both Classical as well as the Baroque features of floating pediments, scrolled shoulders and *oeil-de-boeuf* windows.

However, by the mid-eighteenth century, Rococo became influential in England, with detailing of delicate linear motifs, undulating lines, and natural forms making their way into decorations and buildings. Isaac Ware's book, *A Complete Body of Architecture*, published in 1756, emphasized the use of stucco ornamental material (lime, sand, plaster) for grand rooms. There was indeed a lot of variety in styles, with combinations of Classical, Baroque, and Rococo motifs. Geometric

---

[787] Cited in Blakemore, 247.

patterns in floor design were emphasized in Batty Lagley's 1739 *The City and Country Builder's and Workman's Treasury of Designs* and John Carwitham's 1739 *Kind of Floor Decorations Represented Both in Plano and Perspective*. Casement windows were commonly used, while the double-hung window became standard in upper-class houses. Windows were often rectangular, but some had flattened, arched heads, while some were doubled lancets, representing the Gothic influence during the Rococo phase of the Georgian period. Some windows were more Classical or Palladian, characterized by an arrangement of three openings, with the central window being widest and having a round, arched opening, and the two outer windows flat cornices.

Two cabinet makers, William Ince and John Mayhew, published *The Universal System of Household Furniture*, a 1763 collection of over three hundred finely

Chippendale, commode.

engraved designs in the English rococo style for parlor chairs, claw tables, sideboards, desks, ladies' secretaries, bookcases, writing tables, candle stands couches, draperies, girandoles, and more. The most influential book on furniture was Thomas Chippendale's 1754–62 *The Gentleman and Cabinet-Maker's Director*, an encyclopedic book offering a broad range of furniture designs with 160 plates covering a wide range of different styles, from a simple, undecorated clothing press, to a highly adorned library cabinet with rococo ornaments. Among the wide variety of tables designed during the Chippendale period were the tea table, toilet table, sideboard table for use in the dining room, and a variety of gaming tables for backgammon, cards, and chess. The chest-on-chest (or tallboy) and bachelor chest became typical.

Neoclassic

The Neoclassic style began in France around the 1740s, in reaction to the "excesses, asymmetry, and perceived disorderliness" of Rococo.[788] It came on the heels of major excavations of ancient cities and the emerging study of archeological artifacts and buildings. Jacques Blondel's four volume 1756 work, *Architecture françoise*, was instrumental in consolidating the French Neoclassic movement. While Renaissance and Baroque architecture already represented partial revivals of the Classical architecture of ancient Rome, the Neoclassical movement was aimed directly against the decorative excesses and ritualistic arrangements of the Late Baroque, and the naturalistic ornament of Rococo, in favor of a purer and more authentic Classical style, adapted to the modern Enlightenment world, characterized by reserve, restraint, and self-command.

Walls were designed with symmetrical features and rectilinear treatments. Embellishment reminiscent of the Rococo style persisted, but there was greater discipline and balance. Circular spaces for stairways were frequently used, along with rectilinearity and straight flights of stairs. Various shapes were used for the backs of seat furniture, such as medallion, trapezoid, rectangle, and rectangle with a flattened arched cresting. Commodes were very common in many shapes and sizes; a new type was the demilune commode, which was semicircular in shape

---

[788] Blakemore, 2005, 264.

and featured two drawers in the front and a curved door on each side. Jean-Henri Riesener (1774–1792) was the foremost Neoclassic cabinet-maker in France with a style that was pure Louis XVI, with its rectilinear side view and harmonious ornamentation.

The English Neoclassic period of 1770–1810 also had a predilection for the linear and symmetrical. The furniture designer Robert Adam (1728–92), author of *The Works in Architecture of Robert and James Adam*, was a most influential member of this movement. Adam actually rejected the Palladian style for what he thought was a more archaeologically accurate Neoclassic style. He emphasized the principle of "movement" that has "the same effect in architecture" as in a landscape, to create "an agreeable and diversified contour." Among his many works are the ceiling of the "Red Drawing Room" in Hopetoun House, with its delicate Rococo details composed of foliage, shells, and scrolls in an asymmetrical arrangement, but with some classical motifs. In his furniture designs, Adam combined some Rococo details, but in a more classical direction, as evidenced in his design of chairs with their thin, tapering, fluted legs; and in his lightly scaled and rectangular or semi-oval tables with their round- or square-sectioned legs. George Hepplewhite, 1788 author of *The Cabinet-Maker and Upholsterer's Guide*, was enormously influential as far as the construction of Neoclassic furniture was concerned.

Riesener, commode.

Robert Adam, chair.

Another great furniture designer was Thomas Sheraton, author of the 1803 *Cabinet-Maker's Dictionary*, which included sixty-nine designs for furniture; he strove for lightness, and some characterized his style as feminine in refinement. Sheraton is generally identified with the "late Neoclassic" style, or the "Regency style" of the period 1810–1830, which was more eclectic in absorbing in combination Greek, Roman, Gothic, Egyptian, and Tudor styles. This eclecticism is apparent in the architect John Nash (1752–1835), who consciously combined discordant styles. Thomas Hope, author of the 1807 *Household Furniture*, was inspired in the designs of his Regency interiors and furniture by his travels in Europe, Greece, Turkey, and Egypt. However, these were not borrowings of architectural styles from the East, but reinterpretations of these styles according to European conceptual principles. Europeans freely borrowed certain non-Western motifs, and then integrated them within a European tradition, always searching for new ways while striving for aesthetic perfection. Hope's influence extended beyond the Regency period, into the Regency Revival of the 1920s and 1930s, and even Art Deco design. Hope aimed to express three qualities in his furniture designs: character, beauty, and what he called "appropriate meaning."

Revival Styles in France and England (1830–1901)

Lucie-Smith believes that the period between 1800 and 1850 saw more fundamental changes in furniture design than the preceding two hundred years. It certainly becomes rather complicated to find clearly demarcated styles due to the
combination (and revival) of different styles from Europe's past and from other
cultures, coupled with the persistent creativity and novelties introduced by new
generations of gifted designers.

The French Revival was a continuation and further development of tendencies
already visible during the Napoleonic Empire period (1805–1815), with its mon-
umentality, grand scale, and stateliness. The typical furniture pieces of this Empire
period were heavy, severe, with sharp corners and lack of moldings, imposing,
with uninterrupted flat surfaces, heavy bases for cabinet pieces, and symmetry.
During the reign of Louis Philippe, 1815–30, the Napoleonic style remained paramount through to the Second Empire, 1850–70, with its most successful architect, Charles Garnier, combining the Baroque, Renaissance, and Rococo styles. In
both England and France, the impact of the industrial revolution was felt as machine processes began to replace craftsmen, though high-style furniture continued
to emphasize high quality skill work. There was a lot of variety in the treatment of
chair backs, "upholstered, straight, backward scroll, rounded top, openwork centered with cross bars, arcade revealing Gothic influence with crocketed finials."[789]
Lavish display of upholstery was common, and multiple-seat units were produced;
the tops of tables were round, oval, octagonal, square, or rectangular; and the legs
were carved in the form of colonnettes, chimeras, sphinxes, lions, or human figures.

The historical setting of the English Revival Style was the industrial transformation, the material prosperity achieved by the middle classes, and the opening
of international markets with the spread of railway lines across the world. The
word "eclecticism" is commonly used to describe this Victorian era because more,
than ever, designers combined a variety of past styles adapted to contemporary
uses. This was expressed in books, such as Henry Shaw's 1836 *Specimens of Ancient Architecture*, and Robert Bridgens' 1838 *Furniture with Candelabra and Interior Decoration*, which displayed Grecian Gothic, and Elizabethan designs. A.
W. N. Pugin (1812–52) was a keen advocate of Gothic revival, publishing the

---

[789] Blakemore, 383.

pattern book *Gothic Furniture in the Style of the Fifteenth Century*, and so was Bruce James Talbert, author of *Gothic Forms Applied to Furniture*. Belvoir Castle, completed in 1825, was a mixture of Gothic, Baroque, Rococo, Norman, and Classical. This variety of styles was reflected in chimneys (such as the one in the Drawing Room in the Carlton Towers) and furniture pieces.

Art Nouveau, Art Deco, and Modernism

Art Nouveau (1890–1914), Art Deco (1910–1945), and Modernism (1940s-late 1900s) are difficult to compartmentalize into clear time periods and cultural movements because they evolved from combinations of intersecting artistic currents in different national European cultures, with their own flavors and motifs, beyond buildings and furniture, with the latter two movements influencing the design of multiple industrial consumer items, such as cars, locomotives, radios, and vacuum cleaners. Modernism alone includes many different styles, such as the Bauhaus school, Expressionism, Constructivism, Brutalism, and Metabolism, and in turn inspired Postmodernism.

Art Nouveau aimed at modernizing design and escaping the increasingly eclectic and historically oriented Neoclassic and Revivalist styles.[790] It was modern in its rejection of the traditional hierarchy of the arts, and the aristocratic elevation of painting, sculpture, and architecture over the craft-based decorative arts. We can say that it was democratic in its insistence that art should become part of the everyday life of citizens, and not only the "high" arts, but also ceramics, metalwork, middle class furniture, and interior design, with a view to enhancing the aesthetic sensibilities of the wider public. But, on the other hand, we can say that it was not democratic in its emphasis on high-quality crafts and its criticism of the repetitive designs of mass-produced industrial furniture and decoration. It certainly remained aristocratic in its commitment to aestheticism, the pursuit of art for art's sake, and the exaltation of beauty and individual self-expression over the restrictive conformity and moralism of Victorian Revivalism. Smooth curves, graceful bends, and dancing lines were very significant, sometimes combined with bright colors, from burnt oranges and mustard yellows, to olive greens and soft blues. There is no space to list the numerous artists from all over Europe associated with Art Nouveau. I will mention the Belgian architect and furniture designer

---

[790] Duncan, 1994.

Majorelle, bedroom.

Victor Horta (1861–1947), and Louis Majorelle (1859–1926), who are said to have contributed the most to Art Nouveau furniture.

Art Deco, possibly the most talked-about arts movement in history, is a product of the European modern aesthetic imagination, as well as the first truly international style in art, influencing the architecture of buildings around the world.[791] It was a popular style that influenced not only buildings and furniture, but also jewelry, graphic arts, fashion, cars, gas pumps, trains, ocean liners, and everyday personal objects, such as radios and vacuum cleaners. It seems simple to identify with its sleek, streamlined features, vertical lines, zigzagged patterns and rectilinear shapes. But it is a complex movement influenced by divergent artistic currents, including the bold geometric forms of Cubism, the bright colors of Fauvism, Russian Constructivism, Italian Futurism, and Modernism generally.

While Art Deco was influenced by archeological discoveries in Egypt, and the growing globalization of the European mind and ethnographic interest in the Orient and in African art, it was a movement that looked to the future, not to the past. Art Deco's appearance is overwhelmingly reflective of the invention of industrial machines by Europeans and Americans, their advancements in the use of new materials, such as aluminum, stainless steel, glass, and plastic, and their aesthetic

---

[791] Duncan, 1988.

imagination to create art out of the aerodynamic principles of motion originated by Western scientists. This futuristic orientation was evident in the Streamline Moderne version of Deco, which took off during the 1930s, featuring curving shapes, smooth surfaces, and long horizontal lines, showing up in the industrial design of both moving objects, such cars, trains, ships, and of everyday consumer items, such as kitchen appliances and telephones, giving these products the impression of sleekness, motion, and speed.

Mercury train, Chicago, 1936.

But if Art Deco was characterized by clean lines and smooth surfaces, and no decoration on the facades of buildings, it also saw an explosion of colors of bright and contrasting hues in furniture upholstery, carpets, screens, wallpaper, and fabrics. While Art Deco, similarly to Art Nouveau, emphasized the uniqueness and originality of handmade objects, Deco took the incipient anti-aristocratic impulses of Art Nouveau in a more democratic or consumer-oriented direction. Its aim was less to focus on art for art's sake than to make machine-made objects aesthetically appealing to the increasingly affluent masses of the "roaring 1920s": lamps, clocks, ashtrays, bicycles, and movies in Deco theatres. However, Art Deco did not promote cheaply made products; it certainly used very expensive materials to decorate the first-class salons of ocean liners, deluxe trains, and the lobbies of skyscrapers, though after the Great Depression, the items infused with Deco motifs became less conspicuous consumer items. There are too many names associated with Art Deco to list, if only because of the multiple ways it found expression in ornamental crafts, industrial designs, and consumer products. In furniture

Ruhlmann, commode.

design some of the main names are the cabinet maker Émile-Jacques Ruhlmann (1879–1933), a pure Frenchman, Maurice Dufrène (1876–1955), Jean-Michel Frank (1895–1941), and Paul Follot (1877–1941).

We can date the beginnings of Modernism to Le Corbusier's book, *L'art décoratif d'aujourd'hui*, published in 1925, a polemical treatise against Art Nouveau and Art Deco and in favor of the idea that furniture, buildings, and objects intended for practical uses should be devoid of any decoration and aesthetic motifs. "Modern decoration has no decoration," declared Le Corbusier. A house was simply "a machine to live in." Writing about the deliberately functional, anonymous, and repetitive buildings of Modernism may not be a good way to end a chapter focused on the unsurpassed aesthetic creativity of Europeans. It should be noted that Modernism was the one European movement that not only spread everywhere in the world, but encouraged non-Western architects to make a contribution, with its principle that function, not aesthetics, is what matters.

Modernism was likely an inevitable by-product of the inherent nature of mass industrial societies to value anonymous practicality, culturally neutral technological efficiency, and the power of modernity. Its anonymous, impersonal character is congenial to the belief that the West stands for global modernization. Nevertheless, the best architects of the twentieth century were still Western: Frank Lloyd Wright, Louis Sullivan, Daniel Burnham, Raymond Hood, Cass Gilbert, Hugh Ferriss, William Van Alen, John Mead Howells, Renzo Piano, Adrian D. Smith, John Burgee, John C. Portman, and William Le Baron Jenney. Modernism can be viewed as a realistic expression of an emerging new world of mass industrial society, with huge cities necessitating practical high-rises for millions of inhabitants without the means to pay rent in high-quality architectural buildings.

We also can't ignore the reaction against Modernism in the 1970s and 1980s, starting with the groundbreaking 1966 book, *Complexity and Contradiction in Architecture*, by Robert Venturi. This book, and Postmodernism generally, agreed that in our mass societies, many buildings must serve a function, be practical and efficient in use of energy and materials; however, it rejected the functional purism of Modernism, and called instead for creative mixtures of historic styles from the past, for buildings to be in tune with their environmental settings and in honor of local history and traditions. This call for creative mixtures was itself not new; the revivals and eclectic mixtures we witnessed through the 1800s already testified to Spengler's own view that, by the twentieth century, "the architectural possibilities" of the West had been "exhausted."[792]

The Continuous Creativity of Western Visual Arts and Its Eventual Deterioration/Exhaustion

Not long ago, the celebrated historian Felipe Fernández-Armesto called Kenneth Clark's judgement that Greek art undoubtedly "embodies a higher state of civilization" than African art a "warped perspective," and "a crude perversion of prejudice."[793] No civilization can be said to be "better," Fernández-Armesto insisted, since each culture, from the most primitive to the most advanced, is adapted to a specific environment. We must abandon the "delusions of self-flattery." In contrast, Charles Murray's 2003 book, *Human Accomplishment: The Pursuit of Excellence in the Arts and Sciences 800 BC to 1950* may be read, in its judgment of "excellence" in the arts, as an attempt to establish that, when it comes to the beautiful, there is, as Kant argued, an "ought-ness" implied in our aesthetic judgments, more than an expression of individual taste.

But considering, as Kant understood, that aesthetic judgments are not provable in any scientific way, how can we arrive at universal standards of judgment? Kant's answer was that, first, even though art is a product of human autonomy and reflects personal expression, the true artist is possessed of genius, which is an

---

[792] Spengler, 40.
[793] Fernández-Armesto, 2000, 9.

innate mental disposition through which nature gives rule to art. Second, at the time Kant was living, art and beauty were considered synonymous, and the criteria for the beautiful was based upon and derived from what the elite culture took to be the Greek ideal of nature perfected, and also universal—that is, agreed upon by everyone with taste. As Kant wrote in the *Critique of Judgment*: "For judging of beautiful objects as such, taste is requisite; but for beautiful art, i.e. for the production of such objects genius is requisite."[794] In other words, a great artist cannot but be possessed by an innate disposition for beauty, recognized by those with the requisite taste.

Although Murray does not discuss Kant's aesthetics, this perspective is implied in his conviction that we can make judgments about the relative quality of artistic works in an objective manner. Going by the amount of space allocated to the greatest artists in reference works, encyclopedias, and dictionaries, as decided upon by generations of men with the requisite knowledge and taste for great art, Murray estimates that the absolute number of great visual artists in the West is far higher than the *combined* number of the other civilizations: 479 for the West as compared to 192 for China and Japan combined (with no significant figures listed for India or the Arab World). While acknowledging that it is difficult to apply a uniform standard of excellence, Murray insists that the ability to appreciate the quality of a work of art "varies with the level of knowledge that a person brings to it."[795] Those who know most about an artistic field have a deeper understanding of the intrinsic aesthetic qualities of art works. The strong degree of consensus about the greatest paintings and the painters one finds in reference and encyclopedias, notwithstanding some variations in individual judgements, reflect qualities that are inherent in the work of art. In order to avoid a Eurocentric bias, or impose a Eurocentric conception of beauty, Murray not only relies on sources written by non-Europeans, but creates separate compilations for each of "the giants" in the arts of the non-Western and Western world.

The main flaw with Murray is that the numbers of 479 and 192 leave out a most peculiar characteristic of Western art: its exhibition of a continuous proliferation of highly original artists with new artistic styles, new ways of projecting images on a flat surface, new conceptions of light, new standards of excellence, and new conceptions about nature and man—in contrast to the non-Western world, where aesthetic norms barely changed, or where artists were invariably

---

[794] Kant, 1790/2012, 115.
[795] Murray, 2003, 65.

inclined to follow an established convention without breaking new aesthetic paths. To appreciate the achievement of the West it is not enough to have separate lists comparing great artists across civilizations. Among the 479 great painters compiled for the West, one will find a much higher number of original artists than among the 192 artists compiled for China and Japan.

One need not be an expert to know this. Reading some of the best histories of art, together with decades of research comparing the cultural paths of civilizations, has been enough to convey this startling contrast. This chapter relies closely on four of the most widely-read and authoritative books on the subject: H. W. Janson's *History of Art*, E. H. Gombrich's *The Story of Art*, Arnold Hauser's four-volume book, *The Social History of Art*, and Kenneth Clark's *Civilisation*. To get a perspective from admirers of Chinese art, my reading included the highly re-garded book, *The Arts of China*, by Michael Sullivan, in partial combination with James Cahill's *Chinese Painting*. My focus was on whether China really saw new "isms," or merely continuous refinements and slight alterations within an unbro-ken tradition set in the past. China is the one civilization that can be compared to the West in having exhibited a long continuous line of great painters, with some noticeable changes in artistic styles.

But why does the title of this section say that Western art saw "its eventual deterioration"? Because in the course of the years of thinking about and writing this book, it became clear that the very qualities that made the West the most dy-namic, creative, and dominant civilization in history—its weaker tribal ties, its emphasis on individualism, impartiality, and fairness with anonymous others—have created the conditions for its current demise. This is a subject that will be addressed in the last two chapters. We may ask for now: Why is there such a per-vasive inclination among current academics to downplay European culture, or to insist, in the face of overwhelming counter-evidence, that Greece was no different from other Axial Age civilizations, that the application of Piagetian theory cross-culturally should be suppressed, that the West was created by multiple cultures and races, and that we can make no judgments about the relative quality of the artistic achievements of the cultures of the world?

The suggestion towards the end of this chapter is that the intensification of the ideology of liberalism, with its inherent belief that all collective standards and val-ues should be eliminated, and that the state should only enforce the right of the individual to choose his own values, ultimately worked to undermine the capacity of artists for aesthetic beauty. This was coupled with the deconstruction of Clas-sical and Christian ideals of beauty, and the "progressive emancipation" of

European artists from the conventions of their time, along with the spread of the "democratic" belief that there should be no hierarchy of judgement. We might suggest as well a point already made in regards to music and furniture design: the possibilities for original painting were exhausted by the twentieth century. There was nothing left to originate; European man had reached the end point of his artistic creativity.

Janson, Hauser, Gombrich, and Clark

H. W. Janson's *History of Art*, first published in 1962, with a sixteenth printing in 1971, which was used for this book, and numerous new editions thereafter, is an encyclopedic treatment of the history of art, with millions of copies sold in fifteen languages. Janson came from a Lutheran family of Baltic German stock. His main criterion for choice of great art is originality. "Uniqueness, novelty, freshness," he believes, are the "yardstick of artistic greatness." "An original work must not be a copy, reproduction, imitation, or translation." But it is important to note that Janson warns against a flimsy understanding of what originality entails, making the key point that "without tradition . . . no originality would be possible." Absorbing "the artistic tradition" of one's time, learning the "established ways of drawing, painting, carving, designing" and the "established ways of seeing," is a precondition for creativity.[796] The eventual decline of Western art in the twentieth century can indeed be attributed to the erosion of all traditions and techniques, including the ideal of perfection, with the freeing of the individual from all external constraints and placing him solely in charge of aesthetics.

Janson's book has three opening chapters on "The Art of Prehistoric Man," "Egyptian Art," and "The Ancient Near East." The rest of the book, with the exception of a short chapter on "Islamic Art" and a short postscript with the title "The Meeting of East and West," is entirely about Western art. The non-Western traditions mainly interest him insofar as they "contributed to the growth of the Western artistic tradition." He ignored China, Japan, and India until the end, because they were not a "vital source of inspiration for Western art" except in contemporary times. He believes short sections on Egyptian, Near Eastern, and Islamic art are sufficient to convey the aesthetic qualities of these traditions, with their ceremonial forms and eventual repetitiveness after a period of creativity. The

---

[796] Janson, 1971, 12–15.

East Asian tradition had a "refined style," but this style was characterized by "many centuries of *continuous* development."[797]

It can't be denied, however, that this marginal treatment of Chinese art is a limitation of Janson's book. We will see that there were some variations in artistic styles in China, and many truly great painters. But Janson had to make choices. It is a large book of 600+ pages in small print. Conveying the persistently great originality of the West required full separate chapters on "Greek Art," "Roman Art," "Early Christian and Byzantine Art," "Romanesque Art," "Gothic Art," "Late Gothic Painting and Sculpture," "The Early Renaissance in Italy," "The High Renaissance in Italy," "Mannerism and Other Trends," "The Renaissance in the North," "The Baroque in Italy and Germany," "The Baroque in Flanders, Holland, and Spain," "The Baroque in France and England," "Neoclassicism and Romanticism," "Realism and Impressionism," "Post-Impressionism," and "Twentieth-Century Painting and Sculpture." *History of Art* was determined to convey to students precisely what stood out about the Western tradition: its continuous freshness and ability to generate one artistic epoch after another, rather than a relatively continuous and monotonous tradition.

Arnold Hauser (1892–1978) was a Hungarian Marxist with Jewish ancestry, an admirer of bourgeois norms and sensibilities, writing at a time when students were educated without diversity and equity mandates. *The Social History of Art*, first published in two volumes in 1951, the product of thirty years of labor, opens with eight short chapters on prehistoric, Egyptian, and Mesopotamian art, covering less than fifty pages in a four-volume book that is close to one thousand pages long. This rightfully valued book argues that art became more realistic and naturalistic as Europe became less aristocratic and hierarchical and more bourgeois, urbane, and cosmopolitan. A "naturalistic style" actually prevailed through to the end of the Paleolithic Age in the way animals were depicted in a realistic way, although the art was concerned also with the performance of magical rituals. This naturalistic attitude, which was "open to the full range of experience," gave way in the Neolithic Age to a "narrowly geometric stylization" in which the "artist tended to shut himself off from the wealth of empirical reality." This "formalistic" and "ornamental style" persisted through the history of Egypt and Mesopotamia, with minor variations.[798]

---

[797] Ibid, 569.
[798] Hauser, 1973, Vol 1, 8–21.

The profound changes that accompanied the rise of these civilizations did not occasion fundamental changes to the Neolithic geometrical and formalistic style other than the addition of a monumental quality. We should not "underestimate the spirit of conservatism" of Egyptian art. In Egyptian art, "the person of the artist himself disappeared almost entirely behind his work." Painters and sculptors remained "anonymous" and "undistinguished" craftsmen, "in no way obtruding their own personalities." The art of the early period of Egyptian history was "stereotyped" and "stylized" in the Middle Kingdom (2040–1782 BC), and characterized by "conservatism and conventionalism." "Ancient-Oriental art . . . is an art which both demands and shows public respect. Its approach to the beholder is an act of reverence, of courtesy and etiquette."[799]

There was a bit of naturalism during the reign of Akhenaton (1351–1334 BC), known as the "first prophet" and the "discoverer of monotheism." But while one sees representations of everyday scenes, and some changes from the old monumental style, the art remained "thoroughly ceremonial and formal." The civilizations of Mesopotamia, Babylonian, and Assyria, despite their more dynamic trade, industry and finance, were "more rigidly disciplined, less changeable" in their art than even Egypt. One would have expected the higher urbanization of the Babylonians to have encouraged less rigid forms of art, but Hauser infers that the persistency of despotic rule and "the more intolerant spirit of religion" likely countered any individualistic and naturalistic impulses.[800]

It is only in ancient Crete that Hauser finally encounters a "colorful, unrestrained, exuberant life" in art. Hauser's argument is not that from this point on Western art is persistently creative, never rigid and traditionalist. New artistic epochs emerge (Mannerism, Baroque, Rococo, Classicism, Romanticism, Naturalism, Impressionism) in opposition to prevailing conventions with increasing acceleration from the Renaissance onwards, led by artists who intentionally wanted to break away from the prejudices of their age, innovate and experiment, and demonstrate thereby their own artistic genius.

Gombrich's *The Story of Art*, originally published in 1950, is currently in its sixteenth edition. According to its publisher, it has sold over eight million copies and been translated into over 30 languages, surely making it one of the best-selling art books of all time. Unlike Hauser, who follows a Marxist conception of progress in the arts, Gombrich, born in Vienna into an assimilated family of Jewish origin,

---

[799] Ibid, 31–35.
[800] Ibid.

carefully rejects the idea of progress, believing that "each gain or progress in one direction entails a loss in another, and that this subjective progress, in spite of its importance, does not correspond to an objective increase in artistic value."[801] Achieving originality in one age usually entails sacrificing aesthetic qualities emphasized by preceding generations. At the same time, Gombrich thinks it is possible, much like Charles Murray, to make judgements about the quality of art, as long as it is done by a critic with aesthetic sensibilities developed through years of education.

The Story of Art is a history of art from the beginnings to the present. Gombrich estimates that three chapters, out of twenty-five, are enough to cover the achievements of primitive and non-Western art. His reason for doing this is simple: Western Europe always differed profoundly from the East.

> In the East [artistic] styles lasted for thousands of years, and there seemed no reason why they should ever change. The West never knew this immobility. It was always restless, groping for new solutions and new ideas.[802]

Among European painters there was an "urge to be different," to find a new way to enhance the aesthetic effect of one's work, and convey something different about the world, new life experiences along with permanent aspects of human nature.

Using originality and restless creativity as his central criterion, Gombrich could not help but pay far less attention to an Eastern artistic tradition that remained continuously the same through the centuries. He writes about Egypt's "art of eternity":

> No one wanted anything different, no one asked him to be "original." On the contrary, he was probably considered the best artist who could make his statues most like the admired monuments of the past. So it happened that in the course of three thousand years or more Egyptian art changed very little. . . . True, new fashions appeared, and new subjects were demanded of the artists, but their mode of representing man and nature remained essentially the same.[803]

---

[801] Gombrich, 1967, 3.
[802] Ibid, 131.
[803] Ibid, 42.

About Chinese and Japanese art, he observes:

> The standards of painting remained very high . . . but art became more and more like a graceful and elaborate game which has lost much of its interest as so many of its moves are known. It was only after a new contact with the achievements of Western art in the eighteenth century that the Japanese dared to apply the Eastern methods to new subjects.[804]

Gombrich has a keen eye for what was distinctive about each epoch of Western art and what was original about each of the major painters. So does Kenneth Clark, whose book *Civilisation* is made up of the scripts of a series of television programmes from the spring of 1969. The series, produced by the BBC under the same name as the book's title, consisted of thirteen episodes, each fifty minutes long, singularly focused on European art from the end of the Dark Ages to the early twentieth century. Many were surprised by the "unprecedented viewing figures for a high art series: 2.5 million viewers in Britain and 5 million in the US."[805]

This admiration would dissipate, however, as Britain would go on to embrace multiculturalism and feminism. The objections came down to Clark's "all men" and "all European" cast of great painters, and against Clark's identification of the word "Civilisation" with the creation of great art, combined with his belief that the West produced the greatest art. This may explain why the BBC announced in 2015 a new ten-episode sequel to Clark's series to be called *Civilisations* (plural), with three presenters: "the committed feminist and anti-racist" Mary Beard, the Nigerian immigrant David Olusoga, and the Jew Simon Schama. This new series would emphasize "non-European cultures" to "convey a message of globalism" by "revelling in the variety of our species' ingenuity on an international scale."

Although Clark does not compare Western to non-Western art, and starts with the Dark Ages rather than ancient Greece, the following words in the beginning of *Civilisation* would have disqualified him today from any public appearance:

> Whatever its merits as a work of art, I don't think there is any doubt that the Apollo embodies a higher state of Civilisation than the mask. They both represent spirits, messengers from another world—that is to say, from

---

[804] Ibid, 108.
[805] Hearn, Marcus (2005)

a world of our own imagining. To the Negro imagination it is a world of fear and darkness, ready to inflict horrible punishment for the smallest infringement of a taboo. To the Hellenistic imagination it is a world of light and confidence, in which the gods are like ourselves, only more beautiful, and descend to earth in order to teach men reason and the laws of harmony. . . . Western Europe inherited such an ideal.[806]

It is this conviction that Western art expresses mankind's highest achievements in aesthetics that irks the new diversity-controlled Britain. *Civilisation* is a joy to read for its high-minded learning and enthusiastic appreciation of the sublime originality of Western art in its incessant striving for new forms of aesthetic perfection. Other civilizations remained content with reenacting the perfection they had achieved in the past. The West was different: "The great, indeed the unique, merit of European Civilisation has been that it has never ceased to develop and change. It has not been based on a stationary perfection, but on ideas and inspiration."[807]

What About Chinese Painting?

Before we go on further with Western art, we must assess Chinese painting within the framework of Michael Sullivan's *The Arts of China*, a comprehensive study of Chinese art and a long-standing text for university students, now in its sixth edition. There will be some references to James Cahill's beautiful 1960 book, *Chinese Painting*, with its numerous color transparencies of paintings in plates. One can hardly disagree with Cahill that "the Chinese tradition of painting [is] the richest and most diversified in world art outside Europe."[808] Sullivan is also a keen admirer of Chinese art. The claim that Chinese art was relatively observant of tradition, or attached to old ways, is an interpretation Sullivan would deny as a matter of principle. Cahill less so. Yet, the overall message from Sullivan's *The Arts of China* is that this art was very traditional. Much of Chinese art, it should be said, consisted of bronze casting, ceramics, and jade carving. It was highly sophisticated in technique and decoration, but I hesitate to call it art. It should be categorized

---

[806] Clark, 1970, 2.
[807] Ibid, 74.
[808] Cahill, 1960, 5.

as applied art, the work of highly skilled craftsmen. As H. W. Janson writes, "originality is what distinguishes art from craft."

While paintings with human figures were common from the Han dynasty (202 BC–AD 220) until the end of the Tang (618–907), by the eleventh century, landscape painting was the characteristic product until the end of dynastic rule in the twentieth century. Both the human figure and landscape painting operated within a stable, craft-like tradition, occasionally exhibiting interesting variations, without epoch-making redirections. One might interpolate that there is less individuality and self-consciousness in Chinese portraits. As Cahill observes about the painting below, which is a twelfth-century remake of an earlier eighth-century original, the characters are conscious in their sidelong glances, their postures, the way the hands are poised and the heads tilted, but the picture "tells us nothing about the participants beyond defining their roles in this particular scene … nor is there any of the extraneous overlay—humor, drama, pathos, sentiment—that is so often present in Occidental genre art."[809]

Landscape painting occurred within a cultural matrix that encouraged standardization and regularity, rather than unpredictability and freshness. Sullivan tells us that the "six principles of Chinese painting," which the painter and art critic Xie He wrote about in the sixth century, *remained the pivot around which all subsequent art criticism in China has revolved.*"[810] These six elements were: "spirit harmony," the way of using the brush, "fidelity to the object in portraying forms," "conformity to kind in applying colors," "proper planning in placing of elements," and "transmission by copying." The sixth principle "indicates reverence for the tradition itself, of which every painter felt himself to be a custodian." Overall, this manual told prospective painters that:

---

[809] Ibid, 20–21.
[810] Sullivan, 1999, 95–6; emphasis mine.

Making exact copies of ancient, worn masterpieces was a way of preserving them, just as, at a later date, working "in the manner of" great painters of the past, while adding something of oneself, was a way of putting new life into the traditions.

This passage sums up the underlying nature of Chinese creativity. New trends consisted in breaking from the regimented traditions of one's age by reviving and putting new life into early traditions. Of course, within any tradition, painters were expected to add something of their own, otherwise they would have produced mere replicas. Sullivan mentions Daoist painters who deviated somewhat from "the rigidly traditional way of art and literature," and painters who were influenced by Buddhism late in the Tang dynasty (618–907), who nurtured a "new" tradition in Chinese sculpture that "contained a rich mixture of native and foreign elements."[811]

According to Sullivan, the "great masters of the tenth and eleventh centuries are sometimes called classical because they established an ideal in monumental landscape painting to which later painters were to return again and again for inspiration."[812] Likewise, Zhao Mengfu (1254–1322) "occupies a pivotal position in the history of Chinese landscape painting" because "he united a direct, spontaneous expression of feeling with a deep reverence for the antique." He is said to have gone "beyond the orthodox Song styles" by rediscovering "the brushwork of the long neglected southern manner of [the painters] Dong Yuan and Juran" from the earlier Southern Tang dynasty (937–975). In doing this, Mengfu, "opened the way ... for almost all subsequent scholarly landscape painting up to the present day."[813]

The "urge to penetrate the unknown," identified by H. W. Janson as a hallmark of Western originality, was lacking in Chinese painting. Sullivan indeed tells us that "up until the Yuan, each painter had built upon the achievement of his predecessors in enriching his pictorial vocabulary and drawing closer to nature." But after Mengfu this "succession was broken, as artists began to range back over the whole tradition, reviving, playing variations upon, and painting in the manner of the great masters, particularly those of the tenth and eleventh centuries."[814] Sullivan calls this "a new and indeed revolutionary attitude to painting"—yet it was

---

[811] Ibid, 133.
[812] Ibid, 169.
[813] Ibid, 203.
[814] Ibid, 207.

just a return to an older tradition. In Chapter V, we observed this same type of "revolutionary attitude" in Chinese intellectual history: breaking from a stultified Neo-Confucian tradition by going back to the original Confucian tradition, or by integrating Daoist elements.

With continuous generations perfecting landscape painting, refining and elaborating different variations, Chinese painting could not but be masterful. Since landscapes are inherently diverse, there was always room to paint different things: pictures of flowers, birds, insects and animals. We find Bian Wenjin (1400–1440) specializing in painting birds in fresh ways. Chinese painters also portrayed scholars seated on mountain ledges gazing at some landscape or meditating. All in all, however, these variations occurred within an established tradition. In his *Qingbian Mountains* of 1617, Dong Qichang affirmed his philosophy that "the great Southern tradition must be not only revived and preserved, but creatively reinterpreted, for only thus could it live."[815] A new generation would go back to an older tradition to find ways to express it. Once the "new" way became a tradition, stultification would set in. "The most characteristic intellectual achievement of the Qing dynasty was, like of the Ming, not creative as much as synthetic." The Qing age was "an antiquarian age," and not just in painting, but in its overall obsession with the collection of classic books as well as "paintings, porcelain, and archaic bronzes."[816]

Western Originality: From Ancient to Gothic Times

If you asked someone what exactly makes Greek art great, what was original about the art of Giotto, Michelangelo, Raphael, Velazquez, or Rembrandt, or what's the difference between Renaissance and Baroque painting, or what's new about Mannerism, Rococo, Naturalism, Impressionism, and Surrealism, you would invariably get answers full of generalities without proper distinctions. This

---

[815] Ibid, 229.

[816] Ibid, 246. The highly respected, old-school historian, J.M. Roberts, in *The Penguin History of the World* (1990), has this to say about Chinese art: "It remained profoundly conservative, not only in social and political matters, but even in its aesthetic. The art it esteemed was based on distrust of innovation and originality; it strove to imitate and emulate the best, but the best was always the past. The traditional masterpieces pointed the way.... Restraint, discipline, refinement and respect for the great masters were the qualities admired by the scholar-civil servant who was also artist and patron" (447). This book, originally published in 1976 under the title *The Hutchison History of the World*, is now disregarded by world historians as "Eurocentric."

was the reason for going through the very time-consuming task of distilling some passages from Gombrich, Clark, and Hauser that elucidate what was novel and great about particular Western artists, works of art, and movements. As you read what follows, key in on phrases used to describe unique features of Western art, such as "deeply engaged by the mystery of the human psyche," "all individual expression is unique," "more intense consciousness of being," "an intensity of facial expression," "intensively self-conscious," or "expansion of sensual perception"— for these are reflective of the strong sense of selfhood and interiority permeating Western culture from its beginnings in varying ways and degrees.

Gombrich sees a "great wakening" in Greece, not only in the "discovery of foreshortening," but the striving for personal renown by each artist rather than for repetition of a formula.

> It was here, above all, that the greatest and most astonishing revolution in the whole history of art bore fruit . . . in the sixth century BC. . . . [With the Greeks] it was no longer a question of learning a ready-made formula for representing the human body. Every Greek sculptor wanted to know how *he* was to represent a particular body.[817]

One of the greatest artistic accomplishments of the ancient Greeks was "the discovery of foreshortening," which relates to the way we perceive an object in space depending on the angle from which we see it. It was in Greece that "artists dared for the first time in all history to paint a foot as seen from in front."

> It may seem exaggerated to dwell for long on such a small detail, but it really meant that the old art was dead and buried. It meant that the artist no longer aimed at including everything in the picture in its most clearly visible form, but took account of the angle from which he saw an object.[818]

Then came Hellenistic art with its realistic portrayals of particular characters.

> By the time of Alexander the Great . . . the heads of the statues usually look much more animated and alive than the beautiful faces of earlier works. Together with this mastery of expression, artists also learned to seize the

---

[817] Gombrich, 52; emphasis original.
[818] Ibid, 55–6.

individual character of a physiognomy and to make portraits in our sense of the word. It was in the time of Alexander that people started to discuss this new art of portraiture.[819]

One should not presume, however, that the creativity of Hellenistic art was bound to continue. "The Hellenistics," as Arnold Hauser observes, eventually "reached a dead end and simply went on repeating worn-out formulas."[820] Similarly, after Byzantine art expressed its own style in the fourth century AD, it became rigid and inflexible, and while it experienced a "second golden age" in the ninth and tenth centuries, with some magnificent mosaic paintings, it became, Hauser tell us, "formally stereotyped again … so conservative in fact that in essentials the icons of the Greek Orthodox monasteries were still being painted in the same manner in the seventeenth as in the eleventh century."[821]

Gombrich—who starts with ancient Greece, in contrast to Clark who starts with the "Dark Ages"—ignores the contributions of Roman art, particularly the way in which Roman portraitures raised to a higher level the portrayal of the "real" personality of individuals. But it can't be denied that this art, too, became stereotyped and conventional, including Rome's unique architectural forms of the arch, vault, and dome, although through the passage of time the potential of these forms were fully exploited in the construction of a wide range of engineering structures, theatres, aqueducts, bridges, circuses, and temples.

The term "Dark Ages" is restricted to the period from about AD 400 to AD 1000, rather than covering the full Middle Ages. The Germanic tribes who brought Rome down, such as the Goths, Vandals, and Franks, and later the Northmen or Vikings who raided and pillaged Christian villages and monasteries, included highly skilled craftsmen capable of finely-wrought metalwork and excellent wood carvings with intricately beautiful patterns. At the court of Charlemagne, the tradition of Roman architecture was resurrected in the Palatine Chapel built in Aachen (Aix-la-Chapelle) around AD 800. The notion of creating something different or original was still absent. Gombrich senses, however, an emerging disposition among medieval Christian artists "to express" what they "felt, beyond the Egyptian predilection to express ceremonial and stereotypical images, and the Greek-Roman predilection for a style that alternately emphasized realistic and

---

[819] Ibid, 72.
[820] Ibid, 97.
[821] Hauser, 128.

idealizing elements." Among the great works of art Kenneth Clark includes from the Dark Ages is the Cross of Lothair (about AD 1000), "one of the most moving objects that has come down to us from the distant past … an image of worldly imperium at its most civilized."[822]

The Romanesque period, visible in the tenth century, did not simply resurrect the Roman art of vaulting, large, heavy buildings, but through the eleventh and twelfth centuries was characterized, Clark believes, by "ceaseless experiment" and the realization that "it was not really necessary to make the whole roof so heavy." It was possible to fill the intervals between a number of firm arches with lighter materials, "arches or ribs crosswise between the pillars." This revolutionary idea in architecture can be traced as far back as the Norman cathedral of Durham. This period coincided, from the twelfth century on, with "an extraordinary outpouring of energy, an intensification of existence" across Europe, with the "triumph of the Church" playing a major role. The Chartres Cathedral was a "masterpiece of harmonious proportion." The main portal of the Chartres "is one of the most beautiful congregations of carved figures in the world. The longer you look at it, the more moving incidents, the more vivid details you discover." "One must remember," Clark continues, "that to medieval man geometry was a divine activity." Chartres, indeed, "was the centre of a school of philosophy devoted to Plato, and in particular to his mysterious book called the *Timaeus*, from which it was thought that the whole universe could be interpreted in the form of measurable harmony."[823]

For Gombrich, the Gothic style further revolutionized the Romanesque vaulting method through a device known as flying buttresses, "one of the most remarkable of human achievements." The Gothic style made "stone seem weightless: the weightless expression" of the "spirit" of the individual artist.

For Hauser, "the rise of Gothic style marks the most fundamental change in the history of modern art."

The interior of the Romanesque church is a self-contained stationary space that permits the eye of the spectator to rest and remain in perfect passivity. A Gothic church, on the contrary, seems to be in process of development,

---

[822] Clark, 19.
[823] Ibid, 52, 55.

as if it were rising up before our very eyes; it expresses a process, not a result.[824]

The Gothic sculptor, writes Gombrich, "approached his task in a new spirit," imbuing his statues with "an individual dignity" beyond portraying individuals as representatives of "sacred symbols" copied from religious texts. Gothic statues "look immensely energetic and vigorous." Gothic "knowledge of the human body . . . was infinitely greater than that of the painter of the twelfth century miniature."[825] Clark connects the Gothic world to a new world of chivalry, chastity, and courtly love.

> Of the two or three faculties that have been added to the European mind since the Civilisation of Greece and Rome, none seems to me stranger and more inexplicable than the sentiment of ideal or courtly love. It was entirely unknown in antiquity. Passion, yes; desire, yes of course; steady affection, yes. But this state of utter subjection to the will of an almost unapproachable woman; this belief that no sacrifice was too great, that a whole lifetime might be spent paying court to some exacting lady or suffering on her behalf, this would seem to the Romans or to the Vikings not only absurd but unbelievable; and yet for hundreds of years it passed unquestioned. It inspired a vast literature—from Chrétien de Troyes to Shelley.[826]

The "cult of ideal love" found expression in the "ravishing beauty and delicacy that one finds in the Madonnas of the thirteenth century," identified as "the Gothic Virgin and Child in ivory." Clark notes that Gothic artists also took pleasure in leaves, flowers, and, most of all, birds in manuscript illustrations: "artists drew them with such obsessive accuracy, and I think the reason is that they had become symbols of freedom. . . . Birds were cheerful, hopeful, impudent, and mobile." Clark thinks that before Giotto (1266–1337):

> Italian painting was really only a less polished form of Byzantine painting. It was flat, flowing linear style based on traditional concepts which had changed very little for five hundred years. For Giotto to break away from

---

[824] Hauser, Vol. I, 175, 220.
[825] Gombrich, 137, 139.
[826] Clark, 64.

it and evolve this solid, space-conscious style was one of the feats of inspired originality that have occurred only two or three times in the history
of art.[827]

Italian Renaissance

What was new about the Italian Renaissance? According to Clark, in the perspective painting initiated by Brunelleschi, and improved upon by Ghiberti and
Donatello, in "the belief that one could represent a man in a real setting and calculate his position and arrange figures in a demonstrably harmonious order," we
see "expressed symbolically a new idea about man's place in the scheme of things
and man's control over his own destiny." "The invention of the individual," Clark
believes, "was the source of the Renaissance's creativity." In medieval art, "people
were presented to the eye as figures that symbolized their status," but in Renaissance portraits, the personalities of individuals are revealed with details of their
daily lives. Around 1500–1510, Giorgione, "the passionate lover of physical
beauty," painted a picture entitled *Col tempo* (with time), using extreme realism
to portray an old woman who "must have once been a beauty," her face ravaged
by time.[828] Hauser makes an important observation about the "individualism" of
the Renaissance: while "strong personalities already existed in the Middle Ages,
yet to think and act individually is one thing and to be conscious of one's individuality, to affirm and deliberately to intensify it, is another."[829]

There is no space to go over what these authors say about the originality of
particular painters, about Masaccio (1401–1428) for example, who "brought
about a complete revolution in painting," or about the "entirely new" painter Jan
van Eyck (1390–1441), or about how the equestrian statue Andrea del Verrocchio
made in 1488 of the condottiere Bartolomeo Colleoni was not really a portrait of
Colleoni, but of the idea of a strong and ruthless military commander "bursting
with titanic power and energy," or about Raphael's "perfect and harmonious composition of freely moving figures," or how Correggio (1489–1534) "exploited the
discovery that colour and light can be used to balance forms and to direct our eyes
along certain lines."

We have to say something about Leonardo, of course; Clark believes that he,

---

[827] Ibid, 80.
[828] Ibid, 96–99.
[829] Hauser, Vol. 2, 62.

belongs to no epoch, he fits into no category, and the more you know about him, the more mysterious he becomes . . . he was the most relentlessly curious man in history. . . . Reading the thousands of words in Leonardo's note-books, one is absolutely worn out by this energy.[830]

Meanwhile, for Gombrich, what stands out about *Mona Lisa*,

is the amazing degree to which Lisa looks alive. She really seems to look at us and to have a mind of her own. Like a living being, she seems to change before our eyes and to look a little different every time we come back to her. . . . Sometimes she seems to mock us, and then again, we seem to catch something like sadness in her smile. All this sounds rather mysterious, and so it is; that is the effect of every great work of art.[831]

One thing is certain: Leonardo da Vinci's remark about the indomitable desire of the "wretched pupil" to "surpass his master," was a singularly European attitude, completely absent in China, where the aim was to imitate and reproduce the perfection already believed to have been attained in the past.

Michelangelo is another painter immensely admired by Gombrich. Before Michelangelo, Gombrich believes, no one,

had even come near expressing the greatness of the mystery of creation with such simplicity and force. . . . It is one of the greatest miracles in art how Michelangelo has contrived thus to make the touch of the Divine hand the centre and focus of the picture, and how he has made us see the idea of omnipotence by the ease and power of this gesture of creation.[832]

In line with our emphasis on the self-conscious inner feelings of Europeans, Clark, for his part, sees "the emergence of Michelangelo as one of the great events in the history of western man" for having extended in his art the "powers of mind and spirit to the utmost."[833] It is impossible indeed to extend the powers of the spirit to the utmost unless the artist has achieved a high degree of individuality and aesthetic independence (though at this point in time, societies remained very

---

[830] Clark, 135.
[831] Gombrich, 218–19.
[832] Ibid, 424–27.
[833] Clark, 85.

traditional by current standards, and artists had to follow very strict artistic conventions before they could develop and affirm their creativity). Hauser also thinks
that Michelangelo "rises to absolutely unprecedented heights," but goes further in
seeing him as the first "modern, lonely, demonically impelled artist." How far can
an artist go in relying on his inner sense of artistic genius beyond anything conceived before? Was Michelangelo really "the first to be completely possessed by
his idea and for whom nothing exists but his idea"? Hauser nevertheless recognizes that Michelangelo still felt "a deep sense of responsibility towards . . . his own
artistic genius;" and, one might add, towards the Christian collective outlook still
prevailing in his age.[834]

Clark devotes considerable attention to Albrecht Dürer (1471–1528) a "very
strange character . . . inordinately vain." "No man has ever described natural objects, flowers and grasses and animals, more minutely; and yet, to my mind, something is missing—the inner life." Clark adds, however, that Dürer was "intensively
self-conscious":

> But if Dürer did not try to peer so deeply into the inner life of nature, as
> Leonardo did, nor feel its appalling independence, he was deeply engaged
> by the mystery of the human psyche. His obsession with his own person-
> ality was part of a passionate interest in psychology in general, and this led
> him to produce one of the great prophetic documents of western man, the
> engraving he entitled Melancholia. . . . The figure is humanity at its most
> evolved with wings to carry her upwards . . . holds in her hands the com-
> passes, symbols of measurement by which science will conquer the world.
> Around her are all the emblems of constructive action: a saw, a plane, pin-
> cers, scales, a hammer, a melting pot, and two elements in solid geometry,
> a polyhedron and sphere. Yet all these aids to construction are discarded
> and she sits there brooding on the futility of human effort. Her obsessive
> stare reflects some deep psychic disturbance.[835]

This psychological profile could only be possible in regards to a Western artist.

---

[834] Hauser, Vol. 2, 60.
[835] Clark, 151–55.

Catholic Baroque and Mannerism

Clark sees the Baroque as partly an expression of the Catholic revival of the sixteenth century, the counter-Reformation movement that, in the realm of art, "gave ordinary people a means of satisfying, through ritual images and symbols, their deepest impulses, so that their minds were at peace." He writes that "late Baroque artists delighted in emotive close-ups with open lips and glistening tears." Bernini's The *Ecstasy of St. Teresa* "is one of the most deeply moving works in European art. Bernini's gift of sympathetic imagination . . . is used to convey the rarest and most precious of all emotional states, that of religious ecstasy."[836] Similarly, Gombrich judges that Bernini achieved "an intensity of facial expression which until then was never attempted in art."[837]

There are so many great painters—Holbein, Tintoretto, Titian, Bosch, Grüne-wald, Velázquez, and Rubens—and countless works of art one could spend count-less hours thinking about. Hauser groups "late Baroque" artists under the label "Mannerism," which retained the "passionately expressionistic aims of baroque," while showing "bodies struggling to give expression to the mind . . . turning and twisting, bending and writhing under the pressure of the mind." Within Manner-ism, he sees "two opposed currents—the mystical spiritualism of El Greco and the pantheistic naturalism of Brueghel."[838] Gombrich says that Caravaggio (1571–1610), whom Clark views as "the greatest Italian painter of the period,"

was of a wild and irascible temper, quick to take offence. . . . He had no liking for classical models, nor any respect for 'ideal beauty.' He wanted to do away with convention and to think about art afresh. . . . Consider his painting of St. Thomas: the three apostles staring at Jesus, one of them pok-ing with his finger into the wound in His side, look unconventional enough. One can imagine that such a painting struck devout people as be-ing irreverent and even outrageous. They were accustomed to seeing the apostles as dignified figures draped in beautiful folds—here they looked like common labourers, with weathered faces and wrinkled brows. But,

---

[836] Ibid, 191.
[837] Gombrich, 328.
[838] Hauser, Vol. 2, 92.

Caravaggio would have answered, they were old labourers, common people.[839]

Dutch "Bourgeois" Painting

The seventeenth century, according to Clark, "saw a revolutionary change in thought," most visibly in the Netherlands, "that replaced Divine Authority by experience, experiment and observation."[840] "Amsterdam was the first centre of bourgeois capitalism," with the "first visual evidence of bourgeois democracy." Unlike the art produced in the past, which was feudal, aristocratic, and at the service of a Church that was rich and powerful, the "numerous group-portraits of early seventeenth-century Holland" are of individuals "who are prepared to join in a corporate effort for the public good" of their cities. While excessive capitalist wealth can produce a "defensive smugness and sentimentality" in art, it generated for some time in Holland a society where leading citizens came together to take "corporate responsibility." They could "afford to do so" because they had "leisure," because they had "money in the bank."

Clark includes Rembrandt among "the supremely great figures in history—Dante, Michelangelo, Shakespeare, Newton, Goethe." Among the seven paintings he shows of Rembrandt is *Bathsheba at her Bath* (1654). He judges that "the psychological truth in Rembrandt's paintings goes beyond that of any other artist who has ever lived." In his painting of the Biblical character Bathsheba, he renders her "thoughts and feelings as she ponders on David's letter . . . with a subtlety and a human sympathy which a great novelist could scarcely achieve in many pages."[841] Gombrich also views Rembrandt (1606–69) as "one of the greatest painters who ever lived," writing:

> Creations such as Mona Lisa . . . are convincing and impressive, but we feel that they can only represent one side of a complex human being. Not even Mona Lisa can always have smiled. But in Rembrandt's portraits we feel face to face with real human beings with all their tragic failings and all their sufferings.[842]

---

[839] Gombrich, 290–2.
[840] Clark, 194.
[841] Gombrich, 205.
[842] Ibid, 313, 315.

Included among other great Dutch painters are Frans Hals; Paulus Potter, who painted animals within landscapes with "uncanny realism"; Jacob van Ruisdael, "a master in the painting of dark and sombre clouds, of evening light when the shadows grow, of ruined castles and rushing brooks"; and Vermeer, who painted *The Milkmaid*, "one of the greatest masterpieces of all time . . . something of a miracle."[843]

Rococo, Naturalism, Romanticism, Realism, Impressionism

Rococo "represented a real gain in sensibility . . . and captured new and more delicate shades of feeling," "an art of elegance rather than greatness," writes Clark. For Gombrich, it reflected "the taste of the French aristocracy of the early eighteenth century. . . . The fashion for dainty colours and delicate decoration . . . which expressed itself in gay frivolity." The paintings of Watteau, a sick man who died of consumption at the age of thirty-seven, are seen as the best expression of this new style, with his "visions of a life divorced from hardship . . . a dream life of gay picnics in fairy parks where it never rains, of musical parties where all ladies are beautiful and all lovers graceful in which all are dressed in sparkling silk without looking showy," in the words of Gombrich.[844]

With Naturalism, the painter "lost all consciousness of an independent self" by immersing himself into the totality of nature to gain "thereby a more intense consciousness of being," writes Clark as he examines Rousseau, the poets Coleridge and Wordsworth, and the painters Turner and Constable.[845] He admires Turner above everyone else:

He was a genius of the first order—far the greatest painter that England has ever produced. . . . No one has ever known more about natural appearances, and he was able to fit into his encyclopedic knowledge memories of the most fleeting effects of light—sunrises, passing storms, dissolving mists, none of which had ever been seen on canvas before. . . . [Turner's] new approach to painting . . . consisted of transforming everything into pure colour, light rendered as colour, feelings about life rendered as colour.

---

[843] Ibid, 324.
[844] Ibid, 341.
[845] Clark, 272, 291.

It's quite difficult for us to realise what a revolutionary procedure this was. One must remember that for centuries objects were thought to be real because they were solid. You proved their reality by touching or tapping them. . . . And all respectable art aimed at defining this solidity. . . . Turner declared the independence of colour and thereby added a new faculty to the human mind. [846]

To sustain their originality, and find new ways of conveying our perception of reality, and surpass Turner, the "three great lovers of nature" of the late nineteenth century, Monet, Cézanne, and van Gogh, "had to make a more radical transformation," giving way to a new ism: Impressionism. "An impression of what?"—asks Clark. "Of light." However, for Clark, Monet was the "original unswerving Impressionist," with his view that all a painting can do is give an impression of light. In Monet's words: "light is the principal person in the picture."

Gombrich is fascinated by Impressionism. He believes it was Manet (with an "a") and his followers who

brought about a revolution in the rendering of colours which is almost comparable with the revolution in the representation of forms brought about by the Greeks. They discovered that, if we look at nature in the open, we do not see individual objects each with its own colour but rather a bright medley of tones which blend in our eye or really in our mind. [847]

A novelty about Monet (with an "o") that Gombrich brings up is the "idea that all painting of nature must actually be finished 'on the spot'" which "demanded a change of habits and a disregard of comfort."

"Nature" or "the motif" changes from minute to minute as a cloud passes over the sun or the wind breaks the reflection in the water. The painter who hopes to catch a characteristic aspect has no leisure to mix and match his colours. . . . He must fix them straight on to his canvas in rapid strokes, caring less for detail than for the general effect of the whole. [848]

---

[846] Ibid, 284–5.
[847] Gombrich, 388.
[848] Ibid, 392.

For Hauser, perspective painting reaches its culmination in Impressionism, in "the reproduction of the subjective act instead of the objective substratum of seeing." "Everything stable and coherent is dissolved . . . and assumes the character of the unfinished and fragmentary." Impressionism was indeed an "urban art," a reaction to "external impressions with the overstrained nerves of modern technical man . . . it describes the always ephemeral impressions of city life . . . it implies an enormous expansion of sensual perception."[849]

Renoir's *A Dance at the Moulin de la Galette*, 1876, shows an open-air dance, which appears "sketchy" and unfinished, but the intention, according to Gombrich, was "to conjure up the gay medley of bright colours and to study the effect of sunlight on the whirling throng." The figures remain the focus, however—how the "forms are increasingly dissolved in sunlight and air." "We realize without difficulty that the apparent sketchiness has nothing whatever to do with carelessness but is the outcome of great artistic wisdom."[850]

Clark seems to associate Goya with a new Romantic "pessimism" that emerged in the early 1800s, showing Goya's famous painting of a firing squad called *The Third of May 1808*, and pointing to the poet Byron as the main spokesman of this new feeling, which he contrasts to the romantic naturalism or sentimentalism of Rousseau and his "belief in the beauty and innocence of nature," and Wordsworth's "daisies and daffodils," found in such painters as Constable. Romantic pessimism eulogized the "great forces of nature," the roaring of lions, cataracts, and colossal storms—with the sublime. "Consciousness of the sublime was a faculty that the Romantic movement added to the European imagination."[851]

Hauser, from a perspective that includes the study of literature, thinks that Romanticism "represented one of the most decisive turning points in the history of the European mind." With Romanticism "all individual expression is unique, irreplaceable and bears its own laws and standards within itself." The "intellectual atmosphere created by the [French] Revolution" nurtured an image of the artist as "the lonely human being . . . who feels himself to be different, either tragically or blessedly different, from his fellows," and the idea that art is "an activity of self-expression creating its own standards."[852]

Were the Romantics, then, responsible for starting a dynamic that would eventually undermine (in the twentieth century) the standards of art, with their

---

[849] Hauser, Vol. 4, 158.
[850] Gombrich, 394–5.
[851] Clark, 307.
[852] Hauser, Vol. 3, 144.

excessive subjectivism and preoccupation with their own feelings, with "every-thing dark and ambiguous, chaotic and ecstatic"? Not for Hauser, who ascribes the superiority of Western art over every other artistic tradition to the possibility of "an autonomous art, created from purely aesthetic motives," unlike the anony-mous artists of the non-Western world, who "in no way" were able to express "their own personalities."[853] But how far could Western artists go relentlessly pushing, along with their surrounding modernizing societies, for the deconstruc-tion of every external criterion, conventional custom, and moral and religious standard, including the universally agreed assumption hitherto prevailing that artists must produce "beautiful" works, before they would come to identify art with the deliberate destruction of every standard of beauty?

It can't be denied that the age of romanticism was driven by very high aesthetic standards. It was one of the most creative movements in Western history, com-bining the seemingly contradictory motivations of losing oneself in the unknown, the mysterious natural forces that overwhelm the confidence of the rational self, which Clark also saw in Naturalism, and an individual artist who feels, in the words of Hauser, that sincerity and creativity only come through the creation of one's standards "against the very principle of tradition, authority, and rule."[854] Of great art there still was. Delacroix is the "pessimistic" painter Clark admires most. Delacroix "had the utmost contempt for the age in which he lived, for its crass materialism and complacent belief in progress; and his art is almost entirely an attempt to escape from it."[855] "The abyss did not horrify Delacroix: on the con-trary, he gloried in it." To escape from European civilization, he went to Morocco; and despite "many sordid and grotesque incidents in his life there," he made us believe in the "nobility, dignity, and timelessness" of life in Morocco, with his painting, *Women of Algiers in their Apartment.*

After Delacroix, the one artist Clark holds in the highest esteem is the sculptor Rodin, "the last great Romantic artist," with "abundant animal spirits, creator of the greatest piece of sculpture since Michelangelo." Before the Romantic pessi-mists, he mentions the French painter Jacques-Louis David, as an artist already living, in the midst of the Revolutionary Reign of Terror, at a time that would "darken the optimism of the early Romantics." He shows his famous painting, *La Mort de Marat*, 1793. Marat was one of the leaders of the Montagnards, a radical

---

[853] Hauser, Vol. I, 26.
[854] Hauser, Vol. 3, 142.
[855] Clark, 313.

faction during the Reign of Terror. "Few propaganda pictures made such an impact as a work of art." What he says about David's *Napoleon Crossing the Alps* reveals much about what Clark really thinks about "Civilisation":

> With the appearance of General Bonaparte, the liberated energies of the revolution take a new direction—the insatiable urge to conquer and explore. But what has this to do with Civilisation? War and imperialism, so long the most admired of human activities, have fallen into disrepute, and I am enough a child of my time to hate them both. But I recognize that, together with much that is destructive, they are symptoms of a life-giving force.[856]

Ruskin's sentence—"No great art ever yet rose on earth but among a nation of soldiers"—strikes Clark as "historically irrefutable." Yet he knows there were still many superb and original painters, testimony to the persistently continuous creativity of Europeans: Renoir, Cézanne, van Gogh, Seurat, Courbet, Millet. However, while for Clark artistic greatness continued through the ever more urbane nineteenth century, he observes that the art of this century as a whole can be written "in terms of tunnels, bridges, and other feats of engineering." A new age of machines had arrived, dedicated to the "glory of mammon," money and gain, to which was eventually added a humanitarian feeling, as industrialization brought increasing affluence. Humanitarianism was "one of the greatest civilizing achievements of the nineteenth century." This feeling that "kindness matters most in human conduct" was unprecedented in history.[857] Tragedy and lofty subjects for painting were gone. The post-WWII decades would generate a pleasant atmosphere of "well fed" people along with many public schools and universities engendering a "well read" public, but with the concomitant result of producing, to put it politely, "a little flattening at the top." That is, a generation lacking in glorious subjects, too soft and emasculated for great art.

Gombrich, who takes his survey up to his own time, the first half of the twentieth century, starts to see a decline in that period, though he sees major cultural shifts before eventually leading to a decline in artistic greatness. The period of the "Great Revolution in France" of 1789 "put an end to so many assumptions that had been taken for granted" for centuries, particularly a decisive break with lofty,

---

[856] Ibid, 300.
[857] Ibid, 329.

aristocratic, sublime subjects, leading to a focus on ordinary or everyday subjects. To be sure, in the past, painters like Chardin (1699–1779) had started "to look at the life of the ordinary men and women of their time,"[858] and in the sixteenth century we already had the paintings of Brueghel depicting scenes from daily life, and in some paintings we have shown above. At the same time, while some painters like Joshua Reynolds (1723–92) continued to exhort artists "to strive after lofty and dignified subjects," with "grand and impressive" art, Goya examined the faces of the aristocracy "with a pitiless and searching eye, and revealed all their vanity and ugliness, their greed and emptiness."[859] Great paintings continued, but the "foundations on which art had rested throughout its existence" were being undermined at an accelerated speed as the Industrial Revolution was added to the French revolutionary destruction of monarchical rule and the authority of the Catholic Church by a new middle class "which often lacked tradition" and viewed art as a "perfect means of expressing individuality against all the rules and conventions."

The history of Western art, Gombrich recognizes, has always been characterized by individual expression and the creation of new possibilities for art. The difference now, he seems to be saying, was that the old ideals of beauty and striving for perfection were being rapidly undermined, leaving the individual on his own, without standards other than the standard of doing something new, breaking with the old. The purpose of art was merely to express one's personality, leading to a state of "permanent revolution" as artists contested with each other over who was the most "creative."

It is in the twentieth century, however, that Gombrich sees artists who "proposed to make a clear sweep of all conventions . . . which ultimately led them to a rejection of the whole Western tradition."[860] We saw his admiration for impressionists, who "did not differ in their aims from the traditions of art that had developed since the discovery of nature in the Renaissance. . . . Their quarrel with the conservative masters was not so much over the aim as over the means of achieving it." He judges Cézanne (1839–1906), for example, as one of the greatest of this period: "he was constantly engaged in a passionate struggle to achieve in his painting that ideal of artistic perfection after which he strove."[861] The ancient Greek ideal of striving for the highest in beauty remained during this late age in

---

[858] Gombrich, 353.
[859] Ibid, 365.
[860] Gombrich, 427.
[861] Ibid, 407–08.

Western civilization; but were the fleeting qualities of light, color, and atmosphere in Impressionist art a prelude to the evanescence of aesthetic standards?

Why the Decline of Western Art?

It is in the "experimental art" of the twentieth century—in the quick succession or simultaneous movements of Surrealism, Expressionism, Dadaism, Cubism, and Abstract Art—that Gombrich sees a complete break with the Western tradition. The sole task of the artist was now to create "something new." Many relied on non-Western sources for inspiration, such as African primitivism, Zen Buddhism, Chinese calligraphy, or "Egyptian principles." Abstract and cubist painters wanted "to become as little children" in order to revitalize a spontaneity threatened by mechanization, to reproduce "the memory of childish scrawls." The disregard for harmony and beauty was justified on the grounds of "honesty" for the truth.

There was still great talent, as Gombrich recognizes. One should mention Edward Munch, Picasso, Matisse, and Dali. Gombrich mentions Kokoschka's *Children Playing*, 1909, as a painting that "looked at children with a deep sympathy and compassion. He has caught their witfulness and dreaminess, the awkwardness of their movements and the disharmonies of their growing bodies."[862] But he struggles to find real greatness, as he moves swiftly from one movement to the next, without persuading us that Nicolas de Stael's painting, *Plage à Agrigente* consists of "simple yet subtle brush strokes [which] often give us a sense of light and distance without making us forget the quality of the paint."[863]

Even Hauser (cheerful as he remains through to the end of the nineteenth century, admiring "the person of the artist" still creating authentically original paintings), ends his four-volume work lamenting "the deliberate deformation of natural objects" in "Cubism, constructivism, futurism, expressionism, dadaism and surrealism."[864] Impressionism "prepares the ground for this development insofar as it does not aspire to an integrating description of reality," but these new art forms are nevertheless "fundamentally" different, "ugly art" without the "euphony, the fascinating forms, tones and colours of impressionism."[865] He does not

---

[862] Ibid, 431–2.
[863] Ibid, 460.
[864] Hauser, Vol. 4, 217.
[865] Ibid, 218.

attribute this to the breakdown of social standards of beauty and excessive individualism, but rather to "the deliberate destruction of the unity of the personality."
He sees in Picasso a "complete break with individualism and subjectivism, the absolute denial of art as the expression of an unmistakable personality."[866]

Hauser opines that this "modern art" mirrors "the end of the bourgeois
epoch," the "end of the responsibility that is connected with all rationalism and
individualism."[867] In it we see a "plunging into the unconscious, into the pre-rational and the chaotic," with Surrealism and Dadaism believing that "a new truth
and a new art will arise from chaos, from the unconscious and the irrational, from
dreams and the uncontrolled regions of the mind." In the literary works of Stendhal, Balzac, Flaubert, George Eliot, Tolstoy or Dostoevsky, about which Hauser
writes in great admiration, there was a clear demarcation "between the subject and
object, the self and the non-self"; but in the works of Joyce, Proust, Kafka, and
Gide, about which Hauser barely writes, we have "the kaleidoscopic picture of a
disintegrated world," "the disparagement of man ... in which everything is significant or of equal significance," "the abandonment of the plot, the elimination
of the hero, the relinquishing of psychology."[868]

He closes his book with the rather commonplace view that the only way out of
this decomposition is for the masses to gain a "genuine appreciation of art through
education," training their "capacity for aesthetic judgment" away from the "mo-
nopolizing of art by a small minority."[869] Yet Hauser, the Marxist, writing in the
early 1950s, admits that "film is the only art in which Soviet Russia has important
achievements." It is hard to believe that he would have retained this view after
seeing our contemporary art, despite the explosion in mass education and democratic opportunities for everyone to become an artist.

Western art was bound to decline partly for the reasons Clark and Gombrich
offer. "Without tradition," as H. W. Janson asserted, the "uniqueness, novelty, and
freshness" of Western art would have been impossible. Traditions still sustained
the creativity of the Romantic and Impressionistic eras, but increasingly less at an
accelerating rate through the twentieth century. Kant did not intend to argue in
favor of "art for art's sake," but a future generation of artists, who felt increasingly
adrift without the once pervading traditional Christian culture and patronage of
arts by a "divine" monarchy, found Kant's idea that we should set art free from

---

[866] Ibid, 221–22.
[867] Ibid, 215.
[868] Ibid, 225.
[869] Ibid, 246.

any external norm very appealing and timely. The slogan "art for art's sake" from the latter half of the nineteenth century drew from the Kantian call for the autonomy of aesthetic judgement from other forms of judgement. Art for art's sake says that true art should be independent of all social values, whether moral, religious, utilitarian, or political. Art should be totally "inner-directed" or "self-motivated" by the artist; that is, by the judgment of the artistic genius. As Théophile Gautier famously (though perhaps not the first to do so) wrote: "Art for art's sake means for its adepts the pursuit of pure beauty—without any other preoccupation." The idea of a genius who gives free range to the imagination is congenial with the Enlightenment concept of the individual as a self-legislating being freed from all constraints other than his own expressiveness.

Hauser's view that post-Impressionist art was a revolt against "bourgeois individualism" is unpersuasive. It was, rather, a culmination of the individualism that is inherent to liberalism, its inbuilt progressive drive for the complete "emancipation" of individuals from all "external constraints."[870] The artistic isms of surrealism, dadaism, expressionism, and constructivism, for all their rejection of "bourgeois rationalism" and industrial "de-humanization," were agreeably suited to the bourgeois idea that individuals should be free to decide their own lifestyle, and that a liberal state should refrain from favoring any standard or outlook other than the right of individuals to choose. They reflected the newly emerging asphalt world of capitalism—and in this respect, these isms can be said to be creative in mirroring a new reality completely out of tune with the art of the past. This was a destructive creativity without standards. We will return to this crucial subject in our final chapter in our attempt to understand, beyond the arts, why Western liberal civilization culminated in the current multicultural zeitgeist.

---

[870] Dugin, 2012.

IX

The Rise of the Modern Self, Origins of the Novel, and the Rise and Fall of Children's Literature

I have resolved on an enterprise which has no precedent, and which, once complete, will have no imitator. My purpose is to display to my kind a portrait in every way true to nature, and the man I shall portray will be myself.

– Rousseau, *Confessions*

Is the Novel a Western Invention?

The rise of the modern self is associated with a "new sensibility" or an "affective revolution" detected primarily in the rise of a new literary genre, the novel, in the 1700s. These novels emphasized personal experience and feeling, a spirit of non-conformity towards rigid and "insincere" conventions, and a fascination with the "inner depths" of the affective self. Some believe that sentimental novels were part of a broader cultural movement known as Romanticism, which included such writings as Rousseau's *Julie ou la Nouvelle Héloïse* (1761), Goethe's *The Sorrows of Young Werther* (1774), the poetry of Coleridge, Wordsworth, and Hölderlin, as well as English philosophers who developed the theory of moral sentiments: Francis Hutcheson, Adam Smith, Lord Shaftesbury, and others. These philosophers identified morality with actions done by the right affections based on one's inner sense of right and wrong. They argued that morality should not be about following

449

socially prescribed norms, but about being true to oneself, to one's nature, or the voice of nature within. Rousseau articulated this idea in a very idealistic way with his claim that human beings were naturally authentic and inherently good, and that socialization was responsible for instilling artificial conventions. The term "expressive individuation" is also used to describe this movement, a post-1750 phenomenon associated with the rise of a generalized public culture emphasizing what is original and different in each person, the importance of allowing one's "inner voice" to speak out—in literature, painting, music, and poetry. It was a time when each artist sought to express his own individuated nature; novelists sought to produce genuine characters who would reveal their true feelings, not the type of characters one tended to see in earlier novels, with stereotyped personalities, "one of a genus," made up of what a person had in common with others.

This is the overall idea one might glean from reading Charles Taylor's 1989 *Sources of the Self: The Making of the Modern Identity*, Michael Mascuch's 1997 *Origins of the Individualist Self: Autobiography and Self-Identity in England, 1591–1791*, and Dror Wahrman's 2006 *The Making of the Modern Self: Identity and Culture in Eighteenth Century England*. What was witnessed with the advent of the novel was the portrayal of characters with more complex, differentiated personalities, with highly introspective selves. But there is something incomplete and even misleading about this scholarship in its identification of this "new self" using the language of "man" and "nature." Those who were aware of this "new sensibility," in the 1700s, did write as if they were detecting the expression of a natural disposition in humans as such, a trait that was innate or intrinsic to the essence of man, but which had not been expressed before. Europeans have been invariably inclined to project their experiences onto humanity at large. What is less understandable is that this same mistake has been continued by current academics, even though they know, in Taylor's words, that the authentic or expressive self is a "recent idea in human history" that occurred only in the West. They explain this movement as if it entailed the discovery of the existence of an inner self naturally present in humans. Another weakness in the current scholarship is the absence of any attempt to contrast this new Western self with the rather undeveloped sense of identity we find in the modern non-Western world. As far as I know, no one has directly written about this: whether there was a profusion of differentiated personalities, complex motivations, and richer psychologies in the modern West in ways unparalleled before and outside the West.

It is very difficult for Europeans to fathom the notion that they have an inward awareness, a sense of personhood lacking elsewhere—both because they want to be seen to be nice, caring beings who love all humans, and because most theories in the social sciences today tend to downplay the role of consciousness or individual awareness. Colin Morris, in a book we examined at the end of Chapter II, *The Discovery of the Individual 1020–1200*, insightfully states that having "an inner being" is very "unusual." Westerners take it as a "matter of common sense that we stand apart from the natural order in which we are set . . . and that we have our own distinct personality." They assume that having an inner self "is a common element in human psychology" and that "every adult human being is aware of a distinction between himself and the people and things around him."[871] They don't know that the West is "exceptional among the civilizations of the world." Now, Morris thinks that this "inner self" was already visible in the Middle Ages. But by the 1700s, this inner self had expanded in its depths and variety of expressions, independently from Christian views, particularly among the characters created by novelists, continually self-examining their thoughts, feelings, moods, and conflicting motivations.

It should be abundantly clear by now that the argument of this book is not that human motivation, intentionality, and introspection remain unexamined subjects. We have referenced many works dealing with these topics. The argument is against the prevailing assumption that these attributes belong to humans as humans, or that these attributes emerged at one point in time in the West, rather than over the course of many centuries. There is a school called "methodological individualism" which says that social phenomena must be explained in terms of the intentional states that motivate individual actors, rather than in terms of class or group dynamics. But this methodology is applied to humans across the planet in terms of their self-interests or "rational choices."[872] It has nothing to do with "inner depths" and the differentiation of personalities. The most influential schools of history in the West over the twentieth century and after (to be examined in Chapter X) tend to downplay the very idea that individuals play a role in history and that humans have a free will. The impact of structuralists in this respect can't be underestimated—from Marx to Freud, from Ferdinand Saussure to Roman Jacobson, from Levi-Strauss to Michel Foucault, there has been a persistent devaluation of the importance of individuals in history.[873] Structuralists deny the existence of a "real subject" with a conscious ego. The human subject is "de-centered,"

---

[871] Morris, 1987, 1.
[872] Udehn, 2014.
[873] DeGeorge and DeGeorge, 1972.

constituted by structures and forces beyond his control, unconscious motivations, linguistic structures, capitalist "laws of motion." What requires understanding are the structures that have shaped history and that continue to be in charge of human motivations and behaviors. As Foucault put it: "It's not the assertion of identity that's important; it's the assertion of non-identity."[874]

But this line of thinking, fruitful as it is in conveying the reality that most humans accept the conventions of their time, and are always under the "overdetermination" of many structures, intersecting movements and events, is characterized by an internal contradiction. For if we have become aware of these structures, should we not conclude that our cognition has imbued them with consciousness and that these structures have lost their otherness? Was not the cognitive goal of structuralist knowledge to unveil/reveal the logics of these structures, the forces that have dominated history, in order thereby to free us from their blind control? It is true that some structuralists insisted that one can't step out of these structures, since each discursive interpretation carries its own structures. This is true in the degree to which humans can never be in control of the forces of nature as such, in complete charge of their identities, completely independent of structural realities, both in nature and society. There are nevertheless substantial differences in the degree to which cultures have understood the forces of nature and society, and, in this respect, minimized the "otherness" of these forces and structures, and thus their blind determination over humans. The insights of structuralists would have been impossible without the level of self-consciousness reached in the Western world. In cultures where the psyche is subsumed, barely explored, enveloped by nature and kin-based norms, from which it cannot step outside in a state of critical reflection, you can't have such self-conscious studies as semiotics, for example, which entail a clear-headed attempt to explain the relationship between a sign, an object, and a meaning. Structuralists, after all, are products of a highly self-conscious Western world responsible for the development of all the major fields of knowledge about geological, biological, chemical, economic, and cultural structures.

This chapter welcomes Ian Watt's argument that Europeans invented the "new literary form" known as the novel in the 1700s in reflection of their increasingly "more various, more interesting and certainly more conscious" inner life, in the

---

[874] Cited in Wahrman, 2006, xi. Wahrman does not engage with structuralism of Foucault; in the next chapter I offer a synopsis of Foucault's historiography, and how, for all its apparent radicalism, was easily integrated into the liberal progressive establishment.

market-oriented, urbane, literate, and individualistic culture then spreading in Britain.[875] Watt's book, *The Rise of the Novel: Studies in Defoe, Richardson, and Fielding*, first published in 1957, is still considered "the best book ever written on the early English novel." Its thesis—that there were fundamental differences between the novel and the previous literary forms found, for example, in Chaucer, Spenser, Shakespeare, and Milton—has not gone unchallenged, however.[876] The biggest challenge has come from Steven Moore's two volume, 1800+ page book, *The Novel: An Alternative History*, which argues that novels have been around since ancient times across the world. Whether we accept Moore's claim that his "alternative history" is "not an exercise in multicultural revisionism, but simply an attempt to tell the complete story of the novel," his book undoubtedly suits the multicultural sensitivities of our times, notwithstanding its high scholarly qualities.[877] Before we look further into Moore's argument, let's get Watt's thesis clearly in our mind.

The best way to sum up Watt's thesis is to ask: what exactly was new about the novel, and what does it mean to say that this new form of literature contained characters with deeper and more complex interior selves? We encountered briefly in chapter two Peter Holbrook's claim that "Shakespeare's poetic personality is deeply wedded . . . to fundamentally modern values: freedom, individuality, self-realization, authenticity." How much more "authentic" and preoccupied with their "self-realization" were the characters of eighteenth-century novels? Watt's book was written before Holbrook's, but it draws, nevertheless, a clear difference between Renaissance literature, despite its "growing tendency for individual experience," and the novel. The plots in Shakespeare, Spencer, and Milton, Watt argues, were taken from mythology, history, or previous literature; they were acted out, not "by particular people in particular circumstances," but by "general

---

[875] Watt, 2001, 207.

[876] Some will disagree, believing that Michael McKeon's 1987 book, *The Origins of the English Novel, 1600–1740* is a superior theoretical work, a "more rigorously historical account of the novel's rise." I no longer have the stomach or patience, I must admit, for McKeon's excessively theoretical Marxist approach on the "dialectical constitution of the novel." Ian Watt wears his Marxism lightly, and undogmatically, without swamping his book with pretentious concepts from the latest leftist academics pursuing lucrative careers. As it is, other than McKeon's tracing of the beginnings of novelistic traits back to the 1600s in *Don Quixote* and *Pilgrim's Progress*, and seeking a more "dialectical" explanation," his book agrees with Watt that the English carved a new novelistic path with such novels as *Robinson Crusoe, Gulliver's Travels; Pamela, Shamela* and *Joseph Andrews*.

[877] Moore, 2010, 31.

human types" lacking particularized names. Underlying their use of traditional plots, which was the case among the writers of Greece and Rome, was the acceptance of "the general premise of their times that, since Nature is essentially complete and unchanging, its records, whether scriptural, legendary or historical, constitute a definitive repertoire of human experience."[878]

Watt makes the insightful observation that the characters of the novels were far more "individualised" than in the past, "set in a background of a particularised time and place," due to the accelerating modernization of the 1700s, the emergence of an urbane reading public, and to the way the identity of individuals was coming to be seen in terms of a temporal sequence entailing new personal experiences with individuals continually self-examining their beliefs, inclinations, and feelings, rather than exhibiting ready-made character typologies. He brings up John Locke's definition of personal identity "as an identity of consciousness through the duration of time," a perspective reflected in the way novelists constructed characters inseparable from the temporal dimension of their lives, with a striking "interest in the minute-by-minute and day-to-day temporal setting" of the characters and considerable attention paid to their inner mental states. This was lacking in Shakespeare's "ahistorical outlook," which "allows very little importance to time as a factor in human relationships."[879] The characters of novels are more authentic in their sincere and continual introspective interrogation of their feelings and motivations. It is not that in prior literature one does not find characters with their own peculiar psychologies and personalities, "as authentic as any in the eighteenth-century novel," but that in this earlier fiction, from Chaucer to Bunyan, passages with detailed descriptions of the everyday lives and mental states of characters are "relatively rare" and awkwardly situated within narratives that relied on "timeless stories to mirror the unchanging moral verities."[880]

---

[878] Watt, 14–15.

[879] Ibid, 23.

[880] Ibid, 33, 22. Trying to understand when something new emerges in a civilization undergoing continuous changes, while always under the influence of the past, precludes a simple either-or approach, but calls for a keen antenna to detect subtle variations. Were the characters in Roman literature stereotyped? Well, yes, by the standards of Shakespeare and certainly in comparison to the new literature of the 1700s. The comedy of Terence (186–159 BC), for example, has been criticized for providing plots that are "relatively stereotyped," using "stock characters of comedy" adapted from the comedy of the Hellenistic world. In her introduction to various plays by Terence, Betty Radice (1988), however, warns against this judgement, pointing out that Terence translated Greek comedy "into a different world" and presented characters "as individuals caught up in a complex plot which sets them at cross-purposes and has many comedic possibilities." "His chief original contribution was the double plot . . . the effect of plot on character, and

Steven Moore's mammoth book does not refute anything Watt says. He rarely, if at all, engages with Watt's argument other than asserting that a novel is "a book-length work of fiction," and that fiction has existed since ancient times.[881] This minimal definition of the novel allows him to side-step every argument Watt makes. Moore writes about romances, sagas, tales, pastorals, legends, and folk epics as if they were "novels in everything but name."[882] His book is an "attempt to provide a complete history of the novel"—albeit not of every fiction ever written, but of works that, in his view, have a high aesthetic quality. His choices are determined by such criteria as whether the fiction is "fresh and untraditional," "aesthetically pleasing," "unconventional," "original," characterized by "complexity," and whether they are "innovative," "avant-garde," or "experimental." Yes, he actually insists that "avant-garde, experimental novels," invariably associated with such names as Ezra Pound, T. S. Eliot, James Joyce, and Virginia Woolf, are not a peculiar twentieth-century development. But the notion Moore has in mind with "avant-garde literature" seems to be that of a university undergrad in tune with American pop culture. We are told that the Ancient Egyptian *Contendings of Horus and Seth* "reads like a Monty Python takeoff on Egyptian mythology"; or that in the *Acts of Paul*, "Paul sounds like George Costanza from Seinfeld"; or that the Byzantine *Kallimachos and Chrysorrhoe* strikes one "like a night at the Playboy Mansion."[883]

The criteria Watt uses to define "the novel" are completely ignored in favor of stories that include sleazy behavior or kinky sex. Moore relishes the 2,300-page novel, *The Golden Lotus*, written approximately in the 1590s by "someone who called himself the Scoffing Scholar" for its "hard core" sexual realism, its "epic fornications" and "drug-enhanced bouts." The Scoffing Scholar portrays "well-rounded, completely realized individuals," citing as an example his description of the character P'an Chin-lien:

Painting her brows and making up her eyes,
Applying powder and putting on rouge,
Combing her hair into a chignon,

---

the contrasted reactions of different types of character to the same situation." Still, having said this, Radice recognizes that before the modern era, the "style of acting was declamatory, with formalized gestures, costume was stereotyped, and actors were . . . typical characters."

[881] Moore, vii.

[882] Ibid, 34.

[883] Ibid, 1–36, 44–5, 118, 174.

> *Putting on airs,*
> *And making a spectacle of herself.* [884]

This is merely a third person description of a woman putting on makeup and "putting on airs," completely different from what Watt observes in the novel, the portrayal of the daily experiences of characters "composed of a ceaseless flow of thought, feeling and sensation . . . minute-by-minute content of consciousness, which constitutes what the individual's personality really is." [885]

As Watt says of Daniel Defoe's *Robinson Crusoe*, it reads like a "confessional autobiography and outdoes other literary forms in bringing us up close to the inward moral being of the individual, and it achieves this closeness to the inner life of the protagonist by using as a formal basis the autobiographical memoir." [886] *Robinson Crusoe* is basically an interior monologue by Crusoe externalizing his thoughts for the reader to witness his inner feelings and experiences. Crusoe is portrayed continually self-questioning or re-examining his decisions and actions, seeking confirmation from God about their rightfulness, detailing his daily activities, how he accomplished them, what he learned, how difficult they were, the comforts he attained—always using a first-person point of view. Defoe aimed to put the reader in the shoes of Crusoe, as if they had access to the interiority of his mind. Defoe's 1724 novel, *Roxana,* is almost entirely a psychological drama within the interior of Roxana's mind, a narrative about the turmoil inside her head as she chooses the glamorous but immoral life of a courtesan over the honorable but duller life of a married woman. [887]

Another Chinese novel Moore brings up is *The Three Kingdoms*, also known as *Romance of the Three Kingdoms*, by Lo Kuan-chung, which first appeared in print in 1522, often described as China's oldest novel. Moore identifies it as "the first major Chinese novel." It "might just be the greatest war novel ever written," he thinks. [888] But as Moore knows, the story in this "novel" is not original, but based on the historical *Chronicles of the Three Kingdoms* compiled by the historian

---

[884] Ibid, 640, 659.
[885] Watt, 191–2.
[886] Ibid, 75.
[887] The French prefer to see *La Princesse de Clèves*, authored by Madame de La Fayette in 1678, as the "first novel," or the prototype of the "modern novel," in its depth of psychological analysis and "internal dialogue" But I am inclined to agree with Watt that the characters in this story, and their depiction of passion and love, are less original, drawn from the author's experience of aristocratic society, with its stereotyped mannerisms and forms of verbal expression.
[888] Moore, 605.

Ch'en Shou in 297. In fact, as Robert E. Hegel says in his introduction to the novel, translated by C. H. Brewitt-Taylor, the narrative "shares subject matter with successive generations of plays popular among theater audiences since the middle of the thirteenth century. Likewise, the novel bears a close relation to an illustrated prose narrative that was printed in the 1320s."[889]

Moore eulogizes about how this novel has everything (it is very long, to be sure, over 1300 pages): "from elaborate field maneuvers to one commander chasing another around a tree with a sword, from brilliant strategies to improvised guerilla tactics, along with naval battles, espionage, betrayals, professional rivalries, propaganda and disinformation, diplomatic ploys, supply logistics, a wide a variety of weaponry, brutal executions, and public relations with civilians." But, as Moore then admits, there is barely any character development, and less so any psychological self-examination by the characters. The author, Lo Kuan-chung, is "a laconic writer, emulating the factual style of the historians he drew upon, he rarely comments on his characters' actions, letting their deeds and words speak for them."[890] There are no personalities, as in Shakespeare, and there are no internal monologues, as in Defoe. This is how Chinese novels would remain for the next centuries; Lo Kuan-chung, Moore has to acknowledge, "established the formal template for the classic Chinese novel that would be followed for the next 400 years."[891] Robert Hegel leaves the impression that the characters are indeed stereotypified, "Chang Fei is the model warrior." "Kuan Yu is the embodiment of courage and of faithful service to his lord."[892]

In the end, Moore agrees that, after 1600, the only "fresh and untraditional," "unconventional and original" fiction came from the West. The first volume of *The Novel: An Alternative History*, which is subtitled "Beginnings to 1600," covers in a very balanced way the literatures of the world (though Mesoamerica and sub-Saharan Africa get next to no treatment). However, the second volume, which covers the period from 1600 to 1800, is totally about Western literature. This dramatic change between the contents of volumes 1 and 2 happens surreptitiously, without Moore second-guessing his thesis. Reviews of Moore's two volumes completely ignore this lack of consistency from an author who promises to write a "complete history of the novel" but does not have a word to say about novels in

---

[889] Hegel, 2002, v.
[890] Moore, 607–08.
[891] Ibid, 609.
[892] Hegel, vi.

the non-Western world in the second, and longer, volume (over 1000 pages), which covers the period after 1600.

John Locke's Blank Slate and the Origins of Children's Literature

The study of the rise and fall of children's literature offers a great window into the making of the Western modern self—and its eventual decomposition. This section evaluates the major values reflected in the amazing rise of children's literature, primarily in England, and how this literature exhibited a high level of creativity in content and themes, in pace with continuous liberal changes in society, that would eventually erode all remaining traditions and the persisting hold of Christianity over the minds of the population, and thus create children with "blank slate" interiors, with progressive liberals seeking to fill up their minds, culminating in the domination of a truly "inclusive" multiracial literature.

There is an elective affinity—a relationship of reciprocal attraction and mutual reinforcement—between John Locke's argument that a child's mind initially resembles an "empty cabinet" or a "white paper void of all characters," which can be shaped by controlling the education impressed upon the child's mind, and the origins of a literature specifically written for children in the 1700s in England. John Locke's pedagogical book, *Some Thoughts Concerning Education*, first published in 1692, with its thesis that "children's minds" could be shaped "from without" by "those who have children or the charge of their education" became the moving spirit of the eighteenth century.[893] Samuel Pickering documents in his 1981 book, *John Locke and Children's Books in Eighteenth Century England*, the influence of Locke on the "form, theme, content, and diction" of early children's literature. Pickering does not, however, draw connections between Locke's blank slate thesis and the development of children's literature. Below we will outline the history of children's literature as a singularly Western phenomenon that calls for an appreciation of Locke's blank slate thesis. The focus will be on English and American books, where the influence of Lockean philosophy was greatest, though we should keep in mind that other European nations were originating children's literature around the same period.[894] Folk tales, superstitions, songs, and legends that taught and entertained children have been common throughout the world.

---

[893] Locke, 1996.
[894] Brown, 2008.

Before the early 1700s, however, there were no books written specifically for children.

Children's literature underwent momentous changes in content and theme in the course of time,[895] as the West found itself in a state of continuous modernization and cultural change, driven by new concepts of childhood: from purely instructional stories with practical advice in the 1600s, along with evangelical stories to keep the innate moral sinfulness of children contained, through to stories after 1700 offering both knowledge and recreation that encouraged children to be virtuous and kind to animals; from books in the early 1800s teaching middle-class children the values of thrift, hard work, and family uprightness, through to sentimental stories about the harsh lives of poor Victorian children, and stories encouraging the predilection of children for fantasy and imagination after the 1850s; from stories about heroes and the virtues of loyalty, pluck, and resourcefulness at the time of British imperial greatness, coupled with the rise of girls' stories to prepare them to be wives and mothers during late Victorian times, through to stories about the unchanging trials of adolescent sexuality after the Second World War, combined with science fiction and comic books, to a new agenda of political correctness in matters of sex and race from the 1990s onwards, which brings about a degradation in the quality of children's literature as it becomes a weapon aimed at indoctrinating children into accepting "diversity, equity, and inclusion."

Among conservatives and evolutionary psychologists who believe that humans are born with innate biological drives that explain their behaviors, motivations, and intellectual aptitudes, Locke's blank slate argument is dismissed today as a major error driving the Left's ideology that humans are malleable creatures who can be easily "reimagined" or "reconstructed" anyway one chooses. Everyone knows about the nature versus nurture debate; what they don't know is that the blank slate proponents, for all the "refutations" they have faced in the writings of such prominent scholars as E. O. Wilson and Steve Pinker, have taken complete command of children's books across all the schools, libraries, and publishing houses of the Western world.

They managed to do so because the West has been demolishing its "innate ideas" for centuries now, its kinship-based institutions and norms, and its customs, folkways, and Christian beliefs, while pushing the liberal idea that individuals are inherently rational beings who can decide for themselves their own values. The in-group psychology dominating all traditional societies, as we saw in chapter

---

[895] Hunt, 1995; Alderson, 1982.

seven, was fundamentally altered in Europe into increasingly individualistic habits of thinking and behaving, as Europeans started demolishing their kinship institutions from the Middle Ages onwards, by prohibiting cousin and polygynous
marriages, and promoting monogamous nuclear families. This "liberated" Europeans from their kin-based obligations and encouraged them to create voluntary
(civic) associations, chartered towns, guilds, universities, monasteries, and businesses based on contractual agreements. Kinship ceased to determine the innate
identities and norms of Europeans, their ascribed status and obligations, what values should be transmitted to children, what is sacred or profane. European institutions and associations came to be based on civic norms chosen by anonymous
individuals on their own initiative.

However, for a long time, through the medieval era, Christianity continued to
act as a major collective source guiding Europeans in their families, education,
and overall social life. But as modern Europeans began to talk about the "natural
rights" of individuals to choose their own values and happiness within an increasingly commercialized society, the traditional values of the Church started losing
their influence, particularly after the Enlightenment. This led to the expansion of
Europeans' blank slate interiors, and the rise of ideologies contesting over which
values should command the inner selves of individuals. The West is indeed unique
among civilizations in the origination of ideologies proposing a complete remaking of society: liberalism, socialism, communism, anarchism, feminism, and fascism. Non-Western societies are innately based on their millennia-old traditions.
The West became ideological during the French Revolution, as a new intelligent-
sia consciously set out to remake society anew. Even conservatives became ideologues when they realized they could not restore the old monarchical order and
the old aristocratic class, but had to accept the liberal principle of equality of civic
rights and modern industrial development if they were to preserve in a new form
some traditional values. As we will explain at length in Chapter XI, Western liberalism (which gradually came to include many sub-"isms" within itself, including
modern conservatism) eventually defeated the two major contenders for power,
fascism and communism, proclaiming the "end of history" in the 1990s.

In the England into which Locke was born—a relatively new liberal society
where parliamentary rule had displaced monarchical authority, and where the nation would increasingly come to be seen as a contractually-based covenant among
anonymous individuals with natural rights, rather than based on kinship in-group
loyalties—it made sense to reject innate ideas. The classical liberal disposition to
accept nothing as true unless it was validated by one's "impartial" rational

judgment amplified the West's intellectual creativity. Painters, musicians, sculptors, architects, and novelists were encouraged to rely on their individual aesthetic judgments in the pursuit of the highest forms of beauty and literary expressions.

It is often overlooked, however, that modern Europeans, until recently, notwithstanding their civic institutions, remained attached to their traditions and national heritage, creating nations based on a collective sense of history, memories, and ethnic identity.[896] Christian traditional values continued to play a major role in the parenting and education of children through to the twentieth century. Locke's liberal ideas were not calling for a world without any traditions and common heritage; his liberalism was sensibly aimed at encouraging the initiative, curiosity, and knowledge of children in a world where formal schools for children were just beginning, and most instruction was religiously oriented and paternalistic. Locke argued, with reason, that education should not be despotic and coercive, but should account for children's individual characteristics, encouraging their interest in knowledge while disciplining their habits without indulging their subjective whims.

Locke's Impact in the 1700s

There were books for children before Locke:[897] In 1587 *The Petit Schole* taught the rudiments of English spelling; The 1570 *A Method, or Comfortable Beginning for all Unlearned* was about how to teach reading; and, before these two, there was *Caxton's Book of Curtesye* in 1477 about piety, neatness, and honoring one's parents. Children enjoyed some adult books such as *Plutarch's Lives* of heroic Greeks and Romans—the adventure, the great deeds, and the anecdotes. Richard Mulcaster's 1581 *Positions Concerning the Training Up of Children* actually encouraged laughter among children and the importance of exercise and games. Locke later elaborated upon this view, urging that education should involve "Play and Recreation" as a means of getting "continued Attention" from children, engaging the "liking of Children" for learning, which is "one of the hardest Tasks." Children

---

[896] Smith, 1991.

[897] I do not purport to have read every children's book I am about to examine here, but I have read a high number. The bibliography here is already very extensive, so I decided not to list the children's books mentioned in this chapter. I do reference the scholarly sources cited in this section about children's literature, though not the many Wikipedia and encyclopedia entries, as well as countless online sources I consulted on specific books and authors.

should be free to choose how they play so they discover their individual tempers, inclinations, and aptitudes.

But while England awaited Locke's "monumental educational influence" in the early 1700s, it was the "Good Godly Books" by Puritans that constituted the greater part of books for or about children.[898] There was a "flood of Puritan books" in the 1600s. Puritans advocated literacy among the young for two interconnected reasons: They believed that individuals should have direct access to the Bible, and that encouraging children to read didactic literature was an excellent way to rescue them from their sinful impulses. "Play and idleness" gave children time for devilish temptations without fomenting an upright character. (The historian Percy Muir makes the revealing observation that "the *Cambridge Bibliography of English Literature* lists no children's books of a recreational kind before 1671").

A good example of Puritanism in books was James Janeway's *A Token for Children: being an Exact Account of the Conversion, Holy and Exemplary Lives, and Joyful Deaths of several young Children*, published in 1671. In this book, abstinence from all forms of playfulness was insisted upon, with constant reminders to the parents of the inherent tendency of their children to sin, and the need to raise children guarded against the temptations of Satan by reading the Scriptures. The same, however, cannot be said about John Bunyan's 1678 *The Pilgrim's Progress*. While this book was not intentionally written for children, it was widely read in the nursery and annexed by children as an adventure story about giants and fabulous monsters, sword contests, and a hero overcoming ill fortune. It has been said that Bunyan provided amusement, if unintentionally, and that he preferred to persuade children into righteousness instead of frightening them.

It was in the early 1700s that books expressly written for children came onto the market, guided by the Lockean conception that children were not born with original sin, but resembled an "empty cabinet" that could be shaped according to their education. This Lockean idea was reinforced by a new sensibility attributed to Rousseau's educational novel *Émile*, written in 1762, which argued that children's natural state of being should be valued in itself, rather than viewed as an inferior state requiring the immediate imposition of adult ways.[899] This emphasis on children's "natural" ways of seeing, thinking, and feeling would eventually encourage the writing of books aimed at nurturing the unique imagination of children.

---

[898] Muir, 1969.
[899] Simon, 1995.

With Britain's gradual modernization, there was a growing focus on children's educational maturation. Up until about 1750, roughly speaking, almost one-third of young people died before fifteen years of age.[900] Coping with such regular deaths in their households, combined with the need to have young adults help with farming and craftsmanship, parents barely had time to think about their children's education. But with improvements in agriculture, the rate of infant mortality started to decline slowly but steadily through the 1700s, making parents more optimistic about the prospects of their children surviving into adulthood and the importance, accordingly, of an education in an emerging urban Britain, where a vocational profession was important. Sunday schools that taught reading and writing and some arithmetic were growing in great numbers during the late eighteenth and early nineteenth centuries. In 1800 there were two thousand such schools, with about 10 percent of children between the ages of five and eighteen enrolled. By 1818 some 450,000 children were being educated in Sunday schools.[901]

Apart from books aimed at preparing middle-class children for social accomplishment, such as the 1745 *Circle of the Sciences* series, an encyclopedia published by John Newbery about grammar, arithmetic, and geography, we see a growing emphasis on books that taught moral and religious principles in a more light-hearted, liberal manner, acknowledging playfulness in children's learning. A popular book was Sarah Fielding's 1749 *The Governess; or, The Little Female Academy*, about a girls' village school with a teacher of virtuous character who tells her students that "the true use of books is to make you wiser and better." A 1765 book that inspired a whole genre was *The History of Little Goody Two-Shoes*, written by an anonymous author about a "do-gooder," a poor orphan girl named Margery Meanwell, who goes through life with only one shoe until a rich man gives her a pair, and she tells everyone she has "two shoes," and then becomes a teacher and marries a rich widower, with the story showing that virtue is rewarded.

In *Some Thoughts Concerning Education*, Locke encouraged parents to teach their children kindness to animals, warning that "the Custom of Tormenting and Killing of Beasts, will, by Degrees, harden their Minds even towards Men." This outlook occasioned a debate about the contrasting natures of humans and animals, whether animals had souls, and how the Christian doctrine of universal charity should be applied to animals, with the consensus being that while animals

---

[900] Newton, 2015.
[901] Hunt, 1995.

should not be elevated above humans, they should be put to death only when "necessary either for the food or convenience of man" without cruelty. Thomas Boreman's 1740 *Gigantick Histories*, which would eventually comprise a series of ten separate volumes, was endearing to children in its depiction of animals, with stories about lions, tigers, and leopards, all of which Boreman described and illustrated with woodcuts.[902] A book viewed as "the most representative of children's books," in which animals began to be sentimentalized, is Sarah Trimmer's 1786 *Fabulous Histories*. The book emphasizes the virtue of social hierarchy, according to which parents are above children in their authority, and humans above animals in terms of dominion and compassion, while conveying the message that kindness to animals during childhood can lead to universal benevolence in adulthood. It would take all our space to describe the onrush of children's books during this period.

One of the first and most prolific publishers of books for children and juveniles was John Newbury, who consciously followed Locke in his decision to link "a Knowledge of the Letters" to "Play and Recreation." The first book he published, in 1744, was *A Little Pretty Pocket-Book, intended for the Amusement of Little Master Tommy and Pretty Miss Polly with Two Letters from Jack the Giant Killer*, identified by some as the first children's book in history, consisting of simple rhymes for each of the letters of the alphabet. Newbury "paid great attention to every detail" in the preparation of children's books: the titles, the heroes and stories that would appeal to children, the price, size, and use of pictures.

It is not an exaggeration to say that Europeans invented childhood in the late 1700s as they started showing a keen interest in children's individuality and personalities. Prior to this time, children were depicted as small adults in their clothing, postures, and facial expressions. The appearance of boys at school was that of a small-size adult; it was only at the end of the 1700s that "special dress for children began to appear." Children were expected to think and behave as mature people at about the same age as our children today embark on their primary education. In late eighteenth-century Britain one sees a new artistic interest (headed by the British) in young children aimed at bringing out the distinctiveness of childhood. Children had their own identity already as infants. The paintings of Sir Joshua Reynolds (1723–1792) are very important in this respect. Art historian Ann Higonnet described this new artistic phenomenon as the invention of the innocence of childhood. It was this innocence that defined children's distinctiveness,

---

[902] Barton, 2019.

as conveyed by one of Reynolds' child portraits entitled "The Age of Innocence." An innocent child's body was "defined by its difference from adult bodies." The stages of maturation of children came to be clearly defined sometime between 1780 and 1820: between the infant and the child, the child and the adolescent, with authors delineating the specific educational needs for these stages.

Ellenor Fenn, author of numerous books, stated that "if you expect children to read with spirit and propriety, they must be supplied with lessons suited to their taste, that is, prattle, like their own."[903] Fenn is now acknowledged "as an early advocate of child-centered teaching strategies." A follower of Locke, she opined that "if the mind be a rasa tabula—you to whom it is entrusted should be cautious what is written upon it." Her most popular book, *Cobwebs to Catch Flies*, written in 1783, is a reading primer which consciously differentiated between reading age groups, with parts of the book aimed for children from three to five years, and later parts of the book aimed at those from five and eight. The book met children at their own age, experiences, and interests in how it addressed toys, pets, games, visits to the fair, and other subjects.

Chapbooks, Fairy Tales, *Robinson Crusoe*

The first books written for the delight of children in rural poor homes were chapbooks—that is, half-penny sheets covering a range of subjects from alphabet books and religious stories, to legends of ordinary folk, short biographies, heroic tales, crime news, songs and jests, nursery rhymes such as "Who Killed Cock Robin" and "Little Tommy Tucker," miraculous or ghost stories, prophecies and fortune-telling, and battle or adventure. Fables have always been the oral possession of the illiterate. The development of these fables and fairy tales into books began in the early 1700s. The *Histories, or Tales of Past Times Told by Mother Goose* was a 1729 translation of a book originally published in 1697 in French, a collection of children's tales including *Blue Beard, Sleeping Beauty, Cinderella, Puss in Boots*, and *Little Red Riding Hood*. These stories were original adaptations in prose of preexisting medieval folk tales.

It is worth mentioning that, while folk tales are common to all cultures, being anonymous stories communities passed through the generations by word of mouth, Europeans started a literary scholarship of folklore, collecting and writing

---

[903] Cited in Hunt, 1995.

these tales down in published form during the seventeenth century. The Grimm brothers, Jacob (1785–1863) and Wilhelm (1786–1859), with their background in philology, meticulously recorded the tales from oral sources, writing down every variation, and publishing about three hundred tales into cohesive written forms by 1857. Hans Christian Andersen (1805–1875), a Danish author, not only collected tales, but wrote dozens of original fairy tales—*The Tinder-Box, Thumbelina, The Little Match Girl*—leading some to argue that he invented the literary fairy tale of pure fantasy about magical characters such as wizards, elves, trolls, gnomes, and goblins.[904] By 1800, book publishing had increased substantially with one catalog listing 213 "amusing and instructive books for young minds." Many were adaptations for children of well-known tales, such as *Mother Bunch's Fairy Tales* (1773); nursery rhymes, such as *Mother Goose Melodies;* lullabies; and stories about animals, such as *The Dog of Knowledge* (1801) or *The Adventures of a Bullfinch* (1809). The most popular children's book was *The Comic Adventures of Old Mother Hubbard and Her Dog* (1805) by Sarah Catherine Martin (1768–1826), which sold over 10,000 copies, and is about a mischievous male dog and a female cat who helps with various chores around the house.

Daniel Defoe's 1719 *Robinson Crusoe* was intended for an adult readership, but soon educationists pointed to the story's pedagogical merit and its compatibility with Lockean pedagogical theory providing "instruction with delight."[905] *The New Robinson Crusoe: An Instructive and Entertaining History, for the Use of Children of Both Sexes* by Joachim Heinrich Campe, published in 1788, was the earliest *Crusoe* for children, with more editions, translations, and alternative versions appearing over the years. Rousseau argued that *Crusoe* should be a primary text to raise children "above vulgar prejudices" and encourage them to form their own judgments by imagining themselves as "solitary adventurers" in a natural state, building their own life in circumstances of real utility. James Joyce saw in this book the "Anglo-Saxon spirit . . . the manly independence."[906] Today, *Robinson Crusoe* is condemned as a story that upholds a racist ideology of white supremacy. Crusoe was certainly the embodiment of European individualism, the Lockean ideal of recreating society and oneself out of a blank slate, the quest to become one's own person.

---

[904] Vermont, 2021.
[905] O'Malley, 2012.
[906] Shinagel, 1994.

Victorian Morals, Imagination, and Sentimentalism

In the first decades of Victorian England, 1820–1850, children's books reflected the ideology of the new middle classes: "modesty and moderation, prudence and self-help, respectability and thrift"—a combination of Puritan morality and self-reliance.[907] The father was still the head of the household, and the role of the mother was to attend to the moral well-being of the family, which on average consisted of four or five children brought up on strict gender-based roles, with the sons expected to prepare for success in the public sphere, and the daughters to become ladylike in preparation for a married life, though women did play a public role, including becoming prominent writers of children's books.

Barbara Hofland's writing drew on the hardships of her own life as a widow as well as during her second marriage to an artist without money; in *The Blind Farmer and his Children* from 1816, and *Elizabeth and her Three Beggary Boys* from 1833, she depicted families struggling under hard circumstances (death of parents, bankruptcy) yet prevailing due to their moral integrity and Christian ways. The women in her tales showed strength not by condemning Victorianism (she was a firm advocate of marriage), but as hardy wives and widows willing to set up their own businesses in the face of the father's bankruptcy for the sake of the children.[908] Victorian "rigidity," however, saw more than didactic moral tales. Harriet Mozley's 1841 *The Fairy Bower* and 1852 *Family Adventures* portrayed children as they are, rather than as mere vehicles for adult expectations, enjoying jokes, skating, and arguing about the propriety of their own behaviors. *Peter Parley's Magazine*, an English children's magazine published monthly from 1839 to 1863, contained articles about history, travel, animals, and moral tales about schoolboys, wicked uncles, and other subjects, colorfully illustrated, to instruct and please children.

There were adventure stories about overcoming ordeals, such as *The Settlers at Home* by Harriet Martineau (1802–1876), in which a land is flooded, with mills and barns floating away, farm animals drowning, and everyone in great peril, four children are deprived of their mother and father, the two-year-old baby dies, and they have various struggles for survival—until they are rescued. Frederick Marryat's 1844 *The Settlers in Canada* was about the adventures of an immigrant

---

[907] Hunt, 1995.
[908] Behrendt, 2005.

English family threatened by "Red Indians" and wild animals. His 1847 book *The Children of the New Forest* was about four orphaned children during the Civil War, taught by a forester how to survive by hunting and farming.

This age of realism and railways was also an age of the romantic rediscovery of the imagination. In addition to numerous new versions of Grimm's folktales and translations of Andersen's tales into English, original works of fantasy were written, most notably *Phantasmion* by Sara Coleridge, an 1837 story of a prince who embarks on a journey, taunted and manipulated by mysterious spirits, who finally triumphs over the forces of darkness after multiple trials.

From its Puritan beginnings in the 1700s to 1870, American children's literature experienced significant cultural shifts reflecting changed perceptions of childhood.[909] Between the 1650s and 1750s, children's books were for instruction and a Puritan upbringing—to fight ignorance, the "mother of heresy," and to restrain children's "inborn depravity." A widely-read book was *The New England Primer*, published in the 1680s and illustrated with woodcuts, in verse for easier memorization of its teachings, with its famous opening "in Adam's fall, we sinned all." Thumb bibles decorated with pictures were common; one popular book was *The Duty of Parents to Pray for their Children* (1703) by Increase Mather. The best known was John Bunyan's English classic, *The Pilgrim's Progress*, of which fifty editions were published in America by 1830. Children enjoyed its strong dramatic narrative of Christian, an everyman character, journeying from the "City of Destruction" to the "Celestial City" and seeking deliverance from the burden of his sins. Many new titles came out after 1750s; a publisher in Massachusetts published more than one hundred titles between 1775 and 1800.

While the 1800s saw a gradual shift away from the spiritual intensity of Puritanism and toward a more generalized moralism, the typical children's story before 1850 did not encourage fantasy or imagination: the focus was on moral character, not entertainment. The 1824 *Story of Jack Halyard* was intended "to give an account of one family of superior excellence, as a model to others."[910] After 1850, this moralism came together with a new kind of writing, giving childhood a value in and of itself, an idealized perception of childhood expressed in sentimental stories about children, coupled with messages about the value of self-reliance, humbleness, and the fulfillment of one's duties. The matter-of-fact deathbed scenes of earlier literature gave way to vivid, melodramatic narratives, such as *The Angel*

---

[909] Hunt, 1995; MacLeod, 1975.
[910] Cited in MacLeod, 1975.

Mother in 1854, about a mother's death and the prolonged mourning of her children. Stories of poor children, "filthy, ragged, barefoot even in winter," such as Alice Bradley Haven's *Nothing Venture, Nothing Have* (originally published in 1854) about a girl who had never been to school, and was sent to live with her grandmother by her "poor laboring" father with "a large family and a sickly wife" were common.[911] With the rise of cities, there was a focus on secular subjects and characters: shopkeepers, newsboys, Italian boys singing on the streets for pennies. Series books in magazines were launched, often adventure tales for boys. Horatio Alger was best known for his "rags-to-riches" stories of boys rewarded for hard work, acts of bravery, or kindness. The most beloved book was *Little Women* by Louisa Alcott, about the fortunes of four sisters in their passage to young womanhood, which inspired numerous films.

Golden Age in England and America

The history of children's literature points to the English as the most prominent, original writers. The period 1850–1890 has been identified as a "golden age," with writers drawing on translations of the rich repertoire of Hans Henderson's fairy tales and fables, at the same time as Europeans came to view childhood as a crucial phase in personal development, characterized by freedom from accepted conventions, vitality of imagination, and the child's instinctive connection to the natural world, reflecting the earliest phases of the human psyche, and thus a window to the archetypes of the unconscious. Lewis Carroll's 1865 *Alice's Adventure in Wonderland* is judged as possibly the most brilliant and original children's book. By removing the controlling voice of the adult's narrator and having children speak for themselves, *Alice* was the first to allow the child's mind to occupy the center as the adult reenters into their sense of puzzlement. Charles Kingsley's 1855 *Glaucus; or, The Wonders of the Shore* was inspired by nature walks with children, to bring out "the miraculous and divine element underlying all physical nature."

There was a sentimental belief in the child's innate virtues, away from the earlier emphasis on original sin, characterized by a keen concern for the suffering of poor, homeless, vagrant children, the so-called "street arabs." George Sergent's 1857 book, *Roland Leigh: The Story of a City Arab*, concerned a small boy in the

---

[911] Haven, 1862.

London underground, abandoned even by the church. For Hesba Stretton, children were society's victims; her stories of children starved of food and affection were widely imitated; she even popularized "baby talk." Juliana Horatia Ewing, from a family of ten children and with a strong faith, is known for her efforts to depict children's feelings, closeness to one another, and to their animals. Her stories, such as *Mrs. Overtheway's Remembrances* from 1869, are celebrated as the "first outstanding child-novels."[912]

The year 1877 saw the publication of *Black Beauty*, one of the best-selling children's books of all time, written by Anna Sewell while seriously ill—about horses dragged down by harsh masters and vain passengers. It is a horse's autobiography, in which the central character, Black Beauty, is given some human traits such as thinking and talking, although only the readers can hear Black Beauty talking; none of the human characters in the text hear them, and horses communicate with human characters using gestures and actions. Like earlier books about animals, *Black Beauty* is anthropomorphic, with the horse playing the role of narrator and the readers understanding the world through the horse's own perspective. This story is now considered one of the first animal rights books in its exploration of the hardships faced by horses at a time before the invention of automobiles, when society depended on horses for transportation.[913] Europeans have had a strong connection to horses since Indo-European peoples domesticated them on the Pontic Steppes during the fourth millennium, and then invented the techniques of horse riding as well as chariots.[914]

---

[912] Ewing, 2018.

[913] Norris, 2012.

[914] Kelekna, 2009. The animal rights movement is primarily and essentially a product of the white race. Here's a timeline of some major intellectual landmarks in animal rights:

- 530 BCE: Pythagoras was the first in a line of several Greek and Roman philosophers to teach that animals had souls, and to advocate for vegetarianism.
- 1635: First known animal protection legislation passes, in Ireland, "An Act against plowing by the tayle, and pulling the wool off living sheep."
- 1641: The Massachusetts colony's Body of Liberties includes regulations against "Tirranny or Crueltie" toward animals.
- 1776–1798: The Anglophone world sees publication of Humphry Primatt's *The Duty of Mercy and the Sin of Cruelty to Base Animals*; Thomas Young's *An Essay on Humanity to Animals*, and John Oswald's *The Cry of Nature*, an appeal to mercy and justice, on behalf of the persecuted animals.
- 1780: Jeremy Bentham in *An Introduction to the Principles of Morals and Legislation* argued for better treatment of animals on the basis of their ability to feel pleasure and pain, famously writing, "The question is not, Can they reason? nor, Can they talk? but, Can they suffer?"

As England expanded its empire across the world, adventure stories took off. One of the most widely-known is Robert Louis Stevenson's 1883 *Treasure Island*, a story cognizant of boys' love of treasure, pirates, strange noises, seafaring—along with unpredictable characters, an imperfect hero, and a "formidable and smooth" villain. The novels of the French writer Jules Verne, "father of science fiction," were very popular among English boys, including *Journey to the Center of the Earth* from 1864, *Twenty Thousand Leagues Under the Sea* from 1870, and *Around the World in Eighty Days* from 1872, taking his readers across continents, under the oceans, through the Earth, and into space. George Alfred Henry's stories from the 1880s *The Dragon and The Raven*, *For The Temple*, *Under Drake's Flag*, and *In Freedom's Cause* were also enjoyed for their blending of the extraordinary with the probable, eulogizing honesty, loyalty, pluck, and resilience—with his belief that the British were unequalled in these virtues.

The late nineteenth century saw a sudden attraction for boarding school stories, attuned to the different interests and experiences of boys and girls. Talbot Baines Reed was the most popular writer of boys' fiction about rivalry over games, schoolboy humor, and a muscular type of Christianity—*The Fifth Form at St. Dominic* sold 750,000 copies in 1907. The most prolific author of girl's school stories was L. T. Meade; in addition to her books for adults, Meade wrote about 150

- 1800: Immanuel Kant argued that "Cruelty to animals is contrary to man's duty to himself because it deadens in him the feeling of sympathy."
- 1822: British Parliament passes "Act to Prevent the Cruel and Improper Treatment of Cattle."
- 1824: The first Society for the Prevention of Cruelty to Animals is founded in England by Richard Martin, Arthur Broome, and William Wilberforce.
- 1835: The first Cruelty to Animals Act is passed in Britain.
- 1866: The American Society for the Prevention of Cruelty to Animals is founded by New Yorker Henry Bergh.
- 1875: The National Anti-Vivisection Society is established in Britain by Frances Power Cobbe.
- 1892: English social reformer Henry Stephens Salt publishes "Animals' Rights: Considered in Relation to Social Progress."
- 1906: J. Howard Moore published *The Universal Kinship*, advocating for the ethical treatment of all sentient beings, based on Darwinian principle of shared evolutionary kinship and a universal application of the Golden Rule.
- 1940s: Nazi Germany introduced the law Reich Animal Protection Act.
- 1955: The Society for Animal Protective Legislation (SAPL), the first organization to lobby for humane slaughter legislation in the US, was founded.
- 1964: British Parliament Committee concluded that animals should be afforded "sufficient freedom of movement to be able without difficulty to turn around, groom itself, get up, lie down, [and] stretch its limbs."
- 1984: Tom Regan published *The Case for Animal Rights*, a highly influential philosophical argument that animals had rights.

titles for "young readers"; *A World of Girls: The Story of a School* from 1886 was about disruptive emotions, friendship, loyalty, and jealousy, along with Victorian attitudes about the traditional roles of wives and mothers.

The enfeebled liberal West you see today, publishing grooming stories about transsexuals for primary school libraries, was once continuously creative. This was the case because its blank slate individualism was still sustained by traditions, solid monogamous nuclear families, the continuing presence of Christian values, patriarchal authority, and a sense of national heritage. In the late nineteenth and early twentieth centuries, confidence in Western colonial life and empire-making was perhaps past its zenith, but it was not faltering for everyone; certainly not for Rudyard Kipling, in whose stories the ideals of empire and manliness are celebrated, along with the code that public schools should train boys for their future role as rulers of the Empire, as in his 1899 *Stalky and Co.*, which emphasizes the aggressive competitive aspects of boarding school as a preparation for life in the colonial armies.

Yet for others, the strict moralizing lessons of Victorian times were becoming outmoded. There was an emphasis both on playfulness and on nurturing the imaginations of middle-class children, as we see in *A Child's Garden of Verses*, written in 1885 by Robert Louis Stevenson, which describes children absorbed in imaginary "make believe" games in which boys transform their surroundings through fantasy, turning meadows into jungles and populating a desert with pythons, pumas, and kangaroos. There was indeed, through to the early twentieth century, a marked preoccupation with the inner world of children—not merely with childhood as a distinctive phase, but in rediscovering in the interior world of children the lost world of human wholeness, and criticizing thereby the dismemberment of humans from nature in the new industrial age. A much-admired example of this new literature is *The Secret Garden* by F. H. Burnett. This 1911 story has been interpreted in many ways.[915] The story is about Mary, a British 10-year-old born in India, "a self-absorbed child" with a high imagination, who finds consolation, meaning, and happiness in life, after being neglected by her wealthy British parents, through the discovery of a beautiful and intricate "secret garden."

It is hard to identify one clear literary trend. There was too much variety, and intersecting and contrasting cultural trends, from the creative minds of British authors. Kipling also wrote *Just So Stories* in 1902, fantastical tales encouraging children to wonder how animals came to evolve. Use of parody for comic effect

---

[915] Bixler, 1996.

can be seen in E. Nesbit's 1901 *Nine Unlikely Tales for Children*. Nesbit was a founding member of the Fabian Society who gained much attention in 1899 with *The Story of the Treasure Seekers*, about children who overcome perils through pluck, and *The Wouldbegoods* from 1901, about a middle-class family fallen on hard times, which found great appeal for its special touch for depicting how children truly speak, feel, and behave.

Then in 1904 came J. M. Barrie's *Peter Pan*, "a public phenomenon," about a boy who refuses to become an adult in an ideal world of daring and courage, interacting with fairies, pirates, and mermaids in a mythical paradise. Some have connected "Peter's eternal child-like nature" to the beginnings of "the over-solic-itous parent" who, "by trying to smooth away all difficulties and conflicts" in the lives of their children, in a make-believe world of incredible adventures without risks, create children who refuse to grow up and meet life with all its difficulties.[916] There was also Beatrix Potter's 1902 *The Tale of Peter Rabbit*, a bestseller from the beginning, written in order to amuse a sick five-year-old boy, being about a rabbit who disobeys his mother, combining humor, adventure, and a moral lesson.

In the period of 1870–1914, American children's literature is said to have changed radically, both in the proliferation of books with a greater variety of themes and characters, and the high literary quality.[917] There was a liberal trend to avoid "preaching" in children's stories in preference for amusement, story content, and overall optimism about prospects in life and the possibility of finding happiness. Some say it was a golden age, characterized by such classic titles as *The Wonderful Wizard of Oz* of 1900 by Frank Baum, and *The Adventures of Tom Sawyer* in 1876 and *Huckleberry Finn* in 1884 by Mark Twain. There were other classics in their own right. One was T. B. Aldrich's 1870 book *The Story of a Bad Boy*, hailed as a departure from traditional children's literature for showing boys as they were, rather than as they ought to be, and which started a genre of "bad boy" literature, of which *Tom Sawyer* was one example. So were C. D. Warner's 1877 novel *Being a Boy*, W. D. John Habberton's 1880 *The Worst Boy in Town*, and J. O. Kaler's 1877 *Ten Weeks with a Circus*. These stories, with their realistic images of boys as irrational, primitive, and masculine, attracted many readers. This genre is now criticized for encouraging "toxic masculinity" rather than

---

[916] For a variety of interpretations, contemporary reviews, and plays of *Peter Pan*, including Barrie's various and scattered Peter Pan texts, and a previously unavailable version, see Ann Hiebert Alton's edition (2011).

[917] Hunt, 1995.

"nice," "caring," "gender-fluid," and docile boys who listen attentively to their female teachers. In truth, these "bad boys" had an instinctive sense of what was
right, rooted in small town America, and with their own unique personalities built
from hardship and assertiveness outside a standardized suburbia.

Girls' school stories, or coming of age stories, were very popular. One was
Margaret Sidney's 1881 book *The Five Little Peppers and How They Grew*, about a
widowed mother who has to sew all day to pay rent and feed five growing Peppers,
which she does with a stout heart, a smiling face, and the help of her blue-eyed
Ben, the eldest and the man of the house at the age of eleven. America was still a
land that celebrated independence and self-reliance, not from the standpoint of
the isolated, atomistic selves you see today addicted to social media, but within
concrete local communities. *Rebecca of Sunnybrook Farm* by Kate Wiggins was a
1903 novel about a girl who is sent to live with her lonely aunt after her father dies,
and to whom she brings her youthful enthusiasm and imagination with poems
and songs, selling soap to help a poor family, and then growing up to be a proper
young lady with a kind heart.

Another book now considered a classic was *Pollyanna* by Eleanor Porter, with
its innocent formula that we should be "glad, glad, glad" about everything, however hard it may seem, being a 1913 story about an orphan girl who remains positive and animated in spirit despite a hard childhood and later tribulations,
spreading love and joy wherever she goes and finding happiness in the end, thus
demonstrating that a good disposition and positive outlook can compensate for
the hardships we face. This story was followed by eleven more *Pollyanna* sequels
known as "Glad Books." Another popular book was *Little Lord Fauntleroy* from
1886 by Frances Burnett, about a boy who lives with his "dearest" mother in poverty after the death of his father, who then inherits a British fortune and is sent to
live with the cold and unsentimental lord who oversees the trust.

Continuing Creativity Between 1914 and 1980

The period of 1914–1945 in British children's literature is downplayed as less
original than the preceding periods—but what about J. R. R. Tolkien, author of
The Hobbit and *The Lord of the Rings*? British education at this time was still
rooted in tradition, Western-centric standards, and great books. *The Lord of the
Rings* drew on a combination of Christianity and Germanic heroic legend, including the Norse Völsunga saga, the study of Old English literature, *Beowulf*, and on

Celtic, Finnish, Slavic, and Greek mythology. Tolkien gained access to this pagan tradition through early Christianity, where it continued, not by resorting to some neo-pagan New Age version.

The early twentieth century saw many new children's titles: 688 in 1913, which increased to 1,629 by 1938—despite the First World War, the Great Depression, and the Second World War.[918] They were mostly books for the comfortable middle class, not for the children of parents who participated in the General Strike of 1926. Coincidentally, 1926 was the same year the lovely story of *Winnie-the-Pooh* by A. A. Milne was published, about an optimistic, not very intelligent, but friendly and steadfast teddy bear, with many other animal characters for children to identify with: Piglet, Tigger, and Roo. *The Velveteen Rabbit*, written by Margery Williams in 1922, was another popular book about a stuffed rabbit sewn from velveteen who becomes a boy's favorite toy, but is thrown out of the boy's house to become a real rabbit that the boy then encounters in the wild, showing how toy rabbits become real through the affection and imagination of children. Another classic was *The Story of Babar the Little Elephant*, about a baby elephant who flees the jungle after his mother is killed and moves into a big city where he is civilized and dresses in Western attire. The West was still unwilling to devalue its imperial history; post-colonial theory was still in the future. The Lockean call for affection towards animals had nurtured uniquely Western stories of animals that live like humans, with human qualities, coupled with toys in the shape of animals like a Teddy Bear or Babar dressed up like a human.

Long-running series of stories for boys and girls were common: M. E. Atkinson's *August Adventure*, Elizabeth Yates's *High Holiday*, Francis Joyce's *Yes, Cousin Joseph*, and Elizabeth Brent-Dyer's *The School at the Chalet* with its fifty-seven sequels. The trend-setting writer of modern schoolgirls' stories was the British writer Angela Brazil, author of some fifty boarding school books, beginning in 1906 with *The Fortunes of Philippa*. *The Nicest Girl in the School*, published in 1909, sold 153,000 copies. Brazil was raised by a mother critical of the "traditionalism" persisting in Victorian English schooling, determined to raise her children according to the Lockean principle that children who experience a liberal education in literature, music, and science will become creative and nurturing. Notwithstanding the prior influence of Locke, a traditional moralism continued to prevail in Victorian England about self-sacrifice for the nation, the moral virtues of patriarchal families, and the importance of abiding by Christian norms. Brazil's

---

[918] Hunt, 1995.

books portrayed independent-minded female characters who openly challenged authority, were impertinent, enjoyed pranks, and expressed their youthfulness without worrying about adults' rigidified concerns.

Children's literature during the period of 1945–70 is characterized by historical realism, fantasy/science fiction, and "internationalism." Kipling-type books eulogizing British imperial manliness gave way to books in tune with the egalitarian, post-colonial mood of a Britain without an empire. However, despite promotion of "international exchanges" and a few books about minorities, this period remained creative, even as it was undermining the conditions that made this creativity possible. As TV became a major form of recreation, authors came to deemphasize this aspect of children's books in favor of literary quality—for the newly-constructed public schools and libraries. The rising literary status of children's books is reflected in the growth of literary reviews, book awards, and new journals such as *Children's Literature in Education*. It is said that the 1950s and 1960s were "a period of exceptional artistic license for the children's author"—because while the prescriptive morality of the Victorian era had dissipated, the "new agenda of political correctness in matters of sex, class, and race" was still in the future, so authors were "unusually free of pressures to promote approved conformities."[919]

Incorporating historical research became popular. Irene Hunt's 1964 *Across Five Aprils* integrated historical facts into stories she had heard from her grandfather about family experiences during the American Civil War. Elizabeth Speare's 1957 *Calico Captive* was about a girl kidnapped in an Abenakis Indian raid on Charlestown in 1754. Jean Fritz's 1969 book *George Washington's Breakfast* was about a boy determined to learn everything he could about his namesake, including what the first President ate for breakfast. Cynthia Harnett wrote novels such as *The Woolpack* in 1951 and *The Load of Unicorn* in 1959 about daily life in Medieval England. Henry Treece's 1967 book *Dream Time* was set in prehistory, about a boy with a bad leg cast out from his tribe because of his ability to draw wonderful but forbidden pictures, who embarks on a journey in which he meets many peoples, including the last of the Neanderthals. Alan Garner's 1960 novel *The Weirdstone of Brisingamen* uses Norse mythology to bring clarity to a child's perception of the confusions of modern life.

Science fiction also flourished in this period. The beginning of science fiction (not to be confused with the fantasy genre) has been dated to the late nineteenth century, the age of Jules Verne and H. G. Wells, with their imaginary worlds,

---

[919] Hunt, 1995

titanic disasters on Earth, or strange voyages. Adam Roberts has argued that science fiction really came into its own as a distinctly Protestant kind of "fantastic" writing in response to new ideas coming out of modern science, building on older Catholic traditions of magical and fantastic romances and stories. But others insist that it inherited its own literary identity from the Enlightenment with the satires of Jonathon Swifts' *Gulliver's Travels* and Voltaire's *Micromégas* via the "voyage extraordinaire" and speculation on the human condition.

The best children's sci-fi books of the 1950s include *The Martian Chronicles* by Ray Bradbury, a fascinating 1950 story about Americans who conquer Mars, the home of indigenous Martians, ending in the apocalyptic destruction of both Martian and human civilizations, instigated by humans consumed by their militaristic scientific power. In contrast, Eleanor Cameron's 1954 *The Wonderful Flight to the Mushroom Planet* reflected an optimistic view about the possibilities of science, being a story about two boys who, upon reading a newspaper advertisement looking for a homebuilt spaceship, decide to build one out of tin and scrap wood which they then bring to the advertiser, an inventor who makes a few improvements, gives them a special fuel, and tells them they must visit the mushroom planet, which is really a tiny habitable moon orbiting the Earth that is invisible to normal telescopes. This moon is covered in giant mushrooms and populated by small men with large heads and light green skin who tell the boys that everyone on their planet is dying of a mysterious illness. The boys end up solving the natives' problem before returning to Earth.

Peter Dickinson's trilogy, *The Weathermonger*, *Heartsease*, and *Devil's Children* depicts a repressive Britain in which machines are banned and people return to a primitive lifestyle. In fantasy, we must at least mention *The Chronicles of Narnia*, a series of seven novels written by C. S. Lewis from 1950–56, which has now sold over 100 million copies in forty-seven languages. These stories call upon children to imagine what would happen in a land like Narnia where the Son of God, who became a Man in our world, became a Lion, seen as a marvelous retelling of Bible stories in a new pagan way.

Post 1970: Blank Slate Children Without Families and Civic Communities

During the 1970s there was a noticeable trend in children's literature towards Black pride, female heroes, interracial friendship, and empathy. In 1965 the *Saturday Review* published an influential article by Nancy Larrick with the title "The

All-White World of Children's Books." This article sounded reasonable. If the US was founded on equal natural rights, and Blacks have been an intrinsic component of this nation, should they not be reflected in children's books? Whites as such were not attacked. The article was asking whether the books at the time reflected the experiences of Black children. This was just the beginning, however, of the intensification of liberalism's push in the post-WWII decades for equality of liberty and opportunities among all races. In the late seventies, some authors of children's books expressed concern about the "censorial imposition" of "guidelines" regarding the use of "non-sexist" and "non-racist" language." These guidelines began as mere "requests for tools" to eliminate "bias" in literature and include nonwhites in stories. A few decades later, these demands would be radicalized into demands across all schools for "Books to Teach White Children and Teens How to Undo Racism and White Supremacy."[920]

The time was ripe for the complete indoctrination of children. Children were becoming more isolated than ever as the nuclear family, the last bastion of blood identity—the "All-American Family" eulogized in the 1950s—was discredited as the US started to embrace more progressive politics. This was a time when the divorce rate started to rise and a growing proportion of young adults began to postpone and then forgo marriage altogether. In *Bowling Alone: The Collapse and Revival of American Community*, Robert Putnam noted a dramatic decline, from the mid-1960s onwards, in membership and number of volunteers across a wide spectrum of civic organizations such as religious groups, labor unions, parent–teacher associations, military veterans' organizations, volunteers with Boy Scouts and the Red Cross, and fraternal organizations. In other words, liberalism was now undermining the very civic (contractually created) communities it had created in place of the old kinship tribal communities.[921]

A few years later, Putnam released the results of a comprehensive survey of over thirty thousand respondents around the United States in which he found that the greater the diversity in a community, the fewer people vote and the less they volunteer, the less they give to charity, or work on community projects. In the most diverse communities, neighbors trust one another about half as much as they do in the most homogeneous settings. The study, the largest ever on civic

---

[920] https://tinyurl.com/5n8tbpbe.
[921] Putnam, 2000.

engagement in America, found that virtually all measures of civic health are lower in more diverse settings.[922]

The minds of children were emptied more than ever of any traditions, family experiences, and even attachments to liberal-created civic communities. Not surprisingly, "chronic loneliness" is now "a modern-day epidemic," with "rates of depression and anxiety among teenagers increasing 70 percent in the past 25 years."[923] Children today are incredibly vulnerable to ideological manipulation, which has coincided with a massive increase in the number of new children's book published in the US: from 2,001 in 1971 to 3,214 in 1979, and to 6,154 in 1991, and then to 21,878 new titles in 2009.[924]

It is not that good writers disappeared after 1970. Richard Adams's highly popular 1972 novel *Watership Down* was an old-style animal adventure story, in which a small band of male rabbits with their own history, language, and mythology set out to start a new warren, facing numerous hardships and rescuing female rabbits from an evil rabbit tyrant in order to bring them to their warren, finally living happily ever after. Roald Dahl, author of the famous *Charlie and the Chocolate Factory* and numerous other stories told from the point of view of a child's imagination, also wrote *The Witches* in 1983, Criticized today for its "misogyny," it is categorized as a "dark fantasy" featuring the experiences of a boy and his grandmother in a secret world of witches who hate children.

High-quality historical fiction continued through the 1970s into the 1990s, even as it came increasingly with some PC motivations. Rosemary Sutcliff, the author of many great 1960s stories such as *Outcast*, which tells the story of an orphaned child in Roman Britain who is shipwrecked on a coast outside of Roman rule, continued to write excellent retellings of myths and legends, including *Song for a Dark Queen*, about the tragic life and military campaigns of Boudicca, Queen of the Iceni, against the Romans. Penelope Lively's 1973 historical fantasy novel *The Ghost Thomas Kempe*, about a ghost of a seventeenth-century resident sorcerer, encouraged children to become aware of "layers of memory of which people are composed." Jill Walsh's 1983 *A Parcel of Patterns* is about a girl living in 1665 in a village who tends her flock and teaches her young suitor to read, when one day a parcel of patterns, meant for a new dress for the pastor's wife, arrives from London, carrying an infection that spreads with horrifying speed.

---

[922] Putnam, 2007.
[923] Bedell, 2016.
[924] Hunt, 1995.

But the seeds of political correctness could not be stopped from giving birth to a generation of "progressive" authors. Robert Leeson's historical trilogy *Maroon Boy*, *Bess*, and *The White Horse* (1975–77) were intended to "fight against the oppression of Black people, of women, and working people" in the present. The literary critic Patrick Parrinder stated in 1980 that the aim of science fiction should be "social criticism" and the creation of a more progressive culture.[925] Richard Peck's 1976 book *Are You in the House Alone?* was about a babysitter raped by one of the most respectable boys in town—that is, a privileged White boy. *Autumn Street* by L. Lowry is a "candid and memorable" story about an interracial relationship. Again, these stories were still reasonable in comparison to what was about to be unleashed upon children's fragile minds. Barbara Ashley's 1974 *The Trouble with Donovan Croft* is about a Black boy who loses his ability to talk when he is raised by a White family because he can't stay at his own house since his mother has gone back to Jamaica to care for her dying father. It deals with racism towards Donovan because of his immigrant Jamaican heritage. William Maynes' 1985 novel *Drift* narrates a journey from the point of view of a White boy, and then from the viewpoint of an Indian girl, with the intention of showing the "often limited quality" of the White view. Mary Hoffman's *Amazing Grace* is an "empowering" 1991 book about an African-American girl, with the message that she can be whatever she wants to be, regardless of what other people say, if she stays true to herself as a Black girl.

But increasingly in the 1990s and 2000s, books instructing children that Blacks were victims of systemic White racism would proliferate. Unimaginative, simplistic children's books "about race and racism" now prevail in school curricula.[926] As the West committed itself to mass immigration, the educational establishment coordinated its efforts to fill up the blank slate minds of children with the slogan that "diversity is our greatest strength."[927] Government offices, the mainstream media, the journals, and everyone in charge of education began to dictate what was "appropriate reading" for children, reaching the conclusion that the most important way to educate them was to produce "Resources for Race, Equity, Anti-Racism,

---

[925] A standing argument by literary critics of children's literature was that this literature had always been permeated by "hidden" ideological biases, and that it was naïve to approach children's books from a politically neutral standpoint. The goal of critics should be to "deconstruct" these biases (sexual, racial, religious) and propose new guidelines towards the creation of a "progressive" temperament among children.

[926] For example Burnett, 2024; Gienapp, 2024.

[927] Reedsy Blog, 2024.

and Inclusion."[928] White children needed to be raised with guilt as a means of preparing them to inhabit a diverse world filled with proud immigrants. With the decline of the family, protests grew against stories that assumed that monogamous nuclear families with married fathers and mothers were "normal" rather than an "illiberal" prejudice. The number of LGBTQ books skyrocketed,[929] coupled with a dramatic decline in the quality of children's literature, which have become fluffy stories calling upon White children to be "kind," "nice," and "empathetic" through vibrant rainbow colors.[930]

This is not to say that good books and great fantasy stories ceased after the 1990s. Many classic stories continued to be published. Books written under the pen name "Dr. Seuss" in the 1950s and 1960s like *The Cat in the Hat*, *Green Eggs and Ham*, and *How the Grinch Stole Christmas* gained in popularity. And who can ignore the explosive epic fantasy series that began in 1998 with the publication of *Harry Potter and the Sorcerer's Stone*, successfully adapted into blockbuster movies, a story about a wizard boy set in a magical boarding school. The *Harry Potter* series authored by J. K. Rowling is far and away the highest-selling series of novels ever, selling over 600 million copies. Despite their length, many children enjoyed them, as well as the movies and merchandise they inspired. Through all the wizardry and sorcery, the series emphasized standard values like friendship, humility, and bravery. *Harry Potter* was also politically correct in its day, even touching on themes such as mental health and homosexuality.

But now the author Rowling is seen as not so correct, provoking controversy in recent years "as a person who sees herself as a progressive due to her feminist values . . . but refuses to extend those values to . . . trans people in general." "It's Time for Progressives to Move on from Harry Potter," opined Miles Schneiderman in a 2020 article. The series, and the movies thereof, also came under criticism for their "outrageous lack of diversity."[931] It is time to embrace Marvel's Black Panther children's book series for "providing a lesson in diversity and representation in its celebration of Black culture with an almost all-Black cast."[932] Ta-Nehisi Coates, the MacArthur Genius and National Book Award winner, joined the Black Panther series in 2016, to become an "avenger of civil rights." One of his much-lauded contributions was *A Nation Under Our Feet*, a story about "the

---

[928] See WNDB, n.d.

[929] Google "children's books lgbtq"; you will get over 31,100, 000 results in less than a second.

[930] Google "children's books teaching empathy"; you will get 26,500,000 results in no time.

[931] Leishman, 2017.

[932] Armbruster, 2018.

indomitable will of Wakanda—the famed African nation known for its vast wealth, advanced technology and warrior traditions."[933]

The Guardian noted in 2019 a "seismic shift" in the number of books by and about "Blacks," "Asians or Asian Americans," "Latinx," and "First Nations."[934] This shift is inescapably tied to replacement immigration. A heavily funded, institutional network with full-time salaried bureaucrats has no other motto but that we need more diverse books.[935] Classic books are barely read in our schools nowadays. Many of the pre-1990s books listed above only survive as subjects in literary analysis about "How to Break Up with Your Favorite Racist Children's Books."[936] The list of books getting cancelled includes *The Secret Garden*, *Huckleberry Finn*, *The Little House on the Prairie*, *Peter Pan*, *Peter Rabbit*, *Cinderella*, and *Charlie and the Chocolate Factory*.

We could go on with this depressing conclusion to the otherwise noble history of children's literature. The way liberalism, through to the modern era and until a few decades ago, encouraged a highly gifted genealogy of children's stories deserves our admiration. It seems that liberalism remained a creative and positive force in the West so long as it was supported by family values, the continuation of traditional Christianity, and strong civic communities and associations. It is a complex subject we have only just touched on: why are Western educators disowning the magnificent legacy of children's literature and replacing it with contrived stories promoting the sexualization of children and hatred towards their ancestors? Was Lockean liberalism bound to culminate in this situation? This question will be addressed in the following chapters.

---

[933] See https://ta-nehisicoates.com/graphic-novels/.
[934] Flood, 2019.
[935] See https://diversebooks.org/.
[936] See NHC Education Programs, 2022.

X

The Progressive Logic of the Historical Consciousness of Europeans

History is for human self-knowledge . . . the only clue to what man can do is what man has done. The value of history, then, is that it teaches us what man has done and thus what man is.

– R.G. Collingwood

The Argument

A most startling historical truth is that Europeans invented the writing of history as "a method of sorting out the true from the false,"[937] as a conscious search for a rational explanation of the causes of events, while rendering the results of their investigations in sustained narratives of excellent prose. The other peoples of the world, including the Chinese, who maintained for centuries a tradition of chronological writers, barely rose above annalistic forms of recording genealogies or the deeds of rulers, devoid of reflections on historical causation. This would not have been judged a controversial view a few decades ago. But in a Western world where universities have made it their mission to promote an "inclusive" educational environment, there is a widespread impetus to acknowledge the "accomplishments" of cultures across the world as equally valuable, including their

---

[937] Gilderfus, 2018.

historiographical traditions. The European historiographical tradition is now seen as one approach among others, such as the Chinese "encyclopedic, synchronic, and official historiography," Australian Aboriginal "dreamings" of past events, and African "oral history" of gathering and preserving the voices and memories of people.[938] Indeed, if there is a key difference, it is that European historians have tended to be ethnocentric and arrogant in their supposition that they invented history. Among recent studies promoting a "global approach" against a "Europe-centered approach" is *Turning Points in Historiography: A Cross-Cultural Perspective*, edited by Edward Wang and Georg Iggers. Academics are cited in this book stating that historical thought is not a monopoly of the West: "On the contrary, interest in the past appears to have existed everywhere and in all periods." Western historiography is "not superior." The claims of European colonialists on the "racial inferiority" of other cultures must be "refuted."[939]

When initially conceptualizing this chapter, the aim was twofold: firstly, to demonstrate that Europeans originated the writing of history, wrote the greatest historical books, brought about the professionalization of history during the 1800s, and then wrote the best histories of the non-western world; secondly, to argue that Europeans were the only people to exhibit a high level of historical consciousness, a sense of the temporal character of human life, and of the way that history shapes our thoughts, culture, psychology, and institutions. However, in the course of researching and thinking about this subject, it became clearer that the idea of progress invented by Europeans (as they become increasingly aware of the unique developmental character of their history) entailed the belief that humans could consciously make their own history by re-organizing societies in a rational or "enlightened" way, eliminating ignorance and prejudices, and allowing thereby for the "full emancipation" and flourishment of the potentialities of individuals.

It also became clearer that this historical consciousness, which reached a high level of cognition in the modern liberal era, would eventually nurture the illusion that humans could overcome human ethnic conflict by "liberating" the individual from all collective constraints—"bigoted" traditions, racial, sexual, and national identities. The liberal idea that humans are alike in their equal right to choose their own values is precisely what lies behind the promotion of the cultural relativism that has persuaded Europeans to negate their own accomplishments, including

---

[938] Hughes-Warrington, 2005.
[939] Wang and Iggers, 2002, 1–14.

their invention of historical writing itself. The consolidation of a multicultural historiography was not an arbitrary or isolated decision taken by "woke" academics or "cultural Marxists" secretly marching through the institutions; it was, rather, an expression of a broader movement unfolding out of Western historiographical thinking itself.

This chapter will seek to explain the following propositions:

- Europeans were responsible for the full development of history writing, surpassing since ancient Greek times the historiography of the other civilizations during their entire histories. The Greeks and Romans did hold a cyclical view of history, as the general consensus has it, according to which the nature of all things was to grow as well as to decay. However, this was a view based on a deep understanding of the varying psychology of human nature from times of simplicity and hardship (in the early stages of cultures) to times of affluence and decadence (in the later stages of cultures).

- The Hebrew Bible did go beyond an annalistic account of the deeds of kings, developing a historiography that was "national," or about a people as a whole, but without matching the historiography of the Greeks and Romans, who also initiated an ecumenical vision of the whole inhabited world, which would later merge with the universal historical vision of the Christians in their preoccupation with the creation of a society that would live up to the moral expectations of Christianity. Only Western peoples, in their cosmopolitanism, and in their Christian belief in the equality of souls in the eyes of God, came to transcend the provincialism that is natural to most cultures and that has prevailed in China throughout its history, despite its Confucian proto-universalist principles.

- The Old Testament did initiate a view of history as a purposeful and directional process from the beginning of Creation to the future expectation of a Messiah; however, the New Testament enhanced the connection of God and history with its concept of the Incarnation, when the eternal Word and Son of God "became flesh and dwelt among us." The subsequent Hellenization and Romanization of Christianity in the first centuries AD led historians to search for stages and directionality in the actual, empirical histories of humans, linking the eschatology of the Bible with the history of the Greeks, the creation of the Roman Empire, and the kingdoms created by the Germanic peoples. This connection reveals a God acting through humans, redeeming them as they open their souls to the work of grace, humility, and continence, and as they exhibit charity towards others and improve the world. This would lead Christians to initiate a "progressive" conception of history, as part of God's providential plan, to search for an intelligible pattern in history depicting the gradual improvement of mankind.

- Modern Europeans developed a true historiography characterized by a history of relatively continuous improvements, rather than by mere repetition of the historical styles of the past, as was the case in other civilizations. This was because only Europe experienced an increasing historical consciousness, a deep awareness of the passage of time, rooted in their Christianity and cosmopolitanism, and in their actual epoch-making transformations, the immense contributions of Greek knowledge, the anticipation of the "Peace of God" in Rome's creation of a universal empire characterized by relative peace and order, the successful spread among barbarians of the "New Message" of Christianity for all humans regardless of ethnicity or status, and the invention of universities in the Middle Ages, among many other novelties, followed by the Renaissance, and the continuous revolutions of the modern era in warfare, art, architecture, science, philosophy, and politics.

- It was during the Enlightenment era that historians began to think systematically about the unique progression of the West in science and technology, as well as in constitutional politics, and in relation to the "rights of man"—against the forces of darkness, ignorance, and vice which Enlightenment historians believed still held a tight grip over Europeans, and which needed to be defeated for the full potentialities of humans to be actualized in a future of plenty, harmony, and happiness. Man was a historical being in the process of achieving his full potentialities in the course of time.

- Modernist historians would secularize, not reject, the Christian idea of progress. They gained a more scientific understanding of history, identifying definite stages in the growth of reason and liberty, and in the manners and morals of humans, in terms of purely natural or man-made causes, rather than in terms of the providential hand of God. This idea of progress would come along with tremendous improvements in archival research and in historical methodologies, while the rest of the world would remain stuck with annalistic historiographies.

- The period between 1918 and 1970 would see the consolidation of a Grand Liberal Narrative, particularly in the wake of the defeat of Fascism in the Second World War and Communism in the Cold War. This narrative—the "Allied scheme of history"—would see in history a rational process of the growth of liberty, along with scientific and capitalist prosperity, with the United States as a model for the rest of the world, a result of thousands of years of Western evolution, combining the Greek democratic and rationalist legacy, Roman law, Judeo-Christian values, the Enlightenment, and free markets.

- The German Historical School of the second half of the nineteenth century, known for raising to a higher level the professionalization and specialization of history, constituted a profound questioning of the liberal idea of progress, with its nationalist advocacy of "the historicity of all knowledge and values" and its emphasis on the priority of the freedom of Germans as a people over the individual rights of abstract individuals. But German historicism would be thoroughly domesticated into a defense of "value-pluralism," according to which we should tolerate within each Western nation different cultural values except values that are intolerant of the "value-pluralism" of liberalism.

- Liberalism has an inbuilt progressive logic continually pressing for the "emancipation" of the individual from all traditional restraints, including sexual and racial collective identities, that infringe on the rights of individuals to choose their own lifestyle. This is backed by a new conception of positive liberty rather than mere negative liberty—a liberalism in which the government came to be assigned the role of reducing inequalities, increasing inclusiveness, and assisting in the self-realization of individuals. During the 1960s, this liberal progressivism would engender a New Left historiography that would judge the Grand Liberal Narrative—the Rise of the West—as an "unfinished project" requiring revision.

- The New Left historiography would come to include many schools—the French Annales historians, the New Cultural History, Microhistory, among others—with undeniably high scholarly achievements. All in all, these schools would attack or seek to transcend the "Eurocentrism" of the Grand Liberal Narrative, with its most radical exponents accusing the West of "under-developing" the rest of the world in its climb to supremacy. Old liberals gradually accommodated themselves to these revisions, confident in their defeat of communism in the early 1990s, announcing the "end of history" while including within their fold postmodern, environmental, multicultural, and global historical perspectives.

- The very civilization that produced the greatest historiographical tradition, with many fascinating schools of thought offering original insights, would come to embrace immigrant diversity and racial equity as a new phase in the progressive emancipation of humans. With the endorsement of diversity mandates would come new efforts to rewrite the history of this civilization as an "inclusive" one created by multiple peoples, with the nations of the West designated as "immigrant nations" from their inception, continually enriched by many races with their diverse historiographical traditions.

The Greek-Roman Historiographical Legacy

Not long ago, before the onset of "progressive" diversity mandates, it was generally accepted that historical writing began with the ancient Greeks. R.G. Collingwood made the argument in 1946 in *The Idea of History*, once the best-known book on the philosophy of history in the English-speaking world, that "history is a Greek word, meaning simply an investigation or inquiry."[940] Michael Grant, the famous classicist author of countless books, noted that the word *histor* in the classical Greek language referred to a learned man who settled legal disputes by looking into the accuracy of the events and the disputed allegations. From this legal term was derived the word *historie* as "a search for the rational explanation and understanding of phenomena."[941] In the "theocratic history" of Mesopotamia, accounts of past events consisted, as Collingwood wrote, of "mere assertions of what the writer already knows," not based on answers arrived after research.[942] The Hebrew scriptures were also theocratic history, in that there was no research to find the truth about the past with authors consciously judging the veracity of sources. It is only with Herodotus' book The Histories, written around 430 BC, that we witness for the first time a real inquiry about the past "to get answers to definite questions about matters of which one recognizes oneself as ignorant."[943] The writings of Homer and Hesiod were likewise mythical legends.

Herodotus was rightfully called "the father of history," for he was the first to write a historical inquiry which asked questions about the past based on the critical evaluation of the reports given by eyewitnesses, as was the practice in Greek courts, where one would cross-question the testimony of witnesses. Herodotus self-consciously wrote that the purpose of his book was to present "the results of the enquiry [history] carried out by Herodotus of Halicarnassus. The purpose is to prevent the traces of human events from being erased by time, and to preserve

---

[940] Collingwood, 1977, 18–19.
[941] Grant, 1970, 15–16.
[942] Collingwood, 14, 19.
[943] Ibid, 18.

the fame of the important and remarkable achievements produced by both Greeks and non-Greeks; among the matters covered is, in particular, the cause of the hostilities between Greeks and non-Greeks."[944] Collingwood elaborates that in theocratic history, "humanity is not an agent, but partly an instrument and partly a patient, of the actions recorded"; in Herodotus on the other hand, we have descriptions of "the deeds of men . . . to discover what men have done and partly to discover why they have done it."[945] He sought to understand the reasons men acted the way they did.

John Burrow, an old stock British scholar, maintains that historical writing "based on inquiry" began with Herodotus. In his book, *A History of Histories*, Burrow makes the assessment that we can only talk about "proto-history" in the ancient civilizations of Mesopotamia and Egypt, and among the Assyrians and Hittites who came later, in the sense that they engaged in "record keeping" and chronological recording of the deeds of rulers and the construction of genealogies. Herodotus "regarded himself as an auditor, a collector, recorder, sifter and judge of oral traditions about the recent or remoter past."[946] According to Mark Gilderfus, Herodotus "checked his information against the reports of eye-witnesses and participants and also consulted the documents available to him—inscriptional records, archives and official chronicles."[947]

Collingwood correctly qualifies that *The Histories* of Herodotus could not but derive very little from written sources or historical records, since there were few of these. This heavy reliance on oral sources restricted the writing of history among Greeks to events that happened "within living memory to people" with whom the author could have "personal contact." The Greeks could not write "all embracing" accounts of the remote past and of the peoples of the world, "ecumenical history, world history." For Collingwood, this absence of a concept of "world history" meant that the ancient Greeks lacked a proper "historical consciousness."

Now, it is true, as Burrow notes, that Herodotus' book "embodied extensive geographical and ethnographic surveys" of a variety of ethnic groups in the Mediterranean, North African, and Persian worlds, their clothing, diet, marriage, funerary customs, health, and treatment of disease.[948] It is for this reason that he is regarded, along with Hecataeus (b. 549 BC), as the originator of ethnography, the

---

[944] Dewald, 2008, xviii.
[945] Collingwood, 15, 19.
[946] Burrow, 2009, 24.
[947] Gilderfus, 1987, 14–15.
[948] Burrow, 25.

study of the cultures of other peoples, for his "indefatigable questioning" of different ethnic peoples about their customs and morals.[949] Still, I am inclined to agree with Collingwood that the unity of the historical mind of Herodotus was "only geographical, not an historical unity."[950] It was only after the conquests of Alexander the Great, and the creation of the Hellenistic and Roman empires, that the world became more than a geographical unity for the onset of a historical consciousness, which presupposes as a major condition an awareness of the histories of other peoples, reflections on the broader patterns of history as a whole. What about contemporary claims that other peoples were just as historically accomplished as the ancient Greeks?

We will address these claims later. For now, it will serve to bring up John Van Seters's thesis, articulated in a superb 1983 book of historical scholarship, *In Search of History: Historiography in the Ancient World and the Origins of Biblical History*, that an Israelite inaugurated the historical tradition of the West in the sixth century BC, roughly a century before Herodotus, in the so-called Deuteronomistic (Dtr) history of the Old Testament from Joshua to 2 Kings. The term "Deuteronomistic history" was coined in 1943 by the German scholar Martin Noth, who argued that the books of the Former Prophets of the Hebrew canon— Joshua, Judges, Samuel and Kings—were a unified history written during the sixth century BC, when the Israelites were exiled from Israel and brought to Babylon.[951] Elaborating this argument, backed by extensive sources, Van Seters uses the following criteria to identify history writing in ancient Israel:

- It has "a specific form of tradition in its own right" (as opposed to being merely incidental) to "explain or give meaning" in a literary way to the way things are, showing thereby "some awareness of the historical process" "to account for social change," and "provide new legitimation."
- History writing is not primarily about the accurate reporting of past events, but involves recalling the significance of past events, as we find in Dtr history.

---

[949] Grant (1970, 18, 62) identifies Herodotus as "the pioneer not only of history but of anthropology and ethnology," while recognizing that "around 500 BC a decisive turn was given by Hecataeus of Miletus. In spare but elegant and vigorous Ionic, he wrote two prose works, *Journey round the World* and *Genealogies. . . .* Hecataeus made the subject of geography into a much more serious study than it had been before."

[950] Burrow, 31.

[951] Polzin, 1976.

- While history writing examines the causes of present circumstances, in the world of antiquity at large "these causes were primarily moral"; modern theories of causation or laws of evidence should not be used as criteria.

- History writing has to be national or corporate in character, as was the case in Dtr history; chronological reporting about the deeds of kings do not constitute history.[952]

Van Seters brings out the best of the annalistic form of writing in the Near East; for example, he shows that chronicles did date events rather precisely to day and month of the year, with some chronicles showing evidence of "research" or "a gleaning of materials about the past from various sources." While these chronicles do not yet constitute history writing proper, they "created the potential for the historical 'research' and reconstruction of the past that is indispensable to the development of history writing."[953] What made Dtr history more than a chronicle was, "above all," the fact that it was a history of a "people's past," of the founding of a "nation under Moses, through the conquest under Joshua and the rule of judges, to the rise of the monarchy under Saul and David."[954] In Dtr history, "the royal ideology is incorporated into the identity of the people as a whole" (rather than the ruler alone). "The doctrine of Israel's election as the chosen people of Yahweh set the nation apart from other peoples. . . . All other callings and elections, whether to kinship, priesthood, or prophecy, were viewed in association with the choice of the people as a whole. . . . Nowhere outside of Israel was the notion of special election extended to the people as a whole."[955]

Van Seters shows similarities between the Dtr historian and Herodotus. If the former "gathered his own material . . . in the form of disparate oral stories," so did Herodotus derive "very little" from written sources, or "historical" records; his work was mostly "based on eyewitness accounts."[956] All Hebrew historiography is written from "a theological perspective," but so is the book of Herodotus, *The Histories*, strongly interested in divine providence. "Like Herodotus, the Old Testament exhibits a dominant concern with the issue of divine retribution for unlawful

---

[952] Van Seters, 1983, 4–5.

[953] Ibid, 80, 85, 357.

[954] Ibid, 359.

[955] Ibid, 359–60.

[956] Ibid, 40–7.

acts as a fundamental principle of historical causality."[957] Both works are characterized by a thematic unity and a sustained prose narrative about a people conscious of their national identities (though Van Seters barely says anything about
the emergence of a Greek national identity centered on personal freedom in contrast to Asiatic despotism).

In reply to Van Seters: It is true that in Herodotus' account the deities did play
a role in human affairs, dreams, oracles, and omens. But all in all, it is easier to
accept John Gould's judgement that Herodotus "took the possibility of supernatural causation in human experience as seriously as he took the involvement of
human causation."[958] In fact, Herodotus was "cautious in admitting" the presence
of gods at work in human actions, not because of religious disbelief, but because
of his "uncertainty" or "implicit acknowledgement of the limitations of human
knowledge in such matters," sometimes offering alternative possibilities for the
occurrence of the events, or declining to identify the particular god involved. Herodotus' list of reasons for the Persian war emphasized human motives: arrogance,
excessive pride, blind enjoyment of riches, and lust for power, which brought the
wrath of the gods and their intervention, but which nevertheless pointed to historical explanations relatively free of divine influence, which was not the case in
Deuteronomistic history.

By the time we get to Thucydides' *History of the Peloponnesian War*, written a
few decades after Herodotus' Histories (430 BC), the gods ceased to directly influence the course of events; history is entirely caused by the actions of human beings, even if the historical actors remained guided by a belief in gods, oracles, or
divinations. Thucydides amplified the call for accuracy in the reporting of events,
contrasting his inquiry with that of "prose chronicles, who are less interested in
telling the truth than in catching the attention of the public, whose authorities
cannot be checked." He willfully restricted himself to contemporary history and
eyewitness accounts, knowing that the passage of time made accounts of early
Greek history unreliable. This is the point. Even if we were to agree with everything Van Seters says, Herodotus was just the beginning of Western historiography. While Near Eastern and Israelite historiographical traditions ceased, stagnated, or barely improved, Europeans would go on to build upon their earlier
achievements. They eventually developed a full historical consciousness, which is
incredibly hard to achieve.

---

[957] Ibid, 39.
[958] Gould, 1994, 91–106.

For Nietzsche, Thucydides was "the grand summation, the last manifestation of that strong, stern, hard matter-of-factness instinctive to the older Hellenes."[959] What Nietzsche admired, though, was not Thucydides' neutral impartiality per se, but that his values were not those of a Platonist seeking to escape the harsh reality of human struggle and conflict in a realm of perfections. It was Thucydides' realism, his ability to deal with the world as it was, and his rigorously clinical assessment of human nature that appealed to Nietzsche. Edith Hamilton, author of the once very popular book, *The Greek Way*, originally published in 1930, insists that Thucydides wrote his book "because he believed that men would profit from a knowledge of what brought about that ruinous struggle precisely as they profit from a statement of what causes a deadly disease."[960] Hamilton elucidates Thucydides' concern with the causes of the war, and how he differentiated triggering incidents affecting the timing from the ultimate cause of the war. The confrontation between Athens and Sparta was not generated by misguided humans who could have been dissuaded into a different course of action; no, the Athenians were driven to imperialism, seeking threatening alliances against Sparta, by the natural human obsession with dominating others; and Sparta was driven to react, knowing that lack of action would simply invite further hostilities by the Athenians and others. This is why Thucydides wrote a book "written not for the moment, but for all time."

This clinical analysis of human nature in history would never find expression in the historiographical traditions outside the West. There are many timeless insights in Thucydides about the natural impulses of humans and their varied expressions in different characters and circumstances. He and Herodotus started a historiographical tradition that would last continuously for over a thousand years. We can only go over the surface. Diodorus Siculus (first century BC), known for writing his *Bibliotheca Historica* in forty books, of which fifteen survive intact, mentions many historians on whose works he relied. Some refer to this book as a "Universal History," both for its comprehensive coverage (from the mythic history of the destruction of Troy up to the death of Alexander the Great, including the early centuries of Rome), and for its worldly geographical descriptions of Egypt, India, and Arabia to Europe. He called it "Bibliotheca" in acknowledgment that he was assembling a composite work from many sources. This was not a

---

[959] Jenkins, 2011.
[960] Hamilton, 1942, 184.

history based on eyewitness accounts, but a history based on the authority of prior historical authors/sources.

Siculus, however, was really a compiler rather than a universal historian, because his work was descriptive in character, lacking an interpretative scheme. His predecessor Polybius (200–118 BC) can be said to be the original ecumenical or universal historian, in full awareness that in trying to answer the question in his book, *Histories*, why "the Romans succeeded . . . in bringing under their rule almost the whole of the inhabited world" and writing about how "the affairs of Italy and of Africa are connected with those of Asia and of Greece and all events bear a relationship and contribute to a single end," he was indeed, in his words, the first "to examine the general and comprehensive scheme of events" and to look at history as an "organic whole."[961] In answering this question, Polybius raised the analysis of historical causality to a higher level of precision and analysis, by adding the "how and why" to the "who, what, where, and when" of Thucydides.[962] He sought "to record with fidelity what actually happened," with profuse references to prior historical accounts. Because Polybius covered a long-time span of history, 264–146 BC, unlike Herodotus and Thucydides, he could not rely on eyewitness accounts only. Fortunately, in his time, there were already many authoritative "works of previous historians who had already written the histories of particular societies at particular times," including Rome's own careful preservation of memorials and ancestral portraits.[963]

Polybius' universal perspective was also visible in his effort to provide a sweeping explanation of the rise and fall of civilizations in general, expressing for the first time, in a cohesive manner, the principle of cyclical history.[964] States experience a natural cycle similar to biological organisms, characterized by growth, zenith, and decay. Primitive kinship first emerges and develops into monarchy, monarchy devolves into tyranny, and eventually tyranny is replaced by the aristocratic rule of the best (the men of virtue, piety, and courage who created Rome). This rule then degenerates into oligarchic privilege and excess, followed by democracy, and finally mob rule. He believed that the Roman state was superior to all prior forms of government in combining the best of three forms of rule, monarchical (elected consuls), aristocratic (senate), and democratic (popular assemblies). But,

---

[961] Walbank, 1979, 41–43.
[962] Derow, 1994.
[963] Collingwood, 33.
[964] Champion, 2013.

in his estimation, while this mixed policy could slow down the cycle, it could not avert the eventual disintegration of Rome.

Another revealing quality of ancient Western historiography was its preoccupation with the moral character and personality of great men. Who can forget the famous *Parallel Lives* of Plutarch (AD 46–120), mandatory reading for every young European man not long ago? Nineteenth century positivists, who believed that historians should remain objectively preoccupied with the facts alone without judgments, downplayed Plutarch as a historian for his moralistic judgements about the virtues to be emulated and the vices to be avoided in his illustrations of great men. Yet Plutarch "read voraciously, and faithfully reported what he found in a wide variety of sources."[965] He was "one of the most educated men of antiquity" who knew and quoted "all the major Greek historians," and supplemented his narratives with information from letters, inscriptions, and public documents.[966] His *Lives* were an effort to demonstrate the importance of rational self-restraint against irrational passions, exhibiting a high sensitivity to the dynamics of human motivation, the interaction of contrasting traits, and how they can complement each other within the same character, combined with keen observations about the physical appearance of the characters, thereby showing insight into the variety and complexity of human behavior.

It has been said, nevertheless, that Greek/Roman historiography was limited by its view of an unchanging human nature. Michael Grant, in *The Ancient Historians*, says that "Plutarch has no idea of dynamic biography. . . . The ancients were still mostly convinced that a man's character is fixed; at any point in his life, he is what he always was and always will be."[967] But it is more complicated than that. Herodotus did imply in his ethnographic observations that human nature manifests itself differently (in terms of customary practices) in different geographical settings. The claim that the cyclical view of history "was entailed by a belief in an unchanging human nature" forgets that this view postulates a dramatic alteration in the characters of humans, from virtuous qualities during the rise of states, to decadent traits as wealth, peace, and ease become the new reality. The decline of the Roman character is a pervading theme of Roman historiography; already apparent in Cato the Elder (234–149 BC), author of *Origins*, of which only fragments survive, about the beginnings of Rome up until the victory over Macedonia

---

[965] Cornell, 2004, 3.
[966] Stadter, 1999; Tatum, 2013.
[967] Grant, 317.

in 168 BC. Cato eulogized the "Spartan" austerity and simplicity of the early men who built Rome, and lamented the effeminate influence of Greek learning. Sallust (86–35 BC) saw the old Roman virtues of frugality and piety decline under the influence of luxury and Asiatic indulgences and taste in the first century BC.[968] But, for Sallust, it was not all about character decomposition; he also saw an intensifying civil strife in late republican Rome between two factions: the old patrician class in control of the Senate, and the plebeians in control of the popular assemblies. Sallust, the most widely read ancient historian between 1450 and 1550, a *"popularis"* and supporter of Caesar, praises Tiberius Gracchus in his *The Jugurthine War* (41–40 BC), recognizing the Gracchi brothers as "vindicators of the liberty of the people" against the "shamelessness, bribery and rapacity" of the old aristocracy, as he put it in *Catiline's War,* grabbing the spoils of war and leaving citizen farmers landless, as they were burdened with prolonged military service.[969]

Along with its psychological portraits, Western historiography was characterized by an "elaborated, secular, prose narrative" combined with a literary ability to draw the reader into the events and personalities, in striking contrast to the bureaucratic, impersonal, and annalistic reporting that persisted for centuries in non-western historiography. Roman historians were educated with strict rules for prose composition, and in the art of literary rhetoric. They took delight in their character portraits. Criticizing them for their moralizing judgements betrays a lack of appreciation for their psychological insights, the inevitability of judgements in historical writing, and the importance of bringing out the dramatic character that is actual history. Not until Gibbon's *History of the Decline and Fall of the Roman Empire,* published in the late 1700s, would anyone see the need to supersede the historiography of ancient Romans.

Livy (59 BC–AD 17), immortalized for his monumental history of Rome in 142 books, of which thirty-five survive, from the earliest legends of Rome before the traditional founding in 753 BC through the reign of Augustus in Livy's own lifetime, is widely acknowledged as a "superb narrator." He understood that his accounts of early Rome have "more of the charm of poetry than of sound historical record," although future antiquarians have learned much about the foundational myths of Rome from these accounts. As in Sallust before him, in Livy, as John

---

[968] Breisach, 1983, 55.

[969] Sallust, 2007; Swidzinski, 2007. Cornell (2004) also provides a good account of the reliability of ancient Roman historical works.

Burrow writes, "the question of moral fibre, nurtured by war, weakened by peace and ease, became the core of Roman history."[970]

Livy raised to a higher level of explanatory sophistication the social historical perspective incipient in Sallust, by accentuating the significance of the conflict between the old patricians and the plebeians, which he traced back over the centuries, recounting how these two classes had managed to get along with the abolition of debt enslavement, the redistribution of land, and the eventual opening of the highest offices (consulships, censorships) to wealthy plebeians. He records how in the first century BC this consensus broke down as an elite of rich plebeians allied with the patricians could not resolve their differences with a poor class of smallholders, who were the backbone of the citizen army. Upon returning from military service to their neglected farms, these smallholders, as they struggled to pay debts and taxes, would lose their farms, which made the practice of citizen soldiers obsolete, and led to the rise of private professional armies.[971]

It was Livy's view that Rome had managed to rise and survive major threats, such as the disaster of Cannae, insofar as the upper classes had acted in moderation, bringing the plebeians to rule alongside them, and redistributing the spoils of war. Roman "firmness" and "sternness" were rooted in this social reality, whereas Roman decadence was rooted in the lustful rapacity of a wealthy

---

[970] Burrow, 93.

[971] Morato, 2017. The fall of "the class of yeomen," or independent farmers, and the rise of large landowners relying on servile labor, many of whom were "absentee landlords" living in Rome, is an argument adopted and developed by M. Rostovtzeff in his 1927 classic, *A History of the Ancient World*, subsequently republished in two separate books, *Greece* and *Rome*. I don't want to give the impression that this social history was well-developed already in Livy, a historian who, by the standards of today, can "reasonably be charged as unscientific," as Betty Radice writes in the Introduction to *The War with Hannibal, Books XXI–XXX of The History of Rome from its Foundation* (1972). This readable book, full of dramatic detail, was written for a moral purpose, much as other Roman historians wrote their histories. As Livy himself told his readers: "The study of history is the best medicine for a sick mind; for in history, we have a record of the infinite variety of human experience plainly set out for all to see: and in that record you can find for yourself and your country both examples and warning: fine things to take as models, base things, rotten through and through, to avoid." But the effort Livy puts in trying to get the history right, his description of the actions of countless personalities and events, is astounding; and we should take him at his word when he says "I do hope my passion for Rome's past has not impaired my judgement." Livy tries throughout to offer different perspectives, among the participants, on the nature of the events, over which course of military or political action to follow, always trying to get the dates right, the months and years of the events—in a "novelistic" way, yes, but always in vivid detail, not by way of empty generalities, and backed by a deep grasp of human nature.

oligarchy expropriating the citizen farmers. At the same time, Livy also pointed to demagogues who stirred up the plebs towards mob rule out of their tyrannical ambition. It has been said that the historiography of ancient times contained truths valid "for all time." In his *Discourses on Livy* in 1517, Machiavelli explained, after a close reading of Livy, that all forms of government—monarchical, aristo-cratic, and democratic—are flawed, and that it was the good fortune of the early Roman republic to combine traits from these three. The inherent conflict of in-terests between the nobles and the people can turn out to be constructive, as long as there is an institutional balance of power in which tribunes of the people can wield power. There is never an ideal political order in which conflict is avoidable.

Perhaps the most admired Roman historian is Publius Cornelius Tacitus (AD 56–120). Tacitus enjoyed a very high reputation from the late sixteenth to the late seventeenth century, admired by Gibbon for "the force of his rhetoric . . . to in-struct the reader by sensible and powerful reflections." He wrote primarily about the relations between the Emperor and the Senate, not the wider world of the Em-pire, based on the testimony of eyewitnesses, published transactions of the Senate, news of the court, collections of emperors' speeches, and memoirs. In his didactic concern "to ensure that merit is recorded, and to confront evil deeds and words with the fear of posterity's denunciation," it has been said that he was a moralizing historian.[972] His focus was on the motives of the characters, exposing hypocrisy and dissimulation. Some praise the brevity of description of his Latin style, its "ep-igrammatic" character, or lack of ornamentation. The period he covered, mostly the first century AD, offered only meager examples of virtue—which may be why he praised the Germanic peoples in what may be his best-known work, the fasci-nating ethnographic essay titled *Germania*. Linked to the Third Reich, this essay would also play a key role in the construction of a historiography identifying free-dom as the most important ideal of Western history.[973] Tacitus observed the Ger-mans on their own terms rather than in light of Roman values, showing admira-tion for German sexual temperance, dignity, courage, and loyalty—without falling prey to the modern myth of the noble savage, describing as well their drunken-ness, idleness, and quarrelsomeness. It was this lack of discipline, he believed, that gave Romans an advantage over the formidable German warriors.

[972] Burrow, 26.
[973] Krebs, 2011.

The Emergence of a Christian Historical Consciousness

For all we have said about Greek and Roman historiography (and there were other historians, such as Suetonius, Appian, and Casius Dios), contemporary scholars invariably agree that the ancients remained a "non-historical" people. Herbert Butterfield is convinced "the Greeks did not achieve historical mindedness, and never could have achieved it, because they had the wrong view of time and the time process." The Greeks "only knew of a comparatively short history behind them—they thought that the historical past extended back for only a very few hundred years."[974] But even in the case of the Romans, despite some of their long-term accounts, including a 1400-year history by Casius Dio, Collingwood insists that Roman historians thought of Rome as an "unchanging substance," "the eternal city," experiencing cyclical changes but no identifiable stages of development.[975] Livy never sought to explain how Roman institutions came to be, how they changed over time, other than noticing, if we may add to Collingwood's explanation, the virtues that made possible its rise and the vices bringing about its decline. It was a history without periodization about a city that seemed to be ready-made before history began.

Roman historiography was also particularistic, self-centered around Rome, without grasping the historical dynamics of other people and their place within the historical process. Tacitus distorted history, Collingwood adds, by "representing it essentially as a clash of characters" portrayed as either "exaggeratedly good" or "exaggeratedly bad."[976] As talented as Tacitus was in his character-drawings, his approach encouraged the narrowly circumscribed perspective of seeking the causes of historical events in the personalities of the main actors—a retrogression from the world-historical perspective of Polybius.

The Marxist historian E. H. Carr, author of a fourteen-volume work covering only the first twelve years of the history of the Soviet Union, argues similarly that "the classical civilization of Greece and Rome was basically unhistorical." For Thucydides, "nothing significant had happened in time before the events which he described and nothing significant was likely to happen thereafter." He goes on to explain in his small but insightful 1961 book, *What is History?* that a cyclical

---

[974] Butterfield, 1981, 118, 122.
[975] Collingwood, 44–45.
[976] Ibid, 39.

view of history, the sense that history is "not going anywhere," is devoid of a proper historical consciousness. One must have a sense that there is a "direction in history" to interpret the past properly. While a historian does not have to believe that history is progressing "towards the goal of the perfection of man's estate on earth," without a conception of progress, which entails a history that is characterized by development, such as an increasing capacity to understand and master the laws of nature and improve the living standards of people, we can't speak of "historical consciousness." Carr believes that "it was the Jews, and after them, the Christians, who introduced an entirely new element by postulating a goal towards which the historical process is moving—the teleological view of history." It was "Jewish-Christianity" that gave history "meaning and purpose."[977]

According to Collingwood, Christianity contributed the following to the eventual rise of a modern historical consciousness: the universalism that all persons are equal in the sight of God, that "all peoples are involved in the working out of God's purpose," and that therefore a Christian can't remain content with the particularistic history of one people, but must strive for a universal history. The events that occur in the world must be ascribed to the workings of Providence, which means that one must try to detect an intelligible pattern in the overall history of humans, and treat earlier events as leading up to, or preparing for, God's ultimate plan. This means, we might add, that in order to make sense of history's pattern, history must be divided into epochs, each identified for its contribution to progress and for the ultimate plan.[978]

The flaw in this interpretation is that it does not draw a distinction between the Old and the New Testament view of history, and the subsequent Hellenized and Romanized Christian conception articulated in the first centuries AD. The Old Testament, to be sure, offered a purposeful and directional view of history from the beginning of time, from the Creation and the expulsion from Paradise of Adam and Eve, as a result of their original sin, to the second beginning of mankind with Noah after the flood, followed by God's promise of land to Abraham, demonstrated in the liberation of Jews from Egyptian captivity, followed by numerous events with references to peoples and civilizations in the Near East: Egypt, Babylonia, Assyria, Persia, and Jerusalem. The Hebrew Bible, Van Seters is correct, offered a dramatic long-term narrative of a people intensively preoccupied with their past, the first accounts to go beyond the royal annals of the

---

[977] Carr, 1974, 31–48; 109–132.
[978] Collingwood, 46–52.

Mesopotamian/Egyptian empires to produce a history of a people seeking a national identity with quasi-universalist aspects in its account of the Creation and the Flood. The Hebrew people were unique in rejecting the prevalent belief in recurrent cycles among the religions of Mesopotamia and the peoples of the Hellenistic-Roman world, by looking forward to a future world when the injustices and evil in this world would be corrected.

The Old Testament conception, nevertheless, was about a particular people, the Jews, and, in this respect, it was not universal. It was a conception that remained preoccupied with the Jewish historical experience, leading to a final act of God that would signal the end of history, with dreams of a Messianic kingdom— this in a historical context of loss of political independence, destruction of the Temple, and eventually the dispersion and exile of Jews in foreign lands. The Bible as a whole, both Old and New Testament, did not try to make sense of actual human historical events beyond the experiences of Jews; it did not try to discover a meaningful pattern in the empirical happenings of world history. History in the Bible is meaningful because it is oriented toward some transcendent purpose (the future expectation of a Messiah), but this expectation is not seen to be developing through successive historical stages, because the truth has already been revealed. This is a view that Karl Löwith holds in his 1949 philosophical meditation *Meaning in History*. History is directed by the providence of God's supreme insight and will, but God's ways are hard to make out, and cannot be comprehended by reason. The message of the Bible is that we must trust God's justice in spite of manifest evil in the world, and faithfully wait for justice to be done on Judgement Day. The Biblical conception is similar in some respects to the Greek cyclical acceptance of fate, in the way it looks at history through all the ages as a story of mere genesis and disintegration, action and suffering, as a "continuous repetition of painful miscarriage and costly achievements which end in ordinary failures."[979]

But Löwith is rather indifferent towards the historiography of subsequent Christians who sought to discover in actual history the spiritual unfolding of salvation. Even though the New Testament does not seek to make sense of the actual history of the Hellenistic-Roman world from which it emerged, subsequent Christians, as Butterfield says in *The Origins of History*, "could not help vindicating the idea of the Jesus of History, Jesus the man who had lived at a certain time and in a definite place."[980] The religion of Christianity "was fastened to the hard earth"

---

[979] Löwith, 1949, 182–90.
[980] Butterfield, 172–3.

through "their continuing concern about the possible imminent coming end of the world, and their contact with Greek philosophy"; and, I would add, through the very concept of the incarnation and the cross. Christianity departs from the Old Testament in the consummated advent of Jesus, which signifies that God has given His grace through the hands of His Son who in His sacrifice has brought redemption to all humankind. Humans are no longer fully corrupted, but are newly capable of achieving ethical and eschatological goals in this world. The Christian God is not impersonal, totally unknowable, and separate from our world. He is both transcendental and immanent, for in the incarnation, and the idea that Christ is both fully God and fully human, the unfathomable God of the Old Testament finds concrete expression in history. Christianity recognized the dignity of the material world and its ability for expressing the spirit. Christ is the image of the invisible deity here on earth, and human action can bring about the world's transformation.

In line with the incarnation and immanence of God on Earth, Jesus added an "ethics of love, or compassion," which cultivated "a new sensitivity to human suffering." This motivated Christians to struggle against evil in this world, which set in motion a historical process of moral progression.[981] This religion brought the hope that it was possible to create a better world, for it was a religion that no longer saw suffering as unchangeable, but called upon believers to feel responsibility for the suffering of others. In contrast to Greek pagan ethics and Roman stoicism, which held that it was folly to struggle against the destiny of human limitations and the natural inequalities between aristocrats and ordinary people, there was a feeling of hope and improvement embedded in the ethics of Christianity, according to which all humans on this Earth were equally capable of moral improvement through faith in Christ, and through charitable human relationships and benevolence to strangers.

In its goal to improve the human condition, Christianity would indeed go on to promote a new sexual morality against cousin and polygynous marriage, sexual activity outside marriage, sex with minors, divorce, infanticide, and abortion, in favor of monogamy, freedom to choose one's husband and wife, and affectionate family relations.[982] Non-western religions conceived of salvation as something to be achieved by escaping into the "world behind" or the "world beyond." But

---

[981] Nemo, 2006, 29–38.
[982] Harper, 2013.

among Christians, a sense emerged that history was not a cycle of time but a for-ward-moving process, a linear movement from Creation to the end of time.

However, it was only with the Hellenization and Romanization of Christianity in the first centuries AD that we see philosophers and historians trying to make sense of the connection of God and world history. The New Testament taught that God had connected himself to the happenings of the world through the historical figure of Jesus in the flow of time from the Creation to the eventual Second Com-ing, which made it impossible for Christians to view history as cyclical, but instead postulated a beginning, a central event, and an ultimate goal. The historians of the first centuries AD would take this idea further by interpreting the history before the coming of Jesus and the history of their own times through a Christian lens. Irenaeus (130–202) thus interpreted the Old Testament as the preparation for the New, as an "upward" development which demonstrated the divine "education of mankind."[983]

God, by becoming man through Christ, restored humanity to being in the like-ness of God, which humans had lost in the Fall of Adam. He saw an upward move-ment from the period of infancy in which Adam failed God's command and elic-ited God's punishment, to that of Christ (the new Adam), who represents the new head of humanity and undoes Adam's disobedience. This idea of the "education of mankind" was developed further as Christians wrestled with the historical meaning of Greek philosophy as well as the meaning of Rome as a universal em-pire in God's providential plan. Early Christians neither rejected outright nor ac-cepted Greek philosophy completely, but took a historical view by arguing, as Jus-tin Martyr (100–165) did, that Greece represented a stage in the growth of truth towards fullness in the revelation of Christ. Christ was thought to be "known in part even by Socrates." Clement of Alexandria (150–215), likewise, wrote about God planting the seeds of Christian revelation in Plato and Aristotle.

As the expectation of the Second Coming weakened, Christians developed a conception of historical time that went beyond the finality of the Last Day, guided instead by the promise of redemption in the course of time, for the Creation was not perfect to begin with, but needed time to grow and mature. Before the Last Day, Christians had a historical role to play: "the good news must be preached to all the heathens."[984] For God to accomplish his mission to mankind, a long span of time may be required. Origen of Alexandria (185–253) and his disciples strove

---

[983] Breisach, 77–106.
[984] Breisach, 1983.

to give meaning to the history of Rome. The seeds of Christianity had been sown by Christ in every human since Creation; God had attended to the best in Greece as deliberately as he had revealed the Law to the Jews. The universal peace created by Rome was intended to create the conditions for the foundation of a universal Christian Church. Christians could not therefore discard as futile, as part of a meaningless cycle, the histories of Greece and Rome, for these histories were also part of the divinely ordained progress of humanity.

With the conversion of the emperor Constantine the Great (272–337), the Pax Romana came to be widely accepted as God's instrument for the dissemination of the Gospel over secure roads and seas. It was the historian Eusebius (260/265–339), a close advisor of Constantine, who integrated Rome into Christianity's "upward" education of mankind, generating thereby the possibility of a truly universalist conception of the concrete history of humans. He did so in his Chronicle and his Ecclesiastical History, within a time scale and a chronological timeline that included the rulers and dynasties of the Assyrians, Egyptians, and other peoples, as well as the main figures and events of the Old Testament, the work of the Apostles to the deaths of St. Paul and St Peter, through to the making of Christianity into an officially recognized religion by Constantine in 313. Eusebius provided a chronology of the major world-historical events, placing the birth of Christ in the year 5198 from Adam or 2015 from Abraham, on the basis of many documents and textual sources to ensure a proper record. He was the author of many books based on carefully collected materials, though we must not assume he was a better historian than the Greeks/Romans, who were literary masters of prose, engaging narrators, and insightful psychological analysts. In the words of Michael Grant, Eusebius' narrative was "uninspiring," "dull, muddled and haphazard," with a "cumbersome, obscure and slovenly Greek." [985]

While Saint Augustine (354–430) was not a historian, he offered a profound expression to the idea that truth is inseparable from historical time and that history points towards an end entailing "the education of the human race." Augustine rejected the Greek idea that history goes on repeating itself endlessly through time, and that nothing new emerges with each cycle. Any cyclic view is inherently unable to grasp the meaning of time. In his Confessions, he asked: "For what is time?" He answered: "If nothing passed away, there would not be past time; and if nothing were coming, there would not be future time; and if neither were, there

---

[985] Grant, 357.

would not be present time."[986] Therefore, humans could not have conceived of time if history was characterized by cycles repeating themselves throughout endless ages. In *The City of God*, he argued that God created time: "For, though Himself eternal, and without beginning, yet He caused time to have a beginning; and man, whom He had not previously made He made in time, not from a new and sudden resolution, but by His unchangeable and eternal design."[987] From this initial creation of man in time, we can witness thereafter, in the flow of historical time, "the education of the human race."

Nisbet, however, pushes too far the argument that an idea of progress in a linear and cumulative way can be found in Augustine's writing.[988] Löwith may be more judicious in his claim that "for Augustine the historical task of the Church is not to develop the Christian truth through successive stages but simply to spread it, for the truth as such is established."[989] And while it is hard to deny that Augustine was interested, in the words of Butterfield, "in the whole drama of human life in time," Nisbet underestimates Augustine's break with the Greek idea that man can attain perfection through renunciation of the material world and embracement of a life of pure reason. For Augustine, human perfection, even among Christians, was impossible, for even the most faithful can't overcome the temptations of the flesh, vanity, and selfish anger. Nevertheless, Augustine did not call for an escape from this world, but for humans to show humility, continence, and charity towards others in this world. Moreover, other Christians, including Pelagius (born 354 BC), a contemporary of Augustine, accepted the Aristotelian idea that there is in nature a *telos*, a striving towards the actualization of perfection, and that humans are capable of moral perfection so long as they create a truly Christian society.[990] It is also the case that Augustine, influenced perhaps by Eusebius' attempt to write the actual history of humans within a Christian scheme, did write of epochs, with eight stages referring to the resurrection of Christ and history culminating in a last stage, a blissful period on Earth, prior to entry of the blessed into heaven. Conflict, suffering, torment, fire, and destruction would be endemic, until the attainment of the heavenly city, where humans would be "delivered from all ill, filled with all good, enjoying indefeasibly the delights of eternal

---

[986] Augustine, 1961, Book XI, Chapter 14.
[987] Augustine, 2009, Book XII, Chapter 14.
[988] Nisbett, 59–68.
[989] Löwith, 166.
[990] Brown, 1967.

joys, oblivious of sins, oblivious of sufferings."[991]

Other historians would follow, such as Paulus Orosius (AD 375/385–420), a pupil of Augustine, who wrote *The Seven Books of History Against the Pagans*. These are "considered to be one of the books with the greatest impact on historiography during the period between antiquity and the Middle Ages," integrating into a Christian scheme the history of humanity starting with the Creation up to the times in which he lived.[992] Scholars acknowledge him as "the first Christian universalist in history" with his argument that there were four successive historical empires—Babylonia, pagan Rome, Macedonia and Carthagecato th—followed by a fifth empire, that of the Christian Rome of his time, as the inheritor of all the achievements of the past. But something was missing in the early medieval Christian universalist histories: integration of the superior historical inquiries of the ancient Greeks (Herodotus, Thucydides, Polybius) and Romans (Livy, Sallust, Tacitus), with their higher preoccupation, with checking the trustworthiness of their sources, explaining the reasons for the occurrence of events, and writing detailed narratives in elegant prose. One can indeed say that the ancients would not be surpassed until modern times.

But we must not thereby neglect the achievement of medieval historians in their integration of the new barbarian Germanic kingdoms within the Christian scheme, ascertaining the designs of Divine Providence in the events and kingdoms witnessed. The "universalism" of the *History of the Franks*, by Gregory of Tours (539–594), a Gallo-Roman aristocrat, consisted of a few opening pages summarizing Biblical events, the incarnation of Christ, and the history of the Church, before narrowing the focus to Gaul, in what was then a very localized European world of isolated regions. He related many miracles as examples of the ever-present power of God in the occurrence of events, with portents as warnings from God of things to come, such as lights in the sky, comets, and wolves in the city. For Burrow, Gregory can "hardly" be viewed as a "great historian," for his narrative was "too episodic, too uninterested in generalization and context."[993]

But things would improve with the onset of the Carolingian Renaissance, which brought a revival of letters, accompanied by wide-scale copying of classical texts, under the reign of Charlemagne (768–814). A product of this age was Einhard's 830 *Life of Charlemagne*, which became a model for subsequent biographies

---

[991] Augustine, 2009, Book XXII, Chapter 30.
[992] Chisholm, 1911.
[993] Burrow, 201.

such as Bishop Asser's 893 *Life of Alfred the Great*. Einhard was fortunate to have access to the work of Suetonius, a biographer during the time of Tacitus, author of *Lives of Illustrious Men* (the poets Terence, Virgil, and Horace), and *Lives of the Caesars*. Suetonius is known for avoiding the heavy moralizing of Plutarch, "looking at personages with a cooler and more disenchanted eye," and for attributing to Julius Caesar the famous phrase "the die is cast" when he crossed the Rubicon.[994] Einhard offered keen insight into Charlemagne's political success, battlefield strategy, foreign and domestic policies, friends, enemies, and personal habits. But the Carolingian empire soon disintegrated into separate feudal kingdoms and, in the overwhelmingly rural world of this age, we find instead a type of historical writing that paid homage to a few Christian universalist principles, before focusing on the episodic events of local and national regions.

It is hard for humans to have a historical consciousness without discerning a developmental pattern in history, accumulation of innovations, continuous growth of knowledge, improvement in manners and morals, to allow them to transcend a conception of time in terms of the natural cycles of the seasons and the cyclical succession of civilizations and dynasties. Traditional cultures tend to be, by their very nature, unhistorical, and therefore not able to develop a proper historical consciousness. Nevertheless, there was progress, if intermittent and slow.

Countless chronicles, which laid the groundwork for the nationalist histories of ethnic Europeans in the future, were produced during the Middle Ages: the *Anglo-Saxon Chronicle*, written in the late 900s, now recognized as a key historical source during the period following the Roman presence and preceding the Norman invasion in 1066; the *Chronicle of the Slavs* of 1170; the *Chronicle of Livonia*, describing the conquest and conversion of Latvia and Estonia; the *Chronicle of Prague*, completed in 1119, starting with the creation of the world, then describing the legendary foundation of the Bohemian state, and ending in 1038; the *Chronicle of the Poles*, and *Chronicle of Novgorod* from the 900s to 1400; this is to mention just a few. These chronicles, as Breisach says, "usually reported events, item by isolated item, and their reason for recording an event was not its effects on the subsequent course of events but its being noteworthy in its own right or for instructing human beings about the spiritual cosmos they lived in."[995]

---

[994] Grant, 335–6.
[995] Breisach, 77–106.

The emerging concept of causality, in which a given state of affairs was accounted for in terms of antecedent factors or events, evident in the work of Thucydides and Polybius, was abandoned in medieval historiography. Great historical works were produced, but they were few and far between. One of the most respected is Bede's *Ecclesiastical History of the English People*. Although the aim of this work was didactic, to record examples of goodness and wickedness, Bede is acknowledged as a "measured" historian "completely in control of his theme," producing a history of the English peoples "generally chronologically lucid ... [and] scrupulous in giving his sources."[996] Covering the history of England from the time of Julius Caesar to the date of its completion in 731, this book is considered one of the most important primary references on Anglo-Saxon history.

Otto of Freising's *The Two Cities: A Chronicle of Universal History to the Year 1146*, followed Augustine in seeing in world-historical events the development in time of a divine plan. As time passed, "the minds of men were suited to grasp more lofty precepts about right living." He was looking forward to a golden age of happiness—without, however, offering any details about the progress of men during the Middle Ages.[997] St. Bonaventura (1221–1274) argued in his *Breviloquium* that God could have brought perfection in a "single instant" but "chose instead to act through time, and step by step" in prefiguring the future—without identifying step by step the actual progression of man in history.[998]

Geoffroy de Villhardouin's *The Conquest of Constantinople*, an eyewitness account of the Fourth Crusade (1199–1204) is estimated by Burrow to be a proper history book in having a "coherent continuous narrative" rather than being a mere chronicle of events.[999] Likewise, Burrow sees Jean Froissart's *Chronicles*, depicting the Anglo-French rivalry during the Hundred Years War, as the work of "a master of fluent, controlled and relevant narrative."[1000] Brereton judges Froissart to be "the first of the great war-reporters," whose "overriding preoccupation," notwithstanding the limitations of records at the time, "was undoubtedly to present the factual truth."[1001] William of Malmesbury's *The Deeds of the Kings of the English* is judged by Breisach as an "encyclopedic survey," widely read for its vigor and learning, and for "reaching a literary level superior to that of preceding

---

[996] Burrow, 205.
[997] Baumer, 1978, 97.
[998] McFarland, 2009, 19.
[999] Burrow, 48.
[1000] Ibid, 252.
[1001] Brereton, 1978.

chronicles." With the Roman historian Suetonius as his model, Malmesbury was a "careful, accurate, and conscientious writer" who portrayed historical actors vividly.[1002]

But as much as medieval Christian historians tried to make sense of the course of history, they were frustrated in their inability to establish a clear connection between the idealized City of God and the chaotic and violent City of Man. Augustine, when asked why God allowed the city of Rome to be sacked by the Visigoths in AD 410 if the history of man was guided by Providence, drew a sharp contrast between the City of God—eternal, heavenly, awaiting us in the future—and the City of Man, characterized by pride, self-aggrandizement, and endemic conflict. He did not see in the City of Man, which reflects the actual history of man, a process of cumulative improvement, but a "shallow and corrupt reflection of the heavenly city because its founders" were "sinful men of the world." The City of God, which reflected the ideals that God wanted for this world, would come only after the City of Man had been brought to an end.

Augustine could not integrate the ideals of the City of God with the history of the City of Man. The City of God represented the unchangeable ideals of Christianity, whereas the City of Man represented the indelible values of man in the flesh. Augustine, and medieval Christian historians, could not overcome this dualism, because they could not detect actual progress in the City of Man. They were men, to use a Hegelian phrase, with an "unhappy consciousness"—a consciousness that experiences itself as divided within and against itself, frustrated by its inability to see the unity of God and human history.[1003] The historical consciousness of medieval Christians would have to await the modern era to see this unity, at which time it was secularized into a liberal idea of progress.

The Stalled Development of Chinese and Islamic Historiography

Did Chinese historians, before they came under the strong influence of European historians in the late 1800s, write better histories than ancient Europeans? Hegel said that "no other people has had a series of historical writers succeeding one another in such close continuity as the Chinese." In academia today, students are being asked to "substitute a global approach for a Europe-centered approach"

[1002] Breisach, 115.
[1003] Burbidge, 1978; Pinkard, 1996, 62–81.

to correct a Western bias that assumed "that the Western style of historical writing is superior in every way." We now have books (such as "the impressive two-volume *Global Encyclopedia of Historical Writing*") in which students learn how the historiography of Africa, Asia, and Latin America "rivals that of Western historiography."[1004] The edited collection, *Turning Points in Historiography: A Cross-Cultural Perspective*, tells us that "it is well known that history and its writing did not begin in Greece" but "further to the east and earlier."[1005] It depends how we define history writing. Herodotus himself praised the Egyptians for "their practice of keeping records of the past." The point is that the Chinese annal-biographic form of dynastic historical writing (deemed to be the only real competitor to the West), established in ancient times, with its moralistic tales as to whether or not Tao was present in a certain period of history, persisted with minimal changes for centuries, right until Europeans brought their historical professionalism.

China is indeed the only civilization that can be said to have generated a continuous historiographical tradition, as Hegel understood. This same Hegel, however, would go on to say that it is nevertheless the case that their annals "fail to show any development." In *Turning Points in Historiography* there are two very scholarly chapters seeking to show "new directions" in China. The first, by Lee, merely shows that in the period 960–1126 there was a renewed emphasis on moral teaching based on the reaffirmation of Confucian values, coupled with an increased emphasis on historical criticism. We are initially made to believe that this criticism amounted to rigorous questioning to determine the validity of the sources. But Lee, who supplies eighty-nine bibliographic notes at the end of his chapter, soon admits, after a tortuous effort to show "new directions," that "although Chinese historians were committed to recording historical events factually, they never developed a theory of historical criticism, at least until the end of the eighteenth century."[1006]

The Greeks, Thucydides in particular, started historical criticism of sources, but it was really during the Renaissance that Europeans began to conduct a systematic study for the verification of sources. Lee admits, moreover, that Chinese history books in the period he examines "had yet to exhibit any tendency in employing causal interpretation" beyond showing an awareness that "events were related."[1007] As much as Lee tries to bring Chinese historians closer to the standards

---

[1004] Woolf, 2014.
[1005] Wang and Iggers, 2002, 3.
[1006] Lee, 70, in Wang and Iggers, 2002.
[1007] Ibid, 68.

of modern Western historiography, telling us that the Chinese understood that "when all the relevant facts are put together, and carefully collated and criticized ... the truth will then reveal itself," he cannot but conclude: "I admit that I have searched in vain for this analytical approach. The idea of causation, incipient as it was, did not continue to attract historical thinkers in imperial China; concern for supra-historical causes prevailed and overwhelmed the post Song thinkers."[1008] By "supra-historical causes" he means the ancient Chinese idea that history writing should be about the revelation of Tao in history—that is, with the didactic aim of showing that those dynasties that were successful had received the Mandate of Heaven, and those dynasties that were failures had lost the Mandate. The Chinese did not even develop a theory of dynastic cycles properly speaking, in the sense of identifying the causes for the rise and fall of dynasties, as the Romans did in their examination of the corruption and decadence of human nature.

Not even in the eighteenth century did the Chinese manage to transcend the Mandate of Heaven view of history. This can be established by examining the very words and conclusions of the second chapter in *Turning Points in Historiography*, which ostensibly seeks to demonstrate that China's historiography underwent a major turning point in the 1700s, leading to a historiography comparable to that of the West during the Enlightenment. The title of this chapter, authored by the respected scholar Benjamin Ellman, is "The Historicization of Classical Learning in Ming-Ch'ing China." In tedious detail, trying to squeeze every drop of evidence he can, with 113 bibliographical notes, but only barely filling a spoon, Elman concludes that by 1800 we see in China the use of "inductive methods by evidential scholars [that] indicated that they had rediscovered a rigorous methodology to apply to historiography," entailing "analysis of historical sources, correction of anachronisms, revision of texts."[1009] Yet, he has to acknowledge, for otherwise he would have been dismissed as delusional, that this so-called "evidential research" of the Chinese "did not yet equal the 'objective' premises of German historicism" or manage to "resemble their European Enlightenment contemporaries."[1010]

We will get to the Enlightenment and German historicism later. Let it be said now that the "evidential research" of Chinese historians did not resemble the Enlightenment at all. Historians of the non-Western world like to give themselves airs about how they have deeper historical insights by implying that they know

---

[1008] Ibid, 76.
[1009] Ellman, 130, in Wang and Iggers, 2002.
[1010] Ibid, 103, 135.

both Western and non-Western histories. In truth, their knowledge of the West rarely rises above generalizations informed by their recollections of one or two undergrad surveys. The "evidential research" of the Chinese had nothing to do with an emerging scientific attitude. It was, rather, an attempt to ensure a more accurate determination of the ancient Chinese classics as part of a revival of the authority of these texts in the name of a ritualistic conservative reaction. It was for the sake of ensuring the authenticity of ancient texts that Chinese historians cultivated a philological reading to determine which of many editions of the classics were original and which were copied or forged additions of later centuries. It is true that these "evidential" scholars were tired of the bookish Song and Ming Neo-Confucians, their endless "rationalistic" commentaries on books, and thus they called for the study of "concrete subjects": philology, history, astronomy, geography, and the like. But there was no resemblance between this and the Enlightenment.

The Western-educated Chinese historian Kai-wing Chow questions the bandied-about phrase "evidential research" in his 1994 book *The Rise of Confucian Ritualism in Late Imperial China*, arguing that this period witnessed not a philological revolution but the "rise of Classicism, ritualism, and purism." The "evidential" movement was a response to the threatened position of the Chinese gentry, an effort to restore an elite culture which had been considerably weakened by Ming commercialization. The vision of this movement was conservative, recovery of the "original" or "pure" Confucian norms and language. "Filial devotion, loyalty to the monarch, and wifely fidelity"—these were their mottoes, combined with "punctilious observance of hierarchical relationship, and the exaltation of the ritual authority of the Classics."[1011]

As it is, the "philological revolution" Elman saw emerging in seventeenth- to eighteenth-century China had already been pioneered by fourteenth-century Italian humanists in their rediscovery of lost ancient Roman classics. This started with Petrarch (1304–74), who discovered several texts of Cicero, including letters, and verified that these were actually written by him. Lorenzo Valla (1407–54) carried to maturity this philological program by developing sophisticated methods of linguistic analysis to determine age and authenticity. The best-known example of this textual analysis was his determination that the Donation of Constantine, a testament in which Constantine bequeathed his power and wealth to the Church, was actually a forgery.

[1011] Chow, 1994, 3, 227, 230.

Turning Points in Historiography has a chapter on the "ascendancy" and "inspirational" work of the contemporary Subaltern School of Indian historians—without asking why India, a civilization thousands of years old, never generated a historiography until Western historians brought their professionalism to it. The *Times of India* cited the following words from R. C. Majumdar, a highly respected historian of Indian history: "One of the gravest defects of Indian culture, which defies rational explanation, is the aversion of Indians to writing history. They applied themselves to all conceivable branches of literature and excelled in many of them, but they never seriously took to the writing of history, with the result that for a great deal of our knowledge of ancient Indian history we are indebted to foreigners." The journalist who wrote this article went on to say: "For a country that claims to have a 5000-year-old civilization. . . . There was little recording of the past, only a retelling and that too by poets who mixed fact with fiction and myth with reality."[1012] In the words of Oswald Spengler, "in the Indian culture we have the perfectly ahistoric soul."[1013]

Stephen Humphreys, in his contribution to *Turning Points in Historiography*, praises Islamic historiography "for its richness and variety" and calls for European-centered approaches to be "denounced" as "pure Orientalism of the most invidious kind." He opposes the "imposition of modern Western concepts and categories on another culture" while relying on Western protocols of scholarship, careful referencing of sources, to make his case, and admitting in the end that Islamic historiography "never became a systematic science or even a subject of formal academic study among medieval Muslims." In his book *Islamic Historiography*, Robinson claims that many Muslim historians "were alert to contradictory evidence, to fabrication, exaggeration and bias." It was important for them to be true to the history of their religion. But as Humphreys recognizes, Muslim historians "never show any real awareness of change and development" in their chronologies. "Events were in a real sense timeless . . . conceived and presented as moral exempla, not as links in a continuous narrative or as part of a historical

---

[1012] Saxena, 2010.

[1013] Spengler (1988, 11–2) adds: "There is no pure Indian astronomy, no calendar, and therefore no history so far as history is the track of a conscious spiritual evolution." The key word here is "conscious." Humans became conscious in the course of history, and there is history as long as consciousness emerges, as it did in ancient Greece, which resulted in a more directional history, with man-made institutions relatively freed from blood kinship ties, such as city-states and republican institutions.

process. . . . The Qur'anic understanding of history is cyclical rather than linear."[1014]

Moreover, Muslims did not offer explanations for the cycles of history (as we saw in Polybius, Sallust, Livy). The point of their moral teaching was to illustrate, not to explain, whereas for the ancients the point was to instruct about the nature of human beings, and why this nature underlies the cycles of history. And, as Humphreys admits, Muslims had no conception of change and development—unlike Christians, who initiated a history of development and started to identify the main stages of history. Finally, and this is very important: we do not find, among Muslims or Chinese, actual historical narratives, as contrasted to mere chronicles—that is, there are no controlled, sustained monographs, with a coherent and continuous narrative, as we see in Thucydides, Polybius, Livy, Tacitus, and in some late medieval European historians.

The Achievement of the Renaissance Through to the 1600s

The historiographical thinking of the Renaissance is often viewed as a return to the Roman model of history writing, with Rome praised less for creating a Pax Romana that facilitated the spread of Christianity than for being a city that embodied patriotic republican virtues that could be imitated by the Italian city-states. The Renaissance term "humanities" referred to an education in Latin rhetoric based on a close imitation of ancient models of writing found in Cicero and Seneca, and in Sallust and Livy. The purpose of history was to learn political lessons, as Roman historians had advocated, about the inherently cyclic character of history, how strong men and order emerge out of ruin and hardship, and how weak men and disorder emerge out of comfort and ease; and about the role of fate (*fortuna*) in human action, how even leaders with courage and intelligence may nevertheless be overwhelmed by chance events beyond their control. In Machiavelli's words in *Discourses on Livy*: "those who read my remarks may derive those advantages which should be the aim of all study of history." While few, if any, questioned the role of God as the first cause of all events, Christ's central role, or the Last Judgement, Renaissance historians, like the Romans, accounted for events in

---

[1014] Humphreys, 89–92, in Wang and Iggers, 2002.

terms of the motivations and interests of individuals, appealing to constants in human nature to explain the rise and fall of leaders and states.[1015]

It is also argued that the famous Renaissance division of history into the Ancient Period, the Dark Ages, and the Renaissance, was a direct refutation of the Christian idea that history is characterized by developmental stages. Robert Nisbet contends in his very informative book, *The History of the Idea of Progress*, first published in 1980, that the humanists viewed the Middle Ages as "a thousand years of desuetude, of sterility and drought, and worse, of a vast thicket of ignorance, superstition, preoccupation with the hereafter, and unremitting ecclesiastical tyranny."[1016] For Nisbet, this Renaissance judgement about the past goes against the idea of progress in not seeing a process of cumulative progression, and in viewing the Middle Ages as a long dark age that contributed nothing to history.

What Nisbet misses is, firstly, that the Renaissance does see major accomplishments in historiography, along with developmental achievements in art, technology, commerce, including the discovery of the world, which would make possible a global perspective; and secondly, that the idea of progress does entail a rejection of the prejudices and false opinions of the past. In addition to the proliferation of chronicles on the history of Italian cities, great national histories were written. One example is Guicciardini's *History of Italy*, a detailed account covering forty-four years of history, from 1490 to 1534, which is seen as quite original in its own right, committed to the complexity of historical causation, rather than applying, in formulaic fashion, a cyclic explanation. Rather, it is concerned with the "interaction of many motives, intentions, calculations, misconceptions, irrational impulses and fleeting or enduring psychological dispositions."[1017] Admittedly, it is hard to disagree that Guicciardini's History of Italy was one where fortune,

---

[1015] Machiavelli's *Discourses*, actually, is not only the most insightful historical explanation of Rome's rise and the nature of its republican government since Polybius' work, but the most insightful study of the motives behind the actions of great men, or men who need to be recognized as superior to others, since Thucydides. "For, whenever there is no need for men to fight, they fight for ambition's sake; and so powerful is the sway that ambition exercises over the human heart that it never relinquishes them, no matter how high they have risen. The reason is that nature has so constituted men that, though all things are objects of desire, not all things are attainable; so that desire always exceeds the power of attainment, with the result that men are ill content with what they possess and their present state brings them little satisfaction." Cited from the edition with an introduction by Bernard Crick, listed in the bibliography, and translated as *The Discourses*.

[1016] Nisbet, 1998, 103.

[1017] Burrow, 276.

chance, and evil doings dominated the narrative. The West would have to wait until the 1700s to propound a definite linear conception of history.

Nevertheless, Paolo Giovio's 1550 *Histories of His Own Times* had a somewhat universal character, with its impressive description of the wars of France, Germany, and Spain, and the sack of Rome, and its integration of the entire Mediterranean world, including the contemporary history of the Muslim nations, into his vivid narrative, by an author with an encyclopedic mind.[1018] Moreover, the Renaissance saw the invention of philology, the science of verifying and authenticating old manuscripts, which permitted the identification of forgeries and alterations in old manuscripts and documents. Lorenzo Valla's 1440 *Discourse on the Forgery of the Alleged Donation of Constantine* is now seen as initiating the study of modern philology and a scholarly spirit that would ensure a scientific approach to the use of historical sources, and a more critical attitude towards age-old authoritative writings.[1019]

All in all, Western history was characterized by a developmental pattern both through the Middle Ages and through the Renaissance. Nisbet correctly points to the many achievements of medieval man in Romanesque and Gothic architecture, in the invention of major technologies, such as very efficient water mills, reading glasses, universities, and indeed mechanical clocks, with a new conception of time no longer based on the daily and yearly cycles, but as a "continuum of successive moments" moving in a straight line towards the future. He forgets that the Renaissance sees new developments occurring at an accelerating pace beyond what we generally witness in traditional agrarian civilizations (growth in population, extension of agricultural lands, larger cities), such as the discovery of the Americas, the mapping of the world, the gunpowder revolution, and the Copernican heliocentric breakthrough. Some historians were indeed beginning to realize that the Renaissance was a new epoch in world history, while others began pushing for new conceptions of the natural rights of man across the world.

Francisco López de Gómara, in his 1553 *General History of the Indies*, called the discovery of the Americas the greatest event since Creation, in full awareness that the Christian idea of history, if it was to live up to its universalist ambitions, required the incorporation of the peoples of the Americas and the East Indies. Christian universalism was premised on the belief that its moral message, and its vision of the progression of truth in time, was universally true for all human beings

---

[1018] Zimmerman, 1996.
[1019] Nauta, 2021.

irrespective of ethnic or cultural origin. For this reason, Christians must make sense of the histories of all peoples. Christians had worked hard incorporating the civilizations of Mesopotamia, Egypt, Greece, Rome, and the peoples of Europe, but now a whole New World with very different values confronted them.

Bartolomé de las Casas, in his *History of the Indies* (completed in 1561), insisted that the discovery of the New World actually fulfilled the universal aspirations of Christianity: the unity of mankind anticipated by this religion was becoming a reality through the conversion of the Indians and the salvation of their souls. In *A Short Account of the Destruction of the Indies*, he condemned the atrocities committed by the colonizers against the Indians, and argued that they were fully human in the eyes of God, and that subjugation was a moral crime.[1020] He was indeed the first to extend the Christian view of the unity of mankind to the New World, stating that "All people of the world are humans," with a natural right to liberty, an idea that combined Aquinas' natural law principle that "the light of reason is placed by nature [and thus by God] in every man to guide him in his acts" with the Augustinian "education of the human race."[1021]

In 1566, Jean Bodin published *Methods for the Easy Comprehension of History*, declaring that the unity of mankind was a project of the future, not a reality of the past. Prior universal histories had merely affirmed the unity of human history in terms of the Biblical account of the Genesis, incorporating the histories of unconnected nations without properly fitting them within a cumulative historical path.[1022] Bodin, as Nisbet recognizes, emphasized progression from a time when "men were scattered like beasts in the fields and woods . . . until . . . the refinement of customs and the law-abiding society we see about us."[1023] Pointing to the invention of printing, the mariner's compass which allowed for the circumnavigation of the world, the accumulation of geographical knowledge, Bodin affirmed the superiority of the moderns over the ancients. He recognized the cyclic path of both Greece and Rome as they were eventually overtaken by decay and decline, but added that within the broader context of a universal history one could detect new historical cycles on a higher level of achievement.[1024] He opposed slavery in the New World as unnatural, and envisioned a strong state that would guarantee personal liberty and private property. Beyond this, he envisioned the world as a

---

[1020] Perez, 2020.
[1021] Varacalli, 2016.
[1022] Breisach, 180–86.
[1023] Nisbet, 121.
[1024] Bury, 1960, 37–44.

universal state, with the peoples of the world working in solidarity towards the common good.[1025] He also called for a new universal history that would compare and contrast the different laws and customs of all nations, based on primary sources—thus pointing towards a universalist multicultural history.

Before the 1800s, however, the knowledge Europeans had of the past was extremely sparse for lack of archival historical research, which spoke of their undeveloped historical consciousness. We may date the beginnings of a trend toward systematic archival collections to the late sixteenth century, when King Francis II of France entrusted Jean du Tillet with the reorganization of the royal archives. Without primary sources, historians could not but remain dependent on their own memories and those of eyewitnesses, and on earlier historians and chroniclers. During the Renaissance and through the 1700s, historians still held as their ideal in historical writing the revered ancient models. Tacitus was the most admired model during the 1600s.

Great historical accounts were still being written using and improving upon this ancient model in the psychological analysis of the motivations of human actors and the high literary style of narratives. Edward Hyde, Earl of Clarendon's *The History of the Rebellion and Civil Wars* in England, published between 1702 and 1704, is judged to this day as one of the greatest historical narratives, the standard for all future histories of the revolution. Like the ancients, Clarendon offered keen insights into the ways in which one could find conflicting traits in different men, making for admirable characters. This type of psychological analysis was non-existent outside the West, where the annalistic traditions, with their impersonal form of history writing, barely changed, and where an unchanging atmosphere produced stereotypical historians and historical personalities.

Meanwhile, the historical consciousness of Europeans would experience a steady progression in archival research from the 1600s on. The most outstanding work was Jean Mabillon's 1681 *De Re Diplomatica*, known for establishing the methodology for determining the authenticity and dates of medieval manuscripts in its examination of ink, parchment, and handwriting style.[1026] This revolution in archival methods, which came on the heels of the invention of printing and which facilitated access to archival documents, was essential to the very possibility of studying the past in a scientific and systematic manner. It encouraged a keen interest in the Middle Ages, moving away from the Renaissance notion that it was

---

[1025] Heller, 1994.
[1026] McDonald, 1979.

an ignorant "dark age." These studies in medieval history would eventually lead to a new periodization of history into Ancient, Medieval and Modern, as historians in the 1700s came to acknowledge the significance of the Middle Ages in laying the foundations for modern Europe, and as they came to the realization, with the birth of Galilean/Newtonian science, that they were living in an age that was superior in knowledge to that of the Ancients.

That Bossuet's 1681 *Discourse on Universal History* was "completely anticipated" in Augustine's *City of God*, published over 1200 years earlier, testifies to the immense influence of the Christian conception of history. Bossuet's book was an updated, more historically self-aware attempt to demonstrate the omnipresence of Providence over the course of world history.[1027] Only by postulating the unfolding of God's designs in the course of time and events could humans make sense of their history. Bossuet, advisor to Louis XIV, wanted to show that in history one can detect a progression of epochs—from the Creation itself, the Flood, the law of Moses, the rise and fall of Egypt, Assyria, Babylonia, Persia, Macedonia and Rome, through the coronation of Charlemagne, to his own time. All these seemingly separated peoples were constitutive of one universal process. He praised the Egyptians for their inventive genius, their law-abiding disposition, their advancement in science, their art, education, and agriculture. The divine purpose was anticipated by the prophets in the case of Assyria, Babylonia, and Persia. Providence charged the Jewish people with defending the worship of the true God throughout the pagan centuries.

The extension of Roman peace across the known world facilitated the conversion of the world to Christianity. It was Providence that brought order to the Germanic barbarians, creating kingdoms that would reconcile the Christian framework inherited from Augustine with the classical rhetoric and civic morals of the Greek/Roman world under the law of Christ. While the Almighty sustains and directs the secondary causes, and sometimes interferes directly, Bossuet traced, in some degree of historical detail, the course of events without bringing in God, appealing to the role of geographical conditions, climate, fertility, and the influence of one country on another, while offering many secular economic, social and cultural insights on the rise and fall of empires.

[1027] Wiater, 1940.

Enlightenment Consolidation of the Idea of Progress

It was around the mid-1700s that Europeans began to identify a clear, empirically based sequence of stages independent from the Biblical narrative, depicting a progressive improvement in actual laws, forms of government, economic systems, and in the manner and morals of humans, in terms of purely natural or man-made causes—thus secularizing, not rejecting, the idea of progress in Augustine, Orosius, and Bossuet. This was originally an achievement of the "Scottish Enlightenment,"[1028] with the most notable books including Lord Kames's 1758 *Historical Law Tracts* and *Sketches on the History of Man* from 1774, Adam Ferguson's 1767 *The History of Civil Society*, William Robertson's 1769 *The History of the Reign of the Emperor Charles V*, John Millar's 1771 *Origin of the Distinction of Ranks*, Adam Smith's 1776 *The Wealth of Nations*, and James Dumbar's 1780 *Essays on the History of Mankind in Rude and Cultivated Ages*.

This "modern" stage theory of history began with the observation that increasing commercialization and advancement of human knowledge (now apparent in the rise of Newtonian science) countered the Hobbesian and Calvinist vision of human nature as innately depraved and inclined to permanent violence unless men subordinated themselves to an absolute authority capable of preventing an inevitable "war of all against all." The moral philosophers, the Englishman Lord Shaftesbury and the Scot Francis Hutcheson, began to argue, under the influence of Locke's blank slate argument, that the moral character of humans was not permanently fixed, but capable of improvement. They observed an increasing "refinement" and "politeness" in the urbane and enlightened culture of their times, concluding that humans were born with an innate moral sense, which God granted to them in His own image: a benevolent "fellow-feeling" and a "delight in the good of others." Humans desire happiness, and helping others gratifies them—"approbation of our own action denotes, or is attended with, a pleasure in the contemplation of it." Humans are thus self-interested in the well-being of others for the satisfaction it brings them. Hutcheson agreed with Locke that humans are born naturally free and equal everywhere regardless of origin or status, while going even further by attacking slavery and calling for the maximization of the "natural rights" of man to "life, liberty, and honestly acquired property." The

---

[1028] Herman, 2001; Spadafora, 1990.

pinnacle of social morality would be achieved when each individual was allowed to live his life as he peacefully chooses while respecting the equal rights of others.

But the question remained: If the desire for happiness and freedom is universal, and humans have an innate moral sense, why have these attributes come to fruition only in modern times rather than across societies throughout history? The implied answer appeared to be that the nature of man had been gradually refined in the course of history. Lord Kames was the first to provide a schematic four-stage theory of history—hunting and gathering savagery, pastoral nomadism, agriculture, and commerce—showing how the way people think, act, and govern their lives changes depending on their stage of economic development. Before the rise of commercial society, the natural inclination that humans have to the appropriation of the fruits of their labor as their private property, and to the augmentation of their "opulence," could not find free expression. The reasons were that property was controlled by clans and tribes, or the fields were cultivated communally. This was before the consolidation of commercial society, the legal protection of private property rights, and the enforcement of contracts by the government to ensure the peaceful exchange of goods, which had the effect of softening and polishing the manners of men. As Robertson put it, "Commerce tends to wear off those prejudices which maintain distinction and animosity between nations. It softens and polishes the manners of men. It unites them, by one of the strongest of all ties, the desire of supplying their mutual wants."[1029]

The idea of progress, however, does not require the idea that human nature is innately good. David Hume, known in his time primarily as the author of the six-volume History of England (1754–62), rejected the Shaftesbury-Hutcheson idea that man had an innate "moral sense." Reason is a "slave of the passions"—of anger, lust, fear, envy, and love of fame. Humans employ their reason as an instrument to advance their self-interests, avoid pain, and increase their pleasure. Yet, while Hume emphasized the "uniformity of human nature," he agreed with his Scottish friends that history showed progress: growth of industry, personal liberty, and peaceful cooperation. Increasing commerce, increasing liberty, increasing creativity in the arts and sciences, and increasing refinement in human manners were all interrelated. The progress witnessed in history, Hume argued, consisted in the re-channeling of human passions in constructive directions through the creation of rules and conventions, internalized by humans into habitual behaviors. While greed on its own, without limits, destroys peaceful coexistence,

---

[1029] Herman, 99.

increasing commercialization entailed the rechanneling of this passion in a constructive direction by encouraging everyone to pursue their self-interest within the framework of a civil society that protected the property rights of individuals.

Adam Smith, without denying that humans have "an original desire to please, and an original aversion to offend his brethren," agreed with Hume that self-interest is an essential attribute of man, coupled with the "natural effort of every individual to better his condition" as long as they are given the opportunity to do so in a free market. His *Inquiry into the Nature and Causes of the Wealth of Nations*, seen as a summation of the Scottish exploration of progress, of the stages of economic and cultural development through which humanity has passed, explained at length how it is that the hidden hand of the market, a competitive setting in which everyone is obligated to supply the goods preferred by consumers, channels the pursuit of private gain into the general welfare of society. The way to maximize general wealth is to allow men to pursue their self-interest by buying and selling without government monopolies and curtailments on the accumulation of wealth. Free markets have an inbuilt tendency for progress: increasing participation in the market increases the division of labor and thus productivity, and the greater the pressures of competitiveness, the more businesses invest in new technologies, which ensures continuous progress.

At this point in the history of Europeans, the idea of progress had risen above the speculative; it was based on and supported by the reality that Europe had been progressing at an accelerating rate in the sciences, in liberty, and in invention of new technologies. The Glorious Revolution of 1688 was seen as a largely consensual (polite) and bloodless success of tempered liberty and limited monarchy. Inventions and innovations were appearing successively through the 1700s, such as Jethro Tull's seed drill, Newcomen's atmospheric steam engine, John Kay's flying shuttle, Benjamin Franklin's lightning rod, John Harrison's chronometer for measuring longitude, Hargreaves's spinning jenny, culminating in an Industrial Revolution that would see a whole new epoch in European history. Without these changes—the Renaissance, the discovery of the New World, the rise of Galilean/Newtonian science, the Glorious Revolution, which firmly established the principles of frequent parliaments, free elections and freedom of speech within Parliament, and the subsequent Industrial Revolution—the historical consciousness of Europeans would have stalled and stagnated back into a purely cyclical conception, or never risen above a Christian millennial anticipation of a Golden Age beyond the earthly realities of the City of Man. The Scottish stage theory of history was a major historiographical accomplishment in advancing knowledge about the main patterns of history.

By the mid-1700s, the idea that we can witness cumulative advancement in history, and that we can envision a future world of universal human rights, came to prevail among historians. Among members of the French Enlightenment, the central message was that history was leading towards the perfection of human nature itself. This movement towards greater perfection was anchored in the belief that history was fundamentally a process involving the emancipation of reason from the blind passions of humans, which had been responsible for their superstition and vices, rather than being anchored, as it was for the Scots, in the mere acquisition of commercial comfort and polite behavior.

Voltaire, in his 1754 *Essay on the Manners, Customs, and the Spirit of Nations*, praised the achievements of the Chinese, Indian, Persian, and Islamic civilizations, while arguing that the superiority of the West consisted in the greater progress of its rationality. While the majority of people may never become fully rational, among Western elites there was a noticeable increase in the reliance on reason rather than religious dogma. Voltaire would go beyond Hume's argument, favoring skeptical and naturalistic principles over the revealed truth-claims of Christianity in openly stating that the priestly class was the greatest purveyor of bigotry and oppression. And Condorcet would take to its logical conclusion this progressive idea in his 1795 essay "Sketch for an Historical Picture of the Progress of the Human Mind," which identified ten distinctive stages in humanity's advancement, from the beginning when men were "united into hordes," through "the agricultural state" and "the invention of alphabetical writing," to the "Invention of the art of printing," right to his own time, the ninth stage, when modern Cartesian and Newtonian science were consolidated, and the French Republic declared the "true rights of man." In the tenth stage, he anticipated the education of the human race with the creation of public schools, the spread of mathematics and the social sciences, and "real improvement" in the "moral, intellectual and physical" faculties of men across the world, bringing about, in the words of Keith M. Baker, "a more decent world for universal human rights, individual autonomy, and a measure of equality between individuals and nations."[1030]

[1030] Baker, 2004; Bury, 1960, 202–16. Bury writes: "Condorcet contemplated equality among all the peoples of the earth . . . and the obliteration of the distinction between advanced and retrograde races."

The Enlightenment age saw an increasing awareness among Europeans that their own time was indeed a new era completely different from any previous epoch, a "modern" era, characterized by its skepticism towards all religious beliefs hitherto accepted as true, by its questioning of the notion of "divine right" and rule by a nobility based on privilege of birth. It called for a government based on the will of the educated commercial and professional classes, which had acquired their positions on merit, by peaceful means. Kant, in an essay titled "Idea for a Universal History with a Cosmopolitan Aim," published in 1784, offered a synthesis of the Scottish and French ideas of progress.[1031] History showed a constant propensity towards progress and liberty: "it has revealed a tendency and a faculty in human nature for improvement." Drawing on Hume's conception of human nature and Adam Smith's explanation about how markets redirect human self-interest into benevolent ends, Kant anchored the dynamic of history in the "unsocial sociability" of humans. While humans are social by nature, in need of cooperating with others, they also have a "thoroughgoing resistance" to this tendency due to their vanity, greed, and self-interest. It was this "unsocial sociability," and the antagonisms it generated, that brought about historical change. "Without those qualities of an unsocial kind, out of which antagonism arises . . . men might have led an Arcadian shepherd life in complete harmony, contentment and mutual love, but in that case their talents would have forever remained hidden in their germ." It was as if Providence had implanted this trait in humans as part of a "hidden plan of nature" to bring about the Enlightenment, out of which the rational capacities of men would be fully developed. In his essay "Perpetual Peace," Kant proposed a federation of republics, a "universal civic society which administers law among men," uniting nations into one great supreme body that puts in place constitutions and treaties capable of ensuring liberty, peace, security, and rights within and between nation-states.

These were "philosophic histories," rather than actual historical narratives. One of the first narrative histories of this liberal view was Thomas Macaulay's five-volume *History of England from the Accession of James II*, published in 1846–61. The focus was on England, and its argument was that the Glorious Revolution of 1688, and the liberal progressive history of this nation thereafter, demonstrated that the England of Macaulay's time was not an accidental creation, but the result of centuries of development marked by the gradual march of liberty, beginning in its free Germanic institutions, through to the Magna Carta of 1215, and leading

---

[1031] Rorty, 2009.

to Victorian England as the industrial workshop of the world. Macaulay's book, one of the best-selling historical works ever written, celebrated the peculiarly British achievement for progress without totally breaking with the past, reconciling past, present, and future, as witnessed in the relatively peaceful Glorious Revolution which created a constitutional monarchy while preserving the House of Lords, followed by the Reform Act of 1832, actively supported by Lord Macaulay, a Whig politician.[1032] This Reform Act, he argued, had saved Britain from the radical revolutions experienced on the continent, particularly in France. Herbert Butterfield would call it in 1931 "the Whig interpretation of history." This was a history in which the agent of progress was the middle class, the urbane commercial classes the Scottish Enlightenment had celebrated the previous century for their "politeness."

While Macaulay's "Whig interpretation" would be subsequently developed in a historically "professional" direction (criticized as he was for his unsophisticated use of sources, despite general admiration for his "vivid, dramatic, eloquent and exhilarating" narrative style), the Whig interpretation is seen today as a short-lived effort that barely anyone would accept in subsequent decades, discredited by historical events themselves, the WWI disaster, the rise of fascism, and the cultivation of sophisticated historical methodologies. Butterfield's criticism that Whig narratives were inherently teleological in understanding the past in light of present values, rather than on its own terms, was indeed widely accepted.

Yet, what was really rejected was an oversimplified version of the liberal progressive narrative. We can start to realize this by simply witnessing the widespread acceptance of liberal values throughout the Western world into our own times, and the continued persistence of progressive historians, who now come in multiple shapes, with diverse methodologies, diverse historical agents, freed from any form of Anglo/European centrism. Butterfield's own best-known book, *The Origins of Modern Science, 1300–1800*, published in 1965, was itself quite Whiggish in tracing a cumulative line of scientific advancement in Europe. Because the West was actually seen to increase scientific knowledge, raise productivity, improve standards of living, and achieve greater equality of rights, this progressive liberal view could not be easily dismissed.[1033] Macaulay was one among many. Francois

---

[1032] Breisach, 250–51.

[1033] Although Kant was thinking about a "republic of nations" coexisting in a state of peace, without implying that cosmopolitanism was about integrating millions of immigrants from multiple cultures inside the West, this is how current liberal defenders of the Enlightenment interpret him. Martha Nussbaum deduces from Kant's cosmopolitanism the argument that, since "the

Guizot, France's greatest nineteenth-century constitutional historian, wrote a *History of Civilization in Europe* in 1828, arguing that Europe's dynamism, as contrasted to the theocratic and despotic civilizations of the East, derived from its Germanic love of aristocratic independence, its Roman civic republicanism, and its Christian idea of separation of spiritual and secular powers.

William Stubbs, relying mainly on primary sources, a true antiquarian editor of nineteen volumes of medieval chronicles, known for his dense scholarly rigor, authored *The Constitutional History of England in Its Origins and Development* (1873, 3 vol.), arguing that England had a history of liberty beginning with the Teutonic freeholding of land and self-government of village communities, through medieval local representative bodies, to the fully developed national parliamentary constitution of the modern era. The triumph of the liberal idea of progress cut across ideological, national, and religious differences, notwithstanding the emerging tensions between those who adopted the Scottish/Anglo commercial version of progress (which tended to hold a realistic view of human nature as unchangeable even if capable of "improvement in manners"), and those who believed that progress entailed the "perfection of human nature" itself. The former liberal version would become identified with "conservatives," whereas the latter would be identified with "radical liberals." The most utopian liberal may have been William Godwin, convinced that a time would be reached when "there will be no war, no crimes, no administration of justice . . . and no government . . . neither disease, anguish, melancholy, nor resentment. Every man will seek, with ineffable ardor, the good of all."[1034] Both sides, however, belonged to the same European Christian root, and despite their many quarrels, would eventually, with the defeat of fascism in the 1940s and communism in the 1990s, coalesce as two sides of the same triumphant "end of history" liberalism.

Few could escape the reality of progress in the West, including the Catholic authoritarian Auguste Comte. In his exhausting six-volume treatise *Course in Positive Philosophy* published 1830–1842, Comte would focus on the intellectual history of Europeans in light of the "peculiar capacity of European countries to serve

---

accident of where one is born is just an accident [and] any human might have been born in any nation," European nations should open their borders to replacement immigration if they are to live up to Kant's ideals. See her essay "Kant and Cosmopolitanism" in Bohman and Lutz-Bachmann (1997), p. 31. Liberals believe that the progressive logic of their ideas allows them to read into past progressives the ideas of future progressives.

[1034] Godwin, 1798.

as the theatre of the preponderant evolution of humanity."[1035] This does not mean that his theory, as Karl Löwith implies, was not universal. The Occident was increasingly coming to be seen as the torchbearer for the future course of human history. This "Eurocentrism" would only come to be repudiated as inappropriate for a progressively improving Western world after about the 1950s. Comte explained how the mind had progressed through three stages: the theological, the metaphysical, and the positive or scientific stage, detailing this three stage evolution for each of the major sciences, and how this evolution occurred first in astronomy, physics, chemistry, biology, and, in his time, was occurring in the sciences of man, leading to the development of sociology as the last and most comprehensive positive science, which would work to make society totally rational, with scientists as the rulers, bringing about the perfect realization of all the potentialities of human nature, to a future of peace, harmony, and happiness.

A few decades after Comte, Herbert Spencer, in the wake of Darwin's progress in biological knowledge, would argue that the "law of progress" was inscribed in the evolutionary struggle for survival as witnessed in the natural world, and in the struggle of individuals and nations for supremacy. To ensure the survival of the fittest, the best thing the state could do was to stay out of education, manufacturing, public health, and sanitation. "All deficiency would disappear," all "unfitness to the conditions of existence," as societies left individuals to pursue their interests on their own spontaneous efforts, forming voluntary associations if they so wished, to achieve success or failure.[1036] In societies with minimal state interference, "imperfection would disappear," and "the ultimate development of the ideal man" would be "logically certain." Spencer would eventually be caught up within the very logic of progress he endorsed, as a new generation of progressives would condemn him as a "racist reactionary" to be discarded from the pantheon of great sociologists.

Nisbet contends that up until the 1970s, the idea of progress exerted a powerful influence on Western civilization since ancient times. J. B. Bury, in his classic 1920 work *The Idea of Progress*, referenced earlier, traces its origins to the 1600s.[1037] It seems that this idea originated with Christianity, notwithstanding its undeveloped character, which awaited the reality of actual progress for this idea to be

---

[1035] Breisach, 272.

[1036] Francis 2007, 67–89.

[1037] As Butterfield acknowledged in the last chapter of this book, "Ideas of Progress and Ideas of Evolution," it was hard to deny the "accumulation" of knowledge in the sciences in the modern era, and how scientists were building on the observations and ideas of their predecessors (1965).

articulated in a conscious, empirically based way in the 1700s. Nisbet believes that, by the 1970s, what were once solid sentiments about "the value and promise of Western civilization" came to be "severely challenged by doubt and disillusionment, even outright hostility." Western history was now interpreted as a long travail of follies, colonial wars, despoliation of the world's ecology, enslavement of peoples, and racial inequalities.[1038]

But if the idea of progress was rejected, how come Western elites today (across political lines) are so committed to the "improvement of the human condition" through the maintenance of public goods to reduce the harmful effects of economic inequality, as well as "institutional racism," while advocating for environmentally conscious policies, gender equality, minority rights, and political correctness? What Nisbet misses is that this idea presupposes, by its very normative impetus, progression in the way that we think about progress. Conviction in the superiority of Western civilization, coupled with the designation of less developed peoples as "savages" and "barbarians," is a "Eurocentric prejudice." The idea of progress could not sustain itself merely by repeating that things have been progressing as they should in a harmonious manner leading to the best of all possible worlds at each point in time.

Karl Marx articulated a radically new progressive ideology, according to which liberal capitalism would be replaced by a new modern communism that would overcome the exploitation of man by man, which still prevailed within capitalism. Marx admired the progressive impact of capitalism, writing in 1867 in *Das Kapital* that "the country that is more developed industrially only shows, to the less developed, the image of its own future."[1039] But he criticized liberal capitalism for recognizing only the formal equality of workers, while keeping them in a state of subjugation within the workplace, where capitalists controlled the labor process and extracted surplus value. Humans would develop their full potentialities only when private property in the means of production came to be abolished and a new society created, in which workers would own the means of production and everyone would receive wages according to their effort and merit. Communism was a major challenge to liberalism for many decades, to be eventually defeated by liberalism at the end of the Cold War. The so-called "Western Marxism," which emerged in academia after WWII, would also be eventually incorporated into liberalism as a safe theoretical outlook acknowledged for its "contribution to our understanding

---

[1038] Nisbet, 317–51.
[1039] Marx, 1906, 13.

of history" and supported by career opportunities and huge government grants.[1040] We shall address this later.

So many great books were written in the 1800s that it is difficult to offer a proper summary. Europeans were the only people who gradually became conscious of the temporality of human experience, how each people and epoch are characterized by their own values, concepts of truth, and sense of reality and time. It was around the seventeenth century that Europeans began to employ the tripartite periodic division: Ancient, Medieval, Modern—as they became historically conscious of path-breaking novelties emerging in time.[1041] It was within this historical context that Jacob Burckhardt wrote his celebrated 1860 book, *The Civilization of the Renaissance in Italy*, which aimed to capture the spirit of this epoch, its unique style of politics, its manners, its form of Christianity—through the study of its art.

Burckhardt's argument was that the Renaissance gave birth to modernity because it gave birth to individualism. In the Middle Ages, "man was conscious of himself only as a member of a race, people, party, family, or corporation."[1042] Among the humanists, the scholars, the nobles, artists, and rulers, he observed "an unbridled subjectivity," men obsessed with fame, status, and appearances. This nurtured an intense self-awareness, unlike their medieval forebears, who were trapped within a collective identity, unaware of themselves as possessing individual subjectivity. This will to self-expression fueled the cultural creativity of the Renaissance. We may point today, in light of newer scholarship, to emerging signs of individualism among the ancients and during the Middle Ages.[1043] But this should not distract us from Burkhardt's immense accomplishment as the author who taught us that modernity is fundamentally about the separation of the self from a collective identity, within which humans cannot but remain unconscious. We will see that liberal progress is about intensifying this separation of the self from all traditional restraints including sexuality, racial and national identities, and from human nature itself, in the name of a new and improved humanity.

The discovery of the New World generated numerous historical accounts showing an increasing awareness among Europeans of the multiplicity of customs, manners, and beliefs among the peoples of the world, including the palpable reality that different areas of the planet have followed different historical paths.

[1040] Anderson, 1979.

[1041] Or perhaps earlier, starting with Bodin (1530–1596), as we saw above.

[1042] Burckhardt, 1958, 143.

[1043] Morris, 1987.

We should mention Francis Parkman (1823–1893), an American historian known for *The California and Oregon Trail, Pioneers of France in the New World, The Jesuits in North America, Montcalm and Wolfe*, and his multi-volume *France and England in North America*, published between 1865 and 1892. Theodore Roosevelt dedicated his four-volume history of the frontier, *The Winning of the West*, written 1889–1896, to Parkman. I first learned about him about five years ago when I saw *France and England in North America* with the stamped words "discarded" outside a university library. It did not matter that this book was based on extensive archives in England, France, and North America, written from primary sources, letters, memoirs, dispatches, and first-person observations. This is one of the most enjoyable, best-written, intensely dramatic historical books I have read. Parkman, despite being dogged by lifelong ill health and severe eye trouble, undertook extremely physically demanding expeditions in the New World, living among Indians, admiring them for their bravery, dignity, and fortitude, while pointing to their "fickleness" and lack of fixity of purpose. He saw life as an incessant struggle for existence. John Burrow opines that Parkman was a "sensitive literary artist, a master of evocative, sensuous prose." Historians like Parkman can't be found in any university in our times. He came from an early America, in what ancient Roman historians would identify as a relatively early stage in the cycle of this civilization, when life was hard and men were inevitably strong in character, not from the pampered world of our present "woke" universities.

Science and progressivism have been tightly aligned in the West since the Enlightenment, when science came to be seen for its contribution to the "improvement of humanity." The scientific establishment and the progressive left pushed for the Covid lockdowns and vaccine mandates. The magazine *Scientific American*, which has stated recently that science must never accept studies about IQ differences between races, but instead work towards diversity and racial harmony in the West, announced in August 2021 that "Vaccine mandates are lawful, effective, and based on rock-solid science." It agreed with the call by liberal progressives for "mandatory and punitive vaccination certificates for public activities and firing employees who refuse vaccination."[1044] There is, of course, science going on independently of political aims. But on the most crucial issues of our times, such as race differences, vaccinations, and environmentalism, science is ideologically progressive—rather than progressive in the pure scientific sense of bringing about

---

[1044] Gostin, 2021.

new knowledge. Knowledge that may put limits on or negate the progressive agenda is invariably marginalized or caricatured.

The right does not adequately understand this, believing that science, by its very objective logic, is on their side. If the evidence is laid out in the open, they naively believe, politicians will follow "the data" and choose the right policies. They have failed to realize that Western science has been part of a wider cultural progressivist matrix within which it must find justification and validation. Since progressivism has an inbuilt nature, according to which the present and the future are superior to the past, it cannot but judge the progressives of the past as lesser versions of the progressives of the present. In his time Herbert Spencer was seen as a progressive who believed in the right of free speech, and "the right to ignore the state." His "social Darwinism," very influential through the early 1900s, was used by progressives (along with the Mendelian science of heredity) as a justification for eugenics to solve social problems (crime, alcoholism, prostitution), and as a justification for the civilizing influence of Anglo imperialism on the non-White races. At the time, this was well within the bounds of liberal-minded scientific progressivism. Now it is condemned by a new generation of progressives as a rationalization for the inequality of classes, European colonialism, and claims about the cultural and biological superiority of the West.[1045]

The impact of science on historiography has followed such a pattern, with political progressivism framing the way a science of history ought to be constructed. Initially, it all seemed to be about learning to use the scientific method to understand history better. Henry Thomas Buckle wrote his *History of Civilization of England* in 1857 under the influence of Comte's argument that the task was to search for regularities in social phenomena based on generalizations through the systematic observation of the facts. He called upon historians to give up the Christian view of progress that "in the affairs of men there is something mysterious and providential." Historians should focus on "tracing the progress of science . . . of the fine arts, of useful inventions and . . . of the manners and comforts of the people."[1046] Buckle, who had spent seventeen years working ten hours a day to write his book, would soon be forgotten and displaced by a new generation of Americans known as "Progressive Historians," who believed that the social sciences of economics and sociology were crucial to the understanding of history and acknowledged their debt to Marx's economic interpretation of history.

[1045] Hofstadter, 1992.
[1046] Breisach, 274–5.

Charles Beard, a Fabian socialist, became famous with his *An Economic Inter-pretation of the Constitution of the United States* in 1913, arguing that the financial interests of the Founding Fathers shaped the values of the Constitution. For these historians, progress was a result of rational planning, not of a providential plan. Only "activist" research that grasped the "real" laws governing history could teach the masses how to create a truly democratic and harmonious immigrant America pervaded by a spirit of equality and rationalism. Simultaneously, the progressive jurists Roscoe Pound, Louis Brandeis, and Wendell Holmes proclaimed law to be a means for social reconstruction. Even when Beard rejected the possibility of "sci-entific objectivity" in history, shaken by WWI and the Great Depression, and de-spite his own view that ideas were products of a specific class, period, or national-ity, he affirmed that history aimed at fulfilling the American dream of a just and democratic society, planned by socialist rationalists.

German Historicism: The Defeated Alternative to Liberal Progressivism

Peter Watson's comprehensive 2010 book *The German Genius* demonstrates that from 1750 to the 1930s, Germany was the dominant intellectual force in Western civilization. Among its forty-two chapters you will find one with the title "German Historicism: A Unique Event in the History of Ideas." The educated lay-man invariably identifies Germany's greatest achievements with philosophers, musical composers, and scientists—never hearing about the highly original His-toricist School which peaked in the second half of the nineteenth century. One of its members, Friedrich Meinecke, believed that this School was Germany's great-est contribution to Western thought since the Reformation, "the highest stage in the understanding of things human attained by man."[1047] This School finally pro-vided Europeans with a historical consciousness by explaining how humans are historically conditioned, not within a history conceived as a linear progression following universal scientific laws, but as members of a particular land, nation, and culture. There is no universal "man." Humans can only be understood in terms of their unique history and customs. Historians cannot transcend their own time and culture, but should be aware that their approaches to history reflect the varying cultural frameworks within which they write.

[1047] Watson 2010, 263.

German historicism is also known for its scientific insistence on the critical analysis of documents, commitment to factual accuracy, as well as for raising to a higher level the professionalization and specialization of history as a university discipline—while arguing that the methods of the natural sciences (as Giambattista Vico had hinted at earlier) are inadequate for the study of historical phenomena. The historical sciences deal with purposeful humans and with unique and unrepeatable events, whereas the natural sciences deal with phenomena devoid of intentionality and characterized by recurrence. History is a continuous flux of unpredictable events, and although one can study the nature of institutions and the inner structure of cultures and religions, the peoples of the world each possess their own culture, language, and trajectories, not amenable to schematic theories. Insofar as historians become aware of their historical situation, they can learn to leave their own present context to understand the unique context of other peoples at other times. This is known as hermeneutics—that is, the art of interpreting the historical contexts of events in the past and in other cultures. The idea of progress is wrong, for it imposes one standard of development.

Today, in the academic world, it is almost a truism to say that we are historically and culturally conditioned. German historicism thus appears to have been incorporated into the acceptable tradition of liberal historiography. But it is important to note that claims about "the historicity of all knowledge and values" amount to no more than a domesticated version of German historicism cleansed of its deepest and most controversial ideas—to be easily fitted within the liberal idea of progress. Herder (1744–1803), for example, one of the earliest historicists, has been thoroughly re-interpreted by Western liberals, such as Isaiah Berlin and Charles Taylor, as one of the founders of multiculturalism, even though Herder actually called for the appreciation of the distinctiveness of each nationality and the ways in which each culture can strive for its own perfectibility, and contribute thereby to the fullness of humanity.[1048]

What has been suppressed, or at least thoroughly rejected, about German historicism is that it was an expression of the particularity of an emerging German national identity. Whereas nineteenth-century nationalism in France, Britain, and America came along with liberal universal values about the natural rights of man and the sovereignty of the people against monarchical and aristocratic traditions, German historicists advocated a nationalism with values culture-bound to

---

[1048] Duchesne, 2017–2018.

Germans' particular history. It also emphasized the priority of the freedom of Germans as a people over the abstract rights of individuals.[1049]

The historicist rejection of the universalist pretensions of Enlightenment liberalism, it seems, did not amount to a rejection of what Europeans had achieved in history. The same German historicists who rejected the liberal idea of progress were also the most emphatic in arguing that humans are deeply historical beings, that the laws of a people, their values, and their conception of truth, reflect the unique history and traditions of each region or race. The Germans after the 1850s were the most advanced Europeans in science, technology, military power, levels of education, and culture generally. Essentially, German historicists were the first to posit that a nation can follow a different path to modernity in reaction to the Enlightenment path. German nationalism and geopolitical power in the mid-nineteenth century coincided with modernization. The difference is that the Germans wanted a path that would be balanced with its unique history, respect for aristocratic authority, and a propertied and cultured middle class working in unison with a powerful state acting as the common point of the German people. They sought the highest capacity for independence and strength among the competing powers of the world, rather than a state acting at the behest of a dominant capitalist class pursuing its own interests, or at the behest of a democratic mob easily controlled by private interests. To be somebody, a people must have a strong state, united and independent of other states.

Along with the historicist school came a group of German economists who consciously articulated an alternative economic theory and program to the Anglo-liberalism of Adam Smith and French Enlightenment universalism, while embracing modernization and liberal values judged to be consistent with the collective interests of the nation.[1050] The major thinkers of the German Historical School of economics included Adam Muller (1779–1829), Friedrich List (1789–1846), Wilhelm Roscher (1817–1894), Karl Knies (1821–1898), and Bruno Hildebrand; (1812–1878). Although it would be a great simplification to identify these economists with a common set of principles, they all rejected the liberal idea that economics was a science capable of generating principles and policies with universal validity without considering the particulars of each nation. Treating citizens as faceless producers and consumers, as if they had no bond with a national community, was a mistake. They accepted, generally speaking, the Aristotelian doctrine

---

[1049] Iggers, 1983.
[1050] Shionoya, 2001.

that man is inconceivable outside the State, that no man is an island, but interwoven from birth with a national culture. The State is not, as Locke and Smith saw it, a conglomeration of individuals seeking their self-interest, but a reflection of the need of man to belong in a community. A nation-state can't be concerned only with material production, but must concern itself with the totality of life, with the cultural wellbeing of the members of the nation. The factors of production are not merely "land, labor and capital," but also the "spiritual capital" of the nation: its language, heritage, and traditions. The duty of the State is to utilize the economy to augment national wealth and power, but this wealth is not strictly physical; it is also spiritual, and includes as well the contribution made by past generations to the present race, the arts, the constitution, the laws, and history. But this school, which dominated German thought and economic policy in the second half of the 1800s to the mid-1900s, would be discarded as "fascist" and replaced by Anglo-American-Jewish economic thought in the post-WWII era.

Germans during this period of the mid nineteenth to early twentieth centuries enjoyed considerable individual liberties, universities open to merit, a constitutional monarchy, rule by established procedure, a high degree of economic freedom, and a truly dynamic cultural atmosphere which encouraged the full development of individuality in culture. German historicists believed in a society in which the individual was free, while being simultaneously integrated into the German nation. They did not want a contractual society consisting of atomistic individuals pursuing their private happiness in a state of alienation from the historical heritage of Germany. German historicism rejected the notion that there is meaning in history manifested as a process of increasing rationality, happiness, and freedom. Historians can learn to see how different epochs are connected to each other and gain a wider perspective of history beyond their time and place, but it is a mistake to think that prior epochs or peoples exist entirely for the sake of future epochs, or that there is a seed in the past that contains the future, or that history is heading toward a future bliss of complete rationality and happiness. There is no rational end, but a multiplicity of ways of being. As Humboldt said, a man tends to express the "highest degree of strength and inner unity," the highest dignity, precisely at times when he is also "closest to misery"—not when he is closest to happiness and comfort.[1051] Men have expressed their potentiality, their "Best and Highest," at many moments in history and in different cultural settings.

[1051] In Iggers, 47.

German historicism did not view history as a process of rising perfection. Man's rationality exists within a "total soul" characterized by irrationality, will, and poetic imagination. To treat man as a rational animal is to cut him off from the forces of nature, which are likewise the sources of his creativity. There are many elements in history that cannot be explained in terms of rational factors, and there is much in nature that is vitalist, elusive, and hidden from reason. The truth is sometimes better apprehended in a poetic or artistic manner. A historian should be thorough in the use of sources, but historical writing involves imagination combined with the ability to enter into the world of the past. Contrary to common perceptions, German historicists were not romantics. They rejected the idea of progress, knowing that it inevitably implies a judgement or a standard, inculcating historians to stray away from what Ranke said should be their task: not to pass judgments, but simply to investigate how things happened according to the documentary records.

We have thus far identified very few members of the German historical school other than Ranke and Humboldt, without addressing any of their particular books. Ranke's historical writing alone amounted to over sixty volumes. German historicists were generally prolific, and included some very important philosophers of history such as Wilhelm Dilthey (1833–1911), author of *The Critique of Historical Reason*, an attempt to "investigate the nature and conditions of historical consciousness." He knew he was caught in "a seemingly insoluble contradiction," claiming that, on the one hand, the first condition for "the possibility of historical science" lies in knowing that one's perspective is historically conditioned by the finitude of one's time and place, which means that every view is historically relative, while on the other hand arguing that this historical awareness "has liberated the human spirit from the last chains which natural science and philosophy have not yet torn asunder," by allowing humans to finally realize that a mind that is aware of its historical finitude is a mind that can provide us with a proper knowledge of social and human realities.[1052] Dilthey, however, was also influenced by Auguste Comte's progressivist argument that in history we see the liberation of the human intellect from religious mythologies and metaphysical assumptions, leading to the development of the natural sciences and proper methodologies for the study of history in a factually accurate manner, though he could not accept the scientific idea that reason could stand above historical time to reach absolute truths.

[1052] Bambach, 1995.

This line of historical reasoning triggered countless debates about the possibility of historical objectivity, the relativity of truth, whether there are laws of development in history that could be studied using the methods of the natural sciences, or whether we could, through a comparative historical approach, reveal characteristics that are common to all societies across time, based on human nature, as Darwinian social scientists argue today, allowing us to reach a certain cross-cultural objectivity.[1053] Two things are certain: the first, that there were still no debates whatsoever about the nature of historical knowledge outside the West, this late in history; the historiography of the non-western world remained the same as it had always been: annalistic in form, though Western ideas were starting to reach them. The second, that what Western historians today call "the crisis of German historicism," with unresolvable arguments about the historical relativity of truth, has obscured the fact that the true crisis faced by this school, leading to its domestication and denaturing into a safe theory about how we are historically conditioned, is the suppression of its powerful critique of liberalism and its defense of a unique collectivist path to modernity by Germany.

The crisis was less a result of epistemological conundrums than a result of the defeat of Germany in WWI and WWII. Johann Gustav Droysen said: "The creation of German unity required the presence of a power which could challenge other powers."[1054] He stressed the importance of German national unity, not for the sake of creating an international order based on "brute force," for he believed that this state had to be an ethical reality, but for the sake of defending the uniqueness of German history against the liberal attempt to impose a uniform order of nation-states based on individual rights. The German nation was not reducible to a contractual arrangement by abstract individuals dedicated to private gain and happiness. Individual rights should not take priority over community ties. Germans had always existed within the natural communities of the family, the tribe, and the Volk, and also within "communities of ideals" based on their language, arts, sciences, and religion.

After WWII, western historians reached the conclusion that only nations founded on individual rights were progressive, to the exclusion of "intolerant"

[1053] The topics "Relativism in History" or "Can History be Objective" were the subject of endless debates from the 1950s on. Half the readings in Meyerhoff (1959) concern this topic, with contributions from the most prominent historians and philosophers of the day, such as Benedetto Croce, R.G. Collingwood, Arnold Toynbee, Charles Beard, John Dewey, Ernest Nagel, among others.

[1054] In Iggers, 108.

German historicist ideas about the Volk. They argued that National Socialism and anti-Semitism had deep roots in German historicism. Germans needed a thorough re-education in Enlightenment progressivism. The domestication of German historicism began in earnest during the 1960s in Germany. The contributions of this school to the professionalization of history, its argument that the primary aim of historical narrative is to reconstruct events in their unique individuality, together with its claim that history deals with human intentionality, which is irreducible to the methods of the natural sciences, were happily integrated into the accepted liberal historiographical tradition. But the historicist notion that Germany's "authoritarian" path to modernity constituted its own contribution to the development of the "potentiality of humanity" at a given place and time was utterly rejected—in light of "the catastrophic course of German politics in the first half of the twentieth century."

These words come from Georg Iggers, who fled Germany with his family in 1938, author of a very solid book, *The German Conception of History* and, more recently, *Historiography in the Twentieth Century* from 2005. According to this latter book, a "younger generation of historians ... trained academically after 1945" and "closely linked in their eagerness to confront the German past critically and their commitment to democratic society," turned to the social sciences (away from the historicist preoccupation with diplomacy, the centrality of the state, and political history) to explain why German historians had surrendered "their liberal convictions during the process of German unification under Bismarck."[1055]

The question in the air was whether German expansionist policies from the Wilhelminian years to the Nazi period could be understood within the framework of the authoritarian institutions created in Germany in the 1800s. Fritz Fischer was the first to propose an answer in *Germany's War Aims in the First World War*, published in 1961, and now considered a classic work of scholarship among countless books published on the origins of WWI. His thesis was not that Germany's unsurpassed economic expansion between 1870 and 1914 incited the elites to pursue an aggressive foreign policy. Such an argument would have remained within the framework of Thucydides' no-blame view that the passion for power among leaders is the underlying motivation in geopolitical relations. In the new world of liberal internationalism, Germany needed to be blamed on ideological grounds. Fischer's aim was to show that Germany was aggressive because its

---

[1055] Iggers, 2005, 65–77.

"conservative leadership" had "retarded democratisation."[1056] His student Immanuel Geiss would push this thesis further, in explicit terms, in his 1967 book *July 1914: The Outbreak of the First World War. Selected Documents*: "The determination of the German Empire—then the most powerful conservative force in the world after Czarist Russia—to uphold the conservative and monarchic principles by any means against the rising flood of democracy, plus its Weltpolitik, made war inevitable."[1057]

It was Hans-Ulrich Wehler (Sheehan, 2014), the most influential German historian of the post WWII era, who explicitly argued that the "catastrophic course" of twentieth-century Germany was rooted in its incomplete modernization and retention of "autocratic traditions." By applying the social sciences, Weber's political sociology, Marx's class conflict analysis, and American modernization theory (which held that industrialization naturally engenders political democracy), Wehler concluded that Germany's path to modernity had been incomplete in that its "progressive economic modernization" was not accompanied "by a modernization of social relations and politics." The central aim of historical studies should be to show how economic and social structures are modernized, and how politics and culture should be modernized in a democratic direction. *The Guardian*, for Wehler's obituary in 2014, notes that he fought against "inequality in modern Germany . . . against racism and Holocaust denial, and much more besides."[1058] A major influence upon Wehler was the Frankfurt School's conception of "Critical Theory" as interpreted by Jürgen Habermas, with whom "he remained intellectually close for the rest of his life." It was Habermas' view that the Enlightenment should be seen as an "emancipatory project," with universal ideals that should serve as a normative criterion for the critical examination of past and present societies. There should be no dichotomy between scholarship or science and politics and morality. Historians should offer explanations for why things happened, as well as nurture progressive values.

[1056] Fischer, 1970, 285.
[1057] Geiss 1974, 17.
[1058] Evans, 2014.

The "Grand Liberal Narrative" of the Twentieth Century

Despite a wide variety of historical schools, a centrist liberal historiography committed to the ideals of rationalism, meritocracy, and the global spread of human rights dominated the writing of history until about the 1980s—while subsequently integrating within its fold the more progressive schools of New Left, feminist, multicultural, and postmodernist historians, within a "new liberalism" determined to ensure equal rights for everyone against the continuing racism, sexism, and ignorance of old liberals. But we must avoid judging the historiography of this century in purely ideological terms. Very high-quality history books based on extensive research were written during the twentieth century. We would be mistaken to view these books as opinionated tracts. The historiographical achievement of Western peoples during the twentieth century was outstanding, although in its closing years, and in our century, the progressivist agenda has engendered many below-average books. Not only did Europeans write excellent histories of art, mathematics, architecture, the sciences, and exploration; they wrote histories of every nation in the world while developing all the methodologies, such as paleography (study of historical handwriting), diplomatics (study of documents, records, and archives), chronology (establishing the dates of past events), epigraphy (study of ancient inscriptions), genealogy (study of families), numismatics (study of coins), including ethnography, archeology, and linguistics.

What David Gress insightfully calls "the Grand Narrative," and its ideology of centrist liberalism, "permeated education, public opinion, and political doctrines in much of Western Europe and the US from the 1940s to the 1980s."[1059] There were variations of this narrative, with the "WASP West" and the "Allied scheme of history" gaining the upper hand in the United States, the "Atlantic community" seen as "the pinnacle of human progress," the result of thousands of years of social evolution from ancient Greece and Rome through Judeo-Christianity, Newtonian science, the Enlightenment, and the Industrial Revolution. Daniel Bell saw the 1960s as the coming of "the end of ideology," with only piecemeal technocratic adjustments remaining to be disputed by a relatively affluent population.[1060]

Of course, as Bell said this, the activists of the sixties burst onto the scene. The Vietnam War, the Black civil rights movement, Third World poverty and

---

[1059] Gress, 1998, 21.
[1060] Bell, 2000.

revolutions, and the threat of nuclear war appeared to have brought to an end the 1940s to 1960s family-oriented, idyllic, and still puritanical centrist liberalism. But what these events and movements demonstrated was that a lot more improvements in human affairs remained to be made. This was the task of the next progressive generation.

This essay has been examining this phenomenon in two ways: pointing to the progressive side of past ideas and how they laid the groundwork for new progressive ideas in the next generation, while at the same time showing how new generations sought to rethink the course of history in light of new developments in knowledge and historical methodologies. Consider George Bancroft (1800–1891), the most influential American historian of the nineteenth century. By the standards of later generations, and certainly today, this man would be considered a fascist for his acceptance of the basic moral norms of his day about marriage, Christianity, and for his identification of the greatness of America with its "Anglo-Saxon" character. Yet, contained in his ten-volume *History of the United States* are ideals with a strong connection to contemporary Neoconservative (and current Leftist) policies about spreading democratic rights to the world. Bancroft believed that America was created "for the advancement of the principles of everlasting peace and universal brotherhood." With the spread of American values, the "ages of servitude" and "inequality" would end. The prime longing of all humans, he believed, is for liberty. While this love of liberty was Anglo-Saxon in origin, it had become in America the "breath of life to the people." Americans "heard the glad tidings [of liberty] which promised the political regeneration of the world."[1061] The Declaration of Independence was the "announcement of the birth of a people" dedicated to the spread of liberty to the world. Slavery, Bancroft insisted, was an institution that had originated outside the American ideal of liberty, and that's why it was eventually abolished.

The new progressive historians of the early twentieth century rejected Bancroft's liberal conception in favor of a social or economic historical approach focused on the role of the masses, workers, new immigrants, and women. They were merely addressing the persistent impediments to the actualization of the ideal of liberty, driven by a longing for a more democratic society, by advocating reforms to lift up the masses that had not benefitted from the limited liberties of the past

---

[1061] Breisach, 1983, 256–7. See a long passage online from Bancroft's *History of the United States* with the apt title "American Liberty Enlightening the World": https://tinyurl.com/bc8fwspu.

due to lack of public education and exploitative working conditions. Bancroft was himself an advocate of public schools.

Charles Beard portrayed Americans in *The Rise of American Civilization*, published in 1927, as a democratic people struggling for greater equality and inclusion of immigrants against the propertied interests of big business defended by Bancroft's classical liberalism. The Puritans that Bancroft celebrated for creating a WASP-oriented America were increasingly seen by this new generation of progressive historians as adherents of an outdated America, out of touch with the new realities of a racially diverse immigrant America. And the progressives after Beard, New Left historians, would go on to push for historical narratives that didn't prioritize a White male America, writing books such as Eugene Genovese's 1974 *Roll, Jordan, Roll: The World the Slaves Made*, which won none other than the Bancroft Prize, for its new research about how the antebellum South was a paternalist society that exploited and sought to dehumanize the slaves.[1062] Other historians insisted that culture and ideology were as important in determining the course of history as economic change, and a new generation of students wanted to overturn the "paternalistic" and "stifling" world of their parents in the name of individual "authenticity."

This dialectic within progressivism is quite apparent in the historiography of the twentieth century. Will Durant's colossal twelve-volume, nine-thousand-page *The Story of Civilization* published 1935–1975, a popular work many bought, none read, and specialized academics envied, was seen in its day as an urbane, post-WWII liberal effort to spread knowledge widely among an educated lay population. Having possession of some of these volumes, and reading segments from them, the judgment of Gress seems to be correct that Durant's work is an "immensely learned, vividly written" treatise in which history is seen as "tending to more freedom, greater equality, and broader rights."[1063] Durant experienced this progressivism in his own life, growing up as a New Deal liberal, and becoming a Kennedy liberal in later years uncomfortable with the ethnocentrism of his bestseller, *The Story of Philosophy*, for leaving out Asian philosophers, as he says in the preface to the second edition.[1064] The *Story of Civilization*, even though it started with a first volume dedicated to the "Oriental World," remained

---

[1062] *The New York Times* said in 1974 that "Genovese's magnum opus . . . is also the most profound, learned and detailed analysis of Negro slavery to appear since World War II." Today, in our yet more progressive times, using the word "Negro" would have disqualified this article.

[1063] Gress 1998, 35–6.

[1064] Durant, 1965.

nevertheless a story of Western civilization through the next eleven volumes. Durant belonged indeed to a generation still comfortable with social Darwinism. In a short 1968 book written with his wife, *The Lessons of History*, they wondered whether "Oriental fertility, working with the latest Occidental technology, would bring the decline of the West," and noted that "the first biological lesson of history is that life is competition" and that humans "are subject to the . . . struggle for existence and the survival of the fittest to survive."[1065] Social Darwinism had not yet been fully rooted out from liberalism.

It may seem a stretch to argue that a liberal triumphalist "Grand Narrative" dominated the historical vision, considering the many specialized historians who were ill at ease with sweeping generalizations about the course of history, and rather pessimistic about the future after the disastrous experience of two world wars and the possibility of nuclear annihilation. As a history student myself, I was warned against the assumption that there was a *telos*, purpose, or direction in history leading towards a better future in a cumulative way. Arthur Herman, in *The Idea of Decline in Western History*, published in 1997, argued that a coherent ideology of cultural pessimism could be seen emerging in the late nineteenth century in the writings of Nietzsche, Spengler, DuBois, Freud, Germany's national socialists, through to the 1960s counterculture, the existentialist philosopher Sartre, the world historian Arnold Toynbee, America's multiculturalists, and Afrocentric historians. For Nisbet1, as we saw earlier, the idea of progress persisted until about the 1960s. It is the view of Gress as well that, while the Grand Narrative dominated American elite culture from the 1920s to the 1960s, this narrative "began its fall" in the 1970s, to be successfully deconstructed "by the 1990s" by a successful rebellion of New Left, multicultural, and postmodernist historians.[1066]

A strong case can be made that what was really rejected was a Western-centric idea of progress that was insufficiently progressive. In its classical liberal version, this idea was "biased" in viewing the WASP world of the United States as the culmination of history, to the exclusion of the progressive contributions of other civilizations and races. This narrative was an "unfinished project" requiring revision, starting with an acknowledgment of the way the West had "underdeveloped" the rest of the world in its climb towards supremacy, and the way slaves, indigenous peoples, and working classes had endured oppression in the march of progress. An "honest conversation" about the racial injustices still prevailing in the West

---

[1065] Durant and Durant, 2010.
[1066] Gress, 37.

was required if the Western world was to live up to its ideals of democracy, individual rights, and equality. It was necessary to propose a new, revised, multicultural liberal idea of progress pointing towards a new universalism of human rights and a world history without a triumphalist West.

There was no "long march through the institutions" by a distinct ideology called "cultural Marxism" as is commonly supposed. After the crimes of Stalinism, the failures of communism, and the successes of Keynesian capitalism, Western Marxists gradually abandoned the idea of expropriating power from the capitalists, to focus on socialistic reforms and changes in the cultural attitudes of people, becoming the "New Left," with its members successfully integrated into academia and other institutions by centrist liberals agreeing with them about the need for more progress and more equality.

Jürgen Habermas, a second-generation member of the Frankfurt School, disagreed with Horkheimer and Adorno's argument about the decay of Western rationalism into a self-destructive "instrumental reason," by locating within the Enlightenment a second rational discourse, a "communicative intersubjective rationality" that escaped the narrow means-ends logic of instrumental reason, and that came to fruition in the eighteenth century within the "bourgeois reading public" in places such as salons and coffee-houses, a "public sphere" which set limits to the illegitimate use of power and nurtured a rational-critical culture, where citizens were bound only by the force of the better argument.[1067]

Habermas' own lack of universalism in tracing the history of this emancipatory discourse in "Judeo-Christianity" and in the European Enlightenment, without including the contributions of non-Western peoples, notwithstanding his efforts to see emancipatory impulses in other religions, could be easily remedied, as it has been, with a "global history." A global history has indeed emerged across the Western world, displacing the teaching of Western Civilization courses that had prevailed up until recently. It "moves beyond the obsession with the Enlightenment's European origins," and shows that ultimately it was a "process of global circulation, translation, and transnational co-production that turned the Enlightenment into the general and universal that it had always purported to be."[1068]

A doubly confounding dilemma of liberal progressivism in the twentieth century is that, firstly, it has sometimes entailed a new generation attacking the "conservative" liberalism of prior generations, giving thereby the illusion that "new

---

[1067] White, 1989; Habermas, 1991.
[1068] Conrad, 2012.

historians" with "radical" ideologies (Cultural Marxists, Postmodernists, Feminists) have taken over, instead of constituting the latest versions of a continuously progressing liberalism. It has occasioned, secondly, an underestimation of the incredible historiographical creativity (and progression) of the West in the twentieth century. Generally speaking, the West sees the following historical schools in the post-war decades: 1) continuation of the Grand Liberal Narrative; 2) the rise of a highly influential Marxist/New Left historiography; 3) the French Annales School founded by Lucien Febvre and Marc Bloch; 4) the "New Cultural History" and "Postmodernist" approaches principally associated with Michel Foucault; 5) the Quantitative or "Cliometrics" school, sometimes called "New Economic History;" 6) the Historical Sociology of Barrington Moore, Theda Skocpol, Randall Collins, and Michael Mann; 7) the History of Everyday Life and Microhistory; 8) the Cambridge School, with its historicist or contextualist interpretation, placing primary emphasis on the intellectual context of the discourse of a given historical era, associated with Quentin Skinner and J. G. A. Pocock; 9) the Cambridge Group for the History of Population, founded by Peter Laslett and Tony Wrigley; and 10) World History Connected, or "World History for Us All," currently a mandatory approach to the teaching of history to children across the US. There are yet other schools, which include as well the increasingly influential evolutionary/cultural psychological approach to historical explanations, as currently exemplified by Joseph Henrich and Steven Pinker.

All historians belonging to these schools, in varying degrees and modes of expression, are considered progressive liberals, either in their own time or today. This is equally true of evolutionary psychologists like Pinker, who believes that cosmopolitanism, diversity, and the application of Enlightenment reason have allowed the "better angels in our nature" to shine through. The one school that was not progressively liberal was German Historicism, which was rejected for its attempt to defend the unique "authoritarian" path of German modernization, at the same time that its "historicism" was thoroughly domesticated. The "contextualist" or historicist thought of Quentin Skinner is seen by leftists as "centrist liberal." He is known for his "revival of interest in Roman republicanism," a tradition in political theory that emphasizes individual freedom "understood as non-domination or independence from arbitrary power."[1069] These "republicans," however, cannot decide whether migration controls by a given state would constitute an "arbitrary" or "non-arbitrary" form or state power. None of the members of the historical

---

[1069] Lovett, 2022.

schools identified above has spoken against the imposition of "diversity, equity, and inclusion" as the overriding mission of the universities where they happily teach.

This political flaw should not be used as an excuse to downplay the historiographical achievements of these schools, but, by the same token, we cannot ignore the liberalism within which these schools were fashioned, and how this liberalism has influenced the choice of subjects and the way history is interpreted. The Western historiographical tradition is far superior to the non-Western tradition that multicultural historians are outrageously judging as equal in quality. Take the Annales School: it aimed at a "total history," merging various disciplines—geography, social history, psychology, and demography—and in the work of Fernand Braudel, it saw the differentiation of three historical times, each with its own speed: the *longue durée*, or the slow time of land, sea, recurring seasons, topography, and collective mental structures prevailing among peoples for centuries, which change so slowly they appear as immobile, and which have shaped the history of most humans; this is followed by the conjunctural time of economic cycles and trends in prices, which last for decades; and then there is the fast time of political events, wars, diplomacy, and personalities. If one looks at the everyday life of humans, the things that matter to most—lifespan, standard of living, infant mortality, land productivity—barely changed for centuries, until the West brought industrialization. The ideas of intellectuals appear, in the words of Braudel, as mere "surface disturbances, crests of foam that the tides of history carry on their strong backs." Braudel, author of *The Mediterranean and the Mediterranean World in the Age of Philip II*, published in 1949, is seen by some as the greatest historian of twentieth century. But he can be criticized, of course, for underestimating the accumulating power of European ideas leading to the scientific and industrial revolutions. It is worth noting, however, that the Fernand Braudel Center and the official journal associated with it, *Review*, were founded by the Marxist Immanuel Wallerstein, and the books published under its banner are thoroughly multicultural and anti-Western.

This brings up the question: what about the Marxists who went on to have lucrative careers in universities? The Marxist school played a major role in the promotion of liberal progressivism in the twentieth century. At first, its members saw themselves as representatives of a communist ideology in direct confrontation with liberalism, followers of "historical materialism" as articulated by Marx, Engels, Lenin, Plekhanov, Trotsky, and Kautsky—all of whom, we might add, wrote historical works. Many of the British Marxist historians who would gain international prestige within Western academia (Maurice Dobb, Rodney Hilton, Christopher Hill, Eric Hobsbawm, and Edward Thompson) were formal members of the Communist Party, though they eventually broke ranks after the Soviet invasion of Hungary in 1956. Their goal as scholars was to show the truthful relevance of Marxism to the study of the past, which they did with great success.[1070]

The books of the British names (and, of course, of the founders of Marxism) became required reading across Western academia. Hill, who acted at Oxford as "Senior Member of the exclusive Stubbs Society" (that is, the Stubbs we met earlier for his "Whig" interpretation of history which dominated the Victorian Era) was celebrated for his "history from below" perspective in such books as *The World Turned Upside Down: Radical Ideas During the English Revolution* from 1972, and his 1970 biography, *God's Englishman: Oliver Cromwell and the English Revolution*. E. Thompson, on the strength of his widely-read 1963 book *The Making of the English Working Class*, which "still endures as a staple on university reading lists," was named in a 2011 poll by the liberal *History Today* magazine as the second most important historian of the previous sixty years, behind only Braudel.

Hobsbawm, "a life-long Marxist" who was appointed in 1998 to the very prestigious Order of the Companions of Honour, is best-known for his compound work, the first three of which were required reading during my own undergrad courses, *The Age of Revolution: Europe 1789–1848, The Age of Capital: 1848–1875, The Age of Empire: 1875–1914*, and *The Age of Extremes: The Short Twentieth Century, 1914–1991*. He is also known for the influential idea of "invented traditions," which argues that many European "traditions" which purport to be old are often recent in origin and sometimes "invented." We could go on naming many renowned Marxist historians. G. E. M. de Ste. Croix's 1989 *The Class Struggle in the Ancient World: From the Archaic Age to the Arab Conquests*, which many liberals praised for "establishing the validity of historical materialist analysis of the ancient world," is said to have received more scholarly attention than almost any other work of ancient history since George Grote and Theodor Mommsen. The narrative and analyses of these books are first rate. Ste. Croix's book contains over 120 pages of detailed notes.

This should not surprise us. Marxist historians were operating within the institutional framework of Western universities produced by a progressive world dedicated to the advancement of knowledge and the improvement of society. Centrist liberals were still the majority and did not feel threatened by Marxists. There

---

[1070] Kaye, 1984.

was an implicit recognition among them that the post-WWII world was quite successful in achieving progress, better working conditions, women's right to vote, "racial justice," and so on. Liberalism was showing a progressive capacity to stay apace with the more progressive demands of Marxists. Liberals could not disagree with Hobsbawm's concluding words of hope in *The Age of Empire*: "the actual achievements of the twentieth century in material and intellectual progress—hardly in moral progress—is extraordinarily impressive and quite undeniable. Is there still room for the greatest of all hope, that of creating a world in which free men and women, emancipated from fear and material need, will live the good life together in a good society? Why not?"[1071]

The old liberalism, concerned with ensuring the negative liberties of citizens against the "coercive" powers of the state, had lost touch with the needs of a Keynesian state in charge of keeping capitalism afloat by improving the "effective demand" of workers. Liberals were now agreeing that the West had previously been racist, sexist, and exploitative, and that the government could play a positive role in eliminating these problems. American liberals, such as John Rawls, Donald Dworkin, and Michael Sandel, articulated a new liberalism in which equal rights also meant reduction of inequalities and promotion of the "self-realization" of individuals. Meanwhile, Marxists were moving in directions that challenged the metanarrative of class struggle and the overthrow of capitalists, for a "New Cultural History" that argued, with Michel Foucault replacing Marx as the historical analyst of power, that the sources of power are not limited to the coercion of a capitalist state, but are everywhere, diffused and embodied in "discourses of truth" wielded by heterosexuals, patriarchal men, Whites, scientists, et cetera. Liberal Postmodernism had arrived.

The New Cultural Historians, which included practitioners of "microstoria" and the "history of everyday life," are sometimes categorized as "postmodern," even though few accepted the postmodernist tenet that the construction of narratives is fundamentally determined by aesthetic and rhetorical standards. They were practitioners of rigorous archival research to illuminate the past. What they rejected, though some came from a Marxist background, was the claim that one could understand the full complexity of the past merely by writing about the dynamics of macrostructures, modes of production, class conflict, or the transition from feudalism to capitalism. They sought to understand the everyday life of common people through the study of small villages or singular individuals. The

---

[1071] Hobsbawm, 1987, 340.

cultures of the past could not be framed within a grand narrative about "the story of liberty" or the breakthrough ideas of great scientists.

With the work of Michel Foucault, we may be dealing with a postmodern historian who anticipated, and embodied in his sexual life, the current nature of progressive liberalism. His influence on academic scholarship has been pervasive in anthropology, sociology, criminology, cultural studies, literary theory, feminism, and history. His books, *The History of Madness* in 1961, *The Birth of the Clinic* in 1963, *The Order of Things* in 1966, *Discipline and Punish* in 1975, and *The History of Sexuality* in 1976, are among the most cited ever. He rejected every liberal tenet about the directionality and meaning of history, the concepts of impartial reasoning, the notion that the individual can be a free agent, and the idea that historical research gives us access to an external reality.[1072] Every conception of history is a construct constituted by a language that is permeated with hierarchical relations of power. There are no authors in rational control of their narratives, and there is no conscious intentionality. The idea of free subjectivity is itself a construction created by power. The claim that gender identity is based on the biology of sex is a form of power that aims to normalize as correct certain forms of sexual and gendered behavior, while pathologizing other forms. There can be no liberation of sexuality, a natural form of sexuality, freed from capitalistic or traditional oppression, because sexuality is always a result of cultural and power mechanisms. The liberation of one type of sexuality from the oppression of one group merely engenders another form of sexuality controlled by another group. Foucault, nevertheless, insisted on "critical thinking" against hegemonic institutional norms that have excluded certain ways of thinking and sexuality as demonic, irrational, heretical, or criminal.

A Marxist in his early life, he soon rejected its illiberal authoritarianism and homophobia, influenced by a wide spectrum of thinkers including Husserl, Heidegger, Nietzsche, Marquis de Sade, Kafka, Durkheim, Margaret Mead, Beckett, and many others, while entertaining himself with drugs and sado-masochistic sexual activities. His work has been summarized as a long exploration of transgression against those who control the production of knowledge and define what is human and what is ethical. He thus explored how medical science was used in the eighteenth century to categorize and stigmatize the mentally ill, as well as the poor, the sick, the homeless, or anyone who deviated from the norms of those in

---

[1072] A great overview with selections from each of Foucault's work can be found in Foucault and Rabinow (1984). For an intelligent overview of his thought, see Gutting and Oksala (n.d.).

power. He came up with the concept of "disciplinary power," about how institutions reconstruct the thoughts, habits, skills, and desires of humans in factories, schools, hospitals and prisons, by using rules, surveillance, exams, and punishment.

We have no standards to judge what are "good" and "bad" forms of being a human, because there are no subjects existing outside the contingencies of historical time and power relationships. All we can do is engage in "discourse analysis" so as to uncover existing hierarchies by analyzing the fields of knowledge through which they are legitimated. We can engage in questioning how we came to be the humans we think we are, such as how we came to think that we have natural rights to life, liberty, and happiness, but such a questioning can only show us how our current way of being human is historically contingent and thus changeable. Because the current way of being is not rooted in biology, it is also possible to reconstruct new ways of being.

Yet, while denying progressive concepts of freedom, justice, liberation, and improvement of the human condition, Foucault was a leftist activist who regularly protested abuses of human rights, participated in anti-racist campaigns, and, all in all, was committed to questioning abuses of power. It was this reliance on an implicit Enlightenment form of "critique" of power that prompted Habermas to argue that Foucault's thinking does not self-examine its liberal moral-normative assumptions. [1073] We can add that from Foucault we can see that liberal progressivism is no less driven by a power dynamic than other ideologies. His *History of Sexuality* has been very influential in queer theory, the deconstruction of maleness and femaleness, and the imposition of new relations of power against traditional forms of biological sexuality and marriage. The very notion that humans are totally "constructed" by society, that ideas do not refer to reality, and that there are no principles of morality outside power relations, cannot but lead the Foucauldians to seek to win the contest for power by reconstructing humans as they wish. Universities today are the epitome of the disciplinary society Foucault condemned, in their effort to produce docile students who take all their COVID boosters while wearing masks and writing essays about the blessings of transsexualism and diversity.

The professionalization of history, along with academic specialization in archival research, persuaded historians to abandon philosophical speculations about the laws of history, its purpose or goal, through much of the twentieth

---

[1073] Habermas, 1990.

century. We would have to wait until about the 1970s or 80s to witness the re-emergence of the uniquely Western tradition of seeking to explain the broad patterns of history. However, whereas the earlier accounts by the Scottish historical school, Condorcet, Kant, Comte, and Hegel remained almost entirely focused on Western history, the post-1970s universal histories would be intentionally aimed at "provincializing" the West, by emphasizing, above all else, the study of past connections in the human community, mass migrations, imperial links, long-distance trade, as well as how much the West borrowed from other civilizations and how the world-capitalist system of exploitation made possible the rise of the West. The progression of history would now be premised on the common biological nature of humanity, the universal ecosystem of the Earth, and how the integration of humanity, economic and cultural globalization, the internet, smartphones, international trade agreements, mass migration, and the spread of human rights were leading to the unification of humankind under a progressive world government.[1074]

We could say that the first major attempt at a new universal history that would relegate the West to a provincial place, based on a growing number of specialized works, was Oswald Spengler's *The Decline of the West*, published 1918-23. Spengler consciously set out to provide a new world history which "admits no sort of privileged position to the Classical, or the Western culture as against the cultures of India, Babylon, Egypt," identifying eight world civilizations that "count for just as much in the general picture of history" and that have indeed surpassed classical culture or the West "in spiritual greatness and soaring power."[1075] In Arnold Toynbee's ten volume *A Study of History*, published 1934–54, which distinguished twenty-six civilizations in the course of history, the West was not at the center of human progress, and the driving force of history was the fact that civilizations are energized to respond to challenges from other civilizations.[1076]

While there were still centrist liberals around who believed in the centrality of the West, most attempts to explain the meaning and logic of history would start

---

[1074] Numerous books can be cited covering these topics; suffice it to cite the major bestseller, Yuval Noah Harari, *Sapiens: A Brief History of Humankind* (2014), which has made Harari into some sort of guru in the liberal West. Its argument is that the trend in history is towards large-scale human cooperation leading to the unification of humankind, with the implied message that Western nations need to welcome millions of migrants to increase cooperation.

[1075] Spengler, 1988, 15–26.

[1076] The work Toynbee accomplished is incredible but, unfortunately, this book is way too long to be read in an age when there are so many other books to read. I am happy to say that in my huge library I have an excellent abridged and illustrated version by Caplan (1972).

coming after the 1970s and 80s from leftist progressives and multicultural world historians. J. M. Roberts, a centrist liberal admirer of the Allied powers, unabashedly asserted in his 1995 book, *The Penguin History of the World*, that the history of Africans and Amerindians was not central to world history, and that the modern era saw the "triumph of the West."[1077] But Roberts' liberalism was already old, incapable of withstanding the proliferation of women's history, Black history, ethnic history, peasant history, the history of homosexuals and third world peoples, and the postmodern progressive decentering of everything Western.

The Grand Liberal Narrative that reigned supreme in the US between 1920 and 1970 came to be seen as manifestation of "odious" assumptions of White racial superiority—supposing that the Aryans are peculiarly the race of progress— that belittled the histories of non-Western peoples. It was no longer persuasive for a new generation in the 1970s to be satisfied with the view that developments within Europe (Newtonian science, Enlightenment, Industrial Revolution) were liberating the human mind from superstition and obscurantism. The idea that the central motor of historical change was the interaction between civilizations, reawakening and fertilizing each other, was now very popular—an idea that would be further radicalized, pushed in a more progressive direction, by the historical researches of "dependency" theorists, with their claim that it was the systematic exploitation of the Incas and the Aztecs, and the extraction of gold and silver from the Americas in the sixteenth century, that boosted the fortunes of Europe to begin with, including the brutal importation of African slaves to work in plantations from about 1600 to 1850, coupled with the colonial trade, which allowed Europe to earn massive profits to be reinvested in industrial development. A. G. Frank gained worldwide fame when he coined the term "the development of underdevelopment" to argue that Europe developed by under-developing the rest of the world and blocking their developmental paths.[1078]

The three-volume work *The Modern World System*, published 1974–89 by Immanuel Wallerstein, elaborated this idea into an argument that history needs to be understood along global-systemic lines that recognize how, since the era of world empires, the world had been tied together through wide networks of trade

---

[1077] The "centrist liberalism" of Roberts (circa 1995) is already quite progressive when compared to the "centrist liberalism" of H. A. L. Fisher's book *A History of Europe* (1976), originally published in 1935, critical of what was happening in Germany at the time, but nevertheless willing to use phrases such as "the life-giving inrush of the Aryan peoples." It is a more lively read than the rather dry and neutered prose in Roberts' book.

[1078] Duchesne, 2006.

supported by military and political coercion, and how the world capitalist economy originated by Europe in the 1500s was structured by a new division of labor,
wherein the West forced its colonies to provide cheap labor and raw materials as
well as markets for its manufactures, which kept the non-Western world in a state
of impoverishment while allowing the West to stay at the top. This attack on the
Grand Narrative was the work of many groups: feminists fighting Western patriarchy, Frankfurt School critical theorists, postmodernists, Foucault-inspired new
historicists, and anthropologists pushing the multicultural idea that no culture
should be deemed to be superior. World multicultural history thus came to predominate in the 1980s and 1990s, with Western civ courses fading out. *The World
History Association* was founded in 1982 and the *Journal of World History* in 1990,
with one of its founders, Patrick Manning, acknowledging Wallerstein as one of
the "fathers of world history" in his 2003 historiographical survey *Navigating
World History*.[1079]

It would take too long to go over the countless books published in the last
decades about how Europeans came to establish hegemony over the world, and
how non-European cultures sometimes succumbed to European numbers, weapons, and disease, but sometimes fought heroically against European "decultura-
tion." The end result was that the idea of progress was inverted. Now, the main
pattern of historical evolution was "largely regressive": the standard of living, the
quality of work, and the degree of social equality had deteriorated for most of the
peoples of the Earth; hunters and gatherers and simple horticulturalist tribes were
"the truest democracies."[1080] This argument was initiated by Marshall Sahlins with
his celebrated thesis that the "original affluent society" was hunting and gathering.
Jared Diamond completed it by arguing that "agriculture was the worst mistake
in the history of the human race," and that Europe's uniqueness consisted in its
"guns, germs, and steel."[1081] Martin Bernal's 1991 book *Black Athena: Afro-Asiatic
Roots of Classical Civilization: The Fabrication of Ancient Greece*, despite being
thoroughly refuted by worthy scholars, managed to persuade an establishment

---

[1079] For a review essay of Manning's historiographical book, see Duchesne (2005).
[1080] Duchesne, 2005.
[1081] His book *Guns, Germs, and Steel* (1997) has been, and still is, a bestseller. Ian Morris, author
of the widely acknowledged book, *Why the West Rules* (2010), also dismisses the achievements
of the West, accusing the settlers of the Americas for killing "the enormous majority of the native population with their disgusting European germs"; see my review of his book (2011).

committed to inclusiveness that the "Greek miracle" was a product of Egyptian and Semitic influences, rather than a home-grown "Aryan" phenomenon.[1082]

The idea of progress was not rejected, however. What we had was a more progressive idea against the "ethnocentrism" of the Grand Narrative for a newly emerging diverse America that would fulfill what multiculturalists would call the universal human need for equal cultural recognition. As liberalism progressed in a multicultural, postmodernist, environmentalist, and globalist direction, and as Western governments formally declared that the continued improvement of the West required immigrant diversity, centrist liberals who wished to avoid accusations of racism and stay relevant were compelled to redefine their conservatism in a neoconservative direction in the 1980s and '90s, by arguing that the directionality of scientific, technological, and democratic progress was not a manifestation of Western peoples per se, but a manifestation of the deepest needs and aspirations of humanity, leading to the creation of a "Universal Civilization" where race, ethnocentrism, and tradition would be displaced by adherence to liberal universal values. This idea was originated by Leo Strauss and his pupils.[1083] The major text of this neoconservative interpretation was Francis Fukuyama's *The End of History and the Last Man*, published in 1992.

Fukuyama gave expression to a resurgent optimism among centrist liberals that the American defeat of the Soviet Union in the Cold War signified the triumph of liberalism over its last ideological adversary, communism, after having defeated its other enemy, fascism, in WWII. While this was a victory for the West over the Soviet Union, it meant that the ideology of liberalism was now destined to be universal and without major ideological rivals. Fukuyama anticipated that in the future, more and more governments would adopt liberal democratic institutions, and that we would thus witness the actualization of Kant's project of a "universal history from a cosmopolitan point of view," with nations less concerned about their traditions than about increasing their wealth through capitalism and scientific knowhow. National identities would be diluted in a way resembling what the EU was already doing in Europe, transcending, in his words, "sovereignty and traditional power politics by establishing a transnational rule of law."

Fukuyama defended the idea of history as progress toward more scientific knowledge and more democracy and individual rights. He insisted, against multicultural relativists, that it was possible to construct a "coherent and directional

---

[1082] Gress, 1989.
[1083] Duchesne, 2014.

history of mankind that will eventually lead the greater part of humanity to liberal democracy.[1084] This was not, however, a victory of the "rise of the West," with its uniquely Greek, Roman, Christian, Renaissance, Newtonian, and Enlightenment heritage. Rather, it was a victory for the universal aspirations of humanity. Fukuyama offered two reasons why this history was universal. First, there was already a general consensus in the world, among former communists, fascists, or traditional nations, that science was cumulative and directional, and that it augmented the power and wealth of nations. The scientific method was no longer "Western," but universally accepted. The social and economic effects of technological change were similar in every society, and were thus a demonstration of its universality. Second, the decision of an increasing number of nations to adopt, if partially and slowly, liberal democratic institutions, was a reflection of a universal human need for recognition—that is, for all humans to have their voices heard, their property protected under the law, and their right to seek their own happiness.

Fukuyama was confident that traditionalism, governments, and institutions operating according to long-standing customs and religious beliefs would give way to liberalism, as societies embraced a universal education based on science, and thus encouraged a rational understanding of all things. "Modern education ... liberates men from their attachments to tradition and authority. ... This is why modern man is the last man."[1085] Even if this last man of history loses his ancestral ties, or can no longer live a life of Nietzschean heroism, he will be content with technical advances, entertainment, therapy, consumerism, longevity, and freedom of choice, while still having the opportunity, if he so desires, to engage in "risky" sports. Postmodernists and leftists were furious. But Fukuyama correctly saw that his universal liberalism recognized the individual rights of everyone regardless of race and gender, that it contained the institutional framework for the extension of individual rights to transsexuals and the like, that it accommodated the valuing of the environment, that it allowed individuals to create their own civic associations for a sense of belonging and identity, and that it met the postmodernist rejection of Eurocentrism by recognizing the multicultural right of immigrants to enjoy their customs as citizens within the framework of liberal institutions. Fukuyama has always been an advocate of mass immigration and diversity. His main preoccupation today is support for the "liberation of Ukraine" and the

---

[1084] Fukuyama, 1992, xii.
[1085] Ibid, 306.

extension of these universal values against Russian "authoritarianism and traditionalism."[1086]

The inbuilt progressive tendency of both Neocon and Postmodern liberalism
lies in their commitment to free the individual from the traditional restraints of
society, or any institution, norm, custom, or "prejudice" that constricts the right
of the individual to choose his own beliefs and happiness, as long as they do not
infringe on this principle of liberalism. It should be stated parenthetically that
postmodernism did provide non-western historians, including the philosopher
Alexander Dugin, with concepts to interpret their traditions in a positive light by
decentering the "totalizing" narrative of the "logocentric" West. Postmodernism
in the West, however, encouraged the affirmation of non-Western ways inside the
West, not the reaffirmation of Western traditions inimical to progressivism.

Socialistic liberalism aimed at enlarging the scope of free action on the part of
those who lacked the economic means to exercise their freedom of choice. Its protagonists called for the "positive" right to a good education, right to work, paid
parental leave, adequate standard of living, and medical care. Freedom was no
longer defined as "negative freedom," protection from an oppressive government,
but as the right of everyone, including foreign immigrants, to be afforded by the
government "positive" freedoms for their self-actualization. The civil rights movement that abolished racial segregation and disenfranchisement for being contrary
to the equal protection of the laws guaranteed by the Fourteenth Amendment,
would be seen as insufficient to a new generation of progressives believing that the
only way to overcome persisting inequalities in Black educational and professional achievement was through affirmative hiring to remedy the "injuries of the
past" and persistent "systemic racism." While every liberal politician across Western settler states previously felt no qualms about White-only immigration policies,
by the 1960s and 70s such policies were condemned by a new generation of multicultural liberals for violating both the principle that all human beings across the
world are born free and equal in dignity and rights, and the pluralist principle that
the government should not mandate any cultural values, but should allow individuals from diverse nationalities and races to choose their own values as long as
they don't infringe on the choices of others.

Postmodernist demands for gender equality were also framed in terms of the
liberal right of individuals to choose their sexual identities, rather than being

---

[1086] Believing that liberalism is unstoppable in the world, he predicted the "outright defeat of
Russia" and "the end of Putin's rule" in March 2022, one month into the war (Fukuyama, 2022).

restricted by a male-female collectivist "binary." For all the bickering against post-modernists, the emancipatory project of the Enlightenment, despite its ostensible defense of the "totalizing narrative" of rational progress, shares with postmodern-ism an attempt to overcome the "ethnocentric" power, or lack of racial cosmopol-itanism, of European peoples.[1087] Habermas after all, is an ardent supporter of im-migrant diversity in Germany.[1088]

The same progressive logic applies to the way critical race theorists use racial categories. They believe that in our current society, minorities are "racialized" by dominant Whites, and that overcoming this racial hierarchy necessitates racial identity politics. By giving nonwhites pride in their race and its "achievements," and making Whites aware of their unequal "racialization" of "the Other," they aim to create a future world of equality, including a race-mixed society, that will trans-cend any form of racial identity for the sake of a society in which everyone is judged as an individual. The aim of multiculturalism is to afford immigrant mi-norities with resources to enhance their opportunities for individual integration, while encouraging members of the "dominant" Western culture to respect the ethnic identity and customs of newcomers as long as the principle of individual rights is not trampled upon. The replacement of Whites simply means that indi-viduals with equal rights and dignity who have a different skin color will replace individuals of another skin color.

This explains why not a single historian today, no matter what school of his-tory he/she belongs to, has cared or dared to examine critically what is undeniably the most radical transformation ever witnessed in human history: the complete disenfranchisement and demonization of the indigenous populations of the West at the behest of their own liberal ruling classes. There are no conceptual tools available in the West for such a critical stand. Historians can certainly complain about some perceived negative consequences, about illegal immigration, about the inadequacy of public schools to handle endless arrivals of new immigrants, lack of public housing and the like, but liberalism denies them the right to question immigration in principle. The arrival of millions of immigrants has been going on at an intense level for about three decades, offering enough time for historians to start reflecting about its origins, nature, and consequences. They have, but not a single one has deviated from the accepted liberal narrative.[1089]

[1087] Verovšek, 2022.

[1088] Duchesne, 2015.

[1089] It is hard to think of a book in the West by an academic working at a university critical of immigration as a matter of principle and for the sake of defending the cultural interests of

A standard argument is that immigration is about overcoming the persistence of "nativism" and bringing about a more inclusive Western culture. Another favorite claim is that opposition to immigration in the name of nationalism "threatens to undermine the fundamental values of liberal democracies." Similarly: "anti-immigration" sentiments are a "painful reminder" of the long history of immigration restrictions rooted in the "racist fears of Whites." They also claim, very deceptively, that there is nothing new about current immigration patterns: after all, the US, Canada, Australia, and New Zealand were founded by immigrants. They refuse to examine the evidence showing that the founders of these nations were settlers and families with very high fertility rates. They are actually teaching students that England, France, Germany, Sweden, Italy, Spain, et cetera were also founded by migrants over the course of their histories, and that their "original inhabitants" came out of Africa, the Near East, and the Eurasian steppes. One argument both left and right liberals have embraced is that, due to the decline of fertility rates across the West, mass immigration is necessary to avoid permanent labor shortages, a declining GDP, lower tax revenues, collapse of pension schemes, and declining social services. [1090]

Today, every mainstream politician, across the West (both right and left), and every academic and approved journalist, be they liberals, socialists, environmentalists, Christians, Jews, Muslims, Blacks, Hindus, postmodernists, conservatives, or feminists, accept the mandate that "diversity is our greatest strength," and agree that opposition to immigration is a "white supremacist" view that must not be permitted in the public square. This is the case even among so-called "populist" parties, though some of these want to restrict immigration, and a few countries in Eastern Europe have not yet embraced in full multicultural liberal values. My view is that progressivism is inherent to liberalism, and that liberal progressivism is the

---

Western peoples besides my book *Canada in Decay: Mass Immigration, Diversity, and the Ethnocide of Eurocanadians* (2017). The price for this approach is very high. While this book was a major bestseller, I experienced an academic mobbing in 2019, which forced me to take early retirement, not to mention many other forms of suppression and exclusion from multiple social media venues (PayPal, YouTube, Twitter), including the deletion of about seventy customer reviews of *Canada in Decay* at Amazon.

[1090] Recent books expressing these views include: Reece Jones's White Borders: The History of Race and Immigration in the US from Chinese Exclusion to the Border Wall (2021), Peter Gatrell's The Unsettling of Europe: How Migration Reshaped a Continent (2019), Roger Daniels's, Coming to America: A History of Immigration and Ethnicity in American Life (2022), Andrew Rosenberg's Undesirable Immigrants: Why Racism Persists in International Migration (2022), and Bryan Caplan, Open Borders: The Science and Ethics of Immigration (Macmillan, 2019).

dominant ideology in the West. What exactly is the nature of this ideology, why it is deeply rooted in Western history, and why this ideology inevitably comes with multiculturalism, gender fluidity, and racial diversity, will be the subject of our last chapter.

XI

LIBERAL PLURALISM AND THE TRANSFORMATION OF THE WEST INTO A MULTIRACIAL CIVILIZATION

All forms of collective identity—ethnic, national, religious, caste, and so on—impede an individual's awareness of his individuality. Liberalism encourages the individual to become himself, that is, to be free of all those social identities and dependencies that constrain and define the individual from outside.

– Alexander Dugin

Liberalism or Cultural Marxism?

How did it come about that the most creative civilization in history, the one that called upon individuals to have the courage to use their own rational faculties—Dare to know! *Sapere aude!*—has now imposed upon everyone the mandate of "diversity, equity, and inclusion," punishing those who question this mandate, flying the rainbow flag everywhere, covering up the failures of Black integration in the US as "misinformation," encouraging millions of illegal immigrants to become citizens, and insisting that individual freedom and enlightenment are incompatible with any form of European ethno-cultural identity? The animosity against Whites in their own created nations is so egregiously beyond reason that reasonable people cannot but believe it is the product of some malevolent force acting from the outside, rather than a product of the West itself, a hidden agenda concocted by cultural Marxists "marching through the institutions," a "Kalergi plan" enacted by a mysterious Austrian-Japanese politician, the product of nihilistic and self-destructive "spiteful mutants,"[1091] or "psychopathic narcissists" with a zeal for "social justice,"[1092] or a grand strategy conducted by a minuscule group of Jews in secret since ancient times without Europeans ever noticing it.[1093]

My own view is that the ultimate reason for the current ethnocidal path of the West is to be found within the ideology of liberal pluralism uniquely nurtured by Europeans peoples. The essential tenet of this ideology is that all humans are alike in their inalienable freedom to decide for themselves their values and lifestyles. Liberalism, with its deep roots in the ancient Greek discovery of the self, and the abolition of kinship networks in the Middle Ages, has brought the West incredible success. This long-term perspective does not preclude the role of shorter-term factors in accelerating, intensifying, or spreading this ethnocidal path. The weakening of sentiments of ethnic affiliation and nationalism in the West through the sheer reality of modernization, migration, urbanization, and globalization should not be underestimated. The acceleration of liberal progressivism through the powerful impact of socialists, feminists, and postmodernists is a factor we cannot ignore either. The very success of liberal individualism in creating relatively affluent lifestyles, with lots of entertainment and enticing pleasures, has undoubtedly produced a complacent psychological disposition among many Whites, weakening even further the natural ingroup instincts that liberal values tend to dilute. (As we were warned long ago by the aristocratic ancient Romans: comfort breeds weakness and effeminacy). The zealotry of Jews in the pursuit of cultural pluralism and their adamant opposition to White identity, as Kevin MacDonald has systematically demonstrated, may be identified as the major proximate factor in the radicalization of liberalism in the United States in the post-WWII era.[1094]

[1091] Dutton, 2022.

[1092] Peterson, 2023.

[1093] Guyenot, 2020. This is a friendly questioning. Guyenot is a prolific writer at *The Unz Review* meriting serious attention. Dutton has established himself as a key intellectual in the dissident right. For a careful articulation of the "Kalergi plan," see Clare Ellis's book, *The Blackening of Europe*, published by Arktos in three volumes, based on a dissertation she wrote under my supervision at The University of New Brunswick. The first two volumes have been published under the subtitles: *Volume I: Ideologies and International Development* (2020), and *Volume II: Immigration, Islam, and the Migrant Crisis* (2022). The third volume is forthcoming. The chapter on Kalergi is in the first volume.

[1094] We will return to MacDonald's argument towards the end of this chapter; remember for now that MacDonald frames the role of Jews within his long-term theory that Europeans were selected for individualism, openness to outgroups, and universal moral principles.

The emphasis here, however, will be on liberal pluralism, which is based on the principle of equality of rights, as the ultimate cause, or the "real reason" for the current ethnocidal path of Europeans. The events, policies, institutional changes, and ideas we identify with wokeness and progressivism, as will be explained below, have demonstrated, for many decades, a remarkable parallelism in multiple Western nations; this parallelism points to some common underlying factor operating across all these nations, not necessarily to the exclusion of other local factors, but in conjunction with them.

This is not a matter of reviving James Burnham's 1964 argument that "liberalism is the ideology of Western suicide," already articulated some sixty years ago. What concerned Burnham was the West's global retreat from its colonial empires and lack of confidence in the face of Communist expansion. He viewed this retreat as a product of the naive liberal view that humans are potentially a perfectible species capable of relying on their rational capacities to create a world of nations coexisting in a state of mutual economic prosperity and equality. Westerners were attacking their own history for its shortcomings instead of exhibiting confidence about their unparalleled achievements. Liberals were under the illusion that the problems of the world were mere products of backward customs and irrational prejudices that could be eliminated with a proper rationalist education.

The view developed here will be very different. While there is an intellectual current within liberalism believing it is possible for members of a society to reach a rationally-based consensus on what the good life is, the cardinal principle of contemporary liberalism is simply that every citizen should have the same right, as a naturally free moral agent, to decide what to believe and what way of life to pursue in a state of mutual respect. It would be a mistake to state unequivocally that liberalism is a substantive doctrine that tells its believers what the good life is, what the nature of reality is, or which religion will bring humans closer to God. Liberalism does not mandate, in principle, any system of beliefs and practices, be they Christian, existentialist, or Buddhist. The liberal pluralism dominating the West today holds the view, rather, that humans, with their varying personalities and upbringings, can't be expected to reach a consensus about the good life and the values they should endorse, and that they are reasonable enough to decide for themselves their beliefs. Given this reality about human diversity, the best humans can do is to create a political setting within which every person is equally free to make decisions about the good life based on their conscience, as long as they don't seek to undermine the political setting within which this pluralism is possible.

In this respect, liberalism is unlike any other ideology or traditional normative order in that it lacks a metaphysics about the ultimate nature of reality, about the highest values of life, or what ends individuals should pursue. But this is not all there is to liberalism. Liberalism is not only the child of the idea of progress, as we argued in the last chapter, but embodies within it the very essence of this idea in its commitment to the elimination of every bias, hierarchy, "backward" habits, traditions, and persisting inequalities it deems to be obstructive to the equal liberty of individuals. It is also an ideology dedicated to the socialization of individuals who are "liberal-minded" in their overall personalities, preferences, and choices. It is, therefore, a highly politicized ideology, not the neutral arbiter it purports to be in theory.

We will see below that liberalism, as it came to be institutionalized across the West, does not make equal allowance for all viewpoints within the public sphere, but expects everyone to be "tolerant," "open-minded," and, in our times, in favor of "diversity and inclusiveness." It is now highly unsympathetic and, indeed, intolerant towards views it deems to be insufficiently liberal, even when these views show tolerance towards other perspectives and accept open debate within the public sphere.

This does not mean that liberalism, as it currently exists, is best described as a "totalitarian" ideology with a "communistic" agenda. It is understandable why there is an inclination among dissidents (and conservatives) to blame "cultural Marxism," or the Left generally, for the "cancel culture" that now pervades the West. The Right, lacking an ideology of its own, an alternative doctrine with fully developed concepts and moral values, is fundamentally dependent on liberalism, wishing to return to an earlier version of this ideology. Marxism, fascism, and liberalism are "world-outlooks"—that is, systematic accounts of the nature of the world, with their own economic doctrines, anthropologies, accounts of history, epistemologies, ethical theories, and aesthetics, offering meaning and purpose to their followers. The contemporary dissident world is an inconsistent mixture of views, borrowings from fascism along with populist feelings rooted in natural sentiments and instincts, without a theoretical framework, feeding off liberalism itself, an earlier "classical" version, sustained by race realism.

Race realism is not an ideological worldview but a scientific theory. Dissidents know that fascism is no longer able to garner mass support, both because of its identification with militarism and warfare among Europeans, and its outright defeat by liberalism in WWII. What most dissidents want, including White nationalists, is a liberalism that accepts race differences and understands ingroup ethnic behaviors. They point to the acceptance of slavery by the "classical liberal" found-ing fathers and to the persistence, just a few decades ago, of White-only immigra-tion policies in all Western settler states. This stance betrays a misunderstanding of the ideals and progressive logic of liberalism.

Traditionalists have been the only ones—think of De Benoist, Kerry Bolton, Alexander Dugin—to carry a frontal attack on liberalism as such, holding its in-herent individualism responsible for undermining every cultural, racial and sex-ual identity in the West. But traditionalists have not been able to grapple consist-ently with the ways in which the traditionalism of the West has always coexisted with some degree of individualism, monogamous families freed from polygamous kinship networks, equal civic status, and participation in politics for free adult males—what is now known as a "civic-republican" form of liberalism, in complete contrast to the non-western world. They have been unwilling to admit, moreover, that traditional non-western societies became relatively stagnant intellectually af-ter their Axial Age (800–200 BC) cultivation of Confucianism, Hinduism, Juda-ism, and Zoroastrianism, and that the celebrated aristocracy it identifies with "tra-ditionalism" in the West had been transformed by the 1700s into mere courtiers of the absolutist states, parasitically collecting rents from a backward peasantry, devoid of its former heroic ethos of sacrifice, outcompeted by an entrepreneurial bourgeoise marching through history with its modern liberal ideals. Traditional-ists also tend to view liberalism as an economic doctrine of capitalist individual-ism, without adequately appreciating the nature of liberal pluralism and its ideal of the equal right of human beings to decide for themselves their values.

Not long ago, I myself accepted the claim that cultural Marxists had success-fully carried out a "long march through the institutions" against an otherwise sen-sible liberal culture prevailing before World War II in the West, when individual rights were understood in a libertarian and ethno-nationalistic way. Liberalism, before this march, I argued at length in *Canada in Decay*, guaranteed powerful liberties, freedom from arbitrary arrest and seizure of property, open scientific inquiry on all subjects, including freedom to express views about racial differ-ences, sustained by monogamous traditional family values. This was indeed a lib-eralism in which freedom of association was understood to include the right to refuse to associate with members of certain ethnic groups, the right of leaders to decide which immigrants were best suited to Western culture, even the right to discriminate in employment practices. But this nationalistic liberalism, I believed, had been gradually infiltrated by leftist ideologues in the post-WWII decades, leading to a very different illiberal landscape characterized by the imposition from above of politically correct beliefs, multicultural relativism, gender pronouns, and group-identity politics for "racialized" minorities.

The idea that cultural Marxists are in charge, originally articulated by dissidents, is now widespread among mainstream conservatives in their opposition to "critical race theory."[1095] It is also common among those who identify the heavily Jewish Frankfurt School as one of the intellectual agents behind cultural Marxism. Paul Gottfried was one of the early popularizers of the term cultural Marxism, observing that the ideas of the Frankfurt School "encouraged a war without quarter against bourgeois institutions and national identities."[1096] Gottfried, however, blamed cultural Marxists in general, or the post-WWII New Left, not just the Frankfurt School, for the defeat of liberalism. In his 2001 book *After Liberalism: Mass Democracy in the Managerial State*, he carefully explained that the Left did not just topple the old state, but almost imperceptibly over the twentieth century managed to create a whole new form of governance, a "managerial" or "therapeutic" state with a capacity to engage in the engineering of souls via multiple educational and social programs imposed from above by centralized authorities, along with regulations and speech codes dedicated to the modification of behavior, with trained bureaucrats exacting major penalties against employees deemed to be in violation of anti-racist, anti-sexist, and pro-gay codes. He insisted recently that liberalism reached its "heyday in the 19C" and "has been growing ever weaker since," away from its "biblical morality, a strong nuclear family, and constitutional government."[1097]

Rawls's Theory of Political Liberalism

My own views on the subject have evolved. What is often called "cultural Marxism"—devaluation of traditional family, promotion of racial integration, criticism of European ethnocentrism, promotion of gender fluidity—is rooted in the fundamental principles of liberalism. The conception of liberalism we will be putting forth in this section closely follows John Rawls' theory of political pluralism. Rawls is recognized as the most substantial and influential political

---

[1095] Rufo, 2023.
[1096] Gottfried, 2011.
[1097] Gottfried, 2023.

philosopher of the twentieth century.[1098] A national survey of political theorists conducted in 2008, based on 1,086 responses from university professors in the United States, voted Rawls first on the list of "Scholars Who Have Had the Greatest Impact on Political Theory in the Past 20 Years."[1099] When he died in 2002, over three thousand articles specifically about Rawls had been published;[1100] and his main book, A Theory of Justice, had been cited about sixty thousand times, ranked eighth among the most cited books in the social sciences and philosophy.[1101] He has been regularly cited as an authority in American court opinions, more than sixty times, according to an article published in 2005 in the Harvard Gazette.[1102] Yet, in the abundant writings of dissidents, Rawls rarely gets a mention, never mind a study. The focus is invariably on Frankfurt intellectuals, postmodernists, globalists, feminists, critical race theorists, antifa lunatics, or politicians of the moment.

Strictly speaking, Rawls' "theory" is not about how society ought to be organized, but a systematic treatise on the best way to think about the nature of contemporary pluralist Western democracies.[1103] It is a treatise developed in response to the "new moral sensitivities"[1104] of Westerners after WWII, after the deadly ideological and ethnic conflicts between fascism, communism, and liberalism, the student protests of the 1960s, the civil rights movement, widespread talk about human rights, women's demands for full equal rights, disillusionment with capitalist consumerism, the spread of the New Left on university campuses, and demands by minorities for cultural diversity. The theory aims to show that actually existing political pluralism, and the principles of fairness and equal opportunity that already guide Western jurisprudence,[1105] if properly understood and acted upon, provide the best moral framework for Westerners to coexist in a state of relative concord despite their religious, racial, cultural, and political differences.

[1098] Martha Nussbaum (1999) calls him "the most distinguished political philosopher of our century." This is a generally held view among the numerous academics who have written books about him. See, for example, Audard (2007) and Freeman (2007).

[1099] Moore, 2010.

[1100] Laden, 2003.

[1101] Weinberg, 2003.

[1102] Parker, 1979; Scanlon, 2005.

[1103] The point is not that Rawls, his ideas and books, constitute the intellectual foundation of the liberal pluralist West. It is that his ideas reflect the institutional normative reality of present-day Western societies, although, as we will see, he understates the post-1960s fanatical progressivism of this ideology and, to this extent, underestimates its politicized character.

[1104] Audard, 2007.

[1105] Lawrence, 2016.

The underlying moral premise of Rawls' liberal pluralism is drawn directly out of the Western intellectual tradition with its persisting individualism. It says that each individual has an innate inviolability, a dignity, by virtue of being rationally capable of deciding his own beliefs and self-governing his own life. Given the moral equality of humans as agents capable of autonomy, they should never, in the words of John Locke, be "subjected to the Political Power of another without his own Consent." The public-political sphere should be characterized by value-pluralism, with everyone enjoying the following "basic liberties": liberty of conscience, freedom of belief on all subjects, freedom of association, equal right to participate in politics, equality under the law, right to health care, right to an education, and the right to live free of poverty. When Rawls writes that in our current times these liberties are "reasonably taken as fixed" and "correctly settled once and for all," he means that they are now accepted across the West as indisputably true in the mainstream world of politics.[1106] Doctrines that directly threaten political pluralism and its moral premise of equality of rights will be suppressed or kept on the margins without much influence.

Classical liberals will counter that Rawlsian liberalism, or the liberalism currently practiced across the West, is not at all what the early founders of liberalism believed, and not what many Western governments and most people believed until recent times, before the Left successfully "marched through the institutions." They will argue that classical liberalism is all about the protection of the natural rights of individuals to freedom of speech, freedom of the press, freedom to choose one's beliefs, and the right to private property, and that the government should exist to protect these rights. But this classical liberalism gradually evolved into the progressive liberalism we see in the West today, because the principle of equality of liberty contains within it the principle of equality of opportunity. Progressive liberals, who came onto the horizon early on in the history of liberalism, and did actually carry out a successful march through the institutions during the 1800s and 1900s, consistently argued that humans cannot enjoy equality of freedom, freedom to express their human talents, freedom to think for themselves and to choose their political beliefs, without enjoying equality of opportunity, access to health care, education for their children, and protection from discrimination on the basis of sex and ethnicity. Progressives successfully persuaded the established institutions of the West that, in order to attain equality of opportunity, and avoid the excessive concentration of wealth in the hands of big businesses, and mitigate

---

[1106] Rawls, 2005, 151.

the recessionary tendencies of capitalism due to lack of effective demand by poorer members of society, the nations of the West needed a welfare state. They also needed some degree of social engineering to create a population no longer inclined to discriminate and violate the rights of "excluded minorities."

The majority of so-called "classical liberals" in the nineteenth century, as will be argued below, did not think that this ideology was fundamentally about self-interested competition, or laissez-faire economics. From its beginnings, classical liberalism, despite its revolutionary novel character, remained under the influence of ancient Greek and Roman republican concepts of civic virtue, which persisted through the medieval era, in symbiosis with the Christian idea that every human life is of equal value. Republican civic notions of the common good and the importance of government championing selflessness and benevolence continued to be held by modern classical liberals through both the Glorious Revolution of 1688 and the American Revolution of 1776. By the time we reach J.S. Mill, and the "new liberalism" of the late 1800s, we have a fusion of ancient ideals of civic virtue, dedication, and self-sacrifice, with socialist ideas about the indispensable role of the state in creating fairer opportunities, such as public schools and sanitation, for the positive expression of equal liberties among the poorer members of society. By the time we reach Rawls, the "politically correct" liberalism of the 1990s, and the wokeness of our time, the word "virtue" would come to be redefined as a "public-oriented" citizen who actively promotes a "community" of tolerance towards all races, immigrants, and gender identities.

The intolerance we are currently witnessing is best understood as a product of the essentially progressive nature of liberal pluralism itself. Liberalism aims to liberate individuals from all collective constraints, including "unfair conditions for freedom," such as lack of economic opportunities, classism, racism, or sexism. There is much truth in Rawls' argument that liberalism does not call for states to promote one way of life, but for conditions that allow for the mutual flourishment of whatever lifestyles individuals choose. The task is to understand how the intolerance of wokeness grew out of this pluralism. How did it come about that Western states that purport to respect multiple perspectives are now regulating and suppressing beliefs and actions that counter gender fluidity and immigrant diversity?

The key to understanding the nature of liberal pluralism, its progressivism, and its culmination in liberal intolerance of those who are "not tolerant," is John Rawls' theory of "political liberalism." While in his first book, *A Theory of Justice*, published in 1971, Rawls did set out to articulate a conception of liberalism that was universally true and most capable of promoting perfectionism or human excellences in art, science, and culture, his later work, *Political Liberalism*, originally published in 1993, argues instead that it would be unreasonable for a true liberal society to impose any common ideals about the good life upon citizens.[1107] Rawls insightfully argues that a liberal order must show equal respect for the decisions of individuals about their own conception of the good life and the pursuit of happiness. Liberalism should accept value pluralism as an inescapable reality in a world in which individuals with different personalities and cultural backgrounds are likely to disagree about the fundamental values of life, and should therefore be allowed to decide for themselves, on the basis of their naturally given capacities for free deliberation, to choose their values.

Under conditions of freedom, individuals will always endorse incompatible "comprehensive doctrines," religious, philosophical, or moral world views, about what they sincerely think is the best way to find a purpose in life. Given the commitment of liberalism to the equal dignity of humans to think for themselves, rather than be coerced to follow a particular doctrine, the only consistent political setting for a liberal society to endorse is one in which a plurality of viewpoints is accepted. Rawls believes that the best way for just cooperation among citizens holding different values is for the government to set up rules of engagement and participation in the public sphere that are accepted as fair by everyone, without preference for any one way of life.

Western nations have shown themselves to be fair, Rawls believes, insofar as the political domain within which people express their views has been characterized as "freestanding" (or "self-standing"), wherein the government abstains from imposing the truthfulness of any doctrine, but instead justifies itself to citizens through the equal rights it grants to everyone to express their views, as long as no one tries to infringe upon the equal rights of others. It is Rawls' claim that citizens will endorse political liberalism for themselves as compatible with whatever view they hold to the degree that the state respects their liberties as human beings capable of holding their own doctrines in a state of mutual respect, reciprocity, and civility. Thus, even though citizens hold fundamentally different metaphysical

---

[1107] In *A Theory of Justice*, he aimed to develop "a comprehensive liberal doctrine" from the social contract tradition represented by Locke, Rousseau, and Kant, superior to the utilitarian tradition within liberal thought. The theory of "political liberalism," in contrast, has no comprehensive metaphysical ambitions, but seeks to explain what kind of society would be just and fair to individuals who hold different comprehensive doctrines, including to those who believe in value pluralism.

and religious views, their views will overlap and partly intersect in their shared political conception about the pluralistic character of the public domain.

Rawls thus makes a crucial distinction between "reasonable" and "unreasonable" doctrines. Doctrines are reasonable insofar as they are committed to fairness in the political domain, even if such doctrines hold illiberal religious views or Platonic metaphysical views about what constitutes "human perfectibility." Doctrines are unreasonable if they seek to impose collective or illiberal values upon the political domain, or express views that challenge the autonomy and equal liberties of ethnic minorities, women, or LGBT members. Individuals are free to hold doctrines that affirm traditional values about family life, adhere to the "five pillars of Islam," or to follow a strict Hassidic lifestyle of never changing one's traditional clothing, strict marriage norms, and keeping "spiritually clean" in separation from outsiders. Individuals are also free to create their own private spaces, clubs, engage in group sex or the swapping of sexual partners, join motorcycle gangs, play video games all day, become a mystic, or a hedonist—so long as they do not infringe on the rights of others, or advocate illiberal political views that aim to undermine the pluralist liberal domain. The doctrines that question political pluralism and the basic liberties of all individuals regardless of sex, race, and religious beliefs, are "unreasonable" and should not be allowed in the public sphere except as marginalized and nonthreatening ideas.

Rawls also makes a distinction between his political pluralism and "comprehensive doctrines," including the view of Mill and Kant that an educated elite should decide for citizens how they should "self-actualize" their "true natures" as "rational human beings," or the civic republican view (in its current version as articulated by Charles Taylor, for example), with its claim that humans can only express their freedom and highest faculties as active public citizens, rather than as private individuals dominated by their base instincts.[1108] One of the main purposes of Rawls' *Political Liberalism* is to argue that defending liberal principles of justice, the right of each person to equal liberties, does not require a comprehensive foundational strategy, as he still believed in *A Theory of Justice*. A liberal order that is just or fair to every citizen does not mandate any collective conception, be it Hegelian, cultural Marxist, or Buddhist; it only offers, or so Rawls insists, a "freestanding political conception" according to which a well-ordered liberal society is one that guarantees reciprocity and tolerance between citizens holding different

---

[1108] The debate between Rawlsian and Republican liberals was quite intense through the late 1990s and early 2000s; see Patten, 1996.

world views. It is for citizens to decide individually, as part of their political conscience and dignity as humans, what they wish to think and do with their lives.

Religious parents can teach their children the traditional view that a woman's place is in the home attending to her children, rather than pursuing a career; however, if parents teach their children illiberal political views that deny the equal civic status of women or any other group, encouraging their children to advocate and act on these views in the public sphere, then the government would have legitimate grounds to take actions against such ways of raising children. Traditional doctrines, such as Catholicism and the Mormon religion, which do not allow women to be priests, and advocate many illiberal views, will be counted as reasonable to the extent that the adherents of these religions tolerate the right of others to hold different views in the public domain, without seeking, for example, to undermine women's equal civic rights. [1109]

This does not mean, Rawls cautions, that a liberal government is completely neutral. Liberal governments can promote those values that "make a constitutional regime possible," namely, the virtues of tolerance and reasonableness, the values of equal political and civil liberty, fairmindedness, mutual respect and reciprocity between citizens. [1110] As we will explain later, the point of entry for my criticism of Rawls is that he downplays the degree to which the very cultivation of tolerance, reasonableness, and open-mindedness entails creating a political culture, across all institutions, within families and private businesses themselves, wherein liberal attitudes and behaviors are validated, celebrated, and incentivized, at the same time as non-liberal perspectives and behaviors are discouraged and marginalized. He underestimates as well the progressive logic of liberalism—that is, how this ideology (in its combination with capitalist competition and growth, as we shall see below) is continually pushing to eliminate every remaining tradition and religious belief, while disrupting older ways of life, swamping small rural towns with globalist retail stores and progressive advertisements.

The history of "emancipation" we have witnessed in the modern West is a history of the unfolding of the immanent logic of liberal progressivism. The common

---

[1109] Catholicism remained unreasonable, in Rawls' estimation, until "the Council's Declaration of Religious Freedom—*Dignitatis Humanae*" in 1965 when it "committed itself to the principle of religious freedom as found in a constitutional democracy," and "declared the ethical doctrine of religious freedom resting on the dignity of the human person; a political doctrine with respect to the limits of government in religious matters; and a theological doctrine of the freedom of the church in its relations to the political and social world. According to this declaration, all persons, whatever their faith, have the right of religious liberty on the same terms" (2001, 21–22).

[1110] Rawls, 2005, 157, 192.

argument among dissidents that our current liberal societies are violating freedom of association and rights of economic contract, and behaving in "communistic" ways, with the enactment of laws prohibiting private discrimination in hiring and educational decisions, fails to understand that discrimination in employment violates the liberal principle of fair equality of opportunity for humans deemed to have equal moral worth. Laissez-faire liberalism, or libertarianism, never a majority view in the West, was decisively defeated by the end of the nineteenth century, or at least never adopted as a program by liberal governments, precisely because it was deemed to be inconsistent with liberal principles. Advocacy for minimum wage laws, for health and safety laws, and for elimination of discrimination in hiring on the basis of sex and race, was justified on liberal grounds, as policies that enhanced opportunities for equality of liberty.

Whites Have Been Psychologically "Wired" for Liberal Pluralism Through a Long Historical Journey

One must agree with Alexander Dugin's 2012 thesis that the twentieth century witnessed only three major ideologies: liberalism, fascism, and communism. These ideologies grew in the West, with modern liberalism emerging first in the 1600s, and subsequently defeating the other two younger contesting ideologies in WWII and the Cold War respectively. Alain de Benoist is right: "liberalism is the dominant ideology of our time."[1111] A flaw in De Benoist and Dugin, however, is that they identify liberalism with a narrow version of classical liberalism, a laissez-faire liberalism;[1112] they associate, without fine distinctions, with the names of Locke, David Hume, and Adam Smith, and, in more recent times, with Friedrich von Hayek, Ludwig von Mises, and Milton Friedman, with their emphasis on economic rights of property, freedom of contract, freedom of speech, and a government that ensures these freedoms and limits public spending.[1113] This flaw is compounded by their heavy reliance on Marx's critique of liberalism, which barely addresses the moral ideals of liberalism. They reduce liberalism, in the words of de Benoist, to a worldview that sees "man as a being essentially driven by the desire to maximise his personal interest and private profit."[1114] Nevertheless, I will

---

[1111] Cited in Walker, 2019.
[1112] De Benoist, 2012.
[1113] Dugin, 2021.
[1114] De Benoist, 2023.

defend the Marxist argument that liberalism emerged in close association with capitalism, and that capitalism has an internal dynamic that motivates the relentless accumulation of capital involving the investment of profits with the goal of increasing the competitiveness of firms—and that this dynamic has played a major role, along with liberalism, in the dissolution of Western traditions and national identities, coupled with the promotion of open borders and mass immigration.

De Benoist and Dugin ignore two major components in the Western liberal tradition. Firstly, they leave out the powerful influence of the "high liberal tradition" espoused by Rawls that we have just elaborated, which goes back to the contract tradition of Locke, his moral ideals, and which draws on Immanuel Kant and J. S. Mill's liberal philosophy, with its ideal of free self-governing persons who develop their human rational capacities and pursue ways of life that give expression to their autonomous nature. Although Rawls' political liberalism objects to the Kant-Mill view that the government should promote human perfectionism, he accepts the emphasis these thinkers put on the ideal of persons as self-governing agents. His theory takes it as established by the liberal tradition, and as a presupposed view of actually existing Western states, that humans are sufficiently reasonable and rational to work out their differences in a consensual manner, treating each other as free and equal in the public sphere.

The second, and more important component neglected by de Benoist and Dugin, as well as traditionalist dissidents at large, is the long historical evolution of liberalism from ancient times to the present, before capitalism was born, and its association with the greatness of the West. This is the dilemma we are trying to explain: why is an ideology that is intimately connected to the supreme creativity the West now responsible for its ethnocidal path? Liberalism is almost epigenetically rooted in the historically evolved psychology of Europeans. Kevin MacDonald, as we argued in Chapter VII, is an exception in the dissident right in connecting the weak ethnocentrism of Whites today back to the way evolutionary pressures in the northern climes of Europe in prehistoric times selected for weaker kinship networks, leading to the predominance of nuclear families, exogamous and monogamous marriage, and trust with anonymous strangers based on an individual's reputation. In Chapter I, we traced the primordial roots of liberalism to the aristocratic masculine culture of horse-riding, highly mobile Indo-Europeans, with their uniquely contractual band of warrior brothers, consisting of dignified free men of honor unwilling to submit to despotic rulers, in which the leader was seen as "first among equals." We called this an aristocratic form of liberalism.

With the emergence of civilization in ancient Greece, this aristocratic but still clannish ethos was expanded into a civic republican ethos "befitting any free born person" belonging in a city-state. Although the ancient world retained its belief in the natural inequality of men and the superiority of the aristocracy, it did recognize the freedom of independent farmers, including them as equal citizens of the city-state, and allowing them to take an active civic role in their states.[1115] The essential idea of this civic/republican form of freedom, articulated from Aristotle through to Cicero, was that man's highest nature was most fully realized through his participation in a public civic community wherein politics was conceived as the locus of the good life. The aim of an education in the "liberal arts" cultivated by the Romans was to teach *humanitas*, what is proper for a noble man, magnanimity, disinterestedness, and a spirit of sacrifice for the well-being of the community.

During the Middle Ages, this aristocratic-civic liberalism was substantially influenced by the Christian idea that "every human being had been made equally by God and endowed by Him with the same spark of reason." Tom Holland, from whom these cited words are taken, eloquently insists, in a recent book, *Dominion: How the Christian Revolution Remade the World*, that the current Western liberal values of tolerance, equality, and inclusiveness are "firmly moored" in this civilization's Christian past. Even if we think, as I do, that he draws too straight a line from early Christian beliefs to the current multicultural West, it is hard to deny the transformative power of Christianity in ancient times through the very progression of modern liberalism. In Christianity, one already finds "the oneness of the human race, the obligation of care for the weak and the suffering," and the principle that every human was "equally beloved of God" and therefore possessed an "equal dignity." Among the many examples Holland offers to demonstrate that Christianity infused the moral progression of liberalism is Las Casas' initiation of the idea of human rights from his Christian belief that Indians did not deserve to be treated as inferior to the Spaniards because, in Las Casas' words, "all the peoples of the world are humans, and there is only one definition of all humans and of each one, that is that they are rational."[1116]

Larry Siedentop makes a similar argument, but with a more philosophically oriented emphasis on the Christian creation of freedom of conscience, "beyond the Jewish law or mere rule-following," and beyond the Greek conception that

---

[1115] Hanson, 1999; Thornton, 2000.
[1116] Holland, 13, 347, 481.

only some men should have the privilege and duty to be citizens. Freedom of conscience laid the moral groundwork for religious pluralism and eventually for secularism itself. Siedentop asks: "What is the crux of secularism?" The crux is that religion should not be forced upon anyone, for it goes against the very principle of personal conscience and the conviction that "there is a sphere in which each should be free to make his or her own decisions, a sphere of conscience and free action." Siedentop insists that this belief is inherent in the commitment to "equal liberty" of classical liberalism and its "firm belief that to be human means being a rational and moral agent, a free chooser with responsibility for one's actions."[1117] The argument is not that once Europeans converted to Christianity, they reached the conclusions of Lockean liberalism. It is that Christianity laid the foundation for the separation of spiritual power from temporal power, and for freedom of thought, even though European theologians for many centuries did not understand the full implications of the principles they began to advocate during the Middle Ages. The Popes who called for the autonomy of the Church from secular interference could not anticipate that the premise of individual conscience would be used by future generations of "Protestants" to attack the religious authority of the Catholic clergy in favor of the "priesthood of all believers." And the Protestants could not anticipate that their premise of religious conscience would lay the groundwork for liberal secularism.

Both de Benoist and Dugin, it should be qualified, do recognize the importance of early Christianity, but they avoid detailed historical accounts. Holland and Siedentop go through many historical changes and revolutions during the medieval and modern eras, in full awareness that the institutionalization of Christian principles was a long-drawn-out movement before it evolved into liberal secularism. We have seen many of these developments in prior chapters, including what a mistake Henrich makes in his otherwise impressive book, *The WEIRDest People*, ignoring the civic institutions of the ancient Greeks and Romans, the analytical mind of Aristotle, the relatively rationalized system of Roman law, while trivializing the early Christian moral commitment to monogamy. At the same time, we should not fall into the trap of assuming that changes in ancient times were the "crucial" ones. The institutionalization of monogamy and the rise of voluntary associations in the Middle Ages, together with countless other legal changes, what Berman calls "the Papal revolution" of the twelfth century, were

---

[1117] Siedentop, 2014, 361.

also very important.[1118] Berman believes that this revolution established the roots of modern Western secular legal systems, starting with the canon law of the church, which established the church's corporate autonomy from state interference, and its newly acquired right to exercise legislative, administrative, and judicial powers within its religious domain, including the right to levy taxes and cultural dominion over wide areas of civil and family affairs. Ecclesiastical scholars would indeed cultivate, in the emerging universities, the revival of Roman law, analyzing and synthesizing all authoritative statements concerning the nature of law, the royal law of the major kingdoms, the urban law of the newly emerging cities, feudal law, manorial law, and mercantile law. This amounted to a legal revolution that also conceded corporate status to a variety of groups and associations of individuals to make contracts, to enact their own ordinances and statutes, "to own property, to sue and be sued, and to have legal representation before the king's court."[1119]

These changes were accompanied by what Brian Tierney has identified as "the origins of the idea of natural rights" in objection to the idea of natural law, which had prevailed in ancient times and was still predominant in the writings of Thomas Aquinas (1225–1274). The natural law tradition held that what is naturally just and good was objectively ordained and pre-established by God, and that only educated men, either an aristocratic elite, as was the case in ancient Rome, or a Catholic theological elite, as was the case in Christendom, were sufficiently rational, and with the rightful authority, to apprehend the meaning of natural law, as conveyed in Roman jurisprudence, in Platonic and Aristotelian texts, or in the Bible. The idea of natural rights, the beginnings of which Tierney detects among a group of medieval canonists in the twelfth century, held that all humans are equal moral beings with a rational ability and a free will to discern for themselves what was the right thing to do. This idea, Tierney notes, came within the context of many economic and cultural changes, such as the rise of commerce and cities, and the revival of Roman law. Siedentop agrees with Tierney that this period saw a transition from natural law to natural rights thinking, though he maintains that the idea of natural law as it was articulated by Christians, with their new emphasis on conscience, already contained in principle the idea of natural rights in its belief that natural law is written in the hearts of all men, in that reason is in principle accessible to humans. Canonists basically recast natural law as a system of natural

---

[1118] Berman, 1984.
[1119] Huff, 1993, 119–38.

rights inherent to the individual, rather than to some objectively given order existing externally as part of the natural order of things. Everyone was the equal child of God, and, therefore, everyone should have an equal moral standing and a natural right to liberty, based on personal conscience.

We should avoid, however, postulating an embryonic modern liberalism inside the New Testament, or even in the Middle Ages, for which both Holland and Siedentop can be faulted, notwithstanding the immense significance of these developments, combined with the immense significance of ancient Greece and Rome, and of the prehistorical world of the Indo-Europeans. John M. Headley, in *The Europeanization of the World: On the Origins of Human Rights and Democracy* shows that the European discovery of the world during Renaissance times "decisively and effectively prepared" for the liberal "idea of a common humanity" and an emerging sense of "the human race," and the notion that humans are created equal in certain inalienable rights for life, liberty, and the pursuit of happiness.[1120] Yet Headley knows that the idea of a common humanity had deep roots in pre-Renaissance Europe. He draws the following connections effectively: the mathematized geography started by Ptolemy and others, which "treated the celestial and territorial globes as equivalent, applying the same grid system to each," and which "posited a continuous and essentially uniform surface to the globe"; the Roman principle of universal inclusion and incorporation, which gave practical realization to the Stoic notion of *cosmopolis*, and which persuaded Roman jurists to speak of *ius gentium*, or a common "natural law" for all men, which eventually coalesced in the new citizenship of Christian baptism; the medieval university's rationalizing curriculum of arithmetic, geometry, music, and astronomy; the rationalization of space during the Renaissance, with its linear perspectival painting; and the discovery of the world in the sixteenth century, "which brought the entire globe within its survey," and which revealed that there were similar biological humans spread through the earth. These currents, he believes, reached a certain completion in the modern idea of natural rights as articulated by John Locke and others.

Rawls' theory of justice as fairness presupposes indeed a long historical movement leading to a world in which individuals are "psychologically rewired" with a new set of "weird" dispositions for reduced ingroup favoritism, for greater fairness and cooperation with anonymous strangers, for analytical over contextual thinking, for impartial moral principles and objectivity, and for love of choice and

---

[1120] Headley, 2008, 11, 41.

personal fulfillment. It presupposes a Western reality in which individuals are pre-disposed, in Rawls' words, for "deliberative rationality," with an analytical capac-ity to "draw inferences, weigh evidence, and balance competing considerations," with "the virtues of fair social cooperation" with anonymous strangers holding different doctrines. As much as Rawls may assume that these traits are part of hu-man nature, or easily taught to non-Westerners, his theory of liberal pluralism tacitly assumes a Western world that is already liberal in its psychology.[1121] His interpreters persistently ignore this historical background, either because they take them as valid beyond further inquiry, or under the assumption that they are dealing with natural rights that are inherent to humans as such. This psychological profile, and the liberal pluralism it generated, is at the root of political correctness and White dispossession.

Aristocratic, Civic/Republican, and Classical Liberalism

Although it is correct to talk about a "commercial revolution in the Middle Ages,"[1122] and the rise of a variety of innovative business techniques, such as bills of exchange and double-entry bookkeeping, coupled with the emergence of social structures based on freedom of contract rather than relationships derived from social status, the republican conception of liberalism, with its emphasis on civic public duties, continued to be championed among intellectuals during the Renais-sance right through the Glorious Revolution of 1688, and the Founding of the United States in 1776. As the meticulous research of J. G. A. Pocock (1975), Ber-nard Bailyn (1967), and Gordon S. Wood (1969) has shown, republican liberalism and its ideal of the primacy of the public good over individual self-interest, in-cluding its mistrust of capitalism as a corrupting influence, and its preference for the stable yeomen capable of being industrious without sacrificing the ideals of civic humanism, exercised a powerful influence on the political and intellectual leaders of the English and American revolutions. It is hard to deny, however, Joyce Appleby's contention in *Liberalism and Republicanism in the Historical Imagina-tion*, published in 1992, that this old civic liberalism, which saw history in cyclical

---

[1121] Rawls, 2005, 55. Another of his books, *The Law of Peoples* (2001), is about how liberals in the West should conduct international affairs with people living in non-liberal societies, that is, peo-ple who, by the criteria Rawls employs, are not "reasonably" willing to tolerate views that go against their deepest beliefs.

[1122] Lopez, 1976.

terms and equated change with degeneracy, was increasingly co-existing with a new conception of liberty, today known as "classical liberalism," which reflected the emerging reality of market individualism.

A new generation of thinkers, some associated with the origins of economics as a discipline, including Thomas Mun (1571–1641), Edward Misselden (1608–1654), John Locke (1632–1704), David Hume (1711–1776), and Adam Smith (1723–1790), looked with wonderment at how individuals pursuing their self-interests, rather than civic virtues, were bringing about a general increase in the wellbeing of society by increasing the volume of trade, manufacture, and new technologies during the 1600s and 1700s. Adam Smith would develop a full theory explaining how the hidden hand of the market, a competitive setting in which everyone is obligated to be efficient in supplying the goods preferred by consumers, works to channel the pursuit of private gain into the general welfare of society.

Classical liberalism, in its inception, was partially (not singularly) conceived as an economic doctrine of free markets and private ownership of the means of production, emerging hand-in-hand with the rise of capitalism, in which self-adjusting markets on their own could bring about an increase in the happiness, comfort, and welfare of the majority, without a state having to inculcate common civic-humanist values. From the perspective of the behavior of self-maximizing individuals in the market, we can thus agree with de Benoist. Capitalism on its own, as Marx would go on to explain in the mid-1800s in his grand treatise *Capital*, treats human relationships as commodity exchanges, and abstracts individuals from all social connections other than those created through contractual arrangements for the pursuit of gain. Capitalism does not recognize the autonomous status of peoples, cultures, or nations pre-established on the basis of kinship norms, traditions, or heritage. It is in the nature of capitalism, left to function on its own, without a strong political state dictating other values, or a strong background culture of civic commitment, to break traditional values and national identities, promote globalization, and instill individualistic values that are commensurate with its law of accumulation. As Marx famously observed in *The Communist Manifesto*: "Constant revolutionising of production, uninterrupted disturbance of all social conditions, everlasting uncertainty and agitation distinguishes the bourgeois epoch from all earlier ones. All fixed, fast-frozen relations, with their train of ancient and venerable prejudices and opinions, are swept away, all new-formed ones become antiquated before they can ossify. All that is solid melts into air, all that is holy is profaned."[1123]

The classical liberal idea that all individuals are born with the same natural rights for life, liberty, and the pursuit of happiness irrespective of cultural background is thus a perfect fit for capitalism. There is more, however, to classical liberalism than a theory of free market individualism. Helena Rosenblatt's 2018 book, *The Lost History of Liberalism: From Ancient Rome to the Twenty-First Century* persuasively shows that the identification of liberalism with market individualism per se was an ideological construct of post-WWII Americans in response to the rise of totalitarian communism and the expanding Keynesian state across the West. Many of the names commonly identified with classical atomistic individualism, including Adam Smith, framed their market individualism within the old civic (and Christian) values of selfless patriotism, the common good, and the importance of promoting civic virtue among citizens. This should not surprise us. The world of John Locke and Adam Smith, and of the founders of the US, was still very agrarian, with the vast majority of people living in an unchanging landscape dominated by the alternation of the seasons, going to church, creating large families in customary ways, rarely moving out of their place of birth. Capitalism, if we may quote a few more words from Marx's *Manifesto*, had not yet "put an end . . . to all idyllic relations . . . pitilessly torn asunder the motley" communal ties that bound men to each other, leaving "no other nexus between man and man than naked self-interest."

A flaw in Rosenblatt's thesis, on the other hand, is that she tends to assume that every idea and policy in the nineteenth century in favor of encouraging the common good was a continuation of Roman civic republicanism. It is more sensible to side with Appleby in emphasizing the co-existence of this old civic liberalism with an emerging classical liberalism that reflected the reality of growing commerce and manufactures. But we should also look beyond Appleby, whose study ends with the late 1700s, to new ideas of the common good espoused by democrats and socialists during the 1800s and 1900s, which many "new liberals" in the late 1800s would come to see as a fulfillment of the ideals of classical liberalism itself. The essential argument of these new liberals was that the mere legal recognition by the state of the natural rights of individuals was insufficient for citizens lacking economic and cultural means to express their basic liberties. They also pointed to the prevalence of many forms of discriminatory behaviors and

---

[1123] Marx, 1985.

prejudices against certain groups of citizens on the basis of social class, sex, and religious beliefs.

We should caution against seeing this new liberalism as a negation of the supposed "laissez-faire" nature of classical liberalism. Classical liberalism has always been more than a mixture of laissez-faire and civic republicanism. The central figure in classical liberalism is John Locke, and the central idea in Locke is not laissez-faire, but the idea that all men, by virtue of their capacity to reason, are born with an equal right to natural freedom and that among the fundamental rights to freedom are life, liberty, and property, and that the authority of governments springs from the consent of individuals born with these rights, and that, therefore, governments have an obligation to respect the liberties of individuals, and citizens a right to rebellion if these rights are violated. Locke is a major exponent of the cardinal principle of liberty of conscience, which is at the root of the liberal pluralism that Rawls accentuates, which says that men, by virtue of their natural rights, have a right to decide for themselves what doctrines they wish to follow. The classical liberalism of Locke was indeed a reaction against the violent, authoritarian impulses of Christendom witnessed during the religious wars of the 1600s, when governments sought to enforce religious uniformity as a way of terminating religions divisions believed to be the cause of civil war. Locke argued, to the contrary, that it was government meddling in religion that caused civil war. "It is not the diversity of opinions, which cannot be avoided; but the refusal of toleration to those that are of different opinions . . . that has produced all the bustles and wars that have been in the Christian world, upon account of religion."[1124]

The Long March of Liberals Through the Institutions

Glorious Revolution 1688

Classical liberalism, then, is a complex ideology that emerged in connection with the rise of capitalism, while remaining attached for some time to civic republican values, and articulating ideals that went beyond private economic rights and civic republicanism, that is, the ideals articulated by Locke and the ideals of liberal socialists and democrats. Liberalism can't be defined in terms of how it was

---

[1124] Locke, 1983, 55.

understood and actualized at one point in history.[1125] It can only be understood in terms of its historical evolution, from its roots in the Indo-European aristocratic principle of "first among equals," through the distancing of individuals from tribal identities with the Greek discourse of citizenship,[1126] to the beginnings of legal definitions of personhood in the Roman principle that both land and movable property could be owned absolutely by individuals,[1127] through the Christian notion that humans are morally equal and the "birth of a truly individual will," through the creation of freedom of conscience,[1128] to the systematic effort by the Catholic Church to abolish kinship and promote monogamous families,[1129] the medieval nurturing of civic associations based on voluntary contracts, and beyond into the modern era.

The common thread of this "emancipation of the individual" has been the removal of collective identities, and, in the case of post-Lockean liberalism, of every obstacle, prejudice, tradition, property qualification, economic conditions, including discrimination against women and minorities—preventing individuals from exercising their equal right to freedom. My argument is not that this was an inevitable process, but rather that we can trace in historical actuality, *ex post facto*,

---

[1125] We see this in Paul Gottfried, for whom liberalism has to mean "classical liberalism," though he is not clear when this liberalism commences or ends; sometimes he uses the term liberalism for everything that came before the "political correctness" of the 1990s. Sometimes he gives the impression, and this is true of conservatives generally speaking, that the US broke with true liberalism with Franklin Roosevelt's New Deal, but sometimes Gottfried and others blame Lyndon B. Johnson's Great Society; at other times they insist that it was Obama who launched the US in a direction that can no longer be categorized as liberal in the old sense. Nowadays some conservatives believe that a new ideology, "wokeness," did finally break through liberalism under Biden's presidency. These conservatives and libertarians, much like Gottfried, refuse to see a progressive logic in liberalism as such. In the case of Gottfried, if someone connects John Stuart Mill, for example, to feminism or to post-1990 liberalism, he easily replies that Mill was still a traditionalist who would not have approved of the spread of "political correctness" across campuses in the 1990s; Mill, after all, did not advocate for same-sex marriage. What this line of thinking, this effort to see liberalism in terms of a fixed set of principles, never ponders about is why so many 1970s liberals have gone happily along with the progression of liberalism since, becoming avid supporters of the "emancipatory" policies of the post-1990s, including Biden's open-borders policies of recent years. Think of Paul Krugman, Laurence Tribe, George Soros, Keith Olbermann, or of individuals like Richard Rorty, who easily traversed from New Deal Liberalism to the Great Society, all the way to 1990s political correctness, as great steps bringing about the fulfillment of liberal ideals.

[1126] Thornton, 2000.

[1127] Stein, 1999.

[1128] Siedentop, 2014.

[1129] Henrich, 2020.

this "progressive" logic across the Western world, generally speaking, from the vantage point of what we can learn about history today and witness in our times. This march would eventually lead to the emergence of political correctness and the right of liberal institutions to exclude, or limit the influence of "illiberal discourses" that "threaten" open pluralist societies. What follows is a quick journey through the legislative history of liberalism from the time of Locke to the present to convey the "liberating" logic of this ideology. The focus will be on Britain, the nation most closely identified with the origins of classical liberalism, but also on the United States, the heartland of racial integration, and on Canada, the heartland of multicultural liberalism.

We can start with the liberalism of the Glorious Revolution of 1688, which saw a parliament representative of nobles and prosperous members of the bourgeoisie recognized as the supreme power, with the authority of the monarch limited to executive functions. This parliament came along with a Bill of Rights that established the principles of frequent parliaments, free elections, and freedom of speech within parliament without fear of being questioned in any court or place out of parliament, as well as the principle of no right of taxation without parliament's agreement, and just treatment of people by courts. The Toleration Act of 1688 started a trajectory that eventually terminated the authoritarian Christian unity of the Middle Ages by extending toleration to nonconformists who did not belong to the established Anglican Church who had pledged loyalty to the British monarch. This act did not apply to Catholics, Jews, nontrinitarians, or atheists. Nevertheless, it was revolutionary in its own right, constituting the beginnings of liberty of conscience, a new conception of freedom unknown in ancient Greece, in civic-republican Rome, and in the Middle Ages. In the language of Rawls, or with the benefit of his theory of pluralism, we can say that it launched a new conception of the public sphere as a "freestanding" domain freed from any authoritarian creed, wherein individuals who are "deeply divided by cultural, religious, and moral beliefs" may coexist in a state of tolerance and reciprocity. Freedom of the press was formally enacted in 1695.

Paleoconservatives like to point to Edmund Burke's interpretation of this revolution as one that sought "to preserve our ancient indisputable laws and liberties . . . derived to us from our forefathers and to be transmitted to our posterity; as an estate specially belonging to the people of this kingdom without any reference whatever to any other general or prior right." The Bill of Rights, they tell us, recognized the rights of the British, not the rights of man.[1130] This is true; the language of liberty used by liberalism during this revolution, from "time immemorial," was not based on Enlightenment ideals of equality and liberty taken in the abstract, as universal rights belonging to man as such. English political thinking in the seventeenth century was not dominated by Locke; he was one among a more influential group of men, known as the Harringtonians, influenced by the republican civic liberalism of ancient Rome, and its Renaissance interpreters, Cicero and Machiavelli, and the writings of the foremost English political theorist of classical republicanism, James Harrington (1611–1677), who spoke in terms of civic virtues, citizens dedicated to the commonwealth, the ancient constitution, customs and rights imbedded in English common law.[1131]

Yet one cannot overlook that this revolution did enact a new conception of liberty not valued by the ancients or previously present in English common law: liberty of conscience, the right to hold and profess what principles we choose, which is the keystone of liberal pluralism. The acceptance by the ancient Romans of foreign religious cults was due to the polytheistic character of their pagan religion, which lacked any sacred text or religious dogma, and should thus not be attributed to any principle of religious toleration based on philosophical arguments about liberty of conscience. In his 1689 *Letter Concerning Toleration*, Locke made a philosophical argument, not an argument based on ancestral rights of a particular people: that every man has a right to profess any opinion as long as it is not seditious or dangerous to society.[1132] Men have a right to reach their own views by the use of their reason. Liberty of conscience is therefore a natural right which man possesses by virtue of being capable of choice. Faith cannot be compelled.[1133]

[1130] Edwards, 2000.

[1131] Pocock, 1965.

[1132] Locke, 1983.

[1133] Robert Woolhouse, in *Locke: A Biography* (2007), informs us that in 1659, when Locke was twenty-seven years old, he was sent a copy by Henry Stubb of a recently published book authored by John Owen advocating "against the idea of any religious imposition by the state . . . as there was no agreed and infallible reading of the Bible" (31). While Stubb agreed with Owen's defense of "liberty of conscience," Locke was ambivalent about the possibility that people of different beliefs could "quietly unite under the same government" (as cited by Woolhouse, 32). Nevertheless, the young Locked agreed that faith should not be under the jurisdiction of the magistrate; beliefs "cannot be wrought into the hearts of men" by any power other than God's; "conscience is tenderly to be dealt with," Locke wrote, "and not to be imposed on" (as cited by Woolhouse, 42). In his *Letter Concerning Toleration*, Locke would explicitly state that the proper role of the government was solely with "the quiet and comfortable living of men in society one with another," and not with men's choice of religion. Locke, however, retained his mistrust of Roman

Arguments for religious toleration were not original to Locke, but emerged slowly from the sixteenth century onwards, starting with Erasmus, Sebastian Castellio, Roger Williams, and Thomas More. Roger Williams (1604–1683), an immigrant in New England, may have been the first to make the argument that the best path towards civil peace was for governments to permit religious tolerance, rather than mandating a specific form of Christianity, for every man is equal in their subjective conscience and conviction. Thus, the argument is not, as Locke explained, that every man is equal in talents and physical abilities, but that there is a law of nature, ordained by God, and discoverable by reason, according to which all men are born equally free to make their own decisions, with a right to life, liberty, and "quiet and comfortable living."[1134] The cause of endless bloodshed was not religious pluralism, but the refusal of governments to allow men to make up their own minds in a state of mutual respect.[1135] Future generations of liberals would extend this argument beyond the domain of religion to argue that it is for individuals to decide their culture, not governments; and that the best way to ensure cultural choice is through the enactment of "multicultural citizenship." Rawls does not say much about the history of liberalism; however, he does state unequivocally in his book *Political Liberalism* that "the historical origin of political liberalism (and of liberalism more generally) began in the aftermath of the religious wars of the sixteenth and seventeenth centuries," and that "something like the modern understanding of liberty of conscience and freedom of thought began then."[1136]

Catholics, questioning their loyalty and potential threat to civil peace, even arguing that they should not be granted toleration since they don't permit freedom of religion to those who dissent from their religion (84–5). Was Locke, the supposed believer in negative liberties, voicing from the very beginning arguments against the toleration of beliefs that are "intolerant"?

[1134] Woolhouse, 2007.

[1135] This was the view Locke expressed in *A Letter Concerning Toleration*; the imposition of religious uniformity, not toleration, would put an end to religious enmity.

[1136] Rawls, 2005, xxiv. It is not that Rawls is unaware that his pluralist ideals have roots in Christianity; his argument is that Christianity had an inadequate (illiberal) understanding of what its principle of personal conscience entailed politically. "Christianity punished heresy and tried to stamp out by persecution and religious wars what it regarded as a false doctrine. . . . The inquisition instituted by Pope Gregory IX was active throughout the Wars of Religion in the sixteenth and seventeenth centuries. . . . Heresy was widely regarded as worse than murder. This persecuting zeal has been the great curse of the Christian religion." And "it was shared by Luther and Calvin and the Protestant Reformers, and was not radically confronted in the Catholic Church until Vatican II," that is, until 1965 when the Catholic Church finally "committed itself to the principle of religious freedom as found in constitutional democracy" (2001, 21).

American Founding Liberal Principles

By the time of the American Declaration of Independence in 1776, notwithstanding the persisting influence of civic republicanism among the founders, we have a more definitive statement of the Lockean doctrines of natural rights and of government under social contract. "We hold these truths to be self-evident, that all men are created equal, that they are endowed by their Creator with certain unalienable rights, that among these are life, liberty and the pursuit of happiness." The contractual statement in this Declaration meant that the citizens agreeing to the social contract chose the terms of their association based on the presumption that each regards all others as free and equal persons. The Bill of Rights of 1791 explicitly limits the government's authority to infringe on citizen's right to religious freedom, thought and assembly, and distinctly states that citizens have a right to hold property free from usurpation by the government without compensation, and to equal rights under the law. The relentless dynamic of American capitalism, rising prosperity and education, would sweep away the old civic republican notion that seeking private goods was incompatible with the general welfare of the majority.

A common argument among dissidents wishing to blame cultural Marxism, or the left generally, for the current ills of American society is that the founders, including many of the authors of canonical founding texts of liberalism, had racial views or held slaves themselves. They point to John Jay's statement in the Federalist Papers in 1787–88 that Americans are "a people descended from the same ancestors, speaking the same language, professing the same religion, attached to the same principles of government, very similar in their manners and customs." It can't be denied that there existed a "racial subtext," or a taken-for-granted awareness that only White people, or British descendants, were parties to the social contract.[1137] For a long time, as late as the 1950s, a sizable proportion of Americans did not regard Blacks as full moral persons capable of rational autonomy. The descendants of the people who proclaimed the Declaration, the Constitution, and Bill of Rights, remained segregationists until the 1960s.

Yet, from the very beginning, liberals in the US and Europe noted that, while the American Constitution was "more liberal" than the British, its principle that "all men [are] alike free and equal" was inconsistent with the enslavement of

---

[1137] Taylor, 2012.

Blacks. We should think of the racialist attitudes of the founders as "prejudices" rather than as attitudes that were intrinsic to an earlier, and "truer" interpretation of the founding principles. The American founding principles did not sanction slavery, but they did provide the principles for its abolition, and for equal civil rights regardless of sex and race. By the time Lincoln came along, as he himself wrote, "the liberal party throughout the world" disapproved of slavery and thought that it contradicted the values endorsed in the Constitution. There was no need for a new constitution; "amendments" to the original founding documents were enough to set Blacks free (Thirteenth Amendment in 1865), guarantee citizenship (Fourteenth Amendment in 1866) and the right to vote regardless of race (Fifteenth Amendment in 1870). For a long time, the Supreme Court did justify the legality of segregation under the "separate but equal" law, and identified skin color as a determining factor in many landmark cases; nevertheless, slowly and inevitably, the Supreme court would reach the conclusion that skin color or race can never be a legitimate ground for legal or political distinctions, deciding unanimously in 1954 that segregation was contrary to "the equal protection of the laws guaranteed by the Fourteenth Amendment" and that "separate educational facilities are inherently unequal." The inspiration for these legal changes was the argument that the Constitution was inherently "color-blind."[1138] As President Calvin Coolidge (1923–29), known for his conservative probity, already understood before the civil rights movement: "Our constitution guarantees equal rights to all our citizens, without discrimination on account of race or color. . . . A colored man is precisely as much entitled to submit his candidacy in a party primary, as is any other citizen."[1139]

New Liberalisms: Democracy and Socialism

Whatever claims one may make about the "civic republican motivations" of British Harringtonians and American founders, it would only take a few more years for a new liberal revolution in France in 1789 to justify itself "much more forcefully" in terms of the universal "Rights of Man," freedom of conscience for non-Catholics and Jews, with a constitution in 1791 granting the vote to all adult males over twenty-five years old who paid the equivalent of three days' wages in

[1138] Kull, 1993.
[1139] Bean, 2018.

direct taxes, and which abolished "slavery among the negroes in all our colonies."[1140] Although there would be reactions against the radical Jacobin phase of this revolution, in the course of the 1800s France would come to endorse the incipient principle of fair equality of opportunity advocated by the Jacobins, universal suffrage, and taxation levels to assure everyone their daily bread, a plan for general education for all, and a plan for national welfare and social security. Liberals were concluding that formal legal equality and careers open to talent could never be more than a hollow sham when one class of men can starve another with impunity.

This was not solely a French affair. Burke's prediction that Britain would avoid France's path of subverting its established institutions (because English claims to liberty were rooted in ancestral rights and the accumulated wisdom of the past) would be disproven many times over during the 1800s. Not only would the British go on to embrace Locke, rather than Burke, they would go beyond Locke's liberalism, though not against the spirit of his belief that men have a fundamental right to profess any belief they choose, but beyond his prejudicial views—for example, that Catholics cannot be loyal, or that men who don't believe in God are unfit for society. The Catholic Emancipation Act was passed by parliament in 1829. Then came the momentous English Reform Bill of 1832, which reduced property qualifications for voting to include small landowners, tenant farmers, and shopkeepers. This Bill came after years of liberal criticism that parliament was neither fair nor representative. It was only a matter of time before this same argument was used to end the exclusion of women and most workers from voting.

In 1833, slavery was abolished in the colonies as an inhumane practice that violated the equal moral worth of all humans. In 1846, free trade was established with the repeal of the Corn Laws, at the behest of the Manchester School, which was convinced that free trade, as opposed to mercantilism or imperialism, would have the effect, in the words of Richard Cobden, of "drawing men together, thrusting aside the antagonism of race, and creed, and language, and uniting us in the bonds of eternal peace.[1141] The same year of 1846 saw parliament enact the Religious Disabilities Act, which removed the last restrictions against those who dissented against the Church of England and extended to Jews the same rights on education and property, to be followed progressively by the granting of full political and civil rights to Jews in 1858.

[1140] Soboul, 1975.
[1141] Cited in Spall, 1988.

Yet the free trade mentality of the Corn Laws, the early classical liberal notion that property owners have a right to use their property as they please, was already under criticism when it came to the employment of children and women, as witnessed in the Factory Laws of 1842 and 1847. Despite fierce opposition by free trade liberals, these laws prohibited all females and boys under ten years old from working underground in coal mines, and restricted the working hours of women and young persons age thirteen to eighteen in textile mills to 10 hours per day. The major proponents were Quakers and Anglicans. The Christian and liberal rationale was that such working conditions were damaging to the "moral state" of children, and that without secular and religious instruction, children would be deprived of the right to form "habits of order, sobriety, honesty, and forethought, or even to restrain them from vice and crime." This conforms with Rawls' argument that the basic liberties of liberalism presuppose the right of the individual to be able to develop the capacities for deliberate decision making about their interests and goals in life that allow them to be truly free persons.

John Stuart Mill (1806–1873), who entered parliament as a Liberal in 1866, would go on to renounce all remaining property qualifications for voting, on the grounds that when a segment of the population, in this case the working classes and women, are excluded from representation in the government, their interests and ideas as individuals with the same natural rights cannot find equal expression. As O. Kurer wrote in 1989, J.S. Mill also "consistently proposed" socialistic policies on education, land reform, poor laws, factory acts, and redistribution of income, "derived from his [liberal] ethical principles." He also justified, in his 1859 essay *On Liberty*, unlimited liberty of thought as a way of encouraging humans to employ their rational capacities freed from the constraints of social taboos and dogmatic prejudices. In the words of Nicholas Capaldi, for Mill "freedom consists in living according to rules that are self-imposed, not imposed by others and not imposing on others."[1142] Mill agreed with most of Harriet Taylor's feminist arguments, writing in 1869 in *The Subjection of Women* that the Victorian relations between the sexes violated a basic principle of liberalism: the denial to women of "the equal moral right of all human beings to choose their own occupations . . . according to their own preference, at their own risks."[1143]

It was illiberal for men to decide for women their role in society as if they lacked the moral autonomy given equally to all humans and should have an

---

[1142] Capaldi, 1983.
[1143] Cited in Gordon and David Louzecky, 2023.

inferior civic status to that of men. The Frankfurt School argument that patriarchal families engender "authoritarian personalities," because children are made to fear parental disapproval and to idolize the superior authority of the father, was already implied in Mill's overall commitment to female equality, and his view that the Victorian family of his time was "a school of despotism" in which unequal power-relations between husband and wife perpetuated evil by inculcating boys to believe that "by the mere fact of being born male he is by right the superior of . . . an entire half of the human race." To create a future generation of progressives, the family had to be re-imagined as "the real school of the virtues of freedom," "grounded . . . on equal . . . [and] sympathetic association."[1144]

As Mill was articulating these ideas, the Reform Bill of 1867 was passed, granting the vote to industrial workers—a Bill put through by the Conservative Party. It needs to be added that by this point in time in the late nineteenth century, across Western Europe, traditional conservatism, as a short-lived ideology that emerged in the wake of the French Revolution of 1789 in defense of clericalism, aristocratic privilege, and the divine right of monarchy, had been thoroughly defeated by liberalism. Conservatives would henceforth accept all the fundamental premises of classical liberalism, and its progressive implications, even as they moved at a slower pace. By 1867, conservatives and progressives alike in England had reached the conclusion that democracy is fundamental to give voice to every citizen and to allow them to safeguard their individual rights, and to provide greater parity between individuals in their opportunities to develop their own faculties as human beings. The consensus had emerged that democracy, as Mill argued, was the natural development and consequence of liberal individual rights. Soon the consensus would be, including among conservatives, that without some "socialist" distribution of economic power, or fairer equality of opportunity, the right to vote amounted to a mere formal/juridical equality without substance.

The spread of progressive democratization would inspire a new conception of "positive freedom," in which the government is seen as a vehicle in charge of levelling the playing field by affording greater opportunities to poorer members of society to express their basic liberties, beyond the "negative freedom" of laissez-faire, with its focus on the threats to liberty of an arbitrary and tyrannical state. A foremost British liberal philosopher of this period, Thomas Hill Green (1836–1882), in a well-known 1880 speech, "Liberal Legislation and Freedom of Contract," contrasted two kinds of freedom, negative and positive, arguing that

---

[1144] McCabe, 2015.

individuals cannot become fully free unless the government creates economic and cultural conditions aimed at encouraging their highest nature as autonomous rational beings capable of shaping their own lives, rather than being under the compulsion of their hedonistic or irrational impulses.[1145] Green would thus advocate for sanitary laws, factory inspections, and public education, among many other socialist policies. Most liberals would eventually agree that negative liberties on their own (freedom from arbitrary arrest, freedom of speech and association, equal right to participate in politics) are purely formal if the government does not ensure, in the words of Rawls, "a certain fair equality of opportunity," "meaningful work," "basic health care," and "a decent distribution of income and wealth." As another leading liberal of this period, L. T. Hobhouse (1864–1929), would write: "true Socialism serves to complete rather than to destroy the leading Liberal ideals." "Freedom to choose and follow an occupation, if it is to become fully effective, means equality with others in the opportunities for following such occupation."[1146]

However, we should draw a distinction between the positive conception of freedom advocated by Green, and possibly by Hobhouse with his idea that the state should be conceived as an "ethical community devoted to the promotion of the common good,"[1147] and the Rawlsian conception, which can still be framed in terms of the principles of negative liberty. Rawls endorses socialist programs insofar as they are aimed at removing constraints (harmful working conditions, lack of opportunities in jobs and education, and harmful sanitary conditions) for the proper exercise of one's liberties. Central to his political liberalism is the idea that the government should not hinder individuals in deciding their own values and lifestyles. The state must leave individuals to do or be what they wish to do or be, without dictating any common doctrine. The question, to be addressed shortly, is whether this Rawlsian view is consistent with the current woke view that the government should promote politically correct beliefs against the prevalence of "sexist," "racist," "homophobic," or "Islamophobic" attitudes.

In late nineteenth century Britain, there was a considerable acceleration in the liberal march through the institutions. The Elementary Education Act of 1870 established a national system of free public schools for children aged five to thirteen, stating that attendance should be compulsory, that religious teaching should be

---

[1145] Green, 2015.
[1146] Hobhouse, 1994, 15.
[1147] Meadowcroft, 1995.

non-denominational, and that parents have the right to withdraw their children from religious instruction. Among other notable liberal reforms were the Workmen's Compensation Act of 1906, providing for compensation to workers for injury during employment; the Old Age Pension Act of 1908, the Minimum Wage Act of 1909, and the National Insurance Act of 1911, giving benefits to workers during sickness and unemployment. The Reform Bill of 1918 granted equal suffrage to men aged over twenty-one, whether or not they owned property, and to women aged over thirty. Legislation in the next few years brought equality to women in inheritance rights and unemployment benefits. The Sex Discrimination (Removal) Act of 1919 categorically stated that "a person shall not be disqualified by sex or marriage from the exercise of any public function, or from being appointed to or holding any civil or judicial office or post, or from entering or assuming or carrying on any civil profession or vocation, or for admission to any incorporated society." Divorce was made easier by the Matrimonial Causes Act of 1923, and the Marie Stopes mail-order service made contraception more readily available.[1148] As L. T. Hobhouse clearly stated in 1911, it is a contradiction to have a constitution that affirms the equal rights of all citizens without "rendering the wife a fully responsible individual, capable of holding property, suing and being sued, conducting business on her own account, and enjoying full personal protection against her husband." All these acts are consistent with Rawlsian liberalism.[1149]

The post-WWII decades would see an expansion of these "new liberal" programs, aimed at ensuring a minimum level of subsistence for all, "from the cradle to the grave." The National Health Act of 1946 provided free medicines and medical services to all, "from duke to dustman." These acts went beyond civic and

---

[1148] For key dates in the long march of feminism in the UK, see UK Parliament. "Relationships: Key Dates." https://tinyurl.com/yv62xvzk.

[1149] I have only scratched over the surface of the progressive transformation "classical liberal" England underwent during the nineteenth century. Simon Heffer's sweeping book, *High Minds: The Victorians and the Birth of Modern Britain* (2022), recounts in great detail how in the four decades between 1840 and 1880, "British life changed almost beyond recognition," not only due to industrialization and innovation, but to the emerging consensus among elite members across political lines that "Britain could only be effectively governed – and its prosperity safeguarded – if the State made certain strategic decisions and enforced them through Acts of Parliament" (765). From an impoverished liberal Britain where most of the poor were illiterate with barely any means to improve themselves as individuals, with children working up to 12 hours a day, living in crowded housing without basic sanitation, to a more progressive Britain where one could see "whole suburbs of housing, town halls, museums, concert halls, art galleries, schools, colleges, hospitals, libraries, railway stations, market halls and Gothic Revival churches" (xvi).

political equality; they were economic rights. The English sociologist T. H. Marshall (1893–1981) articulated this idea in a famous essay, "Citizenship and Social Class," written in 1949, arguing that citizens could not fully exercise their civic and political freedoms without a basic level of economic and cultural well-being to equip them with living conditions and an education for intelligent and autonomous choices in life.[1150]

Immigrant Multiculturalism and Liberal Global Capitalism

The "post-war consensus" which began in the 1930s would continue through to the 1960s, when liberal intellectuals led by John Maynard Keynes and William Beveridge formulated the concept of a welfare state based on the widely accepted argument that markets on their own have a tendency to get stuck with high unemployment unless governments promote effective demand through spending. "True individual freedom," as Franklin D. Roosevelt would tell Congress in 1944, "cannot exist without economic security and independence." With the rise of Margaret Thatcher in the 1970s, there was a slight return to some laissez-faire principles, but the path of Britain and the Western world would remain progressively tilted towards the "expansion of freedom." It was from the 1960s on that liberals would start a hard drive for equal rights in all respects for different genders and races. In 1965, the Race Relations Act banned racial discrimination in public places, and made the promotion of hatred on the grounds of "colour, race, or ethnic or national origins" an offence.

The Equal Pay Act of 1970 prevented discrimination, "as regards terms and conditions of employment," between men and women. The Gender Recognition Act of 2004 allowed people to legally change gender. The Same Sex Couples Act of 2013 made same-sex marriage legal. The Equality Act of 2010 brought together many pieces of liberal legislation into one single Act "to protect the rights of individuals and advance equality of opportunity for all," regardless of gender or race, as well as giving women "equal pay for equal work." The Race Relations Amendment Act of 2000 made it "unlawful for any public authority to discriminate on racial grounds—directly, indirectly or by victimisation," and requires, as a

---

[1150] Marshall, 1992.

"general duty," governments, schools and the police, to promote "equality of opportunity and good relations between people of different racial groups."[1151]

While multiculturalism in Britain has not been formally recognized in any
constitutional act, the liberal elites in charge, as in almost every other nation in
the West, came to the conclusion that governments needed to ensure equal rights
for minorities and embrace their ethnic diversity, leading both Canada and Australia in the early 1970s to identify themselves as "multicultural." What seemed at
first a call for undoing "the lingering presence or enduring effects of older . . . ethnic and racial hierarchies" in the West, soon turned into a call for developing "a
new model of multicultural democratic citizenship," away from an identity in
Western nations centered around "Eurocentrism" and "Whiteness" by restructuring them as "immigrant nations."[1152] Before we get into how liberalism came to
justify this profound remaking of the West, it is imperative that we reassert the
intrinsic relationship between liberalism and capitalism. The spread of multicultural immigration across the West coincided with the realization among corporate
business leaders that the Keynesian regime of accumulation, which had brought
effective demand and economic stability from the late 1940s to the early 1970s,
and which involved a "class compromise" between the White working class and
the capitalist elites, together with wife-supporting wages, job protection, and rising incomes across the board, was no longer suitable for the requirements of financial capitalism.

The elections of Thatcher in 1979, Reagan in 1980, and Mulroney in 1984
should be seen less as a return to a laissez-faire that never really existed, than a
concerted effort by business-oriented liberal elites to develop a new regime of accumulation known as "post-Fordism," involving globalized financial markets and
free trade zones, making it easier for businesses to move across national borders
in search of lower wages and less regulations.[1153] This new regime entailed an emphasis on service industries, pursuit of markets without national characteristics,
new communication technologies for up-to-the-minute financial information
and investment decisions, as well as the intensification of a feminized and diversified workforce with stagnant real wages and dual-income families. It is a mistake
to identify these policies with classical liberalism, or "conservatives." Conservative
politicians were enthusiastic pawns within the wider web of global capitalist

---

[1151] Commission, 2000.
[1152] Will Kymlicka, 2007.
[1153] Amin, 1994.

forces, while subsequent New Labour governments would happily go along with this regime, in combination with new norms of multicultural and immigrant human rights, which conservatives would promote as well.[1154]

The opening of Western borders was not orchestrated by cultural Marxists or by high liberal ideals on their own. Multicultural liberalism came hand in hand with the development, in the words of Sam Francis, of a new managerial transnational Western elite "detached and disengaged from—and actually hostile to—any particular place or group or set of beliefs that supports particular identities."[1155] This new globalist liberal elite is indifferent to church-attending family businesses rooted in particular communities. What they aim for, as Theodore Levitt observed in 1983, are products with a generic identity for consumers across the globe, markets without national boundaries, and "globally standardized products that are advanced, functional, reliable." They don't want consumers with "deeply ingrained local preferences of taste"; they want to sell "in all national markets the same kind of products sold at home . . . on the basis of appropriate value—the best combinations of price, quality, quantity, reliability, and delivery." They want "products that are globally identical with respect to design, function, and even fashion." National identities are inefficient, slow-moving, and inconsistent with the new technologies of communications. Rootless individuals endlessly seeking pleasures in a "homogenized world market" is what our current mega-retailers such as Costco, Walmart, Best Buy, Target, Home Depot, and Walgreens cherish above all else.

There is an effective affinity between this globalized capitalism and the liberal leftist goal of creating "post-national" citizens. Leftists want "deterritorialized" individuals without "xenophobic" attachments to ethnic groups, "emancipated" from pre-given sexual, cultural, and racial identities—that is, individuals who construct their identities completely out of their free will. By the end of the twentieth century, both the left and right would instruct citizens that continuously high levels of immigration are essential to sustain the long term economic and social viability of Western civilization.[1156] Below-replacement fertility rates, they would tell

---

[1154] Heath, Jowell, and Curtice, 2001.

[1155] Francis, 2019.

[1156] John J. Mearsheimer's 2018 book, *The Great Delusion: Liberal Dreams and International Realities* also makes the observation that "progressive liberalism," with its emphasis on positive rights, has "triumphed" over classical liberalism, what he calls "modus vivendi liberalism," with its emphasis on negative liberties. He sees in American foreign policy, particularly after the fall of the Soviet Union, an intensification in the "crusader mentality" that is "hardwired" into liberal states, a "universalist logic" that pushes liberal states, with the United States at the helm, to fall

their constituents, demand the importation of millions of immigrants to over-come a shrinking labor force coupled with an aging population, if the West was to avoid permanent labor shortages, a declining GDP, lower tax revenues, and thus declining government services. This convergence of the left and liberal right was most visible in their agreement to redefine Western culture as inherently "multicultural." Whether a right-wing liberal or a left-wing liberal was in power, the end results were in the direction of "diversity, equity, and inclusion," three words now inscribed in every institution and corporation in the West.

Canada, the largest landmass of the West, would stand as a paradigmatic showcase for multiculturalism. The same conservative government of Brian Mul-roney (1984–1993) which promoted a "post-Fordist" regime of accumulation, also brought mass-scale immigration and the implementation of multiculturalism into "all aspects of Canadian society." The Conservative Party would henceforth, Mul-roney announced, cease to be identified as "the Party of White Anglo-Saxon Protestants." "Racism must be stamped out wherever it rears its ugly head." Three key legislative measures were implemented to this end: the Equity Act of 1986, which mandated federal employers to implement affirmative hiring policies for "disadvantaged minorities"; the Multiculturalism Act of 1988, which set out to give Canadians a new multicultural identity away from its British or European-centered identity; and the Five Year Immigration Plan, 1990–1995, which encour-aged continuously rising levels of immigration per year, regardless of fluctuations in the unemployment rate.[1157]

Similar legislative acts were implemented across numerous Western nations during this period or in subsequent years with the complete support of main-stream political parties, the corporate media, and intellectuals in academia. Vari-ations in forms of liberalism between France, Germany, Sweden, Canada, the

---

under the illusion that they can spread liberal rights across the world with little regard for the realities of international power politics, and the nationalist interests of non-Western nations. American, and NATO, policy toward Ukraine is motivated by this "liberal logic." He under-stands as well that conservatives in their actions are just as caught up in the progressive logic of liberalism. He points out that the "annualized growth of federal spending since 1982 grew more under Republican presidents ... by 8.7% under Reagan between 1982 and 1985, but only 1.4% under Obama between 2010 and 2013." "Reagan also signed the Emergency Medical Treatment and Active Labor Act, which prohibits hospitals from turning away people who come to an emergency room for treatment. ... Republican presidents oversaw the beginnings of the Inter-state Highway System, the Environmental Protection Agency, and the Department of Homeland Security. Republicans, in short, are deeply committed to the interventionist state and the exten-sive social engineering that comes with it" (69–70).

[1157] Duchesne, 2017.

United States, Australia, and New Zealand do not obviate this pattern of multi-cultural liberalism. There is also truth in the Marxist argument that "irresistible and relentless pressures for growth are functions of the day-to-day requirements of capitalist reproduction in a competitive market, incumbent upon all but a few businesses."[1158] As fertility rates dropped in the 1960s, immigration came to be seen as the key vehicle to keep the population growing, avoid rising wages due to labor shortages, and ensure a sufficient supply of skilled workers and "labor market flexibility." The principal aim of immigration, in societies with low fertility rates, is to keep the GDP growing. Critics of immigration are right that simply maximizing GDP does not automatically translate into rising GDP per person. There is abundant evidence that higher immigration levels across the West have actually resulted in decreases in GDP per capita for the resident population, overcrowding of hospitals, schools, and recreational facilities, a deteriorated environment, increase in cost of services and cost of housing, and a net drag on government budgets. But the fact remains that mass immigration in the West has been a critical factor responsible for major increases in the workforce and in the size of the economy. In a capitalist economy, the expansion of GDP and the earnings of investors are viewed as the key metric of success.

It happens to be the case that most of the total income gains generated by the expansion of GDP since the 1970s and 80s, right as immigration was intensifying across the West, have accrued to the top percentiles of households—that is, to the major owners of capital. The Pew Research Center reported in 2020 that "income growth was the most rapid for the top 5%" of Americans between 1971 and 2019.[1159] Another study showed that the bottom 50 percent income share of Americans "collapsed from about 20% in 1980 to 12% in 2014," whereas the income share of the top 1 percent "increased from about 12% in the early 1980s to 20% in 2014."[1160] Just as immigration was intensifying, from 1979 to 2019, according to the Economic Policy Institute, the wages for the top 1 percent in the United States "skyrocketed 160%," while the "share of wages for the bottom 90% shrunk."[1161] In England, the top 1 percent of earners increased their share of income from 7.1 percent in 1970 to 14.3 percent in 2005 just as the ruling classes of this nation started to embrace mass immigration.[1162] In more recent years, as England came

---

[1158] Smith, 2010.

[1159] Horowitz et al., 2020.

[1160] Piketty, Saez, Zucman, 2016.

[1161] Mishel and Kandra, 2020.

[1162] Ramesh, 2011.

to be officially identified as "an immigrant nation,"[1163] the wealth of billionaires "skyrocketed by over 1000% between 1990 and 2022," and "the number of billionaires exploded" from 15 in 1990 to 177 in 2022.[1164]

Even France, considered to be an "egalitarian country," has experienced a sharp rise in inequality since the early 1980s, just as the borders were widened for cheaper labor.[1165] In Canada, between 1980 and 2009, right as immigration was intensified, disposable (after taxes and transfers) income inequality increased by 13 percent; the share of market income held for the top 1 percent and 0.01 percent "increased dramatically" from 8.1 percent to 13.3 percent and 2 percent to 5.3 percent respectively.[1166] Australia, Sweden, Germany, and other pro-immigration Western countries have seen similar trends, including Italy, where "the wealth share held by the top 0.1 percent, the richest 50,000 adults, almost doubled from 5.5 percent to 9.3 percent from 1995 to 2016."[1167]

Capitalism in the non-Western world generally still operates within a non-liberal ideological order. Accordingly, businesses in such countries as Japan, China, India, and Saudi Arabia have remained rooted to their national communities, despite their multinational operations, governing in unison with a political elite in charge of national interests, with a clear sense of the friend-enemy distinction, a strong collective identity, a strong sense of heritage, racial identity, customs, and rituals. This is very different from the liberal capitalist West, where the state is envisioned as an association created by individuals with natural rights in abstraction from any prior community, and where it is believed that humans and nations can overcome deadly conflict through the creation of a "new world order" which grants everyone individual freedom and the possibility to improve themselves through market competition, humanitarian works, and geopolitical consensus through diplomacy.[1168] To reach this end, liberal nations are prepared to fight wars against illiberal nations that don't recognize human rights and the equal rights of women and homosexuals, or that refuse to be part of a liberal world order dedicated to the termination of all collective identities.

The argument is often made that multiculturalism goes against both the "Western" character and heritage of Western liberal nations, and against the

---

[1163] Shabi, 2017.
[1164] Wittams, n.d.
[1165] Goupille-Lebret et al., 2018.
[1166] Labonté et al., n.d.
[1167] Acciari et al., 2021.
[1168] Mearsheimer, 2018.

principle of equal rights regardless of race, sex, and nationality, in granting "special group rights" to immigrant minorities—affirmative hiring, public funding of cultural activities, exemption from dress codes, and dual citizenship. This view is mistaken. First, multiculturalism is consistent with the principle of pluralism, the idea that the government should not be in charge of imposing any cultural values other than the value of tolerance and respect for the decisions of equally free individuals to choose their values. The Prime Minister of Canada, Pierre Elliot Trudeau, the first Western leader to make multiculturalism the official identity of a nation in 1971, understood this. A key argument behind Trudeau's decision was that WWII had proven the deadliness of nationalist cultural pride, and that the way out of persisting tensions between the Anglos and the Quebecois was to remake Canada into a multicultural state, away from any form of cultural nationalism.[1169] This is the same rationale underlying the claim that the cause of the religious wars of the sixteenth and seventeenth centuries was the imposition of one Christian creed, and that the way out of this violence was to make religion a private decision based on conviction.

Second, in regard to group rights, liberals would go on to articulate in the 1990s, on the basis of liberal principles, a "multicultural theory of citizenship," arguing that individual members of minorities need to emphasize their group identity in order to overcome centuries of discrimination and "racialization" inflicted on them, and thereby have the same opportunities for liberty and equality. Its most prolific proponent has been the Canadian Will Kymlicka, who has spent most of his career on visiting professorships across Europe selling the "Canadian model of multiculturalism," and was appointed in June of 2023 to the Order of Canada for his "extraordinary contribution to the nation" in "his application of liberal theory to multiculturalism and minority rights."[1170] He elaborated that majorities throughout history have shown a tendency to behave in illiberal ways towards minorities and that, for this reason, minorities and immigrants should be afforded "external protections" against majority decisions that may discriminate against them, as well as resources to enhance their opportunities for individual success within the majority society.

Allowing immigrants to express their ethnic and religious identities, rather than forcing assimilation to the "dominant" Western culture, is consistent with

---

[1169] See Trudeau's famous essay, "The New Treason of the Intellectuals," first published in *Cité libre* (April 1962), readily available online.

[1170] See: https://www.gg.ca/en/order-canada-appointees-june-2023.

the inherent value-pluralism of liberalism, in that it affords everyone the right to their own cultural and religious choices, as long as immigrant groups do not seek to create their own full-scale cultures, or limit the equal rights of individuals within their groups, by engaging, for example, in female circumcision and forced marriages. This policy came to be called "reasonable accommodation" in Canada, possibly in awareness of Rawls' argument that a liberal society has an obligation to be flexible and accommodate different worldviews, even when they are illiberal, as long as these doctrines are likewise reasonably flexible in abiding by the principles of pluralism and tolerance in the public sphere.

It may be replied, admittedly, that Rawls' liberalism does not call for mass immigration as such, but for equal treatment and fair equality of opportunity for citizens within a nation-state. The reality is that, in our globalized capitalist Western world, the Rawlsian case for open borders is very popular. Western law does not allow Western leaders to make any distinctions among potential immigrants on the basis of race, religion, and nationality. White-only immigration regulations were rejected across the West as unconstitutional in the sixties and seventies. Moreover, Western nations are morally guided, in the aftermath of their war against the "racism" of fascism, by their Universal Declaration of Human Rights of 1948, that "all human beings" across the world "are born free and equal in dignity and rights . . . endowed with reason and conscience" and that nations "should act towards one another in a spirit of brotherhood" without making any distinctions "on the basis of the political, jurisdictional or international status of the country or territory to which a person belongs."

Given these liberal realities, it was only a matter of time before someone would draw from Rawls an argument for open borders. We thus find Joseph Carens arguing in 1987 (just as businesses were pressuring for higher levels immigration) in "Aliens and Citizens: The Case for Open Borders," that "there is little justification for restricting immigration" in Rawlsian liberalism, including in the libertarian and utilitarian variations of liberalism, for "each of these theories begins with some kind of assumption about the equal moral worth of individuals. In one way or another, each treats the individual as prior to the community. These foundations provide little basis for drawing fundamental distinctions between citizens and aliens who seek to become citizens." This argument would become common in academia, expressed in books and articles, some relying on liberalism generally or directly on Rawlsian principles to justify mass immigration.[1171]

[1171] Mendoza, 2017; Lindauer, 2021.

The Paradox of Liberal Intolerance: Popper = Marcuse

Conservatives and dissidents at large attribute political correctness, the cen-
soring of "offensive" speech and behavior, to the actions of cultural Marxists. They
believe that before liberal nations experienced a "march through the institutions"
by communists, the principles of scientific impartiality and free speech prevailed
across a liberal West. We cannot deny that important differences exist between
"right wing" and "left wing" liberals, or between Enlightenment liberals who endorse science, and postmodern liberals who emphasize cultural relativism. The
right has shown strong opposition to speech codes and the banning of "controversial" speakers from campuses. They have also identified Herbert Marcuse's theory of repressive tolerance as the ideological originator of PC mandates, and have
argued indeed that this "cultural Marxist" was the first one who proposed a theoretical justification for the suppression of conservative views and the dedication
of universities to a "liberating tolerance" to bring about social justice.

But the reality is that Marcuse's argument in favor of "intolerance against
movements from the Right and toleration of movements from the Left" is consistent with the progressive pluralistic logic of liberalism. Firstly, it is worth noting
that Marcuse, from his young age, had an ambivalent, if not contentious relationship with Marxism, writing a rather bleak account of the USSR in 1961 under the
title *Soviet Marxism: A Critical Analysis*, while sharing "rationalism's protest and
critique" against the "unfreedom and inequalities" still prevailing in the "material
conditions of existence" of bourgeois society beyond the German "idealistic" solution of making oneself free and rational only "in the realm of thought."[1172] The
withdrawal of tolerance he called for was aimed at ideas, groups, and movements
that promoted militarism, corporate capitalist control of the media, chauvinism,
and discrimination on the grounds of race and religion. He was for a progressive
politics aimed at expanding liberal rights through the removal of all structures in
society that prevented Blacks, women, and gays from exercising their free will,
including the removal of sexually repressive norms in order to awaken the erotic
drives of humans.[1173]

Secondly, I am in agreement with the rigorously argued 2020 paper by Sandra
Dzenis and Filipe Nobre Faria, "Political Correctness: the Twofold Protection of

---

[1172] Marcuse, 1969.
[1173] Marcuse, 1962.

Liberalism," and its argument that right-wing critics of "PC intolerance" defend open inquiry under the assumption that it is the best way to protect and validate liberal values, while ultimately agreeing with the left, if tacitly, that "illiberal" findings and conclusions that contradict or invalidate liberal values, even if scientifically based, should be kept outside the mainstream or relegated to the margins. This view is akin to Rawls' exclusion from the pluralist sphere of views which seek to undermine the already "settled" principle of equal freedom for all humans. This explains the general attitude among liberals of paying no attention to, or excluding outright, studies showing average genetic differences between racial groups, including scientific studies demonstrating that in-group favoritism would be a good evolutionary strategy for Europeans.

As Dzenis and Faria also observe, Enlightenment liberals, such as Steven Pinker and Daniel Dennett, don't necessarily call for "legally forbidding" research that threatens the sacred cows of liberalism, but for what may be identified as "soft-censorship": ignoring, caricaturing, or portraying "illiberal" claims as "the product of bad science," creating thereby social pressures "towards conformity." The very few academics who have published scientific papers on IQ differences between races, or the benefits of ingroup ethnocentrism for Europeans, have been either fired from their academic positions or heavily restricted from the public sphere.

Thirdly, the idea that liberals should not tolerate illiberal claims that threaten to undermine liberal values was articulated back in 1945 by the Enlightenment liberal Karl Popper in the widely known 1945 book, *The Open Society and Its Enemies*, listed as one of the Modern Library Board's "100 Best Nonfiction books of the twentieth century." In what has been termed "the paradox of tolerance," Popper argued that a liberal society cannot be tolerant without limit, for this would entail tolerating the intolerant—that is, those who don't believe in liberal tolerance, which would threaten the existence of political pluralism. Rawls' theory of political pluralism says as much.[1174] The essence of liberal tolerance is succinctly articulated by Andrew Kernohan:

[1174] This paradox was already implied in Locke's argument that Catholics, with their religious intolerance, should not be tolerated. Locke held the same view about atheists, stating in his 1689 *Letter Concerning Toleration* that "those are not at all to be tolerated who deny the being of God. Promises, covenants, and oaths, which are the bonds of human society, can have no hold upon an atheist." The logic of this argument is very similar to Rawls' view that those who hold "unreasonable" views and seek to impose a collective conception of the good, and deny thereby the right of individuals to choose their own lifestyles, should not be tolerated.

Liberalism requires tolerance of all manner of views on how to lead a worthwhile life, but not of views that deny the fundamental assumption of moral equality.... Liberal tolerance comes to an end for views (that are) inconsistent with liberal principles, and [that] threaten significant harm to society as a whole.... Therefore, the liberal state *must take an active role in reforming culture and combatting the cultural oppression of groups.*[1175]

It is quite revealing, moreover, that as much as Enlightenment liberals have objected to Marxists, including Popper, who was a critic of the Frankfurt School,[1176] they have never called for them to be banned from liberal society. For Rawlsian liberalism, and for Popper, the ultimate enemy of the West is ethnic European nationalism, or any ideology which seeks to inculcate among European peoples a sense of peoplehood, by virtue of their belonging, through birth and historical experience, to a particular nation. Rawls identified ethnic nationalism, or any form of racial identity among Whites, as "odious." Popper's *Open Society and Its Enemies* is quite sympathetic towards Marx for his "burning desire to help the oppressed" and "his sincerity in his search for truth and his intellectual honesty,"[1177] whereas he despised German nationalism, the "windbaggery" of Fichte and Schelling, and the "charlatan Hegel." Just to be clear, this does not mean that liberal pluralism will tolerate leftists no matter how far they go. All movements are subject to repression if they break the law and call for violence. It does not mean either that conservative liberals cannot challenge or retroact against current woke policies. The point is that leftist radicals tend to be seen in a positive moral light because, in spite of their occasional excesses, they adhere to the fundamental principle that all humans are morally equal.[1178]

Of course, the question arises, if the "liberal state must take an active role in reforming culture," as we just read in Kernohan's words, striving to make the culture "liberal-minded" and opposed to doctrines or religious beliefs that are perceived to be "illiberal," then Rawls may be wrong in arguing that liberalism does

---

[1175] Kernohan, 1998, emphasis mine.

[1176] Keuth, 2015.

[1177] Popper, 1945, 77–8, 25–6.

[1178] As Tom Holland has argued, a key reason why Western peoples have been far less critical of the crimes committed by the Soviet government than of what Rawls calls "the demonic conception of the world" of the Nazis (2001, 20), is that the former promulgated communism in the name of the moral equality of humans, whereas the latter rejected liberalism on the assumption that it equalizes the naturally unequal differences between races and cultures.

not promote any substantive doctrine of the common good. It seems that liberalism aims for a lot more than merely ensuring a neutralized level playing field for all, but instead is actively committed, through its control of the institutions, to the engineering of liberal souls. This progressive impetus, inherent to liberalism, is amply demonstrated in the "long march through the institutions" we outlined in this chapter, and in the continued march in the last decades by "wokeists" for same sex marriage, transgenderism, continuously higher levels of immigration, the complete elimination of "Whiteness" from Western culture, as well as the determination of the United States and NATO to create a "New World Order" dominated by liberal values. Thus, while liberalism wants individuals to decide their own lifestyles, and objects to the "authoritarian imposition" of a worldview, it has shown itself to be very authoritarian, as evident not only in its censorship culture and hate speech laws, but in the very fact that almost all institutions and private businesses now mandate a culture of "diversity, equity, and inclusion," without allowing any dissenting voice. This imposition of a liberal culture—which has come along with continuous denunciations of "White supremacy"—cannot be categorized as a mere effort to exclude the "intolerant"; it should be more accurately described as an effort to create human beings and nations that are pervasively liberal in every respect, with very little room for doctrines and individuals holding "illiberal" values.

The work of the American Catholic philosopher Adrian Vermeule conveys with clarity and rigor how liberal pluralism, despite its claim that it does not impose a comprehensive doctrine, carries within it an authoritarian logic. His critique of liberalism is rooted in his Catholicism; he is known for his "common good constitutionalism" and "integralism," which calls for the abandonment of the separation of church and state, in favor of a political order in which a Catholic conception of the "Highest Good," based on natural law, precedes the rights of individuals.[1179] While his criticism is not directed against Rawls directly, he rejects the notion that liberalism provides a "depoliticized" or a neutralized public political setting where individuals can freely express their choices.[1180] He cites the important insight from Carl Schmitt that "liberalism must be understood as a consistent, comprehensive metaphysical system" in its belief "that the truth can be found through an unrestrained clash of opinions and that competition will

---

[1179] Vermeule, 2018.
[1180] Vermeule, 2019b

produce harmony."[1181] This seems to be basically correct, although we should still draw a distinction between the belief that the common good emerges through a plurality of contesting values, and the communist and fascist advocacy of a "new man." The liberal worldview is relativistic in its belief that, given the inherent inclination of individuals to disagree about lifestyles and the good life, the good can only come from a political setting that allows for the proliferation (as well as contestation) of multiple perspectives, which makes liberalism intrinsically agnostic to values *other than the value of being open-minded*. Nevertheless, we can agree with Vermeule that liberalism carries an aggressive impetus to make everyone accept a liberal progressive world.

Vermeule thinks Schmitt was also the first who grasped "the peculiarly restless and dynamic character of liberalism and its relentless quest for progress," not only in its pursuit of individual emancipation, but also in its capitalist and scientific disruption of traditional communities and cherished ways of life. Vermeule calls liberalism a "secularized soteriology and eschatology" that has come to entail, in our current woke times, "its own cruel sacraments—especially the shaming and, where possible, legal punishment of the intolerant or illiberal—and its own liturgy, the Festival of Reason, the ever-repeated overcoming of the darkness of reaction."[1182] In its emancipatory quest, liberalism has in fact politicized every aspect of life. Vermeule does not blame "cultural Marxism" for this, but thinks (similarly to Dugin, though he does not reference him directly) that liberalism "remains the world's first and last remaining ideology," and that "liberal intolerance represents not the self-undermining of liberalism, but a full fulfillment of its essential nature."[1183]

Kevin MacDonald's Liberal "Moral Communities" and the Jewish Question

What about the Jews? MacDonald and I agree that liberal individualism (though I prefer to emphasize value pluralism) is the dominant ideology of the Western world. MacDonald's central focus, as an intellectual and scholar, has been on the highly influential role Jewish intellectual and media elites have played in accelerating and intensifying the universalist tendencies of liberalism against

---

[1181] Cited in Vermeule, 2019a.

[1182] Vermeule, 2017.

[1183] Ibid.

every remaining collective identity and traditional way of life in the United States, and other Western nations. The liberal culture of the West, he believes, was a necessary but not sufficient condition to bring about the current anti-White "woke" order. Jews played a vital role in the radicalization of liberalism away from its co-existence for many centuries with some degree of in-group Christian identification and, for some decades in the twentieth century, a clear Darwinian awareness of racial differences, coupled with a high degree of Anglo-Saxon cultural nationalism in the United States.

Another key difference, as we saw in Chapter VII, is that MacDonald approaches liberalism from an evolutionary perspective, as a naturally selected behavior that emerged in prehistoric times in two varieties: an egalitarian individualism among northwestern hunter-gatherers, and an aristocratic individualism among the Indo-Europeans. It is the case, moreover, that MacDonald defines liberalism as an evolutionary psychological disposition for monogamous marriages, prohibition of polygamy, weak kinship networks, household settlement independently of parents and extended families, and marriage based on individual choice rather than as decided by close kin, all selected-for by particular environmental pressures in Europe.

My emphasis, rather, is on the emergence of self-consciousness among Europeans, and the modern belief, as Kant articulated, that it is possible for humans to generate norms applicable to all societies, "universally and necessarily valid," rooted in "reason's interests," rather than any "external goal." Humans can learn to govern themselves according to goals not rooted "in anything other than" in "reason itself."[1184] For MacDonald, however, liberal norms are explainable in evolutionary terms, naturally selected under the environmental pressures of the northern climes of Europe, and the relatively weaker kinship networks and monogamous ties that Europeans were selected to create, in varying degrees, across Europe. I do not deny these environmental pressures, but another unique component in the history of Europeans was their higher level of self-consciousness and explicit use of reason, their ability to act according to "reason's interests" in a state of relaxation from Darwinian pressures. MacDonald realizes that Whites today are acting in ways that are contrary to what one would expect from the standpoint of evolutionary psychology, against their own interests. Before Jews came to dominate American intellectual life, media, and finance, there was a strong and healthy Darwinian current among Americans. But under Jewish pressure, liberalism came

---

[1184] Kant, 1993.

to acquire, in recent decades, a cultural Marxist quality. The West today, in his estimation, is dominated by illiberal, politically correct norms imposed from above by extremely powerful "moral communities" in the media, universities, civil rights organizations, political parties, and business groups, with powerful incentives to encourage conformity and penalties against those who dissent.

My view is that liberal intolerance is ultimately a product of the essential progressive tendency of this ideology, and that the Jews have been assiduously effective, obsessively committed, and quite smart in articulating arguments to bring to its conclusion the progressivist logic built into liberalism. Our difference, then, is that MacDonald seems to imply that liberalism was on the right track and capable of co-existing with ethnocentric attitudes and race realism, until powerful Jewish groups undermined these beliefs and pushed liberalism in a cultural Marxist direction, whereas I see Jews bringing to fruition at an accelerated pace tendencies intrinsic to liberal pluralism. Liberalism cannot co-exist long-term with race realism.

MacDonald's argument in *Individualism and the Western Liberal Tradition*, however, is a complex one, and not reducible to simple claims about how "cultural Marxists" are in charge today thanks to Jewish influence. First, it is his view that the individualism of the West has always co-existed with powerful collective norms. He criticizes Joseph Henrich precisely for assuming that the prohibition of collective kinship networks by the Church in the Middle Ages automatically released individuals to choose their own civic associations and norms.[1185] Moral communities were visible among Christians with their many churches, monasteries, and heterodox religious associations, open to individuals as individuals, but based on strong religious norms. The Church took on the role of building in the West "a strong sense of group identification and commitment." The "collectivism of European society in the High Middle Ages was real," but it was a pan-European ideological-Christian form of collectivism set up against the in-group biological collectivism of kinship groups.[1186] It was a collectivism of moral precepts operating at the conscious "higher brain centers located in the cortex," rather than at the instinctive biological/kinship level. The Church had the resources to provide incentives to individuals to join its expanding and revenue-generating institutional structure.

[1185] MacDonald, 2021.
[1186] MacDonald, 2019, 189–191.

Likewise, the Puritans who founded the US combined individualistic tendencies with strong social controls over the education of children, the raising of families, and the overall "acceptable" behavior of individuals in their towns, schools, churches, and civic associations. Their American descendants also managed to create a very powerful nation-state with a strong in-group WASP ethnic identity. MacDonald identifies the long period from 1880 to 1965 as a period of "ethnic defense," in acknowledgement of the considerable influence that Social Darwinian ideas (developed by Arthur de Gobineau, Houston Stewart Chamberlain, Gustave Le Bon, Herbert Spencer, Madison Grant, and Lothrop Stoddard) played in ensuring the Immigration Act of 1924 and keeping the borders closed to large influxes of non-White peoples until 1965. These men were in favor of capitalist individualism, open to talent and to individual outsiders willing to conform to WASP values, but they were also intellectual Darwinians who believed that racial differences were real, that the races were "in competition with each other for supremacy," and that it was necessary for the US to have a collective WASP identity.

This openness, MacDonald explains, made the US (and the West generally) susceptible to ideological infiltration. WASP America would indeed come to be undermined for two key reasons: 1) because it lacked a strong racial ingroup identity, but propagated instead the idea that, as long as immigrants "assimilated," Americans could co-exist in harmony; and 2) because this WASP culture was, in fact, infiltrated by Jewish groups determined to radicalize the concept of liberal openness. Backed by his extensive studies of Jewish intellectual groups, MacDonald explains how Jewish intellectuals successfully radicalized the Anglo-Saxon "sense of fairness and egalitarianism." While the Jews retained a very powerful ingroup identity, they consciously promoted multiculturalism in WASP America as a very effective evolutionary group strategy to protect themselves from "racist" WASPs, who might identify Jews as not sufficiently American. They argued, similarly, that it was illiberal to compel immigrants to assimilate to a dominant Anglo-Saxon culture, a violation of their individual rights and human dignity. America, as a liberal nation, was meant to be a "polycentric" culture characterized by the right of individuals regardless of race and ethnicity to choose their own values.

This intellectual displacement of the Darwinians (and the American intellectuals who emphasized their Anglo-Saxon cultural heritage) came together with the "unseen power" of Jewish international finance, academic influence, control of the media, and outright ownership of major newspapers. Examples of this Jewish power include the ability of Franz Boas and his followers to assume control over the American Anthropology Association, and of every major department of

anthropology, by 1926, displacing the Darwinians. During the post-WWII decades, with the unimpeded augmentation of Jewish influence, any form of eth-
nic/cultural nationalism among Europeans and North Americans was effectively
discredited as inherently belligerent and genocidal. More than any other group,
Jews pushed the idea that Western nations were founded on racism, patriarchal
domination, exploitation of the Third World, and that the mere existence of Western nations without racial diversity was a form of "White supremacy." The result
is that today, according to MacDonald, moral communities shaped by leftist values have become "pervasive throughout the institutional structures of the West."
The "conventional morality and intellectual discourse" of the West is dominated
by "leftist ideologies of race and ethnicity." While the "cohesion" of these communities is not grounded in ethnic ties, it is still "tribal" in the sense that those
who dissent from its values are "socially ostracized" and curtailed in their ability
to make a living.

Another powerful argument MacDonald makes is that while these communities are not grounded in ethnic ties, they do have a biological basis in an evolved
psychological need humans have to seek a "social identity" inside groups where
they are positively valued. The members of these moral communities are no less
inclined than kin groups to view outgroup members in negative terms. The nega-
tively evaluated outgroup, in our times, is defined primarily as Whites who have
an ingroup attachment to their race. The individual rights of those who dissent
from these moral communities can be curtailed, since they are members of a hated
outgroup. The average White person finds it hard to take a stand against these
moral communities, for Whites evolved an unusually high preoccupation with
their moral status and reputation well beyond their family, friends, and professional partners, across classes, races, and religious groups, for "honesty, trustworthiness and fairness." Whereas in societies with strong kinship norms, concern for
one's reputation ended "at the border of the family and the wider kinship group,"
among Whites today, one's reputation as a moral citizen hinges on one's ability to
treat foreigners who come illegally to the nation as equal partners. This preoccupation with one's moral reputation comes along with highly charged emotional
feelings of moral righteousness, which are very pleasurable, and may lead to an
irrational addiction to incessant moral approval from one's ingroup members.
The "empathy" Whites have for nonwhites, moreover, is backed up by "a very
elaborate infrastructure" that provides multiple opportunities for them. Whites
have been "incentivized" both economically and emotionally.

MacDonald ends his evolutionary psychological analysis on the positive observation that Whites still have ethnocentric tendencies. He draws a distinction between implicit and explicit processing of social or ingroup identities among Whites. Whites have retained an instinctive inclination to prefer members of their own race, as is evident in White flight, choice of neighborhoods and schools, and preference for the Republicans in the United States. But since these biases are prohibited, these behaviors are manifested implicitly rather than expressed openly or explicitly. Their ethnocentric inclinations are kept in check by their conscious "higher brain centers located in the cortex," which is the area of the brain that reasons and assimilates the values of society. MacDonald anticipates that, as Whites become aware of their "impending minority status," they will start gravitating towards White ethnocentrism. Whites will come to the realization that their culture of individualism, rule of law, and social trust require them to create moral communities that are "adaptive in a Darwinian sense." They will come to the realization that in nations that are committed to multiculturalism and the celebration of the ingroup identities of nonwhites, their only hope for survival is to create strong ingroups based on moral principles that value White history, traditions, and family—and exclude those who seek the destruction of Whites.

This is one of the strongest explanations out there on the current plight of Whites. I will end this section by reiterating my view that what Jews effectively did was to push the implications of liberal pluralism to their logical conclusion, by showing, for example, that "exclusionary" immigration policies on the basis of race or nationality violate the liberal principle that humans should be treated as morally equal in their dignity and capacity for free deliberation. The Darwinians were defeated for trying to hold on to the illiberal idea that some races are inherently superior, and that the founding WASP culture should be enforced as the ideal culture, holding thereby, from the standpoint of liberalism, "a conception of the good requiring the repression or degradation of certain persons on racial, or ethnic, or perfectionist grounds."[1187] Big businesses and conservative parties across the West have gone along with progressivism because they have come to accept that a liberal society cannot mandate racial and cultural collective identities. A few may admit that Jews (and other nonwhites) are indeed more ethnocentric, nepotistic, and thus hypocritical when they accuse Whites of "exclusionary" attitudes or practices. But, in the overall estimation of powerful White men: 1) Jewish financial power is consistent with capitalist-liberal meritocratic values; 2)

[1187] Rawls, 2005, 196.

the leading role of Jews in the articulation of leftist ideas and policies has been consistent with liberal moral ideals, which is why the foremost White liberal philosophers have gone along with these ideas, developing them together with Jews; and 3) it is widely expected that everyone, including Jews and nonwhites, will increasingly overcome their "ethnic biases" and become as individualistic and pluralistic as Whites—once the younger generations are properly socialized.

Conclusion: Liberalism Has Already Eaten Its Own Tail

The liberal West, the most accomplished civilization in history, the progenitor of all the disciplinary fields of knowledge, the greatest musicians, painters, furniture designers, writers of children's books, mathematicians, philosophers, et cetera, is now decomposing before our eyes. Past societies had huge problems: generalized poverty, endemic violence, mass illiteracy, and few opportunities for individual expression. Modern capitalist liberalism was not a failure from its inception. On the contrary: it has been responsible for the rule of law, open scientific inquiry, relatively peaceful resolution of political conflict, freedom of religious expression, numerous innovations, and sustained growth characterized by the efficient allocation of scarce resources and satisfaction of consumer choice.

What makes the internal decay of liberalism substantially different from prior civilizational declines is that it is a product of the progressive actualization of its own ideals. The result has been the creation of a contemporary Western world characterized by: 1) increasing racial discord coupled with relentless anti-White campaigns in schools and media; 2) persistent weakening of the institution of marriage, along with the demonization of maleness and the celebration of transsexualism; 3) high levels of inequality since the 1970s/80s despite massive growth in government spending; 4) decline of trust and community cohesion, isolation and anomie; 5) erasure of the history of the liberal West itself, its heroes and its symbols; 6) a state of complete paralysis in the face of the arrival of millions of migrants enticed by the principles of equal rights; and 7) suppression of open Enlightenment discourse in our universities and media in order to hide the reality that liberalism has failed for these reasons, and that there is now a growing body of scientific evidence refuting its fundamental premise that all human beings are born naturally equal, and that diversity ensures civil peace.

It is not necessary to elaborate on these claims, which are well-known in dissident circles, except to point out that liberalism, with its ontological claim that the individual is the measure of all things, with a natural right to demand "freedom from any collective identity whatsoever"—to use the words of Dugin—has deconstructed its very own civic communities, refuting its claim that individuals on their own can create a shared sense of identity and purpose. As noted in Robert Putnam's 2000 book, *Bowling Alone: The Collapse and Revival of American Community*, the US saw a dramatic decline, from the mid-1960s onwards, in membership and number of volunteers across a wide spectrum of civic organizations, such as religious groups, labor unions, parent–teacher associations, military veterans' organizations, volunteers with Boy Scouts and the Red Cross, and fraternal organizations, while becoming increasingly disconnected from family, friends, and neighbors. Despite widespread promises from liberal academics that with more grants and billions dedicated to "community development" they could reverse these trends, Putnam went on to recount twenty years later, in *The Upswing: How America Came Together a Century Ago and How We Can Do It Again*, a worsening state of affairs: "deep and accelerating inequality," "unprecedented political polarization," "vitriolic public discourse," "a fraying social fabric," "public and private narcissism." Putnam left readers with the hope that a more communitarian "We" society could emerge, if only American liberals learned to see what they had in common, by embracing their shared sense of liberal identity. He came to the same conclusion in an earlier study he conducted showing that diversity had substantially reduced social trust and community cohesion in the United States.[1188]

Putnam is drawing from a very influential form of "liberal communitarianism" that originated in the 1980s and 1990s, which included such prominent academics as Michael Sandel, Michael Walzer, Will Kymlicka, Allen Buchanan, and Charles Taylor. These academics consciously set out to improve Rawlsian liberalism, or what they called the "abstract individualism" of classical liberalism, by arguing that individuals can never be seen as isolated decision makers since they are always "culturally embedded" and "socially engaged" in their societies. Relying on civic republican motifs, they called upon Western governments to encourage the pursuit of "the good life" as a shared common goal, by crafting a balance between individual rights and social responsibilities. They encouraged governments and other institutions to promote "communitarian values," such as affection for the nation's history, caring for one's neighborhoods and civic associations, in combination with individual flourishing. In the end, though, after endless conferences, articles, books, and millions in government grants, this communitarian liberalism

---

[1188] Putnam, 2021; 2006.

would amount to nothing more than a push for a shared celebration of liberal progressivism, a shared belief that "diversity enriches us all," promotion of multicultural citizenship, celebration of gay parades, along with a shared commitment to the exclusion of "racism" as an attitude that no "decent" individual should be allowed to hold in public.

You cannot create a community by government fiat at the same time that you are promoting the liberation of individuals from all traditional constraints, family life, ethnic attachments, and demonizing their past history as "genocidal" and "systematically racist." The liberalism of the 1940s through to the 1970s, roughly speaking, worked relatively well in the degree to which it continued to be sustained by healthy sentiments and instincts rooted in human nature, acceptance of male/female distinctions, collective norms of motherhood, countless small towns with deeply rooted family businesses, high church attendance, customary regulation of sexual behavior, as well as respect for ancestors, symbols, and authoritative hierarchies. In other words, liberalism "worked" because it was still sustained by important non-liberal qualities from the past. The 1960s, however, saw a final push by liberalism to discredit, mock, devalue, and identify as oppressive these remaining traditions, leading to the liberal world of today populated by dead souls with barely any community ties, in charge of "reimagining" themselves and their societies as their "free" creations.

The result has been that, for all the billions spent by governments on communitarian projects, a higher proportion of citizens across the West are experiencing higher rates of loneliness, stress, anxiety and depression. The birth of loneliness, Fay Bound Alberti tells us in his 2019 *Biography of Loneliness*, is a unique product of the ideology of modern Western individualism. "Before 1800," he observes, "the English word 'loneliness' did not exist. People lived in small communities, they tended to believe in God (which meant they were never really alone, even when they were physically isolated), and there was a philosophical concept of the community as a source of common good. There was no need for a language of loneliness." Fast forward to today. A Surgeon General's Advisory released in 2023 admitted that loneliness or social isolation is an urgent health issue. Americans are lacking "relationships and interactions with family, friends, colleagues, and neighbors."[1189] A 2020 Harvard study on loneliness, reported that "36% of all American—including 61% of young adults and 51% of mothers with young

---

[1189] Murthy, 2023.

children—feel serious loneliness."[1190] Accompanying this social isolation are rising levels of depression and drug dependency. According to a 2019 Pew Research
Center report, "the total number of [American] teenagers who recently experienced depression increased 59% between 2007 and 2017."[1191] Prescription of an-
tidepressants in children aged five to twelve years "increased by more than 40%
between 2015 and 2021," according to *The Pharmaceutical Journal*.[1192] Deaths
from opioid use have skyrocketed.[1193] Similar trends in mental health issues and
drug abuse have been observed across EU countries.[1194]

And the isolation is going to get a lot worse: Only 22 percent of twenty-five-
year-olds were married in 2021, compared with 63 percent in 1980. It was reported
in 2017 that "40 percent of births in the United States occur outside of marriage,
up from 28 percent in 1990."[1195] The rate is almost double among Blacks. The
breakdown of the family, the primary institution of socialization, is accompanied
by the deterioration of the most important civic institution in the socialization of
children: schools. "Crime and violence have become common in schools today"
despite endless promotion of diversity and LGBT love, with students defecating
on floors and rubbing feces on the walls, using "hateful speech targeting teachers'
ethnicities and uttering homophobic slurs."[1196] School integration in the US has
failed.[1197] The one solution liberals can seem to come up with is blaming Whites
and lowering standards to keep White students at the same level as Blacks.[1198]

We could go on with additional statistics showing a serious breakdown in social cohesion, and increasing riots, looting, and sexual assaults. The only "progress" left for liberalism to accomplish is to continually "fix" the problems it continually creates. The West has no choice but to find an alternative ideology. I believe it has to be some form of traditionalism, as Dugin has been arguing, a "fourth
theory" beyond fascism, communism, and liberalism. It is called a "fourth theory"
for it does not advocate specific principles and policies for mankind as such, but
calls upon different cultures/civilizations in the world to find within themselves
their own alternative paths to modernity. This traditionalism rejects liberal

---

[1190] Weissbourd et al., 2021.
[1191] Geiger and Davis, 2019.
[1192] Robinson, 2021.
[1193] See NIH's "Drug Overdose Deaths: Facts and Figures."
[1194] Stewart, 2023.
[1195] Fry, 2023.
[1196] Chang, 2024; Macdonell, 2023.
[1197] TC Newsroom, 2020.
[1198] García, 2020.

unipolarism, the American/NATO effort to impose its liberal model upon all societies, in favor of what Dugin calls a multipolar world, where different civilizations and cultures construct their polities as they see fit within the millennial framework of their own heritage and values. For Russia in particular, Dugin has called for a complete break with liberal universalism and individualism in favor of a strong cultural nationalist state in charge of common values for Russian people. Although he rejects a racial nationalism based on biological criteria, he favors a cultural nationalist Russia in which children are brought up to feel Russian, to respect the traditions of their ancestors, "and everything is Russian—education, professions, way of life, social structure, patriotic spirit."[1199]

Re-creating traditionalism in the West will be an immensely difficult task, for the obvious reason that liberal pluralism is deeply rooted in the history and psychology of European peoples, ensconced in the deep state, in every institution, every political party, school, university, and countless written laws. The only realistic option may be for the West to revive an earlier version of liberalism, what Dugin calls "Liberalism 1.0," which emphasizes negative liberties, freedom of thought, without excessive "wokeness," without seeking to obliterate sexual differences, without critical race theory, and without anti-Christian attitudes. But this is not easy given the almost complete control leftists have over our institutions, the continuously high levels of immigration, and the in-built progressive tendency of liberalism writ large. This is a subject beyond the scope of this book.

I will conclude this arduous intellectual journey by saying that Western nations must legally guarantee the collective freedom of European ethnic groups to preserve and enhance their identity over and above the rights of abstract individuals. They should recognize the best values and practices of the Western aristocratic ethos of heroism, honor, and in-group loyalty. They should draw on the civic-republican and natural law principles of ancient Rome and medieval Europe. Citizens must be socialized not to be tolerant of all lifestyles and cultures, but to learn to appreciate both the highest and the everyday historical world of Europeans. They should be educated to be public citizens rather than mere private beings seeking their own lifestyles. Many things about the European past—small towns, family life, home cooking, local customs, small roads, folk beliefs, customs, architecture, civic associations, and modern popular culture—should be cherished, under the guidance of a collectivist state, rather than continually allowed to be dissipated and intermixed with corporate "ethnic" motifs, sounds, and smells.

[1199] Dugin, 2023.

A Heideggerian might counter that deep in Western history, in Platonism, Aristotelianism, the Catholic concept of natural law, through to modern philosophy and the principle of natural rights, one finds a metaphysics that has grounded the "progressive" dynamic of the West, driving this civilization towards modernity and beyond, with its notion that the whole world can be remade according to knowable, universal, and manipulable reason-based values and laws.[1200] In Plato, as Heidegger explains, one sees the first and most influential effort in Western history to transcend one's time and traditions through the construction of ideas aiming to be true for all time and in all contexts. While for the Presocratics the nature of things, what Heidegger calls "Being," retained a mysterious quality, a hiddenness despite all the inquiries of the mind, with Plato and after, Western reason comes to define itself as the light upon the nature of the universe, as the only agent capable of revealing what is the best political order and all that there is, by going beyond surface appearances and apprehending the unalterable and eternal. Rawls' argument that a pluralist society does not require a metaphysics that instructs citizens as to what the good life is, but merely calls for a pluralist setting within which diverging viewpoints are expressed in mutual respect, could not escape insisting that citizens must be socialized to become liberal-minded and progressive, and that a liberal lifestyle is superior to a non-liberal lifestyle. Thus, from a Heideggerian perspective, efforts to return to the pre-modern metaphysics of ancient or medieval times, and efforts to pretend that pluralism offers a door out of Western foundationalism, will make it incredibly difficult for Westerners, at this advanced stage when science and industrial growth have been given such enormous powers, to escape the metaphysics of liberal progressivism.

But a solution must be found, or Europeans will perish as a world-historical people, and their incomparable history will be slowly forgotten, cannibalized, or redefined as multicultural from its beginnings. This is a major reason for writing this book. Current and future generations may hopefully be inspired to defend and enhance European Civilization by this book's persistent emphasis on the incomparable achievements of their ancestors.

[1200] See Colin Cleary's carefully constructed multipart article at *Counter Currents*, "Heidegger's History of Metaphysics" (2020/2021).

Bibliography

Abraham, J.H. (1973). *Origins and Growth of Sociology*. Penguin Books.

Adams, Marcus P. (2023). Hobbes' Philosophy of Science. *The Stanford Encyclopedia of Philosophy*. In Edward N. Zalta & Uri Nodelman. (Eds.). https://plato.stanford.edu/archives/sum2023/entries/hobbes-science/.

Alberti, Fay Bound. (2019). *A Biography of Loneliness*. Oxford University Press.

Al-Daffa', Ali Abdullah. (1977). *The Muslim Contribution to Mathematics*. Humanities Press.

Al-Khwarizmi. (2024, September 28). In *Wikipedia*. https://en.wikipedia.org/wiki/Al-Khwarizmi.

Alderson, Brian. (Ed.). (1982). *Children's Books in England: Five Centuries of Social Life*. Cambridge University Press.

Alexander, Richard. (1979). *Darwinism and Human Affairs*. University of Washington Press.

Allentoft, Morten, E., et al. (2015). Population Genomics of Bronze Age Eurasia, *Nature*, 522(June 11), 167–172.

Alton, Hiebert Ann. (Ed.). (2011). *Peter Pan. J.M. Barrie*. Broadview Editions.

Amin, Ash. (Ed.). (1994). *Post-Fordism: A Reader*. Blackwell Publishers.

Anderson A, Chilczuk S, Nelson K, Ruther R, Wall-Scheffler C (2023), The Myth of Man the Hunter: Women's contribution to the hunt across ethnographic contexts. PLoS ONE, 18(6) https://doi.org/10.1371/journal.pone.0287101.

Anderson, P. (1979). *Considerations of Western Marxism*. Verso.

Anthony, David W. (2007). *The Horse, the Wheel, and Language*. Princeton University Press.

Anthony, David W. (2023). The Yamnaya Culture and the Invention of Nomadic Pastoralism in the Eurasian Steppes. In Kristiansen, Kristian; Guus Kroone, and Eske Willerslev. (Eds.). *The Indo-European Puzzle Revisited. Integrating Archeology, Genetics, and Linguistics*. Cambridge University Press.

Anthony, D. W. & Brown, D. (2017). The Dogs of War: A Bronze Age initiation ritual in the Russian Steppes. *Journal of Anthropological Archaeology*, 48, 134–148.

Anthony, David and Ringe, Donald. (2015). The Indo-European Homeland from Linguistic and Archaeological Perspectives. *Annual Review of Linguistics*, 1(1), 199–219. doi:10.1146/annurev-linguist-030514-124812.

Antweiler, Christoph. (2018). *Our Common Denominator: Human Universals Revisited*. Translated from the German by Diane Kerns. Berghahn Books.

Appleby, Joyce. (1992). *Liberalism and Republicanism in the Historical Imagination*. Harvard University Press.

Aquinas, Thomas. (1998). *Selected Writings*. Edited with an Introduction by Ralph McInerny. Penguin Books.

Ardrey, Robert. (1976). *The Hunting Hypothesis: A Personal Conclusion Concerning the Evolutionary Nature of Man*. Atheneum.

Aristotle. (1941). On the Soul. In Richard McKeon. (Ed.). *The Basic Works of Aristotle*. Random House.

Armbruster, Emilee. (2018, February 28). A Reflection of Me: Finding the Black Panther in Children's Books. DIBS. https://tinyurl.com/2f7acamx.

Armstrong, D. M. (1968). *A Materialist Theory of the Mind*. Routledge and Kegan Paul.

Arnason, Johann, S. N. Eisenstadt and Björn Wittrock. (2005). Introduction: History, Theory and Interpretation. In Johann Arnason, S. N. Eisenstadt and Björn Wittrock. (Eds.). *Axial Civilizations and World History*. Brill Publishers.

Arnheim, M.T.W. (1977). *Aristocracy in Greek Society*. Thames and Hudson.

Arnsdorf, Jeffrey Allan. (2020). *New Perspectives on Johannes de Muris and his Notitia artis musicae*. Dissertations and Theses. Paper 5624. https://doi.org/10.15760/etd.7496.

Arrian, Lucius Flavius. (1971). *The Campaigns of Alexander*. Penguin Classics.

Assmann, Jan. (2005). Axial 'Breakthroughs' and Semantic 'Relocations' in Ancient Egypt and Israel. In Johann P. Arneson, S. N. Eisenstadt, and Björn Wittrock. (Eds.). *Axial Civilizations and World History*. Brill Publishers.

Audard, Catherine. (2007). *John Rawls*. McGill-Queen's University Press.

Babb, Jeff. (2015). Mathematical Concepts and Proofs from Nicole Oresme. *Science and Education*, 14.

Bailyn, Bernard. (1967). *The Ideological Origins of the American Revolution*. Harvard University Press.

Baker, K. M. (2004). Sketch for a Historical Picture of the Progress of the Human Mind: Tenth Epoch. *Daedalus,* 133(3).

Balazs, Etienne. (1964). *Chinese Civilization and Bureaucracy*. Yale University Press.

Ball, Rouse, W. W. (1893). *A Short Account of The History of Mathematics*. Internet Archive: https://archive.org/details/117770582.

Ball, Warwick. (2016). *Rome in the East: The Transformation of an Empire*. Routledge.

Ball, Philip. (2002). *The Elements: A Very Short Introduction*. Oxford University Press.

Baluška F, Reber. (2019). A. Sentience and Consciousness in Single Cells: How the First Minds Emerged in Unicellular Species. *Bioessays*, 41(3).

Bambach, C. (1995). *Heidegger, Dilthey, and the Crisis of German Historicism*. Cornell University Press.

Bambach, C. (2003). *Heidegger's Roots. Nietzsche, National Socialism, and the Greeks*. Cornell University Press.

Barnes, Jonathan. (1982). *The Presocratic Philosophers*. Routledge.

Barton, Jeff. (2019). More "Gigantick Histories" that "altered the concept of children's books." https://blogs.princeton.edu/cotsen/tag/gigantic-histories/.

Barzun, Jacques. (2000). *From Dawn to Decadence: 500 Years of Western Cultural Life*. HarperCollins.

Baumer, F. (1978). *Main Currents of Western Thought: Readings in Western European Intellectual History from the Middle Ages to the Present*. Yale University Press.

Bean, Jonathan. (2018). Towards a New History of Civil Rights in U.S. History. In Michael J. Douma, Phillip W. Magness. (Eds*.*). *What Is Classical Liberal History?* Lexington Books.

Beckwith, Christopher. (2009). *Empires of the Silk Road: A History of Central Eurasia from the Bronze Age to the Present*. Princeton University Press.

Bedell, Geraldine. (2016). Teenage mental-health crisis: Rates of depression have soared in past 25 years. *Independent* (July 27).

Behrendt, Stephen, C. (2005). Women without Men: Barbara Hofland and the Economics of Widowhood. *Eighteenth-Century Fiction*, 17(3).

Bell, D. (2000). *The End of Ideology*. Harvard University Press.

Bell, Eric Temple. (1951). *Mathematics: Queen and Servant of Science*. McGraw-Hill Book Company.

Bellah, Robert. (2011). *Religion in Human Evolution: From the Paleolithic to the Axial Age*. Harvard University Press.

Bellah, N. Robert, Richard Madsen, William M. Sullivan, Ann Swidler, Steven M. Tipton. (2007). *Habits of the Heart: Individualism and Commitment in American Life, with a New Preface*. University of California Press.

Bellah, Robert and Hans Joas. (Eds.). (2012). *The Axial Age and Its Consequences*. Belknap Press.

Bellis, Mary. (2019). The History of Sports, from Ancient Times to Modern Day. *ThoughtCo* (25 May).

Belsky, Gary, Neil Fine. (2016). *On the Origins of Sports: The Early History and Original Rules of Everybody's Favorite Games*. Artisan.

Bendix, Reinhard. (1977). *Max Weber: An Intellectual Portrait*. University of California Press.

Benoist, de Alain. (2023). Deconstructing Liberalism. *Arktos Journal* (June 20).

Bentley, Jerry. (1993). *Old World Encounters: Cross-Cultural Contacts and Exchanges in Pre-Modern Times*. Oxford University Press.

Berlinghoff William and Fernando Gouvêa. (2015). *Math Through the Ages: A Gentle History for Teachers*. Dover Publications.

Berman, Harold J. (1983). *Law and Revolution, The Formation of the Western Legal Tradition*. Harvard University Press.

Biran, Michal, and Reuven Amitai. (Eds.). (2005). *Mongols, Turks and Others: Eurasian Nomads and the Sedentary World*. Brill Publishers.

Bisson, Thomas, N. (1973). *Medieval Representative Institutions, Their Origins and Nature*. Dryden Press.

Bixler, Phyllis. (1996). *The Secret Garden: Nature's Magic*. Twayne Publishers.

Blackmore, Robbie G. (2005). *History of Interior Design & Furniture: From Ancient Egypt to Nineteenth-Century Europe*. Wiley.

Bo, Cheng. (2014). Six Groups of Paradoxes in Ancient China From the Perspective of Comparative Philosophy. *Asian Philosophy*, 24(4), 363–392.

Bolander, Thomas. (2017). Self-Reference. In Edward N. Zalta. (Ed.). *The Stanford Encyclopedia of Philosophy*. https://tinyurl.com/ybm7vfb8.

Bolton, Kerry. (2017). *The Decline and Fall of Civilisations*. BlackHouse Publishers.

Bonner, Gerald. (2002). *Augustine of Hippo*: Life and Controversies. Canterbury Press.

Borden, Daniel, et al. (2008). *Architecture: A World History*. Harry N. Abrams.

Bourgeois, Quentin, and Eric Kroon. (2023). Emergent Properties on the Corded Ware Culture: An Information Approach. In Kristiansen, Kristian; Guus Kroone, and Eske Willerslev. (Eds.). *The Indo-European Puzzle Revisited. Integrating Archeology, Genetics, and Linguistics*. Cambridge University Press.

Boy, John. (2015). The Axial Age and the Problems of the Twentieth Century: Du Bois, Jaspers, and Universal History. *The American Sociologist, 46(2)*.

Boyer, Carl and Uta Merzbach. (1989). *A History of Mathematics*. Wiley.

Bozio, Antoine, Bertrand Garbinti, Jonathan Goupille-Lebret, Malka Guillot, and Thomas Piketty. (2024). *American Economic Journal: Applied Economics*, 16(2): 31–65.

Braudel, Ferdinand. (1980). *On History*. University of Chicago Press.

Braudel, Ferdinand. (1984). *Civilization and Capitalism. Vol 1: The Structures of Everyday Life*. Harper and Row.

Breisach, E. (1983). *Historiography. Ancient, Medieval & Modern*. University of Chicago Press.

Bremmer, Jan. (1983). *The Early Greek Concept of the Soul*. Princeton University Press.

Brereton, G. (1978) Introduction. In Geoffrey Brereton. (Ed.). *Jean Froissart Chronicles*. Penguin Books.

Brotton, Jerry. (2014). *Great Maps: The World's Masterpieces Explored and Explained*. Smithsonian Institution, DK History Changers.

Brown, P. (1967). *Augustine of Hippo*. University of California Press.

Brown, Penelope E. (2008). *A Critical History of French Children's Literature Volume One: 1600–1830*. Routledge.

Brown, Donald. (1991). *Human Universals*. Temple University Press.

Brown, Richard, Hakwan Lau, and Joseph E. LeDoux. (2019). Understanding the Higher-Order Approach to Consciousness. *Trends in Cognitive Sciences*, 23(9).

Burbidge, J. (1978). 'Unhappy Consciousness' in Hegel — An Analysis of Medieval Catholicism. *Mosaic: A Journal for the Interdisciplinary Study of Literature*, 11(4).

Burckhardt, Jacob. (2007). *Judgements on History and Historians*. Routledge Classics.

Burkhardt, Jacob. (1958). *The Civilization of the Renaissance in Italy, Volume I*. Harper TorchBooks.

Burkert, Walter. (1992). *The Orientalizing Revolution*. Cambridge University Press.

Burkert, Walter. (2004). *Babylon, Memphis, Persepolis, Eastern Contexts of Greek Culture.* Harvard University Press.

Burnett, Christie. (2024, August 23). 65 Picture Books About Diversity & Difference. Childhood101. https://tinyurl.com/5tbeay3f.

Burnham, James. (1964). *Suicide of the West: An Essay on the Meaning and Destiny of Liberalism.* The John Day Company.

Burrow, J. (2009). *A History of Histories: Epics, Chronicles, Romances and Inquiries from Herodotus and Thucydides to the Twentieth Century.* Vintage Books.

Bury, J. B. (1960). *The Idea of Progress: An inquiry into its growth and origin.* Dover Publications.

Butterfield, Herbert. (1965). *The Origins of Modern Science.* The Free Press.

Butterfield, H. (1981). *The Origins of History.* Eyre Methuen.

Butterfield, H. (1973). *The Whig Interpretation of History.* Penguin Books.

Cahill, James. (1960). *Chinese Painting.* The World Publishing Company.

Callaway, Ewen. (2014). Ancient European genomes reveal jumbled ancestry. *Nature* (02 January). https://doi.org/10.1038/nature.2014.14456.

Capaldi, Nicholas. (1983). The Libertarian Philosophy of John Stuart Mill. *Reason Papers*, 9.

Caplan, J. (1972). *Arnold Toynbee. A Study of History. A new edition, revised and abridged.* Oxford University. Press.

Carens, Joseph H. (1987). Aliens and Citizens: The Case for Open Borders. *The Review of Politics*, 49(2).

Carneiro, Robert. (2012). The Circumscription Theory: A Clarification, Amplification, and Reformulation. *Social Evolution & History,* 11(2).

Carr, E. H. (1974). *What is History?* Penguin Books.

Chadwick, Henry. (2001). The Early Christian Community. In: John McManners. (Ed.). *The Oxford Illustrated History of Christianity.* Oxford University Press.

Chadwick, John. (2005). *The Mycenaean World.* Cambridge University Press.

Champion, C. B. (2013). Polybius on Government, Interstate Relations, and Imperial Expansion. In Hans Beck. (Ed.). *A Companion to Ancient Greek Government.* John Wiley & Sons.

Chan, Wing-Tsit. (Ed.). (1970). *A Source Book in Chinese Philosophy.* Princeton University Press.

Chisholm, H. (Ed.). (1911). Orosius, Paulus. *Encyclopædia Britannica.* (11th Edition). Cambridge University Press.

Chow, Kai-Wing. (1994). *The Rise of Confucian Ritualism in Late Imperial China.* Stanford University Press.

Christian, David. (2005) *Maps of Time: An Introduction to Big History.* California University Press.

Churchland, Paul M. (1988). *Matter and Consciousness, A Contemporary Introduction to the Philosophy of Mind.* The MIT Press.

Cipolla, Carlo. (1967). *Clocks and Culture 1300–1700.* W.W. Norton & Company.

Clark, Gregory. (2007). *A Farewell to Alms: A Brief Economic History of the World.* Princeton University Press.

Clark, Kenneth. (1970). *Civilisation: A Personal View*. British Broadcasting Corporation.

Clark J. and Johnson, M. P. (2015). *The Incarnation of God: The Mystery of the Gospel as the Foundation for Evangelical Theology*. Crossway.

Cleary, Colin. (2020/2021). Heidegger's History of Metaphysics. *Counter Currents*.

Cochran, G. & Harpending, H. (2009). *The 10,000 Year Explosion: How Civilization Accelerated Human Evolution*. Basic Books.

Cohen, David. (2002). *How the Child Mind Develops*. Routledge.

Coleman, Daniel. (2006). *Social Intelligence: The New Science of Human Relationships*. Batam Books.

Colish, Marcia. (1998). *Medieval Foundations of the Western Intellectual Tradition 400–1400*. Yale University Press.

Collingwood, R. G. (1973). *The Idea of History*. Oxford University Press.

Collins, Randall. (1990). Weber's Theory of the Family. In Randall Collins, *Weberian Sociological Theory*. Cambridge University Press.

Conrad, S. (2012). Enlightenment in Global History: A Historiographical Critique. *American Historical Review*, 117(4).

Copleston, Frederick. (1963). *Aquinas*. Pelican Book.

Copleston, Frederick. (2003 [1946–1975]). *A History of Philosophy. Volumes 1 to 11*. Continuum.

Cornell, T. J. (2004). *The Beginnings of Rome*. Routledge.

Cotesta, Vittorio. (2015). *King into Gods: How Prostration Shaped Eurasian Civilizations*. Brill Publishers.

Courtland, Shane, D., Gerald Gaus, and David Schmidtz. (2022). Liberalism. In Edward N. Zalta (Ed.). *The Stanford Encyclopedia of Philosophy*. https://tinyurl.com/ybfd7p6d.

Crane, Nicholas. (2003). *Mercator. The Man Who Mapped the Planet*. Phoenix.

Crossan, John & Reed, Jonathan. (2004). *In Search of Paul: How Jesus's Apostle Opposed Rome's Empire with God's Kingdom*. Harper.

Cullen, C. (1976). A Chinese Eratosthenes of the Flat Earth: A Study of a Fragment of Cosmology in Huai Nan Tzu. *Bulletin of the School of Oriental and African Studies*. 39(1).

Dantzig, Tobias. (1956). *Number. The Language of Science*. A Double Day Book.

Dasen, P. (1994). Culture and cognitive development from a Piagetian perspective. In W. Lonner and R.S. Malpass. (Eds.). *Psychology and Culture*. Allyn and Bacon.

Dasgupta, Surendranath. (1922–1955). *A History of Indian Philosophy*. Cambridge University Press.

De Benoist, Alain. (2012). Critique of Liberal Ideology. *Counter Currents*, (May 28).

De George, Richard, T. and Fernande M. De George. (Eds.). (1972). *The Structuralists: From Marx to Levi-Strauss*. Anchor Books.

Dennett, Daniel. (2017*). From Bacteria to Bach and Back: The Evolution of Minds*. Norton.

Dennett, Daniel. (2020, September 12). Why Are We in the West So Weird? A Theory. *The New York Times*.

Descartes, René. (2008). *Discourse on the Method and Meditations*. Translated by John Veitch. Cosimo Classics.

Dewald, Carolyn. (Ed.). (2008). *The Histories by Herodotus.* Translated by Waterfield, Robin. Oxford University Press.

De Vries, Jan. (1994). The Industrious Revolution and the Industrial Revolution. *Journal of Economic History,* 54 (2), 249–270.

Diamond, J. (1999). The Worst Mistake in the History of the Human Race. *Discover* (May 1).

Diamond, J. (1997). *Guns, Germs, and Steel.* Norton & Co.

Domínguez-Rodrigo, M. (2002). Hunting and Scavenging by Early Humans: The State of the Debate. *Journal of World Prehistory,* 16(1), 1–54

Donald, Merlin. (1991). *Origins of the Modern Mind: Three Stages in the Evolution of Culture and Cognition.* Harvard University Press.

Donald, Merlin. (2001). *A Mind So Rare: The Evolution of Human Consciousness.* W.W. Norton.

Donald, Merlin. (2012). An Evolutionary Approach to Culture: Implication for the Study of the Axial Age. In Robert N. Bellah and Hans Joas (Eds.). *The Axial Age and Its Consequences.*

Donovan, Jack. (2012). *The Way of Men.* Dissonant.

Drews, Robert. (1989). *The Coming of the Greeks. Indo-European Conquests in the Aegean and the Near East.* Princeton University Press.

Duchesne, R. (2005). World history—for Africa, against Europe. *The European Legacy,* 10(1).

Duchesne, R. (2005). Centres and Margins: The Fall of Universal History and the Rise of Multicultural World History. In Marnie Hughes Warrington. (Ed.). *Palgrave Advances in World History.* Palgrave MacMillian.

Duchesne, R. (2006). Globalization, the Industrialization of Puerto Rico and the Limits of Dependency Theory. *Austrian Journal of Development Studies,* XXII.

Duchesne R. (2011). *The Uniqueness of Western Civilization.* Brill Publishers.

Duchesne, R. (2011b). Review of *Why The West Rules – For Now: The Patterns of History and What they Reveal about the Future,* (review no. 1091). https://tinyurl.com/2x5ykrup.

Duchesne, R. (2014). The Straussian Assault on America's European Heritage. *The Occidental Quarterly,* 14(3).

Duchesne, R. (2015). Germany Abolishers Itself. *The Salisbury Review,* 33(3).

Duchesne, R. (2015). The Greek-Roman Invention of Civic Identity Versus the Current Demotion of European Ethnicity. *The Occidental Quarterly,* 15(3).

Duchesne, R. (2017–2018). Johann Gottfried Herder: Advocate of European Perfection, Opponent of Multiculturalism. *The Occidental Quarterly.* 17(4).

Duchesne, R. (2017a). *Canada in Decay: Mass Immigration, Diversity, and the Ethnocide of Eurocanadians.* Blackhouse Publishers.

Duchesne, R. (2017b). *Faustian Man in a Multicultural Age.* Arktos.

Dugin, Alexander. (2012). *The Fourth Political Theory.* Arktos.

Dugin, Alexander. (2021). Liberalism 1.0. *KATEHON,* (13 April). https://katehon.com/en/article/liberalism-20.

Dugin. 2023. Making Russian Children. *Postil* (1 August).

Duncan, Alastair. (1994). *Art nouveau.* Norton.

Duncan, Alastair. (1988). *Art Deco.* Thames and Hudson.

Durant, W. (1965). *The Story of Philosophy: The Lives and Opinions of the Greater Philosophers.* Washington Square Press.

Durant, Will & Ariel. (2010). *Lessons of History.* Simon & Schuster.

Dutton, Edward and Charlton, Bruce. (2020). *The Genius Famine: Why We Need Geniuses, Why They're Dying Out and Why We Must Rescue Them.* University of Buckingham Press.

Dutton, Edward. (2022). *Spiteful Mutants: Evolution, Sexuality, Religion, and Politics in the 21st Century.* Radix.

Dzenis Sandra and Filipe Nobre Faria. (2020). Political Correctness: The Twofold Protection of Liberalism. *Philosophia,* 48(1), 95–114.

Earle, Timothy. (1997). *How Chiefs Came to Power.* Stanford University Press.

Edson, Evelyn. (2007). *The World Map, 1300–1492: The Persistence of Tradition and Transformation.* John Hopkins University Press.

Edwards, Owen. (2000, June 16). Edmund Burke on Rights: Inherited, Not Inherent. *The Imaginative Conservative.*

Ehrenberg, Victor. (1964). *The Greek State.* Norton Library.

Eisenstadt, S.N. (2000). Multiple Modernities. *Daedalus,* 129.

Elkana, Yehuda. (1986). The emergence of second-order thinking in classical Greece. In Eisenstadt, S.N. (Ed.). *The Origins and Diversity of Axial Age Civilizations.* State University of New York Press.

Ellman, B. (2002). The Historicization of Classical Learning in Ming-Ch'ing China. In E. Wang and G. Iggers. (Eds.). *Turning Points in Historiography: A Cross-Cultural Perspective.* University of Rochester Press.

Elvin, Mark. (2006). *The Retreat of Elephants: An Environmental History of China.* Yale University Press.

Erb-Satullo, N.L. (2019). The Innovation and Adoption of Iron in the Ancient Near East. *J Archaeol Res,* 27 (21 February), 557–607. https://doi.org/10.1007/s10814-019-09129-6.

Esolen, Anthony. (2002). *No Apologies: Why Civilization Depends on the Strength of Men.* Simon & Schuster.

Evans, R. J. (2014). Hans-Ulrich Wehler obituary. *The Guardian* (July 18).

Evelyn Reed. (1972). Introduction. In Engels, Friedrich. *Origin of the Family, Private Property, and the State.* Pathfinder Press.

Ewing, Juliana Horatia. (2018). *Jan of the windmill. A story of the plains.* CreateSpace Publishing.

Fadiman, Clifton. (1942). Foreword. In: Leo Tolstoy, *War and Peace.* Simon and Schuster.

Fairbank, John King. (1992). *China: A New History.* Harvard University Press.

Fallows, David. (2001). Ars nova. *The New Grove Dictionary of Music and Musicians.* Edited by Stanley Sadie and John Tyrrell. Macmillan.

Fazio, Michael, Marian Moffett, Lawrence Wodehouse. (2004). *A World History of* Architecture. McGraw-Hill.

Feinberg, Todd and Jon M. Mallatt. (2017.) *The Ancient Origins of Consciousness: How the Brain Created Experience.* The MIT Press.

Feng, Jiren. (2012). *Chinese Architecture and Metaphor: Song Culture in the Yingzao Fashi Building Manual.* University of Hawaii Press.

Fernandez-Armesto, Felipe. (2007). *The World—A History*. Pearson Prentice Hall.

Finley, M.I. (1954). *The World of Odysseus*. Viking.

Fisher, H.A. L. (1976). *A History of Europe*. Fontana/Collins.

Fisher, F. Fritz. (1970). Economic Expansion and World Power. In Sheppard B. Clough et al. (Eds.). *The European Past, Vol II. Reappraisals in History Since Waterloo*. The MacMillan Company.

Fletcher, Peter. (2004). *World Musics in Context: A Comprehensive Survey of the World's Major Musical Cultures*. Oxford University Press.

Flood, Alison. (2019). Campaigners hail 'seismic shift' in diversity of US children's books. *The Guardian* (22 March).

Foucault M. and Rabinow, P. (1984). *The Foucault Reader*. Vintage.

Francis, M. (2007). *Herbert Spencer and the Invention of Modern Life*. Routledge.

Francis, Sam T. (2019). Why the American Ruling Class Betrays Its Race and Civilization. *American Renaissance* (August 24).

Frank, A.G. (1998). *Re-Orient: Global Economy in the Asian Age*. University of California Press.

Fraser, Chris. (2020). Paradoxes in the School of Names. In Fung Yiu-Ming. (Ed.). *Dao Companion to Chinese Philosophy of Logic*.

Freeman, Samuel. (2007). *Rawls*. Routledge.

Frost, Peter. (2020). The Large Society Problem in Northwest Europe and East Asia. *Advances in Anthropology*, 1 (3), 214–234.

Fukuyama, F. (1992). *The End of History and the Last Man*. The Free Press.

Fukuyama, F. (2022). Preparing for Defeat. *American Purpose* (March).

Fung Yu-Lan. (1948). *A Short History of Chinese Philosophy*. The Free Press

Gabbay, Dov M. (Ed.). (2002–2012). *Handbook of the History of Logic, 11 vols*. Elsevier.

Garrison, James, W. (1987). Newton and the Relation of Mathematics to Natural Philosophy. *Journal of the History of Ideas*, 48(4), 609–627.

Gat, Azar. (2011). *Nations: The Long History and Deep Roots of Political Ethnicity and Nationalism*. Cambridge University Press.

Geertz, Clifford. (1974). From the Native's Point of View: On the Nature of Anthropological Understanding. *American Academy of Arts and Sciences*, 28(1).

Geiss, I. (1974). *July 1914. The Outbreak of the First World War. Selected Documents*. Norton & Co.

Gellner, Ernest. (1992). *Postmodernism, Reason, and Religion*. Routledge.

Gibbons, Ann. (2017). Thousands of horsemen may have swept into Bronze Age Europe, transforming the local population. *Science* (21 February).

Gibbons, Ann (2015). How Europeans Evolved White Skin. *Science News* (April 2).

Gienapp, Rebekah. (2024, February 16). 42 Powerful Children's Books about Race and Racism. Blog. https://www.rebekahgienapp.com/childrens-books-about-race/.

Gilderfus, M. (1987). *History and Historians: A Historiographical Introduction*. Prentice Hall.

Gill, Christopher. (1996). *Personality in Greek Epic, Tragedy and Philosophy. The Self in Dialogue*. Oxford University Press.

Gillispie, Charles Coulston. (1973). *The Edge of Objectivity. An Essay on the History of Scientific Ideas*. Princeton University Press.

Gilmore, David. (1990). *Manhood in the Making: Cultural Concepts of Masculinity*. Yale University Press.

Gimbutas, Marija. (1997). *The Kurgan Culture and the Indo-Europeanization of Europe. Selected Articles from 1952 to 1992*. Edited by Mirriam Dexter and K. Jones-Bley. *The Journal of Indo-European Studies Monograph Series* No. 18.

Ginsburg, H. P. and Opper, S. (1988). *Piaget's theory of intellectual development*. Prentice-Hall, Inc.

Gleason, Harold, Warren Becke. (1981). *Music in the Middle Ages and the Renaissance*. Alfred Publishing.

Gohau, Gabriel. (1991). *A History of Geology*. Rutgers University Press.

Goldhill, Simon. (2002). *The Invention of Prose*. Cambridge University Press.

Goldstone, Jack. (2009). *Why Europe? The Rise of the West in World History, 1500–1850*. McGraw Hill.

Gombrich. E.H. (1967). *The Story of Art*. Phaidon Publishers.

Goodwin, W. (1798). *An Inquiry Concerning Political Justice*. http://knarf.english.upenn.edu/Godwin/pj87.html.

Gordon, Lynn and David Louzecky. (2023). Stuart Mill & Harriet Taylor Mill on Equality in Marriage & Family. *Philosophy Now*, 154 (February/March).

Gordon-Roth, Jessica. Locke on Personal Identity. (2020). In Edward N. Zalta. (Ed.). *The Stanford Encyclopedia of Philosophy*.

Gostin, Lawrence. (2021). Vaccine Mandates Are Lawful, Effective and Based on Rock-Solid Science. *Scientific American* (August 5).

Gottfried, Paul. (2011). Yes Virginia [Dare], There Is a Cultural Marxism *VDare* (15 October).

Gottfried, Paul. (2001). *After Liberalism: Mass Democracy in the Managerial State*. Princeton University Press.

Gottfried, Paul. (2023). Woke Liberalism? *American Greatness* (20 April).

Gould, J. (1994). *Herodotus and Religion*. In Simon Hornblower. (Ed.). *Greek Historiography*. Clarendon Press.

Goupille-Lebret, Jonathan Thomas Piketty, Bertrand Garbinti. (2018). Income inequality in France: Economic growth and the gender gap. *Vox CEPR* (September 5).

Grant, M. (1970). *The Ancient Historians*. Weindenfeld and Nicholson.

Gray, Aysa. (2019). The Bias of 'Professionalism' Standards. *Stanford Social Innovation Review* (June 4).

Grayling, A.C. (2019). *The History of Philosophy*. Penguin Press.

Green, Thomas. (2015). *Works of Thomas Hill Green*. Edited by R. L. Nettleship. Cambridge University Press.

Gregersen, Erik. (2011). *The Britannica Guide to the History of Mathematics*. Rosen Education Service.

Gregory of Tours. (1974). *History of the Franks*. Translated with an Introduction by Lewis Thorpe. Penguin Books.

Greif, Avner. (2006). Family Structure, Institutions, and Growth: The Origins and Implications of Western Corporations. *American Economic Review*, 96(2), 308–312.

Gress, D. (1998). *From Plato to NATO: The Idea of the West and Its Opponents*. The Free Press.

Gress D. (1989). The case against Martin Bernal. *The New Criterion*, 1.

Gribbin, John. (2002). *The Scientists: A History of Science Told Through the Lives of Its Greatest Scientists*. Random House.

Griffin, Jasper. (2006). The True Epic Vision" review of Gilgamesh: A New English Version. *New York Review of Books* (9 March).

Guest, Ann Hutchinson. (1998). *Choreo-Graphics: A Comparison of Dance Notation Systems from the Fifteenth Century to the Present*. Gordon and Breach.

Gunther, Hans. (2001). *The Religious Attitudes of Indo-Europeans*. Historical Review Press.

Gurevich, Aaron. (1995). *The Origins of European Individualism*. Blackwell.

Gutting, Gary and Johanna Oksala. (2022). Michel Foucault. In Edward N. Zalta & Uri Nodelman (Eds.). *The Stanford Encyclopedia of Philosophy*. https://plato.stanford.edu/archives/fall2022/entries/foucault/.

Guyenot, Laurent. (2020). How Yahweh Conquered Rome. *The Unz Review*. (25 December).

Haak, Wolfgang, et al. (2015). Massive Migration from the Steppe Was a Source for Indo-European Languages in Europe. Nature, 522 (11 June), 207–211. https://www.ncbi.nlm.nih.gov/pmc/articles/PMC50482192.

Habermas, Jurgen. (1979). Moral Development and Ego Identity. In Jurgen Habermas, *Communication and the Evolution of Society*. Beacon Press.

Habermas, Jurgen. (1981). *Theory of Communicative Action, Volume One: Reason and the Rationalization of Society*. Translated by Thomas A. McCarthy. Beacon Press.

Habermas, Jurgen. (1991). *The Structural Transformation of the Public Sphere: An Inquiry into a Category of Bourgeois Society*. MIT Press.

Habermas, Jurgen. (1990). *The Philosophical Discourse of Modernity: Twelve Lectures*. MIT Press.

Hajnal, John. (1965). *European marriage pattern in historical perspective*. In D.V. Glass and D.E.C. Eversley. (Eds.). *Population in History*. Routledge.

Hall, A.R. (1960). *The Scientific Revolution, 1500–1800: The Formation of the Modern Scientific Attitude*. Beacon Press.

Hall, David L., and Roger T. Ames. (1998). *Thinking from the Han: Self, Truth, and Transcendence in Chinese and Western Culture*. State of University New York Press.

Hallpike, C.R. (1979). *Foundations of Primitive Thought*. Clarendon Press.

Hamilton, E. (1942). *The Greek Way*. Norton & Co.

Hamilton, Sue. (2001). Indian Philosophy: A Very Short Introduction. Oxford Paperbacks.

Hanel, Andrea, Carsten Carlberg. (2020). Skin colour and vitamin D: An update. *Experimental Dermatology*, 29(9).

Hansen, Chad. (1983). *Language and Logic in Ancient China*. University of Michigan Press.

Hanson, Victor Davis. (1999). *The Other Greeks, The Family Farm and the Agrarian Roots of Western Civilization*. California University Press.

Harari, Y. N. (2014). *Sapiens: A Brief History of Humankind*. Random House.

Harman, Graham. (2007). *Heidegger Explained. From Phenomenon to Thing*. Open Court.

Harper, Kyle. (2013). *From Shame to Sin: The Christian Transformation of Sexual Morality in Late Antiquity*. Harvard University Press.

Harris, Marvin. (1971). *The Rise of Anthropological Theory*. Thomas Y. Crowell Company.

Harris, William V. (1989). *Ancient Literacy*. Harvard University Press.

Hart, Michael. (2007). *Understanding History*. Washington Summit Publishers.

Hartmann, Nicolai. (2012 [1952]). *New Ways of Ontology*. Reprinted with a new introduction by P. Cicovacki. Transaction Publishers.

Harvey, F.D. (1966). Literacy in the Athenian Democracy. *Revue des Études Grecques*, 79, 585–635.

Hatch, Edwin. (1895). *The Influence of Greek Ideas on Christianity*. C. Green and Son.

Hauser, Arnold. (1973). *The Social History of Art. Volume One: From Prehistoric Times to the Middle Ages*. Routledge & Kegan Paul.

Hauser, Arnold. (1972). *The Social History of Art. Volume Two: Renaissance, Mannerism, and Baroque*. Routledge & Kegan Paul.

Hauser, Arnold. (1973). *The Social History of* Art. *Volume Three: Rococo, Classicism, and Romanticism*. Routledge & Kegan Paul.

Hauser, Arnold. (1972). *The Social History of* Art. *Volume Four: Naturalism, Impressionism, The Film Age*. Routledge & Kegan Paul.

Hauser, Marc. (2000). *Wild Minds: What Animals Really Think*. Henry Holt and Company.

Havelock, Eric. (1963). *Preface to Plato*. The Belknap Press of Harvard University Press.

Haven, Alice Bradley. (1862 [1854]). *Nothing Venture, Nothing Have*. D. Appleton and Company.

Headley, John. (1987). Review: The Reformation in Historical Thought. *Journal of the History of Ideas*, 48(3).

Headley, John. (2008). *The Europeanization of the World: On the Origins of Human Rights and Democracy*. Princeton University Press.

Hearn, Marcus (2005). *Civilisation*. London: BBC. OCLC 778343652.

Heath, Anthony F., Roger M. Jowell, and John K. Curtice. (2001). *The Rise of New Labour: Party Policies and Voter Choices*. Oxford University Press.

Heath, Thomas. (1921). *A History of Greek Mathematics*. Clarendon Press.

Heffer, Simon. (2022). *High Minds. The Victorians and the Birth of Modern Britain*. Pegasus Books.

Hegel, G.W.F. (1956). *The Philosophy of History*. Translated by J. Sibree. Dover Publications.

Hegel, G.W.F. (1971). *Philosophy of Mind. Being Part Three of the Encyclopedia of the Philosophical Sciences*. Translated by William Wallace and A. V. Miller. Oxford University Press.

Hegel, G.W.F. (1977). *Phenomenology of Spirit*. Translated by A.V. Miller. Oxford University Press.

Hegel, G.W.F. (2003). *Introduction to the Lectures on the History of Philosophy*. Translated by T.M Knox and A.V. Miller. Clarendon Press.

Hegel, G.W.F. (1995). *Lectures on the History of* Philosophy. *Volume 1: Greek Philosophy to Plato, Volume 2: Plato and the Platonists, Volume 3: Medieval and Modern Philosophy*. Translated by H.S. Haldane and Frances H. Simson. University of Nebraska Press.

Hegel, Robert E. (2002). Introduction. In Kuang-chung, Lo. *Romance of the Three Kingdoms. Volume 1 and 2*. Translated by C.H. Brewitt-Taylor. Tuttle Publishing.

Heidegger, Martin. (1961). *Introduction to Metaphysics*. Anchor Books.

Heiner, Roetz. (1993). *Confucian Ethics of the Axial Age*. State University of New York Press.

Heller, H. (1994). Bodin on Slavery and Primitive Accumulation. *The Sixteenth Century Journal*, 25(1).

Hengel, Martin. (1974). *Judaism and Hellenism: Studies in Their Encounter in Palestine During the Early Hellenistic Period*. Fortress Press.

Henrich, Joseph. (2010). *Polygyny in Cross Cultural Perspective: Theory and Implications*. https://www.vancouversun.com/pdf/affidavit.pdf.

Henrich, Joseph. (2020). *The WEIRDest People in the World: How the West Became Psychologically Peculiar and Particularly Prosperous*. Farrar, Straus and Giroux.

Henrich, Joseph. (2021). *Why Immigration Drives Innovation. Evonomics: The Next Evolution of Economics* (9 January).

Henss, Ronald. (2024). "The Intelligence of Nations. National IQs and Correlates" *Qeios*, CC-BY 4.0 (May 6).

Herman, A. (2001). *How the Scots Invented the Modern World*. Three Rivers Press.

Herman, A. (1997). *The Idea of Decline in Western History*. The Free Press.

Higonnet, Anne. (2005). *Pictures of Innocence: The History and Crisis of Ideal Childhood*. Thames and Hudson.

Hill, Kim. (1982). Hunting and human evolution. *Journal of Human Evolution*, 11(6), 521–544.

Hillar, Mirian. (2012). *From Logos to Trinity: The Evolution of Religious Beliefs from Pythagoras to Tertullian*. Cambridge University Press.

Ho, Norman. (2017). Natural Law in Chinese Legal Thought: The Philosophical System of Wang Yangming. *Yonsei Law Journal*, 8(1 & 2).

Hobbes, Thomas. (1985). *The Leviathan*. Penguin Books Limited.

Hobhouse, Leonard. (1994). *Liberalism and Other Writings*. Edited by James Meadowcroft. Cambridge University Press.

Hobsbawm, E. (1987). *The Age of Empire: 1875–1914*. Weidenfeld and Nicholson.

Hobson, John M. (2004). *The Eastern Origins of Western Civilization*. Cambridge University Press.

Hoffman, Philip T. (2015). *Why Did Europe Conquer the World?* Princeton University Press.

Hofstadter, R. (1992). *Social Darwinism in American Thought*. Beacon Press.

Holbrook, Peter. (2013). *Shakespeare's Individualism*. Cambridge University Press.

Holland, Tom. (2019). *Dominion: How the Christian Revolution Remade the World*. Basic Books.

Hollingdale, Stuart. (1989). *Makers of Mathematics*. Penguin Books.

Holmes, Bob. (2003). Man's early hunting role in doubt. *New Scientist* (6 January).

Hosch, William L. (Ed.). (2010). *The Britannica Guide to Numbers and Measurement*. The Rosen Publishing Group.

Hough, Richard. (1995). *Captain James Cook: A Biography*. W. W. Norton.

Hu, Shih. (1953). The Natural Law in the Chinese Tradition. In CP. Chou. (2013). *English Writings of Hu Shih*. China Academic Library. Springer. https://doi.org/10.1007/978-3-642-31181-9_21

Hubner, Wolfgang. (2000). "The Ptolemaic View of the Universe" *Greek, Roman, and Byzantine Studies*, 41.

Huff, Toby. (1993). *The Rise of Early Modern Science: Islam, China, and the West*. Cambridge University Press.

Hughes, Patrick and George Brecht. (1984). *Vicious Circles and Infinity: An Anthology of Paradoxes*. Penguin Books.

Humphrey, Nicholas. (1992). *A History of the Mind. Evolution and Birth of Consciousness*. Simon & Schuster.

Humphrey, Nicholas. (1986). *The Inner Eye. Social Intelligence in Evolution*. Oxford University Press.

Humphreys. (2002). Turning Points in Islamic Historiographical Practice. In: E. Wang and G. Iggers. (Eds.). *Turning Points in Historiography: A Cross-Cultural Perspective*. University of Rochester Press

Hunt, Peter. (Ed.). (1995). *Children's Literature: An Illustrated History*. Oxford University Press.

Hunt, Morton. (2007). *The Story of Psychology*. Anchor Books.

Hutton, Sarah. (2023). *The Cambridge Platonists*. Routledge.

Iggers, G. (1984). *The German Conception of History. The National Tradition of Historical Thought from Herder to the Present*. Wesleyan University Press.

Iggers, G. (2005). *Historiography in the Twentieth Century: From Scientific Objectivity to the Postmodern Challenge*. Wesleyan University Press.

Jackson, Roland John. (2023). Counterpoint Music. *Encyclopedia Britannica* https://www.britannica.com/art/counterpoint-music.

Jaeger, Werner. (1986) [1939–1944]. *Paideia: The Ideals of Greek Culture. Volume 1: Archaic Greece and the Mind of Athens, Volume 2: In Search of the Divine Centre, Volume 3: The Conflict of Ideals in the Age of Plato*. Oxford University Press.

Jaeger, Werner. (1961). *Early Christianity and Greek Paideia*. Harvard University Press.

Janson, H. W. (1971). *History of Art: A Survey of the Major Visual Arts from the Dawn of History to the Present*. Prentice Hall.

Jarzombek, Ching, and Prakash. (2017). *A Global History of Architecture*. Wiley.

Jaspers, Karl. (1965 [1947]). *The Question of German Guilt*. Fordham University Press.

Jaspers, Karl. (1965). *The Origin and Goal of History*. Yale University Press.

Jaynes, Julian. (1976). *The Origins of Consciousness in the Breakdown of the Bicameral Mind*. University of Toronto Press

Jenkins, S. (2011). What Does Nietzsche Owe Thucydides? *Journal of Nietzsche Studies*, 42(1), 32–50.

Johnston, Ian. (1988). *The Ironies of War: An Introduction to Homer's Iliad*. University Press of America.

Johnston, Ian. Published English Translations of Homer's Iliad and Odyssey http://johnstoniatexts.x10host.com/homer/homertranslations.htm

Johnstone, Mark A. (2014). On 'Logos' in Heraclitus. In Brad Inwood. (Ed.). *Oxford Studies in Ancient Philosophy*, 47.

Johnstone, Christopher Lyle. (2009). *Listening to Logos: Speech and the Coming of Wisdom in Ancient Greece*. University of South Carolina Press.

Jones, Alexander and Liba Taub. (Eds.). (2018). *Science after Aristotle: Hellenistic and Roman Science*. Cambridge University Press.

Joseph, George Gheverghese. (2000). *The Peacock: Non-European Roots of Mathematics*. Princeton University Press.

Joseph, George Gheverghese, and Julian Williams. (1993). *Multicultural Mathematics*. Oxford University Press.

Jullien, Francois. (2004). *Detour and Access, Strategies of Meaning in China and Greece*. Zone Books.

Jung, C.G. ([1921] 1971). *Psychological Types, Collected Works, Volume 6*. Princeton University Press.

Jung, C. G. (1933). *Modern Man in Search of a Soul*. Harvest Book.

Kain, Philip J. (2005). *Hegel and the Other. A Study of the Phenomenology of Spirit*. Albany University Press.

Kaku, Michio. (2014). *The Future of the Mind: The Scientific Quest to Understand, Enhance, and Empower the Mind*. Doubleday.

Kant, Immanuel. (1950). *Prolegomena to Any Future Metaphysics*. The Bobbs and Merrill Company.

Kant, Immanuel. (1963) "Idea for a Universal History from a Cosmopolitan Point of View". In Lewis White Beck. (Eds.). *Kant On History*. The Bobbs-Merrill Co.

Kant, Immanuel. (1993). *Grounding for the Metaphysics of Morals*. Translator James Ellington. Hackett Publishing.

Kant, Immanuel. (2012). *Critique of Judgment*. J.H. Dover Publications.

Kant, Immanuel. (1999). An answer to the question: What is enlightenment? In Mary J. Gregor. (Ed.). *Practical Philosophy. The Cambridge Edition of the Works of Immanuel Kant*. Cambridge University Press.

Kaye, H. J. (1984). *The British Marxist Historians*. Polity Press.

Keegan, John. (1996). *A History of Warfare*. Vintage Books.

Keetle, Martin. (2013). Wagner bicentenary: the music is still what matters most. *The Guardian* (May 22).

Kelekna, Pita. (2009). *The Horse in Human History*. Cambridge University Press.

Kenny, Anthony. (2006). *The Rise of Modern Philosophy, Volume 3 of A New History of Western Philosophy*. Clarendon Press.

Kernohan, Andrew. (1998). *Liberalism, equality, and cultural oppression*. Cambridge University Press.

Kertzer, David I and Marzio Barbagli. (2001). *The history of the European family*. Yale University Press.

Keuth, H. (2015). "The positivist dispute in German sociology: A scientific or a political controversy?" *Journal of Classical Sociology*, 15(2).

King, Katherine. (1987). *Achilles: Paradigms of the War Hero from Homer to the Middle Ages*. University of California

Kirk, G.S., and J.E. Raven. (1957). *The Presocratic Philosophers*. Cambridge University Press.

Klecel W, Martyniuk E. (2021). From the Eurasian Steppes to the Roman Circuses: A Review of Early Development of Horse Breeding and *Management Animals*, 11(7).

Kline, Morris. (1972). *Mathematical Thought from Ancient to Modern Times*. Oxford University Press.

Kline, Morris. (1978). *History of Western Mathematics*. Oxford University Pres.

Kolenda, Konstantin (1974). *Philosophy's Journey: A Historical Introduction*. Addison Wesley Publishing Company.

Knox, Bernard. (1990). Introduction. In *Homer: The Iliad*. Translated by Robert Fagles. Viking.

Knox, Bernard (1994) *The Oldest Dead White Males*. Norton.

Kohlberg, Lawrence. (1971). From Is to Ought. In Theodore Mischel. (Ed.). *Cognitive Development and Epistemology*. Academic Press.

Kojève, Alexander. (1999) *Introduction to the Reading of Hegel: Lectures on the Phenomenology of Spirit*. Translated by Raymond Queneau and edited by Allan Bloom. Cornell University Press.

Kovačev, ASja Nina. (2009). Return to the Origins – Wagner, Jung, and Symbolic Forms. *Musicological Annual*, 45(1).

Kramer, Samuel. (1959). *History Begins at Sumer*. Anchor Books.

Krebs, C. (2011). *A Most Dangerous Book: Tacitus's Germania from the Roman Empire to the Third Reich*. Norton & Co.

Kristiansen, Kristian; Guus Kroone, and Eske Willerslev. (Eds.). (2023). *The Indo-European Puzzle Revisited. Integrating Archeology, Genetics, and Linguistics*. Cambridge University Press.

Kristiansen, K., et al. (2017). Re-theorising mobility and the formation of culture and language among the Corded Ware Culture in Europe. *Antiquity*, 91(356), 334–347.

Kristiansen, Kristian. (1991). Chiefdoms, States, and systems of social evolution. In Timothy Earle. (Ed.). *Chiefdoms: Power, Economy, and Ideology*. Cambridge University Press.

Kuehn, M. (2001). *Kant, A Biography*. Cambridge University Press.

Kuhn, Thomas S. (1970). *The Structure of Scientific Revolutions*. University of Chicago Press.

Kulke, Hermann and Dietmar Rothermund. (1995). *A History of India*. Routledge.

Kull, Andrew. (1992). *The Color-Blind Constitution*. Harvard University Press.

Kurer, O. (1989). John Stuart Mill on Government. *History of Political Thought*, 10(3), 457–480.

Kymlicka, Will. (2007). Ethnocultural Diversity in a Liberal State: Making Sense of the Canadian Model(s). In Keith Banting, Thomas Courchene and Leslie Seidle. (Eds.). *Belonging? Diversity, Recognition and Shared Citizenship in Canada*. Institute for Research on Public Policy.

Lacy, W.K. (1968). *The Family in Classical Greece*. Cornell University Press.

Laden, A. S. (2003). *The House That Jack Built: Thirty Years of Reading Rawls. Ethics*, 113(2).

Laks, André. (2018). *The Concept of Presocratic Philosophy: Its Origin, Development, and Significance*. Princeton University Press.

Lal, V. (2002). The Subaltern School and the Ascendancy of Indian History. In Edward Wang and George Iggers. (Eds.). *Turning Points in Historiography: A Cross-Cultural Perspective*. University of Rochester Press.

Landes, David. (1983). *Revolution in Time: Clocks and the Making of the Modern World.* Harvard University Press.

Larrick, Nancy. (1965). The All-White World of Children's Books. *Saturday Review* (September 11).

Lawrence, Michael, Anthony. (2016). Justice as Fairness as Judicial Guiding Principle: Remember John Rawls and the Warren Court. *Brooklyn Law Review*, 81(2).

Lawrence, Mishel, and Jori Kandra. (2020). Wages for the top 1% skyrocketed 160% since 1979 while the share of wages for the bottom 90% shrunk. *Economic Policy Institute* (1 December).

Lazaridis, Haak, W. I. Patterson, N. *et al.* (2015). Massive migration from the steppe was a source for Indo-European languages in Europe. *Nature*, 522, 207–211. https://doi.org/10.1038/nature14317.

Le Doux, Joseph. (2019). *The Deep History of Ourselves: The Four-Billion-Year Story of How We Got Conscious Brains.* Viking.

Lee, T. (2002). New Directions in Northern Sung Historical Thinking (960–1126). In E. Wang and G. Iggers. (Eds.). *Turning Points in Historiography: A Cross-Cultural Perspective.* University of Rochester Press.

Leishman, Rachel. (2017). Harry Potter and the Lack of Diversity in the Film Franchise. https://culturess.com/2017/04/30/harry-potter-lack-diversity/.

LePan, Donald. (1989). *The Cognitive Revolution in Western Culture.* Macmillan Press.

Leonhardt, David. (2017). Our Broken Economy, in One Simple Chart. *New York Times* (7 August).

Levin, Flora R. (2009). *Greek Reflections on the Nature of Music.* Cambridge University Press.

Levinson, David, Karen Christensen. (Eds.). (1999). *Encyclopedia of World Sport From Ancient Times to the Present.* Oxford University Press.

Levitt, Theodore. (1983). The Globalization of Markets. *Harvard Business Review* (May).

Levy, Joel. (2011). *The Bedside Book of Chemistry: From Molecules to Elements: The Chemistry of Everyday Life.* New Burlington Books.

Lévy-Bruhl, Lucien. (2018 [1923]). *Primitive Mentality.* Forgotten Books.

Lindauer, Matthew. (2021). Entry by Birth Alone? *Social Theory and Practice* 47(2).

Lloyd, Dennis. (1979). *Introduction to Jurisprudence.* Stevens & Co. 4th ed.

Locke, John. (1996). *Some Thoughts Concerning Education* Grant. Edited by Ruth Weissbourd Grant and Nathan Tarcov. Hackett Publishing.

Locke, John. (1983). *A Letter Concerning Toleration.* In Tully, James H. T. (Ed.). Hackett Publishing.

Locke, John. (1998). *Two Treatises of Government.* Edited by Peter Laslett. Cambridge University Press.

Long, A. A. & Sedley, D. N. (1987). Free Will. In Long, A. A. & Sedley, D. M. (Eds.). *The Hellenistic Philosophers, Volume 1: Translations of the Principal Sources with Philosophical Commentary.* Cambridge University Press.

Lopez, Robert, S. (1976). *The Commercial Revolution of the Middle Ages, 950–1350.* Cambridge University Press.

Lord, L. (1925). Tacitus the Historian. *The Classical Journal* 21 (3).

Love, John. (2000). Max Weber's Orient. In Stephen Turner. (Ed.). *The Cambridge Companion to Weber*. Cambridge University Press.

Lovejoy, Arthur. (1960) [1936]. *The Great Chain of Being: A Study of the History of An Idea*. Harper Torchbooks.

Lovett, F. (2022). Republicanism. In Edward Zalta & Uri Nodelman. (Eds.). *The Stanford Encyclopedia of Philosophy*. https://tinyurl.com/23p93mj8.

Lowith, K. (1949). *Meaning in History*. University of Chicago Press.

Luce, J.V. (1975). *Homer and the Heroic Age*. Harper & Row.

Luce, J.V. (1988). Greek Science in its Hellenistic Phase. *Hermathena*, 145 (Winter), 23–38.

Lukes, Steven. (1971). The Meanings of 'Individualism.' *Journal of the History of Ideas*, 32(1).

MacDonald, Kevin. (1990). *Mechanisms of Sexual Egalitarianism in Western Europe. Ethology and Sociobiology*, 11(3), 195–237.

MacDonald, Kevin. (1995). The Establishment and Maintenance of Socially Imposed Monogamy in Western Europe. *Politics and Life Sciences*. 14(1), 3–23.

MacDonald, Kevin. (2019). *Individualism and the Western* Liberal Tradition: *Evolutionary Origins, History, and Prospects for the Future*. Kindle Direct Publishing Edition.

MacDonald, Kevin. (2021). Understanding Western Uniqueness: A Comment on Joseph Henrich's The WEIRDest People in the World. *Mankind Quarterly*, 61(3).

Macfarlane, Alan. (1978). *The Origins of English Individualism: The Family, Property and Social Transition*. Cambridge University Press.

Machiavelli, N. (1998). *The Discourses*. Edited with an Introduction by Bernard Crick, and Translated by Leslie Walker. Penguin Books.

MacIntyre, Alasdair. (2003). *After Virtue*. University of Notre Dame Press.

MacLeod, Anne Scott. (1975). *A Moral Tale Children's Fiction and American Culture, 1820– 1860*. Archon Books.

Mallory, J. P. (1989). *In Search of Indo-Europeans. Language, Archeology, and Myth*. Thames and Hudson.

Mallory, J. P. (2006). Indo-European Warfare. *Journal of conflict archaeology*, 2(1), 77–98.

Mallory, J. P. (2023). From the Steppe to Ireland: The Impact of aDNA Research. In Kristiansen, Kristian; Guus Kroone, and Eske Willerslev. (Eds.). (2023). *The Indo-European Puzzle Revisited. Integrating Archeology, Genetics, and Linguistics*. Cambridge University Press.

Mallory, J. P. and D. Q. Adams (Eds.). (2006). *The Oxford Introduction to Proto-Indo-European and the Proto-Indo-European World*. Oxford University Press.

Malm, William P. (2021, November 22). Chinese music. *Encyclopedia Britannica*. https://www.britannica.com/art/Chinese-music.

Manco, John. (2013). *Ancestral Journeys: The Peopling of Europe from the First Venturers to the Vikings*. Thames and Hudson.

Manning, P. (2003). *Navigating World History: Historians Create a Global Past*. Palgrave MacMillan.

Marcuse, Herbert. (1962). *Eros and Civilization: A Philosophical Inquiry into Freud*. Vintage.

Marcuse, Herbert. (1961). *Soviet Marxism: A Critical Analysis*. Vintage.

Marcuse, Herbert. (1969). *Negations: Essays in Critical Theory*. Beacon Press.

Marcuse, Herbert, Rober Wolff, and Barrington Moore. (1969). *A Critique of Pure Tolerance.* Beacon Press.

Marias, Julian. (1967). *History of Philosophy.* Translated by Stanley Appelbaum and Clarence C. Strowbridge. Dover Books.

Marsh, Robert M. (2000). Weber's Misunderstanding of Traditional Chinese Law. *American Journal of Sociology,* 106(2), 281–302.

Marshall, T.H. (1992). *Citizenship and Social Class.* Edited by Tom Bottomore. Pluto Classics.

Martin, Henri-Jean. (1994). *The History and Power of Writing.* Translated by Lydia Cochrane. The University of Chicago Press.

Marx, K. (1906). *Capital: A Critique of Political Economy. The Modern Library.*

Marx, Karl and Friedrich Engels. (1985). *The Communist Manifesto. With an Introduction by A. J. P. Taylor.* Penguin Classics.

Mascuch, Michael. (1997). *Origins of the Individualist Self: Autobiography and Self-Identity in England, 1591–1791.* Polity Press.

Mason, Stephen. (1967). *A History of the Sciences.* Collier Books.

Mauss, Marcel. (1997). A category of the human mind: the notion of person; the notion of self. In Michael Carrithers, Steven Collins, and Steven Lukes. (Eds.). *The Category of the Person: Anthropology, Philosophy, and History.* Cambridge University Press.

May, Timothy. (2012). *The Mongol Conquests in World History.* Reaktion Books.

McCabe, Helen. (2015). John Stuart Mill, Utility and the Family: Attacking 'the Citadel of the Enemy.' *Revue internationale de philosophie,* 2 (n° 272).

McCullough, Michael. (2020). *The Kindness of Strangers: How a Selfish Ape Invented a New Moral Code.* Basic Books.

McDonald, P. (1979). Mabillon and the birth of diplomatics. *Studies in Religion/Sciences Religieuses,* 8(4).

McFarland, I. A. (Ed.). (2009). *Creation and Humanity: The Sources of Christian Theology.* John Knox Press.

McKeon, Michael. (1987). *The Origins of the English Novel, 1600–1740.* The Johns Hopkins University Press.

McKeon, Richard. (Ed.). *The Basic Works of Aristotle.* Random House.

Mead, George Herbert. (1972 [1934]). *Mind, Self, and Society from the Standpoint of a Social Behaviorist.* Edited with an Introduction by Charles Morris. University of Chicago Press.

Meadowcroft, James. (1995). *Conceptualizing the State: Innovation and Dispute in British Political Thought 1880–1914.* Oxford Historical Monographs.

Mearsheimer, John. (2018). *The Great Delusion: Liberal Dreams and International Realities.* Yale University Press.

Melchert, Norman. (1991). *The Great Conversation: A Historical Introduction to Philosophy.* Mayfield Publishing Company.

Mendoza, Jose Jorge. (2017). *The Moral and Political Philosophy of Immigration: Liberty, Security, and Equality.* Lexington Books.

Meyerhoff, Hans. (Ed.). (1959). *The Philosophy of History in Our Time: An Anthology.* Doubleday Anchor.

Mill, John Stuart. 1956 [1859]. *On Liberty.* Macmillan Publishing.

Miller, John. (1997). *The Glorious Revolution*. Routledge.

Miller, Stephen G. (1991). *Arete: Greek Sports from Ancient Sources*. University of California Press.

Miller, Judith. (2010). *Furniture: World Styles from Classical to Contemporary*. Dorling Kindersley Ltd.

Miles, Margaret R. (2005). *The Word Made Flesh. A History of Christian Thought*. Blackwell Publishing.

Mitchell, Lynette. (2007). *Panhellenism and the barbarian in Archaic and Classical Greece*. Classical Press of Wales.

Mitchell, Stephen. (2000). Introduction. In Stephen Mitchell (Ed.). *Bhagavad Gita: A New Translation*. Three Rivers Series.

Mithen, Steven. (1996). *The Prehistory of the Mind: The Cognitive Origins of Art and Science*. Phenix.

Moeller, Hans-Georg. (2001). *The Philosophy of the Daodejing*. Columbia University Press.

Montagu, Ashley. (1999) [1953]. *The Natural Superiority of Women*. Rowman Altamira.

Moore, Christopher. (2015). *Socrates and Self-Knowledge*. Cambridge University Press.

Moore, John C. (2019). *A Brief History of Universities*. Palgrave.

Moore, Steven. (2010). *The Novel: An Alternative History. Beginnings to 1600*. Continuum.

Morato, J. (2017). Praecipitia in Ruinam: The Decline of the Small Roman Farmer and the Fall of the Roman Republic. *Brewminate: A Bold Blend of News and Ideas* (April 26). https://tinyurl.com/2jb65xfy.

Montagu, Ashley. (1999). *The Natural Superiority of Women*. AltaMira Press.

Morgan, David. (1986). *The Mongols*. Blackwell

Morgan, Lewis Henry. (1997 [1871]). *Systems of Consanguinity and Affinity of the Human Family*. Introduction by Elisabeth Tooker. University of Nebraska Press.

Morris, Ian. (2010). *Why the West Rules—For Now: The Patterns of History, and What They Reveal About the Future*. Profile Books.

Morris, Colin. (1987). *The Discovery of the Individual, 1050–1200*. University of Toronto Press.

Mortenson, Terry. (2007). The Historical Development of the Old-Earth Geological Timescale. *Answers in Depth*, 2, 120–137.

Mote, Frederick. (1999). *Imperial China, 900–1800*. Harvard University Press.

Mote, Frederick. (1989). *Intellectual Foundations of China*. McGraw Hill.

Mousourakis, George. (2003). *The Historical and Institutional Context of Roman Law*. Ashgate

Muir, Percy. (1969). *English Children's Books, 1600–1900*. B.T. Batsford.

Muller, Hebert. (1961). *Freedom in the Ancient World*. Harper & Brothers.

Murray, Charles. (2003). *Human Accomplishment: The Pursuit of Excellence in the Arts and Sciences 800 BC to 1950*. Harper Perennial.

Murray, Oswyn. (1980). *Early Greece*. Fontana Paperbacks.

Multhauf, Robert. (1967). *The Origins of Chemistry*. Oldbourne.

Myers, A. R. (1975). *Parliaments and Estates in Europe to 1789*. Thames and Hudson.

National Geographic Magazine. 2019. The first Europeans weren't who you might think. (August).

Nature Index. (2018, March 2). Not so fast. Who really leads the world in science?" https://tinyurl.com/45dwp96c.

Nauta, L. (2021). Lorenzo Valla. In Edward N. Zalta & Uri Nodelman. (Eds.). *The Stanford Encyclopedia of Philosophy.* https://tinyurl.com/3zsc444t.

Mead, Lawrence. (2019). *Burdens of Freedom: Cultural Difference and American Power.* Encounter Books.

Needham, Joseph. (1995). *The Shorter Science & Civilization in China: 1. An abridgement by Colin A. Ronan of Joseph Needham's original text.* Cambridge University Press.

Needham, Joseph. (1997). *The Shorter Science & Civilization in China: 2. An abridgement by Colin A. Ronan of Joseph Needham's original text.* Cambridge University Press.

Needham, Joseph. (1995). *The Shorter Science & Civilization in China: 3. An abridgement by Colin A. Ronan of Joseph Needham's original text.* Cambridge University Press.

Nemo, P. (2006). *What is the West?* Translated by Kenneth Casler. Duquesne University Press.

Netz, Reviel. (2009). Imagination and Layered Ontology in Greek Mathematics. *Configurations,* 17 (1–2).

Neumann, Erich. (1973). *The Origins and History of Consciousness.* Princeton University Press.

Neumann, Erich. (1951). *The Great Mother.* Princeton University Press.

Newton, Hannah. (2015). The Dying Child in Seventeenth-Century England. *Pediatrics,* 136(2), 218–220.

NHC Education Programs. (2022, January 24). NHC Education Programs. YouTube. https://www.youtube.com/watch?v=Eogj05OlbOw&t=3092s.

Nicolson, Adam. (2015). A new translation of the Iliad. Review of The Iliad, Homer: A New Translation, by Peter Green. *The Spectator* (August).

Nilsson, Martin. (1968). *Homer and Mycenae.* Metheun and Co.

Nisbett, Richard E., Incheol Choi, Kaiping Peng, and Ara Norenzayan. (2001). Culture and Systems of Thought: Holistic Versus Analytic Cognition. *Psychological Review,* 108(2), 291–310.

Nisbett, Richard E. (2003). *The Geography of Thought: How Asians and Westerners Think Differently . . . And Why.* Free Press.

Nisbet, Robert. (1998). *History of the Idea of Progress.* Transaction Publishers.

Nitis, T. (1989). Ego differentiation: Eastern and Western perspectives. *The American Journal of Psychoanalysis,* 49(4), 339–346. https://doi.org/10.1007/BF01252262.

Norris, Michele. (2012). How 'Black Beauty' Changed The Way We See Horses. https://tinyurl.com/mrx39nzw.

North, Helen. (1966). *Sophrosyne: Self-Knowledge and Self-Restraint in Greek Literature.* Cornell University Press.

Nussbaum, M. (1997). Kant and Cosmopolitanism. In James Bohman and Matthias Lutz-Bachmann. (Eds.). *Perpetual Peace: Essays on Kant's Cosmopolitan Ideal.* MIT Press.

Nussbaum, M. C. (1999). Conversing with the Tradition: John Rawls and the History of Ethics. *Ethics,* 109(2).

O'Connor, Timothy, Emergent Properties. (2021). In Edward N. Zalta. (Ed.). *The Stanford Encyclopedia of Philosophy.* https://tinyurl.com/543fzsrf.

Onians, Richard. (1973). *The Origins of European Thought.* Arno Press.

Oesterdiekhoff, G. (2016). Child and Ancient Man: How to Define Their Commonalities and Differences. *The American Journal of Psychology*, 129(3).

Oesterdiekhoff, Georg. (2015). Evolution of Democracy. Psychological Stages and Political Developments in World History. *International Journal of Philosophy of Culture and Axiology*, 12(2).

Oesterdiekhoff, Georg. (2014). The rise of modern, industrial society. The cognitive developmental approach as key to disclose the most fascinating riddle in history. *The Mankind Quarterly*, 54(3/4).

Oesterdiekhoff, Georg. (2014b). Can Childlike Humans Build and Maintain a Modern Industrial Society? *The Mankind Quarterly*, 54, (3).

Oesterdiekhoff, Georg W. (2012). Was pre-modern man a child? The quintessence of the psychometric and developmental approaches. *Intelligence*, 40, 470–478.

Offer J. (2019). Herbert Spencer, Sociological Theory, and the Professions. *Frontiers Sociology*, 4.

O'Malley, A. (2012). Crusoe's Children: Robinson Crusoe and the Culture of Childhood in the Eighteenth Century. In: Gavin, A.E. (Eds.). *The Child in British Literature*. Palgrave Macmillan.

Ong, Walter J. (1981). *Fighting for Life. Contest, Sexuality, and Consciousness*. Cornell University Press.

Ong, Walter J. (1982). *Orality and Literacy: The Technologizing of the Word*. Methuen & Co.

Osier, Peter. (Ed.). (2016). *The history of Western sculpture*. Britannica Educational Publishing in association with Rosen Educational Services.

Overview: Mathematics 700–1449. (2019). In *Encyclopedia*. https://tinyurl.com/mryxacrp.

Ozment, Steven. (1980). *The Age of Reform, 1220–1550. An Intellectual and Religious History of Late Medieval and Reformation Europe*. Yale University Press.

Pace, Ian. (2021). How the culture wars are killing Western classical music. *Spectator* (09 October).

Paglia, Camille. (1992). *Sex, Art, and American Culture: Essays*. Vintage.

Paglia, Camille. (1990). *Sexual Persona: Art and decadence from Nefertiti to Emily Dickinson*. Yale University Press.

Paglia, C. (2006). Erich Neumann: Theorist of the Great Mother. *Arion*, 13(3).

Parker, Geoffrey. (1988). *The Military Revolution: Military Innovation and the Rise of the West, 1500–1800*. Cambridge University Press.

Parker, Richard B. (1979). The Jurisprudential Uses of John Rawls. *Nomos*, 20, 269–95. http://www.jstor.org/stable/24219140.

Parrinder, Patrick. (1980). *Science Fiction: Its Criticism and Teaching*. Routledge.

Parsons, Talcott. (1968 [1937]). *The Structure of Social Action, Volume II: Weber*. The Free Press.

Parthasarathi, Prasannan. (2011). *Why Europe Grew Rich and Asia Did Not: Global Economic Divergence*. Cambridge University Press.

Patten A. (1996). The Republican Critique of Liberalism. *British Journal of Political Science*, 26(1), 25–44.

Patterson, Cynthia. (2001). *The Family in Greek History*. Harvard University Press.

Pedersen, Olaf. (1997). *The First Universities: Studium Generale and the Origins of University Education in Europe*. Cambridge University Press.

Pen, Ronald. (1992). *Introduction to Music*. McGraw-Hill.

Perez, R. (2010). Las Casas' Articulation of the Indians' Moral Agency. *Ethnic Studies Review*, 43(2).

Periodic table. (2023, November 20). In *Wikipedia*. https://tinyurl.com/4htanchz.

Peristera Paschou et al. (2014). Maritime route of colonization of Europe. Proc Natl Acad Sci, 111(25).

Peters, F. E. (1970). *The Harvest of Hellenism: A History of the Near East from Alexander the Great to the Triumph of Christianity*. Simon and Schuster.

Peterson, Jordan. (2023). The radical Left is guilt-tripping the West into oblivion. *Telegraph* (16 July).

Pickering, Samuel. (1981). *John Locke and Children's Books in Eighteenth Century England*. University of Tennessee Press.

Piketty, Thomas, Emmanuel Saez, and Gabriel Zucman. (2016). Distributional National Accounts: Methods and Estimate for the United States. *Working Paper 22945* (December). National Bureau of Economic Research http://www.nber.org/papers/w22945.

Pinkard, Terry. (1996). *Hegel's Phenomenology. The Sociality of Reason*. Cambridge University Press.

Pinkard, Terry. (2014). *German Philosophy 1760–1860. The Legacy of Idealism*. Cambridge University Press.

Pinkard, Terry. (2017). *Does History Make Sense? Hegel on the Historical Shapes of Justice*. Harvard University Press.

Pinker, Steven. (2003). *The Blank Slate: The Modern Denial of Human Nature*. Penguin Books.

Pinker, Steven. (2011). *The Better Angels of Our Nature: Why Violence Has Declined*. Penguin Books.

Pinker, Steven. (2010). Art and Adaptation. In Brian Boyd, Joseph Carroll, and Jonathan Gottschall. (Eds.). *Evolution, Literature, and Film: A Reader*. Columbia University Press.

Plaks, Andrew. (1987). *The Four Masterworks of the Ming Novel: Ssu Ta Ch'i-Shu*. Princeton University Press.

Plato. (1987). *Theaetetus*. Edited with an Introduction by Robin H. Waterfield. Penguin Classics.

Plato. (1977). *The Republic*. Translated with an Introduction and Notes by Francis Conford. Oxford University Press.

Pocock, J. G. A. (1965). Machiavelli, Harrington and English Political Ideologies in the Eighteenth Century. *The William and Mary Quarterly*, 22(4).

Pocock, J. G. A. (1975). *The Machiavellian Moment: Florentine Political Thought and the Atlantic Republican Tradition*. Princeton University Press.

Polzin, R. (1976). Martin Noth's A History of Pentateuchal Traditions. *Bulletin of the American School of Oriental Research*, 221, 113–120.

Pomeranz, Kenneth. (2000). *The Great Divergence: China, Europe and the Making of the Modern World Economy*. Princeton University Press.

Pope, Alexander. (1943 [1720]). *The Iliad of Homer in the English Verse Translation.* The Heritage Press.

Popkin, Richard. (1999). The Columbia History of Western Philosophy. Columbia University Press.

Popper, Karl. (1945). *The Open Society and Its Enemies. Volume II: The High Tide of Prophecy: Hegel, Marx, and the Aftermath.* George Routledge and Sons.

Pound, Ezra. Homer or Virgil. In *Homer: A Collection of Critical Essays.* Edited by George Steiner. Prentice Hall.

Priest, Graham; Berto, Francesco; Weber, Zach. (2023). Dialetheism. In Edward N. Zalta & Uri Nodelman. (Eds.). *The Stanford Encyclopedia of Philosophy.* https://tinyurl.com/3c2hma5v.

Pronk T.C. (2021). Indo-European secondary products terminology and the dating of Proto-Indo-Anatolian. *Journal of Indo-European Studies,* 49(1&2), 141–170.

Putnam, Robert. (2007). E Pluribus Unum: Diversity and Community in the Twenty-first Century The 2006 Johan Skytte Prize Lecture. *Scandinavian Political Studies,* 30(2).

Putnam, Robert. (2000*). Bowling Alone: The Collapse and Revival of American Community.* Simon & Schuster

Putnam, Robert. (2021). *The Upswing: How America Came Together a Century Ago and How We Can Do It Again Deep.* Simon & Schuster.

Randeep, Ramesh. (2011). Income inequality growing faster in UK than any other rich country, says OECD. *The Guardian* (5 December).

Ravignani, A., Delgado, T. & Kirby, S. (2017). Musical evolution in the lab exhibits rhythmic universals. *Nature Human Behavior* https://doi.org/10.1038/s41562-016-0007.

Rawls, John. (1971). *A Theory of Justice.* Harvard University Press.

Rawls, John. (2001). *The Law of Peoples.* Harvard University Press.

Rawls, John. (2005). *Political Pluralism.* Columbia University Press.

Reber Arthur, S., & František Baluška. (2023). Where minds begin: a commentary on Joseph LeDoux's the deep history of ourselves. *Philosophical Psychology* 36(4), 745–755.

Reedsy Blog. (2024, September 15). 60 Children's Books About Diversity To Read With Little Ones. https://reedsy.com/discovery/blog/childrens-books-about-diversity.

Reich, David. (2018). Ancient DNA Suggests Steppe Invasions Spread Indo-European Languages. *Proceedings of the American Philosophical Society,* 162(1), 39–55. https://www.amphilsoc.org/sites/default/files/2018-08/attachments/Reich.pdf

Rensberger, B. & Farquhar, M. (1995). *The Birth and Death of Democracy. Washington Post* (September 13).

Ricketts, Glenn, Peter Wood, Stephen Balch, and Ashley Torne. (2011). The Vanishing West: 1964–2010. The Disappearance of Western Civilization from the American Undergraduate Curriculum. A Report by The National Association of Scholars.

Ringe, Donald. (2006). From Proto-Indo-European to Proto-Germanic. *A Linguistic History of English. Vol. 1.* Oxford University Press.

Robbins, Philip. (2017). Modularity of Mind. In Edward N. Zalta. (Ed.). *The Stanford Encyclopedia of Philosophy.* https://tinyurl.com/ww77k5h6.

Roberts, Adam. (2005). *The History of Science Fiction.* Palgrave.

Roberts, Julian. (1988). *German Philosophy: An Introduction.* Humanities Press.

Roberts, J.M. (1995). *The Penguin History of the World*. Penguin Books.

Robinson, C. F. (2003). *Islamic Historiography*. Cambridge University Press.

Robinson, Cyril. (1983). *A History of Greece*. Methuen.

Rooney, Ann. (2017). *Mapping the Universe: Exploring and Chronicling the Cosmos*. Sirius.

Rorty, A. O. and James Schmidt. (Eds.). (2009). *Kant's Idea for a Universal History with a Cosmopolitan Aim: A Critical Guide*. Cambridge University Press.

Rosenblatt, Helena. (2018). *The Lost History of Liberalism: From Ancient Rome to the Twenty-First Century*. Princeton University Press.

Rossi, Paolo. (2000). *The Birth of Modern Science*. Blackwell.

Rudwick, Martin, J.S. (1976). *The Meaning of Fossils: Episodes in the History of Palaeontology*. University of California Press.

Rufo, Christopher. (2023). *America's Cultural Revolution: How the Radical Left Conquered Everything*. Broadside Book.

Rushton, Phillippe J. (1997). *Race, Evolution, and Behavior: A Life History Perspective*. Charles Darwin Research Institute.

Russell, Bertrand. (1974). *History of Western Philosophy*. George Allen & Unwin LTD.

Russo, Lucio. (2004). *The Forgotten Revolution: How Science Was Born in 300 BC and Why It Had to Be Reborn*. Springer.

Sachs, Curt. (1940). *History of Musical Instruments*. Norton & Company.

Safranski, Rudiger. (2002). *Martin Heidegger*. Harvard University Press.

Sailer, Steve. (2006). Debating the Unmentionable: The Black-White IQ Gap. *VDare* (26 November). https://tinyurl.com/mvsk9pyb.

Sainsbury, R. M. (1995). *Paradoxes*. Cambridge University Press.

Saint Augustine. (1961). *Confessions*. Translated with an Introduction by R. S. Pine-Coffin. Penguin Books.

Saint Augustine. (2009). *The City of God*. Translated with an Introduction by Marcus Dods. Hendrickson Publishers.

Saller, Richard P. (1994). *Patriarchy, Property, and Death in the Roman Family*. Cambridge University Press.

Sanders, N.K. (1981). *The Epic of Gilgamesh*. Penguin Edition.

Sassi, Maria Michela. (2018). *The Beginnings of Philosophy in Greece*. Princeton University Press.

Saxena, S. (2010). Why is our past an area of darkness? *The Times of India* (17 October).

Scheidel, Walter. (2009). A peculiar institution? Greco-Roman monogamy in global context. *The History of the Family*, 14(3).

Scheidel, Walter. (2008). Monogamy and Polygyny in Greece, Rome, and World History. *Princeton/Stanford Working Papers in Classics* (June).

Schiappa, Edward. (2003). *Protagoras and Logos: A Study in Greek Philosophy and Rhetoric*. University of South Carolina Press.

Schneiderman, Miles. (2020). It's Time for Progressives to Move On from Harry Potter. (2 August). https://tinyurl.com/mwsrrpp5.

Schofield, Louise. (2007). *The Mycenaeans*. The Paul Getty Museum.

Schofield, M. (1986). Euboulia in the Iliad. *Classical Quarterly*, 36, 6–31.

Schonberg, Harold. (1997). *The Lives of the Great Composers*. Abacus.

Schwartz, Benjamin. (1975). The Age of Transcendence. *Daedalus*, 104(2).

Schwartz, Benjamin. (1985). *The World of Thought in Ancient China*. Harvard University Press.

Schwarzmantel, John. (1997). *The Age of Ideology: Political Ideologies from the American Revolution to Postmodern Times*. Bloomsbury Publishing.

Schweitzer, Peter. (1996). Kinship. In Adam Kuper and Jessica Kuper. (Eds.). *The Social Science Encyclopedia, Volume One*. Third Edition. Routledge.

Searle, J. (1980). Minds, Brains and Programs. *Behavioral and Brain Sciences*, 3, 417–57.

Searle. J. (1994). *The Rediscovery of the Mind*. MIT Press.

Seguin-Orlando A, et al. (2021). Heterogeneous Hunter-Gatherer and Steppe-Related Ancestries in Late Neolithic and Bell Beaker Genomes from Present-Day France. *Current Biology*, 31(5).

Sheehan, J. (2014). WEHLER: 1931–2014. Perspectives *on History: The News Magazine of the American Historical Association* (1 October).

Shabi, Rachel. (2017). Britain Is an Immigrant Nation. *New York Times*. (9 March).

Shcheglov , Dmitriy A. (2005). Hipparchus on the Latitude of Southern India *Greek, Roman, and Byzantine Studies*, 45, 359–380.

Shen Kuo. (2023, November 9). Shen Kuo. In *Wikipedia*. https://tinyurl.com/23e5jbh9.

Shinagel, Michael. (Ed.). (1994). *Robinson Crusoe. Daniel Defoe. An Authoritative Text. Contexts. Criticism*. W.W Norton.

Shionoya, Yuichi . (Ed.). (2001). *The German Historical School: The Historical and Ethical Approach to Economics*. Routledge.

Siedentop, Larry. (2015). *Inventing the Individual: The Origins of Western Liberalism*. Penguin Books.

Signoracci, Gino. (2017). *Hegel on Indian Philosophy: Spinozism, Romanticism, Eurocentrism*. Ph.D. Dissertation. The University of New Mexico.

Simon, Julia. (1995). Natural Freedom and Moral Autonomy: Emile as Parent, Teacher, and Citizen. *History of Political Thought*, 16(1), 21–36

Simonsuuri, Kristi. (1979). *Homer's Original Genius. Eighteenth-century notions of the early Greek epic 1688–1798*. Cambridge University Press

Skinner, J. E. (2012). *The Invention of Greek Ethnography. From Homer to Herodotus*. Oxford University Press.

Smith, Richard. (2010). Beyond growth or beyond capitalism? *Real-world Economics Review*, 53. http://www.paecon.net/PAEReview/issue53/Smith53.pdf.

Smith, Anthony D. (1991). *The Ethnic Origins of Nations*. Wiley-Blackwell.

Smith, D.E. (1954). *History of Mathematics. Volume I and II*. Dover Books.

Smith, David E., and Yoshio, Mikami. (1914). *A History of Japanese Mathematics*. Dover Books.

Smith, Lucie. (1979). *Furniture: A Concise History*. Oxford University Press.

Smith, Steven. (1991). *Hegel's Critique of Liberalism: Rights in Context*. University of Chicago Press.

Snell, Bruno. (1960). *The Discovery of the Mind: The Greek Origins of European Thought.* Harper TorchBooks.

Soboul, Albert. (1975). *The French Revolution 1787–1799: From the Storming of the Bastille to Napoleon.* Trans. by Alan Forrest and Colin Jones, Vintage Books.

Sorensen, Roy. (2003). *A Brief History of the Paradox: Philosophy and the Labyrinths of the Mind.* Oxford University Press.

Southern, R. W. (1953). *The Making of the Middle Ages.* Yale University Press.

Spadafora, D. (1990). *The Idea of Progress in Eighteenth-Century Britain.* Yale University Press.

Spall Jr. Richard Francis. (1988). Free Trade, Foreign Relations, and the Anti-Corn-Law League. *The International History Review,*10(3).

Spengler, O. (1988). *The Decline of the West. Volume I: Form and Actuality.* Alfred Knopf Publisher.

Speth, J.D. (2010). Big-Game Hunting in Human Evolution: The Traditional View. In: The Paleoanthropology and Archaeology of Big-Game Hunting. *Interdisciplinary Contributions to Archaeology.* https://doi.org/10.1007/978-1-4419-6733-6_3.

Staden, Heinrich von. (1975). Experiment and Experience in Hellenistic Medicine. *Bulletin of the Institute of Classical Studies,* No. 22.

Stadter, P. (1999). Introduction and Notes. In Robin Waterfield, trans. *Plutarch Roman Lives.* Oxford Univ. Press.

Ste. Croix, G.E.M. (1989). *The Class Struggle in the Ancient World: From the Archaic Age to the Arab* Conquests. Cornell University Press.

Stein, Peter. (1999). *Roman Law in European History.* Cambridge University Press.

Steiner, George and Robert Fagles. (Eds.). (1962). *Homer: A Collection of Critical Essays.* Prentice-Hall.

Stenberg, Robert. (2003). *Cognitive Psychology.* Nelson Thompson Learning.

Steinhardt, Nancy. (Ed.). (2002). *Chinese Architecture.* Yale University Press.

Steinhardt, Nancy. (2019). *Chinese Architecture: A History.* Princeton University Press.

Struik, Dirk. (1948). *A Concise History of Mathematics.* Dover Books.

Sullivan, Michael. (1999). *The Arts of China.* California University Press.

Swidzinki, A. (2007). *Tiberius Gracchus: A Study.* https://tinyurl.com/bf9jcdd8.

Tao Te Ching. A New Translation (2005). Translated by Sam Hamill. Shambhala Classics.

Tarasti, Eero. (1979). *Myth and Music: A Semiotic Approach to the Aesthetics of Myth in Music.* Mouton.

Tatum, J. (2013). Introduction and Notes. In *The Rise of Rome. Twelve Lives by Plutarch.* Penguin Classics.

Taylor, Charles. (1989). *Sources of the Self: The Making of the Modern Identity.* Harvard University Press.

Taylor, Charles. (1979). What's Wrong with Negative Liberty. In A. Ryan. (Ed.). *The Idea of Freedom.* Oxford University Press.

Taylor, Henry Osborne. (1919). *The Medieval Mind: A History of the Development of Thought and Emotion in the Middle Ages, Vol. 1.* The Macmillan Company.

Taylor, Jared. (2012). What the Founders Really Thought About Race. *American Renaissance* (17 February).

Tessier, Marie. (2016). Should Philosophy Departments Change Their Names? Readers Join the Debate. *New York Times*. (May 17).

Tierney, Brian. (2004). *The Idea of Natural Rights-Origins and Persistence. Northwestern Journal of Human Rights*, 2(1). https://tinyurl.com/396esw47.

The Editors of the Encyclopaedia Britannica. (2023). "Philippe de Vitry". *Encyclopedia Britannica* (27 October). https://www.britannica.com/biography/Philippe-de-Vitry.

Thiel, Udo. (2011). *The Early Modern Subject: Self-Consciousness and Personal Identity from Descartes to Hume*. Oxford University Press.

Thornton, Bruce. (2000). *Greek Ways: How the Greeks Created Western Civilization*. Encounter Books.

Thucydides. (1972). *History of the Peloponnesian War*. Translated by R. Warner with Introduction and Notes by M. I. Finley. Penguin.

Tiger, Lionel. (1969). *Men in Groups*. Random House.

Tolstoy, Leo. Homer and Shakespeare. In *Homer: A Collection of Critical Essays*.

Toulmin, Stephen, and June Goodfield. (1982). *The Discovery of Time*. University of Chicago Press.

Trautmann, Martin, et al. (2023). First bioanthropological evidence for Yamnaya horsemanship. *Science Advances*, 9(9).

Trigger, Bruce. (1993). The State-Church Reconsidered. In Henderson, J. S., and Netherly, P. J. (Eds.). *Configurations of Power*. Cornell University Press.

Trudeau, Pierre. (1962). The New Treason of the Intellectuals. *Cité libre*. https://tinyurl.com/yh2vap8e.

Tye, Michael. (2021). Qualia. In Edward N. Zalta. (Ed.). *The Stanford Encyclopedia of Philosophy*. https://plato.stanford.edu/archives/fall2021/entries/qualia/.

Udehn, Lars. (2014). *Methodological Individualism: Background, History and Meaning*. Routledge.

Vamvacas, Constantine J. (2009). *The Founders of Western Thought: The Presocratics*. Springer.

Van Norden, Bryan. (2017). *Taking Back Philosophy: A Multicultural Manifesto*. Columbia University Press.

Van Norden. (2016). If Philosophy Wont Diversify, Let's Call it What it Really Is. *The New York Times* (May).

Van Norden. (2018). The Ignorant Do Not Have a Right to an Audience. *New York Times* (June 25).

Van Seters, J. (1983). *In Search of History: Historiography in the Ancient World and the Origins of Biblical History*. Yale University Press.

Varacalli, T. F. X. (2016). The Thomism of Bartolomé de Las Casas and the Indians of the New World. LSU Doctoral Dissertations. 1664. https://tinyurl.com/y9c7ap4v.

Venturi, Robert. (1966). *Complexity and Contradiction in Architecture*. Double Day.

Vermont, T. (Ed.). (2021). *50 Classic Tales. The Western Folk and Fairy Tale Tradition*. Newly Translated by Paul Marlais. The White Peoples Press.

Vermeule, Adrian. (2017). A Christian Strategy. *First Things*, (November).

Vermeule, Adrian. (2018). Integration from Within. *American Affairs*, 2(1).

Vermeule, Adrian. (2019a). Liberalism and the Invisible Hand. *American Affairs*, 3(1).

Vermeule, Adrian. (2019b). All Human Conflict Is Ultimately Theological. *Church Life Journal*, (July 26).

Verovšek, P.J. (2022). The Reluctant Postmodernism of Jürgen Habermas: Reevaluating Habermas's Debates with Foucault and Derrida. *The Review of Politics* 84(3).

Wagner, Peter. (2005). The Axial Age Hypothesis, European Modernity and Historical Contingency. In Johann Arnason, S. N. Eisenstadt, and Björn Wittrock. (Eds.). *Axial Civilizations and World History*.

Wahrman, Dror. (2006). *The Making of the Modern Self: Identity and Culture in Eighteenth Century England*. Yale University Press.

Walbank, F. W. (Ed.). (1979). *Polybius. The Rise of the Roman Empire*. Translated by Ian Scott-Kilvert. Penguin Books.

Walker, Michael. (2019). Alain de Benoist's Against Liberalism. *Counter-Currents* (12 November).

Wang E. and George Iggers. (2002). Introduction. In E. Wang and G. Iggers. (Eds.). *Turning Points in Historiography: A Cross-Cultural Perspective*. University of Rochester Press.

Warrington, M. H. (2005). World Histories. In Marnie Hughes.

Warrington. (Ed.). *Palgrave Advances in World Histories*. Palgrave MacMillan.

Waterson, James. (2006). The Mamluks. *History Today*, 56(3).

Watson, Burton. (2007). Introduction. In *The Analects of Confucius*, Columbia University Press.

Watson, P. (2010). *The German Genuis: Europe's Third Renaissance, The Second Scientific Revolution, and the Twentieth Century*. Simon & Schuster.

Weber, Max. (1951). *The Religion of China: Confucianism and Taoism*. The Free Press.

Weinberg, Justin. (2016). Most Cited Philosophy Books in the Social Sciences. *DailyNous* (May 19).

West, M.L. (2007). *Indo-European Poetry and Myth*. Oxford University Press.

White, S. K. (1989). *The Recent World of Jurgen Habermas. Reason, Justice & Modernity*. Cambridge University Press.

Whitefield, Peter. (1998). *New Found Lands. Maps in the History of Exploration*. Routledge.

Wiater, A. M. (1940). Bossuet and His Discourse on Universal History. A thesis submitted in partial fulfillment of the requirements for the degree of Master of Arts in Loyola University. https://ecommons.luc.edu/luc_theses/597.

Wilde, Sandra, et al. (2014). Direct evidence for positive selection of skin, hair, and eye pigmentation in Europeans during the last 5,000 years. PNAS, 111(13), 4832-4837.

Wilford, John Noble. (1981). *The Mapmakers*. Alfred Knopf.

Wilson, Edward. (2004). *On Human Nature: Twenty-Fifth Anniversary Edition, With a New Preface*. Harvard University Press.

Windelband, Wilhelm. (1958). *A History of Philosophy. Volume I: Greek, Roman, Medieval. Volume II: Renaissance, Enlightenment, Modern*. Harper & Row Publishers.

Wirszubski, Chaim. (1968). *Libertas as a Political Idea at Rome During the Late Republic and Early Principate*. Cambridge University Press.

Witte, John. (2015). *The Western Case for Monogamy Over Polygamy*. Cambridge University Press.

Wittfogel, Karl. (1957.) *Oriental Despotism: A Comparative Study of Total Power.* Yale University Press.

WNDB. (n.d.). "Resources for Race, Equity, Anti-Racism, and Inclusion." Diverse Books. https://diversebooks.org/resources-for-race-equity-and-inclusion/.

Woltermann, Chris. (1993). Liberty's Aristocratic Roots and Modem Democracy. *Humanitas,* VI(2).

Wood, Allan. (1990). *Hegel's Ethical Thought.* Cambridge University Press.

Woodley, Michael and A.J. Figueredo. (2014). The Biosocial Model of the Rise of Western Civilization: A Counter-Point to Oesterdiekhoff. *The Mankind Quarterly,* LIV(3&4).

Woolhouse, Robert. (2007). *Locke: A Biography.* Cambridge University Press.

Wong, Kate. (2014). How Hunting Made Us Human. *Scientific American,* 310(4).

Wood, Gordon, S. (2002). *The American Revolution: A History.* New York: The Modern Library.

Wood, Gordon, S. (1969). *The Creation of the American Republic, 1776–1787.* University of North Carolina Press.

Woodman, A.J. (2007). Translated, Introduction and Notes, Sallust, *Catiline's War, The Jugurthine War, Histories,* Penguin Books.

Woolf, D. R. (2014). *Global Encyclopedia of Historical Writing.* Routledge.

Young-Bruehl, Elisabeth. (2010). Hannah Arendt's Jewish identity

In Roger Berkowitz, Jeffrey Katz & Thomas Keenan. (Eds.). *Thinking in Dark Times: Hannah Arendt on Ethics and Politics.* Fordham University Press.

Zagorin, Perez. (2003). *How the Idea of Religious Toleration Came to the West.* Princeton University Press.

Zeruneith, Keld. (2007). *The Wooden Horse. The Liberation of the Western Mind from Odysseus to Socrates.* Overlook Duckworth.

Zimmerman, T. C. (1996). *Paolo Giovio: The Historian and the Crisis of Sixteenth Century-Italy.* Princeton University. Press.

INDEX

Ricardo Duchesne is the author of three books, *The Uniqueness of Western Civilization* (2011), *Faustian Man in a Multicultural Age* (2017), and *Canada in Decay: Mass Immigration, Diversity, and the Ethnocide of Euro-Canadians* (2017). Duchesne was a professor at The University of New Brunswick, Canada, until 2019 when he took early retirement after an academic mob of over 100 professors subjected him to harassment and negative media campaigns for his refusal to accept without critical thinking the university mandate of "diversity, equity, and inclusion."

ENJOYED THIS BOOK?

TO READ MORE, VISIT US AT

ANTELOPEHILLPUBLISHING.COM